COLONIALISM AND THE JEWS

THE MODERN JEWISH EXPERIENCE

Deborah Dash Moore and Marsha L. Rozenblit, editors

Paula Hyman, founding coeditor

COLONIALISM AND THE JEWS

Edited by Ethan B. Katz, Lisa Moses Leff,

and Maud S. Mandel

Indiana University Press
Bloomington and Indianapolis

This book is a publication of

Indiana University Press
Office of Scholarly Publishing
Herman B Wells Library 350
1320 East 10th Street
Bloomington, Indiana 47405 USA

iupress.indiana.edu

Manufactured in the United States of America

Library of Congress Cataloging-in-Publication Data

Names: Katz, Ethan, editor. | Leff, Lisa Moses, editor. |
Mandel, Maud, 1967– editor.
Title: Colonialism and the Jews / edited by Ethan B. Katz, Lisa Moses Leff,
and Maud S. Mandel.
Description: Bloomington and Indianapolis : Indiana University Press, [2017] | Series:
The modern Jewish experience | Includes bibliographical references and index.
Identifiers: LCCN 2016035063 (print) | LCCN 2016036190 (ebook) |
ISBN 9780253024503 (cloth : alk. paper) | ISBN 9780253024572 (pbk. : alk. paper) |
ISBN 9780253024626 (ebook)
Subjects: LCSH: Colonies—History. | Colonialism—History. | Jews—History. |
Zionism—History.
Classification: LCC JV185 .C625 2017 (print) | LCC JV185 (ebook) |
DDC 325/.3089924—dc23
LC record available at https://lccn.loc.gov/2016035063

1 2 3 4 5 22 21 20 19 18 17

CONTENTS

ACKNOWLEDGMENTS

THIS VOLUME EMERGED from a rich scholarly conversation begun in November 2012 at the workshop, "Jewish History after the Imperial Turn: French and Comparative Perspectives," sponsored by Brown University's Program in Judaic Studies. The editors and contributors would like to thank Tracy Miller, department manager of the Program in Judaic Studies, for her integral role in the success of the workshop. In addition, our thanks goes to all workshop participants for their thoughtful feedback and incisive interventions, including Nathaniel Berman, Paris Chronakis, Jonathan Gribetz, Mary Lewis, Richard Parks, Rachel Rojanski, Joshua Schreier, Sarah Abrevaya Stein, and Adam Teller.

The workshop would not have been possible without financial support from key units at Brown, including the Department of History, the Cogut Center for the Humanities, the Office of International Affairs, The Office of the Provost, The Arthur B. and David C. Jacobson Lecture Fund, and the Elga and the K. Stulman Memorial Lecture Fund. Additional support came from the American University Jewish Studies Program, the Salo W. and Jeannette M. Baron Foundation, the Lucius N. Littauer Foundation, and the University of Cincinnati Department of Judaic Studies and Faculty Development Council.

At Indiana University Press, we received immediate and enthusiastic support from Deborah Dash Moore and Marsha Rozenblit, as well as from Dee Mortensen, who steadily shepherded this project through the editorial process and offered important structural and conceptual suggestions that made this a better book. We are also grateful to the two anonymous reviewers for their useful and productive feedback. We would like to thank the Centre de documentation juive contemporaine for providing the photo incorporated into the book's cover image as well as Kevin Lewin from Brown University Graphic Services for designing the poster that became the book's cover. We owe a special thanks to Derek Penslar and the editors at Taylor and Francis for enabling us to republish his essay "Is Zionism a Colonial Movement?"

Books of this nature are meant to reflect and spur scholarly conversation. We are grateful to all of the contributing authors for their sustained and stimulating engagement around challenging issues of colonial history and Jewish history over a period of four years.

COLONIALISM AND THE JEWS

1

INTRODUCTION

ENGAGING COLONIAL HISTORY AND JEWISH HISTORY

Ethan B. Katz, Lisa Moses Leff, and Maud S. Mandel

WHERE ARE JEWS in colonial history? Where is colonialism in Jewish history? In many ways, these unasked questions haunt contemporary Jewish and often world politics. Indeed, in the twenty-first century, the relationship between Jews and colonialism has been present in debates about not only Zionism but Jewish–Muslim relations, the wider Middle East, the future of European identity, and the aims and roots of American empire. And yet, typically, the subject of Jews and colonialism is hidden in plain sight, more polemicized or avoided than probed, let alone illuminated. If statesmen, activists, and pundits have difficulty addressing colonialism and the Jews, they are not alone. Until recently, scholars have offered little help.

Indeed, despite the recent outpouring of fruitful scholarly attention to modern colonialism, Jewish historians have been surprisingly reticent to explore the complex ways in which Jews interacted with nineteenth- and twentieth-century overseas empires. Prior to the early 2000s, most historians of European Jewry sidestepped the issue or ignored it altogether. Like most of their colleagues in the wider field of European history, many specialists in Jewish history saw nation-states, rather than empires, as the framework within which the great changes that characterized modern Jewish life took place.[1] In addition, scholars of Jewish history were particularly resistant or late coming to many of the methodological developments that proved crucial to the so-called Imperial Turn. These included critiques of positivism and empiricism; attention to metanarrative and the subjectivity of archival sources; and an emphasis on language, reflecting the influence of Foucauldian ideas about the nexus of knowledge and power.

Undoubtedly, the greatest elephant in the room has been Zionism. During the very period in which postcolonial studies emerged, debates raged over the place of colonialism in the history of Zionism and the State of Israel.[2] This rendered colonialism a veritable minefield for Jewish studies scholars. From the vantage point of postcolonial studies, Jews and colonialism frequently became reduced to polemics over Zionism, flattening the issue rather than taking account of its nuances.

In fact, the modern Jewish experience connects to the history of colonialism by virtue of a number of its central components: mobility and exchange, diaspora, internationalism, racial discrimination, and Zionism, to name but a few. Little wonder that specialists of Jews in North Africa and the Middle East, by contrast with those of Europe, have always made colonialism part of the stories they told. And yet there, too, early work tended not to interrogate the distinctive roles Jews played in colonial societies, economies, and politics. Rather, scholars often simply celebrated the impact of European colonialism by explicitly or implicitly depicting colonial rule as a harbinger of "progress" for non-European Jews, whether in the form of emancipation at European hands or Zionist migration to Palestine and then Israel. In this sense, earlier generations of scholars tended to work within the linear narrative of modernization that characterized the field of European Jewish history, in which colonized Jews became increasingly "modern" by virtue of their contact with Europeans. Such work typically saw colonialism's role in Jewish history and Jews' role in colonial history as a "gentler" one, that is, distinctively benevolent in the scheme of the broader history of European colonialism. Even when these historians revealed a colonial society far more complex than they explicitly recognized, they generally overlooked the ambiguities of colonial Jewish life.[3]

In failing to grapple with colonialism, Jewish historians disregarded essential dimensions of the modern Jewish experience. In European colonies from the British antipodes to French North Africa, Jewish economic, religious, and social life was transformed in important ways by the encounter with empire. Moreover, the effects of empire were as important in metropolitan Europe as they were in the colonies. As explored in this introduction and exemplified in the chapters that follow, a handful of scholars have taken Frederick Cooper and Ann Stoler's dictum that "Europe was made by its imperial projects, as much as colonial encounters were shaped by conflicts within Europe itself," as a spur to new approaches to Jewish history. They have begun to explore the multifaceted ways in which European Jews engaged with empire.[4] Their studies reveal that Jewish modernization was not, in fact, simply an effect of the Jewish encounter with the nation-state, as was long assumed. Rather, the encounter with imperialism—its legal forms, its economic structures, and its cultural and intellectual underpinnings—shaped the contours of European Jewish modernization as well.

This book is inspired by what appears to be the start of a "Jewish Imperial Turn."[5] The book's contributors—scholars in Jewish, European, and Middle Eastern history—have, from their different vantage points, all thought critically about the interpretive potential of bringing the study of colonialism and the study of Jewish history to bear upon one another. Such work yields new insights beyond Jewish history. In recent years, scholars of imperialism have focused on revealing and making sense of the contradictions at the heart of modern European empires. The imperial ventures of nineteenth- and twentieth-century Britain, France, and Germany were highly inegalitarian, characterized by violent conquest, exploitation of resources, and subjugation of peoples. Yet they were frequently undertaken in the name of the universalist values of the Enlightenment, the French Revolution, and modern liberalism. These warrants cannot be dismissed as mere hypocrisy; rather, they reveal the formative contradictions that helped to shape modern European political cultures. Indeed, debates over imperialism were critical for shaping Europeans' understanding of the universal principles by which polities should be organized, such as popular sovereignty, the primacy of the nation-state, and the pursuit of the public good. Such debates were also sites for defining how far universalist principles should extend, and the criteria by which some groups would be included and others excluded (e.g. race, religion, gender, and wealth).[6] The fundamental contradictions at the heart of modern European imperialism—and Jews' frequent place in the crosshairs—have also animated much of the new scholarship on Jews and empire. In many ways, this work challenges scholars to question some of their fields' most basic assumptions and categories of analysis.

We center our discussion on France and its empire. Some of the reasons for this focus are historical. As the seat of the French Revolutionary tradition and a vast global empire, France offers a particularly important instance of the paradoxes of inclusion and exclusion. Furthermore, in the nineteenth and twentieth centuries, France's Jewish population was as significant in its colonies as it was in the metropole. By the late 1940s, there were nearly half a million Jews total in French Morocco (250,000), Tunisia (100,000), and Algeria (140,000), a number that dwarfed not only mainland France's postwar Jewish population of a quarter million but also the pre-war peak of 330,000.[7] Moreover, Jews played an important role in shaping France's imperial history in both metropole and colony. There are historiographical reasons for this focus as well. In recent decades, scholarship in French and French imperial history has been dramatically reshaped by the Imperial Turn. Correspondingly, French Jewish historians have found the new directions particularly fruitful, and historians of French colonialism have begun to give greater attention to Jews.

But this volume looks well beyond the francophone sphere. Our comparative approach places essays treating diverse regions alongside one another, providing the opportunity to isolate what was unique in each setting and to identify themes and patterns that crossed national and imperial borders. To this end, our chapters tell stories that span six continents. The comparative lens pushes us to consider how transnational and nonnational factors, including not only colonialism but also international organizations and transregional economic connections, shaped Jewish modernity. In turn, it permits us to reflect upon the ways in which Jews shaped those larger systems as well.

Why Jewish Historians Need the Imperial Turn

As the essays in this volume show, the Imperial Turn has begun to transform our understanding of modern Jewish history in important ways. For too long, European Jewish historians remained wedded to a theory of Jewish modernization, first explicitly articulated by Salo Wittmayer Baron and later popularized by Hannah Arendt, that depicted the nation-state as the key political formation that shaped modernization for Jews everywhere.[8] The enduring power of this perspective is clear in studies that trace the different "paths of emancipation" that Jews followed in various European nation-states. Indeed, in spite of the variety and complexity of Jewish experiences they have described, Jewish historians have nonetheless largely agreed that the assimilationist demands of liberal nation-states shaped the paths of Jews' transformation in the modern world, which led (albeit in different ways and following different timelines) from communal autonomy to increased political, sociocultural, and economic integration.

Much of this scholarship has treated France as paradigmatic. For the revolutionaries who emancipated the Jews, Rousseauian logic dictated that there could be no legal distinctions among members of the nation. This meant that gaining political rights was predicated on the legal dissolution of Jews' semiautonomous corporate bodies and the minimizing of their social and cultural differences from other Frenchmen. In much early historiography, emancipation was thus depicted as leading to the full abandonment of a distinctive public Jewish identity in exchange for inclusion in the national community.[9] Subsequent scholarship challenged portrayals of modernization as leading toward the *complete* absorption of Jews into their wider national contexts, stressing instead the multiple "paths to, of, and from emancipation."[10] As they rejected a single story of assimilation, scholars sought greater nuance by employing notions of "acculturation," "integration," and the development of Jewish "subcultures."[11] Even this scholarship, however, rarely challenged the primacy of the nation-state in driving the social, cultural, political, and economic transformations of Jewish life in Europe.[12]

Katz, Leff, and Mandel

For the Jewish historians who saw the French model as normative, the experiences of Jews in the Habsburg and Russian empires represented, all too often, cases of delayed or even failed modernization.[13] But by the 1990s a growing rejection of modernization theory across the disciplines led Jewish historians to question the one-size-fits-all approach to the history of Jewish modernization as well, leading away from these stark conceptions.[14] Part of this shift, still ongoing, has involved recognizing that in Eastern European Jewish history, change unfolded within the framework of empire rather than the liberal nation-state.[15] New studies have revealed that the Habsburg and Tsarist empires treated minorities in a different manner than nation-states. Indeed, both tended on some level to cultivate rather than destroy diversity in order to rule more effectively, and these empires were often predicated on the inequality rather than the equality of the governed.[16] Thinking of modernization as an imperial rather than national project has proven a productive framework for understanding Eastern Europe, where rights were granted to Jews by enlightened monarchs with a vested interest in ruling *through* the institutions of religious, ethnic, and national minorities rather than in dissolving them.[17] In this way the notion that the nation-state represents the key political formation for understanding modern Jewish history has been substantially revised, and we now find ourselves in a moment where we have multiple models, a nation-state framework still treated as generally applicable in Western Europe, and an imperial framework that applies to Eastern Europe.

But these two models may be less different than we once thought. France, too, was an empire in the nineteenth and twentieth centuries. As an overseas empire, it has generally been considered distinct from the multiethnic land-based empires referred to earlier, because its colonies were far from the metropole and ruled with separate legal regimes. The presumed distance and separation between colonies and metropole long allowed French and French Jewish historians to imagine a republic based solely on the integrationist model of the modern nation-state. Yet Imperial Turn historiography has shown that even metropolitan France was, from the time of the Revolution, never simply a nation-state committed to the eradication of difference in the name of political equality. It was always also an empire, or, as Gary Wilder calls it, "an imperial nation-state."[18] As such, it was governed by two different logics that were in many ways at odds with one another yet nonetheless coexisted and even fed off each other in important ways. Works like Wilder's that examine France's republic and empire in a common frame have shown that modern France embraced not only universalism but also particularism; not only an ideology of equality but also an ideology of inequality predicated on racial and religious difference; not only liberalism but also, and no less fundamentally, illiberalism.[19] The paradox of the simultaneous embrace of two contradictory sets of ideas is not re-solved by assigning one set to the empire and the other to the metropole; in fact, both tendencies within French political culture were present in both settings.[20]

By recognizing that the very nation-state that emancipated the Jews was al-ways *also* an empire, a handful of scholars—many of them among those contrib-uting to the present volume—have begun to explore the role that empire played in the history of the Jews of France and other colonial metropoles, such as Great Britain and Germany.[21] Such recognition suggests that it is time to rethink the sharp contrast between Western Europe, where Jews lived in nation-states, and Eastern Europe, where they lived in empires. Extending this thinking to French Jewish history specifically and European Jewish history more generally allows us to return with new eyes to some of the fundamental paradoxes that scholars of Jewish modernization have long recognized, providing new ways to understand how and why throughout modern European history, two logics regarding the Jews developed simultaneously: on the one hand, a universalist, assimilating, and egalitarian rhetoric, and on the other, a logic of particularism, difference, and inequality.[22]

As our frame of reference shifts, so too does our understanding of the key terms that shaped the paradigm of Jewish modernization. For example, scholars have long recognized a connection between the secular Enlightenment and the Jewish Haskalah, with recent work even going so far as to show a reciprocal re-lationship between them.[23] Moving to the larger framework of the imperial nation-state focuses our attention on the concept of the "civilizing mission," a term related to the Enlightenment notion of "regeneration." The work of Jay Berkovitz and Alyssa Sepinwall illuminates the importance of the latter concept for both wider French and internal Jewish debates about the process and mean-ing of emancipation.[24] Pushing beyond the boundaries of mainland France, Lisa Moses Leff, Joshua Schreier, and Michael Shurkin have emphasized how for French administrators and Jewish leaders alike, the question of regeneration was vital in assessing possibilities and implementing measures for Jews in French Al-geria and the wider Francophone orbit.[25] The civilizing mission, although decid-edly less egalitarian-minded than regeneration, was a concept every bit as central to European Jewish self-understanding, politics, and philanthropy in the era of imperialism.[26]

A new imperial frame for Jewish history also highlights the multifaceted meanings of the concepts of the "Orient" and the "oriental." Sometimes the im-age of the Oriental was one that European Jews as diverse as Benjamin Disraeli and Abraham Geiger proudly embraced to distinguish themselves from their non-Jewish neighbors. At other times, the Oriental was a trope European Jews disavowed and applied strictly to "Others" in order to bring themselves closer to gentiles in Europe. This was, for example, the case with the Russian Jewish ethnographer Nahum Slouschz's depiction of North African Jews, and in many French Jewish writings that distinguished Algerian Jews from their Muslim neighbors. For all its many-sided meanings, the term proved as central to Jewish modernization as to European discourse more broadly.[27]

Moreover, as we turn our attention to the importance of such concepts to Jewish history, we find that we cannot simply borrow from established methods of analysis and neatly apply them to the Jewish case. Take, once more, the example of Orientalism. Although we have long known that individual Jewish scholars helped to shape the discourse of Orientalism, in order to understand how and why they did so, we need to move beyond the analytic strategies established by Edward Said. The binaries that Said made essential to analyzing the discourse of Orientalism do not work for understanding how it was used by European Jews; Jews positioned themselves on both sides of the dichotomy between "East" and "West" that Said and those he inspired regard as central to Orientalism.[28] As such, studying the Jewish engagement with Orientalism not only helps to add nuance to our understanding of the transformation of Jewish self-identification but also requires us to add complexity to the Saidian framework, or perhaps to reject it altogether.[29]

As we move to integrate empire into the story of Jewish modernization, we find that we are forced to rethink not only the concepts and the political forms that structured it but also the periodization within which modern European Jewish history unfolded and the processes that it entailed. With regard to emancipation in France, for example, a focus on empire points to Napoleonic expansion rather than the 1789 Revolution as the more crucial turning point for understanding the evolution of European Jewish modernity. The first post-Revolutionary empire offered Jews legal equality far beyond the bounds of France proper while not necessarily erasing difference, which Napoleon and his agents often instrumentalized in the service of state power. Moreover, Napoleon's empire not only solidified Jews' rights as citizens, it established new institutions that guaranteed that Judaism as a religion would be publicly recognized.[30]

Attention to the impact of colonialism also raises new questions about the evolution of modern Jewish politics. Beginning in the nineteenth century and continuing well into the twentieth, the empire became a privileged site for working out the meaning and the contours of Jewish identity and Jewish politics. The social and economic practices adopted by metropolitan Jews as they modernized in various Western European countries also often originated in the colonies rather than the metropole. Exploring such phenomena forces us to rethink fundamentally the nature and geography of agency, power, and borders in the history of Jews across Europe.

* * *

The Imperial Turn has been equally thought provoking for scholars working on the history of North African Jews. Earlier work tended to celebrate the relationship between North African Jews and the French state, seeing in imperialism an agent of progressive Jewish modernization or, as in the case of Eastern European Jewish history, conceptualizing the poorer, more traditional, and "oriental" Jews of colonial North Africa as "not yet" modernized. Recent scholarship, however, has begun to challenge those frameworks. Shaped by new perspectives on power relations in colonial territories, the agency of indigenous actors, and the intertwining of metropolitan-colonial historical developments, scholars have reexamined core assumptions regarding the North African Jewish past. As a result, linear narratives of Jewish progress have given way to far more nuanced assessments of the impact of European intervention on Jews, as scholars have re-conceptualized Muslim–Jewish relations so as to account for the impact of French colonial policies. With this work, historians have also begun to challenge the long-held assumption that Jews were subject to a "softer" form of colonialism.[31]

The earliest attempts to write the history of Jews in North Africa were decisively marked by the colonial contexts in which they were produced. Written by local religious and cultural figures or others embedded within the colonial infrastructure, these works served both scholarly and ideological ends, presenting the history and ethnography of North Africa's Jewish population as a means for both supporting the colonial project and promoting the modernization and emancipation of the Jewish populations under study.[32]

The decolonization of North Africa brought a new critical lens to the study of local Jewish life. As Emily Benichou Gottreich and Daniel J. Schroeter have discussed elsewhere, much of this initial work was carried out by Israeli scholars who used the tools of anthropology and historical ethnography to explain the rituals and practices of rural Maghrebi Jews to their European-born, urban co-nationals.[33] By the 1970s and 1980s shifting intellectual and social trends in Israel saw a new generation of North African–born scholars challenge the Eurocentric focus of Israeli academic life with studies on the linguistic and literary heritages of Maghrebi Jews. This paved the way for historians such as Michel Abitbol, Richard Ayoun, and Paul Sebag to craft new narratives that brought the colonial and even the postcolonial period under scholarly scrutiny for the first time.[34] Such work began to integrate the history of North African Jews into the broader story of Jewish modernity by examining the impact of such

Katz, Leff, and Mandel

forces as westernization, antisemitism, and the Holocaust on Jewish life in the Maghreb.

These scholars of the 1970s and 1980s paid more attention to context and historical change than did their predecessors, taking up the colonial and postcolonial periods as serious subjects of analysis. Yet many still accepted without challenge a relatively linear reading of Jewish modernity inherited from the wider field of Jewish history, rarely questioning French republican claims of Jewish betterment through the nation-state's assimilatory embrace. Other scholarship was shaped by a Zionist interpretive lens—of longstanding Jewish decline amidst Muslim persecution, leading to mass migration to Palestine or Israel.[35] Subsequent analysis by scholars such as Moshe Bar-Asher, Yossef Charvit, Joseph Chetrit, and Yaron Tsur challenged the teleological perspectives in this earlier work by tracing the continuities rather than the ruptures of North African Jewish culture over time and problematizing binary views of tradition and modernity. Historical accounts such as these, however, have typically treated Jews in a vacuum rather than as part of the wider colonial landscape.[36]

Indeed, like their Europeanist colleagues, scholars of the North African Jewish past have been reluctant until recently to challenge the triumphalist narrative of European colonialism. Even as scholars have begun increasingly to emphasize colonial violence, inequities, and exploitation and thereby to undermine the simplistic links between European liberalism and a progressive modernity, rare still are works that provide a more complex picture of the deeply entangled relationships among the different social groups that comprised European colonial societies in North Africa and the Middle East. As Sarah Abrevaya Stein has noted recently, we still have much to learn about the processes by which Jews worked with, struggled against, supported, and benefited from the colonial order and the process of decolonization.[37]

In recent years, Stein and others—including many contributors to this book—have begun to address this lacuna by placing Jews and Muslims within a single analytic frame in order to reconceptualize the strategies of colonial rule and the boundaries of communal identities. For instance, Emily Gottreich and Richard Parks have underscored how colonial authorities redrew traditional spatial divisions in colonial Morocco and Tunisia, respectively, and, in the process, reconfigured communal boundaries between Jews and Muslims.[38] Such scholarship compels us to rethink our understanding of antisemitism in the region by unpacking the ways in which French colonial authorities used animosities against one group to govern the other.[39]

This new scholarship in Jewish history has increasingly been in conversation with work in wider French and French colonial history. In the latter fields, scholars have shown how porous metropolitan and colonial boundaries could be, highlighting in particular the ways pre- and postcolonial frameworks regarding religion, ethnicity, and race crossed the Mediterranean and informed developments on both of its shores.[40] In opening up new ways of thinking about colonial geography, these scholars have also reconceptualized the historical rupture between the colonial and the postcolonial moment. Still other scholars working in this field have focused on transregional intersections, demonstrating the way North African Jewish history was shaped by developments throughout the wider French empire and beyond.[41]

Why Colonial History Needs Jewish History

If Jewish historians have, until recently, done little to engage colonial studies, the absence of Jews from the wider field of colonial history has been equally stark. Such a lacuna is, on the surface, difficult to explain. Indeed, in the immediate post–World War II period and during the era of decolonization, several early analysts of the colonial situation made Jewish history critical to their narratives by drawing connections between antisemitism and the Holocaust on the one hand, and colonial racism and violence on the other hand. If Hannah Arendt saw the nation-state rather than the empire as the key framework for Jewish life in France, she also saw histories of antisemitic persecution and colonialism as inextricably linked in a common logic. Likewise, anticolonial thinkers like Frantz Fanon, Aimé Césaire, and Jean-Paul Sartre and early Holocaust memoirists such as Jean Améry and Primo Levi thought about the colonial condition and the Jewish condition together.[42] Yet since the postwar interest in colonialism and antisemitism did not translate into a body of critical scholarship, the initial connections were not fully developed.[43]

When colonial history and postcolonial studies finally exploded in the 1980s and 1990s, Jews posed uncomfortable problems for many historical sources, theoretical frameworks, and political assumptions central to the field. These problems long served to marginalize Jewish history within colonial history. Yet accounting for Jews refigures key questions in colonial history, particularly in the French empire. Since Jews so often fell in between many of the classificatory schemes used by colonial authorities, studying them at once advances and further complicates recent scholarship on interstitial groups under colonial rule. Moreover, Jews offer an exceptionally rich entry point for new efforts to write comparative and transregional accounts of empire, in particular with regard to histories of status, economy, and difference. In addition, Jewish history raises critical terminological issues for colonial history as a field.

The primary reasons for Jews' longstanding absence in colonial history are at once historical and historiographical. Jews' relatively small numbers and minority status in most imperial settings is surely a key factor. But the issues are not merely demographic. Colonial powers and anticolonial nationalists, and later, their historians and theorists relied heavily upon binaries to chart plans for the future and offer observations about the past and the present. The place of Jews in colonial history does not fit neatly into such dichotomous frameworks. Very often Jews were neither exactly masters nor victims of colonial exploitation. Instead, they often circulated between physical spaces of metropole and colony and enjoyed a status somewhere between equal citizens and oppressed subjects. Moreover, they could be both orientalist and orientalized, and frequently knew the life of both the colonizer and the colonized.

During the colonial era, Jews never controlled nor collectively represented a metropolitan European power. At the same time, they were rarely situated on the bottom rung of colonial hierarchies. As essays in this volume show, their political status ranged from that of elite power brokers in the French or British metropole, to Europeanized indigenous instructors in Jewish schools in North Africa, to vulnerable Moroccan Jewish subjects of both the French resident-general and the Muslim sultan, to simultaneous national agents and undesirables on Russian imperial frontiers. Rarely, even in a single colonial territory, did all Jews' legal and social position fit a single category.

Because of their uncertain political status, Jews as a category have remained difficult to classify on several other lines as well. Ideologically, Jews often both sympathized with the discrimination faced by native colonial subjects and perceived a sense of possibility in the promise of European liberal citizenship. This was the case not only in overseas empires like the French and British but also in land-based empires like the Russian. Jews' economic position, meanwhile, was frequently that of an intermediary between metropolitan-based officials or businesses on the one hand and products, services, and menial laborers of the colonies on the other. Furthermore, many Jewish intellectuals perceived imperialism as a potential means of liberation in which Jews could play a critical role; others, however, saw it as a forcible oppressive occupation. Even culturally, particularly in French North Africa, Jews' simultaneous attachments to the clothing, food, language, music, and aesthetics of a native culture they shared with Muslims, and to the French education and culture increasingly shaping their lives, defied dichotomous categories. Jews were thus particularly unsuited to what Cooper and Stoler have lamented as "the Manichaean dichotomies" that "had such sustaining power" for "contemporary actors [and] latter-day historians."[44] As Stoler has emphasized elsewhere, many of these dichotomies were deeply woven into the colonial archive itself.[45]

Meanwhile, Jews have posed thorny problems for postcolonial theory. As Bryan Cheyette has argued, postcolonial thinkers rejected discussing Jewish suffering and the Holocaust for a number of reasons. Many had an "anxiety of appropriation" with regard to Holocaust comparisons; that is, they feared that by making the Holocaust universal and the Jews metaphorical for all victims, other histories of suffering would be subsumed or ignored. Others cast aside histories of antisemitism and the Holocaust as part of "a dominant white 'Judeo-Christian' culture"; they likewise saw Jewish cosmopolitanism as rootless and unprincipled, in contrast to the transnational anticolonial cosmopolitanism valorized in postcolonial studies.[46] Finally, due to the triumph of Zionism and the persistence of the Israeli–Palestinian conflict, these general patterns became inseparable from Middle East politics. Particularly under the formative influence of Edward Said, many postcolonial scholars tended to assume a rapid and dramatic evolution from Jews as, like Arabs and Muslims, leading victims of Western persecution to Jews as violent, indeed Western imperialist persecutors of Arabs and Muslims.[47]

New directions in the field of colonial history, however, make Jews' more complex, uncertain, and uneven relationship to colonialism of growing interest. Scholars have begun to appreciate the fluid, contested, and ever-shifting nature of colonial boundaries and categories, and how those "in-between" groups offer crucial insight about the tensions and contradictions within colonial society more broadly.[48] This has taken a number of forms. In her study of Dutch colonial archives, Stoler focuses on the *inlandsche kinderen*, which meant at various times those of mixed descent, Dutch born in the Indies, or impoverished whites. She argues that this group shows that supposedly fixed colonial categories, including those of "Europeans" and "natives," were actually unstable and ever-shifting, a fact of which colonial administrators themselves were well aware.[49] Yet what do trenchant new studies like this one tell us about European colonialism more broadly or in a comparative context? Here we would do well to ask: How similar or different from these "native whites" of the Dutch East Indies were the French-emancipated Jews of Algeria or their modernizing coreligionists in the schools of the Alliance israélite universelle in Morocco and Tunisia?

Recent scholarship on Jews in the Maghreb offers suggestive starting points. Even though these Jews' ethnic status appears on the surface less ambiguous than that of the *inlandsche kinderen* in Dutch Java, Ethan Katz has found parallels between the reports examined by Stoler and those of French police in the 1950s on migrants from North Africa living in Paris. In these reports, Jews are present but in hiding. That is, the authors oscillate seamlessly between terms like "Algerians" and "Muslims" to describe people, cultural traits, neighborhoods, and cafes. Sometimes, administrators unwittingly lump Jewish individuals or establishments under such headings; at other times they mention Jews in passing in a manner that makes them seem at once included within and exceptional to the report's general categories and observations.[50] In a similar vein, Sarah Abrevaya Stein's study of the Jews of the Algerian Sahara reveals the contrast between French administrators' view of them as "indigenous" and the rest of Algerian Jewry as "French." Such work further illustrates the contingency in the colonial categories assigned to Jews even within a single territory. Likewise, Maud Mandel's depiction of the emergence of the "North African Jew" as a political and discursive category during the years of decolonization shows how colonial officials and international Jewish actors wrestled with Jews' uncertain place in the colonial order at a moment of great change.[51] At the same time, certain North African Jews' place between binaries looks more ideological and less ethnic when we consider the formulation of one of the most insightful early observers of colonialism, the Tunisian Jewish writer and anti-colonialist Albert Memmi:

> I know the colonizer from the inside almost as well as I know the colonized. . . . Like all other Tunisians I was treated as a second-class citizen, deprived of political rights, refused admission to most civil service departments, etc. But I was not a Muslim. . . . The Jewish population identified as much with the colonizers as with the colonized. They were undeniably "natives," as they were then called. . . . However, unlike the Muslims, they passionately endeavored to identify themselves with the French. To them the West was the paragon of all civilization, all culture.[52]

Such a characterization brings to mind the situation of the Egyptians in the Sudan studied by Eve Troutt Powell, who were at once colonized by the British and themselves aspiring colonizers.[53] Memmi reminds us that, even absent the official license of their own colonial state, Jews in these territories resembled in certain respects what Powell calls "colonized colonizers." Indeed, the precise nature of Jews' interstitial positionality in many colonial empires could vary tremendously according not only to time and place but also authorial rendering.[54]

These examples suggest that a focus upon the uncertain, contradictory position of Jews can substantially complicate and enrich colonial history. Scholars of the French empire have started to give attention to Jews along these lines, from their complex position in webs of colonial and anticolonial politics in the interwar Maghreb to their shifting position at the moment of decolonization.[55] Such histories begin to unravel the "us" versus "them" paradigm that have long dominated colonial and postcolonial studies.

Yet, as these cases reveal, thinking across multiple colonial situations opens further possibilities, providing useful material for comparison. Stoler dubs the history of indigenous whites in the Dutch East Indies a "minor history" for the way that their in-betweenness is at once nonrepresentative and deeply revealing. Along these lines, bringing Jews into the picture enables us to chart what we might call a "comparative minor history" of empires, through which historians use the periphery of the colonial experience to rethink the heart of imperial ideology and practice. In the process, we could address better the important question of how Jews' experiences of empire either tracked or diverged from those of non-Jews.

Because Jews lived in nearly all modern European empires in significant numbers and in diverse roles, the comparative history of empires stands to gain a great deal from paying closer attention to them. The proposition is particularly timely, as scholars are more interested than ever in understanding the differences between land-based and overseas empires and between "multiethnic" empires and those grounded in racialized thinking.[56]

Looking at the case of Jews is especially fruitful in another realm of comparative imperial history: economic history. As recent work has shown, Jews have often acted as economic "middlemen": from the merchant Jacob Lasry in the early years of French colonization in Oran to the wealthy British protectee Silas Aaron Hardoon in late nineteenth- and early twentieth-century Shanghai.[57] The ubiquity of this pattern lends itself to a comparison of economic structures of trade, exchange, labor, and exploitation not only between empires but across multiple territories of a single empire. Furthermore, the networks that often linked Jews from one empire to the next open up perspectives in the transregional and borderlands history of empires and the interconnections across them. Studying the numerous Jewish families and firms that crisscrossed multiple imperial contexts also offers the opportunity to bridge early modern and modern histories of empire, whose supposed fundamental differences appear less certain once we begin to compare them.[58]

Finally, Jews offer crucial cases for comparison for colonial historians interested in the histories of difference, race-thinking, exclusion, and genocide. Most scholars agree that matters of difference, particularly racial difference, were critical to all modern empires, but they have only recently begun to emphasize the degree to which ideas and practices varied across historical periods and contexts.[59] Of late, scholars have turned to the highly sensitive questions that initially attracted students of colonialism and antisemitism to one another in the immediate postwar period. To better understand how race and other forms of difference operated in the French and British empires, some historians have begun to bring together the history of Jews with that of other subjects living under colonial rule—in particular, Muslims of French North Africa.[60] Some have approached these questions through the lens of memory studies, examining how memories of colonial atrocities and the Holocaust informed one another.[61] While the willingness to draw such comparisons and connections can be refreshing, scholars do so at their peril if they do not concurrently work through the place of Jews in colonial history. That is, if scholars are to offer critical perspectives on the articulation of memory strands, they need the requisite tools with which to understand the history that such strands purport to represent.

It is perhaps unsurprising that parallels and interconnections between the position of Jews and colonized native populations have been undertaken most directly in German history. These have revealed both tantalizing continuities and crucial differences between the ideas and actions of the German state toward the natives of colonial Africa under the Kaiserreich and Jews under the Nazis. Relocating Jews at the heart of the earlier story of German Orientalism and expanding colonial ambitions complicates the question even further. Susannah Heschel's work here and elsewhere is exemplary of a related push from within Jewish studies to bring Jews together with other historically oppressed minorities in colonial contexts, examining sensitive topics such as the relationship between Jews and Orientalism or between racial ideologies in Europe and Zionist ideas about Arabs in Palestine.[62]

Indeed, for scholars of colonialism and postcolonialism, ultimately, Zionism cannot be ignored. The relationship of Zionism to colonial empires and colonialism has been historically complex and ever-shifting, as several of the essays in this book illustrate.[63] Because Zionism emerged in an imperial context that cut across numerous metropolitan and colonial spaces, and it took up colonial, anticolonial, and postcolonial postures and alliances at various moments, studying it requires grappling with the full ambiguity of Jews' place in colonial history. In many ways, Zionism defies the binaries in which much of colonial history has been written as well as the starkest assumptions of postcolonial studies. The colonial history of Zionism is best written in the type of comparative and transregional contexts that Jewish history demands of colonial history. The history of Zionism and, more broadly, Jews and empire should force a series of reckonings about the meaning of words like "colonial" and "imperial"; "colonizer" and "colonized"; and "metropole" and "colony." Such discussions, however difficult, have the potential to advance the field substantially.

The Stakes of Mutual Engagement

For too long the fields of colonial history and Jewish history paid little attention to one another. A leading factor in this missed encounter is the very reason it has become so pressing: scholars of Jewish and colonial history were blinded to one another by the prevailing narratives and paradigms in their respective fields. Systematic incorporation, they feared, could lead to major disruptions. Recently some scholars have begun to rectify the situation, but substantial work remains to be done. This book seeks to build upon such efforts: we call for major reappraisals in both Jewish history and colonial history through sustained mutual engagement.

This book's structure reflects the areas in which the bringing together of Jewish and colonial history poses the greatest challenges to both fields. Each of this book's three parts revolves around a central question meant to provoke conversation between the two subfields. The essays in part 1, "Subjects and Agents of Empire," proceed from the question: in their various roles in colonial empires, are Jews best understood as subjects or agents of empire? In their diverse approaches and subject matter, the scholars contributing to this section each reveal how Jews fall in between the two categories, eliding such simple characterization. The first two chapters focus on intellectuals, Colette Zytnicki's on Jewish historians of colonial North Africa, and Susannah Heschel's on German Jewish scholars of Islam. Taken together, the essays reveal the complex ways in which Jews both participated in constructing the discipline of Orientalism and stretched its binary frameworks, sometimes to the point of defying them.

Adam Mendelsohn, Frances Malino, and Israel Bartal take a different approach to the question of whether Jews are best understood as subjects or agents of empire in their respective chapters. Mendelsohn shows how deeply connected the histories of distinct groups of Jews were across the British empire. Similarly, Malino examines the women teachers of the Alliance israélite universelle school system, showing that they too were neither fully "metropolitan" nor fully "colonial." Finally, Israel Bartal's essay offers a fresh perspective on the Russian empire by comparing it to the French one, showing how fruitful the Imperial Turn can be for rethinking the position of Jews under the tsars. From Australia to Russia to Morocco, these chapters demonstrate the artificiality of the divide between colonies and metropole. The Jewish actors examined here circulated widely not only due to their ambiguous statuses but also, in many cases, because of their links to inter- and intra-imperial Jewish networks.

Attention to the impact of the colonies also raises new questions about the evolution of modern Jewish politics, for beginning in the nineteenth century and continuing well into the twentieth, the empire became a privileged site for working out the meaning and the contours of Jewish political identities. The essays that form part 2, "Jews in Colonial Politics," thus ask: Politically, how did Jews become defined and define themselves in the colonial venture and in anticolonial struggles? Ethan Katz's chapter looks at three important French Jewish colonial policymakers, revealing a significant colonial reformist strand in French Jewish politics. Tara Zahra's chapter on Zionism as a form of emigration politics illuminates a previously overlooked imperial dimension of early-twentieth-century eastern European politics. David Feldman's chapter on the British Labor

Party's position on Zionism provides new insight into the history and memory of British imperialism.

Turning from metropolitan to colonial politics, Daniel Schroeter's and Maud Mandel's chapters compel us to rethink our understanding of antisemitism and philosemitism in late colonial North Africa by unpacking the ways in which French colonial authorities used animosities against one group to govern the other. Schroeter provides a fresh perspective on Moroccan king Mohammed V's policies toward Jews under Vichy as part of his larger political agenda. Mandel's chapter offers a carefully nuanced rereading of the 1952 Muslim–Jewish riot in Tunis that forces us to rethink colonial antisemitism and the politics of international Jewish organizations. Taken together, the essays in this section illustrate how a sharp opposition between colonial and anticolonial politics becomes difficult to sustain once Jews enter the picture. Jews appear here as liberal reform advocates, symbols in power struggles over the future of colonial territories, by turns colonizers, natives, and foreigners in various metropolitan and native settings. We also see how Zionism itself emerged within a host of wider imperial contexts, including those of the British Labor Party's distinct colonialism and the migration schemes of land-based empires. For Jewish historians, the lines between Jewish and general politics become a good deal fuzzier than conventionally assumed.

The book's final section tackles the vexing question of Zionism's historical relationship to colonialism. The stakes of this question go far beyond the academy, of course, and increasingly so in recent years. The scholars contributing to this section see a rigorous scholarly approach as necessary for adding depth to contemporary polemics. In particular, they favor a comparative historical approach. The section begins with a republication of Derek Penslar's now-classic essay, "Is Zionism a Colonial Movement?" which appeared previously in his book, *Israel in History: The Jewish State in Comparative Perspective* (Routledge, 2006). Two scholars of European imperialism in North Africa and the Middle East, Joshua Cole and Elizabeth F. Thompson, offer critical responses to Penslar's piece. Penslar has in turn contributed a chapter responding to their comments, updating his earlier essay with new reflections and an expanded comparative framework. The authors as a whole find that the relationship between Zionism and colonialism was a historically moving target, so much so that Zionism's complex position may throw into question the utility of labels such as colonial, anticolonial, and postcolonial, which are often as political as they are scholarly.

The themes at the heart of this book point to the potentially enormous implications of the engagement of Jewish history and colonial history for both fields. In Jewish history writ large, the late twentieth and early twenty-first century have witnessed an extended rejection of grand narrative. This has taken the form most often of studies of Jews in individual nation-states or their leading Jewish centers. Despite the immense achievements of this scholarship, it has also bred reluctance among most Jewish historians to frame their studies in the kinds of comparative or transnational terms that assign causality to larger international forces, such as the rise, expansion, and decline of empires. "Thinking like an empire" about Jewish history, to borrow Frederick Cooper's evocative phrase, can enable the recovery of wider patterns of history that have too often become buried under the insularity of single-country studies.[64]

By the same token, colonial history needs Jewish history. The postcolonial critique that has had such a productive effect on both colonial and metropolitan histories has, at times, been harshly critical of modernity and the West in an undistinguishing manner. An equally misplaced nostalgia for empire has emerged from other, more conservative quarters of colonial history. The complex position of Jews within the cracks of colonial history, if taken seriously, forces reassessments that can move beyond stale debates about the demonic or benevolent character of colonialism and the modern West more broadly. Comparative history is one of the methodologies essential to this more nuanced approach; here, the long history of Jewish geographic diversity and trans-imperial connectedness offers an exceptional set of tools from which to build the field.

The importance of mutual engagement is hardly merely academic. Few questions animate current political debates about Jews more than the character of Zionism and the meaning of rising antisemitism. In each instance, conversations more often than not turn on absolutist assumptions about Jewish power or powerlessness, and about the place of Jews within or outside of liberal politics. The histories of Jews and colonialism presented here not only defy such polarized understandings; they also offer essential context that can be fodder for suppler approaches in future discussions.

Notes

1. Frederick Cooper has analyzed the chronology of colonial studies. See Cooper, "The Rise, Fall, and Rise of Colonial Studies, 1951–2001," in Cooper, *Colonialism in Question: Theory, Knowledge, History* (Berkeley: University of California Press, 2005): 33–55.

2. The latter was the case regarding relations not only with the British and American empires and with Palestinian Arabs but also with Israel's own Mizrahi Jews, sometimes referred to as "Arab" Jews.

3. We thank Sarah Abrevaya Stein for sharing with us her unpublished paper, "Jews and European Imperialism," from which we draw some of our insights on this literature.

4. Ann Laura Stoler and Frederick Cooper, "Between Metropole and Colony: Rethinking a Research Agenda," in *Tensions of Empire: Colonial Cultures in a Bourgeois World*, ed. Ann Laura Stoler and Frederick Cooper, 1–53 (Berkeley: University of California Press, 1997), 1.

5. In particular, it grows out of discussions among the group of scholars who gathered at Brown University in November 2012 at an international workshop called "Jewish History after the Imperial Turn: French and Comparative Perspectives." Most of the contributors here took part in the workshop. Two other notable organized efforts to discuss many of the questions here have been the theme of "Jews and Empire" for the fellows of the Frankel Center of Judaic Studies at the University of Michigan during the 2014–15 academic year, and a symposium on "Jews, Colonialism, and Postcolonialism" at the University of Cape Town, South Africa, in 2013.

6. Stoler and Cooper, "Between Metropole and Colony," 1–53; Cooper, "Introduction: Colonial Questions, Historical Trajectories," in his *Colonialism in Question*: 3–32, esp. 27.

7. Figures for North Africa from Michael M. Laskier, "Between Vichy Antisemitism and German Harassment: The Jews of North Africa during the Early 1940s," *Modern Judaism* 11, no. 3 (October 1991): 343–69, here 366. For French Jews, prewar figure from Renée Poznanski, *Jews in France during World War II*, trans. Nathan Bracher (Hanover, NH: University Press of New England, 1997), 1; postwar figure from Maud S. Mandel, *In the Aftermath of Genocide: Armenians and Jews in Twentieth-Century France* (Durham, NC: Duke University Press, 2003), 11.

8. Salo Wittmayer Baron, "Ghetto and Emancipation," *Menorah Journal* 14, no. 6 (1928): 515–26; and Hannah Arendt, *Origins of Totalitarianism* (New York: Harcourt, Brace & Jovanovich, 1951).

9. See, most notably, Michael Marrus, *The Politics of Assimilation: The French Jewish Community at the Time of the Dreyfus Affair* (New York: Clarendon, 1971). For some scholars, such as Arthur Hertzberg, the adoption of the French republican model was the forerunner of modern antisemitism. See his *The French Enlightenment and the Jews: The Origins of Modern Anti-Semitism* (New York: Columbia University Press, 1968), 360–64; see also Shmuel Trigano, "From Individual to Collectivity: The Rebirth of the 'Jewish Nation' in France," in *The Jews of Modern France*, ed. Frances Malino and Bernard Wasserstein, 245–81 (Hanover, NH: Brandeis University Press, 1985). For a more recent and nuanced analysis of the logic of emancipation, see Ronald Schechter, *Obstinate Hebrews: Representations of Jews in France, 1715–1815* (Berkeley: University of California Press, 2003).

10. Pierre Birnbaum and Ira Katznelson, "Emancipation and the Liberal Offer," in *Paths of Emancipation: Jews, States, and Citizenship*, ed. Pierre Birnbaum and Ira Katznelson, 3–36 (Princeton, NJ: Princeton University Press, 1995), 24.

11. The literature on the complexities of Jewish acculturation in modern Europe is vast. Some important examples for the French case include Jay Berkovitz, *The Shaping of Jewish Identity in Nineteenth-Century France* (Detroit: Wayne State University Press, 1989); Jay Berkovitz, *Rites and Passages: The Beginnings of Jewish Culture in Modern France* (Philadelphia: University of Pennsylvania Press, 2004); and Paula Hyman, *The Emancipation of the Jews of Alsace: Acculturation and Tradition in the Nineteenth Century* (New Haven, CT: Yale University Press, 1991).

12. The primacy of the nation-state is particularly visible in several important comparative edited volumes in modern European Jewish history from the 1990s and early 2000s. See, notably, Birnbaum and Katznelson, eds., *Paths of Emancipation*; Michael Brenner, Vicki Caron, and Uri R. Kaufmann, eds., *Jewish Emancipation Reconsidered: The French and German Models* (Tübingen: Mohr Siebeck, 2003); Jonathan Frankel and Steven J. Zipperstein, eds., *Assimilation and Community: The Jews of Nineteenth-Century Europe* (Cambridge: Cambridge University Press, 1992); and Frances Malino and David Sorkin, eds., *From East and West: Jews in a Changing Europe, 1750–1870* (New York: Basil Blackwell, 1990).

13. See the discussion of this point in Benjamin Nathans, *Beyond the Pale: The Jewish Encounter with Late Imperial Russia* (Berkeley: University of California Press, 2002), 370 and passim.

14. Such diversity was already implicit in Jacob Katz, ed., *Toward Modernity: The European Jewish Model* (New Brunswick, NJ: Transaction, 1987); and was embraced more wholeheartedly in works like Birnbaum and Katznelson, *Paths of Emancipation*; Brenner, Caron, and Kaufmann, *Jewish Emancipation Reconsidered*; Frankel and Zipperstein, *Assimilation and Community*; and Malino and Sorkin, *From East and West*. Of course, even as these works pointed away from the one-size-fits all approach to Jewish

modernization, they nonetheless still generally assumed a national, rather than imperial framework for its unfolding.

15. Marsha Rozenblit's *Reconstructing a National Identity: The Jews of Habsburg Austria during World War I* (Oxford: Oxford University Press, 2004), for example, shows how Jews in the Austro-Hungarian empire were among the most fervently loyal to the imperial monarchy precisely because that form fostered a "comfortable tripartite identity" for them in ways that were only possible in an imperial, rather than a strictly national setting (128). Benjamin Nathans also shows how important Russia's imperial framework was in shaping Jews' path to modernization in that setting, in his *Beyond the Pale*, 367–81.

16. See Frederick Cooper and Jane Burbank, *Empires in World History: Power and the Politics of Difference* (Princeton, NJ: Princeton University Press, 2010), esp. 347, where they discuss the modernization of Jews in the Habsburg empire in these terms.

17. The same observation could fruitfully be extended to the millet system under the Ottoman Empire. See, for example, Esther Benbassa and Aron Rodrigue, *A History of the Judeo-Spanish Community, 14th–20th Centuries* (Oakland: University of California Press, 2000); and Bruce Masters, *Christians and Jews in the Ottoman Arab World: The Roots of Secularism* (Cambridge: Cambridge University Press, 2004).

18. Gary Wilder, *The French Imperial Nation-State: Negritude and Colonial Humanism between the Two World Wars* (Chicago: University of Chicago Press, 2005), 3.

19. Ibid., 22.

20. There is a growing literature that demonstrates this point. For a few illustrative examples, see Alice L. Conklin, "Colonialism and Human Rights: A Contradiction in Terms? The Case of France and West Africa, 1895–1914," *American Historical Review* 103, no. 2 (1998): 419–42; Lynn Hunt, ed., *The French Revolution and Human Rights: A Documentary History* (New York: Bedford St. Martins, 1996); Clifford Rosenberg, *Policing Paris: The Origins of Modern Immigration Control between the Wars* (Ithaca, NY: Cornell University Press, 2006); and Todd Shepard, *The Invention of Decolonization: The Algerian War and the Remaking of France* (Ithaca, NY: Cornell University Press, 2006).

21. For examples of work that has begun to lay the groundwork in this field, see Sara Abrevaya Stein, "Dividing South from North: French Colonialism, Jews, and the Algerian Sahara," *Journal of North African Studies* 17, no. 5 (2012): 773–92; Sara Abrevaya Stein, "Protected Persons? The Baghdadi Jewish Diaspora, the British State, and the Persistence of Empire," *American Historical Review* 116, no. 1 (February 2011): 80–108; David Feldman, "Jews and the British Empire, C. 1900," *History Workshop Journal* 63, no. 1 (2007): 70–89; Abigail Green, "The British Empire and the Jews: An Imperialism of Human Rights?" *Past & Present* 191, no. 1 (2011): 175–205; and Christian S. Davis, *Colonialism, Anti-Semitism and Germans of Jewish Descent in Imperial Germany* (Ann Arbor: University of Michigan Press, 2011).

22. See on this point esp. Alyssa Goldstein Sepinwall, *The Abbé Grégoire and the French Revolution: The Making of Modern Universalism* (Berkeley: University of California Press, 2005).

23. See, for example, Schechter, *Obstinate Hebrews*; and Jonathan M. Hess, *Germans, Jews and the Claims of Modernity* (New Haven, CT: Yale University Press, 2002).

24. Berkovitz, *Shaping of Jewish Identity*; and Sepinwall, *Abbé Grégoire*.

25. Lisa Moses Leff, *Sacred Bonds of Solidarity: The Rise of Jewish Internationalism in Nineteenth Century France* (Stanford, CA: Stanford University Press, 2006); Joshua Schreier, *Arabs of the Jewish Faith: The Civilizing Mission in Colonial Algeria* (New Brunswick, NJ: Rutgers University Press, 2010); Michael Shurkin, "French Nation Building, Liberalism and the Jews of Alsace and Algeria, 1815–1870" (PhD thesis, Yale University, 2000).

26. On Jews and the civilizing mission, see Leff, *Sacred Bonds of Solidarity*; Aron Rodrigue, *French Jews, Turkish Jews: The Alliance Israélite Universelle and the Politics of Jewish Schooling in Turkey 1860–1925* (Bloomington: Indiana University Press, 1990); and Schreier, *Arabs of the Jewish Faith*.

27. Adam Kirsch, *Benjamin Disraeli* (New York: Schocken, 2008). On the way that Geiger and certain other Jewish scholars of Islam in some cases used their scholarship to mark Jews as oriental and at

other times to "de-orientalize" Jews, see Susannah Heschel, "German-Jewish Scholarship on Islam as a Tool of De-Orientalization," *New German Critique* 117 (Fall 2012), 91–117. On Slouschz's orientalism, see Harvey E. Goldberg, "The Oriental and the Orientalist: The Meeting of Mordecai Ha-Cohen and Nahum Slouschz," *Jewish Culture and History* 7, no. 3 (2004): 1–30. For important initial work on Jews and Orientalism, see ibid; Ivan Davidson Kalmar and Derek Penslar, eds., *Orientalism and the Jews* (Waltham, MA: Brandeis University Press, 2005).

28. Edward Said, *Orientalism: Western Conceptions of the Orient* (New York: Penguin, 1978). For more on this point, see also Kalmar and Penslar, *Orientalism and the Jews* and Goldberg, "The Oriental and the Orientalist."

29. Said's *Orientalism* faced significant critiques from an early date. Notable examples include Sadiq Jalal al-Azm, "Orientalism and Orientalism in Reverse," *Khamsin* 8 (1981): 5–26; Bernard Lewis, "The Question of Orientalism," *New York Review of Books*, June 24, 1982; and Emmanuel Sivan, "Edward Said and His Arab Reviewers," *Jerusalem Quarterly* 35 (Spring 1985): 11–23.

30. Phyllis Cohen Albert, *The Modernization of French Jewry: Consistory and Community in the Nineteenth Century* (Hanover, N.H.: Brandeis University Press, 1977). For a useful discussion of Napoleon's varying impact on Jewish institutions in lands he conquered, see Bart Wallet, "Napoleon's Legacy: National Government and Jewish Community in Western Europe," *Simon Dubnow Institute Yearbook* 6 (2007): 291–309.

31. For a discussion of "soft" colonialism and the Jews in Algeria, see Stein, "Dividing South from North," 784. In her careful study of the development and operation of the consistories in Algeria, Valerie Assan, *Les consistoires israélites d'Algérie au XIXe siècle:"L'alliance de la civilization et de la religion"* (Paris: Armand Colin, 2012), has laid out what might be considered a kind of middle-ground position. Assan acknowledges that the rabbis of the Algerian consistories, brought from the mainland, seemed like other colonial functionaries to native Algerian Jews and that the consistories operated according to colonial hierarchies between metropolitan French and "indigènes"; yet she also emphasizes that the consistories' regeneration project had its own more idealistic goal of emancipation for Algerian Jewry, setting it apart in its aims from French colonization more broadly.

32. For fuller development of many of these issues, Colette Zytnicki, *Les Juifs du Maghreb: Naissance d'une historiographie coloniale* (Paris: Presse universitaire Paris-Sorbonne, 2011).

33. For an in-depth historiographical review of the scholarship on North African Jewish life, from which the following two paragraphs are drawn, see Emily Benichou Gottreich and Daniel J. Schroeter, "Rethinking Jewish Culture and Society in North Africa," in *Jewish Culture and Society in North Africa*, ed. Emily Benichou Gottreich and Daniel J. Schroeter, 3–23 (Bloomington: Indiana University Press, 2011). For examples of the early scholarship on rural North African Jews, see Shlomo Deshen, *The Mellah Society: Jewish Community Life in Sherifian Morocco* (Chicago: University of Chicago Press, 1989); Shlomo A. Deshen and Moshe Shokeid, *The Predicament of Homecoming: Cultural and Social Life of North African Immigrants in Israel* (Ithaca, NY: Cornell University Press, 1974); Harvey E. Goldberg, *Cave Dwellers and Citrus Growers: A Jewish Community in Libya and Israel* (Cambridge: Cambridge University Press, 1972); Mordekhai Ha-Cohen, *The Book of Mordechai: A Study of the Jews of Libya: Selections from the Haghid Mordekhai of Mordechai Hakohen: Based on the Complete Hebrew Text as Published by the Ben Zvi Institute Jerusalem*, ed. and trans. with introduction and commentaries by Harvey E. Goldberg (Philadelphia: Institute for the Study of Human Issues, 1980); Moshe Shokeid, *The Dual Heritage: Immigrants from the Atlas Mountains in an Israeli Village* (Manchester: Manchester University Press, 1971); and Alex Weingrod, *Reluctant Pioneers: Village Development in Israel* (Ithaca, NY: Cornell University Press, 1966).

34. Michel Abitbol, *The Jews of North Africa during the Second World War* (Detroit: Wayne State University Press, 1989); Michel Abitbol, *Tujjar al-sultan: 'ilit kalkalit Yehudit be'Maroko* (Jerusalem: Institut Ben-Zvi, 1994); Michel Abitbol, *Le passé d'une discorde: Juifs et Arabes depuis le VIIe siècle* (Paris: Perrin, 1999); Richard Ayoun and Bernard Cohen, *Les Juifs d'Algérie: Deux mille ans d'histoire* (Paris:

Jean-Claude Lattès, 1982); and Paul Sebag, *Histoire des Juifs de Tunisie: Des origines à nos jours* (Paris: L'Harmattan, 1991).

35. See for example, Michael M. Laskier, *The Alliance Israélite Universelle and the Jewish Communities of Morocco, 1862–1962* (Albany: State University of New York Press, 1983); Michael M. Laskier, *North African Jewry in the Twentieth Century: The Jews of Morocco, Tunisia, and Algeria* (New York: New York University Press, 1994); and Norman A. Stillman, *Jews of Arab Lands: A History and Source Book* (Philadelphia: The Jewish Publication Society, 1979).

36. All of these scholars have written several important books and articles. For some examples, see Joseph Chetrit's numerous articles on North African Jews in his journal *Miqqedem Umiyyam [mi-Kedem u-Miyam]*. For some of Tsur's important contributions, see Yaron Tsur, "L'époque coloniale et les rapports 'ethniques' au sein de la communauté juive en Tunisie," in *Mémoires juives d'Espagne et du Portugal*, ed. Esther Benbassa (Paris: Publisud, 1996); Yaron Tsur, "Haskala in a Sectional Colonial Society: Mahdia (Tunisia) 1885," in *Sephardi and Middle Eastern Jewries: History and Culture in the Modern Era*, ed. Harvey E. Goldberg, 146–67 (Bloomington: Indiana University Press, 1996); Yaron Tsur, "Jewish 'Sectional Societies' in France and Algeria on the Eve of the Colonial Encounter," *Journal of Mediterranean Studies* 4 (1994): 263–77; Yaron Tsur, "Yehadut Tunisya be-shilhe ha-tekufah ha-teromkolonialit," *Miqqedem umiyyam* 3 (1990): 77–113; Moshe Bar-Asher, *La composante hébraïque du judéo-arabe algérien: Communautés de Tlemcen et Aïn-Témouchent* (Jerusalem: Hebrew University Magnes Press, 1992); Moshe Bar-Asher, *Masorot u-leshonot shel Yehude Tsefon-Afrikah* (Jerusalem: Mosad Bialik; Ashkelon: Ha-mikhalalah Ha-ezorit, 1999); Bar-Asher's articles in the journal *Massorot*; Yossef Charvit, *La France, l'élite rabbinique d'Algérie et la Terre Sainte au XIXe siècle: Tradition et modernité* (Paris: Champion, 2005); and Yossef Charvit, *Elite rabbinique d'Algérie et modernization, 1750–1914* (Jerusalem: Editions Gaï Yinassé, 1995).

37. Stein, "Protected Persons?," 84.

38. Emily Gottreich, *The Mellah of Marrakesh: Jewish and Muslim Space in Morocco's Red City* (Bloomington: Indiana University Press, 2007); and Richard Parks, "The Jewish Quarters of Interwar Paris and Tunis: Destruction, Creation, and French Urban Design," *Jewish Social Studies* 17, no. 1 (Fall 2010): 67–87. For other work that has fruitfully placed Jews and Muslims in a single analytic frame, see Joëlle Bahloul, *The Architecture of Memory: A Jewish-Muslim Household in Colonial Algeria, 1937–1962*, trans. Catherine du Peloux Ménagé (Cambridge: Cambridge University Press, 1996); Elizabeth Friedman, *Colonialism & After: An Algerian Jewish Community* (Boston: Bergin & Garvey, 1988); Claude Hagege and Bernard Zarca, "Les Juifs et la France en Tunisie: Les bénéfices d'une relation triangulaire," *Le Mouvement social* 197 (October–December 2001); Schreier, *Arabs of the Jewish Faith*; Daniel J. Schroeter, "French Liberal Governance and the Emancipation of Algeria's Jews," *French Historical Studies* 33, no. 2 (2010): 259–80; Daniel Schroeter and Joseph Chetrit, "Emancipation and Its Discontents: Jews at the Formative Period of Colonial Rule in Morocco," *Jewish Social Studies* 13, no. 1 (2006): 170–206; Daniel J. Schroeter, *The Sultan's Jew: Morocco and the Sephardi World* (Stanford, CA: Stanford University Press, 2002); and Benjamin Stora, *Les trois exils* (Paris: Stock, 2006).

39. See also Joshua Cole, "Constantine before the Riots of August 1934: Civil Status, Anti-Semitism, and the Politics of Assimilation in Interwar French Algeria," *Journal of North African Studies* 17, no. 5 (December 2012): 839–61; and his "Antisémitisme et situation coloniale pendant l'entre-deux-guerres en Algérie: Les émeutes antijuives de Constantine," *Vingtième siècle* 108 (October–December 2010): 2–23.

40. See esp. Wilder, *French Imperial Nation-State*; Rosenberg, *Policing Paris*; Shepard, *Invention of Decolonization*; and Naomi Davidson, *Only Muslim: Embodying Islam in Twentieth-Century France* (Ithaca, NY: Cornell University Press, 2012). Works that treat Jews in France that reflect an engagement with this wider scholarship include Ethan B. Katz, *The Burdens of Brotherhood: Jews and Muslims from North Africa to France* (Cambridge, MA: Harvard University Press, 2015); Leff, *Sacred Bonds of Solidarity*; Lisa Moses Leff, "The Impact of the Napoleonic Sanhedrin on French Colonial Policy in Algeria," *CCAR Journal* 54, no. 1 (2007): 35–54; and Maud S. Mandel, *Muslims and Jews in France: History of a Conflict* (Princeton, NJ: Princeton University Press, 2014).

Katz, Leff, and Mandel

41. Ethan Katz, "Tracing the Shadow of Palestine: The Zionist-Arab Conflict and Jewish-Muslim Relations in France, 1914–1945," in *The Israeli-Palestinian Conflict in the Francophone World*, ed. Nathalie Debrauwere-Miller, 25–40 (New York: Routledge, 2010); Maud Mandel, "Transnationalism and Its Discontents during the 1948 Arab-Israeli War," *Diaspora* 12, no. 3 (2003): 329–60; Joshua Schreier, "From Mediterranean Merchant to French Civilizer: Jacob Lasry and the Economy of Conquest in Early Colonial Algeria," *International Journal of Middle East Studies* 44 (2012): 631–49; and Schroeter, *Sultan's Jew*.

42. Several scholars have recently made a similar point. See, esp., Bryan Cheyette, *Diasporas of the Mind: Jewish and Postcolonial Writing and the Nightmare of History* (New Haven, CT: Yale University Press, 2013). For close analysis of several of the same thinkers and questions, see Michael Rothberg, *Multidirectional Memory: Remembering the Holocaust in the Age of Decolonization* (Stanford, CA: Stanford University Press, 2009).

43. Cooper cites the trauma of the colonial wars and decolonization, postcolonial efforts to write indigenous histories of Africa and elsewhere from a distinctly noncolonial standpoint, and overriding narratives of progress as among the reasons that there was a lag of decades before the burst of scholarly interest in colonial history. Cooper, "Rise, Fall, and Rise of Colonial Studies."

44. Stoler and Cooper, "Between Metropole and Colony," 8.

45. Ann Laura Stoler, *Along the Archival Grain: Epistemic Anxieties and Colonial Common Sense* (Princeton, NJ: Princeton University Press, 2009).

46. Cheyette, *Diasporas of the Mind*, 37–38.

47. Said's book *Orientalism* proved a fundamental text in the emergence and direction of postcolonial theory. Said, *Orientalism*. Despite his acknowledgment of Jews as frequent victims of Orientalism, Said focused considerable attention elsewhere on Zionism as an example of Orientalism tied to Western colonialism. See, esp., Edward W. Said, "Zionism from the Standpoint of Its Victims," *Social Text* 1 (1978): 7–58. Here we draw on Ivan Davidson Kalmar and Derek Penslar, "Introduction: Orientalism and the Jews," in Kalmar and Penslar, *Orientalism and the Jews*, xv. At the same time, as Said complained, many of his Jewish critics, rather than glean insight from the conceptual and empirical links between antisemitism and Orientalism, "have seen in the critique of Orientalism an opportunity for them to defend Zionism, support Israel and launch attacks on Palestinian nationalism." Edward W. Said, "Orientalism Reconsidered," in Alexander Lyon Macfie, ed., *Orientalism: A Reader* (New York: New York University Press, 2001), 353. For an argument for the importance of Said's pro-Palestinian politics to *Orientalism* itself, see James Pasto, "Islam's 'Strange Secret Sharers': Orientalism, Judaism and the Jewish Question," *Comparative Studies in Society and History* 40, no. 3 (1998): 437–74, esp. 472.

48. On this point, see Stoler and Cooper, "Between Metropole and Colony," 6.

49. Stoler, *Along the Archival Grain*, 6.

50. For further discussion on these lines, see Katz, *Burdens of Brotherhood*, introduction and chapter 4. For related observations about Jews in the colonial archives, see Sarah Abrevaya Stein, *Saharan Jews and the Fate of French Algeria* (Chicago: University of Chicago Press, 2014).

51. Stein, *Saharan Jews*; Mandel, *Muslims and Jews in France*, 35–58.

52. Albert Memmi, *The Colonizer and the Colonized*, trans. Howard Greenfeld with a new introduction by the author, preface by Jean-Paul Sartre (New York: Orion, 1965), xiii–xiv.

53. Eve M. Troutt Powell, *A Different Shade of Colonialism: Egypt, Great Britain, and the Mastery of the Sudan* (Berkeley: University of California Press, 2003).

54. Stoler and Powell are hardly alone in recent efforts to focus on groups that defy simple classification in the colonial context. Among other examples are Engseng Ho, *The Graves of Tarim: Genealogy and Mobility across the Indian Ocean* (Berkeley: University of California Press, 2006); Linda Colley, "Going Native, Telling Tales: Captivity, Collaborations and Empire," *Past and Present* 168 (2000): 170–93; Shompa Lahiri, "Contested Relations: The East India Company and the Lascars in London," in *The Worlds of the East India Company*, ed. H. V. Bowen, Margarette Lincoln, and Nigel Rigby (Woodbridge,

UK: Boydell, 2002); and Laura Tabili, "Outsiders in the Land of Their Birth: Exogamy, Citizenship, and Identity in War and Peace," *Journal of British History* 44, no. 4 (2005): 796–815.

55. In the first instance, see Cole, "Constantine before the Riots"; Cole, "Antisémitisme et situation coloniale"; Mary Lewis, *Divided Rule: Sovereignty and Empire in French Tunisia, 1881–1938* (Berkeley: University of California Press, 2013); and in the second, Shepard, *Invention of Decolonization*, chap. 6. Jonathan Wyrtzen addresses elements of each of these in the history of Moroccan anti-colonial movements and decolonization in *Making Morocco: Colonial Intervention and the Politics of Identity* (Ithaca, NY: Cornell University Press, 2015).

56. For two good discussions of the problems of definition of colonialism and empire, see Cooper, "States, Empires, and Political Imagination," in his *Colonialism in Question*, 153–203; and Ania Loomba, "Situating Colonial and Postcolonial Studies," in her *Colonialism/Postcolonialism* (New York: Routledge, 1998), 7–23.

57. See, respectively, Schreier, "From Mediterranean Merchant to French Civilizer"; and Stein, "Protected Persons?"

58. For further important efforts from a Jewish history perspective regarding Jews and economics in imperial contexts, see, for example, Rebecca Kobrin and Adam Teller, eds., *Purchasing Power: The Economics of Jewish History* (Philadelphia: University of Pennsylvania Press, 2015); Schroeter, *Sultan's Jew*; Sarah Abrevaya Stein, *Plumes: Ostrich Feathers, Jews and a Lost World of Global Commerce* (New Haven, CT: Yale University Press, 2008); and Francesca Trivellato, *The Familiarity of Strangers: The Sephardic Diaspora, Livorno and Cross Cultural Trade in the Early Modern Period* (New Haven, CT: Yale, 2009).

59. On this point, see Cooper's introduction to *Colonialism in Question*, esp. 23, 29; and for a more sustained treatment, Stoler, *Along the Archival Grain*.

60. For histories of colonialism and decolonization where Jews are incorporated for significant comparison or relations, see Shepard, *Invention of Decolonization*, chap. 6; and Davidson, *Only Muslim*. For more sustained discussions of Jews along with other groups in the colonial and postcolonial context, see Cole, "Antisémitisme et situation coloniale"; Kimberly Arkin, *Rhinestones, Religion, and the Republic: Fashioning Jewishness in France* (Stanford, CA: Stanford University Press, 2013); Mandel, *Muslims and Jews in France*; Aamir Mufti, *Enlightenment in the Colony: The Jewish Question and the Crisis of Postcolonial Culture* (Princeton, NJ: Princeton University Press, 2007); Katz, *Burdens of Brotherhood*; Gil Anidjar, *The Jew, the Arab: A History of the Enemy* (Stanford, CA: Stanford University Press, 2003); Cheyette, *Diasporas of the Mind*; Rothberg, *Multidirectional Memory*; Schreier, *Arabs of the Jewish Faith*; and Feldman, "Jews and the British Empire, c. 1900."

61. See esp. Cheyette, *Diasporas of the Mind*; Rothberg, *Multidirectional Memory*; and Maxim Silverman, *Palimpsestic Memory: The Holocaust and Colonialism in French and Francophone Fiction and Film* (Oxford: Berghahn, 2013).

62. In these often interrelated fields, see, among others, Davis, *Colonialism, Anti-Semitism*; Annegret Ehmann, "From Colonial Racism to Nazi Population Policy: The Role of the So-Called Mischlinge," in *The Holocaust and History: The Known, The Unknown, The Disputed, and The Reexamined*, ed. Michael Berenbaum and Abraham J. Peck, 115–33 (Bloomington: Indiana University Press, 1998); Eric Ames, Marcia Klotz, and Lora Wildenthal, eds., *Germany's Colonial Pasts* (Lincoln: University of Nebraska Press, 2009); Susannah Heschel, "Revolt of the Colonized: Abraham Geiger's Wissenschaft des Judentums as a Challenge to Christian Hegemony in the Academy," *New German Critique* 77 (Spring–Summer 1999): 61–85; Hess, *Germans, Jews, and the Claims of Modernity*; Isabel Hull, " 'Final Solutions' in the Colonies: The Example of Wilhelmine Germany," in *The Specter of Genocide: Mass Murder in Historical Perspective*, ed. Robert Gellately and Ben Kiernan, 141–61 (Cambridge: Cambridge University Press, 2003); Kalmar and Penslar, *Orientalism and the Jews*; Aziza Khazzoum, "The Great Chain of Orientalism: Jewish Identity, Stigma Management, and Ethnic Exclusion in Israel," *American Sociological Review* 68, no. 4 (2003): 481–510; Suzanne L. Marchand, *German Orientalism in the Age of Empire: Religion, Race and Scholarship* (Cambridge: Cambridge University Press, 2009); Pasto, "Islam's 'Strange Secret Sharers' "; and

Katz, Leff, and Mandel

Achim Rohde, "Der innere Orient: Orientalismus, Antisemitismus und Geschlecht im Deutschland des 18. bis 20. Jahrhunderts," *Die Welt des Islams* 45, no. 2 (2005): 370–411.

63. Efforts to discuss Zionism in comparison with other imperial contexts have only begun recently in earnest. Particularly thoughtful contributions include those in the volume of Caroline Elkins and Susan Pedersen, eds., *Settler Colonialism in the Twentieth Century. Projects, Practices, Legacies* (New York: Routledge, 2005); and the work of Lucy Chester, e.g., "Boundary Commissions as Tools to Safeguard British Interests at the End of Empire," *Journal of Historical Geography* 34, no. 3 (July 2008): 494–515.

64. See Cooper, "States, Empires, and Political Imagination." For salient related arguments about the need to look toward international historical forces and networks as a way to move beyond nationally and locally focused accounts of modern Jewish history, see Abigail Green, "Old Networks, New Connections: The Emergence of the Jewish International," in *Religious Internationals in the Modern World: Globalization and Faith Communities Since 1750,* ed. Abigail Green and Vincent Viaene, 53–81 (Basingstoke: Palgrave Macmillan, 2012).

PART 1

SUBJECTS AND AGENTS

OF EMPIRE

2

THE "ORIENTAL JEWS" OF THE MAGHREB

REINVENTING THE NORTH AFRICAN JEWISH PAST IN THE COLONIAL ERA

Colette Zytnicki

As is well known, the term "Orientalism" has multiple meanings. To start with, it refers to a discipline that studies what Europeans have long termed "the East," and that slowly emerged in major centers of Western thought and culture during the centuries following the Middle Ages. It reached its zenith in the nineteenth century, especially in France, in the Académie des inscriptions et des belles lettres and the Société asiatique, founded in 1822. In this sense, Orientalism comprises scholarly texts, institutions, and researchers. Jewish intellectuals played a significant part in its French version.[1] A second definition, which does not contradict the first, emphasizes the ideological and political aspects of this current. Here one may refer to the works of Edward Said, for whom Orientalism is also a project to impose Western hegemony over the East—first cultural and then political.[2] As he sees it, the object of Orientalism is to lay the groundwork for and then to legitimize the domination of one part of the world by another. It gives rise to biases, prejudices, and preconceived notions and implies a hierarchy of peoples and cultures.

This is not the place to repeat the various criticisms of Said's thesis, especially the short shrift he gives to the Jewish dimension.[3] But we can address the ongoing discussion that bears simultaneously on where Jews fit into Orientalism and on their relationship to the so-called East. For a number of years now these questions have been posed on both sides of the Atlantic. The contributors to a volume edited by Michel Espagne and Perrine Simon-Nahum analyzed the position of Jewish intellectuals in the field of Oriental studies.[4] The earlier work of Ivan Davidson Kalmar and Derek J. Penslar, published in the United States, took up similar questions while also raising another issue: the link to "the East" as it was experienced and formulated by Jews in the nineteenth and twentieth centuries.

Kalmar and Penslar also explored the participation in orientalist thought of scholars from "oriental" lands. The involvement of Jewish intellectuals and scholars in Orientalism was not merely as contributors to the discipline. They also asked, note Kalmar and Penslar, about the allegedly "Eastern" aspect of Jewish identity, seen by many as oriental: "The Jews are identified, both by themselves and by the Western world, with the ancient Israelites who established themselves and the monotheistic tradition, in the same 'oriental' location. It is this latter identification with the biblical lands that allowed Jews to be seen during the centuries as an 'oriental people', a perception challenged only in the twentieth century as the result of Jewish-Arab strife in the Middle East."[5]

The present chapter examimes Jewish scholars' view of the Jews of the Maghreb from the double perspective of Orientalist and Orientalized. In 1830 the colonialist project began efforts to incorporate the Maghreb, heretofore seen as Eastern, into the West. Following the lead of Michel de Certeau, I begin by analyzing what he called places of knowledge: "In history every 'doctrine' which represses its relation to society must be regarded as abstract. . . . 'Scientific' discourse which *does not speak* of its relation to the social 'body' could never establish a practice. It would no longer be scientific. Here I face a question central to the historian's labors. This relation with the social body is specifically the object of history."[6] I ask myself to what extent the academies in Europe and the colonies, as well as the scholarly periodicals associated with them, included Jews as both authors and objects of study in a body of knowledge that can be described as orientalist.

I then proceed to examine the content of this discourse, with the focus on how the Jews of North Africa were perceived. Clearly, these images were multifaceted. What Orient was represented by Maghrebi Jewry? How was its alleged Eastern identity described: as archaism, tradition, renewal, an authentic Judaism preserved from modernity? In their wider conception of North Africa as Eastern, what role did scholars ascribe to the Jews? Were Jews seen as a marginalized people, a civilizing influence, or a bridge (a set of views that could be held in succession or overlap)?

Unlike previous scholarship, I will not focus on texts written in Europe about "Eastern" peoples but on works inspired by the past of the Jews of North Africa and produced in the colonial Maghreb and metropolitan France in the nineteenth and twentieth centuries. A rich if modest historical literature was produced in the century between roughly 1860 and 1960 by scholars who were fascinated by the past of Maghrebi Jewry.[7]

This study makes no pretense of being exhaustive. I pose questions but provide only partial answers. In a word, here I sketch out a few lines for a history that remains to be written.

A History Produced as Part of French Orientalism

L'Académie des inscriptions et des belles lettres

Orientalism emerged as a scholarly discipline at the turn of the nineteenth century.[8] Silvestre de Sacy, one of the first scholars in this field, taught at the École des langues orientales, founded in 1795, held a chair at the Collège de France under the Bourbon Restoration and was one of the founders of the Société asiatique, which rapidly became the crown jewel of research on the Orient. So-called Eastern peoples and their cultures were also central to the work of some members of the Académie des inscriptions et des belles lettres, a prestigious institution founded in 1663. It was there, in 1867, that Ernest Renan established the Collection of Semitic Inscriptions (Corpus inscriptionum semiticarum), which includes Hebrew texts.

One of the students of Renan's successor, Philippe Berger, was responsible for the Maghrebi Jews' discreet penetration of that erudite assembly. Berger began as Renan's secretary and then succeeded him at the Académie des inscriptions et des belles lettres and the Collège de France, where he was installed in the chair in Hebrew in 1910. It was through him that one of his students, Nahum Slouschz, became acquainted with the world of North African Jewry. Born in Vilna in 1872, Slouschz was raised in Odessa, where his family was closely involved in the emerging Hebrew cultural renaissance. His father, a rabbi, was a member of the proto-Zionist Hibbat Ziyyon movement. The young Slouschz visited Palestine multiple times (in 1891–1892 and 1896–1897) before leaving Russia, first for Switzerland and then for France.[9] In 1903, after settling in Paris, he submitted a thesis with the translated title "Renaissance of Hebrew Literature, 1743–1885," still considered a relevant and learned analysis of a field with which he had a deep personal acquaintance.[10]

Sent out by the Moroccan Scientific Mission and supported by Philippe Berger, who provided him with letters of introduction, as well as by the Alliance israélite universelle, Slouschz traveled to Libya in 1905, officially in order to collect Semitic inscriptions.[11] He was led to the question of the origins of the Jews of North Africa, which had not previously been part of his life or scholarly interests: "My studies led me by chance, in 1905, to take up, as a Hebrew scholar under the auspices of the scientific mission of Morocco, the history of the Jews of Morocco. I was struck by the great importance of the problem of the ethnic and historic origin of the various groups of the African Jews."[12] This expedition provided him with material for a number of articles.[13] He returned to North Africa in 1910, on behalf the Institut des inscriptions et des belles lettres, to collect documents about ancient Phoenicia. It was then that he discovered just how much, in his estimation, Carthage owed to ancient Israel.[14] He crossed the Mediterranean again in 1912, funded by the Collection of Semitic Inscriptions, which gave him a grant of 1,500 francs to collect Punic and Hebrew inscriptions, and by the American banker Jacob Schiff, on behalf of the Jewish national cause. Slouschz himself was a member of the Jewish Territorial Organization.[15]

At the same time, Slouschz began work on a thesis about the ancient past of the Jews of North Africa, under the direction of Philippe Berger.[16] This work, which includes many findings open to debate, nevertheless ushered the history of Maghrebi Jewry into the shrine of Orientalism that was the Académie des inscriptions et des belles lettres. It should be noted, too, that Slouschz's unsystematic work and impressionistic and incomplete use of the ancient literature meant that it was unlikely to elicit the emergence of a robust scholarly literature.

The Study of the History of the Jews of North Africa by the Colonial Scholarly Institutions

Although some attention has been paid to the scholarly institutions created by the French in their North African colonies, they have not been sufficiently examined alongside the orientalist current in metropolitan France to permit an accurate assessment of both the links and the differences. One might assume that the scholarly societies established in Algeria were wholly engaged, as institutions, in the field of Orientalism. Their subject, after all, was indeed "the East," now nearby, mundane, domesticated—in a word, colonized. The objective of these academies, which were based on the French model, was to study the peoples and land of Algeria in both their historical and contemporary dimensions. The trans-Mediterranean ties between the colonial institutions and the scientific societies of metropolitan France brought the former into the sphere of Orientalism.

The colonial academies can certainly be seen as a means for controlling the local population, a control exercised by mastery of their past; of their political, judicial, and religious structures; and of their geographic environment. One must, however, go beyond this utilitarian perspective, which, though far from negligible, does not account for the totality of the work by the learned societies of Algeria. The expropriation of ancient and medieval relics—Pagan, Christian, and Muslim[17]—was part and parcel of the emergence of a scholarly discipline focused on the colonial societies and drew on the same process as the colonizers' symbolic appropriation of the land. The country's past became the colonizers' own; its monuments became part of their national heritage. The members of the colonial academies were viewed as local scholars who embarked on the study of their own towns and regions. This movement can be compared to another process that was in progress at the time: the civilizing mission that the Jews of France assumed with regard to their co-religionists. Consistories based on the French model were created in Algeria in 1845. Rabbis trained in the purest French Jewish mold were sent out to persuade the Jews of Algeria that they had to change and assimilate into the world of the occupiers.

The writings of Abraham Cahen and Maurice Eisenbeth lie precisely at the intersection of these different currents: Orientalism, the symbolic seizure of the Algerian past, and the assimilationist thrust, as expressed by one of the new colonial academies in Algeria. The Archaeological Society of Constantine, of which both were members, was founded in 1852 at the initiative of Léon Rénier and Colonel Creully, the director of fortifications. It focused on the history of the Oran region, and its members were learned "Europeans" (in the sense given to the term in those days), with very few Jews or Muslims among them. The institution managed to achieve some renown. Stéphane Gsell, a specialist in ancient North Africa, was a member from 1892; André Cagnat, Gabriel Esquer, and Georges Marçais and his brother William were members in 1934. All of them were affiliated with the Académie des inscriptions et des belles lettres. They and others constituted a bridge between Orientalism in metropolitan France and the scholarly institutions of the colonies.

This was the setting in which Abraham Cahen wrote the first comprehensive history of the Jews of North Africa. Cahen was born in 1831 to a leading Jewish family of Metz. After completing his studies in the lycée, he attended the rabbinical college in his hometown between 1852 and 1858. After being profoundly shaped by the French Judaism of the metropole, Cahen received a rabbinic pulpit in Constantine in 1863 and was named chief rabbi of the town in 1867.[18] In 1877 he was called to Algiers. His political stands and relations with the local religious authorities triggered a number of conflicts in which he clashed with the Jewish notables of Constantine and Algiers. The resulting outcry eventually forced him to resign his position in 1880. Thus we have an idea of his personality: a learned and a fierce defender of the French brand of Judaism, which he wanted to inculcate—perhaps with a certain degree of condescension—into the local elites, who sometimes resisted him.[19] Admitted to the Archaeological Society of Constantine, Cahen mixed with the local scholarly community, sharing its curiosity about the past of a country that was both foreign—he had only recently taken up residence there—and close at the same time, because it had in the meantime become French soil. Cahen's studies are part of this scholarly appropriation of the colonial worlds and territories, in which true curiosity and the urge to dominate are inextricably mixed. Received with the honors associated with his position as senior rabbi of a major community, Cahen participated fully in the activities of educated society in Constantine. In 1866, he published his first contribution to its bulletin, *Recueil des notices et mémoires de la province de Constantine*; his history of the Jews of North Africa came out in 1867.[20]

Maurice Eisenbeth began his study of local history in the same society. Born in Paris in 1883, Eisenbeth attended the rabbinical seminary there between 1902 and 1908. After serving as rabbi of Sedan before the First World War, he became rabbi of Constantine in 1928 and chief rabbi of Algiers in 1932. Like Cahen before him, he belonged to the Archaeological Society of Constantine. He was welcomed into its ranks in 1931 by its president, who addressed his cordial greetings to "M. Eisenbeth, recently admitted as a member of our society. M. Eisenbeth, by his general culture and profound knowledge of Semitic languages, will certainly render very appreciable services to the archaeological society."[21]

Thus, the history of the Jews of North Africa occupied a place, albeit limited, in the Algerian colonial institutions that were engaged in a utilitarian Orientalism (whose purpose was to enhance the control of the local population by means of an inventory of their culture and history), one that was both scholarly and identity-based. The meager share of attention accorded to the Jews certainly coincided with the space the French authorities conceded to them: an inevitable recognition of their presence along with a desire to limit their influence.

Jews in the Scholarly Institutions of Morocco

In Morocco, the interest in Jews was more sustained. It is evident in the work of the Scientific Mission, established in 1903, before the political colonization of the kingdom. From the later nineteenth century, Morocco was an object of especially strong curiosity, which, as was the rule in the colonial world, mingled scientific with political interests and collective with personal ambitions. Its objective, as defined by the mission's founder, Alfred Le Châtelier, was clear. As he explained it to the institution's first director, Georges Salmon, the objective was to collect masses of materials, the "documentation of details," without preconceived notions or a premature desire to synthesize, in order "to lay the basis for an indigenous policy."[22] It was the Berbers who most interested French scholars then, but they also encountered Jews who shared a presumed Eastern origin, religious rituals, and sometimes even common language with their Muslim neighbors. Thus we can understand how, while studying the Berbers, scholars frequently found themselves facing the mystery of the ancient Jews.

The *Revue du monde musulman* provides evidence of this interest. Established in 1906 under the auspices of the Moroccan Scientific Mission, and claiming to be "neither Orientalist nor colonialist," the periodical, whose focus was the social and political study of Islam, had a target that extended beyond the Maghreb.[23] It set itself the goal of being the most important scholarly journal about a Muslim world that stretched from North Africa to Central Asia and China. It was interested in peoples' past as much as in contemporary political stakes. And, most astonishingly, it allotted significant space to the Jews. Slouschz, who made early contact with the Scientific Mission, played an important role in this. His contributions to the periodical were quite diverse. They included frequent studies on the lot of the Jews in the Near and Middle East and extensive attention to the Maghreb. One type of contribution he made consisted of accounts of his expeditions across North Africa. They offer descriptions, some of them still useful today, of regions that remain little known to Westerners.[24] For example, he turned one trip to Tripolitania in 1906 into an article. What is interesting here, more than the scientific aspect, is his portrait of Jewish cave dwellers. It was deep in the mountains that Slouschz discovered the descendants of the original African Jews of whom he dreamed: "But in the *haras* [Jewish quarters] of small towns where the European penetration has not yet been felt, you might think you were in a ghetto of the Middle Ages; whereas in the mountains, the African Jew, often victimized by the Muslims, resists with greater physical and moral energy. Their villages of cave dwellers or mountain men recall a distant past, whose significance is demonstrated by the abundant ruins. They are also evidence of the vitality of the indigenous element of the Jewish population."[25]

Two of Slouschz's articles of a different kind are devoted to persons who resembled him in some respects. The first is about Samuel Romanelli, a young Italian Jew, born in Mantua, Italy, in 1757, who spent time in Morocco in the late eighteenth century: "Morocco in the Eighteenth Century: The Memoir of a Contemporary, Samuel Romanelli."[26] Describing Romanelli's text as "the best documented, the best observed, and especially the most vivid account we have for the eighteenth century," Slouschz summarizes the work in his typical fashion— a bit sketchily.[27] It is remarkable how closely he identifies with the young Italian scholar. Like Romanelli, he was an outside observer of the Moroccan Jews, who fascinated him at the same time as they amazed and even repelled him. Slouschz had the same troubling experience of being immersed in a world that was simultaneously strange and near. The main difference is that, unlike Romanelli, Slouschz had a certain legitimacy that came with having been officially invited by the colonial authorities. This meant that he stayed on the right side of the social and political barrier (or at least he thought he did): thanks to his links with the Moroccan Scientific Mission and the Académie des inscriptions et des belles lettres, he was affiliated with the future tutelary power in Morocco.

Somewhat later, Slouschz planned a study about an explorer whose works had not been translated into French: "Moses Edrehi, a Moroccan scholar, 1760(?)–1840"—another precursor who could have been his Moroccan twin.[28] Edrehi, born in the Draa Valley around 1760, was educated in Fez and other places in Morocco. After applying himself to "modern languages" he set off for Amsterdam, where he pursued advanced studies in Kabbalah and Hebrew and mastered French, German, English, Spanish, and other languages. He traveled throughout Europe and settled for a time in Paris. There he met Silvestre de Sacy in 1814, became the Arabic interpreter for the local prefect (who was Persian), and joined several scholarly institutes. He pursued a dream shared with so many others before and after him, that of finding the remnants of the lost tribes of Israel.[29] He recorded this quest in the *Book of Miracles*, published in Hebrew in 1818. Later Edrehi crossed the channel to England, where he found employment as a teacher of oriental languages and translated his book into English.[30] This picturesque character resonated with Slouschz, who could not avoid reading his study about lost Jews as a sort of prefiguration of his own quest in North Africa.

An excursion to Debdou in the early 1910s provided the occasion for one of Slouschz's most interesting articles in the *Revue du monde musulman*.[31] In this sociohistoric study, based on field research and abundant literary documentation, he traced the story of the local Jews and left us with a good description, painted from everyday life, of a time when the Westernization process promoted by the colonizer and the Alliance schools had not yet made serious inroads.

Slouschz's involvement with the *Revue du monde musulman* was substantial. It epitomized what became his primary fixation, the desire to demonstrate the Jews' ancient and legitimate presence in North Africa. In a publication devoted essentially to the Muslim world, the past and present of Jews living in Islamic lands found its place through the evocation of several episodes, major figures, and symbolic places of Jewish history.

Hespéris: Archives berbères et bulletin de l'Institut des hautes études marocaines was the other crown jewel of the French cultural presence in Morocco. Founded in 1921, it was the journal of the Institute of Higher Moroccan Studies, itself founded shortly before then, in February 1920, under the auspices of the French authorities in Morocco. Articles about the Jews were fairly common. They covered diverse areas such as history and anthropology, and their authors, too, were of diverse origins, both Jewish and non-Jewish. The former included representatives of what one might call the nomadic Jewish intelligentsia that found a new role in colonial Morocco as interpreters or as headmasters of the Alliance schools.

One of these was Yomtob Semach. Born in Bulgaria in 1868, he taught in Beirut and Baghdad before reaching Morocco, where he served as inspector of the Alliance schools between 1915 and 1939. He contributed two signed articles to *Hespéris*. The first is a biography of the person who guided Charles de Foucauld during his expedition to Morocco, Rabbi Mordechai Aby Serour.[32] At the time, the rabbi was known to the public at large only through the portrait, often far from flattering, painted by the French explorer, who covered up the flamboyant personality worthy of the hero of a picaresque novel. In the second article, Semach presents *Yahas Fez*, a chronicle by Rabbi Abner Hassarfaty.[33] This text serves as a sort of bridge between ancient memorial traditions, rabbinic genealogies, and modern intellectual curiosity. Reissued in the late nineteenth century, the chronicle was the fruit of a European tour by two Moroccan rabbis, Haim Cohen and Jacob Benzimra, in 1878. These emissaries of Moroccan Jewry wrote down the questions they were asked by senior figures of the Alliance, by the chief rabbi of France, and by various English personalities whom they met later in London. When they got back home, the two commissioned Rabbi Hassarfaty, known for his wisdom and erudition, to provide an exhaustive response to a questionnaire drawn up by the Alliance. This work, in Hebrew, consists of a rather short section about the major traits of the Fez community, followed by the genealogy of its rabbis and illustrious families. It concludes with observations about popular culture and valuable information about conditions in the mellah in the 1870s. After describing this text, Semach offers only a summary and a few excerpts from it, in French translation.

Scholars were also sensitive to the changes in Jewish life in the colonial era. The cultural modes that the colonists and the teachers of the Alliance brought with them to Morocco disrupted ancestral rites and customs. Some traditions seemed to be disappearing right before the eyes of contemporary observers. A number of ethnological studies sought to keep them alive in the collective memory. One such is a 1923 article by Ruben Tadjouri, "Jewish Marriage in Salé."[34] Such accounts of wedding ceremonies, with their element of exoticism and unfamiliarity for Westerners, both Jewish and non-Jewish, are a commonplace of travel literature. This article, though, is of a different sort. Extremely detailed, and reporting on the rites of betrothal and the wedding itself, it also provides relevant information about rabbinic law, collected from the works of Chief Rabbi Abraham Encaoua.[35] Tadjouri, like Semach, was employed by the Alliance. Born in Libya in 1895, he began teaching at the Alliance school in Meknes in 1914. From 1919 to 1926 he served as headmaster of the school in Salé, and then of the school in Casablanca. Like Semach, he rose up through the ranks of the organization until, in 1940, he became the Alliance's senior representative in Morocco. Native to North Africa and Westernized by his education, he was acutely sensitive to the disappearance of the ancient traditions:

> In all that follows, we will try to depict the various Jewish wedding ceremonies as they took place a decade or so ago, because, since the French occupation, the contact with European elements and the education provided by the school has had an increasing impact on customs. The ancient traditions are gradually being abandoned and usages that are centuries old are increasingly giving way to a timid, awkward, and ridiculous

parody of European customs. Day by day, the variegated scenes of Jewish life in Salé are losing the originality and picturesque nature that gave them their charm and interest for foreign observers. It has become urgent to note down the most typical details of these customs, inasmuch as it is probable that within a few years not the slightest trace of them will remain.[36]

Thus the "Eastern identity" of the Jews of the Maghreb was threatened by the Westernization that followed in the wake of colonization. It was left to Jewish scholars, themselves of Eastern origin, to preserve them in ethnographical texts. This was also the goal of three articles that appeared somewhat later: "Judeo-Arabic Texts from Fez," by Louis Brunot and Élie Malka (1932); and, by Brunot alone, "Notes on the Arabic Dialect of the Jews of Fez" (1936) and "Judeo-Arabic Proverbs from Fez" (1937).[37] The collaboration between Brunot and Malka was fruitful. The former played an important role in the scholarly world of colonial Morocco. After he submitted his thesis, "The Sea in the Traditions and Industries of Rabat and Salé," in Algiers in 1920, the young graduate was sent to Morocco, where he found employment in the civil service. There he met Malka, a student (and later teacher) of Moroccan affairs at the Institut des hautes études marocaines.

In Morocco, the Jews, their past, and their customs became part of colonial Orientalism by means of scholarly journals whose contributors included well-known Orientalists such as Évariste Lévi-Provençal and Émile Laoust, colonial civil servants and teachers in Alliance schools. The space allotted to studies of the Jews stemmed not only from the many persons who knew how to turn them into objects of research but also from the colonizers' interest in the Berbers. That is, French researchers were most interested in studying the Berbers, for not only political reasons (strategies of divide-and-rule) but also scholarly ones. Along the way, however, they could not help but discover Jews who shared with their Muslim neighbors presumed "oriental" origins, piety, and even sometimes a common language. While researching Berbers, scholars thus encountered numerous times the distant and recent past of the Jews of Morocco.

The Eastern Identity of the Maghrebi Jews

If it is undeniable that, due to their geography and the way of life that they shared to a large extent with their Muslim neighbors, North African Jews were in some sense intrinsically different from their French co-religionists, that difference still must be defined. One can put the question differently: In what way were the Jews of the Maghreb perceived, and how did they perceive themselves, as "Eastern"?

Zytnicki

North African Jews' self-perception as "Eastern" may be rooted in their more distant past. This raises the issue of the origins of the Jews of the Maghreb: Are they descended from peoples who migrated from the Near East? Or are they Berbers who converted to Judaism at some point in history? The question remains controversial today in the popular milieu, and I will not resolve it here.[38] Our interest is in trying to understand the political and cultural issues at stake during the colonial period. For, beyond the simple historical enigma, something else is at play here. The assertion of a Near Eastern origin is a source of legitimacy and prestige in the eyes of the Jews of the West as well as of the local Muslims, for whom the Near East is the absolute reference point as the source of the Prophet's message and the original home of the Arabs.

Since the eighteenth century much of both Europe and the Islamic world have believed that civilization was born in the East, the cradle of all civilized societies.[39] The earliest French authors who wrote about the history of Algeria had no doubt that the peoples of Africa originated in the Palestinian East. This belief was reinforced by a whole series of legends and interpretations of the sacred texts. The popular accounts traced the roots of the indigenous peoples of North Africa to a very distant period. The Ghriba Synagogue in Djerba, revered by the Jews of Tunisia, is supposed to have been built by exiles that arrived on African shores after the destruction of the First Temple.[40] Myths of this kind were not specific to the Jews: the Berbers were quite happy to see themselves as descended from the Philistines. The local legends collected by René Basset exemplify this.[41] The belief in a Near Eastern origin was also prominent in the Muslim historical tradition. Ibn Khaldun, often quoted, holds that the Berbers are "the children of Canaan, the son of Ham, the son of Noah. . . . They received Judaism from their powerful neighbors, the Israelites of Syria."[42] It seems, then, that for the peoples of North Africa, both Jews and Berbers, the search for their roots led them to claim the eastern littoral of the Mediterranean as their birthplace. In the rivalry of memories, in the claim to an ancient lineage as the basis for legitimacy and prestige, the wellspring was necessarily in the East, between the river Jordan and the Mediterranean.

The Bible, too, seemed to provide indirect corroboration of the notion of the long-ago origins of the Jews and Berbers of North Africa. Nineteenth-century scholars began poring over the sacred texts, looking for a reference to Carthage that would support the partisans of a Jewish presence in Africa in very distant times. The antiquity of a Jewish presence in North Africa was also treated in the Talmudic literature, which was familiar with Roman Carthage, whose large Jewish population maintained active contacts with Palestine. According to

André Chouraqui, "a Talmudic text, considered to be ancient by the second-century Tosefta, speaks of the migration to Africa of the Girgashites, one of the seven nations of Canaan, in the time of Joshua: 'The Girgashites rose and left of their own accord, and as a reward there was given them a land as good as their own land . . . [in] Africa.'"[43] Both the Jerusalem Talmud and the Babylonian Talmud mention sages who were born in the Punic capital.[44] We know also that Rabbi Akiva spent time in Africa in the second century, as did Rabbi Levi at an unknown date.[45] The Jerusalem Talmud, whose final redaction was in the fourth century, mentions several African rabbis by name (Abba, Adda, Aha, Hanna, and Isaac).[46] The Talmudic sages counted Carthage as among the largest cities in the world. Nineteenth-century authors also cited classical Jewish and Christian authors, such as Flavius Josephus, Eusebius, and Procopius, all of whom believed in the Eastern origins of the Jews of North Africa.

Thus, diverse elements—popular legends as well as biblical and Talmudic texts—handed down among all the ethnic groups in North Africa led to the linkage of the history of both the Jews of North Africa and the Berbers to the far-off East. Edmond Pellissier de Reynaud, in his *Annales algériennes*, held this to be unquestioned, quoting Leo Africanus and "knowledgeable" rabbis. Didn't the Jews refer to the Kabyles as "Philistines" and say that the Moazabites were descended from the Moabites, the offspring of Lot's incest with his daughter? Pellissier did not challenge either the popular legends or the biblical tales and concluded: "The many centuries that separate us from the era in which we place the migration of the Moazabites are no reason to reject the proofs we have discovered for the Asiatic origins of this tribe. Ultimately, it is no more extraordinary to find this small group in Africa than to see the Jews, their ancient persecutors, there. We can thus regard the Canaanites' migration to Africa as factual."[47]

The linkage of Berbers to Philistines and of North African Jews to Hebrews was challenged in the early twentieth century by Stéphane Gsell, who saw them as fabrications by Jewish or Latin authors.[48] Nevertheless, the power of these legends and the authority of ancient and medieval rabbis obliged scholars of the colonial period to substantiate or refute their predecessors' interpretations.

This search for ancestors lies at the heart of Slouschz's work and is prominent in the two theses he submitted in 1909: *Hébraeo-Phéniciens: Introduction à l'histoire des origines de la colonisation hébraïque dans les pays méditerranéens* and *Judéo-Hellènes et Judéo-Berbères: Recherches sur les origines des Juifs et du judaïsme en Afrique*.[49] Slouschz proposes a definitive answer to the question of the ancient origins of the Jews of North Africa and describes the migrations that propelled peoples from the East to the West, from Asia to Africa.

He begins with the point that ancient peoples were themselves mixtures of diverse groups, preserving, in a fragmentary way, an echo of the earliest civilizations. After reviewing the Protosemitic invasions, Slouschz brings on stage a strange group whom he calls the "Hebraeo-Phoenicians," produced by the mixing of all the various groups that lived on the eastern shore of the Mediterranean. The divorce between Melkart (the Phoenicians) and Jehovah (the Hebrews) took place after this age, but some vestiges of the two peoples' former unity remained. These traces were especially prominent (according to Slouschz) in the Tyrian colonies, which were not Phoenician but Hebraeo-Phoenician. His second point is that the founders of Carthage were the heirs of a Semitic civilization common to the Hebrews and the Phoenicians. For him, given the intermixing of peoples, the settlement of Jewish colonists in the Maghreb, carried with the current of Hebraeo-Phoenician civilization, is plausible. This leads to a double conclusion: first, that the Hebrews and Phoenicians shared a common civilization; second, that Jews did indeed migrate to Carthage, but Greek observers failed to note their presence because of the closeness of the two cultures.

Slouschz further developed this theme in an article published in the *Revue tunisienne*, "The Hebrew and Phoenician Civilization of Carthage."[50] Here he tried to demonstrate the likelihood of a Jewish presence in ancient Carthage, despite the silence of classical sources on the subject. Jerusalem and Carthage are two branches of the same tree, whose roots are Hebrew. The goal is less to discover whether there were Jews in Carthage than to estimate the Jewish content of the Punic civilization. He considers the conclusion to be indisputable: both Jews and Berbers descend from ancient immigrants from the East and have equal grounds for claiming a millennial presence in North Africa:

> Those Jews whom African folklore has associated with the destiny of the Berber race since earliest antiquity still exist today and can be found in the fellahin of the Atlas Mountains and among the nomads of the Sahara. With their physical and moral character and their syncretistic beliefs, which bear the traces of all the primitive or sectarian forms of Judaism that have since disappeared, they serve as a pendant to the Berber race itself, it too the result of a mixture of conquering races, both sedentary and nomadic, that passed in several stages from the coasts of the Red Sea to the West and North Africa.[51]

The Judeo-Berbers are supposed to have preserved traces of primordial Judaism, whose imprint Slouschz sought out in cemeteries, language, and customs. He held that they were among the most ancient peoples of Africa:

> What we sought to demonstrate is the three-thousand-year-old relationship that can be found among the three Hebraic races on African soil; the survival of the races that came from both the Red Sea and the Mediterranean; it is their civilizing role in the northern countries as well as among the Berbers that we have demonstrated. Canaanites, Hebraeo-Phoenicians, Hebrews, Judeo-Arameans, Judeo-Hellenes, Judeo-Romans, converts to Judaism, Judeo-Berbers, Judeo-Arabs—this is the genealogy that

underlies our study: This human amalgamation, which reached its apogee with [the Berber queen] Kahina, who epitomizes the epic of the African homeland, is the most indigenous and African of all.[52]

The Eastern origin of the Jews of North Africa, proclaimed by local legends and internal authors, exercised a seductive power on Jewish historians. Slouschz's hypothesis was adopted, with reservations, by Rabbi Eisenbeth, far from a specialist on the subject. The notion makes it possible to affirm the continuity of the Jewish people, who, though scattered and dispersed, nevertheless survive across the centuries and continents. But it also provides a weighty argument to support the claim of a presence in North Africa at least as ancient as the Berbers' and in any case antedating the Arabs'. The Jews, who originated in the East, can thus be viewed as one of the oldest elements of the Maghrebi population.

European Jews' Perceptions of North African Jews

Whether or not authors were persuaded of the Eastern origins of the Jews of North Africa, they certainly held them to be oriental with regard to their lifestyle and culture. How did Western Jews perceive their co-religionists on the other side of the Mediterranean in the late eighteenth and early nineteenth centuries, when Western eyes were fixed on the East and, as a corollary of the Enlightenment, peoples were ranked by their degree of civilization? Did they share their non-Jewish European compatriots' condescension for the peoples of the Maghreb?

For a partial answer to this question, we can consider a book by Samuel Romanelli. Romanelli was one of the intellectuals who took part in the Haskalah in the eighteenth century. Endowed with a solid traditional education in his hometown, which was a major Jewish intellectual center at the time, he also had the benefit of a sterling secular education. An excellent linguist, Romanelli was led by his love for English literature to translate Alexander Pope's *Essay on Man* into Hebrew. He left Italy and discovered France, the Netherlands, Germany, and England, where he mixed with Jewish Enlightenment circles. When a local merchant asked Romanelli to accompany him on a trip to Morocco, Romanelli embarked on an adventure he could not have imagined: Thinking he would be away for several months, he stayed in Morocco for four years. He met curious individuals, lost his job, and gained the favors of an important personage. In his book *Travail in an Arab Land*, Romanelli combines an account of his adventures with profound reflections about Moroccan society.

Romanelli spent four years living among the Jews of Morocco. Initially employed by a merchant from Gibraltar, he subsequently entered the service of a court Jew and frequented the circles of the wealthy traders of the coastal towns.

Zytnicki

He traveled throughout the country, residing in Tetouan, Meknes, Marrakesh, and Mogador. He frequented diverse circles: the rich Jewish merchants whom he served, the scholars in yeshivot with whom he conducted learned disputes, and the wives and daughters of houses that offered their hospitality. His friends were Jews as well as Christians. On the other hand, although he knew Arabic— he went to the schools to learn the literary language and spent time in the marketplace to master the vernacular—he felt no attraction to the Muslim world, which he scorned, and whose oppression of the Jews he decried.

His feelings about his co-religionists were somewhat ambiguous. On the one hand, he praised their fine qualities: "They are good-hearted folk, charitable and hospitable to strangers. They honor the Torah and study it. They hold the European Jews who come there in high esteem and call them 'freemen.' "[53] Aware of the abuse he encountered when he wore Jewish garb—which he did not always do—he felt genuine sympathy for all Jewish Moroccans. But he was not naïve. He paints a pitiless and harsh portrait of his employer, a court Jew— corrupt, cruel to his family, and spineless vis-à-vis the sultan—who ultimately converted to Islam in 1790 during a period of persecutions. Romanelli, a man of the Enlightenment and fully enlisted on the side of education, the source of essential progress, was pained by the backwardness of Moroccan co-religionists. He recognized their undeniable piety and deep knowledge of sacred texts but reproached them for their more or less voluntary enclosure in an outmoded perception of the world and of knowledge: "The sciences are too lofty for them. Their ignorance is bliss, for they say that many victims have been thrown into the pits of heresy and atheism by science. The light of knowledge does not shine upon them, nor has it even reached them until now to eradicate their moral failings and their immature vanities. A veil of obscurantist faith corrupts their hearts and blinds their eyes."[54]

In a discourse full of rhetoric and philosophy, Romanelli condemns his co-religionists' "superstitions" and sometimes makes fun of them, but he always engages them in dialogue. Invited to deliver sermons in a yeshiva, he offers a defense of a symbiosis of Jewish culture and secular culture: "They tested my vision. And how did I reply? By bringing counsels of old. By expounding at length on the fundamental sciences. By confirming each biblical verse I cited on the basis of a philosophical theory and each philosophical theory on the basis of a scriptural verse. In one instance, I cited Plato to elucidate Moses. In another, I showed that Moses' teachings were found in Socrates."[55]

Still, he did not despise his Moroccan co-religionists, whose lot he shared whenever he had to wear their garments. One day, having been struck by an Arab in the street he reacted: "My heart flared within me, and I looked daggers at him. The voice of my vengeance's blood cried out to me from shame. Nevertheless, I remained silent and controlled myself, because my Jewish clothes were my bit and bridle restraining me."[56]

Romanelli's perspective is both external (he was an educated European Jew) and internal because for a time he shared the life of the Jews of Morocco. He was simultaneously rather condescending toward his co-religionists, whom he considered to be backward, and curious about the civilization that he found both foreign and close. Thus, Romanelli evinces an orientalist mindset, in Said's sense of the term, but also perceives a deep nobility, culture, and religious faith in this obscurantist Orient.

The same ambiguity marks the Ashkenazi rabbis Cahen and Eisenbeth. They viewed the Jewish world they visited and whose history they recounted as ossified by centuries of darkness. For both of them, ever since the end of the first millennium the vitality of the Jewish world has come exclusively from the West. According to Cahen, for example, the Jewish emigrants from Spain at the end of the Middle Ages provided the impetus for the rehabilitation of the backward and enervated Jews of the East. The Spanish Jews "brought with them, not only their fortunes, but also their intelligence, their science, their talent for commerce and industry."[57] He depicts them as the precursors of the French colonial occupation, the first European penetration of an Orient that had been sleeping for more than two centuries. Eisenbeth, too, in his *Le Judaïsme nordafricain: Études démographiques sur les Israélites du département de Constantine*, proposed a fairly traditional view of a North African Jewry that had reached its zenith in tenth-century Kairouan and Fez, before sinking into a deep decline.[58] He portrays a society that is willfully superstitious, uncultured, and backward. On two occasions, however, this Eastern world had had a growth spurt: when rabbinic Judaism was spread through the region by "emissaries from Palestine" and again with the arrival of the Jews from Spain in the sixteenth century.[59] But these two episodes "did not produce a deep regeneration of the primitive Judaism."[60] For both Cahen and Eisenbeth, from the European Middle Ages on, all vitality was to be found in the West. The colonial project enabled the revival of a Jewry that was imprisoned in its Oriental shell.

The same point of view was adopted by the Alliance, which, even before France took control of Tunisia and Morocco, aimed to bring the seeds of a renaissance to the Jews of the region by bringing them into contact with Western modernity.[61] The theses defended by the Alliance in this regard are well known:

> What was, what is the goal of the Alliance when it endows primary schools in the communities of the Near East and Africa? First of all, it is to bring a ray of Western civilization to places that have degenerated over centuries of oppression and ignorance; next, by providing the children with the elements of a basic and rational education, to help them find occupations that are more secure and less undignified than

peddling; finally, by opening their minds to Western ideas, to destroy certain prejudices and certain outmoded superstitions that have paralyzed the communities' activity and expansion.[62]

This orientalist attitude is apparent in the writing of a young Jewish woman,
Louise Bornstein, who was sent out from France to teach in Tunisia in the 1890s.
In her first years on the job, there was a total separation between her world and
that of her pupils: "It seems that there had never been [any school], so deep was
the Jews' barbarism, so little awakened their minds, so rare any delicate sentiments. Far from finding anything original in them, an individuality deserving to
be preserved, . . . what I see in them now is hypocrisy, baseness, insolence. Their
faults leap out at you; their good qualities, not at all. The only way we can achieve
anything is by teaching them, by inspiring them to want to live as human beings, to
have human sentiments."[63] She would have to acquire greater familiarity with the
place before she could understand her Tunisian co-religionists and recognize
their good qualities.

The Jews, a "Bridge between East and West"?

In his *Study of the History of Jews and Judaism in Morocco*, Slouschz views the
North African Jewish world with an orientalist eye.[64] He always sees the Muslim
influence as negative; for him, it connotes ignorance and barbarism. By contrast,
all enlightenment comes from Europe: in the past, it was brought by the refugees
from Spain; more recently, by the French, through the Alliance and the colonial
administration. There cannot be any exchanges between the Muslim world and
the West. On the contrary, Slouschz sees an irreducible opposition between
them, which is one reason why the Jews of northern Morocco never assimilated
among their neighbors. Like the overwhelming majority of his fellow Europeans, he had no doubts as to the superiority of European civilization and its mission to educate the peoples of the south, and attempted to demonstrate this in
his study of the Jews of Morocco.

Between the "Judeo-Berbers," as Slouschz called them, who lived in the
southern part of Morocco and shared the lifestyle and language of their Berber
neighbors, and the Jews of the coastal regions, whom he also referred to as the
"Roumi" (the term that the Jews and the Muslims of Morocco applied to their
European co-religionists), he constructed a scale that ranged from backwardness
to civilization.[65] He saw the Jews of Spanish origin as the elite because of their
European identity. They had retained something of Spain in themselves, and,
according to Slouschz, had never mixed with the local Jews (an assertion refuted
by recent scholarship). They were already ripe for the colonial adventure:

They have much in common with Europeans, and especially with what is often called the Mediterranean race: the same surprising faculty for assimilation, a certain mental agility, a more or less obvious indifference to questions of a religious and national order, customs that are often more lenient that those of other Jews, well-developed commercial skills, and a ready tendency to migrate. All these characteristics, which have been heightened since the opening of the Alliance schools, in combination with the waning of their religious sentiments, make the Spanish Jews in Morocco an intermediary not only between the Europeans and the natives, but also with their coreligionists of the interior. The latter will be the first to profit from the benefits of the European penetration and to contribute to the revival of Judaism.[66]

But behind this colonialist declaration, both sincere and inevitable, we must also note the seductive power that the Judeo-Berbers exercised on Slouschz, because he believed they preserved the most ancient heritage of the Jewish people.

In addition to this hierarchy of the different Jewish groups living in Morocco at the start of the twentieth century, which ranks them by the extent of their acculturation to the Western world, Slouschz also underscores their role in Eastern societies. For him, they always play a basic and special function. They partially assimilated with the peoples among whom they lived, such as the Phoenicians, the Romans, and the Berbers, but always maintained their religious identity and transmitted it to their descendants. Always integrating with the dominant group, they played a civilizing role par excellence. Here we come to a unique element of the Eastern identity of the Jews of the Maghreb (and perhaps of the East), as highlighted in the literature we have been looking at. Considered to be the privileged brokers between peoples, they are seen as the specific vectors of the encounter between West and East. This is the role that Cahen and Eisenbeth assigned them for the end of the Middle Ages, when the Jews of Spain took up residence in North Africa and inspired the locals with new life from the West. It is also the function they assigned them in the colonial period. The Jews of North Africa are held to be the best intermediaries between the Arab–Muslim world and the colonizers. This refers to the situation of some of the Jewish elite in Algeria at the start of the French occupation.[67] But it also represents a political stand taken by these authors, who are French Jews imbued with the idea of the civilizing mission of France. The rabbis assume the challenge of westernizing the Jews of Algeria and supporting the home country in its civilizational tasks.[68] The Moroccan-born David Cazès, the first headmaster of an Alliance school in Tunis and author of a history of the Jews in Tunisia, states this explicitly: "Of all the indigenous subjects, [the Jews] are the element that finds it easiest to assimilate; they possess the capital and the commerce of the Regency; they are the most intelligent and most active element of the population, and it is on them that

France can count to introduce its language, its spirit, and its civilization to the Tunisian population."[69]

The Return to the East

The Jews' role as civilizing agents and intermediaries between peoples was highlighted by André Chouraqui, who raised this notion to its greatest prominence in the 1950s. It features centrally in his first study of the history of the Jews of the Maghreb, described as an "advance towards the West" not only by the Jews but by all the peoples of North Africa. In this progression, the Jews, located between the Westerners and the Arabs, played the role of a bridge and catalyzed the movement. Chouraqui's evaluation of the colonial period is complex and has to be placed in the proper context. The Algerian Jewish elite wanted to maintain a levelheaded stance in the conflict that, at first politically and later military, tore the country apart. Caught between the nationalist claims of the Muslims and the colonialist discourse, they tried to propose a solution that could reconcile these contradictory interests: the extension of full political rights and civic equality to all inhabitants of Algeria, without exception, in which that country, like metropolitan France, would remain loyal to its aspirations for liberty.

A son of the Enlightenment, Chouraqui writes of the "French project" to which, he says, the "rebirth of this country" must be ascribed: "When the French arrived, the Jews, heirs to the longest African tradition, had been reduced, in varying degrees, to the condition of serfdom in the former feudal society. From one day to the next, as if by magic, they found themselves freed from the excesses of their servitude and able to fully adhere to a new order, whose conquest nevertheless did not take place without serious effort."[70]

The book concludes with an analysis of African Judaism, attracted to mysticism, imbued simultaneously with Arabo-Berber influences and the culture of the Spanish exiles, totally distinct from the North African civilization with which it shared the cult of saints and superstitions, languages, and everything that was the deep content of a life that had been so long intermingled. In brief, they were a people who seemed to embody many characteristics of the so-called Orient. Although the French colonization had put an end to legal discrimination against the Jews, their situation remained precarious in the Maghreb of the 1950s. In a colonial empire then in turmoil, they found themselves pulled between a ruling power that continued to marginalize them and the rising nationalist forces, hesitant about what place to allow the Jews in the state they were demanding. The advent of modernity had not been without risks; it could be the road toward assimilation and forgetting the past, self-renunciation, departure for

France or Israel. Although still on a limited scale in 1952, these movements imperiled all Jews. Subsequent events belied the prophecy: when he wrote his book, Chouraqui could not imagine that North African Jewry would soon be extinct.[71] On the contrary, he saw it as destined to play a major role, thanks to its position as an intermediary in a Maghreb that was in the midst of a great transformation:

> We have often noted, in the course of our studies, how the Jewish community is located between the Muslims and the Europeans in every respect; it holds this intermediate position even in its demographic structures. It is the fundamental law of its constitution and evolution. Transferred to the social plane, this position, so often thankless, could become fruitful or even redemptive. From the political perspective, the Jews are a negligible force in North Africa. But their role could be decisive in the sense that they seem to be designated by nature to fill a necessary mediating function. In all their activities they can attempt, in concert with all men of good will, Muslims and Christians, to create a link that will make it possible to find new paths on which North Africa can find its salvation.[72]

After history proved him wrong—and, in any case, after he chose to relocate to Israel in the late 1950s—Chouraqui came to see matters differently. In the revised edition of his work, published in 1987, he assigned a totally different direction to Jewish destiny. The call of the West is no longer inexorably marked in the destiny of North African Jewry. On the contrary, their entry in the thickness of time must be understood as a pendulum swinging between East and West:

> The historian observes the facts: The Jews arrived in North Africa in the second half of the first millennium before the Christian era, borne in the wake of the first conquers of these lands, the Phoenicians, at a time when their homeland fell to foreign domination. At the end of the second millennium of the Christian era, the revolution that chased France, its most recent occupier, from the Maghreb carried back with it most of the Jews of North Africa, a majority of whom returned to the shores of the Land of Israel, abandoned two thousand years earlier.[73]

The book's conclusion confirms the Eastern identity of the Jews of the Maghreb:

> With regard to the East, the Jews of North Africa were enriched by their replanting in the Berber soil, where they preserved, as it were in the pure state, an immemorial past in which the Arab influence predominated, bearing the civilizing values of the East from which they came, to which they always remained loyal and to which they returned at the end of their journey of two millennia.[74]

And so in the twentieth century the Jews of the Maghreb—or at least a majority of those born in Tunisia and Morocco—returned to their oriental roots.

Conclusion

As we asked at the outset: is the history of the Jews of the Maghreb, as written in the context of French colonialism, indeed orientalist? The question pertains both to the settings in which this history was produced and to its content.

With regard to the former, we can certainly answer in the affirmative. The past of the Jews of North Africa gained entry (albeit by the back door) into the emblematic institution of French Orientalism, the Académie des inscriptions et des belles lettres. It also took root in the learned societies established in the colonies and their periodicals, alongside the annals of the Berbers and the Arabs. The history of North African Jewry became an object of orientalist study for rabbis, a nationalist scholar, and teachers in the Alliance schools. Still, as I have emphasized, it occupied only a modest place in this scholarly literature, a limited volume that owes as much to the colonizers' lack of interest in Jewish life (except in Morocco) as to the tiny size of the local Jewish intelligentsia during the period in question.

With a regard to the Eastern identity of the Jews of North Africa, the answer must be more nuanced. There is no doubt that the Jews of Europe, who might well be considered the "Orientals" of that continent, shared their neighbors' condescending view of the peoples of the East, reproached as backward and superstitious. The consistory rabbis and the Alliance directors saw their role as rescuing the Maghrebi Jews from their anomie and leading them to join the West. But this Orientalism is not as clear-cut as it may seem. When non-Jewish scholars described Eastern societies, they drew a demarcation line between Western peoples and Eastern peoples and were skeptical about the latter's capacity to reform. The Jewish intellectuals, by contrast, focused on the Jews' mediating role. According to Slouschz, in Africa the Jews were the civilizing people par excellence. Cahen and Eisenbeth added that they often played the role of cultural broker. As such, they could rapidly find their place in the modern society brought by the colonizers. In a word, for all these authors, Jews are the prized students of Westernization. Colonialism has accelerated their progress toward the West, bringing everything excellent with it. That is the direction in which history is headed. At the same time, in these authors, and especially Slouschz, we can also discern a clear fascination with ancient Judaism, its culture and faith being gradually undermined by modernity. The ethnographic studies deplored both the old superstitions and their disappearance. If the oriental identity of the Jews of North Africa was attacked in the nineteenth century, its loss started to be felt in the twentieth.

Today the return to the East is deeply anchored in contemporary images. It was launched by Chouraqui who, in the 1980s, reversed the course of history sketched out by his teachers and even by his younger self. Not only is the past of the Maghrebi Jews to be found in the East, so is their future, he tells us. Chouraqui is no longer the only one to hold this view. The number of mass-market publications about North African Jewish traditions and the success of Benjamin Stora's book[75] invite us to reevaluate this part of the East that was under assault in the nineteenth century—a North African East of which the Jews were stripped after their forced exodus from the Maghreb that pushed them out of North Africa and which they now invest with music, literature, art, and even history. Will academic Orientalism be succeeded by a nostalgic Orientalism?

Notes

1. Perrine Simon-Nahum, *La Cité investie, la science du judaïsme français et la République* (Paris: Le Cerf, 1992).

2. Edward W. Said, *Orientalism* (London: Penguin, 1978). Throughout this article I use the terms "East" and "Eastern" not as actual descriptions of places or peoples but rather to indicate their place in European orientalist conceptions.

3. On the latter issue, see Ivan Davidson Kalmar and Derek J. Penslar, "Orientalism and the Jews: An Introduction," in *Orientalism and the Jews*, ed. Ivan Davidson Kalmar and Derek J. Penslar (Hanover, NH: Brandeis University Press, 2004). For stimulating critiques of Said's thesis more broadly, see, among others, Sadiq Jalal al-Azm, "Orientalism and Orientalism in Reverse," *Khamsin* 8 (1981): 5–26; Bernard Lewis, "The Question of Orientalism," *New York Review of Books*, June 24, 1982; and François Pouillon and Jean-Claude Vatin, eds. *Après l'orientalisme: L'Orient créé par l'Orient* (Paris: IISMM-Karthala, 2011).

4. Michel Espagne and Perrine Simon-Nahum, *Passeurs d'Orient: Les Juifs dans l'orientalisme* (Paris: Éditions de l'Éclat, 2013).

5. Kalmar and Penslar, "Orientalism and the Jews," xiii.

6. Michel de Certeau, *The Writing of History*, trans. Tom Conley (New York: Columbia University Press, 1988), 62.

7. See Colette Zytnicki, *Juifs du Maghreb: Naissance d'une historiographie coloniale* (Paris: Presses de l'Université Paris-Sorbonne, 2011). The present article is based in part on ideas developed there. See also the rich work of Daniel Schroeter, for example: Daniel J. Schroeter, and Emily Gottreich, eds., *Jewish Culture and Society in North Africa* (Bloomington: Indiana University Press, 2011); and Daniel J. Schroeter, *The Sultan's Jew: Morocco and the Sephardi World* (Stanford, CA: Stanford University Press, 2002).

8. Henri Laurens, "L'Orientalisme français: Un parcours historique?" in *Penser l'Orient: Traditions et actualités des orientalismes français et allemands*, ed. Youssef Courbage and Manfred Krop, 103–28 (Beirut: Presses de l'IFPO, 2004).

9. See Catherine Nicault, "L'émigration de France vers la Palestine (1880–1940)," *Archives Juives, Revue d'Histoire des Juifs de France* 41, no. 2 (2008): 10–33.

10. Nahoum Slouschz, *La Langue et la littérature hébraïques depuis la Bible jusqu'à nos jours, leçon d'ouverture du cours libre* (Paris, 1904).

11. As Slouschz explained, "This expedition was organized under the auspices of the Scientific Mission to Morocco, through the kindness of its delegate, M. Le Châtelier. . . . My eminent teacher, M. Phillipe Berger, furnished me not only with his valuable advice, but also with letters of introduction to

French scholars and authorities to facilitate the task that I have set myself. The Alliance israélite universelle, faithful to its traditions, also contributed to the success of my trip." Nahoum Slouschz, "Un voyage d'études juives en Afrique," *Mémoires présentés par divers savants à l'Académie des inscriptions et des belles lettres* 12, no. 2 (1909): 488. On Slouschz and his work, see also Harvey E. Goldberg, "The Oriental and the Orientalist: The Meeting of Mordecai Ha-Cohen and Nahum Slouschz," *Jewish Culture and History* 7, no. 3 (2004): 1–30.

12. Nahum Slouschz, Foreword to *Travels in North Africa* (Philadelphia: Jewish Publication Society of America, 1927).

13. Slouschz, "Un voyage d'études juives en Afrique."

14. Nahoum Slouschz, *La Civilisation hébraïque et phénicienne à Carthage* (Tunis: Société anonyme de l'Imprimerie rapide, 1911).

15. On the grant, see Unsigned letter from the Ministry of Public Instruction and Beaux-Arts to Jean-Vincent Scheil, Secretary of the Collection of Semitic Inscriptions, in Archives Nationales (Paris), F17/17286.

16. Nahoum Slouschz, *Les Hébraeo-Phéniciens: Introduction à l'histoire des origines de la colonisation hébraïque dans les pays méditerranéens* (Paris: E. Leroux, 1909); and Nahoum Slouschz, *Judéo-Hellènes et Judéo-Berbères. Recherches sur les origines des Juifs et du judaïsme en Afrique* (Paris: E. Leroux, 1909).

17. Nabila Oulebsir, *Les Usages du patrimoine: Monuments, musées et politique coloniale en Algérie (1830–1930)* (Paris: Éditions des sciences de l'homme, 2004).

18. Abraham Cahen, *Les Juifs dans l'Afrique septentrionale* (Constantine: Arnolet, 1867).

19. Jean-Philippe Chaumont and Monique Lévy, eds., *Dictionnaire biographique des rabbins et autres ministres du culte israélite: France et Algérie. 1807–1905* (Paris: Berg International, 2008), 204–7.

20. *Bulletin mensuel de la société archéologique, historique et géographique du département de Constantine* (Constantine: Amolet, 1867).

21. Ibid.

22. Alfred Le Châtelier to Georges Salmon, October 26, Archives du ministère des Affaires étrangères (Paris), NS, correspondance politique et commerciale, 1897–1917.

23. Alfred Le Châtelier, quoted in Edmund Burke III, "The First Crisis of Orientalism, 1890–1914," in *Connaissances du Maghreb, sciences sociales et colonisation*, ed. Jean-Claude Vatin, 213–47 (Paris: Éditions du CNRS, 1984).

24. Nahoum Slouschz, "Les Senoussiya en Abyssinie," *Revue du monde musulman* 1 (1906): 169–82; and Nahoum Slouschz, "Une expédition à travers la Cyrénaïque," *Revue du monde musulman* 8 (1909): 56–65.

25. Nahoum Slouschz, "Les Juifs en Tripolitaine," *Revue du monde musulman* 2 (1907): 34.

26. See below for analysis of Romanelli's book and personality.

27. Nahoum Slouschz, "Le Maroc au XVIIIᵉ siècle: mémoire d'un contemporain, Samuel Romanelli," *Revue du monde musulman* 10 (1909): 452.

28. Nahoum Slouschz, "Moïse Edrehi, un savant marocain: 1760(?)–1840," *Revue du monde musulman* 7 (1909): 53–68.

29. Tudor Parfitt, *The Lost Tribes of Israel: The History of a Myth* (London: Orion Publishing, 2003). See also Tudor Parfitt, "The Use of the Jew in the Colonial Discourse," in Kalmar and Penslar, *Orientalism and the Jews*, 51–67.

30. M. Edrehi, *An Historical Account of the Ten Tribes Settled beyond the River Sambatyon in the East: With Many Other Curious Matters Relating to the State of the Israelites in Various Parts of the World* (London, 1836).

31. Nahoum Slouschz, "Les Juifs de Debdou," *Revue du monde musulman* 22 (1913): 221–69.

32. Yomtob Semach, "Un rabbin voyageur marocain, Mardochée Aby Serour," *Hespéris: Archives berbères et bulletin de l'Institut des hautes études marocaines* 8 (1928): 388–99.

33. Yomtob Semach, "Une chronique juive de Fès: le *"Yahas Fès"* de Ribbi Abner Hassarfaty," *Hespéris: Archives berbères et bulletin de l'Institut des hautes études marocaines* 19 (1934): 79–94.

34. Ruben Tadjouri, "Le mariage juif à Salé," *Hespéris: Archives berbères et bulletin de l'Institut des hautes études marocaines* 3 (1923): 393–420. The article also contains translations of several wedding songs along with their musical notation.

35. Rabbi Encaoua (1810–1860?) published various ritual and mystical works as well as poems and elegies.

36. Tadjouri, "Le mariage juif à Salé," 393.

37. Louis Brunot and Élie Malka, "Textes judéo-arabes de Fès," *Hespéris: Archives berbères et bulletin de l'Institut des hautes études marocaines* 14 (1932): 1–61; Louis Brunot, "Notes sur le parler arabe des Juifs de Fès," *Hespéris: Archives berbères et bulletin de l'Institut des hautes études marocaines* 22 (1936): 1–32; and Louis Brunot, "Proverbes judéo-arabes de Fès," *Hespéris: Archives berbères et bulletin de l'Institut des hautes études marocaines* 24 (1937): 1–100.

38. See Daniel J. Schroeter, "La découverte des Juifs berbères," in *Relations judéo-musulmanes au Maroc: Perceptions et réalités*, ed. Michel Abitbol, 169–87 (Paris: Editions Stavit, 1997).

39. "At the end of the eighteenth century, the idea emerged that such an enterprise [i.e., of knowing peoples' pasts] is possible: all that is required is to study geography. Civilization took its first steps in the East. Since then, culture has been marked by a dual process: it has moved towards the West. At the same time, progress has been frozen in the centers where it began, to the extent that it is in the East that one must now look for the image of Man that came before us." Paul Claval, "Réflexions sur la géographie de la découverte, la géographie coloniale et la géographie tropicale," in *L'Empire des Géographes: Géographie, exploration et colonisation, XIXe-XXe siècle*, ed. Pierre Singaravelou (Paris: Belin, 2008), 21.

40. A. Zaoui, "Djerba ou l'une des plus anciennes communautés juives de la Diaspora," *Revue de la pensée juive* 2, no. 5 (1950): 129–36; and Jacob Pinkerfeld, "Un témoignage du passé en voie de disparition, les synagogues de la région de Djerba," *Byrsa* 7 (1957): 127–37. Both authors support the distant origins of the synagogue. The latter does not exclude the existence of a community before the destruction of the Second Temple, although this idea has been challenged by scholars more recently.

41. René Basset, *Nédromah et les Traras* (Paris: E. Leroux), 1901.

42. Ibn Khaldoun, *Histoire des Berbères et des dynasties musulmanes de l'Afrique septentrionale*, trans. Baron de Slane (Algiers: Imprimerie du gouvernement, 1852), 208.

43. André Chouraqui, *Histoire des Juifs en Afrique du Nord* (Paris: Hachette, 1987), 50, citing *Leviticus Rabba* 17:6.

44. Here I draw on the analysis in ibid., 50, as well as in Richard Ayoun and Bernard Cohen, *Les Juifs d'Algérie, mille ans d'histoire* (Paris: J. C. Lattès, 1982), 33.

45. Claude Aziza, *Tertullien et le judaïsme* (Paris: Les Belles Lettres, 1977).

46. Jean-Marie Lassère, *"Ubique populus": Peuplement et mouvements de population dans l'Afrique romaine, de la chute de Carthage à la fin de la dynastie des Sévères: 146 a.C.–235 p.C.* (Paris: Éditions du CNRS, 1977), 414.

47. Edmond Pellissier de Reynaud, *Annales algériennes* (Algiers: Anselin et Gaultier-Laguionie, 1836), 251.

48. Stéphane Gsell, *Histoire ancienne de l'Afrique du Nord*, vol. 1 (Paris: Hachette, 1913).

49. Slouschz, *Les Hébraeo-Phéniciens*; and Slouschz, *Judéo-Hellènes et Judéo-Berbères*.

50. Slouschz, *La civilisation hébraïque*.

51. Slouschz, *Judéo-Hellènes et Judéo-Berbères*, 247.

52. Ibid., 251–52.

53. Samuel Romanelli, *Travail in an Arab Land*, trans. Yedida K. Stillman and Norman A. Stillman (Tuscaloosa: University of Alabama Press, 1989), 28.

54. Ibid., 28.

55. Ibid., 59.

56. Ibid., 58.

57. Cahen, quoted in ibid., 54.

58. Maurice Eisenbeth, *Le Judaïsme nord-africain: Études démographiques sur les Israélites du département de Constantine* (Constantine: Pierre Braham, 1931).

59. Ibid., 37.

60. Ibid., 38.

61. Aron Rodrigue, *De l'instruction à l'émancipation* (Paris: Calmann Lévy, 1989); and André Kaspi, ed., *Histoire de l'Alliance israélite universelle, de 1860 à nos jours* (Paris: Armand Colin, 2010).

62. Instructions for teachers, 1896, quoted in *Instructions générales pour les professeurs* (Paris, 1903), 94–5.

63. Louise Bornstein to General Secretary of the Alliance Israélite Universelle, November 25, 1900, Archives Alliance Israélite universelle Tunisie XIV E 085; quoted by Marie-Pierre Brau, Mémoire de Master 1, Université de Toulouse-Le Mirail, September 2012.

64. Nahoum Slouschz, *Étude sur l'histoire des Juifs et du judaïsme au Maroc: Première partie. Les origines juives au Maroc* (Paris: E. Leroux, 1906), 162.

65. On the Judeo-Berbers, see Haïm Zafrani, *Two Thousand Years of Jewish Life in Morocco* (New York: Sephardic House; Jersey City, Ktav, 2005); Haïm Zafrani, *Études et recherches sur la vie intellectuelle juive au Maroc: De la fin du 15ᵉ au début du 20ᵉ siècle. Deuxième partie, Poésie juive en Occident musulman*, 2nd ed. (Paris: P. Geuthner, 2003); and Haïm Zafrani, *Juifs d'Andalousie et du Maghreb* (Paris: Maisonneuve et Larose, 1996).

66. Slouschz, *Étude sur l'histoire des Juifs*, 167.

67. Joshua Schreier, *Arabs of the Jewish Faith: The Civilizing Mission in Colonial Algeria* (New Brunswick, NJ: Rutgers University Press, 2010).

68. Valérie Assan, *Les consistoires israélites d'Algérie au XIXᵉ siècle: "L'alliance de la civilisation et de la religion"* (Paris: Armand Colin, 2012).

69. David Cazès, *Essai sur l'histoire des Israélites de Tunisie depuis les temps les plus reculés jusqu'à l'établissement du protectorat de la France en Tunisie* (Paris: Éditions Durlacher, 1888), 7.

70. André Chouraqui, *Marche vers l'Occident: Les Juifs d'Afrique du Nord* (Paris: Presses universitaires de France, 1952), 310.

71. "Without wanting to play the prophet (the 'lessons' of history are too often contradicted by the facts for us to hold on to them), we can nevertheless estimate that Jewish life will continue only as long as it appears to be possible and fruitful." Ibid., 317.

72. Ibid.

73. Chouraqui, *Histoire des Juifs en Afrique du Nord*, 473.

74. Ibid., 522.

75. Benjamin Stora, *Les Trois exils: Juifs d'Algérie* (Paris: Stock, 2006).

3

THE RISE OF IMPERIALISM AND THE GERMAN JEWISH ENGAGEMENT IN ISLAMIC STUDIES

Susannah Heschel

LECTURING TO BRITISH Jews in 1958, the great scholar of medieval Judaism and Islam, Shlomo Dov Goitein (1900–1985), declared, "It was Islam which saved the Jewish people." How did this salvation come about? Because Islam, Goitein stated, provided the conditions, both economic and intellectual, that encouraged the "creative symbiosis" that emerged between medieval Jewish and Islamic cultures.[1] The religion of Islam, Goitein claimed, was a religion of "personal responsibility of man before God," a religion of "ethical monotheism."[2] And Islam is derived from Judaism: "It would be correct to state that Islam is nothing but Judaism in an Arabic pattern of large dimensions. . . . The entire religious typification of Islam as a faith of religious law is nothing but a reflection and extension of Judaism."[3]

The dramatic enthusiasm he expressed for Islam was vectored inward: Goitein focused on how Islam (and, by implicit contrast, not Christianity) had benefited the development of Judaism precisely because it was a religion derived from Judaism and shared its central principles. With this argument, Goitein stood in a long tradition of Jewish scholarship that enjoyed demonstrating extensive Jewish influences on the Qur'an and that often called Islam the "daughter religion" of Judaism. Striking is Goitein's labeling of Islam as a religion of "ethical monotheism," precisely the term used by modern liberal Jews to describe Judaism, and marking a sharp distinction from earlier Jewish views of Islam. In the premodern era, Jews had been far more ambivalent about Islam, acknowledging its monotheism but also claiming Islam had retained pagan rituals, such as the circumambulation of the Ka'aba.[4] Also striking is Goitein's reticence about exploring Islamic influences on Judaism; he speaks of the "impact" of Islamic law on Jewish law but then argues that Islamic influences on Judaism are really a reclamation of elements that were originally derived from Judaism.[5]

Goitein's formulations stand as the culmination of a tradition of European Jewish scholarship that emphasized a unidirectional influence of Judaism on Islam and that celebrated Islam's derivation from Judaism as one of the latter's great contributions to Western civilization. Islamic influences on Judaism were understood by most modern Jewish scholars as providing a context for Jews to flourish in an atmosphere of religious tolerance, international trade, and intellectual pursuit. That Islam may in turn have influenced Jewish belief, Jewish law, or movements of religious change was only rarely considered in the history of this scholarly tradition until after World War II. Goitein himself stands as a major figure who is both a culmination of the European tradition of scholarship and also a marker of the migration of that scholarship out of Europe. Raised in Germany, he received his doctorate under the noted scholar of Islam Professor Josef Horovitz at the University of Frankfurt, then left for Palestine in 1923, bringing both European philological methods and a century-long tradition of Jewish scholarly investigation of affinities between Judaism and Islam to the Yishuv (the Jewish settlement in pre-state Palestine), and, in 1928, to a professorship at the Hebrew University of Jerusalem, and finally, in his later years, to the United States, where he moved in 1957 to become professor of Arabic at the University of Pennsylvania and, in 1970, a fellow at the Institute for Advanced Study in Princeton.

European Jewish scholarship on Islam was an extraordinary achievement that occurred within a relatively short time span, from the 1830s to the 1930s, and during an era when Jews were emancipated, Germany was unified, and Oriental Studies became an academic field at universities. This was also the era of the rise of German nationalism, imperialism, colonialism, and antisemitism. How did German political interests affect the politics of philological scholarship? European imperialism fostered scholarship on Islam in practical ways, but my question is whether we can identify imperialist motifs in the philological arguments regarding Islamic texts. Edward Said, in his highly influential book of 1978, *Orientalism*, called attention to the relationship between scholarship and governmental power and to the many ways Islam was imagined in Europe as an erotic and primitive phenomenon, culturally inferior and yet fascinating to Europeans. In her recent study of the field of Oriental Studies in Germany, Suzanne Marchand also notes the close connections between the work of scholars and the imperial aims of Germany but uncovers the theological concerns about the nature of religion and the origins of Christianity as central motivations of German orientalists. Nineteenth-century Jewish scholars of Islam developed a different kind of Orientalism. Their work was influenced by European imperialism, to be sure, but they generally presented Islam not as primitive or a source of erotic pleasure. Rather, Islam was elevated in their eyes as both a "daughter religion" of Judaism and, as Goitein declared, an environment in which Jews could flourish.

In addressing the influence of imperialist, colonialist, and orientalist politics on Jewish scholarship, I examine the overall Jewish narrative of Islam, the role of imperialism in facilitating access to scholarly materials as well as European travel to Islamicate countries, the popular Jewish understandings of a Golden Age of Spain and the use of Moorish architecture for synagogues, and imperialist influences on Jewish historical narratives of Islam and philological analyses of its texts. Islam began during the first half of this very remarkable century as the projected ideal image of what Judaism ought to become. By the end of the century, Jewish scholars conventionally assumed Islam was Judaism's daughter religion, even as many Christian scholars insisted on the primacy of Hellenistic, rather than Jewish, influences on the Qur'an. By the early twentieth century, a creeping appropriation began to take shape in some Jewish writings that overlooked Islam's distinctiveness, viewing the Qur'an simply as a receptacle of Judaism's teachings, or viewing Muslims as atavistically practicing ancient Israelite traditions that could be reclaimed by Zionists in Palestine. Yet other German Jewish scholars during the first decades of the twentieth century began recognizing the Qur'an as an autonomous agent of interpretation and revision of Jewish (as well as Christian and Hellenistic) ideas, though without breaking Islam's link to Judaism.

Jewish Orientalism

Starting in the 1830s with the publication of Abraham Geiger's groundbreaking book, *Was hat Muhammad aus dem Judenthume aufgenommen?*, German Jewish scholars flocked to the study of Arabic and Islam, translating the Qur'an into German, French, and Hebrew, and producing some of the most important and lasting scholarship on the origins and early development of Islam, especially on the parallels and influences between Judaism and Islam. Popular as well as scholarly Jewish publications spoke of a "Golden Age" of Muslim Spain, where Jews were treated with tolerance and respect, and of the production of important medieval works of Jewish philosophy and poetry written in Arabic. Synagogues were built in Moorish architecture throughout Europe and also in the United States. Within less than a century, Jewish scholars came to play a dominant role at German universities in the field of Islamic Studies. Forced to abandon their positions in Germany after Adolf Hitler came to power, they brought their philological skills and their interest in Jewish–Islamic relations to a diasporic academic world extending from Britain and the United States to pre-state Palestine and, ultimately, to the State of Israel that came into being in 1948.[6]

If Goitein's remarks stand as a culmination of Jewish claims of a "creative symbiosis" of Islam and Judaism, they also reflect a late-nineteenth-century shift in the tone of Jewish writings on Islam. There is no uniform Jewish approach to Islam during the nineteenth century, but some striking features predominate in the narrative. Most Jewish scholarship focused on early Islam rather than modern developments, and concentrated on philological analyses of early Islamic texts, often drawing comparisons with Jewish texts that led them to argue for Judaism's strong influence on Muhammad, the Qur'an, and the legal systems and religious practices of Islam. Jewish scholars practiced historical-critical methods on Islamic texts that they also applied to rabbinic texts, and they brought a historicist sensibility to philological methods that were predominantly linguistic in their day.

The image of a remote, seductive, primitive, fascinating Islam was part of the often-contradictory image that dominated European Orientalism. By contrast, the imagined "Islam" created by European Jewish scholars was primarily a rational religion free of mysticism and apocalypticism. Indeed, just as nineteenth-century Jewish historians considered Kabbalah and Hasidism foreign to the "healthy body" of Judaism, their fantasy (influenced, of course, by Enlightenment traditions) was of an Islam that conformed to the rational, ethical religion of Judaism that they were trying to shape.[7] That was a key reason why most Jewish scholars avoided studying Sufism or Shi'ism until the early twentieth century studies of Israel Friedlaender (1876–1920).[8] Instead, they focused on shared theological traditions, parallels in legal interpretation, and, especially, similarities between Jewish and Islamic interpretations of biblical texts. Islam, for nineteenth-century Jews, was a rational religion, just like their imagined Judaism was supposed to be, so that the study of Islam became a template for the ongoing Jewish de-orientalization of Judaism: both were presented as religions of rationalism, monotheism, rejection of anthropomorphism, and ethical law.[9] The appropriation of Islam as a branch of Judaism does not have a parallel among European Christian theologians, many of whom tended, as Albert Hourani has pointed out, to view Islam less as a theological challenge than as a military threat to Europe.[10] The Protestant theologians of modern Europe who shaped biblical scholarship, for example, wrote extensively about the theological implications of Judaism for Christianity, but said little or nothing about Islam. Among their concerns, for example, was elucidating the differences between Jesus's teachings and the rabbis of the first century, explaining why Jews failed to recognize Jesus as the promised messiah, and distinguishing between Judaism as a religion of law and Christianity as a religion of love and intimacy with God.[11]

By contrast, German Jewish scholars viewed Islam in terms similar to the liberal Judaism of the German world. Both were presented as religions of rationality and moral exhortation, not of mystical exploration; of philosophy and science, not doctrine and dogma. For liberal Jews, Judaism was ethics, and ethics in Judaism, as Sigmund Freud once wrote, is not about renunciation or abstinence, but "is a limitation of instinct, a restriction of instinctual gratification" that is supposedly the mark of the modern European.[12] When European Jews, such as Gustav Weil, Ignaz Goldziher, Gottlieb Leitner, Josef Horovitz, Arminius Vambery, and Max Herz, spent time in Islamicate countries, their travel reports focused on political and theological challenges facing contemporary Islam. Their descriptions of their travel lack both the sexual references and the depiction of Islamic despotism and primitivism found in the travel reports of many other Europeans of the same era, such as Gustav Flaubert, Richard Burton, Gérard de Nerval, Louise Colet, and Anne Blunt.

Yet even as they attempted to de-orientalize Judaism and present a rational Islam, German Jews claimed an Oriental identity for themselves. That Jewish Oriental desire was expressed in the nineteenth century by an imagined Jewish–Muslim symbiosis and expanded during the early twentieth century to a reclamation of an East European Judaism, including Hasidism, that had heretofore been regarded as primitive and inferior to West European Jewish life.[13] While Said identified a modern European discourse he termed "Orientalism" that emphasized Muslims' inferiority to the West and sexual promiscuity, European Jewish scholarship on Islam generally emphasized Islam's affinities with Judaism and even its derivation from Judaism.[14] For Said, scholars of Islam generated a discourse of "Orientalism" that identified Islam as Europe's inferior "other," using that contrast to establish Europe's superior identity. Scholarship functioned as a tool of European imperialism, according to Said, but because he limited his study to England and France, he did not examine German engagement with Islam. Nor did he understand the more complicated politics implied by the development of scholarship on Islam developed by German Jews at a time when, at least in the initial decades, they had not yet been fully emancipated.

Yet, although Jewish scholarship on Islam did not fit the patterns of Orientalism outlined by Said, and although Germany itself was not an imperial power until late in the nineteenth century, cultural as well as political features of European imperialism and Orientalism still played a role in the growth of Islamic Studies in Germany. Jewish scholars in Germany (which became the leading center of such scholarship) benefited from European imperial adventures through the acquisition of manuscripts, the ability to travel to Islamicate countries, and the interest in Islam that grew in part as a response to the increasing German financial and political engagements in the Middle East, the Ottoman

Empire, and North Africa. Equally important is the reflection of a European "culture of imperialism" in the world of scholarship as in the world of belles lettres, opera, visual art, architecture, home decorations, fashion, and beyond. If an ostrich plume in a woman's hat brought empire into the daily attire of European women, and if the novels of Joseph Conrad combine the self-aggrandizement and abjection of imperial conquest, how do Jewish narratives of Islam practice empire? To answer this question, we turn to the scholarly cultivation of Islam as Judaism's receptacle, and to popular use of Moorish architecture as a signifier of Judaism.

Jewish interest in Islam was motivated both by internal and external factors. Like Christian scholars who entered the field of Oriental Studies during the nineteenth century, Jewish scholars were concerned with theological questions, such as the relationship between revelation and historical-critical method. Like their Christian counterparts, they were unwilling to limit themselves to the formal rigors of traditional theological categories and doctrines and turned instead to Oriental Studies as a context for thinking about religious questions. While Ignaz Goldziher, for example, found that his historical analyses of rabbinic texts sparked outrage within the Hungarian Jewish community, he could apply his methods to Islamic texts and be received as a great scholar, both by Europeans and by the faculty of the al-Azhar University in Cairo.[15]

German Jews focused on Arabic and Islam, while most German Christian scholars of the Orient turned to the study of Sanskrit and Persian. For both Jews and Christians, the use of historical-critical philological methods was not an abandonment of theological concerns but an effort to deepen their understanding of religion; during the nineteenth century, German scholars, Jews as well as Christians, were motivated less by the kind of imperial politics and orientalist discourse that Said outlined in relation to France and England than by the theological concerns that Marchand has argued were central to the rise of Oriental Studies as an academic field in Germany.[16] Both Said and Marchand call our attention to the benefits European imperialism provided scholars as manuscripts and archeological data were brought from the Middle East to Europe. Moreover, scholars were participants in a growing popular fascination in Europe with the Orient, though, as Marchand makes clear, Persian and Sanskrit captured German attention through the mid-century. Only in the last decades did attention turn to contemporary Islam, and it took German governmental interference to establish institutes in Hamburg and later in Berlin to train in the languages necessary for the military, diplomatic, and business ventures Germany had begun. These included, for example, arms sales to the Ottoman Empire, the investment in the Baghdad Railway, and the construction of roads, hospitals, and factories in Palestine.[17] If the Berlin conference convened by German chancellor Otto von

Bismarck in 1884–85 marked Germany's emergence as a colonial power, particularly in Africa, Germany had nonetheless long served as a hub of scholarship that influenced both Europe and intellectuals in colonized regions.[18]

Abraham Geiger and the Origins of Jewish Scholarship on Islam

The beginnings of modern Jewish scholarship on Islam were also the beginnings of historical philological methods for reading Islamic texts. Abraham Geiger (1810–74) burst onto the scholarly stage in 1833, at the age of twenty-three, with his "epoch-making" book on the Qur'an that was widely hailed throughout Europe as a landmark, demonstrating an entirely new way to understand the origins of Islam by placing Qur'anic texts into the context of rabbinic texts. Until his book, scholars had been unaware of the parallels Geiger demonstrated between the Qur'an and rabbinic literature, particularly midrashic commentaries on the Bible, and presumed that Muhammad's renditions of biblical stories were influenced by Christian heretics in Arabia who had conveyed false, distorted biblical accounts to him. Geiger's book originated as a prize-winning essay at the University of Bonn, with the topic formulated by his professor, Gustav Freytag: "What Did Muhammad Take from Judaism?"

The comparisons between Islam and Judaism delineated by Geiger inaugurated a tradition of Jewish scholarship on Islam that sought parallels between the two religions; this includes Isaac Gastfreund, *Mohammed nach Talmud und Midrasch* (1875); Hartwig Hirschfeld, *Jüdische Elemente im Koran* (1878); Israel Schapiro, *Die haggadischen Elemente im erzählenden Teil des Korans* (1907); Heinrich Speyer, *Die biblical Erzählungen im Qoran* (1931); and Abraham Katsh, *Judaism in Islam* (1955), among others. Changes in the nature of this body of Jewish scholarship occurred over time, as I describe below, but diverse works retained a basic narrative of Islam as Judaism's receptacle, a narrative carried out of Europe into the diasporas of Israel and the United States, as exemplified by Goitein's writings.

Jewish scholarship on Islam begins with Geiger's extraordinary book, a major work that he completed in a short, intensive period of study at the University of Bonn, where he was part of a small group of Jewish men studying Arabic. The group included two of his close friends, Ludwig Ullmann, who translated the Qur'an into German (published in 1840), and Salomon Munk, who became a leading scholar of Arabic Jewish philosophy and professor at the College de France, in Paris.

What marks the scholarship on Islam developed by German Jews is the extraordinary training in classical Jewish texts that each brought to the field. Each came to university study of Islam from religious Jewish homes and traditional childhood education in rabbinic literature and medieval commentaries that emphasized memorization. When Geiger was writing his book on the Qur'an, for example, there were no critical editions of rabbinic texts, let alone of the Qur'an, and no dictionaries or concordances. He mastered Arabic and the Qur'an in his two years of study at the University of Bonn and drew on his masterful prior knowledge of Jewish literature.

Demonstrating the parallels between Qur'anic passages and texts from the Midrash and Mishnah (e.g., Sura 5:35 parallels Mishnah Sanhedrin 4:5), Geiger argued that Muhammad knew even more of Jewish law than he adopted for Islam, and that he had little intention of imposing a new code of laws but rather wanted to spread new and purified religious (that is, Jewish) views (much as Geiger subsequently argued about Jesus). As an Arab, Muhammad did not want to deviate too far from established custom among Arab pagans, so he limited his introduction of new customs, most of which, Geiger claimed, were derived from Jewish religious practice. Throughout the book, Muhammad is portrayed in language far more sympathetic than was common at the time. He was not an imposter or seducer and certainly not a "madman," as the medieval Jewish philosopher Moses Maimonides called him, but a product of his social context, with a clever political skill and a desire not to create a new religion but to spread monotheism.[19] The narrative Geiger developed concerned not only the ways Muhammad composed the Qur'an to solidify his own position of leadership but also his transmission of Jewish learning that he acquired from rabbis in Arabia who were happy to share their teaching with Arab pagans. Muhammad, Geiger claimed, constructed an image of Abraham in the Qur'an as a prototype of himself—as a public preacher who won converts, was a model of piety, established a monotheistic religion, and became a leader of his community.[20] The spread of Jewish beliefs and practices to pagan Arabia was an example of Judaism's widespread influence on world religion. For Geiger, the significance of Scripture was not so much as the word of God received by Jews but as a religion that the Jews transmitted to the world.

Geiger's study of the Qur'an and its parallels with rabbinic texts introduced historicist methods into what had been a predominantly linguistic philological approach to Islamic texts and launched a small industry of Jewish scholarly writings that compared rabbinic versions of biblical stories with those of the Qur'an. This was Geiger's only scholarly study of Islam, but thirty years later he applied similar methods to his study of early Christianity, which he similarly presented as derived from Judaism. Yet there was a difference: Whereas Christianity was unable to preserve that monotheism and instead developed a Trinitarian theology, Islam, in an argument shared by Geiger and most subsequent German Jewish scholars of Islam, preserved Jewish monotheism. Moreover, Islam maintained, like Judaism, a strict prohibition against idolatry, including anthropomorphism, and adhered to a religious legal system that was, like Jewish law, ethical but also more liberal than Jewish law in certain respects, permitting, for example, eating meat with milk.

Geiger's approach to Jewish law was itself conditioned by his study of the philological methods of the Tübingen School. Shaped by the writings of Ferdinand Christian Baur starting in the 1830s, the Tübingen School distinguished between conflicting "Tendenzen" of Jewish Christians and Gentile Christians reflected in the texts of the New Testament. Those methods were applied by Geiger to Jewish texts of antiquity, including Aramaic, Greek, and Syriac translations of the Bible as well as mishnaic and midrashic sources. In his magnum opus, the *Urschrift und Übersetzungen der Bibel*, a study of Second Temple–era Judaism that he published in 1857, Geiger identified conflicting religious, political, and cultural tendencies expressed in the linguistic nuances of Bible translations and rabbinic literature. He identified these as reflecting conflicts between liberal Pharisees and reactionary Sadducees. Geiger's methods were subsequently applied by Goldziher to his studies of Hebrew myths, later to his lectures on Jewish history, and in particular to his numerous influential studies of the Qur'an, Hadith, and sharia.[21]

Yet in his 1863 lectures on the history of Judaism, Geiger modified his view of Muhammad, coming closer to what we see below as Gustav Weil's characterization of Muhammad's political shrewdness. Geiger wrote of Muhammad's dilution of Judaism as motivated by his own practical goals of conquest and persuasion. Islam triumphed, Geiger wrote, because it was well suited to the Arab people and to the era in which Islam consolidated its empire. That is, lacking an ideal past, Islam focused on the present. Its core teachings, derived from Judaism, retained simplicity and were not complicated with deeper understandings of holiness, purity, and morality. Without a more sophisticated understanding of human nature and of God, Islam brought a simple message to simple people.

Geiger's tone in his writings of the 1860s reflects a wider shift in Jewish scholarship on Islam. Judaism now appears not simply as the source out of which Islam emerged but far more aggressively responsible for all that is good in Islam: "Whatever good elements Islam contains, whatever enduring idea appears in it, it has taken over from Judaism. . . . Judaism is the only fruit-bearing and world-conquering thought contained in Islam."[22] These later claims reflect what entered the more popular multivolume narrative of Jewish history published a few years earlier by Heinrich Graetz: "The best of what the Qur'an contains is borrowed from the Bible or the Talmud."[23] The claim that "there is no God but Allah" was taken from Judaism, Graetz wrote, but Muhammad's subsequent addition, "and Muhammad is his prophet" was simply a reflection of his "arrogance."[24] Islam is not the "son" of Judaism, Graetz wrote, but "nursed at its breast. It was aroused by Judaism to bring into the world a new form of religion with political foundations . . . and it exerted an enormous influence on the shape and development of Jewish history."[25] Yet Islam was also Judaism's "second enemy," Graetz writes.[26] Geiger's claim of Islam's derivation from Judaism was also echoed by subsequent Jewish scholars of Islam, becoming the most common Jewish narrative of Islam and turning Islamic texts into receptacles of Judaism, archives of its teachings.

Gustav Weil: Traveler and Scholar

Gustav Weil (1808–89), a contemporary and friend of Geiger's, also had, like Geiger, a strong education in traditional Hebrew texts. Born to a notable family in Sulzburg, in Baden, he was sent at the age of twelve, in 1820, to live with his uncle, the consistorial rabbi of Metz, and study at the yeshiva in Metz. In 1828 Weil entered the University of Heidelberg, where he studied Arabic and became interested in Islam. He returned to France in 1830 to study in Paris under Silvestre de Sacy, the leading Arabist of his day. Shortly thereafter, Weil traveled with French expeditions to Algeria and then to Cairo, where he spent several years during the 1830s studying Arabic and teaching French. A prolific scholar, Weil went back to Germany in 1836, received a doctorate from the University of Tübingen, and then returned to the University of Heidelberg, where he refused baptism, a condition for professorship. Instead, he served for two decades as an assistant librarian before finally receiving a full professorship in 1861, at the age of fifty-three, thanks to the intervention of the Baden-Württemberg Ministry of Education.[27]

European imperialism clearly benefited Weil, both by facilitating his journey with French troops to Egypt and by acquiring manuscripts that he used for his research in Germany. Weil made extensive use of Islamic manuscripts acquired by the ducal library in Gotha for his numerous publications, including in 1843 the first European biography of the prophet Muhammad based on Islamic sources—the *sira* of ibn Ishaq, as preserved by Ibn Hisham. He also wrote a book on Arabic poetry (1837), a five-volume history of the caliphates (1846–51), and a study of biblical legends as interpreted in the Midrash Yalkut Shimoni and the Tafsir, published in 1845. His most important work, however, was his chronology of the Qur'anic suras, published in 1844.

Weil's scholarship on Islam was extensive and had a wide readership in its day; he was cited by popular writers, including Benjamin Disraeli and Washington Irving, and influenced a next generation of scholars, most notably Theodor Nöldeke, whose chronology of the Qur'an was based on Weil's pioneering study. Weil's biography of the prophet was perhaps the first by a European to be based on Islamic sources—manuscripts at the ducal library at Gotha and in the possession of the noted biblical scholar Heinrich Ewald, professor at the University of Göttingen. Throughout his scholarship, he places emphasis on Jewish sources, comparing Jewish and Islamic biblical legends, for example, and using Jewish-inflected Islamic sources for his biography of Muhammad. Like Geiger, Weil presents Islam as deeply influenced by Judaism, and both as the two great monotheistic religions.[28]

Both Geiger and Weil viewed Islam as a movement of religious reform, a liberalization of Judaism that Geiger also identified as the essence of Pharisaic Judaism. For Geiger, Muhammad was a genuine religious enthusiast who was honestly convinced of his religious message, constructing the Qur'anic image of Abraham as a prototype of himself, a public preacher who won converts, was a model of piety, established a monotheistic religion, and so forth.[29] For Geiger, Islam was derived from Judaism, a "daughter" who spread Judaism's teachings to Arab pagans. Weil's view of Muhammad, though positive, places greater emphasis on his political motivations and achievements, and presents Islam as a purified version of both Judaism and Christianity: "a Judaism without the many ritual and ceremonial laws, which, according to Muhammad's declaration, even Christ had been called to abolish, or a Christianity without the Trinity, crucifixion and salvation connected therewith."[30] Weil constructed Islam after the image of religion of his day: Judaism without law, Christianity without dogma; Islam was a pure Enlightenment religion. At the same time, Weil writes that "Muhammad might be a messenger of God for Muslims, as Moses is for the Israelites, but they [presumably both Muslims and Jews] must recognize Christ as the greatest of all prophets for all human beings and for all eternity."[31] Weil's acclamation of Jesus was not a personal endorsement of Christianity; Weil refused baptism even though it would have radically hastened his appointment to a professorship at the University of Heidelberg.

In contrast to Weil, Geiger, who was a leader among German rabbis in the movement to liberalize Judaism, saw Judaism as the pure, original monotheistic religion and was not interested in promoting Jesus as the greatest of all prophets, nor did he elevate Islam above Judaism; his goal was rather to restore the progressive, liberal agenda that he believed was represented by the Pharisees. Nonetheless, it is clear that Geiger and Weil shared an image of an ideal religious leader, whether prophet or rabbi, who was ethical, inspiring, rational, and liberal. Both Weil's Muhammad and Geiger's Pharisees were ultimately quite similar to the Jesus of liberal Protestantism, or the figure of Nathan in Gotthold Ephraim Lessing's play, *Nathan the Wise*. For Geiger and Weil, Muhammad and the Pharisees were precursors of the contemporary religious and political movements of liberal reform that Geiger and Weil hoped would develop in their day.

Gottlieb Leitner and Ignaz Goldziher: European Jewish Traveler-Scholars

Subsequent scholars also benefited from the opportunities provided by imperialism, combining travel and scholarship. The Hungarian Jew Gottlieb Leitner (1840–99), who studied in Istanbul, Heidelberg, and London, went to Lahore, India, in 1861 with British forces, where he taught himself Urdu and published books on Islamic history in Urdu as well as linguistic studies of Dardic languages. He helped establish the University of the Punjab and, in opposition to the British, argued that the language of instruction at the university should be Urdu, not English.[32] His Hungarian compatriot, Ignaz Goldziher (1850–1921), who came to be considered the foremost scholar of Islam in his day, grew up in Hungary and received his doctorate at the University of Leipzig from Heinrich Leberecht Fleischer (1801–88). He then traveled to the Middle East in the 1870s, visiting Beirut, Damascus, Palestine, and Cairo, where he spent several months studying at Al-Azhar University, where he was warmly received. After joining Friday prayers at a mosque in Damascus, Goldziher wrote: "I became inwardly convinced that I myself was a Muslim." In Cairo, at a mosque, "In the midst of the thousands of the pious, I rubbed my forehead against the floor of the mosque. Never in my life was I more devout, more truly devout, than on that exalted Friday."[33] Such comments were seldom heard from Jewish scholars who visited a church. Judaism's alliance with Islam in contrast to Christianity represents a triangulation that was not uncommon in colonial settings. For example, Avril Powell points out that the Scottish Christian missionary William Muir, who knew Arabic and was a scholar of Islam, encountered Muslims in India who spoke of Christianity's allegedly unfair treatment of the Old Testament and the Jews as a reason not to convert.[34] In discussions involving Judaism and Islam, Christianity became theologically marginalized as the religion resting on miracles, the supernatural, and on dogma contrary to reason—as well as being intolerant of other religions.

Goldziher's scholarly productivity was extraordinary. While breaking with some aspects of the Jewish narrative of Islam, he reshaped others. After earning his doctorate from Fleischer at Leipzig, he spent some months in Berlin, where he met Geiger, whose work he credited with influencing his own understanding of the historicist methods of the Tübingen School, methods Geiger had applied to the study of the Second Temple and rabbinic Judaism. Goldziher used those methods to juxtapose and analyze the Hadith and Qur'an. In Mecca, he argued, Muhammad intensified the religious mood, whereas in Medina, where a large Jewish community lived, Muhammad created rules and institutions. In Mecca the revelation was visionary and Muhammad was a prophet; in Medina the revelation was colorless and Muhammad presented himself in the line of Abraham. Turning to the Hadith, Goldziher recognized that *isnads*, chains of transmission, are not reliable sources of historical data; "Minute study soon reveals the presence of the tendencies and aspirations of a later day, the working of a spirit which wrests the record in favour of one or the other of the opposing theses in certain disputed questions."[35] In other words, *isnads* were used to legitimate later teachings by projecting them into the past. The inability to prove an early dating for the Hadith was, for Goldziher, a sign of Islam's progressive development beyond the Meccan and Medinan periods.

Questions of Jewish and Christian influences on the Qur'an were not the issue, he argued, but rather how Muhammad transformed the teachings of Judaism and Christianity. Still, Goldziher argued, like other Jewish historians, that the transformation Islam brought about in Arabia concerned ethical behavior:

> From the point of view of cultural history it is of little account that Muhammed's teaching was not the original creation of his genius which made him the prophet of his people, but that all his doctrines are taken from Judaism and Christianity. Their originality lies in the fact that these teachings were for the first time placed in contrast to the Arab ways of life by Muhammed's persistent energy. If we consider how superficially Christianity influenced the few Arab circles in which it penetrated, and how alien it was to the main body of the Arab people despite the support which it found in some districts of Arabia, we must be convinced of the antagonism of the Arabs to the ideas which it taught. Christianity never imposed itself on the Arabs and they had no opportunity to fight against its doctrines sword in hand. The rejection of a viewpoint diametrically opposed to their own found its expression only in the struggle of the Arabs against Muhammed's teachings. The gulf between the moral views of the Arabs and the prophet's ethical teachings is deep and unbridgeable.[36]

We see in Goldziher's Islam a template for presenting Judaism to the European Christian audience. Like Islam's Hadith, Judaism has Aggadah; like sharia, Judaism has halakha. Both are religions of monotheism, rejection of anthropomorphism, and emphasize ethical behavior. With Goldziher, Islam's function in modern Judaism reached a pinnacle as the projected image of what Judaism ought to become. Goldziher wrote, "My ideal was to elevate Judaism to a similar rational level [as Islam]."[37] With Judaism's alliance with Islam, Christianity is theologically marginalized; it is the religion that rests on dogma contrary to reason, on miracles and the supernatural. As religions of reason, Islam and Judaism were linked—by Jewish thinkers—in pointing to the alleged anomaly of Christianity, with its dogma of virgin birth, and so on, as a religion in violation of reason. That liberal Protestantism, by now well established in Germany, had long abandoned miracles and supernatural dogma in favor of the teachings of the historical figure of Jesus diverted attention to Catholicism as the religion contrary to reason.[38]

That Jews were more sympathetic to Islam than were Christians may have been due, in part, to Christian missionary efforts that sought to disparage Islam and convince Muslims to convert to Christianity. For example, the Scottish Orientalist and Christian missionary, William Muir (1819–1905), whose writings on Islam are marred by antagonisms—he suggested that Muhammad was inspired not by God but by the "Evil One"—served with British colonial administrators in India from 1837 to 1876 but retained an animosity toward Islam. The contrast offered by Gottlieb Leitner, a Hungarian Jew, is startling. Born in Budapest in 1840, Leitner was raised in Istanbul, where he was able to attend a Qur'an school, and then studied in England, where he was appointed professor of Arabic and Islamic law at King's College in 1859. His scholarship ranged from a history of the rise and development of Islam, written in Urdu, to an overview of Islam in the Middle East prior to the Mongol invasions, to numerous works of linguistics.

After receiving British citizenship in 1861, Leitner worked for the colonial administration in Punjab in an era when Lahore was undergoing rapid change. Lahore had become the new intellectual center following the destruction of Delhi during an 1857 revolt against the British. The shift from Delhi to Lahore also meant a shift from a cultural world focused on Persian to an Anglicized culture. Leitner became increasingly disaffected with the British colonial administrators in Punjab, although he was regarded as a valuable intermediary to the local society. In 1864 he was appointed principal of the newly founded Government College, and the following year he founded Anjuma-e Punjab, the Punjab Society, which provided a free library, sponsored public lectures, and led to the founding of the University of the Punjab in 1882.

During his extensive travels in the region, particularly the unexplored region between Kashmir and Afghanistan, Leitner studied local languages, publishing grammars and dictionaries of Dardic languages, and reports about regions of Central Asia and remote areas of India where he traveled. He also published—in Urdu—an introduction to Arabic and a history of the rise of Islam. Leitner was a leader in debates over educational reform and the language of instruction, insisting that Urdu be the language of instruction at the new university in Lahore, in opposition to those who wanted the language of higher education and scholarship to be English (or at least a European language). After returning to England in 1881, following several years of study in Heidelberg, Leitner raised funds to build a mosque in a suburb of London, Woking, the first in England, and the adjoining Centre for Oriental Studies, where he offered classes in Arabic and Islam. He died in 1889.

Leitner's opposition to aspects of colonialism was matched by his sympathy for Islam. He wrote:

> There is something better than mere knowledge, and that is sympathy: sympathy is the key to the meaning of knowledge—that which breathes life into what would be dead bones. There are instances of eminent scholars who, for want of sympathy, have greatly misjudged Muhammadanism. Sir William Muir, for example, has been led into very serious mistakes in dealing with this religion. . . . "To walk with God," to have God with us in our daily life with the object of obtaining the "peace that passeth all understanding," "to submit to the Divine will"—this we too profess to seek; but in Islam this profession is translated into practice, and is the cornerstone of the edifice of that faith.[39]

That passage stands in striking contrast, for example, to the view of Carl Heinrich Becker (1876–1933), an orientalist and politician who served as Prussian Minister of Culture from 1925 to 1930. While Becker emphasized the importance of Islam to Western civilization, he nonetheless saw it as defective and inferior, lacking a Renaissance and humanism.[40] Similar concerns about Islam's backwardness were expressed by Martin Hartmann (1851–1918), a scholar and diplomat who traveled extensively in the Ottoman Empire and the Middle East and who was encouraged by his friend Goldziher not to be too critical of Islam. Yet each wanted programs to "modernize" Muslims: Hartmann wanted a nationalist awakening among Arabs and Turks, Goldziher hoped for religious reform of Islam, and Becker and the Dutch scholar Christian Snouck Hurgronje wanted a privatization of Islam as a religion.[41]

Leitner was the exception to the Jewish scholars of the era: he did not bring knowledge of Hebrew and rabbinics to his study of Islam. Yet he stood in a marginal position in relation to the British authorities in India. Although his stepfather had nominally converted the family to Protestantism, and apparently did not assert a Jewish background in public, "his British colleagues were aware of his background."[42] Leitner had neither a missionizing interest nor a religious identification with the other British colonial administrators in Punjab and instead fostered relationships with Indian intellectuals, such as Muhammad Hussain Azad. Throughout his writing, Leitner expresses tremendous respect for Islam and a hope for religious tolerance and appreciation. The relationship of Judaism and Islam is most clearly expressed in the Woking mosque he built: its many windows are formed of cut stone, and the open spaces of the stone cutout are in the shape of Stars of David, a concrete representation of a Jewish–Islamic imbrication.

The "Golden Age of Spain" and Moorish Synagogues

Scholarship on the Qur'an was only one aspect of the Jewish interest in Islam. A widespread historical myth of a "Golden Age" of Muslim Spain, a *convivencia* in Andalus, captured the imagination of Jewish scholars, including Goitein, and was used to bolster the notion of a Jewish–Muslim "symbiosis."[43] Even Graetz, so often a curmudgeon on Islam, lauded tenth-century Muslim Spain, in language anticipating Goitein's, as the "only country that provided the fertile ground" on which Judaism was able to achieve its "most beautiful flowering and mature into a higher level of development."[44] By contrast, the portrayal of Christianity by Graetz is of a persecutory religion that brought endless suffering to the Jews.

According to Ismar Schorsch, it was nineteenth-century German Jews' identification with Muslim Spain and Sephardi Jewry that led to the choice of Moorish architecture in numerous European and American synagogues of the modern era.[45] Yet, on closer examination, the connection between historical imagination and aesthetics becomes more complex. Occasional public buildings were constructed in Germany during the nineteenth century in oriental architecture; the Potsdam water pumping station, built in 1841 in Moorish style to look like a mosque complete with a minaret, is a prime example.[46] Yet as the most prominent public displays of Jewish presence in cities and towns, synagogues would be an odd choice for Jews to build in an architectural style evoking an "Orientalism" that was supposedly disparaged as primitive and inferior. Moreover, while many Jews may have been well aware of the Sephardi tradition, few non-Jewish Europeans walking past a synagogue that looked like a mosque would have known about Sephardi Jews or even Muslim Spain. Why, then, would Jews choose that architectural style so often?[47]

Ivan Kalmar points to the opinions articulated by Jewish community leaders and architects (both Jewish and Christian) when they were designing European synagogues. Jews, Kalmar argues, embraced their status as "oriental," expressed by Moorish architecture. For example, at the stone laying of the Hamburg Temple, which opened in 1842, a hymn composed for the occasion proclaimed the union of East and West in a building that combined Moorish and Gothic features.[48] The architecture was certainly not an attempt at assimilation, nor an effort to overcome widespread negative identification of Jews as "oriental." Indeed, as Kalmar notes, in 1881, the distinguished Semitics scholar Paul de Lagarde ranted against the Moorish architecture of the New Synagogue in Berlin: "[Their] alien nature is stressed every day and in the most striking fashion by the Jews—who nevertheless wish to be made equal to Germans—through the style of their synagogue. What is the sense of raising claims to be called an honorary German and yet building the holiest site that one possesses in Moorish style, so as to never ever let anyone forget that one is a Semite, an Asiatic, a foreigner?"[49] Despite such rants, Jews retained Moorish style for their synagogues because, Kalmar argues, they wished to embrace an oriental identity that became increasingly important with the rise of neo-Hasidism and Zionism.

That Jewish embrace of oriental identity was not a generic embrace of the East but a Jewish triangulation with Islam and Christianity. What the Moorish synagogue accomplished was to break the identity of Judaism within Christianity's supersessionist economy. While Gothic architecture was too closely identified with Christianity and allowed little room for the separate identity of another religion, Moorish architecture could point to both Judaism and Islam without swallowing one or the other. Even more important, building a synagogue in Moorish architecture served to balance what was transpiring within. Even as the synagogue services were "Christianized"—the rabbi wearing the robes of a Protestant pastor, giving a weekly hortatory sermon, Hebrew prayers sung to German melodies, and an organ accompanying the service—the building was Islamicized, offering perhaps a balance or at least discouraging a sense of the capitulation of Judaism to the dominant Christianity of Europe.

For nineteenth-century European Jews to identify with Islam, then, constituted an affirmation of Jewish Orientalism but simultaneously an inversion of the conventional understanding of Orientalism introduced by Said. Rather than static, timeless, or regressive, as in the orientalist narrative, Islam and Judaism were linked in the Jewish narrative as religions of scientific and philosophical rationalism; rather than cultures of eroticism and sensuality, Islam and Judaism were religions of ethical law; such was the discourse of German Jews. Islam is a religion to combat paganism by transmitting Jewish monotheism. The German Jewish philosopher Salomon Formstecher (1808–89) commented in his major work, *Religion des Geistes*, published in 1841, "As a mission of Judaism to the pagan world, Islam finds its essence in the essence of Judaism," but in mixing Jewish with pagan thinking, Islam becomes "slavishly submissive to the despotic commands of a power-hungry God, and everyone who represents this submissiveness in his ways of thinking and acting is a Muslim."[50]

Rarely do we hear Jewish voices defining Islam as the negative counterpoint to Judaism or speculating on the sexual mystique of the harem. Rather, Islam becomes in Jewish terms a tool for spreading Judaism's monotheism. In creating that narrative, Jewish scholarship deflected attention from the abject role played by Judaism in Christian supersessionist theology. The emphasis on shared Jewish and Islamic commitments to monotheism, religious law, tolerance, and, in the Middle Ages, explorations of science and philosophy de-orientalized the two religions and linked them in an intimate partnership. Here is the voice of the German Jewish philosopher of the turn of the century, Hermann Cohen: "The Jewish philosophy of the Middle Ages does not grow so much out of Islam as out of the original monotheism. The more intimate relationship between Judaism and Islam—more intimate than with other monotheistic religions—can be explained by the kinship that exists between the mother and daughter religion."[51]

Imperialism within Philology

Josef Horovitz (1874–1931), Goitein's doctoral advisor, was yet another German Jew with a strong background in Hebrew texts. The son of a rabbi who was also a noted scholar, Horovitz studied Islam at the University of Berlin under Eduard Sachau, professor of Oriental Studies from 1876–1930, and then in 1905–6 traveled to Cairo, Damascus, and Istanbul with the Italian Orientalist Leone Caetani (1869–1935) in search of manuscripts.[52] Horovitz then became a professor of Arabic in India from 1907 to 1914 at the Mohammedan Anglo-Oriental College (after 1920, the Aligarh Muslim University), founded by Syed Ahmad Khan in 1877. Horovitz returned to Germany with the outbreak of the First World War, where he became professor at the University of Frankfurt and trained many of the next generation's leading Jewish scholars, including Goitein. One of Horovitz's students in India had been Hamiduddin Farahi, the teacher of Amin Ahsan Islahi, both important scholars of the Qur'an; remarkably, both refer to Hebrew texts in their work, no doubt as a result of Horovitz's teaching.[53] While in India, Horovitz also became close to Muhammad Ali—a scholar, poet, and political activist who helped found the All India Muslim League—and sympathized with his anticolonialist stance.

Horovitz's scholarship turned in many fruitful directions, including a study of the historical development of the Qur'an, which continued the work of Weil and Nöldeke on the contextualization and chronological sequencing of the suras. This was also the era of Wilhelm Dilthey's hermeneutics of sympathy and the rise of the History of Religions School that viewed religion as a phenomenon of human cultural expression. In his studies on the Qur'an, Horovitz shifted attention from the dominant paradigm of Jewish textual influences on the Qur'an, looking instead for a historical dynamic at work within the Qur'an, a dynamic that read and interpreted a wide range of influences. In subtle ways, Horovitz restored some agency to the Qur'an, which he presented as a text that constructed Muhammad, first as a prophet, and in the later, Medinan suras into a more formalized style. He saw a predominance of Old Testament influences on the Qur'an, yet argued that the later suras demonstrate greater influence of the New Testament. Yet, rather than labeling such influences as examples of Jewish or Christian influence, Horovitz painted a more dynamic and syncretistic picture of early Islam. In an article on proper names in the Qur'an, Horovitz breaks with the Geiger-inspired tradition of viewing the Qur'an as a receptacle of Jewish texts and ideas and instead demonstrates the difficulty in identifying a name as Jewish or Christian, given the shared linguistic and cultural traditions of both religions. The Qur'an is not simply a derivative of Judaism in Horovitz's vision but an entity that constructed itself by interpreting its very mixed and complex surrounding cultures.[54]

Horovitz's years of teaching at the Mohammedan Anglo-Oriental College while India was under British colonial rule no doubt influenced his anticolonial stance, expressed, for example, in his 1928 publication that warned of growing opposition in colonized regions to British rule.[55] Those concerns about colonialism had already been brought by Horovitz to Palestine in the 1920s, which was also under British control. Judah Magnes, founder and president of the Hebrew University, asked Horovitz to draw up plans for an Oriental Studies institute. While remaining at the University of Frankfurt, Horovitz wrote a proposal that envisioned an institute at the Hebrew University as a bilingual center, teaching classes in both Hebrew and Arabic. The course offerings would encompass both classical Islamic texts taught by European-trained philologists and courses on Islamic thought taught by imams on contemporary theological and legal debates in the Muslim world. His plan was never implemented.[56] However, during his visit to Jerusalem in 1925, Horovitz was credited with inspiring the creation of Brit Shalom, a bi-national movement of Jewish intellectuals who sought to create a democratic state in Palestine of Jews and Arabs.

Horovitz's anticolonialist stance resonated in his scholarship as well. Islam is not simply the colonized presence of Judaism or Christianity in Arabia but an autonomous religion, and the Qur'an is not simply a passive repository of Jewish and Christian traditions. Rather, he examines developments within the Qur'an, from the Meccan to the Medinan suras, with special attention to changes in language and style, and including pre-Islamic Arabic influences as well as those drawn from Judaism and Christianity. Horovitz's work breaks with the prior scholarship in which Islam was textualized and turned into an archive of Judaism, a receptacle of Jewish, Christian, and pagan ideas; rather, he presents Islam as an interpretative tradition with its own, original perspectives. In some sense, then, Horovitz's politics can be seen as reflected in his work, an attempt to decolonize Islam from Judaism.

However, Horovitz's approach to Islam was not always continued by his many students, who included David Sidersky, Heinrich Speyer, Yosef Yoel Rivlin, Ilse Lichtenstadter, Richard Ettinghausen, Martin Plessner, Gotthold Weil, and Shlomo Dov Goitein, among others. The publications by Jewish scholars of

Islam during the 1920s and 1930s continued to look for Jewish influences on Islamic traditions, returning Islam to the position of receptacle.[57] A prime example is the study of Israel Schapiro, who spoke in his introduction of aggadic influences on the Qur'an, published in 1907, of the Qur'an's "dependence on Jewish texts." The Qur'an elaborated on Jewish texts as a kind of "bejeweling" of the original, Schapiro wrote.[58] A few years earlier, Hartwig Hirschfeld, another Jewish scholar of Islam, had written that the "Qur'an, the textbook of Islam, is in reality nothing but a counterfeit of the Bible."[59] Within the colonialist setting, arguments that Islam was not an original revelation but a distortion of biblical and postbiblical Jewish teachings were used to denigrate Islam and were used by Christian missionaries hoping to convince Muslims to abandon Islam. Indeed, that was the motivation for publishing an English translation of Geiger's book on the Qur'an, undertaken by Christian missionaries in India at the turn of the century.[60]

Jewish scholarship on Islam at the turn of the century was fostered by two major developments: critical editions of rabbinic texts, particularly midrashic sources that were the building blocks of studies of the Qur'an, and the opening of university professorships to Jews. By the 1920s, a disproportionate number of professorships at German universities in Islamic Studies were occupied by Jewish scholars, and by 1933, 25 percent of the chairs in Oriental Studies were occupied by Jews, as the historian Ludmila Hanisch has demonstrated.[61] Many of these positions played key roles; for example, the Jewish Semitics scholar Eugen Mittwoch became director of an institute for the study of Oriental languages at the University of Berlin that offered certification to those seeking military, diplomatic, or business adventures in overseas colonies in Africa and Asia. It should be noted, however, that Mittwoch was not hired for a similar position at the University of Hamburg because he was a Jew; that position went instead to C. H. Becker.

The 1930s brought an abrupt end. Horovitz died suddenly in 1931, interrupting what might have been a major shift in the scholarly tone of Islamic Studies and in the politics of the Oriental Institute of the Hebrew University that ultimately did not implement his proposals. One of Horovitz's most gifted students, Heinrich Speyer, also died suddenly, in 1935, before publication of his book, *Die biblische Erzälungen im Qoran*.[62] Speyer's work opened new vistas by including gnostic and Samaritan sources in his reconstruction of the Qur'an and by expanding Horovitz's method of examining intra-Qur'anic shaping of the text. Speyer further described both Christian and Jewish influences on the Qur'an's reading of biblical texts, and the complex interaction of Jewish and Christian materials. His work was also reliant on significant advances in the field of rabbinics—the numerous midrashic texts published in the 1880s and 1890s by

Salomon Buber, for example, and, later, by Viktor Aptowitzer, among others. Describing the Qur'an's readings of biblical stories, Speyer writes of a "mutual influence on the religious world of imagination of Judaism, Christianity, and Islam." He notes further that Jewish beliefs were picked up by Christianity and transmitted to Islam, and then subsequently appeared in Jewish legendary texts.[63] There is a religious dynamism among the three religions, a scenario of mutual influences and interactions. The radical nature of Speyer's work, which was neglected for decades, is highlighted by its contrast to Goitein, who categorically denied Christian influence on the Qur'an, writing that it is "entirely impossible to assume that Christians, or even Judaeo-Christians, should have been the mentors of Muhammad," as the figure of Christ and "everything else Christian" is absent from the fifty to sixty oldest chapters of the Qur'an.[64] Rather, for Goitein, Muhammad is entirely indebted to Judaism. Though he does not say so explicitly, Goitein's arguments imply that the tolerance of Islam toward Judaism was derived, like all of Islam, from Judaism.

Conclusion

On a concrete level, the impact of imperialism on Jewish scholarship ranged from the availability of data (textual or material) that provided a basis for historical and philological investigations to political and economic engagement in German adventures. Germany did not have colonial holdings until late in the nineteenth century, when it gained pieces of Africa and Asia. However, Germany was a major force within Europe, especially in monetary and diplomatic engagement with France and Britain, starting much earlier, as those countries acquired territories abroad. Germany's influence was exerted in major investments in finance and building projects, including railroads, and in military and political involvement, particularly in the Middle East and the Ottoman Empire. Strongest of all was the supremacy of scholarship exerted by Germany, a scholarly vitality that attracted intellectuals from colonized regions, such as India, as well as Europeans.[65] Layered over these was a German "diplomacy of mediation" that sought to achieve German supremacy within the empires of Europe even without extensive colonial holdings.[66]

Even as Germans observed the extensive colonial reach of other Europeans countries, they engaged in "colonial fantasies" that influenced not only the highest levels of political and economic powers but also everyday practices and patterns of thought, though not without ambivalence. During the nineteenth century, oriental styles in design were exotic and enticingly un-German, but the presence of Jews in Germany was problematic and frequently described as foreign and oriental. After all, as Axel Stähler points out, in nineteenth-century German discourse, Jews were called "deutsch redende Orientalen" by the historian Heinrich von Treitschke, "orientalische Fremdlinge" by the publicist Wilhelm Marr, and "Wüstenvolk und Wandervolk" by the economist Werner Sombart.[67] The historicization of biblical studies by German Protestants in the nineteenth century reinforced the orientalization of Judaism, in the sense of the Orient as a shelter from the vicissitudes of progress; or, better put, Islam was timeless and Judaism was regressing. The philologists Friedrich Max Müller and Ernest Renan spoke of "Semitic monotheism" as the product of desert nomads foreign to European Aryans. The historian Thomas Trautmann has recently argued that the nineteenth-century search for language families quickly led to distinctions of race, Aryan and Semitic. The term "Arya," Trautmann writes, was taken from Sanskrit and applied by Max Müller to the people speaking Indo-European languages.[68]

The concept of the "Semitic" linked Jews and Arabs, Gil Anidjar points out, and participated in the racialization of philology and the study of religion.[69] Linking Jews with a non-European Orient was a tool of marginalization and even exclusion; how, then, did Jews respond and what role did their scholarship on Islam play?

Jews were both targets of an antisemitic rhetoric in Europe that labeled them as foreign Orientals and, at the same time, agents constructing oriental images of their own creation. Leora Batnitzky has recently argued that modern Judaism had to be shaped as a religion appropriate to the nation-state context.[70] Yet those European nation-states were also empires, and Jews adapted to the imperialist and orientalist culture of Europe in a two-sided fashion. On the one hand, European Jews identified themselves with the imperialist tradition by orientalizing the Jews of the East and South—the pious, Yiddish speaking Jews of Poland and the Jews of North Africa and the Ottoman Empire were viewed as primitive, superstitious, and effeminate.[71] On the other hand, they also identified themselves as oriental by linking Judaism with Islam, building synagogues in Moorish architecture but redefining their Islamic and Jewish Orient as a tradition of rationalism, scientific exploration, and, in particular, of religious tolerance. By the early twentieth century, Europeans no longer disparaged the Orient but embraced it as a source of primitive wisdom, insight, and the revitalization of Europe, and Jews, too, embraced Hasidism, cultural Zionism, and other East European Jewish movements as a source of regeneration and even remasculinization.[72] Those European attitudes had a lasting impact; Aziza Khazzoom and Gil Eyal, among others, have demonstrated lines of continuity between European Jewish orientalist attitudes and the social structures and political policies of the State of Israel.[73]

When Goitein arrived in Palestine, he first taught at the Reali School in Haifa, a school that continues to this day to have Jewish and Muslim students. In a pamphlet published in 1946, Goitein wrote that the Zionists were children of the Orient and should learn Arabic: "Learning Arabic is a part of Zionism, . . . a part of the return to the Hebrew language and to the Semitic Orient, which today is completely Arabic-speaking. We desire that our children, when they go out into the world, be able to feel that they are children of the Orient and able to act within it, just as we aspire that they do not lose the precious inheritance of European spirituality that we have brought with us." His apparent disillusionment with the growing Jewish disinterest in Arabic did not lead him, however, to question how the Arab population of Palestine experienced his overtures: were they as interested in a "symbiosis" as he was?[74] After all, Goitein wrote that the State of Israel is "the spearhead of the West in the midst of a still hostile Eastern world." The problem today, he writes, is "whether the culture of the West is strong enough to amalgamate the gigantic masses of the Eastern peoples—from Morocco to Indonesia and the Philippines—who have already adopted not only Western techniques, but also many Western patterns of thought, into one basic global civilization."[75] Surely the West was eager for the amalgamation, but was the East? What Goitein writes of Muhammad may have led him to imagine contemporary Arabs thinking in similar terms: "mentors who guided his first steps and provided him with the material and even the basic ideas of his historic mission."[76] Indeed, he claims that the "ancient parts of the Qur'an had come to him, so to speak, pre-fabricated, as an organic whole. His own contribution was his prophetic zeal."[77]

Further research is needed to trace the transfer of European Jewish scholarship to Palestine and Israel and to determine its cultural and political implications. The Jewish appropriation of Islam as a religion derived from Judaism may have been one factor in the difficulty some of the early Zionists had in distinguishing Islam and Muslim identity. Wearing a kaffiyeh, riding a camel, and assuming that Bedouin had retained an authentic, biblical identity to be recaptured by modern-day Jews may have been influenced in part by assumptions that Islam was simply Judaism in another form and thus available for easy reclamation.

The supersessionist nature of Jewish philological claims in relation to Islam could easily be appropriated for political goals, erasing Islam's originality and independence precisely at the time Jews laid claim to Palestine. Narratives describing a "Golden Age" of a Judeo-Islamic "symbiosis" or of Islam as Judaism's "salvation" could be invoked by some Jewish Orientalists in pre-state Palestine in an effort to suggest that Jewish settlements might bring about a revival of that medieval symbiosis.[78] Those narratives offered an alternative to Christian myths of a Jewish return to biblical land as a fulfillment of Christian theological hopes, but were no less supersessionist. The myths of history, however golden, did not mitigate political conflicts over land and dominion in Palestine, and Zionism could not offer a return to a mythical al-Andalus of Jewish-Muslim harmony.

Notes

1. The use of the term "symbiosis" by modern Jewish historians discussing Jewish history under Islamic rule is analyzed by Steven M. Wasserstrom, *Between Muslim and Jew: The Problem of Symbiosis under Early Islam* (Princeton, NJ: Princeton University Press, 1995).

2. S. D. Goitein, "Muhammad's Inspiration by Judaism," *Journal of Jewish Studies* (1958), 144–62, at 162.

3. S. D. Goitein, quoted in Gideon Libson, "Hidden Worlds and Open Shutters: S.D. Goitein between Judaism and Islam," in *The Jewish Past Revisited: Reflections on Modern Jewish Historians* (New Haven, CT: Yale University Press, 1998), 176.

4. Bernard Septimus, "Petrus Alfonsi on the Cult at Mecca," *Speculum* 56, no. 3 (1981): 517–33.

5. Libson, "Hidden Worlds and Open Shutters," 163–98.

6. Gil Eyal, *The Disenchantment of the Orient: Expertise in Arab Affairs and the Israeli State* (Stanford, CA: Stanford University Press, 2006); and Martin Jay, *Permanent Exiles: Essays on the Intellectual Migration from Germany to America* (New York: Columbia University Press, 1986).

7. As one of many examples of the invocation of Judaism as ethical monotheism, see David Koigen, "Christian Mystery and Jewish Moral Drama: Man's Role in History," *Commentary* 2 (1946): 175–79, at 175: "The power of the ethical is always more obvious in Judaism than in Christianity. The Hebrew consciousness has no need of taking refuge in Hellenic Christian mystery, because for it the great mystery was consummated, the cosmic tragedy already resolved, when the one God created, out of chaos, heaven and earth and all that lives and moves thereon."

8. Israel Friedlaender, "Shiitic Elements in Jewish Sectarianism," *Jewish Quarterly Review*, New Series, 2, no. 4 (April 1912): 481–516.

9. Susannah Heschel, "German-Jewish Scholarship on Islam as a Tool of De-Orientalization," *New German Critique* 117 (Fall 2012): 91–117.

10. Albert Hourani, *Islam in European Thought* (Cambridge: Cambridge University Press, 1991).

11. I might call attention here to the Protestant authors of the lives of Jesus, starting with Hermann Samuel Reimarus; to the surveys of first-century Palestinian religion and the role of Jesus within it, by Theodor Keim, Daniel Schenkel, and Karl von Hase, among others; and to the classic statements of liberal Protestantism, by Albrecht Ritschl and Adolf von Harnack.

12. Sigmund Freud, *Moses and Monotheism*, standard ed., vol. 23 (London: Hogarth, 1939, 1964), 118.

13. Paul Mendes-Flohr, *Divided Passions: Jewish Intellectuals and the Experience of Modernity* (Detroit: Wayne State University Press, 1991), 77–132.

14. Edward Said, *Orientalism* (New York: Pantheon, 1978).

15. Josef Van Ess, "Goldziher as a Contemporary of Islamic Reform," in *Goldziher Memorial Conference*, ed. Eva Apor and Istvan Ormos, 37–50 (Budapest: Hungarian Academy of Sciences, 2005).

16. Suzanne Marchand, *German Orientalism in an Age of Empire* (New York: Cambridge University Press, 2009).

17. For a brief survey of some of these major investments, see Nina Berman, *German Literature on the Middle East: Discourses and Practices, 1000–1989* (Ann Arbor: University of Michigan Press, 2013), 144–52.

18. Kris Manjapra, *Age of Entanglement: German and Indian Intellectuals across Empire* (Cambridge, MA: Harvard University Press, 2014).

19. See Moses Maimonides, "Epistle to Yemen," in *A Maimonides Reader*, ed. Isador Twersky, 437–62 (New York: Behrman House, 1972), 441.

20. Abraham Geiger, *Was hat Mohammed aus dem Judenthume aufgenommen? Eine von der Königl. Preussischen Rheinuniversität gekrönte Preisschrift* (Bonn, 1833; reprint, Osnabruck: Biblio Verlag, 1971), 98–99.

21. There is no complete edition of Goldziher's collected works, which he published primarily in German, but also in Hungarian. Some of his articles are collected in *Muslim Studies*, trans. S. M. Stern and C. R. Barber, ed. S. M. Stern, 2 vols. (New Brunswick, NJ: Aldine Transaction, 2006); and Ignaz Goldziher, *Vorlesungen über den Islam* (Heidelberg: C. Winter, 1963).

22. Abraham Geiger, *Das Judentum und seine Geschichte. In zwölf Vorlesungen. Nebst einem Anhange: Ein Blick auf die neuesten Bearbeitungen des Lebens Jesu* (Breslau: Schlettersche Buchhandlung, 1864), 156.

23. Heinrich Graetz, *Geschichte der Juden*, vol. 5 (Berlin, 1998), 102.

24. Ibid., 101.

25. Ibid., 100.

26. Ibid., 118.

27. University of Heidelberg archives, PA 2423: Personalakten Gustav Weil.

28. Unlike Geiger, Weil did not examine parallels between the two systems of religious law or compare Qur'anic passages to the Talmud.

29. Geiger, *Was hat Mohammed?*, 98–99.

30. Gustav Weil, *The Bible, the Koran and the Talmud* (London: Longman, Brown, Green, and Longmans, 1846), ix.

31. Gustav Weil, *Historische-Kiritische Einleitung in den Qoran* (Bielefeld: Velhagen & Klasing, 1844), 121.

32. Ayesha Jalal, *The Pity of Partition: Manto's Life, Times, and Work Across the India-Pakistan Divide* (Princeton: Princeton University Press, 2013); Robert Ivermee, "Shari'at and Muslim Community in Colonial Punjab, 1865–1885," *Modern Asian Studies* 48, no. 4 (October 2013): 1068–95; and Tim Allender, "Bad Language in the Raj: The 'Frightful Encumbrance' of Gottlieb Leitner, 1865–1888," *Paedagogica Historica* 43, no. 3 (June 2007): 383–403.

33. Martin Kramer, Introduction to *The Jewish Discovery of Islam: Studies in Honor of Bernard Lewis* (Tel Aviv: Moshe Dayan Center for Middle Eastern and African Studies, 1999), 15.

34. Avril Powell, *Scottish Orientalists and India: The Muir Brothers, Religion, Education and Empire* (Woodbridge, UK: Boydell, 2010).

35. Ignaz Goldziher, "The Principles of Law in Islam," in *Muslim Studies*, 2:302. Note that D. S. Margoliouth, a contemporary of Goldziher's, took the argument even further, as did Henri Lammens and Joseph Schacht.

36. Goldziher, *Muslim Studies*, 21.

37. Goldziher, *Tagebuch*, 59, cited by John Efron *German Jewry and the Allure of the Sephardic* (Princeton: Princeton University Press, 2015), 514.

38. That Jews insisted on presenting Christianity as a religion of doctrine contrary to reason, even though Protestants had abandoned such doctrines, is a phenomenon traced by Uriel Tal in his classic work, *Christians and Jews in Germany*, trans. Noah Jacobs (Ithaca, NY: Cornell University Press, 1976). A more recent study focusing on Jewish views of Catholicism is Ari Joskowicz, *The Modernity of Others: Jewish Anti-Catholicism in Germany and France* (Stanford, CA: Stanford University Press, 2013).

39. Gottlieb Leitner, *Muhammadanism* (Woking, England: The Oriental Nobility Institute, 1890), 3, 4.

40. Marchand, *German Orientalism*, 85, 364.

41. On Hartmann and the Arabs and Turks, see Dietrich Jung, *Orientalists, Islamists and the Global Public Sphere: A Genealogy of the Modern Essentialist Image of Islam* (Sheffield, UK: Equinox, 2011), 210.

42. Jeffrey M. Diamond, "The Orientalist-Literati Relationship in the Northwest: G.W. Leitner, Muhammad Hussain Azad and the Rhetoric of Neo-Orientalism in Colonial Lahore," *South Asia Research* 31:25 (2011), 28.

43. For a range of approaches to the question of "symbiosis," see Wasserstrom, *Between Muslim and Jew*; Gil Anidjar, *Semites: Race, Religion, Literature* (Stanford, CA: Stanford University Press, 2008); and Maria Rosa Menocal, *The Ornament of the World: How Muslims, Jews, and Christians created a Culture of Tolerance in Medieval Spain* (Boston: Little, Brown, 2002).

44. Graetz, *Geschichte der Juden*, 336.

45. Ismar Schorsch, "The Myth of Sephardic Supremacy," in *Leo Baeck Institute Year Book* 34 (1989), 47–66.

46. Berman, *German Literature on the Middle East*.

47. For a review of Moorish synagogue architecture, see Hannelore Kuenzel, *Islamische Stilelemente im Synagogenbau des 19. und frühen 20. Jahrhunderts* (Frankfurt am Main: Peter Lang, 1984).

48. Ivan Kalmar, "Moorish Style: Orientalism, the Jews, and Synagogue Architecture," *Jewish Social Studies* 7, no. 3 (Spring–Summer 2001): 68–100.

49. Paul Anton de Lagarde, quoted in ibid., 89.

50. Salomon Formstecher, *Religion des Geistes: Eine Wissenschaftliche Darstellung des Judentums nach seinem Charakter* (Frankfurt am Main: J. C. Hermann, 1841), 398.

51. Hermann Cohen, *Religion of Reason out of the Sources of Judaism*, trans. Simon Kaplan (New York: F. Ungar, 1972), 92. "Die jüdische Philosophie des Mittelalters erwächst nicht sowohl aus dem Monotheismus des Islam, als vielmehr aus dem ursprünglichen Monotheismus, und höchstens kann die Verwandtschaft, die zwischen dieser Tochterreligion und der der Mutter besteht, die innige Beziehung verständlich machen, welche intimer als sonstwo zwischen Judentum und Islam sich anbahnt." *Religion der Vernunft aus den Quellen des Judentums* (Leipzig: G. Fock, 1919), 107–8.

52. Lawrence Conrad, ed., Introduction to *Josef Horovitz, The Earliest Biographies of the Prophet and Their Authors* (Princeton, NJ: Darwin Press, 2002), xxiv.

53. Amin Ahsan Islahi, *Pondering over the Qur'an*, trans. Mohammad Saleem Kayani (New Delhi: Alkitab Publications, 2006), vol. 1, 227–28.

54. That approach is notable in Horovitz's article on proper names in the Qur'an, in which he demonstrates that the culture in which early Islam took shape was multicultural, and Jews, Christians, Parsees, Arabic poets, and others who populated Arabia shared languages and texts, so that identifying a Jewish or Christian source is not clear-cut: "Religious communities made use of entirely identical expressions even for specifically religious concepts. For this reason an expression, concept, or tradition . . . must not necessarily be assumed to have reached Mohammed through Jewish mediation." Josef Horovitz, "Jewish Proper Names and Derivatives in the Koran," *Hebrew Union College Annual* II (1925): 145–229, at 147.

55. Josef Horovitz, *Indien unter Britischer Herrschaft* (Leipzig, Berlin: Verlag von B. G. Teubner, 1928).

56. Menachem Milson, "The Beginnings of Arabic and Islamic Studies at the Hebrew University in Jerusalem," *Judaism* 45, no.2 (Spring 1996): 169–83.

57. David Sidersky, *Les origines des légendes musulmanes dans le Coran et dans les vies des prophètes* (Paris: P. Geuthner, 1933); and Heinrich Speyer, *Von den biblischen Erzählungen im Qoran* (Berlin: Akademie fuer die Wissenschaft des Judentums, 1924).

58. Israel Schapiro, *Die haggadischen Elemente im erzaehlenden Teil des Korans* (Berlin: H. Itzkowski, 1907), Part 1, 5.

59. Hartwig Hirschfeld, Preface to *Composition and Exegesis of the Qur'an* (London: Royal Asiatic Society, 1902), ii.

60. According to the translator's preface, the head of the Cambridge Mission at Delhi requested an English translation for use in his dealings with Muslims. Abraham Geiger, *Judaism and Islam: A Prize Essay*, trans. Anonymous (Madras: SPCK, 1898).

61. Ludmila Hanisch, "Akzentverschiebung—Zur Geschichte der Semitistik und Islamwissenschaft während des 'Dritten Reichs,'" in *Berichte zur Wissenschaftsgeschichte* 18 (1995): 217–26, at 218.

62. The difficulty in publishing Speyer's book in Nazi Germany is recounted by Franz Rosenthal, "The History of Heinrich Speyer's Die biblischen Erzählungen im Qoran," in *"Im vollen Licht der Geschichte": Die Wissenschaft des Judentums und die Anfänge der kritischen Koranforschung*, ed. Dirk Hartwig et al., (Würzburg: Ergon Verlag, 2008), 113.

63. "Jüdische Sagen und Vorstellungen verschwinden, sobald das Christentum sich für seine Dogmenlehre auf sie bezieht, gehen vom Christentum in den Islam über, um auf diesem Umwege spater wieder in der üüdischen Haggada aufzutauchen." Heinrich Speyer, *Die biblische Erzählungen im Qoran* (Hildesheim: G. Olms, 1961), xiii.

64. Goitein, "Muhammad's Inspiration," 158.

65. Manjapra, *Age of Entanglement*, 5.

66. Joern Thielmann, "Islam and Muslims in Germany: An Introductory Exploration," in *Islam and Muslims in Germany*, ed. Ala Al-Hamarneh and Joern Theilmann, (Leiden: Brill, 2008), 2.

67. Axel Stähler, "Orientalist Strategies of Dissociation in a German 'Jewish' Novel: Das neue Jerusalem (1905) and Its Context," *Forum for Modern Language Studies* 45, no. 1 (2008): 51–89.

68. Thomas R. Trautmann, *Aryans and British India* (Berkeley: University of California Press, 1997), 16.

69. Anidjar, *Semites*.

70. Leora Batnitzky, *How Judaism Became a Religion: An Introduction to Modern Jewish Thought* (Princeton, NJ: Princeton University Press, 2011).

71. See, for example, Samuel Romanelli, *Travail in an Arab Land*, trans. Yedida K. Stillman and Norman A. Stillman (Tuscaloosa: University of Alabama Press, 1989).

72. Martin Buber, Max Nordau, Franz Rosenzweig, and Erich Fromm are among those linked to a movement of Jewish "regeneration," though with different meanings for each.

73. Eyal, *Disenchantment of the Orient*; and Aziza Khazzoom, "The Great Chain of Orientalism: Jewish Identity, Stigma Management, and Ethnic Exclusion in Israel," *American Sociological Review* 68, no. 4 (August 2003): 481–510.

74. This question was raised by Professor Walid Saleh, University of Toronto, at a conference on S. D. Goitein held at Brandeis, March 2014.

75. S. D. Goitein, *Jews and Arabs: Their Contacts through the Ages* (New York: Schocken, 1964), 9.

76. Goitein, "Muhammad's Inspiration," 152.

77. Ibid., 155.

78. Yuval Evri, "Translating the Arab-Jewish Tradition: From al-Andalus to Palestine/Land of Israel," *Berlin Essays of the Forum Transregional Studies* 1/2016, 5.

4

NOT THE RETIRING KIND

JEWISH COLONIALS IN ENGLAND IN THE
MID-NINETEENTH CENTURY

Adam Mendelsohn

As BEFITS A nation birthed from a penal colony, Australia and its Jews celebrate Moses Joseph, a convict transported in 1827 for theft, as one of the founding fathers of the Jewish community of Sydney. Within a handful of years of his arrival in the antipodes, Joseph had amassed enough money to open a tobacconist shop—his wife, a free settler who followed him to Australia, was, for legal reasons, his nominal employer—and began a meteoric rise that left him a substantial landowner, pioneering industrialist, shipping tycoon, and leading gold buyer in the early 1850s. Chained migration spurred the unmanacled variety: his success enticed a flotilla of family members to sail for Australia and New Zealand. The fledgling Jewish community in Sydney depended on his energy and largesse, as did a variety of other causes. (His fanciful coat of arms—with "Jerusalem" in Hebrew at its center—appears in stained glass at the University of Sydney, flanked by those of colonial luminaries and Queen Victoria.) He was instrumental in creating and supporting several Jewish institutions in the colonial port town, including its first permanent synagogue and Jewish school. Joseph returned to England as a prosperous merchant—he was granted an absolute pardon in 1848—with his once-sullied image burnished by success. In London he became a patron of Jewish causes, donating money to schools and other institutions in the capital that sought to uplift and modernize Jewish life.[1]

Moses Joseph was not the only Jew who returned to England reinvented as a colonial gentleman and with the newfound means to influence metropolitan Jewish life. He was part of a small cohort of Jewish return migrants who, though now ostensibly men of leisure, were generally not the retiring kind. Elevated in status and sought after for wealth earned under a colonial sun, some became advocates of communal modernization and religious reform in the middle decades of the nineteenth century. Within a Jewish community still dominated by an entrenched communal aristocracy whose authority rested on long-held wealth, prestige, and traditions of noblesse oblige, some of these newly wealthy colonials threw their weight behind efforts to remake the community and its leadership. They were not alone in returning from the colonies with firm ideas about the need for political and social change. Similar patterns were evident among non-Jewish colonials who returned to the metropole. Yet in spite of the high rate of return—by one estimate 40 percent of all emigrants from England, two million in total, returned between 1860 and 1914—and the assertiveness of some of these returnees, relatively little work has systematically assessed their influence.[2]

The impact of members of the new Jewish colonial elite who returned to Albion from the settlement colonies is particularly striking when compared with that of Jews who rose to positions of prominence in the empire's possessions in Asia.[3] With a handful of important exceptions, Jews of Asian origin were more notable for their absence from London society than for their presence. Why did relatively few Jews from Britain's empire in the East decamp to London in the middle decades of the century? The answer is less obvious than it might at first seem. For although Jews who returned from the settlement colonies were generally native-born Englishmen and those who migrated from Asia to Albion were not, the latter were part of a small stream of Indian subjects of the Crown who settled in England.[4] It was not for want of attachment to the empire. In Burma, Aden, and India, Jews embraced the trappings of imperial culture and in many cases sought an education in English for their children. It was not because the colonial elite could ill afford to settle in England. Several Jewish families in India attained wealth unimaginable to the likes of Moses Joseph and his ilk, and sent their sons to the imperial capital to establish branches of their expansive enterprises. Nor was it because they feared rejection by London society. Some achieved a social rank far higher than all but the best of the Anglo-Jewish elite—attaining a status far exceeding that of those who returned from Australia—and were quickly incorporated into the inner circle of the Jewish aristocracy. Yet for all their prosperity and prestige, those who swapped humid Bombay for dank London appear to have been less inclined to press for change within the Anglo-Jewish community than were the returnees from the settlement colonies. So if money, culture, and their potential reception were seemingly not insurmountable obstacles, why did comparatively few Jews from Britain's colonial possessions in Asia resettle in England? And why were they comparatively quiet when it came to promoting reform in the religious and social life of Anglo-Jewry?

Until recently, historians were reticent on the reciprocal influences of empire on Jewish life and Jews on the empire.[5] Although Jews in the British Empire were only a tiny minority, their experience can add to our understanding of several subjects that have attracted considerable notice among those who study the empire.[6] Attention to Jews aids the efforts of those who have pointed to the heterogeneity of the imperial project by identifying the ethnic and religious diversity of the traders, missionaries, officials, and farmers who settled the empire. Recognition of the cultural, religious, familial, and mercantile connections that bound Jews in the metropole to those in the colonies augments the arguments of those attuned to the operation of networks within the imperial realm.[7] And the careers of Moses Joseph and other colonial Jewish returnees offer fresh perspective on the much-debated relationship between Britain and its colonies. Far from being passive carriers of a metropolitan Jewish culture transplanted to distant shores, Joseph and his fellow Jews in the settlement colonies were forced to adapt to the particular challenges of being Jewish in colonial environments distant from major centers of Jewish life. This in turn shaped how they approached Anglo-Jewish society when they returned to England after successful colonial careers.

Anglo-Jewry had already partaken in colonial commerce well before the Victorian age. For more than a century prior, members of the Anglo-Jewish elite made and bolstered fortunes in trading with India, North Africa, the Levant, the Mediterranean, and the Caribbean.[8] Such opportunities required capital and connections; most Jews in England struggled to make ends meet as peddlers, artisans, and petty shopkeepers. Some Jewish hawkers in London were at the bottom end of an international distribution chain that sometimes included Jewish intermediaries. Among the baubles sold by Jewish peddlers in the street trade were sponges from the Levant and Adriatic, ostrich feathers from North Africa, and oranges and lemons, fruits of Mediterranean commerce. Jews were also active in the port towns which serviced the British fleet (Charles Dickens described Portsmouth as a "Seaport Town principally remarkable for mud, Jews and sailors"): cashing pay, acting as bankers and creditors to sailors and their families, selling slops aboard ship, and even press-ganging men into service.[9] Yet in the first decades of the nineteenth century, the impoverished Jewish majority was many times more likely to encounter the colonies as indentured servants, transported criminals, and subjects to be shipped off in elite-sponsored colonization schemes than as direct participants in colonial ventures.[10] This pattern began to shift when an increasingly industrialized (and acquisitive) Britain rediscovered its appetite for colonization, establishing settlement colonies at the Cape (acquired permanently in 1806) and antipodes (beginning with New South Wales in 1788) and steadily accumulating and consolidating territory and control in South Asia and the Far East. This second British Empire presented a far larger set of opportunities to a wider swathe of Jews at home and abroad than did its earlier imperial forays.[11] Demand from the colonies stimulated metropolitan markets; Jews in England were fortuitously positioned in a number of marginal niches that were boosted by the imperial economy. Others were drawn as immigrants to Australia, Canada, and South Africa by the promise of a fresh start away from the slums of London. And in Britain's eastern empire— Aden, India, Burma, and the treaty ports of China—a Jewish population with roots in the East found a lucrative niche servicing the needs of the empire.

Moses Joseph was not alone in starting his life anew in the antipodes as a convict—he was one of at least 384 Jewish chained migrants transported to Australia between 1788 and 1830—but he and his fellow Jewish felons were soon outnumbered by free settlers. A striking percentage of those who joined them in Australia in the 1830s were scions of leading Sephardic and Ashkenazi families. As many as a third of early voluntary Jewish migrants to the antipodes belonged to the British communal aristocracy. The expanding settlement colonies of the British Empire provided an alluring prospect for the sons and daughters of the Anglo-Jewish elite.[12] Unlike the majority of their penurious fellow immigrants to Australia, the scions of the de Pass, Furtado, Mocatta, Montefiore, Phillips, and Samuel clans came as unfettered investors and speculators. For footloose Joseph Barrow Montefiore, impatient at age twenty-five with his position as a broker on the London Exchange (and overshadowed by his more successful and illustrious cousin, Moses), Australia was terra nova. The family was already active in the West India trade; here was the means to establish his own colonial fortune.[13] He arrived in 1829 to take possession of a vast land grant, which he supplemented with a banking and export business in partnership with his brother in London. During the boom years of the 1830s, Montefiore and his fellow pedigreed immigrants prospered, sending Australian produce to London, and trading with the United States, China, and the South Seas.[14] Montefiore's first Australian fortune, however, collapsed in 1841, a victim of his overenthusiastic speculation and the looming economic depression in the colony. The de Pass brothers, also men of elevated pedigree, encountered fewer such headaches at the Cape. Aaron and Elias de Pass arrived in Cape Town in 1846, quickly ensconcing themselves as pioneers of the coastal trade. Alongside interests in shipping, whaling, and copper mining, the brothers dominated the export of phosphorous-rich guano, harvested from the islands that dotted the western coast of South Africa, to England and the United States. This natural fertilizer was much in demand by farmers. The de Pass brothers distanced themselves from this foul enterprise by giving generously to Jewish charities in Cape Town, and did the same when they returned to London.[15]

If these sons of privilege were somewhat insulated from the jolting downturns that periodically disrupted colonial growth—Montefiore returned to stake out a second fortune in South Australia in 1846—they were far from alone in profiting from empire. The settlement colonies were remarkably open to enterprising immigrants drawn to commerce. Although the rate of failure was high, settlers benefited from growing international demand for colonial produce and an expanding domestic market driven by immigration. The settlement colonies provided a relatively fluid economic and social environment, comparatively free of entrenched competition and barriers to entry, enabling legions of Jewish settlers to transcend their humble antecedents. Benjamin Norden and his four brothers, the sons of a petty shopkeeper in Hammersmith, arrived in South Africa in 1820, sent by a scheme funded by the British government to settle close to four thousand settlers as farmers on the disputed eastern frontier of the Cape Colony. After failing as a farmer on soil better suited to grazing than cultivation, Norden and many of his fellow migrants gravitated toward the towns and trading posts of this unsettled province. After he established himself as an auctioneer in Grahamstown in 1829, Norden dabbled in the lucrative trade with the Xhosa and Zulu, bartering beads, ironware and guns for ivory and cattle. In 1840 he moved to Cape Town where he set himself up as a merchant and concession agent, also sniffing opportunity in the guano trade.[16] By the time Benjamin Norden returned to London in 1858, he had firmly established himself as a prosperous colonial gentleman, a patron of local causes, and midwife in the difficult birth of the Cape Town synagogue. His tenure in Cape Town had not been without its setbacks.[17] He left behind a reputation for extraordinarily litigiousness, noteworthy even by the elevated standards of colonial lawsuits. (So important was credit to colonial businessmen that many were quick to resort to the courts to protect their integrity, lest damage to their reputations harm access to money at home and abroad.[18])

Benjamin Norden was by no means the only settler of modest background who returned to Britain with a remade reputation. Several who left London stained by the poverty of the East End returned in triumph as prosperous colonial gentlemen. The colonies provided opportunity for reinvention, enabling a minority of those who left Albion impecunious (or in shackles) to return gilded by success. (As Lady Duff-Gordon, visiting Cape Town in 1861, wryly remarked "a change in hemisphere will reverse reputations."[19]) Others were able to wipe clean the taint of failure. Jacob Phillips, bankrupted when his jewelry business failed in Birmingham in 1832, revived his fortunes in Hong Kong in the 1840s. Phillips imported guns and other Birmingham manufactures to the treaty port, and sent luxuries back home to be sold by his business partner. The firm opened branch offices in Australia and the Philippines, which he staffed with family members. Phillips returned to Birmingham in 1851 as a prosperous merchant, using his new status to become a patron of communal and civic causes.[20] Norden, Phillips, and Moses Joseph were among a cohort of prosperous colonial Jews who retired to England. London exercised a powerful draw for successful colonists, offering access to culture and leisure unavailable in still rough-and-ready colonial port cities as well as promising comfort and prestige to those who returned with ample funds.

A striking number of those who returned to London as colonial worthies became supporters of communal reform, providing funding, leadership, and endorsement to several new welfare, educational, and religious initiatives. Their priorities were Jewish inflections on issues that agitated other colonial returnees. Some colonists who became familiar with responsible and accountable government, free education, and universal male suffrage at the edges of the empire pushed for the same in England.[21]

In several cases, support for religious reform among Jewish returnees involved support for the contentious West London Synagogue of British Jews whose adoption of religious reforms in the 1840s—a shorter prayer service, a new prayer book, and regular sermons in English—created fissures within the communal elite and challenged the authority of the chief rabbinate. Those who had spent decades in the West Indies, antipodes, or at the Cape may have become inured of a less rigid religious environment and accustomed to exercising power within the Jewish community. Distance diluted the authority of religious leaders in London. Moses Joseph, the president of the York Street Synagogue in Sydney in 1845, remonstrated to the British chief rabbi that it was all but impossible to maintain traditional Jewish life in Australia. "So far distant as we, Reverend Sir, are from your guidance and considering the nature of our congregation, you cannot expect we are very orthodox in all matters relating to our faith." Delays in the passage of letters provided congregations with significant latitude while they waited months for responses to their questions. Local realities also demanded compromises. With a gender imbalance in New South Wales weighted at two men for every woman in 1841, the exclusion of the intermarried would doom the already foundering congregations.[22] This problem was not unique to Sydney and its surrounds, nor was it confined to poor members of the community. Benjamin Norden, the leading light and major benefactor of the fractious congregation in Cape Town—and the husband of a Christian wife—apparently saw no contradiction between his communal role and his personal affairs.[23] While intermarriage was the most visible compromise with local circumstances, friction arose between hazans (synagogue officiants) and colonial congregations due to widespread apathy toward kashrut (dietary laws), mikvehs (ritual baths), and synagogue attendance. Many wealthy Jewish colonists had little patience for a meddlesome priest, particularly when they held power over his paycheck and had functioned without the services of a hazan for lengthy periods.

Colonial grandees who returned to Britain swapped the autonomy of a freewheeling and flexible religious environment for a rigid Anglo-Jewish alternative where the wants of the chief rabbinate were harder to ignore. Colonial success may have conferred a degree of confidence and openness to new ideas, increasing their willingness to challenge the structures and norms of Jewish life in the metropolis. Although London high society may have disdained parvenus from the colonies, deep pockets and self-assurance bought influence.[24] While it is less surprising that Joseph Barrow Montefiore—first president of the Sydney synagogue and a scion of a patrician family deeply embedded in communal leadership in London—became one of the two founding wardens of the reform West London Synagogue of British Jews, Benjamin Elkin provides a more illustrative example.[25] Born in Portsea in 1783, Elkin left England at twenty-one for Barbados, where he prospered initially as a watchmaker, first working from a small shed, and later as a successful general merchant. He took a leading role in the organization of the Bridgetown synagogue, insisting that those who had taken slaves as concubines be barred from reading from the Torah, an unpopular edict that threatened the financial position of the congregation. Elkin later returned to England but continued to profit from the West Indian trade. In 1841 he became a founding member of the West London Synagogue of British Jews and a leading polemist on its behalf in the Jewish press in England and the United States. In this latter role he sought to differentiate the reforms undertaken in London as more restrained and halachically acceptable than those initiated by religious reformers in central Europe, and he sought to defend the spirituality, rationality, and egalitarianism of the congregation (boasting that "in our Synagogue there is no more distinction between rich and poor than in the grave" and extolling the education offered to girls) as well as its fidelity to Talmud law. He was far removed in social status and background from the phalanx of the Montefiores and Mocattas and other patricians who made up much of the membership of the renegade synagogue. Even in death he created a headache for the Orthodox establishment: a dispute over the permissibility and form of his burial in the Great Synagogue cemetery in 1848 widened the gulf between the early reformers and the Orthodox establishment.[26] Other wealthy colonists of humble backgrounds also turned their energy and time toward charity and communal reform. Rambunctious Elias Davis, who spent some time in Australia, was also a vocal proponent of the modernization of the management of the synagogue and an early backer of the Sussex Hall, the Jews' and General Literary Institution.[27] Benjamin Norden reestablished himself in London as a well-to-do philanthropist, sponsoring the Soup Kitchen and poor visiting committees. He was a stern proponent of the reform of the newly established Board of Guardians, criticizing its patrician overseers for excluding public accountability.[28]

Although greater in number and more confident in their identity as Englishmen than the handful of Jewish expatriates from the Raj now living in

London, those Jewish colonial gentlemen who had returned from Australia and the Caribbean must have looked in wonder at the prominence achieved by this smaller group of Jews of Indian origin. Their success belies easy assumptions about the role of race in determining status in the metropole. None were more famous than Arthur, Reuben, and Albert Sassoon, the sons of a merchant family that had made an immense fortune trading opium, textiles, and cotton in India and China. Soon after moving to England, the Sassoons started to run in the same dizzying social circles as the Prince of Wales, joined the gentry and were awarded titles, and established a dynasty that intermarried with the Anglo-Jewish elite. Yet for all of their social prestige and tremendous wealth, the Sassoons and scions of other Jewish families with roots in the East arguably had less influence on Jewish life in England than did the likes of Joseph, Norden, and Elkin. Why was this the case? And what might this tell us comparatively about the experience of Jews in various parts of Britain's empire?

The nature of Britain's expansion in Asia made it particularly dependent on middlemen. Britain—operating until 1858 in the guise of the East India Company—maintained a light footprint in terms of personnel but left a deep imprint in terms of power. This was a mercantile empire driven, above almost all else, by profit. Its key centers—Bombay, Calcutta, Rangoon, Singapore, Shanghai, and Hong Kong—bloomed along with the fields of cotton, poppies, and tea cultivated for trade with China and England.[29] Outside of administrators, merchants, and military men, these centers attracted relatively few British settlers, relying heavily on enterprising proxies and intermediaries to operate effectively. This management structure created opportunities for ethnic minorities to flourish by servicing the empire. In return, the colonial authorities provided a relatively stable and liberal political environment and rewarded ethnic elites for their loyalty. The major ports of the eastern empire became multiethnic cities, home to conspicuous and successful trading diasporas. Rival ethnic entrepreneurial networks competed and occasionally collaborated in pursuing mercantile ventures. This cooperation sometimes stretched beyond the business sphere. In 1839 Jewish, Parsee, Hindu, and Muslim business leaders in Bombay sent a joint petition to the governor protesting against proselytizing Scottish missionaries who operated in the city.[30]

A Baghdadi Jewish diaspora that settled in Bombay and Calcutta from the early decades of the nineteenth century onward proved particularly adroit at ministering to the needs of the empire in the East. While earlier generations of Baghdadi merchants had conducted a thriving trade with the East India Company in Surat and Madras, the most entrepreneurial of the recent arrivals benefited from the acquisitive and mercantile-minded new imperial order.[31] By the 1830s Jews dominated the retail trade in Bombay; by the last quarter of the century they controlled parts of the city's trade with China and fed the voracious mills of industrial England with cotton from the subcontinent. Like camp followers behind an advancing army, this Baghdadi diaspora established trading posts in each of the new territories claimed by Britain in the East. Offshoots of this network flowered in Aden, Hong Kong, the five treaty ports in China, and Lower Burma.[32] A small group established a beachhead in Australia, which had trading ties with both China and India.[33] The most visibly successful member of this diaspora was David Sassoon, based in Bombay, who rotated his sons between offices in China, Baghdad, and London. The branches and factories of his sprawling business network were staffed by Jews recruited from Baghdad.[34] The firm shipped opium to China, sent Bombay yarn to Lancashire and finished piece goods to India, exported English textiles to Persia and Persian weaves to England, and supplied tea to the thirsty British market and sugar to sweet-toothed Indians. The global reach and interconnectedness of this commodity trade was amply demonstrated during the American Civil War. When the blockade of Confederate ports interrupted the supply of cotton to the mills of Lancashire, the Sassoons and other exporters rushed lower quality Indian crop to satisfy the demand. Bombay boomed while the war lasted but suffered after Appomattox, when southern cotton returned to market and cotton prices began a precipitous decline.[35]

The Sassoons and other beneficiaries of the empire in the East were heavily invested in its success. The colonial administration was a guarantor of the safety of the mercantile elite and in turn relied heavily on a class known to be well disposed toward the Raj. This codependence tightened during and after the Sepoy Rebellion (1857–58). In a conspicuous act of patriotism, David Sassoon offered to enlist a Jewish legion to support the beleaguered British. When the last vestiges of the rebellion were crushed in July 1858, he instructed the Jews of Bombay to pray for the royal family and to illuminate their homes in celebration. The Baghdadi synagogue in Calcutta held a thanksgiving service. (Sassoon's flamboyant acts of fealty may have also been connected to the British occupation of Bushehr in 1857, a major depot for his trade with Persia. More than ever, his economic position relied on remaining in the good graces of the imperium.) Following the mutiny, a newly installed British colonial leadership in Bombay actively wooed the merchant class, encouraging investment in railroads and wharfage, infrastructure that could serve dual military and mercantile ends. Alongside its substantial capital investment—the Sassoons, for example, took considerable risks developing Bombay harbor—the Baghdadi elite developed a strong psychic attachment to empire and its values. Sir Bartle Frere, governor of Bombay, recognized the utility (and dependence) of the community. Writing in 1862, he noted that they were "like the Parsees, a most valuable link between us and the natives—oriental in origin and appreciation—but English in their objects and associations, and, almost of necessity, loyal."[36]

The Sassoon family exemplified the acculturation of the Baghdadi diaspora. David Sassoon appears to have not learned English and continued to use Judeo-Arabic in his business dealings. He did, however, send his son Abraham to London at age fifteen to be tutored by Hermann Adler (the future chief rabbi) and established ties of friendship and patronage within the English expatriate elite in Bombay. Whatever his private convictions, Sassoon must have been well aware that the appearance of loyalty and patriotism paid dividends. During the boom that accompanied the American Civil War, the Bartle Frere administration pushed merchants to fund civic projects. English and vernacular schools sprung up across the Bombay Presidency, including the Benevolent Institution, sponsored by David Sassoon to serve the Jews of Bombay. The school provided education in both Hebrew and English, employing the latest scientific approach and Western priorities: without vernacular instruction, the children of poor migrants would be "half educated or even quite ignorant" and hence unemployable. Sassoon commissioned Moritz Steinschneider to produce several lavishly illustrated textbooks for the school. Although Sassoon chose a noted German scholar for the task, the books were unabashedly English in tone and object, containing the national anthem, prayers for the government and Queen Victoria, and the Decalogue and Shema in English translation. This emphasis on modern pedagogy squared with Victorian notions of scientific charity: Sassoon also sponsored a bevy of institutions dedicated to self-improvement.[37] So pronounced was his public Anglophilia—parties to welcome arriving governors, substantial donations to patriotic causes, sponsorship of statues to British monarchs—that one Bombay wit proclaimed his surprise that David chose to name his daughter Mozelle rather than Victoria. In fact, there is some evidence of his ambivalence toward acculturation. Tellingly, his sons waited until his death before anglicizing their names: Abdullah became Albert, Abraham Shalom switched to Arthur. Although the family patriarch could slow the tide of anglicization during his lifetime, his sons embraced the trappings and rewards of life as colonial grandees and later when they entered London society.[38]

The process of anglicization advanced apace elsewhere within the Baghdadi diaspora. The trend was accelerated by the strong sense of loyalty that many Baghdadi migrants felt toward a liberal regime that had provided ample space for the exercise of their mercantile skills. Others, who were protectees or subjects of the British Crown, were invested in its success.[39] Their acculturation was expressed in a variety of ways, ranging from the private (brides who signed *ketubot* that compared the sanctity of the marriage contract with an act of Parliament at Westminster) to the public (patriotic celebrations organized by synagogues to mark Victoria's birthday). In Hong Kong, Singapore, Shanghai, and Rangoon, Baghdadis quickly adopted English as their vernacular and sent their children to schools modeled on metropolitan institutions.[40] An unexpected corollary of ac-culturation was a deliberate distancing from the Bene Israel, the community of Indian Jews who claim to have settled on the Konkan Coast before the Common Era. As Baghdadis integrated into colonial society, they became increasingly anx-ious to preserve their status and civic inclusion. This became particularly acute following the mutiny as Britons in India become more race conscious. Yet as early as 1836, David Sassoon attempted to divide the Jewish cemetery in Bombay into separate sections for Baghdadis and Bene Israel. These tensions were replicated elsewhere. Arguments ostensibly relating to religious differences between the two communities sometimes masked the Baghdadis' efforts to underline their differences from their Bene Israel brethren.[41]

If Jews in Asia became eager handmaidens to their colonial rulers, why did relatively few Jews from this portion of the empire settle in England? The success of the Sassoons in India is somewhat deceptive. While Baghdadis were the most conspicuous Jewish beneficiaries of the imperial economy, the Baghdadi dias-pora was itself divided by class and social status.[42] The Baghdadi community in Bombay, the sun around which a constellation of satellite communities in Asia orbited, reflected this internal diversity. David Sassoon and his firm acted as a polestar, drawing poor Jews from Baghdad, Damascus, and Aleppo to Bombay in search of jobs. In 1873 only twenty-nine Jews, the majority presumably Baghda-dis, qualified for a municipal franchise in that city that was based on payment of rates exceeding fifty rupees.[43] Although other Jewish subcommunities also carved out niches that ranged from the menial—railway construction in Man-dalay or as sailors aboard the ships trading with China—to the entrepreneurial, the empire was stinting in doling out riches in Asia. There were, however, manifold ways of servicing the imperial project: in Port Said and Suez, the shunting yard of the British Empire, enterprising Jews pimped prostitutes to sailors and tour-ists bound for India, the Far East, and Australia.[44] The Bene Israel embraced military service in the Sepoy regiments, first for the East India Company and later in the Bombay Army. Male members of the community enlisted in consid-erable numbers—the Bene Israel lived within a major recruiting area—and were deployed in imperial wars in Persia (1855–57), China (1856–60), and Abyssinia (1867–68). Access to Western education opened opportunities outside of India as well. Bene Israel and Cochini Jews parlayed their literacy in English to work as clerks and managers for British and Baghdadi firms in Burma. Others prospered as suppliers and outfitters to the military and civil service: filling contracts (in Burma, E. Solomon and Sons supplied water to the British navy as well as ice to cool the drinks of wilting Englishmen) or selling fine goods to colonials pining for home.[45] But few of these opportunities promised wealth of the kind attained by the Sassoons and a handful of other Baghdadi luminaries.

And not all Jews in the East prospered under British rule. Just as the new economic order presented opportunity for those who were well positioned, it could also bring disruption and hardship for those less prepared for modernity. The introduction of the railway and telegraph in India from the 1860s, for example, eventually allowed British merchants to bypass the agents and middlemen—a significant number of them Jews—who had previously thrived as compradors in the cotton trade.[46] The asymmetrical impact of the empire on Jews is seen most clearly, however, in Aden, a Crown colony annexed by Britain in 1839. An influx of artisans after the annexation undercut local Jewish craftsmen with less sophisticated skills.[47] The government prohibition of the repair and construction of thatch huts, a traditional Jewish occupation, added to the endemic poverty. At the same time, Aden's importance as a strategic port provided numerous new opportunities for enterprising immigrants. The Jewish population grew from roughly 250 in 1839 (a third of the town's population) to 1,070 three years later.[48] Aden attracted Jewish refugees from Yemen as well as merchants drawn by the town's mercantile prospects. The port sat athwart the sea lanes to Asia and Australia, commanding the entrance of the Red Sea and trade routes with the Arabian Peninsula. As a trade depot and coaling station, the constant traffic of steamships presented commercial opportunities for everyone from petty entrepreneurs selling cigarettes and trinkets to ships anchored at Steamer Point to merchants involved in the export of coffee to Europe and America and to international traders such as the Messa dynasty, with offices in England, China, India, and the United States.[49] As an administrative center with close governmental and economic links with the Bombay Presidency, the town housed a sizable population of Bene Israel stationed as civil servants and soldiers.[50] The census of 1872 counted 1,435 Jews from India and Burma living in the town.[51] Instead of solidarity, the Jews of Aden displayed complex communal stratification, much of it a consequence of the heterogeneous composition of a community that included both the native-born and several foreign subcommunities. A rabbinic emissary from Palestine who visited in 1859 noted that the Bene Israel, who lived in a special government quarter with their wives and children, were ostracized by other Jews.[52] Those born in Aden or abroad regarded those from Yemen as religiously suspect and sniffed at their low status occupations as domestic servants, Torah teachers, *shochets* (ritual slaughterers), and laborers.[53]

Despite the economic and social diversity among Jews in Aden, almost the entire community shared the kind of Anglophilia seen among Baghdadis elsewhere. To some extent, they shared this disposition with other groups living within Aden, particularly those who had cause to recall the devastating flooding that beset the town before the intervention of ambitious British engineers. Jews, however, had particular reason to support the imperial presence.[54] Crown rule brought a radical change to Jewish social and legal status by removing legal disabilities and extending civil rights to the Jewish minority. With their new status came agency and opportunity. Jews were free to travel as Crown subjects armed with British passports; some soon visited Egypt, London, and Palestine.[55] They could represent their interests to the Crown and in turn attempt to turn imperial interests to their best advantage. And the British presence opened new sources of livelihood, whether supplying the administration and its officers with labor and goods or catering to the sailors, soldiers, and visitors who passed through the town.

Unsurprisingly many Jews in Aden welcomed the British occupation, and, over time, constructed an elaborate folklore that ascribed the conquest to divine intervention and claimed an apocryphal Jewish role in facilitating the invasion. The community came to stage an annual celebration to mark the British victory. Their public display of loyalty went deeper than pageantry, probably predicated on the knowledge that the British presence protected the community against those who might resent its elevated status. Jews, for example, were key agents in an early British spy network that ensured the colonial administration was apprised of the intentions of inland chieftains.[56] This loyalty was repaid during times of tension. When the Muslim population of Aden rioted in 1872, the British authorities intervened to protect the Jewish minority.[57] While the Jews of Aden threw in their lot with colonial rule, they were also influenced by the culture of the colonizers, over time adopting British naming patterns as well as the English language.[58]

As the example of Aden demonstrates, the British Empire distributed its rewards unevenly in the East. Even as some Baghdadis rose to heights unimaginable at midcentury for Jews in the settlement colonies, they were surrounded by others whose economic ascent was more modest and uncertain. Few among those who were psychically attached to England and its empire could afford to retire to London. In Australia, by contrast, many more Jewish settlers encountered opportunity for advancement, particularly once the discovery of gold transformed an economy dependent on pastoralism into one less sensitive to the welfare of its sheep. Jews, who clustered in the retail trade in Australia and New Zealand, rode a surging wave of demand for clothing, textiles, and other imported goods. Although their earnings were dwarfed by the towering wealth of the Sassoons, more acquired the means to consider a return to England than did the average Jew in India, Burma, and Aden.

However, this still does little to explain why those few Jews from Britain's eastern empire who did settle in London in the middle decades of the century appear, despite their superior wealth and status, to have been less inclined to push for communal change than those who had returned from the antipodes. In large measure because their numbers were so few, returnees from the settlement colonies were a minority among proponents of reform and modernization within Anglo-Jewry at midcentury. They appear, however, to have punched above their weight because of their familiarity with exercising authority, their expectation and experience of greater latitude in religious and communal affairs than was the custom in London, and the relative freedoms granted by carrying a heavy purse. Several had played leading roles in funding and supporting the hesitant growth of synagogues and other communal institutions in the colonies. Energetic, self-made men may have chafed at a conservative communal leadership in London more accustomed to noblesse oblige than to sharing power with new money. They did, however, find allies within an increasingly assertive Jewish middle class and a Jewish press that promoted greater accountability, transparency, and professionalism among the communal organizations that it covered. Yet some, like Benjamin Norden, may have discovered that religious compromises—in his case, intermarriage—that had been largely overlooked in the colonies now acted as an impediment to exercising substantial sway within existing Jewish institutions in England. This may add a further dimension to explaining their propensity toward favoring religious and communal reform. With established avenues of achieving prestige and status within Anglo-Orthodoxy restricted or blocked, they may have sought to challenge a communal elite that thwarted their ambitions and aid the formation of new institutions less judgmental of their religious mores and humble backgrounds. In essence, their behavior may have been motivated at least partly by a strategy of insurgency, seeking to open new venues for social advancement within Jewish communal life in London.

By contrast, the Sassoons and other members of the Jewish colonial elite who moved to the metropole from Asia encountered few of the obstacles that impeded strivers like Norden. Their immense wealth—the Sassoons were regarded as the "Rothschilds of the East"—ensured an eager reception in high society; it helped that they had moved in the most exclusive circles in Bombay and that in London the Prince of Wales liked to be surrounded by men of great wealth. Paradoxically, the Sassoons may have had a smaller impact on the direction of Jewish life in England precisely because of the speed with which they were coopted into an Anglo-Jewish elite that was still defined in large measure by its adherence to religious Orthodoxy and its Sephardi heritage. Baghdadi Jews like the Sassoon may have felt very much at home among those Montefiores and Mocattas, who sought to balance their lives as members of the landed gentry with their commitment to Jewish observance. The traditionalism of Baghdadi Jews in India and England more closely matched that of the Jewish upper crust than did the more freewheeling forms of practice found among Jews in

Melbourne, Sydney, and Cape Town. With the sponsorship of the Sassoons, the Baghdadi community in India had created an elaborate religious infrastructure that allowed for the maintenance of a traditional Jewish lifestyle. They had little reason to support religious reform when they moved to England, and no need to butt heads with an establishment that welcomed them warmly. Wealthy colonial Jews from Asia were, therefore, very much unlike the colonial gentlemen of humbler stamp whose backgrounds and religious compromises generated frustration and rejection when they returned to Albion. Contrary to our expectations, it was not the Sassoons and other migrants from Asia who were interlopers out-of-step with the Jewish life of the London elite but native-born and Ashkenazi Englishmen like Moses Joseph and Benjamin Norden who were the outsiders when they returned to their homeland.

Notes

1. Lawrence Nathan, *As Old as Auckland: The History of LD Nathan & Co. Ltd and of the David Nathan Family 1840–1980* (Takapuna, NZ: Benton Ross, 1984), 17; John Levi and George Bergman, *Australian Genesis: Jewish Convicts and Settlers 1788–1850* (Adelaide, Aus.: Rigby, 1974), 226–27; Hilary Rubinstein, *The Jews in Australia: A Thematic History*, vol. 1, *1788–1945* (Port Melbourne, Victoria: William Heinemann, 1991), 413–14; John Levi, *These Are the Names: Jewish Lives in Australia, 1788–1850* (Melbourne: Melbourne University Press, 2006), 371; and *Journal of the Legislative Council of New South Wales, Session 1872* vol. 21 (Sydney: Thomas Richards, 1872), 746.

2. For an important exception, see Marjory Harper, ed., *Emigrant Homecomings: The Return Movement of Emigrants, 1600–2000* (Manchester: Manchester University Press, 2005). Note, however, that this volume focuses less on the impact of returnees than on the motives and mechanisms of return. See also James Smithies, "Return Migration and the Mechanical Age: Samuel Butler in New Zealand 1860–1864," *Journal of Victorian Culture* 12, no. 12 (Autumn 2007): 203–24; Eric Richards, *Britannia's Children: Emigration from England, Scotland, Wales and Ireland since 1600* (London: Palgrave Macmillan, 2004), 169; John Darwin, "Imperialism and the Victorians: The Dynamics of Territorial Expansion," *English Historical Review* 112 (June 1997): 169; and Gary B. Magee and Andrew S. Thompson, *Empire and Globalisation: Networks of People, Goods and Capital in the British World, c. 1850–1914* (Cambridge: Cambridge University Press, 2010), 31, 64.

3. Scholars distinguish between several patterns of colonial development. Settlement colonies typically were characterized by substantial immigration from the mother country and the creation of elaborate political and social systems often initially modeled on the metropole. Colonies of occupation were typically administered by a relatively small cadre of civil and military functionaries and attracted relatively little permanent settlement of immigrants from the metropole. Within Britain's empire, the development of Australia reflected the first pattern, whereas the Raj and other Asian colonies typically followed the latter model. D. K. Fieldhouse offers an elaborate typology in *The Colonial Empires: A Comparative Survey from the Eighteenth Century* (London: Weidenfeld and Nicolson, 1966).

4. See Michael H. Fischer, *Counterflows to Colonialism: Indian Travellers and Settlers in Britain 1600–1857* (Delhi: Permanent Black, 2004), particularly chapters 7–10.

5. This still applies, for the most part, to studies of the early Victorian period. Neither of the two best recent reevaluations of Anglo-Jewish history—Todd Endelman's *The Jews of Britain, 1650 to 2000* (Berkeley: University of California Press, 2002) and David Feldman's *Englishmen and Jews* (New Haven,

CT: Yale University Press, 1994)—makes any reference to South Africa, Jamaica, or Australia in its index. The latter discusses the importance of empire—but only in the period following 1880.

6. At mid-century there were roughly 35,000 Jews in England, fewer than 500 in British Canada, and around 100 in New Zealand, 5,500 in Australia in 1861, approximately 1,800 in Jamaica in 1871, and 375 in the Cape Colony in 1875.

7. On the heterogeneity of the imperial project, see T. M. Devine, *Scotland's Empire: 1600–1815* (London: Penguin, 2004); John M. Mackenzie and T. M. Devine, eds., *Scotland and the British Empire* (Oxford: Oxford University Press, 2011); Keith Jeffery, ed., *"An Irish Empire"?: Aspects of Ireland and the British Empire* (Manchester: Manchester University Press, 1996); and Magee and Thompson, *Empire and Globalisation*, 135–36. On networks, see Zoë Laidlaw, *Colonial Connections, 1815–1845: Patronage, the Information Revolution and Colonial Government* (Manchester: Manchester University Press, 2005); Alan Lester, *Imperial Networks: Creating Identities in Nineteenth-Century South Africa and Britain* (New York: Routledge, 2001); Kirsten McKenzie, *Scandal in the Colonies: Sydney and Cape Town, 1820–1850* (Melbourne: Melbourne University Press, 2005); and Simon Potter, ed., *Imperial Communication: Australia, Britain and the British Empire* (London: Menzies Centre for Australian Studies, King's College London, University of London, 2005).

8. For a useful summary of Jewish involvement in international commerce, see Harold Pollins, *Economic History of the Jews in England* (Rutherford, NJ: Fairleigh Dickinson University Press, 1982), 43–54. On trade with India, see Gedalia Yogev, *Diamonds and Coral: Anglo-Dutch Jews and Eighteenth-Century Trade* (New York: Leicester University Press, 1978), 124–80, 253–74. On trade with the Maghreb, see Daniel Schroeter, *The Sultan's Jew: Morocco and the Sephardi World* (Stanford, CA: Stanford University Press, 2002), 71–87. On the Caribbean trade, see Stephen Fortune, *Merchants and Jews: The Struggle for British West Indian Commerce, 1650–1750* (Gainesville: University Presses of Florida, 1984), 73–77, 94–98, 130–50; and Eli Faber, *Jews, Slaves, and the Slave Trade: Setting the Record Straight* (New York: New York University Press, 1998), 22–43. On the Levantine trade, see Eliezer Bashan, "Contacts between Jews in Smyrna and the Levant Company of London in the Seventeenth and Eighteenth Centuries," *Jewish Historical Studies* 29 (1986): 53–73; and Todd M. Endelman, *Jews of Georgian England, 1714–1830: Tradition and Change in a Liberal Society* (Philadelphia: Jewish Publication Society of America, 1979), 24. On the Mediterranean trade see T. M. Benady, "The Role of Jews in the British Colonies of the Western Mediterranean," *Jewish Historical Studies* 33 (1994): 48, 52.

9. On Jewish hawkers selling sponges, see Henry Mayhew, *London Labour and the London Poor*, vol. 1, *The London Street-Folk* (London: Griffin, Bohn, 1861), 442–43. On the sale of oranges and lemons, see ibid., 61, 79, 81, 86–89. The peddling of lemons declined as the citrus became a profitable commodity, the result of the passage of a law that required foreign-bound ships to be provided with lemon juice; ibid., 89. On the supply of sponges from Smyrna, Rhodes, Beirut, and Greece, see James McCoan, *Our New Protectorate: Turkey in Asia* (London: Chapman and Hall, 1879), 82, 115, 118–20; and John MacCulloch, *A Dictionary, Geographical, Statistical, and Historical* (London: Longman, Brown, Green, and Longmans, 1851), 968. On Jewish involvement in the wholesale of these products by the 1850s, see Mayhew, *London Labour*, vol. 2, *The London Street-Folk*, 118. On Jewish involvement in the sponge trade see Jonathan Frankel, *The Damascus Affair: "Ritual Murder," Politics, and the Jews in 1840* (Cambridge: Cambridge University Press, 1997), 70; and Pollins, *Economic History*, 107. On the North African Jewish trading network that supplied ostrich feathers to London, see Sarah Abrevaya Stein, "Mediterranean Jewries and Global Commerce in the Modern Period: On the Trail of the Jewish Feather Trade," *Jewish Social Studies: History, Culture, Society* 13, no. 2 (2007): 1–39. For Portsmouth quote, see Charles Dickens to Johann Kuenzel, July? 1838 in *The Letters of Charles Dickens*, ed. Madeline House, Graham Storey and Kathleen Tillotson, 12 vols. (Oxford, UK: Clarendon, 1974), 1:423.

10. The extent of Jewish poverty in eighteenth-century England is discussed in detail in Endelman, *Jews of Georgian England*, 31–32, 166–80. On transportation of Jews to the New World, see Eric Goldstein, *Traders and Transports: The Jews of Colonial Maryland* (Baltimore: Jewish Historical Society of Mary-

land, 1993), 27–36; on colonization schemes, see Eli Faber, *A Time for Planting: The First Jewish Migration, 1654–1820* (Baltimore: Johns Hopkins University Press, 1992), 19–21; and Endelman, *Jews of Georgian England*, 168–69.

11. On this transition, see P. J. Marshall, "Britain without America—A Second Empire?" in *The Oxford History of the British Empire*, vol. 2, *The Eighteenth Century*, ed. P. J. Marshall, 576–94 (Oxford: Oxford University Press, 1998). On the historiographic debate about this periodization, see C. A. Bayly, "The Second British Empire" in *The Oxford History of the British Empire*, vol. 2, *Historiography*, ed. Robin Winks, 60–64 (Oxford: Oxford University Press, 1999). On the economic impact of Empire on Britain, see B. R. Tomlinson, "Economics and Empire: The Metropolitan Context" in *The Oxford History of the British Empire*, vol. 3, *The Nineteenth Century*, ed. Andrew Porter, 31–51 (Oxford: Oxford University Press, 1999). For a useful summary of the changes within the Jewish economy, see Vivian Lipman, *Social History of the Jews in England, 1850–1950* (London: Watts, 1954), 29–34.

12. Levi and Bergman, *Australian Genesis*, 199; and Lazarus Morris Goldman, *Jews in Victoria in the Nineteenth Century* (Melbourne, Aus.: Lazarus Morris Goldman, 1954), 141.

13. He was joined in Sydney by his nephew Jacob Levi Montefiore of Bridgetown, Barbados, in 1837. See *Jewish World*, January 30 and February 2, 1885; and Levi and Bergman, *Australian Genesis*, 175.

14. See Levi and Bergman, *Australian Genesis*, 76, 196–201, 213–14, 297.

15. On their business activities, see Louis Herrman, *A History of the Jews of South Africa, from the Earliest Times to 1895* (Johannesburg: Gollancz, 1935), 123–26; Lawrence Green, *At Daybreak for the Isles* (Cape Town: H. B. Timmins, 1950), 80–82; Israel Abrahams, *The Birth of a Community: A History of Western Province Jewry from the Earliest Times to the End of the South African War, 1902* (Cape Town: Cape Town Hebrew Congregation, 1955), 32–33; Louis Hotz, "Contributions to Economic Development," in *The Jews in South Africa: A History*, ed. Gustav Saron and Louis Hotz (Cape Town: Oxford University Press, 1955), 352. On guano export, see Edward Napier, *Excursions in South Africa, Including a History of the Cape Colony, an Account of Native Tribes, etc.* (London: W. Shoberl, 1849), 324–25; E. Littell, *The Living Age*, volume 12 (Boston: Littell, Son, and Co., 1847), 173–74. For their provenance in London, see Albert Montefiore Hyamson, *The Sephardim of England: A History of the Spanish and Portuguese Community, 1492–1951* (London: Methuen, 1951), 294, 314, 336, 397. On their charitable giving, see London *Jewish Chronicle* (hereafter *JC*), December 25, 1846; July 7, 1854; December 12, 1862; and January 13, 1865.

16. On the 1820 settlers, see Leonard Monteath Thompson, *A History of South Africa* (New Haven, CT: Yale University Press, 2001), 55–56; and Basil Alexander Le Cordeur, *The Politics of Eastern Cape Separatism, 1820–1854* (Oxford: Oxford University Press, 1981), 58. On trade on the Cape frontier, see Timothy Keegan, *Colonial South Africa and the Origins of the Racial Order* (London: Leicester University Press, 1996), 68; and Lester, *Imperial Networks*, 55. For Norden's trading expeditions and his business career, see D. J. Kotzé, ed., *Letters of the American Missionaries, 1835–1838* (Cape Town: Van Riebeeck Society, 1950), 19, 82, 91; and Herrman, *History of Jews in South Africa*, 109–11. For Abraham Norden, Benjamin's father, see Henry Buckler, *Central Criminal Court Minutes of Evidence*, vol. 13 (London: George Hebert, 1840), 605.

17. His public image was more than a little dented in 1849 after he supplied the convict ship *Neptune*, anchored for five months off the port town in a face-off between residents and the government over plans to establish a penal colony at the Cape, in defiance of a local boycott. The ship, hailing from Bermuda, was to disembark convicts, a first step toward establishing a penal colony. After extensive local protest—including an attack on Norden—the government plan was thwarted, and the *Neptune* sailed for Van Dieman's Land. On Norden and the *Neptune* affair, see Milton Shain, *The Roots of Antisemitism in South Africa* (Charlottesville: University Press of Virginia, 1994), 9; Nigel Worden, Elizabeth Van Heyningen, and Vivian Bickford-Smith, *Cape Town: The Making of a City; An Illustrated History* (Claremont, SA: D. Philip, 1998), 175–77; McKenzie, *Scandal in the Colonies*, 172–75; and John Mitchel, *Jail Journal, or Five Years in British Prisons, Commenced Aboard the Shearwater Steamer . . .* (New York: Office

of the "Citizen," 1854), 202–9. On Samuel Rodolf, see Herrman, *History of the Jews in South Africa*, 113; and A Minutes, Vol. 1, Box 1, BC 849, Cape Town Hebrew Congregation Archive.

18. On the importance of personal reputation and litigation to defend personal integrity in the colonial environment, see McKenzie, *Scandal in the Colonies*, 84–86; for court cases involving Jewish businessmen in Cape Town and Sydney, see ibid., 69–89. For a selection of Norden's litigation, see C. H. Van Zyl, *The Theory of the Judicial Practice of the Cape of Good Hope: And of South Africa Generally* (Cape Town: J. C. Juta, 1902), xxi.

19. On colonial self-reinvention, see McKenzie, *Scandal in the Colonies*, 1–4, 9, quote on 51. For other striking cases of colonial economic success see Nathan, *As Old as Auckland*, 48–50; *JC*, July 30, 1897; Bill Williams, *The Making of Manchester Jewry, 1740–1875* (Manchester: Manchester University Press), 321–23.

20. See Birmingham Jewish Local History Study Group, "A Portrait of Birmingham Jewry in 1851," in *Provincial Jewry in Victorian Britain*, ed. Aubrey Newman (London: Jewish Historical Society of England, 1975); Geoffrey Alderman, *Modern British Jewry* (Oxford, UK: Clarendon, 1992), 30; John Alfred Langford, *Modern Birmingham and Its Institutions: A Chronicle of Local Events, from 1841 to 1871* (Birmingham: E. C. Osborne, 1877), 85; Pollins, *Economic History of the Jews in England*, 107; George Elwick, *The Bankrupt Directory: Being a Complete Register of All Bankrupts . . .* (London, 1843), 322; and Caroline Plüss, "Sephardic Jews in Hong Kong: Constructing Communal Identities," *Sino-Judaica* 4 (2003): 63.

21. See Magee and Thompson, *Empire and Globalisation*, 31.

22. Quote from Israel Porush, "The Chief Rabbinate and Early Australian Jewry," *Australian Jewish Historical Society Journal* 2, part 8 (1948): 483, "Chief Rabbinate and Early Australian Jewry": 482. The statistic is cited in McKenzie, *Scandal in the Colonies*, 50.

23. Minutes for January 4, 1852 and May 11, 1856, A Minutes, Vol. 1, Box 1, BC 849, Cape Town Hebrew Congregation Archive.

24. On the disdain for the colonial nouveau riche, see McKenzie, *Scandal in the Colonies*, 5.

25. *JC*, January 7, 1848; January 14, 1848; January 21, 1848. For his status as a founding warden, see David S. Katz, *Jews in the History of England, 1485–1850* (Oxford, UK: Clarendon, 1994), 341. For the early proponents of establishing a separate synagogue, see Hyamson, *Sephardim of England*, 280.

26. For his obituary, see *JC*, January 7, January 14, 1848. For his theological views, particularly on the Oral Law, see his unsigned introduction to Morris Raphall and D. A. Da Sola's *Eighteen Treatises from the Mishna* (London: Sherwood, Gilbert, and Piper, 1843), which he published without their permission. For evidence of his economic success in Barbados, see Jacob Rader Marcus, *Memoirs of American Jews, 1775–1865*, vol 1. (Philadelphia: Jewish Publication Society of America, 1955–56), 209. For his polemics, see Benjamin Elkin, *Rejected Letters* (London: J. Wertheimer, 1842); Benjamin Elkin, *Letters Addressed to the Editor of the 'Voice of Jacob,' Being Replies to the Observations in Nos. xxxvii and xxxix* (London: J. Wertheimer, 1843). For his letters to Isaac Leeser, see the *Occident and American Jewish Advocate* 2, no. 11 (February 1845); 3, no. 3 (June 1845); 2, no. 1 (April 1844).

27. *JC*, October 1, 1847; and Goldman, *Jews in Victoria*, 92.

28. *JC*, January 15, 1858; March 18, 1859; April 6, 1860; February 14, 1862; April 27, 1866; and Vivian Lipman, *A Century of Social Service 1859–1959: The Jewish Board of Guardians* (London: Routledge and Kegan Paul, 1959), 25. Norden adopted other gentlemanly pursuits, including supporting the Horticultural Society. See *Proceedings of the Horticultural Society* 1 (1861): 140.

29. On the growth of Bombay, see Amar Farooqui, *Opium City: The Making of Early Victorian Bombay* (Gurgaon, India: Three Essays Collective, 2006), xiii, 8, 25, 42; and Christine Dobbin, *Urban Leadership in Western India: Politics and Communities in Bombay City, 1840–1885* (London: Oxford University Press, 1972), 1–7.

30. Dobbin, *Urban Leadership*, 20–22.

31. Extensive documentation about early traders at Fort St. George can be found in the Lucien Wolf Papers, HA India folder, Mocatta Library, University College London. See also Yogev, *Diamonds and*

Coral, 67–109, 124–80; Thomas Timberg, "Baghdadi Jews in Indian Port Cities," in *Jews in India*, ed. Thomas Timberg (New York: Advent, 1986), 274–75; David Solomon Sassoon, *A History of the Jews in Baghdad* (Letchwood, England: S. D. Sassoon, 1949), 204–5; Joan Roland, "Baghdadi Jews in India: Communal Relationships, Nationalism, Zionism and the Construction of Identity," *Sino-Judaica* 4 (2003): 1; and Stanley Jackson, *The Sassoons* (New York: Dutton, 1968), 5.

32. On Hong Kong, see Dobbin, *Urban Leadership*, 7, 154; and Caroline Plüss, "Globalizing Ethnicity and Multi-Local Identifications: The Parsee, Indian Muslim and Sephardic Trade Diasporas in Hong Kong," in *Diaspora Entrepreneurial Networks: Four Centuries of History*, ed. Ina Baghdiantz McCabe, Gelina Harlaftis and Ionna Pepelasis Minoglou, 245–68 (New York: Berg, 2005). On China, see Chiara Betta, "The Trade Diaspora of Baghdadi Jews: From India to China's Treaty Ports, 1842–1937," in *Diaspora Entrepreneurial Networks: Four Centuries of History*, ed. Ina Baghdiantz McCabe, Gelina Harlaftis and Ionna Pepelasis Minoglou, 269–85 (New York: Berg, 2005); Chen Zhilong, "Shanghai: A Window for Studying Sino-Indian Relations in the Era of Colonialism and Imperialism," in *India and China in the Colonial World*, ed. Madhavi Thampi, 33–51 (New Delhi: Social Science, 2005). The Jewish community grew in step with the British conquest of Burma, which started with coastal territories ceded in 1826, to the conquest of Lower Burma in 1852, and finally Upper Burma in 1885. Rangoon, a strategic port, administrative center, and transit point on the opium trade route with China was settled by a small contingent of Baghdadis and Bene Israel, some of whom became involved in the export of rice and timber. The community retained strong links to Calcutta. See Ruth Fredman Cernea, *Almost Englishmen: Baghdadi Jews in British Burma* (Lanham, MD: Lexington, 2007), xv–xvi, 5.

33. See Frank Broeze, "A Scottish Merchant in Batavia (1820–1840): Gillean Maclaine and Dutch Connections," in *Diaspora Entrepreneurial Networks: Four Centuries of History*, ed. Ina Baghdiantz McCabe, Gelina Harlaftis and Ionna Pepelasis Minoglou (New York: Berg, 2005), 405–6; Jackson, *Sassoons*, 5; and Levi and Bergman, *Australian Genesis*, 74, 268.

34. The Parsee magnates of Bombay also created extensive business networks of this kind. See Farooqui, *Opium City*, 27; and Chiara Betta, "The Rise of Silas Aaron Hardoon (1851–1931) as Shanghai's Major Individual Landowner," *Sino-Judaica* 2 (1995): 4.

35. For the civil war boom in Bombay, see Dobbin, *Urban Leadership*, 25–26; Cecil Roth, *The Sassoon Dynasty* (London: R. Hale, 1941), 45, 47–50, 98; and Jackson, *Sassoons*, 21, 24, 39–40, 44.

36. Quoted in John Benyon, "Frere, Sir (Henry) Bartle Edward, First Baronet (1815–1884)," in *Oxford Dictionary of National Biography: In Association with the British Academy; From the Earliest Times to the Year 2000* (Oxford: Oxford University Press, 2004). See also Dobbin, *Urban Leadership*, 23; Sassoon, *History of Jews in Baghdad*, 208; Roland, "Jews in British India," 22–23; Jackson, *Sassoons*, 19; and Roth, *Sassoon Dynasty*, 80.

37. See Moritz Steinschneider, ed., *Reshith Hallimud: A Systematic Hebrew Primer* (Berlin: A. Asher, 1860); Sassoon, *Jews in Baghdad*, 207; Anne Cowen and Roger Cowen, *Victorian Jews through British Eyes* (Oxford: Oxford University Press, 1986), 57–60; Roth, *Sassoon Dynasty*, 65; and Roland, *Jews in British India*, 17–18.

38. Roth, *Sassoon Dynasty*, 11–13, 55, 65, 73, 118; Jackson, *Sassoons*, 19, 29, 35, 46–47; Sassoon, *Jews in Baghdad*, 207; and Cernea, *Almost Englishmen*, xxii.

39. See Sarah Abrevaya Stein, "Protected Persons? The Baghdadi Jewish Diaspora, the British States, and the Persistence of Empire," *American Historical Review* 116, no. 1 (2011): 80–108.

40. See Sassoon, *Jews in Baghdad*, 208, 212–13; Jonathan Goldstein, "Singapore, Manila and Harbin as Reference Points for Asian 'Port Jewish' Identity," *Jewish Culture and History* 7, no. 2 (2004): 273–74; Joan Bieder, "Jewish Identity in Singapore: Cohesion, Dispersion, Survival," *Sino-Judaica* 4 (2003): 31; Plüss, "Sephardic Jews in Hong Kong," 63, 73–74; Cernea, *Almost Englishmen*, xxiii, 40; and Chiara Betta, "Baghdadi Jewish Diaspora in Shanghai: Community, Commerce and Identities," *Sino-Judaica* 4 (2003): 94.

41. On this issue, see Roland, "Baghdadi Jews in India," 3–6; Cernea, *Almost Englishmen*, 71–2, 214; and Sassoon, *Jews in Baghdad*, 214.

42. See Betta, "Baghdadi Jewish Diaspora in Shanghai," 82, 90–91.

43. Only 0.6 percent of the city's male population (3,918) met these criteria, including 1,040 Parsees. The turnout of the Jewish vote was miniscule as the election was held on the Sabbath. Cited in Dobbin, *Urban Leadership*, 173, 175; and Joan Roland, *Jews in British India: Identity in a Colonial Era* (Hanover, NH: Brandeis University Press, 1989), 17.

44. Plüss, "Sephardic Jews in Hong Kong," 59; Cernea, *Almost Englishmen*, 4; and Jacob Landau, *Jews in Nineteenth-Century Egypt* (New York: New York University Press, 1969), 37.

45. See Anthony Pamm, "The Military Services of the Bene Israel of India and the Honours and Awards Granted to Them (1750–1918): An Analysis and Compilation," 1992, unpublished manuscript, Jewish National and University Library; Shellim Samuel, "Jews in the Indian Army," *India and Israel* 4, no. 8 (1852): 21–24; Roland, *Jews in British India*, 21–23; and Cernea, *Almost Englishmen*, xx, 4, 8.

46. See Dobbin, *Urban Leadership*, 154.

47. On American designs on a Red Sea trading depot, see Emma Roberts, *Notes of an Overland Journey through France and Egypt to Bombay* (London: Wm. H. Allen, 1841), 103.

48. A census conducted six weeks after the conquest found 301 Jewish women and 267 Jewish men in the town. As Kour points out, the town had already attracted immigrants from Arabia, India and the East African coast. The 1842 census found 590 Jewish males and 480 females. This shift in gender balance almost certainly reflected the arrival of male migrants searching for work. See Zaka Kour, *The History of Aden, 1839–72* (London: Totowa, 1981), 21, 26.

49. See Reuben Ahroni, *The Jews of the British Crown Colony of Aden: History, Culture, and Ethnic Relations* (Leiden: Brill, 1994), 34, 40–41, 46–56, 111, 319; Caesar Farah, *The Sultan's Yemen* (London: I. B. Tauris, 2002), 120–25; Kour, *History of Aden*, 15; and JC, June 17, 1859. On Jews and the coffee trade in Aden, see Michel Tuchscherer, "Coffee in the Red Sea Area from the 16th to the 19th Century," in *The Global Coffee Economy in Africa, Asia and Latin America, 1500–1989*, ed. WG Clarence-Smith and Steven Topik (Cambridge: Cambridge University Press, 2003), 61. On the importance of trade with the United States, see Thomas Marston, *Britain's Imperial Role in the Red Sea Area, 1800–1878* (Hamden, CT: Shoe String, 1961), 368.

50. Aden may have also possessed a population of Beta Israel involved in trade with Abyssinia. Yemeni Jewry's links to India long predated British colonization. In 1836 visiting missionary Joseph Wolff was told by Joseph Alkaree, chief rabbi of Sanaa, that the community was supplied with books from Joseph Samah of Calcutta. See Joseph Wolff, *Journal of the Reverend Joseph Wolff* (London, 1839), 391–92. The account of Beta Israel in Aden comes from JC, July 5, 1867, and is somewhat confused. On Aden's place within the British Empire, see Robert Blyth, *The Empire of the Raj: India, Eastern Africa, and the Middle East, 1858–1947* (New York: Palgrave, 2003). On Yemeni Jewry's medieval trading ties with Arabia and India, see Roxani Margariti, *Aden & the Indian Ocean Trade: 150 Years in the Life of a Medieval Arabian Port* (Chapel Hill: University of North Carolina Press, 2007), 13, 19 , 22, 113, 184–88, 196–97, 203–5.

51. The census also counted forty Persians residing in Aden, some of whom may have been Baghdadi Jews. The census figures are provided in Frederick Hunter, *An Account of the British Settlement of Aden in Arabia* (London, 1877), 26. For Indian military units stationed in the town, see 142.

52. Sappir estimated that three hundred Bene Israel lived in Aden.

53. JC, July 5, 1867; Ahroni, *Jews of the British Crown Colony of Aden*, 108, 147.

54. Ahroni, *Jews of the British Crown Colony of Aden*, 35–37.

55. Ibid., 42, 185; and JC, October 2, 1863.

56. JC, July 6, 1866; Kour, *History of Aden*, 120; and Ahroni, *Jews of the British Crown Colony of Aden*, 43–45.

57. Ahroni, *Jews of the British Crown Colony of Aden*, 89–90.

58. On Westernization, see Ahroni, *Jews of the British Crown Colony of Aden*, 143, 154, 176, 179–80.

5

ORIENTAL, FEMINIST, ORIENTALIST

THE NEW JEWISH WOMAN

Frances Malino

IN AN EMOTIONALLY charged letter written from Tripoli on June 11, 1911, Maïr Lévy pleaded with the Alliance israélite universelle (AIU) to accept his daughter Tamo at one of the three Parisian boarding schools that trained Alliance *institutrices* (primary school teachers). What else can she do, he asked, my "French-speaking, African-born, Jewish daughter?"[1] In his plaintive query, Lévy could hardly capture the "braided identity" of his daughter or of the hundreds of other young women who brought France's civilizing mission—and that of the Jews—to Jewish girls in Muslim lands.

The Alliance, an international Jewish organization that established a network of primary schools in North Africa, the Ottoman Empire and the Middle East, intended its teachers to be French-born. When few Jews chose to leave Europe for the villages and towns of North Africa and the Middle East, the Alliance opted instead to provide the brightest "Orientals" with a normal-school education in Paris.[2] French teaching certificates in hand, they were then to serve the Alliance for at least ten years, just as French-born teachers were required to serve their state. In contrast to those in the metropole, however, and unanticipated by the Alliance, would be the independence, even truculence, of its *institutrices* once they returned to the "Orient."[3]

This chapter focuses on the pioneering generation of French-speaking, North African- and Ottoman-born *institutrices*.[4] It explores how undertaking the civilizing mission of the Alliance also transformed these Jewish women into agents of French colonialism, simultaneously decentering the empire while structurally underscoring their outsider status as Orientals in Europe, and Orientalists and feminists in North Africa and the Middle East. The chapter suggests as well that many of these *institutrices* redefined the feminism they encountered in the metropole to advance their own liberation as well as that of the young girls they taught. Lastly, it concludes that the pioneering generation of *institutrices*, indebted to an emerging "constellation" of new women in fin-de-siècle France, may be seen collectively as exemplars of a New Jewish Woman.

The period examined is from 1892 to 1934, the years of the Alliance's greatest influence. They were also the years when Alsatian-born Jacques Bigart was the central figure (*secrétaire général*) in the functioning and success of the Alliance. Obsessively conscientious and acutely attuned to every minute detail in the lives of "his" teachers—both male and female—Bigart dutifully answered each of their letters, often also correcting their French in blue pencil. The bureaucratization of the Alliance organization subsequent to his death robbed the archives of such personal content.

The women teachers of the Alliance confided in Bigart their dreams, frustrations, and the bitter pain of their losses. Male teachers wrote letters as well, of course, in keeping with the French epistolary tradition. (The Alliance believed that letter writing strengthened loyalty and connectedness among teachers.[5]) But the letters from the women—they exist in the thousands held together with rusting straight pins in the archives of the Alliance—are less self-conscious than those of their male counterparts, more personal, even confessional. Never intended for the public domain, they reveal worlds both intimate and beyond prescriptive dictates. Without them—along with the contents of the Alliance library, they survived removal by the Nazis to Frankfurt during the Second World War—our inquiry into the lives of individual *institutrices* would not have been possible.

Messody Pariente, or the Making of a Feminist Orientalist *Institutrice*

Messody Pariente's letters vividly capture the trajectory of an Alliance *institutrice* as she became feminist in her professional assertiveness, orientalist in her assumptions about her native society, and an outsider in both metropole and colony. Born in Tétuoan in 1877 to an illustrious Sephardi family (its members included her uncle, Semtob Pariente, a major figure in extending the influence of the Alliance in Turkey), Messody Pariente studied at the local Alliance school before departing for Paris to train as an Alliance teacher. In 1895 she returned to Northern Morocco as an *adjointe* (assistant) in the Alliance girls' school of Tangier. Two years later she became an assistant in Tétuan to her former teacher.

Pariente refused to accept the Alliance's presumption that marriage to Amram Elmaleh (born in Tangier in 1879 and also an Alliance teacher) meant an end to her teaching career. "I assumed that in authorizing me to leave with him for

Beirut you intended to give me a post there as well," she explained in her letter to Paris. "If there is no vacancy, I dare hope, Monsieur le Président, that on my return you will procure me one."[6] Three years later (1906), Pariente became the founding director of the Alliance girls' school in Mazagan (El Jedida).

In Mazagan, Pariente demonstrated the traits that would mark the rest of her life—indomitable strength, keen intelligence, and remarkable courage—all of which her pride and sense of self reinforced. Shortly after her arrival in Mazagan, for example, local unrest necessitated that she depart to Tangier. Upon her return she found the Alliance reluctant to send her an assistant. "You express fear for the security of a young girl who would come all alone to Morocco. She would not be alone in Mazagan. She would be with me, staying with me if it is necessary. If the situation becomes so aggravated as to present serious dangers, we shall not remain and my assistant will leave with us. This lack of tranquility could last for years. Is it because of this that you are gong to suspend our work in Morocco?"[7] Unwilling to compromise "her" work in Morocco (like many *institutrices*, Pariente chaffed at the metropole's ignorance of conditions on the ground), she successfully arranged for two French Catholic sisters from Tangier to join her.

Pariente's confident assertion of independence stood in sharp contrast to her assessment of her African-born co-religionists. In 1909 the Alliance sent her to Fez to reopen the girls' school (it had been closed for two years). Her letters to Paris barely hid, indeed, many did not, her dismay at the "retrograde ideas and strange customs" she encountered—a reaction not uncommon among northern Moroccan Sephardi Jews when interacting with their Arabic-speaking co-religionists: "Your schools in Fez," she wrote shortly after arriving, "are too important and the work that we undertake in a milieu as backward as this too interesting for you not to furnish us the means to work actively and fully for the regeneration of this population."[8]

While in Fez, Pariente battled child marriage by charging parents higher fees if they enrolled only their sons in school.[9] She developed a warm working relationship with the local rabbis and a successful and demanding Hebrew program for her students. With the *tricoteuses* (knitting machines) she imported—without permission from the Alliance—she established a successful cottage industry among the women of the *mellah* (Jewish quarter). In April 1912, after the establishment of the French Protectorate and with thousands of rebelling Moroccan soldiers pillaging the *mellah*, Pariente and her husband guided the Jews of Fez to the safety of the sultan's palace. Transforming a local synagogue into a hospital and aided by a Russian Jewish female doctor, they tended the sick and wounded.

The *école ménagère* (domestic training school) that Pariente subsequently established in Rabat was placed under the auspices of the French Protectorate rather than the Alliance. Before long she accused the French authorities—rightly believing they cared little for indigenous Jews—of modifying her programs, reducing her personnel, augmenting her work, and paying her less than her non-Jewish peers. She lost the position in 1922 after a serious illness required she take a leave of absence.

Pariente refused to be silenced. Empowered by notions of republican justice, she brought a formal complaint against the recently appointed and increasingly conservative director of public instruction.[10] In it she demanded the 32,000 francs owed her for the remainder of her contract. After a judgment in her favor and bursting with pride at her defiance and success, Pariente wrote the Alliance: "For once justice has proven itself just. I received everything I requested except for the indemnity that was fixed at one year of my salary [Messody had requested two and a half years]. Mr. Hardy had to pay me 12,000 francs and all the legal expenses. One never anticipated that this little *institutrice* Madame Elmaleh was going to file a complaint against the Directeur de l'Instruction Publique, des Beaux-Arts et des Antiquités. But one sees everything these days . . . *n'est ce pas!*"[11]

Pariente retired to Casablanca in 1924. As a social and political activist, she worked with deaf and blind children, obtained better pension benefits for Alliance retirees, and organized a local chapter of Oeuvre de Sécours aux Enfants. She also home-tutored her nephew Edmond Amran Elmaleh (he would become one of Morocco's most beloved writers) when asthma prevented him from attending school.[12]

In 1958 Pariente left Casablanca to join her children in Paris. Her last letter to Morocco was dated 1962. Her unwavering commitment to the language and ideals of the Republic notwithstanding, she was not at home in France. "You have no idea," she confided to R. Tajouri, Délégué de l'AIU au Maroc, "how much I live in thought and heart for everything that concerns Morocco."[13]

Exile in Paris? A Setting for Education, Outsiderdom, Orientalism, and Feminism

As the odyssey of Pariente suggests, she came to embody many of the ideals, values, and prejudices of the wider French colonial establishment. And yet she was also never fully French. Indeed, from their initial arrival in Paris for their teacher training, Pariente and her generation of Alliance teachers were made aware that their status was that of outsiders, notwithstanding the fact that the education they were to receive was designed for them to play a role in the French civilizing mission.

Until 1922, when it opened its own normal school for girls in Versailles, the Alliance trained its future *institutrices* at two private schools for girls, the *pensions* (boarding schools) of Mme Isaac and Mme Weill-Kahn, and at a vocational and normal school for girls, the École Bischoffsheim, established in 1872 by Louis Bischoffsheim and his wife. At its sixtieth anniversary, the école proudly announced that between 1872 and 1926, 232 *orientales* had successfully studied there.[14]

Regardless of place of origin, once they arrived in Paris, all Alliance-subsidized students were collectively labeled *orientales*—a category associated in the metropole with primitiveness, exoticism, and effeminacy. As late as 1927, for example, when Bischoffsheim's *directrice* bid farewell to the last class of Alliance students, she found it necessary to contrast the "elegance" and "civilization" of the "*orientales*" in the audience with the "lack of hygiene," gaudy rags," and "guttural cries" of those who had come to Paris a half century earlier.[15]

Although Mesdames Isaac and Weill-Kahn refrained from publicly disparaging their students from the Orient, at these *pensions* as well the *orientales* stood apart. On weekends and during long summer holidays, for example, when their European classmates returned to their homes, they remained at school. They remained there as well during the First World War, albeit garnering praise for "bravery," "military discipline in the face of bombardments," "patriotism," and their "French hearts."[16]

The Jewish education they had received as young girls also set the Alliance students apart from their European-born classmates, most notably subsequent to the secularization of the French public school system in 1882.[17] All sixty-nine girls, for example, who took the Alliance exam in 1912 for admission to one of the three normal schools (they came from cities across the Mediterranean, including Adrianople, Aleppo, Beirut, Brousse, Cairo, Cavalla, Constantinople, Damascus, Haifa, Jerusalem, Larache, Monastir, Rhodes, Safed, Salonica, Smyrna, Tangier, Tétouan, Tiberias, Tripoli, and Tunis) could already read and write Hebrew. Some even listed Hebrew as their favorite class.[18] Once in Paris, moreover, they would continue their Jewish education. Indeed, they were tested regularly both in Hebrew and Jewish history. "I was truly surprised at the success of the Hebrew teaching," one examiner wrote in 1905. "Many of the students from the boys' school are inferior to some of these girls."[19]

What these young girls felt about their designation *orientale* is difficult to ascertain (One can only imagine their reactions to the pavilions featured at the Paris Expositions Universelles showcasing "exotic" human and material cultures). A heated dispute between two teachers (each used initials that were not her own) that erupted in 1901 on the pages of the Alliance's *Revue des écoles* suggests that their responses were both emotionally charged and varied.

Mademoiselle B, an experienced *directrice*, had suggested establishing a separate normal school exclusively for Alliance girls comparable to the École normale israélite orientale for boys. Its mandate would be to ensure that in the future teachers returned to the Orient not only with teaching degrees but also with training more appropriate for their profession. Mademoiselle R.S., a newly graduated *institutrice*, rejected her colleague's "reproaches" as well as her "remedies." She acknowledged that a young assistant might not fully understand the complexities of her profession when she first arrived at her post. But this was only natural, she argued, and hardly a reason to deny young girls from the Orient exposure to European classmates, especially when one observed the nefarious effects on the boys who had no such exposure. "It is in contact with these spiritual and playful children, which the little Parisians often are, that we acquire ease, character, the spirit of doing the right thing, and vivacity. In class, emulation stirs us; we wish, as they, to demonstrate some cleverness, a quick retort."[20]

Mademoiselle B had the final word. Girls are always more at ease than boys at this age, she explained; it had nothing to do with their classmates. Now that candidates were carefully selected through exams and recommendations, moreover, the so-called benefits of contact with Parisians belonged to a "truth of yesterday" or merely reflected a "simple prejudice" of today. Simple prejudice or not, for those in the metropole, the *institutrices* retained the designation of *orientales*—although their return to North Africa and the Middle East certainly attenuated its significance. The feminism these *orientales* appropriated while abroad, on the other hand, ensured they became outsiders in their homelands as well.

Transposing Familial Feminism to the Orient

In 1900 Hassiba Benchimol (her ancestors are immortalized in a Delacroix painting) left Tangier for Fez to establish an Alliance school for girls.[21] Her first impressions are notable for their passion and fury—as well as her self-identification as a feminist. "From the moment of her birth, a woman in Fez feels the weight of her inferiority. While cries of joy and endless celebration welcome the birth of a son, for a young girl, whose only sin is to have been born, there are only cries of mourning. I must confess that as a woman and a feminist, these practices revolt me."[22]

Benchimol and her generation of *institutrices* experienced Paris during the early years of *féminisme*, a term broadly used and distinguished at the time by the expressions "familial" (often referred to as "equality in difference" feminism) and "individualist." Individualist feminists repudiated all concepts of women's special nature, espousing instead equality of opportunity for all individuals, regardless of sex, familial considerations or national concerns.[23]

The Alliance, as did many French republicans with whom it had close ties (the *directeur de l'enseignement primaire*, for example, taught pedagogy at its normal school and provided the Alliance leadership with government regulations), supported "familial" feminism. Indeed, familial feminism had informed Adolphe Crémieux's call of a half century earlier to educate the Jewish girls of the Orient. They were to become, he explained in 1865, the type of mother this new generation required.[24] That familial feminism continued to inform the Alliance's mission can be seen in the 1910 address of the president of the Association des anciens élèves of Salonica: "Our Association must create the ideal woman of tomorrow, a noble and intelligent woman, educated and sweet, the woman a young man dreams will become his lifetime companion."[25]

Familial feminism appeared as well in articles the Alliance reproduced in its *Bulletin des écoles* (a separate journal that appeared monthly between 1910 and 1914).[26] "Let us not appear to advocate changing women into men," one such article warned. "We are no longer at a time when one asks himself if a woman has a soul or if the soul of a woman differs from that of a man. What is incontestable is that neither their destination nor their nature is the same."[27] Another concluded: "The fundamental rule of female education must be equality in difference or difference in equality."[28]

The Alliance's decision to reproduce these articles or excerpts from them— at times even adding its own critical commentary and placing them in a special section titled "Questions féminines"—suggests that it struggled with their themes. Were women the same or different from men, and, if the latter, how could one ensure their equality in the area of education and at the same time preserve their essential differences?[29]

Committed to the view that women's lives should be improved (as did many Europeans, the Alliance believed that gender relations were an indicator of a society's level of civilization), the AIU failed to anticipate just how radical even familial feminism might become when transplanted to the Orient. In France, for example, mainstream feminists, eschewing confrontation and conflict, subscribed to the role of preserving political and social stability. Indeed, most children, as Linda Clark has demonstrated in *Schooling the Daughters of Marianne*, were led to expect adult lives "comparable to those of their parents."[30] In the Orient, on the other hand, "equality in difference" feminism had a more destabilizing effect for it presumed radical changes not only within the household but also beyond. "Our task," Hassiba Benchimol's cousin Messody Coriat proclaimed when establishing a school in Marrakesh in 1902, "is to make of our young girls women different from their mothers . . . who will no longer be at the mercy of their husbands' whims."[31]

Historians have argued that feminists in both France and Britain collaborated in strengthening the empire. British feminists, for example, "worked consistently to identify themselves with the national interest and their cause with the future prosperity of the nation-state."[32] The Alliance's espousal of feminism was certainly linked to its political self-representation in imperial France. That of its *institutrices*, on the other hand, was not. On the contrary, even if France loomed large in their endeavor, most *institutrices* sought in feminism personal liberation irrespective of national concerns.

The Oriental New Woman? The Impact of the Parisian Sartorial Revolution

Assertions of autonomy and agency, in spite of retribution from Paris as well as isolation and "exile" from the communities the *institutrices* served, were often indebted to yet another cultural shift in the metropole—the emerging "constellation" of new women. Much to the chagrin of those who feared the masculinization of French culture, these new women publicly pursued a career and explicitly challenged, in print and in dress, the prevailing ideals of femininity. Some new women were feminists: others were not. Among them could be found Marguerite Durand, founder of the newspaper *La Fronde*, the writers Séverine (Caroline Rémy de Guebhard) and Gyp (Sibylle Riquetti de Mirabeau) (her works, despite their antisemitism, could be found on the shelves of the Alliance school library in Tripoli), and the great Jewish actress Sarah Bernhardt. As Mary Louise Roberts has shown in *Disruptive Acts: The New Woman in Fin-de-Siècle France*, this *femme nouvelle* was often linked in the French cultural imagination with the Jew. Both were seen as cosmopolitan or non-French, posing a "menace" in their fluid identity, and as responsible for fin-de-siècle decadence.[33]

Attendance at the theater, daily strolls in the Bois de Boulogne, and the increasing accessibility of journals and newspapers, brought the *orientales* into almost daily contact with the "New Woman." Even after they returned to the Orient, the magazines they subscribed to, paid for by the Alliance, and the catalogs they received from Parisian department stores like Le Bon Marché (which mailed 260,000 catalogues internationally in 1894), kept them informed of the radical transformations in French female fashion that reflected and contributed to changing attitudes toward female identity.[34] Whether in Tétouan or Teheran, Alliance *institutrices* were participants in Paris' evolving sartorial scene as corsets, bustles, and plumes gave way to the masculinized *costume tailleur*.

In the ateliers they established alongside the Alliance schools, the *institutrices* (along with the couturiers they hired from Europe) carefully replicated the liberating Belle Époque styles. "Since the Italian occupation," the *directrice* of the school in Tripoli informed the Alliance on May 5, 1912, "the situation of our young girls is even better. Their work, entirely European, is even more appreciated and thus more remunerative. Some Italian families already living here are surprised to find works of such a marvelous delicacy among *indigènes* they considered savages."[35] Although the teacher in Tripoli sought to attract European or Europeanized customers to her atelier, she made quite clear that she also introduced the new styles with an eye to remaking the self-image of her students and facilitating their new roles as breadwinners and "modern" wives.

The sartorial revolution introduced by the *institutrices* left some Europeans—for example, Elkan Nathan Adler, son of the chief rabbi of the British Empire—nostalgic for the traditional dress of the Orient. "I sighed for the artistic draperies which our émigrés had brought over to Tangiers from Castile," he mused after observing a "smart-looking" Paris frock, in primary colors, being made for a Tétuoanais Jewish bride.[36] Many years later, on visiting Fez (at seventy-one years of age, he made his first trip to Morocco), Bigart also fell prey to the nostalgia of the Orient's rich sartorial past. Young girls from the Alliance school, dressed in the carefully preserved gold- and silver-embroidered outfits of their grandmothers, had welcomed him. "This spectacle of past centuries and vanished souls," he wrote, "offered me a feast for the eyes I shall find nowhere else."[37]

Adler and Bigart may have yearned for the eroticized fashions of a Delacroix painting, but the *institutrice* whose Tétouan workshop Adler visited had a profoundly different image in mind: "We have created such a change in the manner of dress," she proudly announced, "that one thinks himself in Europe."[38] If adopting Western dress signified for Jewish males in nineteenth-century Europe profound changes in their lives ("Clothes alone," the Lithuanian *maskil* Mordechai Aaron Günzburg argued, "constitute the wall that divides Jew and Christian and makes them think the other a different species of man"), it was no less a significant marker for Jewish girls living in Muslim lands.[39]

Adler visited the Tétouan workshop in 1897. Three years later, at that same atelier, a rebellious student absconded with the dressmaking model (she did not want to pay the tariff for clothes made at the atelier). Since the *grand rabbin* (chief rabbi), whose support the *directrice* could have counted on in her punishment of the student, lay gravely ill, the student's father and uncle were able to exploit the incident to mobilize Tétouan's disaffected community members, many of whom, including themselves, had recently migrated from the south, spoke Judeo-Arabic, and were viewed with disdain and distrust by the Sephardim of the north. Within months, the Alliance notified the *directrice* and her husband of their transfer to Tripoli. The *directrice's* response barely hid her fury. The Alliance, she wrote, by ignoring her many accomplishments in Tétouan, had made of her "an abstraction."[40]

Unexpected Empowerment: The *Institutrices* Appropriate the *Mission Civilisatrice*

In her angry response to the Alliance, Tétouan's *directrice* also exposed, intentionally or perhaps not, the paradox of "equality in difference" feminism: grounded in a republican universalism that excluded women, it coded the "abstract individual" as masculine.[41] A similar paradox could be found in France's *mission civilisatrice* (civilizing mission). It, too, expressed universalist aspirations yet simultaneously divided the world into "civilization" and "barbarism," thus invoking a "discourse of difference" between French subjects and those who were colonized.[42] The Alliance incorporated this paradox in its initial 1860 *appel* (call) as well as in Crémieux's 1865 impassioned call to educate the women of the Orient: "Israélites of the Orient and Africa, what have you made of your daily companion, your equal before God? In what subservience do you leave her? What support do you find for the trials of life in this subaltern creature?"[43]

The *mission civilisatrice* permeated the printed instructions and *circulaires* the Alliance sent regularly to all its teachers. Their task, they were told, was to combat "the bad habits" diffused among oriental populations: "egoism, pride, exaggeration of personal feeling, platitudes, blind respect for force or fortune, and the violence of petty passions."[44] The Alliance also honed the republic's pedagogical mandate to be more appropriate for young girls living in the Orient. They should not, for example, be "encumbered" by the official programs in France concerning the learning of the French language. As for the teaching of history, there was no need for young girls to learn facts; an oral discussion of principles and causes, in short, a moral education, was sufficient.

Despite their origins, few were the teachers who escaped viewing their charges through the orientalist lens of the Alliance. Frustration, exhaustion, and lack of success, would find some even referring to their students as *"petites sauvages"* (little savages). It is true, the Salonican-born *directrice* wrote from Rhodes in 1905, "that our little girls have defects but my intention is not to depict them as ugly as the devil. . . . Although sentiment is erased in them as quickly as it is born, I hope to succeed in awakening their sensitivity and educating their heart."[45]

Writing also in 1905 from Tangier, Hassiba Benchimol could not resist comparing her Moroccan students to their more "civilized" counterparts in Tunis. More tellingly, especially given the imperfections of her own French accent—"mon fils le chien" (my son the dog) younger family members recall her saying when referring to her son Lucien—she disparaged the language of her Moroccan co-religionists in contrast to the one she had so proudly adopted as her own: "Tunis is a French city, grand and beautiful; Tangier in contrast appears ugly, even mean. I no longer have the pleasure of hearing French spoken around me, the language I love more than my mother tongue [the Judeo-Spanish spoken in the north of Morocco]. Here one vegetates, is bored and can't help noticing the inferiority of those around us, both in their ideas and their knowledge."[46]

That eradicating oriental habits in their students—whether manifested in their language, clothing, or moral character—was a goal shared by the majority of the *institutrices* is hardly surprising. The Alliance had set the same goal for them during their four-year stay in Paris. And the Alliance succeeded: *institutrices* returned to the Orient Europeanized in language and dress as well as education.

Not surprisingly, undertaking the *mission civilisatrice* was empowering for the *institutrices*. It gave them status and authority both locally and in communications with the metropole. On July 28, 1912, for example, the *directrice* of the school in Tripoli, reporting to Paris on the Italian occupation and the antisemitism that had emerged in its wake, explained why she believed the Jewish community might be transformed "for the better":

> For the first time notables turn their eyes to their unhappy brothers and defend them when the occasion presents itself. These occasions are sadly more frequent as is always the case on the eve of a conquest. While anti-Semitism may be inevitable, the effect seems to have some advantages for our brothers. The Italianized notables understand that there still exists an abyss between themselves and the conquerors and from this deception is born quite naturally a new, solid, serious, and sacred connection between themselves and their previously ignored coreligionists. We have followed this shift with pleasure and already foresee the day when Jewish solidarity in Tripoli will form an important *faisceau* [beam], impervious to attack.[47]

Paradoxically, undertaking the *mission civilisatrice* also inspired the *institutrices* to defy the Alliance, whether by teaching historical facts rather than moral lessons to young girls, importing sewing machines without permission (since the machines took hours to learn, the Alliance wanted girls to learn to sew by hand), or exposing the racial and sexual prejudices of the metropole. Defiance even extended to the teachers' intimate lives. Although required to seek formal approval from the Alliance to marry, they often merely presented Paris with a fait accompli.[48] One *institutrice*, when announcing her decision to wed, merely assured the Alliance that she had not acted lightly and that her husband to be would make her as "happy" as she, for her part, would try to make him.[49] Education may have been "a massive canon in the artillery of empire," but in the hands of the *institutrices* it also became a challenge to patriarchal as well as colonial authority.[50]

In spite of their own orientalism, and often against the mandate of the institution they served, the teachers also used their role as educators to forge solidarities of freedom and choice among themselves and their "disinherited sisters."[51] In so doing, they resembled those "imperial feminists" who, while "hewing closely" to orientalist stereotypes, nevertheless challenged the assumptions justifying the *mission civilisatrice* and its "misogynistic underpinnings."[52] Among these feminists as well, however, Alliance *institutrices* remained structurally apart. "Colonized women, Jews, and foreigners in France could only mimic Frenchness," the radical feminist and ardent supporter of female suffrage Hubertine Auclert proclaimed. "They could become almost French, but not quite."[53]

Conclusion

The pioneering generation of Alliance *institutrices*, "agents" of the empire, albeit never considered French, had an enduring impact on the young girls of the Orient, especially in the areas of literacy, eradication of child marriage, familiarity with Jewish tradition and history, and the acquisition of skills required to earn a living and maintain a "modern" home. Diplomats as well as educators, they also negotiated successfully with colonial authorities, warring factions within the communities they served, and an international organization all too often divorced from the reality on the ground (in this, they had much in common with the pioneering generation of French Catholic women missionaries.[54]) The voluntary associations they founded, moreover, such as the *Sociétés des dames*–in Tétouan, it provided a complete trousseau and food for new mothers—and the *Sociétés scolaires* and *Associations des anciens élèves*, provided public spaces in which former students could express both solidarity and activism. Lastly, had it not been for their network of family and friends, the Alliance's mission, certainly in relation to the young girls of the Orient, would have failed.

The *institutrices* may have also left footprints beyond their own religious community. Everything new pertaining to women, a Moroccan Muslim woman explained long after most Jews had emigrated, is owed to Jewish girls who opened the breaches by letting us believe change was possible. Albeit hyperbolic, this assertion suggests an even broader legacy of the Alliance and its *institutrices*.[55] A legacy, however, that would lay dormant during a protectorate that rejected academic instruction for indigenous Muslim girls. "Overzealous French *maîtresses* [mistresses]," Georges Hardy and Louis-Hubert Lyautey had argued, might "infect their Muslim students with emancipatory ideas."[56]

Neither in their profession nor in their political and social activities do the Alliance *institutrices* resemble the constellation of new women (journalists, actresses, and writers) that emerged in Belle Époque France. Yet, in the cast of their character, impact of person, and fluidity of identity, Messody Pariente and her generation of Alliance teachers—oriental, feminist, and orientalist—were no less unconventional and unsettling in their world than the New Woman of the metropole.

Notes

1. Archives of the Alliance israélite universelle (AIU), Paris, Lybie IV.E.22, June 11, 1911.
2. Since the French Revolution, primary school teachers in France were trained at departmental *écoles normales*. Although from the beginning the Alliance trained all the boys at the École Normale Israélite Orientale, it did not establish a normal school for girls until 1922. Following the Alliance's usage, the terms "oriental" refers to those Jews living in North Africa, the Middle East and the Ottoman Empire.
3. Frances Malino, "Institutrices in the Metropole and the Maghreb: A Comparative Perspective," *Historical Reflections* 32, no. 1 (Spring 2006): 129–43.
4. Although I refer throughout this chapter to the teachers as *institutrices*, many would be promoted to the position of *directrice* (headmistress).
5. Martha Hanna, "A Republic of Letters: The Epistolary Tradition in France during World War I," *American Historical Review* 108, no. 5 (December 2003): 1338–61.
6. Letter dated July 10, 1902, Archives of the AIU, Maroc LXX.E. 1041.
7. Letter dated September 22, 1907, Archives of the AIU, Maroc XXIX. E. 475.
8. Letter dated June 16, 1909, Archives of the AIU, Maroc XV. E. 246.
9. At the beginning of the nineteenth century, child marriage was prevalent among the Jews of Morocco although not always among the same classes. In Tétouan, for example, it existed only among the poorer members of the community, while in Fez child marriages remained the preserve of the wealthy. From the beginning, the *institutrices* refused to admit to their schools students who were married, sadly acknowledging that they were thus denying an education to these very young girls. The alternative, however, was to condone the practice.
10. Georges Hardy would subsequently play an important role in Vichy France.
11. Letter dated January 24, 1924, Archives of the AIU, Maroc XXIX.E. 475.
12. Born in Safi in 1917, Elmaleh fought for Moroccan independence. In 1965 he left Morocco for Paris, not to return until 1980. He died there at the age of ninety-three, having requested that four languages be transcribed on his tombstone: Arabic, Berber, Hebrew, and French. I learned of Elmaleh's relationship to Messody in an interview with him in January 2005.
13. Archives of the AIU, Delegation Casablanca E. 89.
14. *Paix et Droit* (May 5, 1932): 11.
15. Letter dated December 20, 1927, Archives of the AIU, France VI, E. 6d.
16. Ibid.
17. After 1882 the teaching of Hebrew and Jewish history were relegated to private Jewish schools, such as the *écoles consistoriales*. If they chose to, Jewish girls in public schools could attend two classes a week (the boys were expected to attend four) in a supplementary system of religious courses, the *cours d'instruction religieuse*.
18. Archives of the AIU, Moscou 100-3-58.
19. Archives of the AIU, France V.E. 5b. The place of Hebrew in the Alliance curriculum for both boys and girls declined as the Alliance became more directly identified with and indebted to France. Shortly before the Second World War, perhaps in response to the changing political climate in Europe, the Alliance intensified religious instruction in its normal schools in Paris and reintroduced the *brevet d'hébreu* for its teachers. Interviews with female students who attended Alliance schools subsequent to the war, however, as well as from *institutrices* who taught during this period, suggest that Hebrew in the

Alliance curriculum never returned to the place it had occupied in the late nineteenth and twentieth centuries.

20. "Les Adjointes de nos écoles," *La Revue des écoles de l'Alliance*, January–March 1902, 262.

21. Eugène Delacroix, "Saâda, The Wife of Abraham Benchimol and Précidia, One of Their Daughters," Tangier, 1832, New York, Metropolitan Museum of Art.

22. Letter of November 25, 1900, Archives of the AIU, France XIV F25. See also Aron Rodrigue, *Images of Sephardi and Eastern Jewries in Transition: The Teachers of the Alliance Israélite Universelle, 1860–1939* (Seattle: University of Washington Press, 1993), 82–84. For a discussion of *institutrices* in Palestine, see Sylvie Bijaoui, "Un chemin d'émancipation: L'Alliance israélite universelle et les femmes Juives de Palestine—1872–1939," *Archives juives: Revue d'histoire des Juifs de France*, 46, no. 1:107–19.

23. Karen Offen, "Depopulation, Nationalism, and Feminism in Fin-de-Siècle France," *American Historical Review* 89, no. 3(1984): 648–76.

24. "Announcement of the President, Vice-Presidents, Treasurer and Secretary," published in the *Bulletin de l'Alliance israélite universelle*, March 1, 1865: v.

25. *Association des anciens élèves de l'Alliance israélite universelle salonique bulletin annuel*, 1909–1910, p. 8. I thank Paris Papamichos Chronakis for sharing this document with me.

26. For example: "What Differentiates the Education of Girls from That of Boys," "The Qualities of a Woman," "For Our Girls," and "Gymnastics for Young Girls."

27. *Bulletin des écoles* (1910): 66.

28. *Bulletin des écoles* (1911): 95.

29. In these questions concerning the nature and education of women, France's Jews may well have heard echoes from emancipation debates of a century earlier, for example from Berr Isaac Berr's eloquent and impassioned 1791 *Lettre d'un citoyen* in which, after assuring his coreligionists that with the required civil oath they renounced only their servitude, he outlined the educational, linguistic, and professional changes necessary to transform Jews into respected and worthy Frenchmen. Berr Isaac Berr, *Lettre d'un citoyen member de la ci-devant communauté des Juifs de Lorraine, à ses confrères, à l'occasion du droit de citoyen actif rendu aux Juifs par le décret du 28 septembre 1791* (Nancy, 1791).

30. Linda L. Clark, *Schooling the Daughters of Marianne: Textbooks and the Socialization of Girls in Modern French Primary Schools* (Albany: State University of New York Press, 1984), 104.

31. Letter of August 13, 1902, Archives of the AIU, France XIV.F.25.

32. Antoinette M. Burton, *Burdens of History: British Feminists, Indian Women, and Imperial Culture* (Chapel Hill: University of North Carolina Press, 1994), 5.

33. Mary Louise Roberts, *Disruptive Acts: The New Woman in Fin-de-Siècle France* (Chicago: University of Chicago Press, 2002), 13 and 113–15.

34. Michael B. Miller, *The Bon Marché: Bourgeois Culture and the Department Store, 1869–1920* (Princeton, NJ: Princeton University Press, 1981), 35–37.

35. Archives of the AIU, Lybie III.E.20. Were the ateliers replicating the fashionable harem pants? If so, were they, too, engaged in eroticizing the Orient?

36. Elkan Nathan Adler, *Jews in Many Lands* (Philadelphia: Jewish Publication Society of America, 1905), 172. Adler visited Tetouan in 1897.

37. Jacques Bigart, *A la Mémoire de Jacques Bigart, 1855–1934* (Paris: Alliance israélite universelle, 1934), 13.

38. Letter of May 11, 1893, Archives of the AIU, Maroc L.XIV. E. 980.

39. "Maskil" is the term used by contemporaries and historians for individuals who were part of the Haskalah, or Jewish European Enlightenment movement, based upon the older use of maskil as an honorific for scholar or enlightened man. Citation is from Israel Bartal, "Mordechai Aaron Günzburg: A Lithuanian Maskil Faces Modernity," in *Profiles in Diversity: Jews in a Changing Europe 1750–1870*, ed. Frances Malino and David Jan Sorkin (Detroit: Wayne State University Press, 1998), 135.

40. Letter of December 31, 1900, Archives of the AIU, Lybie III E 21.

41. Joan Wallach Scott, *Only Paradoxes to Offer: French Feminists and the Rights of Man* (Cambridge, MA: Harvard University Press, 1996).

42. For a discussion of universalism and the civilizing mission, see Rachel Nuñez, "Rethinking Universalism: Olympe Audouard, Hubertine Auclert, and the Gender Politics of the Civilizing Mission," *French Politics, Culture and Society* 30, no. 1 (Spring 2012): 24–25.

43. "Announcement of the President, Vice-Presidents, Treasurer and Secretary," published in the *Bulletin de l'Alliance israélite universelle* (March 1, 1865): vi.

44. Alliance israélite universelle, *Instructions générales pour les professeurs* (Paris: Alliance israélite universelle, 1903), 27–28.

45. Letter of December 14, 1905, Archives of the AIU, France X.F. 18.

46. Letter of January 7, 1898, Archives of the AIU, Maroc L.I. E. 827. Hassiba's younger relatives, more Europeanized than she, were unable to resist marking her as *orientale*. Interview by the author with Mesdames F.S. and S.H. in Paris on July 9, 2002. When Hassiba's daughter Marcelle, then living in Argentina, was asked by her grandson how many languages she knew (she had just addressed his mother in French), she answered: "Many but not one is useful anymore." David Beytelmann to Frances Malino in an email dated August 20, 2015.

47. Letter of July 29, 1912, Archives of the AIU, Lybie III.E. 20.

48. The Alliance permitted its teachers to marry—as did the French state—and the majority did so (most to each other).

49. Letter of May 22, 1894, Archives of the AIU, Maroc LXIV E. 980.

50. Bill Ashcroft, Gareth Griffiths, and Helen Tiffin, eds., *The Post-Colonial Studies Reader*, 2nd ed. (London: Routledge, 2006), 371.

51. Letter of July 28, 1912, Archives of the AIU, Lybie, III, E. 20.

52. Nuñez, "Rethinking Universalism," 28–29.

53. Quoted in ibid., 34.

54. Sarah A. Curtis, *Civilizing Habits: Women Missionaries and the Revival of French Empire* (Oxford: Oxford University Press, 2010).

55. Emanuela Trevisan Semi and Hanan Sekkat Hatimi, *Mémoire et représentations des Juifs au Maroc: Les voisins absents de Meknès* (Paris: Publisud, 2011), chap. 5. Aomar Boum, in his recent book *Memories of Absence*, provides a fascinating perspective on Muslim memories of Jews. He did not include Muslim women in his interviews. Although he was not refused access to these women, Boum believed the presence of their male relatives prevented them from talking freely. Aomar Boum, *Memories of Absence: How Muslims Remember Jews in Morocco* (Stanford, CA: Stanford University Press), 5.

56. Spencer D. Segalla, *The Moroccan Soul: French Education, Colonial Ethnography, and Muslim Resistance* (Lincoln: University of Nebraska Press, 2009), 110.

6

JEWS IN THE CROSSHAIRS OF EMPIRE
A FRANCO-RUSSIAN COMPARISON

Israel Bartal

IN THE HISTORY of empire, Jews offer a useful tool for in-depth comparison between land-based and overseas empires, entities that remain too rarely examined in concert. Moreover, among the areas where the persistent "East–West divide" of modern Jewish historiography can be broken down most profitably is in the emerging field of Jews and empire. The French and Russian empires offer a striking case in point. The Jews in Imperial Russia in the modern era experienced a series of political, social, economic, and cultural changes that they shared with fellow Jews in other European empires, particularly the French. At the same time, the Russian Jewish encounter with empire was marked by distinct characteristics. Therefore, rethinking the French and Russian Jewish experiences from one another's vantage point, in an imperial key, proves instructive on a number of levels.

Key Differences, Commonalities, and Crosscurrents

Three particular factors left salient imprints on Russian Jewry's imperial experience. First, unlike the French case, Russian imperialism was mostly an overland affair. That is, from the late early modern period onward, the czars gradually pushed back the land borders of their empire, adding new ethnic groups to populations that were already settled on imperial soil. Most Jewish subjects of nineteenth-century Russia inhabited parts of the empire that had been annexed pursuant to the three partitions of the Polish-Lithuanian Commonwealth in 1772–93 and the concurrent Russian–Ottoman wars. Namely, Russian Jews dwelled not in overseas colonies but in districts that, in greater part, belonged to administrative systems that were directly controlled from metropolitan Russia—at least if the government apparatus had its way.

116

Second, French Jewry in the late eighteenth century was a meager fraction of the kingdom's population; even French Jews who lived in the overseas territories that France took over during its colonial expansion in the nineteenth century were a relatively small group. The Jews in the provinces that Russia had annexed from the Polish-Lithuanian Commonwealth, in contrast, were a collective of considerable demographic importance. From a 1772 estimated number of some 400,000 in the territories annexed by Russia, the Jewish population under the czars grew to more than 5 million by 1897.[1] As the dominant urban element in hundreds of cities and towns in the newly annexed territories, Jews cast a socioeconomic net over wide expanses of territory along czarist Russia's western frontiers. The Jews of Alsace, a region annexed by the French monarchy in the late seventeenth century, were the group of French Jews most similar to the population of the western reaches of czarist Russia in demographic, cultural, social, and economic terms.

Third, most of Russian Jewry was inseparable from the rest of the Ashkenazi Diaspora, which spread from Alsace in northeastern metropolitan France, and from England and the Netherlands in western Europe, to Lithuania and Ukraine on the eastern edge of the continent. Thus, the Jews of Imperial Russia were a link in a demographic and cultural chain that crossed geopolitical borders and exposed the Jews of the empire to the influences of processes, currents, and movements that originated in the neighboring countries' religious and cultural centers. By contrast, the impact of the Ashkenazi cultural world on French Jewry in the imperial era was quite modest.

And yet historical comparison of the large Jewish population that dwelled in the czarist empire from the last decades of the eighteenth century with the history of Jewry in imperial France shows that, notwithstanding the differences in geopolitical, demographic, and cultural conditions between the two collectives, the encounter between the Jews and the Russian and French imperial authorities had several commonalities. Both, in fact, were new populations. Neither empire had had a significant Jewish population at the dawn of the early modern period. Expulsions that had taken place hundreds of years before the eighteenth century and bans on Jewish settlement in both empires' territories produced similar demographic outcomes. That is, the Jews reestablished their presence in the Russian Empire and the French monarchy at a rather late point in time, and the reasons for it were migrations and the annexation of territories that already had Jewish populations. For example, Spanish-Portuguese Jewish settlement resumed in several French cities when "new Christians" reached these locations in the century preceding the French Revolution, whereas Imperial Russia absorbed migrants from Galicia, part of Imperial Austria, in its southern provinces in the years following the partitions of Poland.

Another similarity, one that had highly significant implications for relations between the Jews and the authorities, involved the introduction of parallel models of administration by France and Russia. In both countries, the Jews found themselves under centralized rule, whether they had migrated from other lands or inhabited communities in the occupied territories. The France and Russia that the Jews encountered when they first became these countries' subjects were feudal states that were in the midst of a transition to absolutist rule. The various estates in these kingdoms (which also accommodated ethnoreligious urban groups that enjoyed considerable autonomy) were being co-opted into the imperial bureaucracies and steadily lost independence until they ultimately became subordinates of the central regime. During the eighteenth century and the first half of the nineteenth, the Russian government introduced a series of administrative reforms that weakened the status of corporative entities at large and gradually obliterated Jewish autonomy (with pauses in mid-course for special legislation pertaining to the Jews' status in 1791, 1804, and 1835). In France, a centralized revolutionary regime did away with Jewish self-rule (in 1790–91). One may also note conceptual and structural commonalities between the dissolution of the *kahal* under Czar Nicholas I (1844) and the liquidation of the Jewish community institutions in Alsace during the French Revolution.

Toward the middle of the eighteenth century, the absolutist template of governance was influenced by Western Enlightenment thinking and evolved into so-called enlightened absolutism. Frederick the Great in the Kingdom of Prussia, Josef II in Austria (and in the Holy Roman Empire), and Catherine II in Russia conducted a continual and highly insightful discourse with social and economic philosophers and thinkers (most of whom were French subjects) and also accepted their outlooks regarding the Jews, their religion, their customs and, above all, their social conduct and economic behavior.[2] They perceived the Ashkenazi Jewish corporative entity—a cultural, linguistic, and behavioral anomaly—as in need of correction. Within a few decades of the empire's annexation of Belarus and Ukraine (which were inhabited by hundreds of thousands of Jewish subjects of the Polish-Lithuanian Commonwealth), acceptance of European Enlightenment ideas in influential circles in the Russian government led to the adoption of social and economic reform programs in the spirit of physiocracy (a doctrine that also had a definitive influence on French economic policy on the eve of the Revolution). The imperial regime strove to apply the principles of prerevolutionary French economic policy to correct the perceived moral failings and improve the economic conduct of the Jews in the territories that it had annexed from Poland.[3] As historian Adam Teller puts it, "The economic component of this ideology—physiocracy—that valued the natural economy and agricultural work above all, viewed Jewish economic activity negatively. It argued that in order to make Jews useful members of society, their economic life should be reformed to make it more 'productive.' In real terms, this meant causing Jews to abandon petty trade in favor of agriculture, or at least crafts and industrial labor."[4]

Likewise, everything said and written about the economic depredations and vile morality of the Alsatian Ashkenazi Jews in the early going of the French Revolution—remarks that reverberated in discussions about the Jewish question in the Polish Sejm in 1788–91—made its way to Russia under Alexander I. The most conspicuous and influential text in this matter was a tract that the noted Russian poet Gavrila Derzhavin wrote about the famine in Belarus. Derzhavin, a senator, was sent by Czar Pavel I to investigate the reasons for the famine in this area, which had been annexed from the Polish-Lithuanian Commonwealth in the First Partition (1772). In his tract, Derzhavin stated flatly that the Jews' lack of productivity and their exploitation of the rest of the population had harmed the state economy and the welfare of the main population group (the peasantry) and that it was they, the Jews, who had pushed the region into economic crisis. The conclusions in the tract even shaped certain clauses in the "Statute Concerning the Organization of the Jews," which was approved by Alexander I on December 9, 1804. One reason for this, among others, was that two members of the committee that drafted the aforementioned statute, who belonged to the Polish aristocracy (Adam Czartoryski and Seweryn Potocki), retained the physiocratic views that were presented during the debates on the Jewish question in the Polish Sejm several years earlier.[5] This kind of criticism, widely brought against the Jews of Alsace at the turn of the nineteenth century, continued to echo in the Russian imperial discourse on how to integrate the Jews as loyal and useful subjects.

Jewish thinkers and public activists internalized this discourse as well. The Haskalah or Jewish Enlightenment, a factor of marginal influence on economic processes and political changes in eastern Europe, accepted almost unquestioningly the government's criticism of the Jews' role in the old socioeconomic order. Thus, just as the Jews' functioning in the feudal economy had been badly harmed by external processes that they could not possibly change, the image of the Jewish "ancien régime" was thoroughly subverted in the eyes of internal and external critics. Jews had held a set of crucial positions in the feudal agrarian economy of Poland-Lithuania; they retained them under Russian rule as long as this economic system existed.

Jews as Both Undesirables and Agents of Empire

Until the mid-nineteenth century, the *kehilla* system, which persisted under official Russian sanction for decades after the partitions of Poland, anchored the network of Polish noble estates that remained operative across the expanses of eastern Europe. The Polish uprisings against Russia (1830–31, 1863) and the ascendancy of the capitalist economy during Alexander II's reforms (1856–63) converged to undermine the foundations of socioeconomic existence in traditional eastern European Ashkenazi society. The early-nineteenth-century Russian critics of Jewish autonomy aimed neither to abolish feudalism nor to tear down the estate economy. Instead, they proposed to extricate the Jews from economic feudalism and shift them to alternative vocations. In the spirit of the French Enlightenment, they connected the "unproductive" image of the Jew and the ideas of cultural and social "regeneration." On this basis, they sought to transform into farmers and craftsmen the masses of Jews whom they considered parasites who lived off indigenous peasants' labor in the western provinces of the empire. Inducing Jewish mass migration from the northwest of the empire to sparsely populated areas in the south and the east, transferring surplus population that was regarded as unproductive to new areas and establishing agricultural colonies for this population in frontier districts—all of these were consistent with the empire's interest in settling the territories of the "new Russia": the *gubernias* of Taurida, Kherson, and Ekaterinoslav, part of the provinces that had been conquered from the Ottoman Empire.

This marked the birth of an ambitious colonization venture in which thousands of Jews were displaced from the empire's northwest reaches and resettled in farming colonies in the south Ukrainian steppe. The dualism that characterized the empire's attitude toward Jewish internal migration—overland territorial continuity and administrative unity, as we recall—fathered a sociopolitical creature of a new kind. The Jew who migrated to the southern gubernias had been evicted from his former place of residence due to having been labeled as a disloyal nuisance. Concurrently, however, he carried out the imperial mission of a Russian settler and a cultural agent in his new locale. This dualism, which the Jewish subject also accepted, continued to accompany Russian Jewry into the twentieth century. Ever since the First Partition of Poland, the imperial authorities had viewed the large Jewish population, added to the empire almost overnight, both as a useful asset that should be deployed wisely and as a social and economic problem that had to be confronted. The changes that occurred in the Russian state's ambivalence toward the Jews from the late eighteenth century to the eve of World War I reflected vacillations and changes of mind in government corridors. The czars modeled their reforms concerning the Jews' legal status and economic activity after those introduced by the neighboring empires to the west. Conversely, the influence of anti-Jewish traditions from the centuries preceding Catherine's reign persisted well into the nineteenth century.

During Russia's mighty territorial expansion before the 1917 revolutions, the concept of "internal colonization" was widely invoked to describe the migration policy of the Russian government.[6] In this colonization, which combined massive resettlement projects with social reform, the imperial legislators sought to make the Jews part of their campaign to expand the empire's borders. To accomplish this, they allowed, encouraged, and at times even tried to force Jews to emigrate from the northwestern sector of the Pale of Settlement to the new gubernias in the vast territories that the Russian army had annexed from the Ottoman Empire. From the other end, they used legislative means to hinder Jews from moving out of the areas annexed from the Polish-Lithuanian Commonwealth to settle permanently in the Russian interior.

Colonization by Jews who had lived in the northwestern part of the empire was in fact a form of deportation. It was a time when states were habituated to ridding themselves of surplus populations that they considered unuseful, if not harmful, to the political order and economic welfare by systematically exiling them to penal colonies in faraway, uninhabited areas (as in the case of Australia as a destination for criminal convicts from Great Britain). Thus the Russian policy toward the Jews was not exceptional. Large-scale settlement operations that included large numbers of Jews, nearly all of them from Lithuania and Belarus— together with a steady flow of Jews who migrated voluntarily in order to take advantage of the improved economic conditions that the imperial regime was promoting—totally transformed the demography and geography of the new territories. Thus, a network of cities, towns, and villages spread across the sparsely populated steppe and major urban localities sprouted where no man had gone before.

Jewish Colonists on Imperial Frontiers

The Jewish settlers, along with other migrants from central Europe, were agents of Western culture in its Imperial Russian iteration whether they knew it or not. As we recall, French lawmakers regarded the Ashkenazi Jews of that country as a harmful socioeconomic element in need of correction. Ashkenazim who settled en masse in the western gubernias of Imperial Russia during Catherine II's reign were viewed similarly as a "non-European" population group in need of reeducation or eviction to recently conquered frontier areas. The comparison between the Russian case and France on the eve of the Revolution almost begs itself: the Russian authorities in the late eighteenth and early nineteenth centuries, like their counterparts in France, contended with a rather similar population. At both ends of the Ashkenazi diaspora, from Alsace in the west to Lithuania and Ukraine in the east, Yiddish-speaking Jews who had enjoyed self-rule and lived under their religious law encountered policies of a new and unprecedented kind: they were called upon (at least in the reformers' memoranda and the "reform" schemes of experts and *maskilim*, proponents of the Haskalah) to surrender their traditional way of life, their attire, their language, and their sources of livelihood. The Alsatian Jews were the last in France to receive French citizenship, and even then only if they improved their economic conduct. In the Napoleonic era, the regime again demanded that they adopt different economic behavior, using exactly the same words that the Russian legislator used toward the Jews of Lithuania and Belarus.

The Alsatian Jews who underwent French acculturation in the course of the nineteenth century, the era of the "internal colonization" of Russian Jews in the southern provinces, were similar in their social situation and state of mind.[7] In the decades following the French colonial conquest of Algeria in 1830, these Alsatian Jews also played quite similar roles in French Jewish philanthropic activity in North Africa (and elsewhere in the Mediterranean basin). The French colonial regime tended to consider the Jews more deserving of civil rights than the Muslim majority population. Thus, those who in one part of the empire were pariahs marked for "reeducation" became in another part a vanguard of the imperial culture.[8] From a historical perspective, the Jewish migrants in the southern reaches of Imperial Russia continued to serve a function similar to that of their ancestors for centuries in the Polish-Lithuanian Commonwealth: founders of cities and expanders of borders in the frontier regions of the empire. Agricultural colonization, organized with czarist government support, continued until the middle of the nineteenth century. By the end of that century, roughly one hundred thousand Jews were living in farming colonies in the southern parts of the empire. At the time they constituted the world's largest collective of Jewish farmers in the modern period.[9] However, the spontaneous mass migration of Jews to the south from the gubernias of Lithuania and Belarus, mentioned earlier, was several times greater in numerical and geographic magnitude than the agricultural project, itself impressive in size. Hundreds of thousands of Jewish migrants thronged to the southern provinces of Imperial Russia and established hundreds of new communities within a few years. Odessa, the favored imperial port city, hosted a Jewish population of nearly 140,000 by 1897 and had evolved into a leading center of Jewish culture—whereas one hundred years previously it had been home to a handful of Jews next door to the Ottoman hajj bey fortress.

The Jews thus accounted for an important share of the demographic change that Russia underwent in the nineteenth century. Under the czars, they moved to the periphery en masse because the heart of the empire was off limits to them. In the twentieth century, however, after the restrictions established under enlightened absolutism were repealed, the direction of the internal migration reversed. Thus, just as Paris attracted migrants from Alsace, so did Moscow and St. Petersburg lure Jews from the now-defunct Pale of Settlement.

Empires of Revolution

Between the eighteenth and the twentieth centuries, the two empires, the French and the Russian, demarcated the limits of Ashkenazi Jewish settlement in the Old World. That is, the former set the western frontier of the Ashkenazi diaspora and the latter shaped its eastern frontier. The influence of both empires' policies, however, was also evident within the vast geographic space that separated them. From the French Revolution to the 1917 upheavals in Russia, both powers "projected" conceptual and political influences that were definitive in the reshaping of European Jewry. Each of them, in its own turn, underwent a series of revolutionary political changes that unleashed unprecedented changes in Jewish society as well. Furthermore, France in the west and Russia in the east did not merely "project" revolutionary republican, liberal, or socialist ideas; they were also involved, at one time or another, in literally exporting their revolutions to the rest of continental Europe. The French republican army, later to evolve into that of the Napoleonic empire, disseminated the revolutionary model to many neighboring states and countries. Jewish emancipation in Europe began in the wake of France's conquests. French soldiers extricated the Jews of the cities of Italy from their ghettos. When the new revolutionary parliament of the Batavian Republic established in the Netherlands granted the Jews political equality, it followed the lead of the French national assembly. In several German states, the legal status of the Jews changed in the aftermath of Napoleon's conquests.

From 1815 onward, reaction to the French conquests was identified, among other things, with the slowing of the Jews' de jure integration into the countries of the continent. Moreover, in early nineteenth-century Europe the resistance to emancipation (and to the ideas of the Revolution generally) was linked to the struggle for liberation from the French occupier's yoke. At the time of the "Spring of Nations" (the 1848 revolutions), the struggle for the Jews' emancipation was repeatedly associated with the ideas of French-style political equality, prompting resistance among ethnic groups that disapproved of what they considered Jewish identification with the imperial regime. A wave of anti-Jewish riots erupted in France in the winter of 1848 and, within a few months, spread across the continent from the communities of Alsace as far as Bohemia and Hungary.[10] Several decades later, the momentum turned around and the anti-Jewish reactions radicalized.

Arguably, however, the impact of the 1917 revolutions in Russia on European Jewry (and on Jewish migrants to the west and Palestine) was quite similar to that of the revolutionism that France had exported to the continent in the previous century. It even paralleled, to a large extent, the *mission civilisatrice* of French colonialism, for example, the principles of equality under law and the republican freedom like those that the French governors in the West African colonies wished to apply in the period preceding World War II.[11] The discourse of civilizing republicanism left an indelible imprint on the modernization of North African Jewry. Jewish intellectuals and politicians identified with the liberating empire, on grounds of which the autochtonous national movements eventually treated the Jews with estrangement and leveled against them accusations of radicalism, universalism, and collaboration with the foreign Western regime. In both cases, the Russian and the French, imperialistic movements and currents aspired to reform the world and man by political or military means and threatened to undermine the foundations of traditional Jewish society, its ways of life, and its culture. One need not lavish words about the radical totalitarian stage of Russian imperial history that began with the 1917 revolutions, precipitating extreme changes in Jewish society and culture within a few years. Its impact, much like the French republican revolutionism, was disseminated both through "projection" beyond the imperial borders and through the bayonets of the Red Army. Here, too, the phenomenon of identifying with concepts of global and human reform recurred in the service of an imperial regime. The nexus of Jews' revolutionary political activity and the Soviet connection brought on a ferocious reaction in the rest of continental Europe and beyond, with ghastly results that ranged from the slaughter of tens of thousands of Ukrainian Jews in 1919–20 to the mass participation of members of various ethnicities in the murder of the Jews during World War II.

Conclusion: Jewish Imperial Messianism and Its Price

The recurrent and seemingly paradoxical pairing of imperial expansion and the dissemination of ideas of equality, freedom, and fraternity in the modern era is a definitive characteristic of French and Russian history. With respect to Jews, this combination may be interpreted as a radicalized metamorphosis of the enlightened absolutist policy toward the Jews or the fulfillment of the principles of the French Revolution among the Jewish populations that came under the imperial regime's wings. Both empires' governing institutions chose at times to apply Enlightenment-style human engineering to their Jewish subjects as they integrated them (either empathetically or forcibly) into the imperial expansion project. Such an effect is almost totally absent, or at least presents itself much more mildly, in the imperial experience of the Jews in the British Empire and the second German Reich. The Jews' identification with imperial revolutionary projects was pronouncedly messianic from the dawn of the Haskalah movement in central and eastern Europe.[12] Haskalah poetry in the Russian Empire invoked messianic concepts in its depiction of the czars, while some German and Dutch Jews likened the French Revolution to the onset of the Redemption (אתחלתא דגאולה). It goes without saying that Jews' later addiction to French "imperial" republicanism or the vision of the Soviet "world of tomorrow" were very similar manifestations of secular messianism.

In Russian history, internal migrations were definitive in instilling the imperial culture among the diverse population groups that inhabited the newly annexed territories in the 150 years preceding the 1917 revolutions; they also had no small effect on the shaping of the political culture. Russia, an eastern European country that many in Britain, France, and Germany found hard to associate with the West in the nineteenth century, became, for no small number of its new subjects in the annexed territories, a conspicuous agent of Western Enlightenment, science, progressive ways, and European-style centralized administration.[13] From the first decades of the nineteenth century, the *maskilim* in Russia began to see themselves as agents of westernizing trends that they detected (not altogether mistakenly) in the imperial government policy. In the early 1860s, as many Russian Jews embraced Alexander II's reforms with quasi-messianic enthusiasm, the Haskalah poet Judah Leib Gordon (1830–92) commented:

> And now there is no city nor province where the young men of Israel cannot draw cold, flowing waters, defiantly and without shame. You will find thousands in the secondary schools, hundreds in the universities, and scores of specialist physicians in government service! . . . How many of our young men will you now find wielding the pen of an author, fluently speaking the language of the land [Russian] or German and French, and all of them of this new generation, creations of the last decade; how many noble, wealthy Jews will you find now regarded as dignitaries of the government, Jews in their hearts, but in their appearance, clothing, and manners—like Europeans. Now we can remain calm and rely upon the Almighty, for there is great hope for our future.[14]

For Gordon, the impassioned poet, the blessings of Western civilization emanated from the east—from St. Petersburg, capital of the empire. How similar his remarks are to the observation of Ethan Katz regarding Jews' idealized picture of France, its empire, and its culture: "But moreover, France, in the eyes of many enthusiasts of Franco-Judaism, not only offered Jews unprecedented paths to citizenship, opportunity, and success but also had the broader capacity to forge loyal French subjects and citizens across much of the globe."[15]

Thus, at both extremes of the continent, many Jews linked their people's fate to a utopian confluence of political rights, Western cultural superiority, and the empire's political and military might. For two centuries starting in the late 1700s, Paris and St. Petersburg were a Jerusalem for them. When the two empires experienced times of crisis and weakness, however, no small number of Jews paid for their quasi-messianic embrace of the ideas of global human reform, in favor of which they had relinquished old identities.

Notes

1. For a comprehensive study on the demography of Russian Jewry, see Shaul Stampfer, "Aspects of Population Growth and Migration in Polish-Lithuanian Jewry in the Modern Period," in *The Broken Chain: Polish Jewry through the Ages*, ed. Israel Bartal and Israel Gutman, 263–85 (in Hebrew) (Jerusalem: Zalman Shazar Center, 1997).

2. On the French physiocratic debates and its implications for the position of Jews in a state economy, see Arthur Hertzberg, *The French Enlightenment and the Jews: The Origins of Modern Anti-Semitism* (New York: Schocken, 1968), 71–77.

3. For a recent review of the scholarship on physiocratism and Russian imperial policy toward the Jews, see Nathan Hellman, "Trading Freedom in the Russian Empire: The Extent to which Russia Attempted to Solve the Jewish Question by Granting Jews Rights Only in Scenerios that Economically Benefited the State," *Anthós* 5, no. 1, art. 9, doi:10.15760/anthos.2013.97.

4. Adam Teller, "Economic Life," *YIVO Encyclopedia of Jews in Eastern Europe*, accessed June 27, 2016, http://www.yivoencyclopedia.org/article.aspx/Economic_Life.

5. Jolanta T. Penkaz, "To What Extent Did Prince Adam Czartoryski Influence Alexander I's 'Jewish' Statute of 1804?" *Polish Review* 40, no. 4 (1995): 403–14. For the impact of French physiocratic theories on Polish reform projects, see Marcin Wodzinski, "Clerks, Jews, and Farmers: Projects of Jewish Agricultural Settlement in Poland," *Jewish History* 21 (2007): 279–303.

6. Alexander Etkind, *Internal Colonization: Russia's Imperial Experience* (Cambridge: Polity, 2011).

7. See Paula Hyman, *The Emancipation of the Jews of Alsace: Acculturation and Tradition in the Nineteenth Century* (New Haven, CT: Yale University Press, 1991).

8. For a fuller exploration of these issues, see Joshua Schreier, *Arabs of the Jewish Faith: The Civilizing Mission in Colonial Algeria* (New Brunswick, NJ: Rutgers University Press, 2010).

9. Regarding Jewish farming colonies in an international context, see Israel Bartal, "Farming the Land on Three Continents: Bilu, Am Oylom, and Yefe-Nahar," *Jewish History* 21 (2007): 249–61.

10. Jacob Toury, *Turmoil and Confusion in the Revolution of 1848: The Anti-Jewish Riots in the "Year of Freedom" and their Influence on Modern Antisemitism* (in Hebrew) (Tel Aviv: Moreshet, 1968), 24–62.

11. Alice L. Conkin, *A Mission to Civilize: The Republican Idea of Empire in France and West Africa 1895–1930* (Stanford, CA: Stanford University Press, 1998).

12. Olga Litvak, *Haskalah, the Romantic Movement in Judaism* (New Brunswick, NJ: Rutgers University Press, 2012), 89–102.

13. On the image of eastern Europe in the context of modernization, see Larry Wolff, *Inventing Eastern Europe: The Map of Civilization on the Mind of the Enlightenment* (Stanford, CA: Stanford University Press, 1994); and Larry Wolff, *The Idea of Galicia: History and Fantasy in Habsburg Political Culture* (Stanford, CA: Stanford University Press, 2011), 13–62.

14. Judah Leib Gordon, cited in Israel Bartal, *The Jews of Eastern Europe, 1772–1914* (Philadelphia: University of Pennsylvania Press, 2005), 106.

15. Ethan B. Katz's contribution to this volume, "Crémieux's Children: Joseph Reinach, Léon Blum, and René Cassin as Jews of Empire," 131.

PART 2

JEWS IN COLONIAL POLITICS

7
CRÉMIEUX'S CHILDREN

JOSEPH REINACH, LÉON BLUM, AND RENÉ CASSIN AS JEWS OF FRENCH EMPIRE

Ethan B. Katz

IN MARCH 1958, in the midst of the Franco-Algerian War, Algerian Jewish leader Jacques Lazarus addressed a group of community notables gathered in the city of Algiers.[1] Lazarus sought to reassure his co-religionists that their status as French citizens, contrary to certain recent reports, had never been in question under the current republican government; likewise, he defended the Crémieux Decree, the 1870 act that had made Algerian Jews French citizens and that now was the subject of criticism by the Algerian nationalists fighting for independence. Near the end of his speech, Lazarus claimed that the members of his community were, all at once, "French, Jewish, republicans, and liberals." Having grown up in Alsace, earned distinction as a Resistance fighter during World War II, and taken a leading role in Algerian Jewish organizational life since the late 1940s, Lazarus could speak credibly for Jews in both metropolitan France and Algeria. Indeed, in expressing a particularly Jewish sympathy for the nationalist cause, Lazarus exclaimed:

> We understand the aspirations of the Muslim masses, today walled off in silence, to a better life, to complete equality. The Jews, in general, are always against all racisms, against all excesses, whoever the authors, whoever the victims. In this country of Algeria, [the Jews] have always prioritized total equality and the same rights for all, and we remember that the name of a great Jew is linked to a project which, if it had not been torpedoed at the time by certain reactionary antisemites and racists who are in large part responsible for the current situation, would have [saved us] without doubt [from] the [current] grief and even suffering; I am speaking of, as you surely understand, the Blum-Viollette Plan.[2]

Lazarus made an impassioned and elegant case for the credentials of French and Algerian Jews as almost innately liberal and reformist in their colonial outlook.

But was it true? Could a tradition of liberal, reformist colonialism among Jews be traced back over decades? If so, for the figures within that tradition, what was the relationship between their identification as Jews and their liberal colonial politics? Perhaps most importantly, what might this tradition tell us about how Jewish servants of the state squared their deep commitment to the egalitarian republican tradition with the brutal inequalities instituted and long maintained by France in its colonies?

This essay pursues these questions through an assessment of the colonial reform efforts of Joseph Reinach (1856–1921), Léon Blum (1872–1950), and René Cassin (1887–1976). These three Jews were leading French statesmen of their generation and took a substantial interest in empire, including France's most prized colonial possession, Algeria. Despite being major figures in their lifetimes and remaining well known, all three have been relatively little examined in both colonial history and the history of Jewish politics.

By now scholars have had much to say about both the presence of Jews in the French political arena and the relationship between patriotism and Jewishness for many Jews in France. In the first instance, at once historically and historiographically, those whom Pierre Birnbaum influentially deemed the "state Jews" of the Republic have done much to shape understandings of French Jewry.[3] Another strand of scholarship has shown amply how for French Jews in the era of emancipation, traditional Jewish values and modes of thought became intertwined with attachments to the French nation and in particular with support for ideals of the Revolution and the Republic.[4] And yet, until now, scholarship in each of these areas has given almost no attention to two often crucial—and, I argue, interrelated—issues: the place of the empire and the significance of the law as both profession and ideal for large numbers of middle-class, integrated Jews devoted to France. In the process, key facets of many Jews' ideological formation and their wider importance for the history of Jewish politics have been neglected. More recently, a number of scholars have begun to consider the first of these issues, examining intersections between French colonial history and histories of Jews in France, primarily for the nineteenth century.[5] Their work has underscored the connections between Jewish international advocacy in the colonial arena and beyond and Jewish identity and citizenship at home.[6]

The present essay builds upon each of these elements in the historiography but seeks to push them in new directions by engaging more fully with broader developments that have placed the history of mainland France in an increasingly imperial framework. The essay analyzes the role of three leading Jewish political actors at three critical moments in the history of Muslim status in Algeria. These moments—World War I; the Popular Front; and the period from the Allied landing in Algeria to the early Fourth Republic—constituted the three most significant opportunities for major reform in the status of France's colonial subjects in Algeria before the Franco-Algerian War (1954–62). Crucially, each was a moment of not only national and colonial but decidedly international import. In every instance, a leading advocate for liberalizing reforms in Algeria was a visible French Jew of considerable stature. All were critical of existing French colonial policies and practices but rarely if ever questioned the basic assumptions of French colonialism. Such a coinciding of these figures and moments enables us to interrogate if and how these figures' Jewishness intersected with their liberal colonial politics and to thus discern where both continuities and distinctions can be found among them. As suggested by the engagement of numerous other Jews with the question of colonial reform in Algeria, Reinach, Blum, and Cassin were hardly unique cases of what I term Jews of French Empire.

Through this study, we can see how important colonialism was for each of these figures' Franco-Judaism, how important their Jewishness was for their colonial engagement, and how both were inseparable from the development of their internationalism. For my purposes, "Franco-Judaism" refers to an ideology, particularly popular among the Ashkenazi bourgeoisie, of patriotic devotion to a vision of France as a democratic, secular, egalitarian republic. Jews who held this ideology saw themselves and their Frenchness as proudly attached to the heritage of the Revolution of 1789. They saw France as the living embodiment of ethical values that were linked to the teachings of Judaism and the Hebrew Bible. But moreover, France, in the eyes of many enthusiasts of Franco-Judaism, not only offered Jews unprecedented paths to citizenship, opportunity, and success but also had the broader capacity to forge loyal French subjects and citizens across much of the globe. Because Algeria's Jews had acquired French citizenship en masse in 1870 and thereafter integrated substantially to French language and culture, the territory appeared to offer a positive test case. Even in the face of colonialism's persistently brutal inequalities and exploitations vis-à-vis other native populations, many Jews would maintain their hopes for the French civilizing mission, particularly in Algeria, until the bitter end.

Reinach, Blum, and Cassin were among those who lived most acutely the contradictions of being Jewish French imperialists. They had much in common: all were battle-tested republicans, assimilated but proud Jews, internationalists, at once policymakers and intellectuals, and—not least important—lawyers. At three distinct historical moments, they took similar positions on legal status for Muslims in French Algeria. Yet as oppositional politics in the colonies evolved from the early to mid-twentieth century, their liberalism, at one time relatively progressive, became increasingly outmoded.

Thus, this essay does not seek to cast Reinach, Blum, and Cassin as heroes or would-be liberators. All of their proposed reforms fell well short of either autonomy or complete legal equality for Algeria's Muslims. At the same time, depicting the three men as vile colonialist oppressors would obscure a great deal of complexity in both their historical contexts and precise policy positions, particularly when Jewish politics enters the picture.[7] Reinach's conservatism and unceasing commitment to the civilizing mission reflected the late-nineteenth-century republican, imperial, and Jewish communal dynamics on which he cut his teeth. Blum was formed politically as an idealistic socialist and Zionist, questioning colonialism earlier than most and fighting for international disarmament in the interwar years. Wounded in World War I, Cassin became a humanitarian activist for veterans, a resister against Nazism, and a theorist of international law who sought to position France for the post-1945 world of "human rights" talk.

In a longer historical context, these figures were heirs to the man who might be considered the first Jew of French Empire: Adolphe Crémieux.[8] As a young attorney and community leader, Crémieux skillfully led the ultimately triumphant legal struggle against the "Jewish oath." In one of the founding events of modern Jewish internationalism, he played a key role in the successful intervention of European Jews on behalf of their Levantine co-religionists in the 1840 Damascus Affair. Crémieux later served as the president of the Alliance israélite universelle (AIU).[9] At the same time, he rose to the highest levels of national French politics. Léon Gambetta, one of the key architects and early ministers of the Third Republic, had begun his career in law practice with Crémieux and saw him as a crucial confidant and mentor. Gambetta made Crémieux justice minister in the Government of the National Defense of September 1870 that preceded the founding of the Third Republic.[10] It was in this context that Crémieux orchestrated his most famous single act, the October 1870 emancipation law that would forever bear his name and through which the vast majority of Algeria's 37,000 Jews, willfully or not, became full French citizens. This decree would be long remembered with pride by French and Algerian Jews for setting the latter more fully on the path to "Frenchification."

Joseph Reinach: Defending the Republic for Jews and Muslims

In May 1917 at the height of World War I, Joseph Reinach published an article in his regular column in the newspaper *Le Figaro* on an atypical subject entitled "Of Islam in the World War." The piece discussed in detail the unsuccessful propaganda efforts of the Kaiserreich aimed at provoking North African Muslims to revolt or join the Central Powers; Reinach also gave substantial attention to the history of French and German disputed claims in Morocco and the ongoing French colonization under way there. Eventually, the author arrived at one of the earliest known statements of advocacy by a prominent French Jew for greater equality for France's Muslim subjects. As the article reached its rhetorical climax, Reinach asked, "Can our war of liberation of peoples limit itself to Europe?" He answered his own question by quoting enthusiastically the words of Husayn bin Ali, sharif of Mecca, a key leader of the Arab uprising against the Ottoman Empire (and close ally therein of France and England): "from Verdun to the Ka'aba."[11] Reinach then declared:

> Muslims of Asia and Africa, fighting in the English and Russian armies as in ours, mixing their heroic blood with ours, have acquired great rights, from the Ganges to the Volga, and from the Persian Gulf to the Atlantic. Oppressions, which have always been detestable, would be tomorrow frightfully ungrateful. Whoever has shed with us his blood has the right to our liberty and our justice. [Whether] bureaucratic or military, parliamentary or electoral, we must break all resistance [and] produce a vast reform in the status of the Muslim *indigènes*.[12]

This statement appeared in the midst of a wider debate, provoked by the war's unprecedented mobilization of imperial manpower on the part of the French state. From 1914 to 1918, approximately 600,000 colonial subjects served in the French armies, and the plurality were some 250,000 Muslims from North Africa.[13] Under these circumstances, World War I tested, as never before, France's capacity and willingness to extend the assimilationist logic of republican citizenship to its imperial subjects.[14] The patriotic sacrifice of Algerian Muslims in particular, by far the largest group from any single territory, provoked extensive debates among French policymakers about the possibility of rewarding them with naturalization at the war's end.

Despite his relative conservatism on imperial and military issues, Reinach spoke boldly here, at the very least implying strong support for enfranchisement and displaying little of the reservation or hesitation of most French policymakers regarding reforming the status of Algerian Muslims. His position—and the terms in which he articulated it—reflected several dimensions of his persona: an unshakably idealistic vision of France and the heritage of 1789; the experience of the Dreyfus Affair as a national and personal struggle for justice; an ardent belief in the necessity of France being an imperial power with a strong military; interconnected with this imperialism, a view of foreign relations and liberal progress in which notions of international order played a key role; and a deep sense of the progressive movement of history. Each of these elements at once gave voice to and shaped the form of Reinach's Franco-Jewish consciousness.

Born in 1856, Reinach grew up in Paris in a Jewish family of German Alsatian origin; his father had come to Alsace from Germany, drawn by the promise of the ideals of the French Revolution. Hermann-Joseph Reinach, from humble origins, became a major investor in the French railway system; thus, Joseph and his brothers Salomon and Théodore inherited tremendous wealth. Each of these extraordinarily talented and versatile brothers earned major recognition for his intellectual achievements, service to the state, or both. Receiving his law degree from the Paris Law faculty, Joseph Reinach enrolled in the Paris Bar in 1877 at the age of twenty-one. His legal talents quickly became apparent, and he served as secretary for the bar's *conférence* in 1879–80.[15] During the same period, his budding journalistic work caught the eye of Léon Gambetta, one of the Third Republic's founding fathers; by age twenty-five, Reinach was Gambetta's chief of staff at the Ministry of Foreign Affairs. In his proximity to Gambetta's inner circle, Reinach entered the same milieu previously inhabited by Adolphe Crémieux.[16] Later, he was elected deputy to the national parliament from the Basses-Alpes, serving first from 1889–98 then, after being defeated, returning to serve two terms from 1906 to 1914, when he lost the seat once more. Long associated with the so-called Opportunist republicans of Gambetta's coalition, Reinach served his first two terms as a member of the moderate republican Alliance démocratique, and the latter two with the center-right Gauche démocratique. Early in his political career, when he engaged in the fierce struggles to establish republicanism on firm footing, Reinach became a battle-tested public figure who rarely shied from a fight. Strong in not only mental but physical constitution, the stocky Reinach was eventually a veteran of thirteen duels.[17]

While avowedly assimilationist, actively opposed to the Zionist movement from the time of its founding, and extremely reluctant to reference his Judaism in public life, Reinach was deeply grounded in Jewish culture and identity. He had extremely close relationships with much of his family, his brothers in particular; he corresponded with them constantly and turned to them for advice and comfort in times of crisis. What was in many respects a highly insular Jewish milieu provided crucial support for Reinach throughout his career. Under the pressure of family, he married a Jewish woman in accordance with tradition. Like many Jews of French Empire, he participated in the AIU, serving as its secretary in the mid-1880s; longer term, he worked closely with his brothers on behalf of national and international Jewish causes.[18] Meanwhile, in the era of Édouard Drumont, Boulangism, and the Panama scandal, Reinach became a symbol for many ethnic nationalists of the Jews' alleged access to the halls of French political power.[19] He faced repeated and vicious antisemitic attacks that became particularly venomous and unceasing during the Dreyfus Affair.[20]

The affair became the defining episode of Reinach's adult life. Reinach was one of the first public figures to come to Alfred Dreyfus's defense, and remained thereafter a leading Dreyfusard. He published numerous pamphlets, collaborated closely with Dreyfus's family members and other leading advocates such as Bernard Lazare, and worked furiously behind the scenes. His family and the

Dreyfuses became personally very close; his only son, Adolphe, even married Marguerite Dreyfus, the daughter of Alfred's brother and close confidant, Mathieu. From 1901 to 1911, Reinach published a magisterial seven-volume history of the affair that long remained the definitive work on the subject.[21]

In the context of the affair, World War I would become a moment of triumph and vindication for Reinach and many of his fellow French Jews. The war offered an opportunity for Jews to reaffirm their commitment to French patriotism and their full inclusion within the nation. Such affirmation occurred through service in the military, the very institution that had so besmirched its reputation and revealed the widespread antisemitism in its ranks during the affair. In spite of the affair, Reinach, a captain in the army reserves, had never ceased to believe in the military; in 1913 he helped to spearhead the Three-Year Law that extended the length of mandatory military service.[22] Amid the wartime unity of France's "Union sacrée" (Sacred Union), discussions abounded concerning the multiple confessional groups serving in the French forces.[23] Both Jewish and non-Jewish press coverage of the Union sacrée gave substantial attention to the fact that Jewish soldiers were fighting alongside Catholics and Protestants for France. In October 1916 eminent right-wing intellectual Maurice Barrès published a series of articles on the Union sacrée in his regular column in the popular L'Écho de Paris.[24] Barrès, an avowed Catholic, had been a leading anti-Dreyfusard. As a deputy in parliament and celebrated writer, he advocated an ethnic, exclusivist French nationalism frequently tinged with antisemitism. Yet in his discussion of France's "diverse spiritual families," he described "traditionalists," Protestants, socialists, and Jews as the four elements making up the national greatness of France. Barrès's shift in attitude toward Jews had particular significance for Reinach: the latter had been the victim of vicious personal attacks by the former during the affair. Barrès and Reinach, old enemies, now undertook similar wartime pursuits as columnists writing almost daily in support of the French military effort; on at least one occasion, the two even toured the trenches together.[25]

Such newfound recognition for Jews as patriots played a critical part in Reinach's ability to advocate for citizenship for France's Muslim soldiers. French Jews' recognized participation in the Great War and Reinach's own involvement in wartime national unity enabled him to speak from a more credible position than otherwise would have been possible. In addition, the war became a deeply personal trial for Reinach: His only son, Adolphe, went missing at the front in August 1914 and would never return; his son-in-law Pierre would die in action the following year.[26] Therefore, Reinach, like so many of his compatriots, appreciated in the most tangible manner the great sacrifice entailed in wartime service to France.

As Reinach set about advocating for greater Muslim rights, other legacies of the Dreyfus Affair found themselves reawakened as well. Soon after his column appeared in *Le Figaro*, part of it was reprinted in *El Akhbar*, an Algeria-based "indigénophile" newspaper, and one of the only periodicals during the war that sought to speak for Muslim interests. The editor, Victor Barrucand, saluted Reinach for his courage. As a young journalist during the affair, Barrucand had become an ardent Dreyfusard, reporting on Dreyfus's retrial in Rennes for the city's only Dreyfusard newspaper, representing the League of the Rights of Man (Ligue des droits de l'homme, or LDH) locally, and taking part in the journal *La Revue Blanche*, where a number of Jewish Dreyfusards got their start.[27] At the end of June, Reinach responded to Barrucand's enthusiastic reprint with a brief letter praising the newspaper's longtime advocacy for Muslim rights. He exclaimed: "The flag of liberty and of justice, we cannot deploy it here and roll it up elsewhere. [Rather] always and everywhere, we must be firm about the principles of modern France."[28] Reinach and his fellow Dreyfusards had made the motto "Truth and Justice" the byword of their movement. Here, in advocating for another oppressed minority, Reinach tapped into the activist networks and language of the Dreyfusards, which for many had become a permanent part of their political identity and sense of purpose.[29]

Reinach's approving reference to the longstanding reform advocacy of Barrucand's newspaper revealed that he was no casual observer or latecomer on questions of colonialism—as did, in his longer original piece, the detailed level of observation about German Muslim-targeted propaganda and goings-on in French colonial Morocco. Indeed, from early in his career, his unshakable belief in the greatness of France and its capacity to act as a force for the spread of civilization made him a staunch supporter of French Empire.

Reinach consistently linked his support for France's colonies to his internationalism. According to his outlook, when France pursued its true foreign policy interest, it also, by definition, promoted a more just world order.[30] As a member of parliament, he repeatedly promoted the creation of a colonial army and proposed the establishment of a minister of colonies.[31] He strongly endorsed colonial undertakings like the 1881 seizure of Tunis and establishment of Tunisia as a protectorate, writing that a site of "Muslim fanaticism" now would become "a tranquil land, a vast field open to Western civilization."[32] Reinach later co-authored a *Manuel Franco-Arabe* for Algerian Muslim schoolchildren, where in the section on French history, he extolled the virtues of France and its laws and the beneficence of its presence in Algeria.[33] Reinach constantly contrasted France as a benevolent imperial force for civilization, law, and reason, with Germany in particular, as well as the Russian (until World War I) and the Ottoman Empires, treated as epitomizing barbarity, brutal repression, and racial ideology.[34]

Reinach's imperialism was never simply about French might overseas but linked to aspirations of a wider system of international governance. Much of his perspective on foreign affairs appears to have been shaped by an extended trip to the Ottoman Empire in the late 1870s, which resulted in a two-volume work on the "Eastern question." Here Reinach spoke of the need for France and England to work together to promote stability and justice; he discussed various possible confederations, from a Danubian one for central Europe to a Latin one in the Mediterranean. The great underlying principles that would inform these arrangements were constants of his thought: "freedom," "reason" and "law."[35]

Indeed, for Reinach, law remained central to both his understanding of how to advance international institutions and his positivist view of the arc of history.[36] It is little coincidence that in his article on Islam in the Great War, he spoke of reform and legal "status," that is, in the language of rights. Years earlier he had insisted, "Three great ideas dominate history: that of force, that of utility, that of law. In the latter part of the nineteenth century, Germany and in turn, Russia, subsumed law under superior force."[37] With World War I, Reinach believed that the opportunity was emerging to reverse that trend.

Reinach's outlook on imperial and international politics took form in the context of major shifts in international law and relations, what historian Eric Weitz has described as the move from the Vienna system of the nineteenth century to the "Paris system" that would emerge from the peace settlement following World War I.[38] The fundamental changes of this period entailed new conceptions of the connection between national or ethnic groups and sovereignty—including notions of self-determination, minority rights, and the forced displacement of populations—and the development of the "civilizing mission" as a formal program. According to a worldview that developed in the late nineteenth century, certain regimes were uncivilized and needed the tutelage of Europe before they could ever be prepared to enter the "family of nations." The civilized/uncivilized divide was signaled in significant part by one's internationally respected sovereignty or lack thereof. Among European powers, in order to be civilized, a state or empire had to offer basic protections of liberty and equality for its citizens.[39] In this period, France developed its own specific brand of the emerging internationalism, linked to the wider political philosophy of "solidarism" elaborated by Léon Bourgeois. This school of thought saw the spread of the values of the French Revolution as the principal way to promote not only French interests but civilization.[40]

During World War I Reinach drew upon these wider political and intellectual currents but reframed them in ways that reflected his personal views of the historical moment and the status of various groups, including Jews.[41] When Reinach wrote about the war as a contest of liberation not only for the peoples of

Europe, or about the need for France to apply its principles of justice every-where, he suggested that the ideals of civilization could and should already be applied to a wider set of populations. His specific ideas embraced two different facets of such a vision. First, calling for dramatic reform for the status of Muslims in the French colonies implied that through their military service, these sub-jects had proven their capacity for French citizenship, that is, their level of civili-zation, and that France itself, in this war of liberation, needed to show its own level of civilization by extending democratic protections to a wider portion of its people. At the same time, Reinach also appeared to support self-determination for the Arabs long under Ottoman rule. In a passage following his call for colo-nial reform, the author touted the recognition France had already offered for the newly formed Kingdom of Hejaz under the leadership of Husayn bin Ali. Rein-ach framed the uprising in the Hejaz as an effort to restore the area, housing the holy sites of Mecca and Medina, to its rightful character as an Arab, religiously Muslim region, removed from the yoke of Turkish despotism. Muslim civiliza-tion, which had given so much to Europe in the Middle Ages, had since ossified under dogmatic interpretations and oppressive rule. Now, however, Europe could repay its debt by "emancipating Islam from the Turk" and restoring it to its former intellectual and worldly glory. He appeared to view the civilization of France's Muslim subjects internally, and Muslims of the Middle East interna-tionally as of a piece.[42]

While Reinach did not mention the Jewish case here, the history of indige-nous Jews of Algeria, already emancipated by France at this time for almost half a century, offered an implicit example of the French capacity for ongoing civili-zation of new populations in faraway lands. Indeed, Reinach's embrace of inter-nationalist ideas, particularly French solidarism, contained a distinctively Jewish component. By the 1860s, "solidarity" was the term used by the AIU to encapsu-late its specifically Jewish form of French internationalism, which included robust efforts to defend Jewish rights abroad, framed as part of the broader civilizing mission.[43] Indeed, the AIU, where Reinach had briefly played a leadership role, scored its great victory for Jewish rights internationally with article 44 of the Berlin Treaty of 1878. This momentary triumph was only possible in the context of the emerging civilized/uncivilized divide in international law and its manifes-tation in questions of sovereignty and recognition. After years of campaigning, at the Berlin Congress, AIU leaders in France and abroad finally convinced the great powers to condition Romania's acceptance in the family of nations in part on full religious freedom for all of its citizens. While this clause was never en-forced and abuses against Romania's Jews worsened over time, the inclusion of protection for Jewish rights in the Berlin Treaty, as Eric Weitz contends, was nonetheless significant. Article 44 made Jewish rights a formal matter of international concern; furthermore, it signaled how, dispersed over vast territories and frequently facing discrimination, Jews were almost unique in their position in the crosshairs of great power politics and the emerging international system.[44]

By World War I antisemitism was on the rise in eastern Europe and beyond, and the Zionist, Bundist, and autonomist movements had gathered steam. The cause of emancipation was losing its centrality in Jewish politics. Yet Reinach's vision for securing the Jewish future appeared little changed. If the war became a heady moment of advocating Jewish nationalism or minority rights for many others, for him it offered new promise for Jewish integration everywhere, based once more on the great principles and model of French civilization. In September 1916 Reinach composed a letter to the Paris correspondent of a Russian Jewish newspaper that found its way into multiple French Jewish newspapers.[45] The letter reiterated Reinach's opposition to Zionism, dismissing the idea as a fantasy with no chance of realization and insisting that Jews were a religious group, not a nation. Given the principles underpinning the author's own internationalism, this distinction was crucial, for it avoided altogether the question of Jewish self-determination or special status as a national or racial minority.

In the same article Reinach went on to articulate his personal vision—one that strongly echoed the intertwined Franco-Jewish solidarity of the nineteenth century—for how the war could transform Jews' position. He spoke of the need for "absolute religious equality" as "one of the noblest conquests of the Revolution" of 1789 and how Jews were now assimilated as citizens like any others in countries such as France and England. Just as Muslims' military service moved him to support reforming their status, he highlighted Jews' patriotism, which he called second to none, expressing the hope that soon "the equality of all citizens, without distinction of religion before the law, will be established in Russia, in Poland, in Rumania, in all the countries where it has not yet been recognized." Reinach insisted that this "great war for liberty of peoples" should "be crowned by liberty and by equality of all citizens of the same country." He further reminded readers that "the blood of Jews has flowed on all the battlefields of Poland and Galicia," and that Jews were fighting every bit as heroically as the Christians and Muslims of the Russian Empire. Reinach reasoned that in the aftermath of what the French repeatedly termed "a war to save civilization," what had worked for Jews in France should liberate all people everywhere. In this vein, between the war's end and his death in 1921, Reinach would look toward a new world order, supporting the creation of the League of Nations and the international system that he hoped it could forge.[46]

In his discussions of both Muslim and Jewish rights, Reinach spoke as much as anything as a historian who had long believed in France as a republic of ever increasing justice and, following the tradition of Jules Michelet, saw the historian's work as helping to advance the country along its destined path. In the course of the Dreyfus Affair, Reinach had become a masterful historical polemicist. Now he situated World War I on a grand narrative plane, as a turning point in the history of colonial empires and their subjects, Islamic history, and Jewish history. Reinach's histories had frequently valorized suffering; now those soldiers, Jewish and Muslim, who had shed their blood for the great powers became martyrs to the cause of human liberty.[47]

In spite of the distinctive aspects of Reinach's thought, he was hardly alone among French Jews in his support of greater rights for Muslims in Algeria. In November 1917 the LDH, of which Reinach had been a founding member during the Dreyfus Affair, offered a precise proposal: the LDH recommended that all Algerian Muslims who fought for France in World War I and applied for French citizenship should be granted their request, without the pre-condition of having to forfeit their personal status as Muslims.[48] Liberal, largely middle-class Jews remained a sizable contingent of the league's membership and leadership, constituting 10–12 percent of those on its central committee between 1898 and 1940.[49] At the LDH meeting where the reform position gained unanimous approval, Edmond Zadoc-Kahn, son of Rabbi Zadoc Kahn, famous as chief rabbi of France during the Dreyfus Affair, even exclaimed, "I believe that I can affirm that the French *israélites* will come with great satisfaction to confer civic rights to the Algerian *indigènes* who fight so valiantly for France." France's traditionalist Jewish newspaper *L'Univers israélite* urged the league to go further. Arguing that all Muslim soldiers should automatically gain citizenship with or without an application, the newspaper editorial asked, "Isn't it the equitable complement to the Crémieux Decree? We think so and do not hesitate to say it."[50] The words of Zadoc-Kahn and *L'Univers* not only showed a broader Jewish interest in colonial reform for Algerian Muslims; they also highlighted more explicitly than Reinach the distinctively Jewish dimensions of this advocacy. Both the struggles of the Dreyfus Affair and for Jewish citizenship in Algeria became linked with efforts to improve Muslim rights in Algeria. Likewise, Crémieux and Reinach became connected anew.

Reinach's own advocacy for Muslim rights in Algeria evinced a complex set of commitments to the memory of Dreyfus and more broadly to the Republic and its civilizing mission. He saw a certain idea of France as crucial for the freedom of not only the French people broadly but Jews specifically, and for the emancipation of not only the peoples of Europe but those far beyond. Reinach's writings revealed a palpable sense that with the Great War, he was living a hinge point in French, Jewish, and international history.

Ultimately, however, despite the many promises and intimations of greater equality for Algerian Muslim soldiers, the war resulted in only a rather limited set of reforms: the Jonnart Law of February 1919 created a new group of about 400,000 "seminaturalized" adult Muslim men in Algeria. They could vote, but only for Muslim candidates, in local contests, and only in their own, specifically Muslim electoral college. The law actually erected higher barriers to full naturalization (while maintaining the basic requirement of the renunciation of one's "personal status" as a Muslim).[51] It would be another generation before the hopes of more significant reform were rekindled.

Léon Blum: The Popular Front and Reform in Algeria

Unlike Reinach, who would only offer up his thoughts on colonial reform late in life and as a commentator sidelined from actual policymaking, Léon Blum did so at the peak of his career from the height of power: as France's first Jewish prime minister.[52] As state Jews go, Blum and Reinach could hardly have been more different. While, like Reinach, Blum came from a family of Alsatian origin, Blum grew up in the working-class setting of "the Pletzl," the central Jewish quarter in Paris where thousands of Jewish immigrants from eastern Europe came to settle in the late nineteenth and twentieth centuries.[53] In contrast to the physically imposing Reinach, Blum was a slight, effete man always photographed in spectacles (though he would display his own physical courage, including in a number of duels).[54] As a young man, Blum was passionately drawn not to the rough and tumble of politics but to the world of literature and the arts; fascinated by Stendhal, he became an art and literary critic and a poet, and developed a relationship with Marcel Proust.[55] Blum's family was religiously traditional: his mother kept a kosher home and lit Shabbat candles; Léon and his brothers all held Bar Mitzvahs.[56] By temperament and ideology, whereas Reinach was largely a pragmatic conservative, Blum became a socialist idealist.

Blum was trained in both literature and law and was admitted in 1896 to the powerful Conseil d'État. There he would remain for twenty-four years and would rise through the ranks, becoming a commissioner in 1910. By the time of his departure in 1919, he had made a number of notable decisions that favored the general interest or the local collectivity against the free enterprise of big business, or that defended the rights of the individual citizen against "abuses of power"; Blum earned fame for his capability as a jurist.[57] Even more so than Reinach, though he eventually moved to other pursuits, Blum remained steeped in the power of the law and the approaches of the legal profession.

It was as a lawyer that Blum became involved in the Dreyfus Affair, an event by which he was as much shaped in his own way as Reinach. Once his mentor, Lucien Herr, brought him to the cause in 1897, Blum found himself stunned by the evident injustice committed against Dreyfus. During the trial of the famous

French writer Émile Zola, Blum interpreted the law for the defense and even helped to write briefs. Like many young activists, he would be permanently reshaped by the drama of the affair, seeing it ever after as a model for activist "engagement."[58]

Just as importantly, it was through the affair that Blum came to know French socialist leader Jean Jaurès, who would exercise a decisive influence upon him. Blum found himself spellbound by Jaurès's emphasis on principled republican moderation and social justice, and on the vital role of the nation within international socialism. For Jaurès, socialism was democratic, humanistic, and protective of the individual; he rejected violence and embraced compromise within France's democratic system. Beginning in 1898 he took up Dreyfus's cause out of a conviction that the state was an instrument of not only class domination but also law and order. He believed deeply in the Third Republic as the embodiment of the values of the Revolution of 1789; in his vision this revolution would be completed when France became a socialist republic.

Overtaken by the lucidity and reason of Jaurès's arguments, Blum embraced the man's philosophy wholeheartedly. Like his teacher, Blum saw socialism and a belief in French civilization, in particular the tradition of the French Revolution, as inseparable.[59] Devastated by Jaurès's assassination on the eve of World War I, Blum became chief of staff to the socialist minister Marcel Sembat in the wartime "Union sacrée" coalition government. After the war, in 1919, he was elected to parliament representing Paris. The following year, when the Socialist Party undertook a fierce debate about whether to join the Bolshevik movement, Blum led the minority in rejecting this course and remaining part of the Second International. From that moment until his death thirty years later, he became the party's undisputed leader, conscience, and spokesman.[60]

For Blum, his devotion to socialism could not be disentangled from his Jewishness. While he abandoned traditional observance as a young adult, Blum never lost a sense of social justice and Jewish solidarity that could be traced to his upbringing. He repeatedly connected socialism's emphases on justice, redemption, and an equal share for all to the centrality of these in his understanding of Jewish tradition.[61] Indeed, much more often than Reinach, Blum was explicit about the Jewish component of his republican and socialist politics. On the floor of the Chamber of Deputies in 1923, he declared himself at once fully French and proudly Jewish and said: "I have never noticed, between these two aspects of my consciousness, the least contradiction, the least tension."[62] Blum's three marriages were all to Jewish women, and much of his inner social and political circle was made up of Jews. In the mid-1930s, he harshly criticized those who had a harder time being comfortable with a multifaceted identity, attacking wealthy and bourgeois Jews "who [were] afraid of the struggle engaged on behalf of

examples, he took the occasion of Bastille Day in 1920 to write in his newspaper *Le Populaire*:

> A certain number of Tunisians . . . recall the bloody sacrifice of the Tunisian people during the war. . . . And they demand to the old fatherland of the Declaration of the Rights of Man, a written Constitution, the guarantee of rights and public liberties, the full participation of the people, without distinction of race or religion, in the government of the territory, "in the measure compatible with its international obligations," that is to say with French sovereignty. . . . What can we reply to that? Why should the diplomatic fiction of the "Protectorate" maintain under pure tyranny men who can, [like others], demand the right of peoples [to self-determination] and who have shown themselves worthy of freedom?[72]

Here Blum pointed not only to the tensions between French universalism and colonial rule but also to those of the Paris system, between the language of rights and the framework of empire. According to the vision hashed out at Versailles, the great imperial powers—with holdings that were by definition ethnically diverse—formed the basis, in part through an expansion of the civilizing mission into the Mandate system, for a new international order. Yet, within that order, distinct ethnicity conferred newly articulated rights of sovereignty or protection. Such a system was wrought with contradictions that for the colonized had to lead either to full assimilation or independence. Blum demanded that since France possessed colonies, it had to rule them with fidelity to its universal principles. Ultimately, meanwhile, colonialism was indeed only justifiable to Blum, explains one of his collaborators, "insofar as it would prepare peoples to govern themselves."[73] In the late 1920s and early 1930s, Blum harshly critiqued the practices of French colonial rule, even expressing support for the possibility of self-rule in Algeria.[74]

When the Popular Front came to power in 1936, however, Blum took a more cautious approach. His early months in office were spent on another set of politically charged issues—negotiating an end to a wave of strikes across France, through which he delivered landmark socialist reforms like the forty-hour work week and mandated paid vacations. Moreover, his ongoing pacifism meant that above all else he sought to avoid violence in the colonies, either in the form of colonial conquest or repression, or anticolonial resistance.[75] It bears recalling as well that Blum had written countless legal decisions while at the Conseil d'État that reflected his conviction that law possessed the power to create a more just order. In a related vein, like his teacher Jaurès, Blum believed that by accelerating the pace of change, reform could even be revolutionary.[76]

Nonetheless, Blum sought to reshape France's relationship with millions of colonial subjects in North Africa and the Levant. He believed that in order to facilitate reform, he needed to empower liberal policymakers who were far more expert than himself in the specifics of the region. Therefore, he appointed Marius Moutet, a longstanding voice for reform in the empire and his colleague at the League of the Rights of Man (where Blum had been a member since the early 1920s), as minister of the colonies. He placed other liberals, Pierre Viénot and Charles-André Julien, in charge of the mandates in the Levant and the High Mediterranean Committee, respectively. Finally, he tasked former governor-general of Algeria Maurice Viollette—popular among Muslim notables for his liberal reformism but detested by European settlers on the same grounds—with reforming the status of Muslim indigènes in Algeria.[77]

In autumn 1936 the administration formally announced the so-called Blum-Viollette Plan. The bill proposed citizenship for roughly twenty-one thousand Algerian Muslims, based on the attainment of a certain degree of military rank or higher education, without their having to surrender their status as Muslims. This group was supposed to constitute a vanguard for native Muslim citizenship, leading to wider enfranchisement over a period of years. The measure also contained several other reforms to improve the social, economic, and cultural situation of Algerian Muslims. Many Muslims in Algeria and the metropole had greeted the election of the Popular Front with enormous optimism; Blum was seen for a time as a heroic figure. Even as the Blum-Viollette Plan was more modest in its proposals than many had hoped, still it had far-reaching implications and galvanized not only Muslim integrationists but also Islamic religious reformers and communists, who united to support the Popular Front in a "Muslim Congress."[78] Thus, a leading French Jew lent his name to what would quickly become a highly controversial reform proposal meant to liberalize the status of Algerian Muslims. In so doing, Blum was taking the position of the Jew of empire to its full implications.

Indeed, Blum's aspirations for colonial reform in the Maghreb and the Mashriq—which also included a never-ratified independence treaty with Syria and Lebanon and outreach to opposition leaders in Morocco and Tunisia—were linked not only to his socialism and pacifism but also to his Jewishness. When a delegation from the Muslim Congress came to meet with Léon Blum and Jules Moch, secretary-general of the prime minister's cabinet and a fellow Jew, they received the group warmly and Blum exclaimed: "As a French Jew, I am very happy to receive a French Muslim delegation."[79] At a moment of mounting antisemitism, when Blum explicitly attempted to revive the Dreyfusards' energy for justice and the Republic, such a statement sounded like an offering of solidarity from one historically persecuted group to another. With the Arab revolt raging in Palestine, Blum's words also appeared to express his hope that France might become a site of Jewish–Muslim entente amid tumult elsewhere.[80] Blum's Jewishness played out in this context less as a way of asserting ethnoreligious particularity and more in connection to his belief in social justice. When the grand rabbi of Algiers came to warn him about how the Blum-Viollette proposal might create dangers for the Jewish community, Blum responded that his only objectives in Algeria were to establish justice and to move its inhabitants toward equality.[81]

As in Reinach's time, during this period, a number of other Jews on both sides of the Mediterranean supported liberal reforms for Muslims. In Algeria, in March 1936, several young Algerian Jewish leaders published an article in which they specifically faulted the Crémieux Decree for not applying to Muslims, asking rhetorically: "If one wants to attach the [Muslim] population . . . to the Motherland forever, is there any better way than to make them French?"[82] In the metropole in spring 1938, in a front-page interview with *L'Univers israélite*, the young Alsatian Jewish deputy Jean-Pierre Bloch compared the Blum-Viollette bill to the emancipations of French and Algerian Jewry. Reminding readers of a Muslim delegation that had defended the Crémieux Decree, Bloch argued that France's Jews had an opportunity to support a just measure and to show solidarity with Muslims.[83]

Blum raised the connection between his own Jewishness and his advocacy for the colonized in November 1938 at a meeting of the LICA where he made a plea on behalf of accepting further Jewish refugees to France. Blum declared:

> "I will speak to you about the Jewish question, about the tragic Jewish question, and nevertheless I am Jewish . . . For many years now, I do not believe anyone has ever been able to reproach me for hesitating [to speak out] on behalf of the *indigènes* of the colonies of Asia or Africa when they were oppressed by brutal administrators or greedy bosses. Why would I not speak out this evening on behalf of the Jews, just as I have spoken out so many times on behalf of the Vietnamese or the Negroes of the Congo?"[84]

These words suggested a dual motive for advocating on behalf of the colonized: a sense of kinship between ethnic minorities with a history of oppression and a strategy to continue defending Jewish rights without being accused of particularism.

By the time that Blum made this speech, the Blum-Viollette proposal had long been a dead letter. It faced tremendous, indeed, violent settler opposition from the start. Once it reached parliament, Algeria's conference of mayors voted almost unanimously to reject the bill. Many of the Radicals who controlled the French Senate objected to it because they saw the provision that permitted Muslims to keep their personal status as antirepublican.[85] Blum's cabinet was also preoccupied with a host of more immediate economic, social, and political problems that made it difficult to focus intently on the colonial sphere.[86] One member of Blum's policy team later explained that due to his sense of juridical scruples, even in the face of these challenges, the prime minister refused to consider imposing the law as an executive decree.[87] Thus, Blum's reverence for the law became something of a double-edged sword. With the bill stalled at the outset and a spate of other pressing issues, supporters set it aside in the expectation that Blum's government would turn to it later.[88] Instead, Blum resigned abruptly in June 1937, and despite repeated attempts by certain reform advocates to revive the bill, it never even came to a vote.

Yet the Popular Front turned out not to be Blum's last opportunity to speak out on the question of the rights of the colonized, including in Algeria specifically. As part of his wider push for independence within the newly renamed French Union in 1947, he supported Interior Minister Édouard Depreux's proposal for a new status of self-rule for Algeria. He described the bill as an effort "to divide between two peoples (Muslims and Europeans) the free government of the land of Algeria," and to reject at last the "chimera of assimilation." Attacking the repeated intransigence of the settlers in the face of any reform proposals, including the one of a decade earlier that bore his name, Blum dubbed this bill—which in the end did not gain the support of the French parliament—as the "last chance" for France to maintain its "moral and political" influence over the territory.[89]

Ironically, although Blum advocated full autonomy and sounded increasingly pessimistic about the long-term prospects of colonial governance, he seemed unwilling to apply the principles of integration and equality to Algeria. In December 1949, a few weeks before his death, Blum expressed dismay at French opposition to the creation of a United Nations commission to investigate conditions in "non-autonomous territories." Here he wrote of colonial exploitation as "disavowed by modern law and morals," and insisted that colonized territories could not be controlled "against the consent of the governed." He further noted that these principles were consistent with the Charter of the United Nations and "implied" in the Universal Declaration of Human Rights. Even as he saw French decolonization on the horizon, he continued to call for a combination of equal individual rights and collective self-determination in the empire.[90]

René Cassin: Human Rights and the Rights of the Colonized

The tension alluded to by Léon Blum at the end of his life, between the empire and the new international norms that followed World War II, was all the more acute in the thought of our third figure of focus, René Cassin. On the one hand, he was a leading member of "Free France," Charles de Gaulle's antifascist resistance movement that became a shadow government formulating plans for the postwar order. On the other hand, in this very context, Cassin played a key role in charting the future of the empire. This occurred during the final major opportunity for reform in Algeria, which began during the late stages of World War II.

To these questions, Cassin brought his own liberal Jewish outlook shaped by a broad range of experiences. Unlike Reinach or Blum, Cassin never was elected to public office but rather rose to prominence through the civil service.[91] He grew up in Bayonne in a Sabbath-observant home, the son of a "free-thinking" merchant father and a religiously traditional mother. He went on to study law and history at the University of Aix-en-Provence. While these specialties may have foreshadowed a life in public service, Cassin's civic devotion grew most directly out of his experience fighting in World War I: while at the front he suffered a serious wound to his abdomen, and he was awarded both the Croix de guerre and the Médaille militaire. Following the war, Cassin became the chief animator and honorary president of one of France's largest interwar veterans' associations, the Union fédérale des mutilés (UF), where he worked as an indefatigable advocate for the basic rights, care, and pensions of France's wounded warriors and their families as well as war widows and orphans. Beginning in 1919 he also held key administrative posts in both the National Office of the Disabled and Discharged of the War and the National Office of Orphans; such a combination of positions enabled him to coordinate many of the efforts on behalf of France's war victims.

At the same time, looking far beyond France itself, in an early indication of the direction his internationalism would take, Cassin was among a handful of civic leaders in France and around the world who sought to translate the horrors of the war into a movement for humanitarianism.[92] Connecting to the most idealistic impulses and rhetoric around the founding of the League of Nations, the humanitarianism of the post–World War I moment aspired to a different kind of internationalism than that embraced by Joseph Reinach in the previous generation—one driven more by nonstate actors, more transnational in orientation, and more concerned specifically with the rights of the most vulnerable. The movement recognized rights for groups including workers, stateless persons, victims of famine and epidemic, children, and victims of war. Cassin and others repeatedly insisted that all of the war's veterans and their families had earned "rights not charity." With the help of the International Labour Organization, he endeavored to build an international veterans movement that would be equally open to wounded warriors from all states, including those of Germany and the other Central Powers. The resulting organization, the Conférence internationale des associations de mutilés et anciens combattants, undertook two major initiatives: to make individual countries legally recognize the rights of their veterans and to build a transnational pacifist veterans movement to fight for the outlawing of war itself.[93]

Cassin's insistence that there be no hierarchy among the war's victims likely helped encourage the UF to take an interest in veterans and their families of the empire, particularly French North Africa. This included the Muslim *indigènes* of Algeria. In 1923, as a number of veterans' associations already established in North Africa became officially incorporated within the UF, Cassin himself wrote in the association's newspaper to urge the participation of "our brothers of North Africa, in whatever milieu, race or region to which they belong." He exclaimed: " 'One for all,' they should say. From the metropole, we warmly call out to them 'All for one.' "[94] In the early to mid-1920s representatives of the UF in Algeria advocated repeatedly for Muslim veterans and their families to receive "allocations, pensions, and recognition proportionate to their cost of living." UF delegations passed resolutions opposing discriminatory measures against Muslim families, fought efforts to differentiate between European and *indigène* war victims, and sought to better inform *indigène* veterans and their families of their rights.[95] At this formative stage of his legal career and internationalist activism, Cassin addressed the question of the relationship between the sacrifice of colonial soldiers and their rights. While the UF did not tackle the issue of citizenship, it did seek to apply to the colonies a kind of universalism regarding the rights of war victims. For Cassin there appeared to be a set of basic humanitarian needs worthy of attention and legal protection, regardless of one's status within the national community. While defending these rights in North Africa did highlight the shared humanity of colonial subjects, it did little to question their unequal status under French law. For Cassin the uncertain relationship between empire, military service, and rights would resurface more directly a generation later.

Meanwhile, even more so than for Reinach or even Blum, a devotion to the law, both in France and internationally, became a defining part of Cassin's work. Holding a doctorate in law, Cassin became a professor of law in Paris.[96] In 1924 he was appointed a French delegate to the League of Nations. From 1924 to 1938, in that capacity, he spent a month of each year in Geneva, gaining significant exposure to international politics and diplomacy. He began to work on the establishment of an international set of safeguards for peace and democracy. Such efforts would ultimately culminate in his role as a leading author of the 1948 Universal Declaration of Human Rights, which earned him the Nobel Peace Prize twenty years later. By the mid-1930s, following a trajectory similar to Blum's but with greater decisiveness, Cassin had moved away from his earlier hopes for international peace; he, too, grasped already the dangers of Benito Mussolini and Hitler and urged rearmament and greater confrontation. This made him a relatively lonely voice both at the league and in what remained of the substantially pacifist French veterans' movement.[97]

Cassin's knowledge of the brutality of Nazi anti-Jewish measures, and the antisemitism he felt in certain attacks on his "bellicosity," brought him a new kind of Jewish consciousness. In terms of Jewish practice, Cassin took more after his "free-thinking" father than his observant mother, signaling his distance from tradition when in 1917 he married his longtime Catholic companion. At the same time, as for Reinach and Blum, Cassin saw his Jewishness as inseparable from his belief in French civilization. Through most of his childhood and adolescence, the Dreyfus Affair had given him a formative sense of the meaning of antisemitism and the struggle for justice.[98]

Thus it was at once as a devotee of the Republic, an international opponent of fascism, and a Jew that Cassin decided to join Charles de Gaulle and Free France in London following the French defeat in 1940.[99] Cassin played a critical role in de Gaulle's movement: he brought credibility as a well-known, longtime civil servant with a substantial following in the veterans' movement and invaluable experience as an administrator, jurist, and international representative. Beginning in mid-1941 Cassin's position became less political and more policy oriented. He took on numerous administrative assignments, leading and serving on various French and Inter-Allied commissions and committees charged with writing what in many cases become important proposals for the postwar world. Cassin focused his efforts on two areas of planning in particular: outlining the basis for a new international order and discussing how to reestablish republican legality and reform the French state. Here his interests in human rights, the defense of the Jews, and the colonial future would converge in revealing ways.

As the war increasingly became framed as a struggle between democracy and fascism, Cassin was one of a number of statesmen and intellectuals across Europe and far beyond who began to think of how to ensure that a more humane world would emerge once the fighting stopped.[100] Beginning in June 1941, he participated in a series of Inter-Allied conferences at St. James Palace in London, where leaders from governments-in-exile met to plan for a postwar democratic Europe. They also agreed upon principles for how to punish the mounting Nazi atrocities against many of their compatriots, establishing in 1943 the Inter-Allied Commission for the Punishment of War Crimes, where Cassin played a key role as France's representative.[101]

During the same period Cassin reflected upon the future of the French Empire, continuing to see this as a vehicle for—rather than an inhibitor of—both republicanism and internationalism. Already in October 1940, he wrote a note to de Gaulle in which he argued that Free France needed to differentiate itself from Vichy France in part by a politics of "Liberté." Strikingly, Cassin defined this as "liberty for the French people and those of the Empire to organize the way of life of Greater France and to determine [it] within [their own territory]."[102] This suggested already a vision of substantial reforms in the colonies, toward fuller participation among the native populations in both the governing of the empire and of their individual territories, consistent with the oft-cited interwar dream of "Greater France." Not long after, Cassin became first an appointee and soon the permanent secretary of the Free French Council of Defense of the Empire. The only civilian on the council, he served alongside colonial and military officials who had played important roles in the far corners of the empire.[103] Likewise, he would spend much of the war in motion between France and various parts of the francophone world; as the leaders, populations, and resources of the empire proved integral to both the resistance effort and his own wartime itinerary, Cassin acquired a kind of imperial education.

By 1944 Cassin and the commission he led that was devoted to the increasingly discussed question of "human rights" produced a lengthy, soon-to-be-published document entitled "Human Rights and Free France," proposing rights and duties within and beyond France.[104] This document reveals how the war had crystallized Cassin's views on human rights, Jewish politics, and empire as well as their interrelationship. On the document's opening page, Cassin framed the war in no uncertain terms, unwittingly previewing the tensions that would plague "Greater France" in the postwar: "On one side, it is the murderous rage of those who negate national independence and trample the feet of human dignity; on the other, we die for liberty or we prepare the supreme uprising toward all liberations, that of nations like that of human beings." Moreover, he specifically condemned "the universal threat contained in the Japanese, Italian, and German aggressions, perpetrated against yellows, blacks, and whites, against 'Spanish reds,' against Basque or Austrian Catholics, against Jews." Just as he listed Jewish victims as one group among many, when he mentioned Jewish resisters like Victor Basch, the recently slain leader of the League of the Rights of Man, he treated them as martyrs for basic freedom and not as Jews per se.[105]

And yet nonetheless, in the same essay he praised General de Gaulle for reaching out to the World Jewish Congress to express his solidarity with Jews and opposition to all racism. In particular, he dwelled on the general's October 1941 message to Rabbi Stephen Wise, World Jewish Congress president, where he had taken the occasion of the 150th anniversary of the emancipation of French Jews during the Revolution to insist that such equality "still remain[s] in force and cannot be abrogated by the men of Vichy."[106] The Revolution was the historical moment that had long emblematized for French Jewry the inextricably linked destinies of France and the Jews; thus Cassin fused here the causes of Jewish justice and French universalism as part of a single struggle.

The empire's enduring strength was critical to that struggle as well. When Cassin spoke of the crime of "negat[ing] national independence," he specifically meant the invasions and occupations by the Nazis, not the possession of colonial territory overseas. Further on, he mentioned with pride Félix Éboué—with whom he had served on de Gaulle's Council of Defense of the Empire—describing the man as "a great governor of black color, originally from our Antilles," who rallied Chad to the side of Free France, Cassin explained, because he was "impregnated with the human genius of France." Cassin declared confidently that such actions "gave the most dazzling proof of love and grateful fidelity to the mother country that our great ancestors could have imagined, when they sent out to the world the motto: Liberty, Equality, Fraternity, and undertook the struggle for the emancipation of the oppressed races."[107] In the list of thirty-four rights attached to this opening essay, Cassin and his colleagues focused almost entirely on the rights of individuals rather than those of nations.

The words that Cassin used to explain and extol Éboué's work communicated in no uncertain terms his firm belief—renewed through the empire's role in the fight against fascism—in the inherent greatness and justice of France's civilizing mission. This document's framework also reflected the wider evolving terms of international discourse and motivations around human rights. By 1944 the Allied powers and key actors in the formation of postwar international law and institutions were backing away from the Atlantic Charter's broad articulation of a right to self-determination three years earlier; in a marked shift for one of the Paris system's key tenets, they were moving the focus on rights from groups to individuals. The latter could justify rather than throw into question the work of colonialism. Like other architects of the United Nations and the Universal Declaration of Human Rights, Cassin assumed that the empires of the great powers would not only continue but also serve to shape a new imperial internationalism. The eventual 1948 declaration even referred unproblematically in its preamble to "the peoples of territories under jurisdiction" of the UN "Member States" and very carefully included neither a right to self-determination nor protections for minorities.[108] Thus, as with Reinach and Blum before him, Cassin offered a vision for France and the world in which passionate attachment to the legacies of the Revolution and the Rights of Man coexisted with silences about the fundamental inequalities inherent in colonialism.

Each of the aforementioned elements in Cassin's outlook—his republican Jewishness and experience of Jewish vulnerability, his belief in the law, his respect for war veterans, and his understanding of the complementary relationship between the empire's civilizing mission and international human rights—would prove key to the positions he took vis-à-vis colonial reform. Unlike in the moments where Reinach and Blum engaged the issue, Cassin did so at a time of unprecedented Jewish powerlessness in modern French history. His work also occurred largely behind the scenes, rather than in the press or the public eye. Thus he was a relatively solitary Jewish voice for colonial reform in this critical moment.

The unique circumstances of World War II also produced other contrasts between Cassin and his predecessors. Whereas for both Reinach and Blum, the connection between Jewish and Muslim rights in Algeria had been largely implicit and abstract, in Cassin's case, the link became tangible and immediate. On March 14, 1943, Gen. Henri Giraud, French commander in Algeria after the Allied liberation, repealed all Vichy legislation in Algeria but then immediately revoked the Crémieux Decree once more. In his capacity as national commissioner of Justice and Public Instruction, Cassin responded immediately with an internal, private communication (so as not to give any ammunition to the supporters of Giraud, de Gaulle's rival for the leadership of Free France). He declared the act "a veritable racial law, which, under the pretext of re-establishing equality with the Muslim *indigènes*, misunderstands completely the great differences of will [between Jews and Muslims]."[109] Subsequently, Cassin's continued efforts, most influential as head of the Juridical Committee of the unified resistance, helped lead to the reinstating of French citizenship for Algerian Jews in October 1943.

Not coincidentally, during the same period Cassin assumed his most significant activism to date for Jewish causes. By 1943 the war years had witnessed the passing, migration, or deportation of most leaders of the AIU; Free France had taken charge of the Alliance schools in the Levant. In these circumstances, de Gaulle suggested Cassin become the new head of the AIU and seek to revive it. Cassin accepted the charge and would remain president of the organization until his death thirty-three years later. This new responsibility thrust him immediately into the role of an international Jewish personality charged with caring for the welfare of Jewish communities across the francophone world and beyond.[110]

Despite his new duties to the Jewish community specifically, Cassin did not treat Jews' French citizenship in Algeria as a separate question from that of Muslims. In May 1943 Cassin had issued a press release for the National Committee of the Resistance in which he discussed the movement's efforts to restore republican law. He not only condemned Giraud's action against Jews but also made a plea for a reform in Muslim status: "Equality between the indigènes of Algeria, Muslims or Jews, cannot be conceived by a reduction [in status]. Only a major *improvement* in the juridical condition of all the indigènes of Algeria and a revision in a liberal sense of the attribution of political rights can enable us to realize [such equality]."[111] Subsequently, he took part in the reform effort leading to the March 1944 law that opened all civil and military positions to Muslims, gave

Muslim men the right to vote in an enlarged Muslim electoral college, ended the detested "native's code," and gave sixty thousand Muslims full citizenship with the maintenance of their "personal status."[112]

Whereas only ten years earlier these reforms would have been almost unthinkably progressive, by this time positions like Cassin's were rapidly becoming quite moderate by comparison with the wave of anticolonial movements beginning to sweep the world. This became all the more clear in the spring and summer of 1944, when Cassin played a leading role in the commission charged with studying measures for assuring to French colonies their just place in the new French order. Perceiving the ramifications that the war could have for France and for colonialism broadly, Cassin spoke in commission meetings about the need for France to decentralize the empire and give greater rights and autonomy to its imperial territories. He proposed changes both in terms of real power and in the terminology used to describe the imperial relationship. Outlining a system based on what they termed "the federal principle," Cassin and his colleagues stated in their summary report of July 1944 that the expression "France and its colonies," which "implies a legal relationship of possession," needed to "disappear from the vocabulary," to be replaced by a "new legal formula, founded on the spirit of association, or if you will, of fraternity."[113]

Indeed, in the commission's discussions, Cassin expressed views that linked imperial reform to what amounted to an inching forward of French universalism in the empire as well as to respect for veterans and a pragmatic view of international politics. In the meeting of May 16, he spoke of how the subjects of the empire would seek to collect on the metropole's wartime debt to them: "People will have the pride to say, 'hey, well we have strongly contributed to saving France.'"[114] In late June he made the connection more explicit: "The fundamental idea that we must make the French people understand, it is that . . . they owe the Empire significant material assistance. . . . This entire war is the demonstration of how the Empire is able to render services to France. . . . The populations who have so faithfully defended France have the right to [make themselves heard regarding] their security, their well-being and also [their] common interests."[115]

At the same time, Cassin expressed concern for France's international standing, seeming to foresee the potential dangers of both internationalist critiques of the French Empire and anticolonial liberation movements; moreover, he sought to make the French relevant to ongoing discussions about the postwar world order, where currently they did not have a say.[116] Thus, he and his fellow commission members declared in their summary report that France had to face the consequences of having lost some prestige in the war; and of the widespread "mixing" among metropolitan and colonial troops that had occurred. "The project of [a] federation," they argued, would show that France had kept its longstanding promises, and would actualize ethnic intermingling while maintaining France's face as a Western power. In short, it was "in itself, great enough to justify France [and its colonial sovereignty] before the world."[117]

Within a federalist system, Cassin and his colleagues recommended dividing France's overseas possessions into categories and ranked Algeria among the group considered most vibrant, developed, and worthy of significant autonomy. At a meeting in early July, Cassin expressed his specific concerns on this score: "I have told you of the dangers that I see in giving too autonomous of a status to Algeria, due to the [lack of] present maturity of the Muslims of Algeria, and the abuses that the currently ruling French majority could make of an autonomy forced [too quickly upon the population]."[118] Thus, Cassin revealed his basic assumptions about the need to "civilize" further the native populations of the colonies, coupled with fears of the anti-egalitarian abuses of the European settler classes. His particular interest in the fate of Algeria's Jews, increasingly caught in the crosshairs of native oppositional politics and settler antisemitism, may have informed his cautious position here. Regardless, the work of this commission, of which Cassin was an important part, contributed to a substantial legal breakthrough in French colonial rule. The imperial structure that emerged in May 1946 echoed the thrust of the commission's recommendations: the empire was renamed the "French Union"; all subjects were declared equal citizens; and various categories of overseas territories were created, each with representation in local, national, and French Union legislative bodies.[119]

Cassin saw the cause of reform in Algeria in part through the lens of human rights, but for him the colonial context was vital to the implementation of these rights. Colonial reform was the next step forward for France. The country was in his view both the author of human rights and a pillar in an emerging international system that he hoped would defend such rights better than its predecessors. But whereas other natives' rights could become equal at some point in the far-off future, Jewish rights needed to be linked to the broader progress of human rights in real time. While he hoped to improve the lot of the former, he wanted to protect fiercely the latter. For all of his vision as a liberal humanist, when it came to the empire, Cassin fell behind the times. He could not abandon a belief in colonialism as the unproblematic extension of France's liberating gifts to the world. Even after living through Vichy and the Holocaust, he never questioned the notion of a clear fault line between civilized and uncivilized territories, nations, and populations. He saw no apparent relationship between murderous antisemitism and the violation of the rights of the colonized.[120]

With Cassin's longer-term colonial engagement in mind, can we better understand the positions he took during the Franco-Algerian War? Contrary to what some have suggested recently, these positions were not the sudden result of a singular confrontation with colonialism on Cassin's part that revealed a blind spot in his universalism.[121] Rather, they reflected the longstanding considerations, priorities, and contradictions outlined above. During the war Cassin headed the Conseil d'État but did not use this position of judicial authority to raise questions about widespread French human rights abuses in Algeria. Instead, he in fact authored an infamous memo approving "detention centers" for Muslims, even as French law explicitly forbade the use of internment camps. His cooperation with France's counterinsurgency forces was consistent with his longstanding view of the French Empire's essential place in the international system and his lack of support for a universal right to self-determination. He did not perceive the Algerian nationalist forces as representative of a legitimate movement for national independence but rather agreed with most policymakers that this was merely an uprising in a part of France that needed to be defeated; its demands were worthy of liberalizing reforms but not separation. Furthermore, Cassin's actions implied that the Algerian nationalists were unlawful guerillas and therefore unworthy of the respect due to enemy soldiers in a conventional war. After de Gaulle "returned" to power in 1958, Cassin favored the Gaullist approach of finding a practical solution to the conflict in consultation with Algeria's Muslims. Yet once the inevitability of separation became apparent, he joined de Gaulle and others in seeking to exclude Muslims—finally granted equal citizenship in 1958—from postcolonial France. Such a position worked in tandem with Cassin's simultaneous effort to fold Algeria's Jews into the legal category of "Europeans," newly opposed to that of "Muslims." In a manner surprisingly reminiscent of Blum's terms of support for self-rule ten years earlier, he pointedly explained that there were only two groups—"French" and "Muslims"—in Algeria.[122] It appears that for Cassin, the stubborn war for independence in which so many of the latter participated, had proven that they still lacked the "maturity" to join European civilization.

Conclusion

This essay calls on us to take seriously a little-considered but important facet of Jewish politics in modern France through the lives of three major figures in both French and French Jewish history. It is hardly a coincidence that at each of the three major moments of possible reform in Algerian Muslims' legal status in the first half of the twentieth century, a French Jew with considerable political stature strongly supported liberalizing reform within the colonial system. For Joseph Reinach, Léon Blum, René Cassin, and many others, being a French Jew who celebrated the joint heritage of the French Revolution and the Hebrew Bible meant believing in the civilizing mission, particularly in Algeria, where they perceived that French civilization had done so much to elevate Jews. It meant as well believing in the power of law to protect and even transform. Yet it did not mean adhering to a single tradition of imperial or Jewish politics. Reinach's faith in the civilizing mission and assimilation never wavered; Blum saw self-rule as the only justifiable endgame of colonialism and supported Jewish self-determination in Palestine; Cassin hoped that Greater France would be the seat of growing rights, for its citizens and the world, until he concluded it no longer could.

Frederick Cooper and Ann Stoler have argued that "the colonies of France, England, and the Netherlands . . . did more than reflect the bounded universality of metropolitan political culture: they constituted an imaginary and physical space in which the inclusions and exclusions built into the notions of citizenship, sovereignty, and participation were worked out."[123] This was surely the case for Jews as well, with a long history in metropolitan spaces where they had struggled not only to gain legal equality but also to integrate into larger society while maintaining their Jewishness. Like a number of French Jews in public life, Reinach, Blum, and Cassin faced persistent antisemitism and questions about their Frenchness. The opportunity to advocate reform for Algerian Muslims highlighted Jews' own French civic and colonialist bona fides, enabled them to speak about difference and inclusion without focusing on the position of Jews per se, and underscored in their own minds a commitment to liberal, humanistic values that they saw as distinctly French and Jewish.

Empire also became a way to consider the Jewish question on an international plain. Working out the meaning of abstract concepts of citizenship and civilization, and Europe itself and the place of Jews therein, only made sense within the framework of evolving internationalist norms and laws. Reinach, Blum, and Cassin came of age across more than half a century that moved from the Vienna system of the nineteenth century, focused on rulers and nations, to the post–World War I Paris system centered on populations; included an interwar emphasis on humanitarianism, pacifism, and briefly antifascism; and then moved toward an articulation of human rights, however halting, during and following World War II. And in this respect, their story was very much a transimperial one, shared by a number of other Jews of empire in other European capitals, from the British statesman and philanthropist Moses Montefiore, to the Habsburg pacifist and pan-European visionary Alfred Fried. From the midnineteenth century into the 1960s, these and many other Jews of empire linked activism on behalf of internationalist causes with the twinned matters of imperial interests and concern for Jewish welfare. To paraphrase Frederick Cooper, these Jews had come to "think like imperialists."[124] For these figures, liberal imperial internationalism seemed a way to bring together the best interests of their nation-state, humanity, and the Jews.[125]

Katz

Notes

This essay benefited immensely from the comments of a number of participants at the workshop "Jewish History After the Imperial Turn," held in November 2012 at Brown University, and from several careful readers who have generously offered feedback on subsequent drafts. I am particularly grateful to Jessica Hammerman, Nathan Kurz, Moria Paz, Gil Rubin, and my co-editors, Lisa Moses Leff and Maud S. Mandel, for their invaluable comments. Any errors or shortcomings remain mine alone.

1. Archives du consistoire centrale israélite de France (Paris), Fonds Jacques Lazarus, Rapport aux assises du Judaïsme Algérien, Algiers, March 13–14, 1958.

2. Ibid.

3. Pierre Birnbaum, *The Jews of the Republic: A Political History of State Jews in France from Gambetta to Vichy*, trans. Janet Lloyd (Stanford, CA: Stanford University Press, 1996).

4. See esp. Jay Berkovitz, *The Shaping of Jewish Identity in Nineteenth-Century France* (Detroit: Wayne State University Press, 1989); Jay Berkovitz, *Rites and Passages: The Beginnings of Modern Jewish Culture in France, 1650–1860* (Philadelphia: University of Pennsylvania Press, 2004); Lisa Moses Leff, *Sacred Bonds of Solidarity: The Rise of Jewish Internationalism in Nineteenth-Century France* (Stanford, CA: Stanford University Press, 2006); and Ronald Schechter, *Obstinate Hebrews: Representations of Jews in France, 1715–1815* (Berkeley: University of California Press, 2003). Ample material produced by French Jews in this vein is discussed at length in Michael R. Marrus, *The Politics of Assimilation: A Study of the French Jewish Community at the Time of the Dreyfus Affair* (Oxford: Oxford University Press, 1971), despite the author arguing in an almost opposite direction.

5. See esp. Jonathan Frankel, *The Damascus Affair: "Ritual Murder," Politics, and the Jews in 1840* (Cambridge: Cambridge University Press, 1997); Leff, *Sacred Bonds of Solidarity*; Aron Rodrigue, *French Jews, Turkish Jews: The Alliance Israélite Universelle and the Politics of Jewish Schooling in Turkey 1860–1925* (Bloomington: Indiana University Press, 1990); Joshua Schreier, *Arabs of the Jewish Faith: The Civilizing Mission in Colonial Algeria* (New Brunswick, NJ: Rutgers University Press, 2010); and Colette Zytnicki, *Les Juifs du Maghreb: Naissance d'une historiographie coloniale* (Paris: Presses de l'Université Paris-Sorbonne, 2011). Regarding Jews and the law in the international realm, the scholarship is in its infancy but growing. Martti Koskenniemi analyzes the Jewish component of several prominent Jewish theorists of international law in *The Gentle Civilizer of Nations: The Rise and Fall of International Law, 1870–1960* (Cambridge: Cambridge University Press, 2001). An approach that gives attention not only to the field of legal scholarship but also to Jewish history is taken in James Loeffler and Moria Paz, *The Law of Strangers: Critical Perspectives on Jewish Lawyering and International Legal Thought* (Cambridge: Cambridge University Press, forthcoming).

6. On Jewish internationalism as a broader global force, see Abigail Green, "Old Networks, New Connections: The Emergence of the Jewish International," in *Religious Internationals in the Modern World: Globalization and Faith Communities Since 1750*, ed. Abigail Green and Vincent Viaene, 53–81 (Basingstroke: Palgrave Macmillan, 2012).

7. Here I deliberately allude to the salience of Sarah Abrevaya Stein's critique of Abigail Green, *Moses Montefiore: Jewish Liberator, Imperial Hero* (Cambridge, MA: Harvard University Press, 2010). See Stein's review in *Journal of Modern History* 83, no. 3 (2011): 624–26.

8. On Crémieux, see S. Posener, *Adolphe Crémieux: A Biography*, trans. Eugene Golob (Philadelphia: Jewish Publication Society, 1940); and, more recently, Daniel Amson, *Adolphe Crémieux: L'oublié de la gloire* (Paris: Seuil, 1988). Regarding Crémieux's relationship to empire, see Leff, *Sacred Bonds of Solidarity*.

9. Founded in 1860, the AIU was a Paris-based Jewish international humanitarian agency that, largely through a network of hundreds of schools educating thousands of mostly Jewish students in North Africa, the Levant, and the Balkans, sought to spread French language, culture, and values to much of world Jewry.

10. On Crémieux's relationship with Gambetta, see Birnbaum, *Jews of the Republic*, chap. 13.

11. The Ka'aba is the central mosque in Mecca where Muslims are required by traditional Islamic law to make a pilgrimage, or hajj, at some point in their lifetime.

12. Quoted in "Nouveaux Motifs," *El Akhbar*, June 16, 1917.

13. Soldiers from North Africa included roughly 173,000 from Algeria, 50,000 from Tunisia, and 37,000 from Morocco. Pascal le Pautremat, *La politique musulmane de la France au XXe siècle: De l'Hexagone aux terres d'Islam. Espoirs, réussites, échecs* (Paris: Maisonneuve & Larose, 2003), 146, 173. The overall figure for colonial soldiers comes from Tyler Stovall, "The Color Line behind the Lines: Racial Violence in France during the Great War," *American Historical Review* 103 (1998): 737–69, at 766.

14. See Richard S. Fogarty, *Race and War in France: Colonial Subjects in the French Army, 1914–1918* (Baltimore: Johns Hopkins University Press, 2008).

15. Wendy Ellen Perry, "Remembering Dreyfus: The Ligue des Droits de l'Homme and the Making of the Modern French Human Rights Movement" (PhD diss., University of North Carolina–Chapel Hill, 1998), 822.

16. On this period in Reinach's career, see Steve Marquardt, "Joseph Reinach (1856–1921): A Political Biography" (PhD diss., University of Minnesota, 1978), 22–68; Birnbaum, *Jews of the Republic*, 7–19; and Perry, "Remembering Dreyfus," 821–27. At least one later antisemitic account would hypothesize that late in life, Crémieux might have advised Gambetta to take Reinach under his wing. See Robert Launay, *Figures juives* (Paris: Nouvelle librairie nationale, 1921), 187.

17. Details on Reinach's family and personal life are from Michael Burns, *Dreyfus: A Family Affair, 1789–1945* (New York: HarperCollins, 1991); and Ruth Harris, *Dreyfus: Politics, Emotion, and the Scandal of the Century* (New York: Picador, 2010).

18. Harris, *Dreyfus*, 187–88; and Perry, "Remembering Dreyfus," 826. Harris speaks here of a "fierce clannishness" among the Reinach brothers.

19. More specifically, Reinach was also the son-in-law and nephew of one of the key figures implicated in the Panama scandal, Baron Jacques de Reinach.

20. In 1894, Alfred Dreyfus, a French artillery officer who was Jewish, was falsely accused of treason by the French army. Soon he was convicted and sent to confinement on Devil's Island. As evidence mounted that Dreyfus was innocent but the army refused to reconsider its decision, the controversy became a bitter debate that consumed French politics and society until Dreyfus's second trial and pardon in 1899, and in some manner until its final resolution with his full rehabilitation in 1906. Antisemitism played a central role in the affair, but Dreyfus's ultimate exoneration restored many Jews' faith in the Republic. On antisemitism against Reinach, see Birnbaum, *Jews of the Republic*, 7–19; for specifically during the affair, see Burns, *Dreyfus*, esp. 188–89, 277–78, 406–8.

21. Joseph Reinach, *Histoire de l'affaire Dreyfus* (Paris: Revue blanche/Fasquelle, 1901–11).

22. Perry, "Remembering Dreyfus," 824.

23. The term initially was used to describe the national unity government formed at the war's outbreak but soon took on wider symbolism. Monarchist and socialist defections from the government in August 1917 ended the official Union sacrée.

24. Maurice Barrès, *Les Diverses familles spirituelles de la France* (Paris, 1917). *L'Écho de Paris* had the quite sizable circulation of 430,000. Philippe E. Landau, *Les Juifs de France et la Grande Guerre: Un patriotism républicain, 1914–1941* (Paris: Editions CNRS, 2000), 55.

25. Reinach and Barrès's visit to the front is mentioned in "Hier et aujourd'hui," *Archives israélites*, May 25, 1916. On their relationship more broadly, see Antoine Compagnon, "Joseph Reinach et l'éloquence française," *Comptes-rendus des séances de l'Académie des inscriptions et belles-lettres* 151, no. 2 (2007): 1117–40.

26. For the latter, Perry, "Remembering Dreyfus," 821.

27. On Barrucand, see Céline Keller, "Victor Barrucand, dilettante de la pensée," *Histoires littéraires* 8 (2001): 38–47; Christine Drouot and Olivier Vergniot, "Victor Barrucand, un indésirable à Alger,"

Revue de l'Occident musulman et de la Méditerranée 37 (1984): 31–36; on *La Revue Blanche* and the affair, see Venita Datta, "Jewish Identity at *La Revue blanche*," *Historical Reflections / Réflexions historiques* 21 (1995): 113–29.

28. "Une Lettre de M. Joseph Reinach," *El Akhbar*, 1 July 1917.

29. Regarding such language during the affair and how it shaped a tremendous sense of self-righteousness for the movement's activists, often for the rest of their lives, see Harris, *Dreyfus*.

30. This precise formulation appears in Marquardt, "Joseph Reinach," 147–48.

31. Birnbaum, *Jews of the Republic*, 12.

32. Quoted in Marquardt, "Joseph Reinach," 153.

33. Joseph Reinach and Charles Richet, *Manuel Franco-Arabe*, with Arabic text by M. C. Houdas and preface by Victory Dupuy (Paris: Delgrave, 1888); on Reinach's contribution to the book, Marquardt, "Joseph Reinach," 178–82.

34. See Anne Couderc, "Joseph Reinach et *la Question d'Orient* (1876–1879)," in *Les Frères Reinach*, Colloque réuni les 22 et 23 juin 2007 à l'Académie des Inscriptions et Belles-Lettres, ed. Sophie Basch, Michel Espagne and Jean Leclant, 285–307 (Paris: AIBL, 2008), esp. 291–93; and Marquardt, "Joseph Reinach," esp. 212–27.

35. Cited in Couderc, "Joseph Reinach," 298–99; and Marquardt, "Joseph Reinach," 195–98.

36. It bears noting in this context that Reinach appears to have remained an active member of the association of former secretaries of the Paris bar for many years, suggesting an ongoing identification with lawyers. See Launay, *Figures juives*, 187n1.

37. Couderc, "Joseph Reinach," 293.

38. Eric Weitz, "From the Vienna to the Paris System: International Politics and the Entangled Histories of Human Rights, Forced Deportations, and Civilizing Missions," *American Historical Review* 113, no. 5 (December 2008): 1313–43.

39. This account draws substantially from Weitz, "From the Vienna to the Paris System"; and Antony Anghie, *Imperialism, Sovereignty, and the Development of International Law* (Cambridge: Cambridge University Press, 2005).

40. See Koskenniemi, *Gentle Civilizer of Nations*, chap. 4.

41. The precise way that these developments impacted Reinach's foreign policy views requires deeper investigation. Nonetheless, given not only the outlook Reinach articulated on international affairs but also his belief in approaching foreign policy with an academic, even "scientific" grounding, his emphasis on law and his legal training, his longtime engagement in international developments as a policymaker, and the circles in which he moved, it seems reasonable to assume Reinach was familiar with key currents in contemporary French and European thought regarding international law and the international system. On the first point and for some tentative suggestions of specific influence, see Couderc, "Joseph Reinach."

42. For more on these earlier views, see Couderc, "Joseph Reinach"; and Marquardt, "Joseph Reinach," 153, 178–83.

43. As Leff, *Sacred Bonds of Solidarity* shows, the term both had ancient significance for Jewish unity and peoplehood, and was adapted by French republicans since the mid-nineteenth century to signify and in a sense sacralize their liberal, socialist, and anticlerical ideals. See *Sacred Bonds*, chap. 5.

44. See Weitz, "From the Vienna to the Paris System," 1321. He sees Jews and Armenians as similarly positioned in this context. Leff, *Sacred Bonds*, chap. 5, analyzes in detail the process leading to the inclusion of the protections for Romanian Jews in the Berlin Treaty, and their failure of enforcement, and seems less persuaded of any long-term significance. For a comparative discussion of the cases of Romania and Morocco that highlights further the importance of the civilized/uncivilized divide, see Abigail Green, "The Limits of Intervention: Coercive Diplomacy and the Jewish Question in the Nineteenth Century," *International History Review* 36, no. 3 (2014): 1–20.

45. "Une Lettre de M. Joseph Reinach: Contre le Sionisme-Pour l'Émancipation," *L'Univers israélite*, September 8, 1916.

46. See Marquardt, "Joseph Reinach," 523–27; and Couderc, "Joseph Reinach," 306–7.

47. In my discussion of Reinach's view and deployment of history, I am influenced by Harris, *Dreyfus*, esp. 161–68.

48. Gilbert Meynier, *L'Algérie révelée, la guerre de 1914–1918 et le premier quart du siècle* (Librairie Droz, Genève, 1981), 553. The latter portion of this proposal would have marked a key departure from standing policy. Whereas the 1865 *sénatus-consulte*, which remained in effect, required any Algerian Muslim to forfeit his Muslim "personal status" as a precondition for eligibility for French citizenship, the LDH was suggesting that no such compromise should be necessary for any Algerian Muslim veteran of World War I who desired to become a citizen.

49. To give statistical perspective, during this period Jews were well under 1 percent of all those living in France. On the league's history, see Perry, "Remembering Dreyfus"; and William Irvine, *Between Justice and Politics: The Ligue des Droits de l'Homme, 1898–1945* (Stanford, CA: Stanford University Press, 2007). For figures, see Irvine, *Between Justice*, 1, 9.

50. Quote from both Zadoc-Kahn and *L'Univers israélite*'s response is in P.R., "Un acte de justice," *L'Univers israélite*, December 14, 1917. During the affair, Edmond had himself played a role by showing his father that the document attributed to Dreyfus was a forgery. Jean-Philippe Chaumont and Monique Lévy, eds., *Dictionnaire biographique des rabbins et autres ministres du culte israélite, France et Algérie, du Grand Sanhédrin (1807) à la loi de Séparation (1905)* (Paris: Berg International Éditeurs, 2007), 397.

51. Le Pautremat, *La politique musulmane*, 239–41.

52. Concerning Blum's Jewishness, see Pierre Birnbaum, *Léon Blum: Prime Minister, Socialist, Zionist* (New Haven, CT: Yale University Press, 2015).

53. See Nancy Green, *The Pletzl of Paris: Jewish Immigrant Workers in the Belle Époque* (New York: Holmes and Meier, 1986).

54. On the latter point, see, for instance, "Un duel," *Le Petit Parisien*, October 15, 1912.

55. See Léon Blum, *Léon Blum avant Léon Blum: Les Années littéraires, 1892–1914, Cahiers Léon Blum*, Nos. 23–25 (1988).

56. For detail on Blum's Jewish upbringing, see Birnbaum, *Léon Blum*, chap. 1.

57. Jean Lacouture, *Léon Blum* (Paris: Seuil, 1977), 115–20.

58. For the last point, see Harris, *Dreyfus*, 115. On Blum in the affair, see Léon Blum, *Souvenirs sur l'Affaire* (Paris: Gallimard, 1935).

59. See Birnbaum, *Léon Blum*, chap. 4.

60. Here I have drawn on Tony Judt, "The Prophet Spurned: Léon Blum and the Price of Compromise," in *The Burden of Responsibility: Blum, Camus, Aron, and the French Twentieth Century*, 29–85 (Chicago: University of Chicago Press, 1998), at 32–33; 38–39.

61. See Birnbaum, *Léon Blum*, chap. 4.

62. Judt, "Prophet Spurned," 42.

63. Ibid., 43.

64. "La chambre des députés," *L'Univers israélite*, June 12, 1936.

65. Quoted in Judt, "Prophet Spurned," 77.

66. See Birnbaum, *Léon Blum*, chap. 9; and Paula Hyman, *From Dreyfus to Vichy: The Remaking of French Jewry, 1906–1939* (New York: Columbia University Press, 1979), 170, 175.

67. Quoted in Birnbaum, *Jews of the Republic*, 91–92.

68. I draw this characterization from Judt, "Prophet Spurned," 65. On his activism in the Second International, see Lacouture, *Léon Blum*, 249.

69. For the general history of the Popular Front, see Julian Jackson, *The Popular Front in France: Defending Democracy, 1934–1938* (Cambridge: Cambridge University Press, 1988).

70. See his statement to this effect from 1933, quoted in Lacouture, *Léon Blum*, 253.

71. See ibid., 327, 337.

72. "Le droit des peuples," *Le Populaire*, July 14, 1920, reprinted with incorrect publication and date in *Léon Blum, militant des droits de l'homme, Cahiers Léon Blum*, No. 31 (May 1998): 102–3, at 102.

73. Charles-André Julien, "Léon Blum et les pays d'outre-mer," in *Léon Blum, chef de gouvernement*, ed. Pierre Renouvin and René Rémond, 377–90 (Paris: Presses de la fondation nationale des sciences politiques, 1981), 377.

74. For broader critiques, see Lacouture, *Léon Blum*, 576; on Algeria, see Benjamin Stora, *Nationalistes algériens et révolutionnaires français au temps du Front Populaire* (Paris: L'Harmattan, 1987), 52.

75. In part I draw this analysis from Stora, *Nationalistes algériens*, 50.

76. See Blum, "Idée d'une biographie de Jaurès," in *L'oeuvre de Léon Blum, 1914–1928* (Paris: Albin Michel, 1965).

77. Julien, "Léon Blum et les pays d'outre-mer," 377–79; regarding Viollette, see "Interventions sur le rapport de M. Charles-André Julien," in *Léon Blum, chef de gouvernement*, 405.

78. See Benjamin Stora, *Histoire de l'Algérie coloniale (1830–1954)* (Paris: Découverte, 1991), chap. 4.

79. Mahmoud Abdoun, *Témoignage d'un militant du mouvement nationaliste* (Algiers: Dahleb, 1990), 21. See also Archives de la préfecture de police (APP) (Paris), BA 2171, report of July 22, 1936.

80. On Blum's effort to resurrect the spirit of the Dreyfusards in the Popular Front, see Harris, *Dreyfus*, 382.

81. Lacouture, *Léon Blum*, 572. It is unclear here what precisely those dangers were, but one imagines that the most significant concern was that such a proposal under Blum's name could provoke a rise in the already significant settler antisemitism. Soon, indeed, antisemitism, colonial racism, and anticommunism converged in a wave of rhetorical and physical violence. See Samuel Kalman, "Le Combat par Tous les Moyens: Colonial Violence and the Extreme Right in 1930s Oran," *French Historical Studies* 34, no. 1 (Winter 2011): 125–53; for the broader context of imperial reform as a motivation for antisemitism against Blum and others, see Pierre Birnbaum, *Anti-Semitism in France: A Political History from Léon Blum to the Present* (Oxford: Blackwell, 1992), chap. 12.

82. Cited in Benjamin Stora, *Les trois exils: Juifs d'Algérie* (Paris: Stock, 2006), 63.

83. Raymond-Raoul Lambert, "Le problème Algérien: Déclarations de M. Pierre-Bloch, député de l'Aisne, vice-président de la commission d'enquête en Algérie," *L'Univers israélite*, March 4, 1938.

84. Léon Blum, "Discours au XIe congrès de la LICA," November 26, 1938, in *Léon Blum, militant des droits de l'homme*, 79.

85. See Charles-Robert Ageron, *"L'Algérie algérienne" de Napoléon III à de Gaulle* (Paris: Sindbad, 1980): 123–64, at 134–35, 138, 161.

86. Julien, "Léon Blum et les pays d'outre-mer," 379.

87. Ibid., 381.

88. "Interventions sur le rapport," 396.

89. "Le Statut de l'Algérie," *Le Populaire*, August 2, 1947, in *Léon Blum, militant des droits de l'homme*, 120–22; and Lacouture, *Léon Blum*, 580.

90. "Le colonialisme devant l'ONU," *Le Populaire*, in *Léon Blum, militant des droits de l'homme*, 135–37.

91. Cassin attempted, with encouragement from some party leaders, to become the candidate of the Parti Radical for Parliament in the district of Albertville-Moutiers in Savoie in 1931, but after being unsuccessful, never considered seeking elective office again. See Antoine Prost and Jay Winter, *René Cassin et les droits de l'homme: Le Projet d'une génération* (Paris: Fayard, 2011), 107–8.

92. See ibid., chap. 1–2; and Bruno Cabanes, *The Great War and the Origins of Humanitarianism, 1918–1924* (Cambridge: Cambridge University Press, 2012).

93. Regarding Cassin's work to organize veterans and its international and humanitarian dimensions, see esp. Cabanes, *The Great War*, chapter 1; I have also drawn on Antoine Prost, "René Cassin and the Victory of French Citizen-Soldiers," in *The Great War and Veterans' Internationalism*, ed. John Paul Newman and Julia Eichenberg, 19–31 (New York: Palgrave Macmillan, 2013).

94. "L'Union fédérale et nos camarades de l'Afrique du Nord," *France Mutilée: Journal officiel de l'union fédérale* (*FM*), June 3, 1923.

95. Quotation from "Les congrès de Constantine," *FM*, March 11, 1923. For examples of various efforts on behalf of North African indigène soldiers, "Derniers Echos du Congrès de Marseille," *FM*, April 15, 1923; "Les congrès de Constantine," *FM*, March 18, 1923; and "La Justice Militaire," *FM*, June–July 1925.

96. On his interwar veterans' advocacy and work in the law and at the League of Nations, see Prost and Winter, *René Cassin*, chap. 2–3.

97. See ibid., 110–11; 128–32.

98. For examples of Cassin's Jewish consciousness emerging in the face of the rise of fascism, see letters cited in ibid., 128, 132. Regarding the formative nature of the Dreyfus Affair, see ibid, 30–33.

99. Ibid, 140–1.

100. For this broader context, see Mark Mazower, "Blueprints for the Golden Age," in *Dark Continent: Europe's Twentieth Century* (New York: Vintage, 1998), 182–211.

101. See Prost and Winter, *René Cassin*, 184–91.

102. Quoted in ibid., 162.

103. See ibid., 164; 167–77.

104. The January 1942 Declaration of the United Nations, signed by twenty-six countries, framed the war as a struggle "to preserve human rights and justice in their own lands" and marked a signal moment in the emergence of this language. Quoted in Mark Mazower, "The Strange Triumph of Human Rights, 1933–1950," *Historical Journal* 47, no. 2 (2004): 379–98, at 385.

105. Archives Nationales (AN) (Paris), 382 AP, 71, "Les Droits de l'Homme et la France Libre," by René Cassin, marked as forthcoming in the May 1944 issue of "Cahiers antiracists." Quotations here are from p. 1.

106. Ibid., 6.

107. Ibid., 6–7.

108. "United Nations Universal Declaration of Human Rights (1948)," in *The Human Rights Reader: Major Political Writings, Speeches, and Documents from the Bible to the Present*, ed. Micheline R. Ishay, 407–12 (New York: Routledge, 1997), 408. On the broader international context, see Mark Mazower, *No Enchanted Palace: The End of Empire and the Ideological Origins of the United Nations* (Princeton, NJ: Princeton University Press, 2012).

109. Quoted in Marc Agi, *René Cassin fantassin des droits de l'homme*, preface by André Chouraqui (Paris: Plon, 1979), 169–70.

110. Regarding the changes at the AIU during the war, see Catherine Nicault, "L'Alliance au lendemain de la seconde guerre mondiale: ruptures et continuités idéologiques," *Archives Juives* 34, no. 1 (2001): 23–53. On Cassin's work at the AIU and as a major representative for and among Jews in the international setting, see Prost and Winter, *René Cassin*, 368–98.

111. Quoted in Agi, *René Cassin*, 169–70. Emphasis added.

112. Benjamin Stora, *Histoire de l'Algérie coloniale (1830–1954)* (1991; reprint, Paris: Découverte, 2004), 83–84; and Annie Rey-Goldzeiguer, *Aux Origines de la guerre d'Algérie, 1940–1945: De Mers-el-kébir aux massacres du Nord-Constantinois* (Paris: Découverte, 2002), 188. For Cassin's involvement, Agi, *René Cassin*, 172, 179.

113. AN, 382 AP, 71, transcript of commission meeting of May 9, 1944; "Rapport de la commission chargée d'étudier le moyen d'installer les colonies dans la nouvelle constitution française," attached to transcript for meeting of July 4, 1944. Quotations from the latter.

114. AN, 382 AP, 71, transcript of commission meeting of May 16, 1944.

115. AN, 382 AP, 71, transcript of commission meeting of June 27, 1944.

116. On these discussions, see Mazower, "Strange Triumph." On Cassin's broader concern to make France relevant at this time, see Prost and Winter, *René Cassin*.

117. AN, 382 AP, 71, "Rapport de la Commission Chargée."

118. AN, 382 AP, 71, transcript of commission meeting of July 4, 1944.

119. For a good overview of these changes and their significance for France's colonial subjects, see Frederick Cooper, *Colonialism in Question: Theory, Knowledge, History* (Berkeley: University of California Press, 2005), 215–18. On this commission in the context of broader debates at this moment over the recalibration of individual and territorial status in the postwar French empire, see Frederick Cooper, *Citizenship between Empire and Nation: Remaking France and French Africa, 1945–1960* (Princeton, NJ: Princeton University Press, 2014), chap. 1, esp. 40–45. The momentary embrace of federalism in the immediate postwar period—long forgotten in teleological narratives of decolonization—has just begun to receive substantial attention from historians. Its historical viability is a matter of debate. See esp. Cooper, *Citizenship between Empire and Nation*; Todd Shepard, *The Invention of Decolonization: The Algerian War and the Remaking of France* (Ithaca, NY: Cornell University Press, 2006); and Gary Wilder, *Freedom Time: Negritude, Decolonization, and the Future of the World* (Durham, NC: Duke University Press, 2015). For a critique, Samuel Moyn, "Fantasies of Federalism," *Dissent*, Winter 2015, at http://www.dissentmagazine.org/article/fantasies-of-federalism.

120. This hardly made Cassin unique among contemporary legal theorists of human rights, but it did suggest a lack of engagement with other contemporary humanist thinkers like Hannah Arendt, Aimé Césaire, Frantz Fanon, and Jean-Paul Sartre.

121. I take issue with this characterization on the part of both Samuel Moyn, "René Cassin, Human Rights, and Internationalism," in *Thinking Jewish Modernity*, ed. Jacques Picard, Jacques Revel, Michael P. Steinberg, and Idith Zertal, chap. 19 (Princeton, NJ: Princeton University Press, 2016); and Fabian Klose, in his review of the English translation of Prost and Winter, *René Cassin*, in *American Historical Review* 119, no. 5 (December 2014): 1786–87.

122. See Prost and Winter, *René Cassin*, 330–4; and Shepard, *Invention of Decolonization*, chap. 6, esp. 171.

123. Frederick Cooper and Ann Laura Stoler, "Between Metropole and Colony," in *Tensions of Empire: Colonial Cultures in a Bourgeois World*, ed. Frederick Cooper and Ann Laura Stoler, 1–55 (Berkeley: University of California Press, 1997), at 3.

124. See Cooper, *Colonialism in Question*, chap. 6. On Montefiore in this context, see Green, *Moses Montefiore*; on Fried, see Katherine Sorrels, "Pan-Europe's Cosmopolitan Outsiders," *Austrian History Yearbook* 46 (April 2015): 296–327, doi:10.1017/S0067237814000204.

125. For an examination of similar convergences specifically in the nineteenth-century British imperial context, see Abigail Green, "The British Empire and the Jews: An Imperialism of Human Rights?" *Past & Present* 191, no. 1 (2011): 175–205.

8

ZIONISM, EMIGRATION, AND EAST EUROPEAN COLONIALISM

Tara Zahra

IN 1897 O. FADEUHECHT from Kolomea in Austrian Galicia wrote a letter to the Zionist newspaper *Die Welt*, in which he sought to publicize the "miserable situation of Russian Jews in London and their bleak future." Tens of thousands of Jews from the Russian Empire were living in East London, he reported, where they worked long hours for pitiful wages, producing cheap clothing for export to the Levant, Egypt, and Central Africa. They were forced to work on the Sabbath and were unable to raise their children "in a Jewish spirit." The export trade was largely "in Christian hands," he lamented, and workers had little hope of profiting from their own labor. Instead, their arrival depressed wages for all textile workers, provoking antisemitism. In Whitechapel, "where all the Russian Jews live in abominable apartments that mock the most primitive notion of hygiene," a local antisemitic newspaper had recently appeared. In the British parliament, meanwhile, a campaign to restrict Jewish immigration from eastern Europe was gaining traction. Fadeuhecht saw a solution to the plight of his co-religionists in Zionism. "Why should the Russian Jews flock to London, where they struggle against a difficult and hopeless future, and not immediately to southern Palestine," he asked. In Palestine, they could raise their own sheep, spin and weave their own wool, and create a new clothing export industry that would profit Jews. They would be able to retain their Jewish faith and culture. It was a solution that "must succeed, because it links material interests with the highest interests of humanity."[1]

Fadeuhecht's letter reminds us that the rise of Zionism coincided not only with the radicalization of eastern European nationalist movements and the European scramble for colonies. It also took shape in concert with one of the greatest waves of mass emigration in modern history, as millions of people, Jews and non-Jews alike, left eastern and central Europe at the turn of the twentieth century. In the Habsburg Empire and its successor states, this exodus provoked profound anxieties about the place of East Europeans in global racial and civilizational hierarchies. Among both Jews and non-Jews, emigration also shaped new efforts to channel migration toward purposeful forms of "colonization" that would serve collective interests.

The colonial aspirations that developed in east-central Europe in the first half of the twentieth century differed in several respects from the colonial practices of the British and French Empires in the same period. Most significantly, they were not (outside of Bosnia) initially oriented toward formal territorial annexation. East European colonial advocates generally acknowledged that they had arrived too late to the starting line in the race for colonies. There were few unclaimed territories in the world where they could claim formal sovereignty. Instead, their goal was to create autonomous "colonies" of settlers within existing empires or states (in places like Brazil, Argentina, Madagascar, and Palestine). Unlike British and French colonial empires, eastern European settlement projects also took shape in the context of a mass emigration that was already under way. Colonial advocates explicitly sought to replace what they viewed as unplanned, chaotic emigration with what the historian Mark Choate has called "emigrant colonialism."[2]

Austro-Hungarian proponents of emigrant colonialism and their successors in interwar eastern Europe specifically hoped to redirect emigration away from North American cities like Chicago and New York, where migrants were allegedly exploited and quickly assimilated (and therefore "lost" to the empire or nation), toward less-developed regions of South America or Africa, where they would become self-sufficient landowners, farmers, or managers. As in formal settler colonies, these "emigrant colonies" were to work for the economic and political benefit of the nation or empire. Rather than assimilating to their surroundings, settlers were to live in enclosed communities and maintain their cultural, linguistic, and emotional ties to their homeland. Like other European imperial projects, emigrant colonies were also justified by the conviction that European settlers would play a "civilizing" role vis-à-vis natives, expanding the prestige of the sending country. Eastern Europeans would not, however, formerly rule over the territories they settled.

These colonial ambitions may seem, at first glance, like an arcane historical footnote. Aside from Austria-Hungary's 1876 occupation and 1908 annexation of Bosnia, the dual monarchy had few colonial conquests of which to boast. To the extent that postcolonial theory has made its way into scholarship on the history of east-central Europe, it has not generally problematized the relationship of eastern Europeans to the world beyond Europe.[3] Some historians of eastern Europe's multinational empires have adopted postcolonial frameworks to understand the relationship between imperial capitals and their imagined peripheries.[4] Other scholars have deployed a postcolonial framework to understand the hierarchical relationships between different national or linguistic groups within the Russian, Austrian, and Ottoman Empires.[5]

More commonly, however, European historiography positions east-central Europeans as objects of imperial fantasies or victims of colonial conquest by their more powerful and militarized neighbors. A view of east-central Europe as "Germany's India or Algeria" has inspired numerous studies in which German fantasies of the "Wild East" are linked to European imperialism, the rise of Nazism, and the Holocaust.[6] In the wake of the twentieth-century saga of violent occupations in eastern Europe, it is not surprising that the colonial aspirations of eastern Europeans themselves have received so little attention. This would largely be a history of failed or stillborn colonial projects, hatched by states whose own sovereignty was repeatedly violated. Such imaginary colonies appear marginal at first glance both to the history of eastern Europe and to the history of colonialism at large.

One form of eastern European "emigrant colonialism" did take root, however, and that was Zionism. It may therefore be useful to analyze Zionism not only in comparison and relation to British or French colonies but also in the context of the homegrown (if ultimately unsuccessful) colonial aspirations that sprung up in east-central Europe itself between 1880 and 1939. This in turn requires situating Zionism in the context of the general eastern European debates about both emigration and colonialism in this period, as emigration and colonial politics were deeply intertwined.

In recent years, historians of both Jewish life and of eastern Europe have worked to integrate Jewish history and eastern European history more fully. This has entailed more attention to the ways in which Zionism emerged in dialogue with other eastern European nationalist movements at the turn of the twentieth century. Consequently, however, there has actually been a tendency to minimize the importance of emigration itself to Zionist movements. Historians of Jewish political and cultural activism in east-central Europe have rather highlighted the extent to which Zionist organizations and movements in the Habsburg lands, interwar Czechoslovakia, and Poland overlapped with and contributed to the broader project of diaspora nationalism. For many Zionists, the goal of Jewish nation-building within eastern Europe was totally compatible with long-term aspirations for a Jewish homeland in Palestine. Most Zionists did not believe that all Jews could or should emigrate from Europe, moreover. They were torn between a desire to rescue Jews in need and achieve a demographic majority in Palestine and concerns that overly rapid settlement would undermine the entire movement. Many were convinced that the success of the Zionist project depended on selectively recruiting the right kind of settlers. They disagreed, however, about the qualities of the ideal pioneers—were they capitalists who could invest in the economy? Or workers and farmers who would cultivate the land and construct roads and railways? Either way, not all Jews, or even all Jewish emigrants, were considered fit to be pioneers.[7]

This meant that Zionists were generally committed to a struggle on two fronts: the long-term dream of creating a new Jewish home in Palestine and a concurrent goal of protecting and establishing Jewish collective rights (framed as "national" rights) in Europe. In practice, moreover, the boundaries between Zionism and other forms of diaspora nationalism were often blurry. In Habsburg Galicia, for example, Joshua Shanes maintains that Zionism emerged in "conversation and cross-fertilization" with other East European nationalisms (not simply in reaction to them).[8] Like these other nationalist movements, Zionists generally focused on the goals of achieving minority rights and cultural autonomy for Jews living in eastern Europe. In Czechoslovakia, Tatjana Lichtenstein argues, Zionism was a vehicle for Jewish integration into Czechoslovak society rather than a ticket out.[9] James Loeffler suggests that few Zionists imagined the mass emigration of Jews from Europe before the Second World War. The departure of some Jews to Palestine was supposed to enable others to stay, with more secure political and cultural rights as a national minority.[10] Kenneth Moss also stresses the extent to which Zionist ideas circulated well beyond the milieu of committed Zionists in interwar Poland. Jews with diverse political commitments were thinking about the "politics of exit" between the wars.[11] Overall, these works point to the fluidity of political loyalties and the overlapping agendas of Jewish nationalist movements as well as the extent to which they were embedded in local eastern European contexts.

This research has greatly enriched our understanding of Zionism, nationalism, and eastern European history more broadly. Situating Zionism in an eastern European context also requires that we take emigration seriously, however. From the 1880s onward, the unprecedented movement of people out of east-central Europe preoccupied officials, political activists, reformers, and ordinary people from all corners of the Habsburg Empire and its successor states, and from every national, linguistic, and religious community. For Jews and non-Jews alike, the question of how to respond to emigration was immediately linked to concerns about the position of eastern Europeans in multinational communities and colonial projects at home and abroad.

In Austria-Hungary, a colonial society was founded in 1894, followed by a naval association in 1907. The leaders of these colonial pressure groups as well as other emigration reformers immediately justified their colonial aspirations in terms of the perceived emigration crisis. Richard Schroft, a leader of the Austro-Hungarian

Colonial Association, explained that Austrian colonial policy should be formulated "in tight relationship to the organization of emigration" such that Austrian emigrants "not only succeed economically, but through the preservation of their language and nationality, are also able to remain in active national and economic contact with their motherland."[12] Instead of laboring in American factories and mines, colonial advocate Friedrich Hey insisted that Austrian peasants should settle "in the regions of Southern Brazil, Argentina and Uruguay with suitable climates," where they would manage small family farms. "These enclosed colonies would remain in lasting contact and economic relationship with their homeland to the benefit of our industry, our shipping firms, our commerce and trade." Hey, a geometrician employed by the Austrian trade ministry, did not envision the conquest of foreign lands but rather a form of "peaceful" empire building. This was admittedly a consolation prize in the European scramble for colonies, but it would have to do. "Since all of the appropriate parcels of African land have long been in secure hands, we have no choice but to content ourselves with the surrogate of peaceful colonization," he reasoned.[13] Polish economist and emigration expert Leopold Caro likewise praised emigration to South America as "an instrument of national expansion, a means of peaceful extension of national frontiers."[14]

Channeling emigration toward "peaceful" colonization was not an original idea. Austrians self-consciously followed the examples set by Germany and Italy, both also latecomers to the scramble for colonies. In the 1890s the Italian and German governments began to see emigration as a potential substitute for colonial conquest, a way of projecting influence and prestige around the world. Through expanding consular networks, the revision of citizenship laws, and the creation of emigrant banks, schools, and other associations, they aimed to maintain the loyalties and protect the welfare of citizens abroad. By 1908 there were 1,403 Italian associations with more than 200,000 members in America, all partially supported by the Italian government. A 1912 law made it easier for emigrants and their children to retain Italian citizenship.[15] In Germany, nationalist and imperialist pressure groups attempted to steer emigrants toward rural colonies in Africa and South America, where they would ostensibly retain their language and culture. They construed so-called Auslandsdeutsche as a diasporic community that would create new markets for German products and strengthen Germany's global influence. Germany's 1913 citizenship law extended citizenship to children born to Germans abroad, consolidating the ideal of a German diasporic community defined by descent.[16]

Early Zionist movements took shape in this general context. There were, however, both similarities and important differences between Zionist goals and those of other eastern European settlement projects. Zionist and other Jewish nationalist movements responded to a variety of specific concerns about the future of the Jewish community within Europe. Anxieties about the disappearance of Jewish culture and calls for its renewal or reinvention animated many so-called cultural Zionists from the late nineteenth century onward. These concerns were intensified by existential fears about the physical and political security of Jews in Europe as new forms of violent, racial antisemitism swept the continent. The Russian pogroms of 1881–82; the Dreyfus Affair, witnessed by Theodor Herzl as a Viennese reporter for the *Neue freie presse*; the growing popularity of Karl Lueger's antisemitic Christian Social party in Vienna; a proliferation of blood libel trials in central and eastern Europe—all suggested to many Jews that their future in Europe was precarious. Many Zionists coupled their concerns about antisemitism with more positive visions of social, psychic, and political regeneration and transformation in Palestine.[17]

Many factors also inspired eastern European settlement projects, of course. But in contrast to Zionist movements, protean eastern European settlement projects were always geared toward expansion for the benefit of some kind of "homeland" in Europe. The nature of that homeland shifted with the collapse of the Austrian Empire and the creation of self-declared nation-states in 1918. Yet emigrant colonialism was always intended to serve the economic and political interests of a metropolitan state or nation in Europe. Zionists, by contrast, hoped to create a new homeland in Palestine. Many saw settlement in Palestine as a "return" to the native land of the Jews and worried about how to cultivate the attachment of Jews around the world to this homeland. The ideology of "return" versus expansion had significant implications for the place of land and labor in Zionist thinking as well as for attitudes toward and relationships with local populations.[18]

Both Zionism and other East European settlement schemes developed at a moment when more people than ever were leaving eastern Europe. Fantasies of colonial settlement became one strategy for managing the fears of social and national upheaval induced by mass emigration. Before the 1880s relatively few citizens of the Habsburg lands made the long, arduous journey across the Atlantic. Many more people crossed the German-Austrian border for seasonal labor, moved between villages to marry or work, or migrated between the countryside and growing cities like Vienna, Budapest, Cracow, and Prague (and back again). In 1880 only 17,267 Austro-Hungarians immigrated to the United States. By 1892 that number had more than quadrupled, to 76,937. This was only the beginning of the emigration boom. In the first decade of the twentieth century, around 2,145,266 subjects of the dual monarchy landed on American shores.[19] The largest number of migrants departed from the impoverished Austrian provinces of Galicia and Bukovina and from southern and eastern Hungary.[20] The Habsburg monarchy was the top supplier of immigrants to the United States in the first decade of the twentieth century, accounting for 27.9 percent of all newcomers. Caro described villages that became ghost towns overnight. "Entire regiments left in 1907 in order to earn money in America. Many houses stood empty, and in many others only old women and small children remained behind. . . . Everyone believed that America was the Promised Land, a true paradise."[21]

Imperial Russia was also hemorrhaging population in the late nineteenth and early twentieth century. The vast majority of the 2,771,900 Russian citizens who emigrated to North and South America between 1880 and 1910 were members of minority groups. Around 2 million Jews left Imperial Russia between 1880 and 1914.[22] In contrast to Imperial Russia, Jews were not heavily overrepresented among the ranks of emigrants from the Habsburg monarchy, however. Out of a total of 275,693 emigrants from Austria-Hungary in 1905, for example, 17,352 emigrants (6 percent) were Jewish, only slightly more than the percentage of Jews in the total population in 1900 (4.7 percent in Austria, 5 percent in Hungary). Jewish emigration thus formed part of the broader wave of emigration that swept the empire at the turn of the twentieth century. Even in Austria-Hungary, however, there were distinctive aspects to Jewish emigration. The return rate from the United States was as high as 39.6 percent for emigrants from the Austrian half of the Habsburg monarchy and 37.9 percent from Hungary in the first decade of the twentieth century, for example. Among Jewish emigrants from the Habsburg Empire, by contrast, only 20 percent returned home in 1912. Rates of return to Russia were even lower, at 7.6 percent in 1912. This is hardly surprising given the intensive and violent persecution of Jews in Russia and the fact that migrants who left the Russian Empire on so-called emigrant passports were actually deprived of their citizenship and banned from ever returning.[23]

Almost as soon as mass emigration became a reality in the Habsburg Empire, people began to panic about it. Military officials bemoaned the growing number of conscripts who failed to appear for military duty. Landowners worried about where they would find workers to harvest their crops (and the need to pay them higher wages). Catholic and Jewish Orthodox leaders warned of secularization, demoralization, and family breakdown abroad. Family members wondered if they would ever see each other again. To many, "American fever" (and its cousins "Brazilian fever" and "Argentinian fever") threatened to destroy individuals, families, and nations.[24]

Anti-emigration policies were partly grounded in mercantile economic theories, which saw population as a measure of political, economic, and military strength. At the turn of the twentieth century, however, concerns about emigration also reflected new worries about the place of eastern European workers in global civilizational and racial hierarchies.[25] These "Second World" anxieties stemmed from the precarious place of eastern Europe between the imagined "West" and the colonial world. As millions of eastern Europeans left home in order to toil in North American factories and mines, in particular, many Austrian reformers began to fear that they would become the "slaves" or "coolies" of the twentieth century. They believed that freedom of movement constituted a dire threat to free labor as well as to the health and welfare of Habsburg subjects.

In the last decade of the monarchy's existence, authorities thus stepped up efforts to curb emigration both directly and indirectly. They regulated and arrested emigration agents (the people who sold migrants steamship tickets, often Jews), introduced new passport and visa requirements, policed train stations and borders, and used administrative backchannels to hinder emigration. New laws in interwar east-central Europe went even further, empowering the state to limit emigration if it threatened the "public interest." These obstacles to emigration, introduced by democratic governments, prefigured the draconian restrictions on mobility that we tend to associate with the Iron Curtain.[26]

Where some reformers saw a crisis, however, others saw an opportunity, or at least a necessary evil. Proponents of emigration as well as more pragmatic reformers believed that it was futile to attempt to curb emigration through repression alone. Policing borders, they reasoned, only increased clandestine emigration, along with the premiums paid to smugglers and agents. They instead proposed to transform anarchic emigration into new forms of colonial settlement that would serve collective interests. Zionists and non-Zionists alike in eastern Europe shared this aspiration around 1900.

Eastern European colonial fantasies reflected a desire to guarantee that Habsburg citizens play the role of colonial masters in "underdeveloped" lands, rather than being reduced to cheap factory labor in crowded American cities. For emerging eastern European nationalist movements, agricultural settlements were also meant to defend emigrants against the threat of assimilation to "dominant" national majorities. In this vision, emigrants would live in hermetically sealed rural communities with their own schools and churches. They would retain their language and culture as well as their precarious status as "white" Europeans. Sigismund Gargas, an economist from the University of Cracow, recalled that Brazil was chosen for Polish settlement because the "relatively lower culture of Brazil in comparison to the Anglo-Saxon culture of North America . . . poses less of a national threat than immigration to the United States."[27]

The idea of creating enclosed national "colonies" through land-acquisition were adopted from the internal colonization efforts of nationalist activists in Habsburg Austria and Prussia, who sought to populate threatened "language frontiers" with nationally reliable settlers. Zionists, of course, deployed the same strategies in Palestine based on their own experiences in central and eastern

Europe (even if some were open to multilingualism among Jews).[28] Zionist leader Alfred Ruppin, for example, was directly inspired by the colonization efforts of the German Settlement Commission in West Prussia (and Polish counter efforts). The commission purchased large estates from Poles and Germans, divided them up, and then recruited German farmers to settle the land. In both Austria and Prussia, these strategies often backfired, however. In Austria, for example, new German settlers frequently ended up befriending and even marrying their Slavic neighbors, to the great despair of nationalist organizers.[29]

Plans for emigrant colonies crystallized in the 1890s, when an outbreak of "Brazilian fever" swept through the Russian Empire and Austrian Galicia. The Brazilian government, seeking white settlers to populate its vast domain, had begun to offer free transportation to migrants from Europe. Beginning in 1890, over 100,000 citizens of Imperial Russia and Austria set out for Brazil, dreaming of rich farmland, warm weather, and relief from poverty. Many of the emigrants were Polish- or Ruthene-speaking peasants, and the exodus generated intense debate among Austrian social reformers and government officials. Conservative newspapers dispatched reporters to Brazil, who described terrifying attacks by natives, locusts, and ants, and reported that the settlers were working in slave-like conditions on the brink of starvation.[30] Both the conservative press and anti-emigration activists tended to depict the emigrants themselves as ignorant, gullible victims of unscrupulous emigration agents. Caro lamented, "The uneducated are most easily induced to emigrate by agents and village pub-owners; these people are the easiest targets and the most docile material. Illiterates will believe almost anything."[31]

Not everyone shared these negative views of emigration, however. Some Polish nationalists even dreamed of building a prosperous "New Poland" in Brazil. An informational guidebook published in 1896 cautioned prospective emigrants against "ill-considered departure from the land of your fathers" and tried to direct migrants away from the coffee and sugar plantations of Sao Paolo and Espírito Santo, where conditions were considered unsuitable for white Europeans. But the authors saw plenty of opportunity in Paraná, where Poles could acquire land and form enclosed colonies. "Without doubt there are not, in the whole territorial expanse of the state of Brazil, more favorable conditions for European immigrants than in the state of Parana. Its healthy and temperate climate, the condition of its soil, and its present state of development give the European immigrants a guarantee of peaceful and profitable conditions for work," the guide advised. "Build then, fellow countrymen, Polish churches and schools, establish societies and libraries, venture into commerce and industry . . . maintain close spiritual and economic ties with Poland—and God will bless your work."[32]

Zionists in Austria-Hungary shared many of the hopes and concerns of their neighbors about emigration. Early Zionists including Theodor Herzl famously considered options ranging from Argentina to Africa before finally settling on Palestine as their goal. Zionists also advertised themselves as settlers in terms of their potential contribution to colonial projects. At the Sixth Zionist Conference in 1903, British Zionist Israel Zangwill speculated, "If Britain could attract all the Jews of the world to her colonies she would just double their white population . . . with all of Judea helping us . . . we could create a colony that would be a source of strength, not only to Israel but to the British Empire . . . a colony that would co-operate in extending civilization from Cairo to the Cape."[33] Even once Zionists officially set their sights on Palestine, organized movements to establish Jewish colonies in other parts of the world persisted. When Zionists at the Seventh Zionist Congress in 1905 voted against a plan to establish a Jewish colony on British territory in what is today eastern Kenya (the so-called Uganda plan), a group led by Zangwill seceded and established the Jewish Territorial Organization. The territorialist movement continued to promote the settlement of Jews in colonies other than Palestine into the mid-twentieth century.[34]

Zionists themselves represented aliyah (immigration of Jews to Israel) as fundamentally different from immigration to the United States. Zionist demographer Jacob Lestschinsky called emigration to Palestine "a pure, clean current rooted in elevated, distant national and social goals; an organized, planned current that is all idea and vision, and therefore is limited in scope and has never attracted people who are fanatical about making money and getting rich."[35] In reality, however, Gur Alroey has shown that the motivations as well as the social and demographic profiles of Jews who emigrated to Palestine and those who immigrated to the United States during the early twentieth century were strikingly similar.[36] Before restrictive immigration laws drastically limited Jewish immigration to North America and most of western Europe after the First World War, Palestine was one option among several for prospective emigrants. Zionists, meanwhile, advanced their own project in the 1890s by publicizing and sensationalizing the negative experiences of emigrants outside of Palestine.

These attacks were not simply intended to negate life in the diaspora. They were infused with anxieties about the civilizational and racial status of Jews, anxieties similar to those expressed by non-Jewish eastern Europeans as they debated the merits of emigrant colonialism. The debate was particularly intense with respect to settlement in South America at the end of the nineteenth century. In the 1890s Baron Maurice de Hirsch's Jewish Colonization Association (JCA) began to fund Jewish agricultural colonies in Argentina and Brazil as well as North America. By 1896, the year of the baron's death, the JCA had settled 6,757

Russian Jews in Argentina.[37] The Zionist press in Austria launched fierce attacks on the JCA in the 1890s, although the JCA's central office in St. Petersburg was actually run by a Zionist sympathizer, Schmuel Janovsky.[38] Like other Austrian emigration reformers, Zionists feared that Jewish migrants would be reduced to the status of colonial or slave labor. In March 1898, *Die Welt* published a letter from a Jewish emigrant in Ecuador. Many countries in Central and South America were recruiting Russian Jews as emigrants, he reported. Some even offered free land. But he warned prospective migrants not to be seduced by these offers, since "the goal is to attract colonists and use them to cultivate deserted or worthless state lands. And this cultivation is almost impossible for a European." In addition to poor land, settlers in Argentina were allegedly forced to contend with yellow fever, mosquitoes, flies, rats, scorpions, and Indians. The basic problem, however, was that Jews could not compete with native labor. While agricultural labor in South America was not suitable for Europeans, "the Indian, mestizo, and black man can survive, because he does the hardest work in this barbaric climate with ease, and needs no more than some oranges, bananas, a little rice . . . a straw house with a roof of leaves and a hammock inside."[39]

A few months later, reports surfaced that many migrants who had settled in Argentina under JCA auspices were returning to Russia. These emigrants had been relatively well off before their departure. They had left for Argentina five years earlier with one thousand rubles each, full of hope. Upon arrival they purchased land, built houses, and worked hard to render the land fertile, *Die Welt* reported. But insects destroyed their crops, and within a few years they had lost everything. They were now returning "as beggars."[40] Also writing for *Die Welt*, S. Werner depicted the Argentinian colonies as cesspools of misery and hardship. "The grasshoppers which destroy the entire harvest; the storms that kill the cows; the wild natives whose sole occupation is robbery and murder, and finally the [JCA] administration, which sees tormenting the colonists as their calling— those are the conditions under which the settlers must live." According to Werner, a group of colonists had complained to officials in Buenos Aires about their plight. The officials were sympathetic but replied that there was nothing they could do, since it was illegal to interfere in conflicts between "masters and their peons." "What does 'peon' mean?" asked Werner, answering, "Peons are men in bondage, slaves! . . . That's how we learned that we are officially seen as slaves of Baron Hirsch."[41]

When opportunities to emigrate elsewhere dried up in the interwar period, Jewish emigration to Palestine reached its peak. Even then, however, Palestine remained one option among several for prospective Jewish emigrants, alongside western Europe (particularly France, between the wars) and South America. To a certain extent, this suited most Zionists just fine, as they continued to worry about overly rapid settlement and were intent on selectively recruiting the "right" emigrants to Palestine. By the 1920s and 1930s, in recognition of both the practical limits on emigration to Palestine (the pace of which was controlled by the British) and the desperation of Jews seeking to leave Europe, many Zionists came to support the efforts of the JCA, Hebrew Immigrant Aid Society, and other organizations to resettle Jews elsewhere.

The conviction that other emigration destinations competed with and threatened the Zionist project resurfaced again after 1945, however, when Zionists in Europe fiercely opposed efforts to resettle Jewish Holocaust survivors outside of Palestine. In October 1945, for example, leaders of the Central Committee of Liberated Jews in Bavaria rejected a plan, sponsored by British Jewish agencies, to transport one thousand young survivors to Britain for rest and rehabilitation after the war. The Central Committee resolved "to ensure that no one single child should, under any circumstances, be allowed to immigrate to any other country than the only possible haven for them—Palestine." Emigration *from* Palestine/Israel was meanwhile seen as a form of national treason. Jews who voluntarily left or returned to Europe after settling in Palestine challenged a teleological narrative in which arrival in the Promised Land represented a triumphant ending to the saga of Jewish displacement.[42]

Both Zionist movements and other eastern European colonial projects also developed in a context in which controlled emigration was seen as a tool for solving social and political problems. The idea of moving "surplus" populations to imperial outposts was nothing new. In the nineteenth century the French and British Empires had expelled vast numbers of convicts to colonial penal colonies, a form of settlement that Derek Penslar calls "penal colonialism." In the British Empire, champions of emigration also urged the government to "shovel out paupers" in the 1820s and 1830s. Orphans and "surplus" single women later joined the paupers in exile. Emigration, in this context, became a strategy for simultaneously ridding the metropole of unwanted demographic elements and rendering colonies profitable.[43]

Eastern European "emigrant colonialism" also attempted to transform "unwanted" or "surplus" populations into servants of empire. Populations considered "undesirable" at home would paradoxically strengthen the empire or nation abroad. By the end of the nineteenth century, however, "surplus" populations were increasingly defined in national or religious terms. Many nationalist economists and political activists now insisted that achieving demographic "equilibrium" required the emigration of particular ethnic groups. Emigration policy thereby became a strategy for creating homogenous national territories.

The Hungarian government adopted this strategy early on. At the turn of the twentieth century, officials actively encouraged Slovak-, Croatian-, and

German-speaking Hungarians to emigrate while discouraging Magyar speakers from leaving home. As of 1904, two-thirds of emigrants leaving the Hungarian half of the dual monarchy were not native Hungarian speakers. A secret memorandum from the Hungarian under-secretary of state to the Hungarian prime minister was explicit about the aims of this policy: "For the institution of national statehood it is absolutely necessary that the ruling race . . . become the majority of the population. . . . Providence . . . has granted another population factor which has significantly raised the proportion of the Hungarian element at the expense of the nationalities between 1890 and 1900. . . . This important new factor is the mass emigration of the non-Hungarian population."[44]

In Vienna, by contrast, imperial authorities officially mourned the loss of all the kaiser's subjects equally. At the provincial and local levels, however, Polish nationalist activists began to worry about how Polish emigration would affect the demographic balance sheet in Galicia. They specifically feared that Polish emigration would play to the advantage of Ruthene speakers in eastern Galicia. Representatives of growing populist and antisemitic parties, meanwhile, began to suggest that the emigration of Jews to Palestine or North America represented a promising solution to the "Jewish problem." In 1901, for example, after being informed that sixteen thousand Jewish Galicians had emigrated that year, the antisemitic priest and peasant organizer Stanislaw Stojalowski quipped, "a pity there were not three times as many."[45]

In Russia, imperial authorities began to encourage Jewish emigration in the 1890s while restricting the emigration of nationally "desirable" citizens, a policy that Eric Lohr calls "filtration." The Russian government allowed the JCA to set up shop across the empire beginning in 1892, effectively legalizing Jewish emigration, although emigration remained illegal for non-Jewish Russians. The JCA had established four hundred offices through Russia by 1910, providing migrants with information about opportunities to emigrate and assisting with the burdensome paperwork. Imperial authorities even furnished Jewish emigrants with a discounted train ticket to the border. Emigrants who left with JCA assistance were subject to the eternal ban on return, however, with tragic consequences if they failed to prosper in their new homes or were rejected at America's gates.[46]

Zionists clearly did not share the antisemitic view that Jews were an "undesirable" population that needed to be reduced through emigration. If anything, Zionism developed in response to such arguments, which confirmed a sense that Jews needed their own national home if they were ever to live in peace. Some early Zionists did, however, adopt the language of "surplus" population and "saturation" in support of emigration. They hoped that the departure of some Jews from eastern Europe would reduce antisemitism and improve life for those who stayed behind. Leon Pinsker, an early advocate of Jewish emigration from Europe, argued in 1882, "There is a certain point of saturation, beyond which their numbers may not increase, if the Jews are not to be exposed to the dangers of persecution as in Russia, Romania, Morocco, and elsewhere. It is this surplus which, a burden to itself and to others, conjures up the evil fate of the entire people. It is now high time to create a refuge for this surplus."[47] In 1896 Theodor Herzl speculated that channeling emigration toward a Jewish state would benefit those who remained in Europe. "The departure of the dedicated Jews would be even more to the advantage of the 'assimilated' than of the Christian citizens, for they would be freed of the disquieting, unpredictable, and inescapable competition of a Jewish proletariat driven by poverty and political pressure from place to place, from land to land. This drifting proletariat would become stabilized." Once again, the goal was to channel an unruly emigration already in progress toward rational resettlement. "Nor will their exodus in any way be a flight, but it will be a well-regulated movement under the constant check of public opinion."[48]

All of the colonial settlement schemes that emerged from eastern Europe were particularly concerned about maintaining or regenerating the imperial or national loyalties of emigrants, which were supposedly threatened by unplanned emigration. While the Austrian Empire sought to cultivate the supranational Habsburg loyalties of its subjects abroad, growing Hungarian, Polish, and Czech nationalist movements (and later nation-states) increasingly saw planned colonial settlement as a strategy for keeping migrants emotionally bound to a specific national community. Both Zionists and eastern European proponents of colonial settlement justified their projects as a form of self-defense against denationalization and exploitation. Both were linked to hopes for national preservation and autonomy outside of Europe. Rather than being "lost" to the nation through assimilation in North American cities, eastern European emigrants were to preserve their language and culture in isolated agricultural settlements. For Zionist activists, meanwhile, settlement in Palestine was intended to be a bulwark against assimilation in Europe itself, whether understood in religious or cultural terms. Arthur Ruppin, for example, was particularly concerned about the dangers of Jewish conversion, intermarriage, and assimilation in western Europe. He also supported the separation of the Jewish and Arab populations in Palestine out of fear that Jews would otherwise assimilate to Arabs.[49]

Zionists and eastern European nationalists alike argued vociferously about the specific content of the national cultures that they aimed to create or preserve abroad. Zionists, for example, disagreed about whether the Jewish community in Palestine should be secular or religious; whether it should be built around the Yiddish or Hebrew language and culture; and whether it should be socialist, liberal, or conservative in its political orientation. But they generally agreed about the need to maintain some kind of distinctive and autonomous Jewish nation. Palestine was attractive because it was a place where Jews would (theoretically) remain Jewish. In 1903, for example, German Zionist David Trietsch denounced the Jewish Agricultural and Industrial Aid Society (an organization that resulted from a merger of the Baron de Hirsch fund and JCA) for its efforts to disperse Jewish immigrants across rural America. These Jews immediately lost their "national unity" and abandoned their religious faith, he insisted, since they were isolated from one another and could not establish synagogues. "The principle of dispersal," he declared, represented nothing less than the "downfall of Judentum and a continuation of the thousand-year-old wars of annihilation (*Vernichtungskriege*) against the Jews." The only solution, in his view, was to pursue a policy that represented dispersal's antithesis. "It is clear that if we want to replace the thinnest distribution of Jews around the world with the most compact settlement possible in one country, then that country can be no other than our land of Palestine, because the unification of all Jews in any other country is unthinkable."[50]

Zionists directed similar attacks against Jewish rural settlement schemes in Canada, publishing letters from malcontent emigrants to publicize their sad fate. In 1903 one Romanian emigrant reported, "As far as our situation here is concerned, we are doing badly. . . . Many families have already left the country and many more will leave." The emigrant lamented that many colonists "do not know any longer if they are Jews," since it was impossible to observe Jewish dietary laws in the Canadian hinterland. The editors of *Die Welt* once again denounced the JCA, which was responsible for the Canadian settlements. "This is how the JCA helps the Romanian Jews . . . by forcing them to go to Canada, to forget their Jewishness, and by making it impossible to follow Jewish laws."[51]

Although motivated by common concerns about denationalization, eastern European colonialists and Zionists differed significantly when it came to the role of both land and labor in their settlement projects. For most eastern European proponents of colonial settlement, the vision of isolated agricultural colonies was profoundly antiurban. Settling peasants on the land was supposed to prevent their moral and physical degeneration in urban factories and mines. Eastern European advocates of colonial settlement therefore tended to represent colonial settlement as a project of social as well as national preservation. They hoped to sustain what they represented to be the "traditional" values and social structure of the rural peasantry.

In reality, however, eastern European emigrant colonialism was as much about the construction or reform of national communities as about "preservation." There was no unitary "Czech," "German," "Slovak," or "Polish" national community in east-central Europe in the late nineteenth century any more than there was a unified Jewish nation, particularly given the widespread persistence of bilingualism and national indifference in the region. The massive social changes associated with urbanization and industrialization were already well under way by the time mass emigration began (and indeed precipitated emigration). Like the Zionist project, eastern European colonial settlement schemes were vehicles for reimagining and consolidating national communities more than "preserving" preexisting national cultures.[52]

Zionists, however, often adopted a much more explicit rhetoric of social, economic, psychological, and even physical transformation through resettlement. The Zionist ideal of "productivization," in particular, called for the transformation of petty traders and merchants into what one Zionist leader even termed hearty and masculine "muscle Jews."[53] These goals had important implications for Zionist attitudes toward and relations with Arabs in Palestine. Labor Zionists, in particular, who dominated Jewish politics in Palestine from the turn of the century until the 1930s, extolled the virtues of physical labor, maintaining that Jews should render the land fertile by their own hands. "Our settlers do not come here as do the colonists from the Occident to have natives do their work for them," insisted Martin Buber. "They themselves set their blood to make the land fruitful."[54] While other European settler colonies tended to force indigenous populations into the labor market through taxation and other coercive measures, Labor Zionists raised fire for displacing Arab workers and landowners in their effort to employ "Hebrew labor."[55]

Eastern European emigration reformers, by contrast, were typically adamant that eastern Europeans not do work traditionally reserved for native or nonwhite labor. In 1907, for example, rumors spread in Austria that emigrants from the empire were being hired to replace African American plantation workers in the American South. As recruiters from Louisiana and Georgia began to prowl the eastern European countryside in search of cotton pickers, Austrian officials panicked. Polemical denunciations of the emigration business as a form of "human trafficking" reached a new key as rumors spread that Austrian peasants were literally replacing former slaves. Reformers also worried about the supposed threat of racial "degeneration" through intermixing. In 1908 an Austrian consul toured Florida, Georgia, Alabama, and South Carolina to investigate working and living conditions in the South. Since Austrian immigrants would inevitably "live and work with the blacks" on southern plantations, he insisted that "the only possible consequence is that our people will be brought down to the level of the blacks, and that they will hardly be better treated."[56]

There was no unified position toward indigenous populations among either eastern Europeans or Zionists, however. Both early Zionists and eastern European advocates of colonial settlement generally assumed that native populations outside of Europe would welcome them with open arms. Like other proponents of European colonialism, both tended to portray themselves as representatives of European civilization, culture, and progress. Early Zionists commonly held that Arabs would applaud Jews for bringing European civilization to Palestine. "We will endeavor to do in Asia Minor what the English did in India—I am referring to cultural work and not to rule by force. We intend to come to Palestine as the emissaries of culture and to expand the moral boundaries of Europe to the Euphrates," proclaimed Max Nordau at the eighth Zionist conference in 1907.[57]

As the reality of Arab protest was absorbed on the ground, however, some revisionist Zionists declared that conflict (even armed conflict) with Arabs was inevitable—again drawing direct inspiration from other colonial powers. In a speech to the British House of Lords in 1937, Vladimir Jabotinsky went so far as to compare the Zionist need for armed defense to the British Empire's need to suppress native rebellions. "A nation with your colossal colonizing past experience surely knows that colonization never went on without certain conflicts with the population on the spot, so that the country had to be protected. . . . In Kenya until recently every European was obliged to train for the Settlers Defense Force. Why should the Jews in Palestine be forced to prepare for self-defense underhand; as though committing a legal offense?"[58]

At the other end of the political spectrum were visions of cooperation and cultural synthesis. Many Socialist Zionists saw Arabs and Jews as natural allies in a struggle against class oppression. Some even insisted on the ethnic or racial affinity of Jews and Arabs, both of whom they believed to be native to Palestine. In the words of the early Socialist Zionist Ber Borochov, "The local population in Palestine is closer to the Jews in racial composition than any other people." A minority of Zionists even imagined that a new culture would be born of Jewish-Arab synthesis.[59] These disagreements among Zionists, of course, echoed similar disagreements among Habsburg nationalists and among other proponents of emigration in eastern Europe about the desired degree of contact and proper relationship between linguistic and national communities both in eastern Europe and in settlements abroad.

With the collapse of the Austrian Empire into self-declared nation-states in 1918, efforts to channel emigration toward colonization intensified in east-central Europe. This was partly the consequence of the new quota law in the United States, which discriminated against migrants from southern and eastern Europe and sharply reduced opportunities for emigration to the United States. The radical limits placed on immigration to the United States also resulted in a spike in Jewish emigration to Palestine. Between 1924 (when the restrictions took effect) and 1929, around eighty thousand Jews settled in the mandate (although twenty-three thousand ultimately left during the economic crisis of 1926–28).[60]

In 1924 Jan Sykáček, a former diplomat, revived the notion that Czechoslovakia should imitate Italy and Germany by creating enclosed Czechoslovak colonies in South America. "I have seen how other nations deal with this important question, especially the Italians and Germans. They work systematically in every sense, in that the motherland correctly understands the importance of colonies, from both a national and economic perspective." Germany and Italy used their foreign colonies to "promote the motherland" around the world, according to Sykáček. "The motherland is in constant contact with them and they are not held aloof like they are here in Czechoslovakia."[61]

Eastern European officials also continued to worry that their citizens would not be accorded the privileges of white Europeans in these far-flung settlements, however. In the 1920s, for example, French officials increasingly sought to recruit eastern Europeans to work in French colonies and overseas territories (such as Corsica, French Guiana, and Tahiti). In 1927 a delegation of French and Czech authorities actually visited Corsica and then reconvened in Paris to discuss prospects for Czech and Slovak employment there. The French delegation aimed to reassure their Czech colleagues that Corsica was safe for European habitation, promising lush gardens and free wine to Czech workers.[62] But Czechoslovak officials were not convinced that their citizens would be better treated than convicts sent to labor in French penal colonies. They were even less enthusiastic about schemes to export Czechs to Tahiti, where a colony of around ninety Czechoslovaks had already settled in June 1926. "The bad example of the natives, who live off fish and fruit and work only when they need money, negatively influences the immigrants, who often fall to their level. We do not recommend that our people emigrate to Tahiti or any other French Island under any circumstance," Czech diplomats advised. "The position of foreign workers there is the same as that of native workers and Chinese."[63]

In interwar Poland, the desire to channel emigration toward colonization gave rise to a powerful lobby in favor of formal overseas expansion. Polish colonial ambitions took shape as early as 1919, when a group called Polish Bandera began to promote popular interest in maritime navigation. By 1930 the organization had become the Maritime and Colonial League, a pressure group that raised funds for the navy and lobbied the government to pursue colonial interests. The league boasted 1,200 branches and a membership of 250,000 people as of 1934. The Polish lust for colonies intensified after Benito Mussolini's 1935 invasion of Ethiopia. That October leaders of the Maritime and Colonial League insisted, "We Poles, like the Italians, are facing a great problem of accommodating and employing a large population increase. We Poles, like the Italians, have the right to demand that export markets as well as areas for settlement be opened to us, so that we may obtain raw materials necessary to the national economy under conditions similar to those enjoyed by the colonial states." In September 1936, Polish Foreign Minister Józef Beck unsuccessfully appealed to the League of Nations for colonies—preferably those taken from Germany after the First World War. Popular pressure for Polish colonies achieved a frenzied pitch during the Maritime League's "Colonial Days" festivities in April 1938, a series of nation-wide parades and celebrations attended by around 10 million Poles.[64]

Poland continued to lobby the League of Nations for a place in the sun right up until the outbreak of the Second World War. A Polish memo submitted to the League in 1939 proposed that the League's colonial mandate system be extended to Africa, and that African colonies be redistributed among Europe's countries according to "their capacity for colonization and their real economic and demographic needs." Of course, the Polish delegation claimed to be at the top of the list on both counts. In terms of colonizing capabilities, Polish emigrants had already "provided the proof" of their abilities "by transforming the virgin forests and uncultivated plains of Brazil, Argentina, Canada, and Siberia into arable land. . . . In particular the tenacity of labor, love of the land and pioneering spirit of the Polish peasant has rendered him invaluable." In response to British and French objections that redistributing African colonies would harm the "interests of indigenous populations," the Polish delegation invoked the brotherhood of white men. "There exist rural populations in Europe whose economic standard of living are particularly painful, and whose interests are worth at least as much as those of the black population in Africa. By closing off access to colonial territories to overpopulated nations, the great powers betray the interests of the white race. This treason endangers the solidarity and entente among peoples."[65]

Throughout interwar eastern Europe, emigration policies also became a more explicit tool of nationalization after the First World War as trends begun before the war radicalized. In practice this meant that eastern European governments tended to look favorably upon Zionism. In Czechoslovakia, for example, the state officially recognized Jews as a national community by offering Jewish citizens a new option on the censuses of 1921 and 1930: they could declare themselves members of the Jewish nation rather than Czechoslovaks or Germans. The goal of this policy was to reduce the number of Germans counted in the census, as Czechoslovak officials (along with Zionists) hoped that German-speaking Jews would choose to identify as Jews rather than as Germans. Czechoslovak Zionists themselves were not, however, primarily oriented toward promoting emigration, as Tatjana Lichtenstein has demonstrated. They saw the Zionist movement itself as a means of integrating Jews into Czechoslovak society (as an autonomous national community) rather than moving Jews out. The Polish government also expressed its support for the Zionist movement throughout the interwar period, declaring its "special interest in the emigration of the Jews from Poland" (including emigration to Palestine) as early as 1919.[66] New Polish passport restrictions, meanwhile, hindered the emigration of Poles beginning in 1920. The Polish Interior Ministry simultaneously distributed a circular to local government offices informing them that the new restrictions did not apply to Jews. Polish Jews should be encouraged to emigrate "in the interest of the Polish Republic," the circular advised. "Particularly from an economic perspective it is advisable to facilitate their departure."[67]

A view of emigration as the solution to the "minority problem" in eastern Europe had tragic implications for Jews in the late 1930s, and especially with the rise of Nazism and the refugee crisis in Europe. In this context the goal of facilitating Jewish emigration and creating eastern European colonies mutated into fantasies of dumping Jews in a colonial reservoir. Longstanding discussions about the potential of Jewish settlers to thrive as colonial settlers now framed discussions about where Jewish refugees might find a haven from Nazism. In the years leading up to the Second World War, Polish officials increasingly insisted on Poland's right to colonies as an outlet for its "surplus" Jewish population.[68] Both Polish and Romanian officials lobbied Western diplomats and international organizations such as the League of Nations to find an international "solution" to the so-called Jewish problem through mass emigration to a colonial territory.

Advocates of Jewish resettlement found a receptive audience in western leaders, who recognized the growing severity of the refugee crisis in Europe but were not willing to open their own gates to immigrants. "It must be frankly recognized that the larger Eastern European problem is basically a Jewish problem," declared American president Franklin Delano Roosevelt in 1939. "The organized emigration from Eastern Europe over a period of years of young persons . . . is not beyond the bounds of possibility. The resultant decrease in economic pressure; the actual removal over a period years of a very substantial number of persons . . . should reduce the problem to negligible proportions."[69] For Roosevelt, the emigration of eastern European Jews, preferably to someplace in South America or Africa, represented a forward-thinking and "orderly" alternative to chaotic deportation and flight.

Roosevelt was not the author of these visions, however. He simply appropriated ideas that had long been circulating locally in eastern and central Europe, and he attempted to mobilize the international community behind them. Emigration politics and policies thus "trickled up" from eastern Europe into the spheres of international politics and humanitarianism in the 1930s. In the two years before the outbreak of the Second World War, Jewish humanitarian organizations and international nongovernmental organizations scoured the world for a colonial territory—Madagascar, British Guiana, and Angola were among the most serious contenders—to serve as a haven or dumping ground for Jewish refugees. Colonial settlement, along with emigration, was widely considered the first "solution" to the "Jewish problem" in eastern Europe.

As the threats to Jews' livelihood and physical security multiplied in the 1930s, an increasing number of eastern European Jews themselves—including Zionists and non-Zionists—came to see emigration as their best or only hope for a better life (and, ultimately, for survival). Discussions of emigration permeated Polish-Jewish society in the 1930s. By November of 1937 Leon Alter, the director of the Jewish Emigration Society (JEAS, Żydowskie centralne towarzystwo emigracyjne w Polsce), reported "a particularly intense demand for emigration that is taking on the character of a psychosis" among Polish Jews. "At the moment we find ourselves before problems of exceptional severity," Alter lamented. "While our emigration committee is trying not to allow any possibility for emigration to escape, we must simultaneously resist all attempts to provoke a massive, chaotic, forced emigration."[70]

In this desperate context, possibilities for escape were still shaped by the much longer history of emigration policies and colonial politics in eastern Europe. Since the late nineteenth century, eastern European policymakers—including Jews—had seen emigration as a potential solution to a number of political and social "problems" ranging from social inequality and persecution to national and religious conflict. These emigration schemes had always been framed by racial hierarchies and entangled in global colonial politics. Debates about the relative merits of Jewish colonization in Argentina, Brazil, or Palestine intersected with longstanding discussions about the possibilities for Austrian, Polish, or Czech settlement in Brazil, Tahiti, and New Orleans. East European proponents of emigration had long been tempted by the potential opportunity to solidify their status as white Europeans in colonial settings. At the same time, they were persistently plagued by racial anxieties. What if, instead of proving their whiteness, eastern Europeans were reduced culturally, socially, or even biologically to the status of colonial labor?[71]

Jewish territorialist visions, including Zionism, shared many qualities with this specific eastern European variant of emigrant colonialism, even when they took shape in response to persecution. Proponents of Jewish emigration to colonial contexts frequently emphasized that Jews would serve as a European "civilizing" force in their new homes. Opponents of Jewish settlement outside of Europe or Palestine, meanwhile, were as anxious as other eastern Europeans about the imagined dangers of social or racial degeneration. Hans Klein, an Austrian territorialist, opposed Jewish settlement in the tropics in 1937 based on his conviction that Jews would be reduced to colonial labor. "They will sink to the level of Coolies and their wives will mix with the Negroes!" he warned.[72]

Even at the height of the Jewish refugee crisis, organizations like the American Jewish Joint Distribution Committee (JDC), which worked tirelessly to rescue Jews from Nazi-occupied Europe, adopted the tropes of colonial experimentation. Joseph Rosen, vice president of the JDC-sponsored effort to resettle Jews in the Dominican Republic in 1940, predicted that after the war, millions of people would be forced to seek new homes. "Large sections of undeveloped and unpopulated territories may be available for mass settlement with fewer obstacles and less resistance from the existing population than in countries of temperate zones," he speculated. Therefore, the goal of the Dominican colony was to determine concretely whether Europeans could do hard physical labor in subtropical conditions as well as "whether they can be established there on a sufficiently high standard of living, considerably above the standards of the native laboring population, and be able to maintain these standards without continued help from the outside."[73]

James Rosenberg of the JDC agreed in 1940 that the significance of the small Jewish colony in the Dominican Republic was to prepare the ground for future colonies. "Whatever the outcome of the present war, students of world conditions are agreed that in the coming years there are bound to be mass movements of populations from overcrowded, war-torn countries in Europe. If those enslaved people can find new life in such fertile undeveloped lands, some part, at least, of the world's sickness may be cured."[74] Talk of resettling Jewish displaced persons in South America, Africa, or other colonial territories only subsided with the establishment of the State of Israel in 1948.

Understanding the relationship between Jews, Zionism, and colonialism ultimately requires that we consider the multiple varieties of colonialism that flourished in Europe around the turn of the century as well as the multiple varieties of Zionism. Among those colonial projects were the mostly failed and forgotten dreams of transforming emigrants from the Habsburg Empire and its successor states into colonial settlers. These eastern European dreams of settlement abroad were linked to anxieties about the national loyalties and civilizational status of eastern Europeans in the context of mass emigration and a globalizing labor market. Zionism shared many of these concerns even as it responded to the distinctive threat of antisemitism. It was ultimately one of the only eastern European colonial schemes to be realized in practice, outlasting the very states and societies that incubated it.

Notes

1. O. Fadeuhecht, "Kleiderconfection in den Colonien," *Die Welt*, June 11, 1897, 9.
2. Mark Choate, *Emigrant Nation: The Making of Italy Abroad* (Cambridge, MA: Harvard University Press, 2008).

3. There are a few recent exceptions, notably, Benno Gämmerl, *Staatsbürger, Untertanen und Andere: Der Umgang mit ethnischer Heterogenität im Britischen Weltreich und im Habsburgerreich, 1867–1918* (Vienna: Vandenhoeck & Ruprecht, 2010); Simon Loidl, "Kolonialpropaganda und Aktivitäten in Österreich-Ungarn, 1885–1918" (Ph.D. diss., University of Vienna, 2012); Walter Sauer, ed. *K. u. k. kolonial: Habsburgermonarchie und europaische Herrschaft in Afrika* (Vienna: Böhlau, 2007); and Alison Frank, "The Children of the Desert and the Laws of the Sea: Austria, Great Britain, the Ottoman Empire, and the Mediterranean Slave Trade in the Nineteenth Century," *American Historical Review* 117, no. 3 (June 2012): 410–44.

4. See Larry Wolff, *The Idea of Galicia: History and Fantasy in Habsburg Political Culture* (Stanford, CA: Stanford University Press, 2010).

5. For a discussion of this issue, see Tara Zahra, "Looking East: East Central European Borderlands in German History and Historiography," *History Compass* 3, no. 1 (2005): 1–23.

6. David Blackbourn, "Das Kaiserreich Transnational: Eine Skizze," in *Das Kaiserreich Transnational: Deutschland in der Welt, 1871–1914*, ed. Jürgen Osterhammel and Sebastian Conrad (Göttingen: Vandenhoeck & Ruprecht, 2004), 323; Mark Mazower, *Hitler's Empire: How the Nazis Ruled Europe* (New York: Penguin, 2009); Kristin Kopp, *Germany's Wild East: Constructing Poland as a Colonial Space* (Ann Arbor: University of Michigan Press, 2012); Vejas Liulevicius, *The German Myth of the East: 1800 to the Present* (Oxford: Oxford University Press, 2009); and Elizabeth Harvey, *Women in the Nazi East: Agents and Witnesses of Germanization* (New Haven, CT: Yale University Press, 2003).

7. Gur Alroey, *An Unpromising Land: Jewish Migration to Palestine in the Early Twentieth Century* (Stanford, CA: Stanford University Press, 2014), 96–103.

8. Joshua Shanes, *Diaspora Nationalism and Jewish Identity in Habsburg Galicia* (Cambridge: Cambridge University Press, 2012), 2.

9. Tatjana Lichtenstein, *Zionists in Interwar Czechoslovakia: Minority Nationalism and the Politics of Belonging* (Bloomington, IN: Indiana University Press, 2016).

10. James Loeffler, "Between Zionism and Liberalism: Oscar Janowsky and Diaspora Nationalism in America," *Association for Jewish Studies Review* 34, no. 2 (November 2010): 289–308.

11. Kenneth Moss, "Thinking with Restriction: Immigration Restriction and Polish Jewish Accounts of the Post-Liberal State, Empire, Race, and Political Reason 1926–1939," *East European Jewish Affairs* 44, nr. 2–3 (December 2014): 205–224.

12. Richard Schroft, *Das Programm der Österreichisch-ungarisch Colonial-Gesellschaft* (Vienna, 1895), 15.

13. Friedrich Hey, *Unser Auswanderungswesen und seine Schäden* (Vienna: Fromme, 1912), 13–17.

14. Caro, quoted in Benjamin P. Murzdek, *Emigration in Polish Social-Political Thought, 1870–1914* (Boulder, CO: East European Quarterly, 1977), 170.

15. On Italian emigration policies and their relationship to imperialism, see Choate, *Emigrant Nation*; see also Caroline Douki, "The Liberal Italian State and Mass Emigration, 1860–1914," in *Citizenship and Those Who Leave: The Politics of Emigration and Expatriation*, ed. Nancy Green and François Weil, 91–113 (Urbana: University of Illinois Press, 2007); and Philip V. Cannistraro and Gianfausto Rosoli, "Fascist Emigration Policy in the 1920s: An Interpretive Framework," *International Migration Review* 13, no. 4 (Winter 1979): 673–92.

16. On German emigration and nation-building, see Sebastian Conrad, *Globalization and the Nation in Imperial Germany*, trans. Sorcha O'Hagen (Cambridge: Cambridge University Press, 2010); Krista O'Donnell, Renate Bridenthal, and Nancy Reagin, eds., *The Heimat Abroad: The Boundaries of Germanness* (Ann Arbor: University of Michigan Press, 2005); and Donna R. Gabaccia, Dirk Hoerder, and Adam Walaszek, "Emigration and Nation Building during the Mass Migrations from Europe," in *Citizenship and Those Who Leave*, 63–90.

17. For accounts of the origins of Zionism in turn of the century Europe, see Michael Brenner, *Zionism: A Brief History*, trans. Shelley L. Frisch (Princeton: M. Wiener, 2003); David Engel, *Zionism* (New York: Pearson/Longman, 2009); and Ezra Mendelsohn, *Zionism in Poland: The Formative Years, 1915–1926*

(New Haven, CT: Yale University Press, 1981). On the rise of racial antisemitism, see Peter G. J. Pulzer, *The Rise of Political Anti-Semitism in Germany and Austria* (New York: Wiley, 1964).

18. For a comparative discussion of settler colonialisms in the twentieth century, see Caroline Elkins and Susan Pedersen, "Settler Colonialism: A Concept and Its Uses," in *Settler Colonialism in the Twentieth Century. Projects, Practices, Legacies*, ed. Caroline Elkins and Susan Pedersen, 1–20 (New York: Routledge, 2005).

19. Annemarie Steidl, Wladimir Fischer-Nebmaier, and James W. Oberly, "The Transatlantic Migration Experience: From Austria-Hungary to the United States, 1870–1950," unpublished manuscript, printed manuscript, October 2012, 137; Samuel L. Baily, *Immigrants in the Lands of Promise: Italians in Buenos Aires and New York City, 1870–1914* (Ithaca, NY: Cornell University Press, 1999), 54; and Heinz Fassmann, "Die Bevölkerungsentwicklungen," in *Die Habsburgermonarchie 1848–1918*, vol. 9, Teil 1 (Vienna: Österreichische Akademie der Wissenschaften, 2010), 173–75.

20. For numbers, see Josef Ehmer, Annemarie Steidl, and Hermann Zeitlhofer, "Migration Patterns in Late Imperial Austria," Working Paper 3, Commission for Migration and Integration Research (Vienna: Austrian Academy of Sciences, 2004), 6–7; and Michael John, "Push and Pull Factors for Overseas Migrants from Austria-Hungary in the 19th and 20th Centuries," in *Austrian Immigration to Canada: Selected Essays*, ed. Franz A. J. Szabo (Ottawa: Carleton University Press, 1996), 59–60.

21. Leopold Caro, *Auswanderung und Auswanderungspolitik in Österreich* (Leipzig: Duncker & Humblot, 1909), 8.

22. On emigration from Imperial Russia, see Eric Lohr, *Russian Citizenship: From Empire to Soviet Union* (Cambridge, MA: Harvard University Press, 2012), 83–114, for numbers, see p. 195; Alison K. Smith, "The Freedom to Choose a Way of Life": Fugitives, Borders, and Imperial Amnesties in Russia," *Journal of Modern History* 83, no. 2 (June 2011): 243–71; Murzdek, *Emigration in Polish Social-Political Thought*, 35–78; Tobias Brinkmann, *Migration und Transnationalität* (Paderborn: Schöningh, 2012), 61–91; and Tobias Brinkmann, "Points of Passage: Reexamining Jewish Migrations from Eastern Europe after 1880," in *Points of Passage: Jewish Migrants from Eastern Europe in Scandinavia, Germany, and Britain 1880–1914*, ed. Tobias Brinkmann, 1–23 (New York: Berghahn, 2013).

23. Leopold Caro, "Der Los unserer Auswander," *Volkswirtschaftlichen Wochenschrift* 23 (1907), 6; and Annemarie Steidl, Wladimir Fischer-Nebmaier, and James Oberly, "The Transatlantic Migration Experience from Austria-Hungary to the United States, 1870–1950," printed manuscript, October 2012, 72. On the myth of "no return," see Jonathan Sarna, "The Myth of No Return: Jewish Return Migration to Eastern Europe, 1881–1914," *American Jewish History* 71 (December 1981): 257. On return migration in general, see Mark Wyman, *Round-Trip to America: The Immigrants Return to Europe, 1880–1930* (Ithaca, NY: Cornell University Press, 1996).

24. On anti-emigration policies in Austria-Hungary, see Tara Zahra, *The Great Departure: Mass Migration from Eastern Europe and the Making of the Free World* (New York: W.W. Norton, 2016).

25. On the transnational consolidation of an imagined "white" community and its effects on global migration politics, see Marilyn Lake and Henry Reynolds, *Drawing the Global Colour Line: White Men's Countries and the International Challenge of Racial Equality* (Cambridge: Cambridge University Press, 2008); On whiteness and US immigration, see Mae Ngai, *Impossible Subjects: Illegal Aliens and the Making of Modern America* (Princeton, NJ: Princeton University Press, 2004); Matthew Frye Jacobson, *Whiteness of a Different Color: European Immigrants and the Alchemy of Race* (Cambridge, MA: Harvard University Press, 1998); David R. Roedinger, *Working Toward Whiteness: How America's Immigrants Became White: The Strange Journey from Ellis Island to the Suburbs* (New York: Basic, 2005); Karen Brodkin, *How Jews Became White Folks and What That Says about Race in America* (New Brunswick, NJ: Rutgers University Press, 1998); and Thomas Guglielmo, *White on Arrival: Italians, Race, Color, and Power in Chicago, 1890–1945* (New York: Oxford University Press, 2004).

26. For more on efforts to restrict emigration in East Central Europe, see Zahra, "Travel Agents on Trial."

27. Sigismund Gargas, Das polnische Auswanderungsproblem, Berlin 1919, Sig. 3, f. 1162, Panstowy Urząd Emigracyny, Archiwum akt nowych (AAN), Warsaw.

28. Liora Halperin's recent work suggests, however, that early-twentieth-century Zionists were more open to multilingualism (among Jews) than previously recognized. Halperin, *Babel in Zion: Jews, Nationalism, and Language Diversity in Palestine, 1928–1948* (New Haven, CT: Yale University Press, 2014).

29. On Zionism and the Prussian model, see especially Yfaat Weiss, "Central European Ethnonationalism and Zionist Binationalism," *Jewish Social Studies* 11 (September 2004): 108–10. On internal colonization efforts in Austria and Prussia (and their failures), see Pieter M. Judson, *Guardians of the Nation: Activists on the Language Frontiers of Rural Austria* (Cambridge, MA: Harvard University Press, 2007); and Thomas Serrier, *Entre Allemagne et Pologne: Nations et identités frontalières, 1848–1914* (Paris: Belin, 2002).

30. Murzdek, *Emigration in Polish Social-Political Thought*, 61–69.

31. Caro, *Auswanderung und Auswanderungspolitik*, 53, 65–67.

32. Manoel F. Ferreira-Correia and Serro Azul, *Opis stanu Parana w Brazylii wraz z informacyami dla wychodzow*, trans. Jozef Siemiradzki (Lwow, 1896), 56–58, 80.

33. Zangwill quoted in Meri-Jane Rochelson, "Zionism, Territorialism, Race, and Nation in the Thought of Israel Zangwill," in *The Jew in Late-Victorian and Edwardian Culture: Between the East End and East Africa*, ed. Eitan Bar-Yosef and Nadia Valman (New York: Palgrave Macmillan, 2009), 150.

34. On the Jewish Territorial Movement and the intersections of colonialism and Zionism, see the dissertation in progress of Laura Almagor, "Forgotten Alternatives: Jewish territorialism as a movement of political action and ideology (1905–1965)" (PhD diss., European University Institute, 2015); and David Glover, "Imperial Zion: Israel Zangwill and the Origins of the Jewish Territorial Movement," in *The Jew in Late-Victorian and Edwardian Culture: Between the East End and East Africa*, ed. Eitan Bar-Yosef and Nadia Valman, 131–44 (New York: Palgrave Macmillan, 2009).

35. Cited in Alroey, *An Unpromising Land*, 9.

36. Alroey, *An Unpromising Land*, Chapter Two

37. On the JCA, see Theodore Norman, *An Outstretched Arm: A History of the Jewish Colonization Association* (London: Routledge, 1984), 70.

38. Alroey, *An Unpromising Land*, 67.

39. "Aus Südamerika," *Die Welt*, March 4, 1898, 7.

40. Josef Zipfer, "Rückkehr jüdischer Colonisten aus Argentinien," *Die Welt*, May 27, 1898, 8; and "Die Colonisten aus Argentinien," *Die Welt*, June 17, 1898, 12.

41. S. Werner, "Die argentinischen Greuel," *Die Welt*, July 15, 1898, 7–8.

42. On this conflict, see Margaret Myers Feinstein, *Holocaust Survivors in Postwar Germany, 1945–57* (New York: Cambridge University Press, 2010), 159–98, quote at 173. On displaced persons and Zionism, see also Avinoam Patt, *Finding Home and Homeland: Jewish Youth and Zionism in the Aftermath of the Holocaust* (Detroit: Wayne State University Press, 2009); Atina Grossmann, *Jews, Germans, and Allies: Close Encounters in Occupied Germany* (Princeton, NJ: Princeton University Press, 2007). On emigration from Palestine/Israel, see Ori Yehudai, "Forth from Zion: Jewish Emigration from Palestine and Israel, 1945–1960" (Ph.D. diss., University of Chicago, 2013).

43. On British emigration policies in the nineteenth century, see David Feldman and M. Page Baldwin, "Emigration and the British State, 1815–1925," in *Citizenship and Those Who Leave*, 135. On penal colonies, see, for example, Stephen A. Toth, *Beyond Papillon, The French Overseas Penal Colonies, 1854–1952* (Lincoln: University of Nebraska Press, 2006); and Cassandra Pybus, *Epic Journeys of Freedom: Runaway Slaves of the American Revolution and their Global Quest for Liberty* (Boston: Beacon, 2007). On British child emigration schemes, see Ellen Boucher, *Empire's Children: Child Emigration, Welfare, and the Decline of the British World, 1869–1967* (Cambridge: Cambridge University Press, 2014). On the emigration of "surplus women," see Kathrin Levitan, *A Cultural History of the British Census: Envisioning the Multitude in the Nineteenth Century* (New York: Palgrave Macmillan, 2011), 134–38. The phrase "penal

colonialism" comes from Derek Penslar, chapter 12 of the present volume: "Is Zionism a Colonial Movement?"

44. Cited in Julianna Puskás, *Ties That Bind, Ties That Divide: 100 Years of Hungarian Experience in the United States* (New York: Holmes & Meier, 2000), 90. See also Caro, "Der Los unserer Auswander," 6; and Monica Glettler, *Pittsburg-Wien-Budapest: Programm und Praxis der Nationalitätenpolitik bei Auswanderung der Slowaken um 1900* (Vienna: Verlag der Österreichischen Akademie der Wissenschaften, 1980), 401–6. Out of 163,703 emigrants from Hungary to the United States in 1905, 52,368 (31 percent) were Slovak-speakers and 35,104 (21 percent) Croatian-speakers, 7,261 (4 percent) Romanian-speakers, and 2,579 (1.5 percent) speakers of Serbian.

45. Stojalowski quoted in Murzdek, *Emigration in Polish Social-Political Thought*, 174.

46. Lohr, *Russian Citizenship*, 94–107.

47. Leon Pinsker, "Auto-Emancipation: An Appeal to His People by a Russian Jew" (1882), in *The Zionist Idea: A Historical Analysis and Reader*, ed. Arthur Hertzberg (New York: Jewish Publication Society, 1959), 196.

48. Theodor Herzl, "The Jewish State," in *The Zionist Idea: A Historical Analysis and Reader*, ed. Arthur Hertzberg (New York: Jewish Publication Society, 1959), 212, 214.

49. Weiss, "Central European Ethnonationalism," 106–7.

50. David Trietsch, "Die jüdische Emigrationsfrage," *Die Welt* January 2, 1903, 10–12.

51. "Von den rumänischen Emigration," *Die Welt*, February 6, 1903, 7.

52. Judson, *Guardians of the Nation*; and Tara Zahra, *Kidnapped Souls: National Indifference and the Battle for Children in the Bohemian Lands, 1900–1948* (Ithaca, NY: Cornell University Press, 2008).

53. See, among others, Todd Samuel Presner, *Muscular Judaism: The Jewish Body and the Politics of Regeneration* (New York: Routledge, 2007); Arieh Bruce Saposnik, *Becoming Hebrew: The Creation of a Jewish National Culture in Ottoman Palestine* (New York: Oxford University Press, 2008).

54. Martin Buber, "From an Open Letter to Mahatma Gandhi," (1939), in *The Zionist Idea*, 465.

55. Elkins and Pedersen, "Settler Colonialism," 10–11.

56. General-Consul Baron Hoening, Bericht über seine Bereisung der Südstaaten, April 12, 1908, Carton 53, Fach 15, Administrativ Registratur (AR), Ministerium des Auessern (MdA), Haus-Hof-und-Staatsarchiv (HHstA).

57. Nordau quoted in Yosef Gorny, *Zionism and the Arabs* (Oxford: Clarendon, 1987), 35.

58. Vladimir Jabotinsky, "Evidence Submitted to the Palestine Royal Commission" (1937), in *The Zionist Idea*, 564–65.

59. Cited in Gorny, *Zionism and the Arabs*, 35, 48, 119. On Polish Zionists and Arabs, see Mendelsohn, *Zionism in Poland*, 347–50.

60. Brenner, *Zionism*, 84–86.

61. Memo from Jan Sykáček, 20 September 1924, Carton 3797, Ministerstvo sociální péče (MSP), Národní Archiv (NA), Prague.

62. Francousko-česká komise, najímaní čsl. Zemědělského dělnictva a dílcích kolonů na Korsiku. March 16, 1928, MZV, V. Sekce- 6. bězná spisovna, Carton 486, MAE.

63. Informace o vyhlídkách pro vystěhovalce na Tahiti, 1928, MZV, V. Sekce- 6. bězná spisovna, Carton 486, Archives des affaires étrangères, Paris (MAE).

64. Marek Arpad Kowalski, *Dyskurs kolonialny w Drugiej Rzeczypospolitej* (Warsaw: Widawn, 2010), 72.

65. Memorandum sur la question de l'extension aux territoires coloniaux d'Afrique des principes des mandats, May 23, 1939, Sig. 9737, B26147, MSZ, AAN.

66. On Zionism and the interwar Czechoslovak census, see Lichtenstein, *Making Jews at Home*, chap. 3. On Zionism in interwar Poland, see Mendelsohn, *Zionism in Poland*, 112.

67. Wydanie paszportów zagranicznych do Ameryki obywatelstom polskim wyznanie mojzeszowego, May 19, 1920; Opis Ministerstwo spraw wewnętrznych, June 28, 1920, W sprawie wydawania

paszportów do Ameryki, Sig. 411, Starostwo Grodskie Krakowie, Archiwum państowe w krakowie (APKr).

68. Wydawnictwo Ruchu Miecz i Pług, *Polska kolonialna*, Warsaw, 1943, 5–6; Notatka do rozmowy z Ministrem Delbosem na temat polskich zainteresowań kołonialnych, Sig. 2/322/0/9593 - B 26003; Ideologja Towarzystwa Popierania Osadnictwa Polskiego na Madagaskarze, sygnatura: 2/322/0/9826 - B 26236, Ministerstwo Spraw Zagranicznych, Archiwum akt nowych, Warsaw. On Polish colonial ambitions, see Taras Hunczak, "Polish Colonial Ambitions in the Inter-War Period," *Slavic Review* 26, no. 4 (December 1967): 648–56, at 650.

69. Telegram from Cordell Hull to Myron Taylor, January 14, 1939, Folder Portugal and Angola, Records of the Intergovernmental Committee on Refugees, 1938–1947 (IGCR).

70. Rapport sur l'état actuel du problème de l'émigration juive de Pologne, November 23, 1937, Reel 487, 1967; and Memo from Leon Alter, November 19, 1937, Reel 485; RG 11.001M94, HIAS—Paris, USHMMA.

71. On the link between population transfer, ethnic cleansing, colonialism, and humanitarianism in interwar Europe, see especially Eric D. Weitz, "From the Vienna to the Paris System: International Politics and the Entangled Histories of Human Rights, Forced Deportations, and Civilizing Missions," *American Historical Review* 113 (December 2008), 1313–343; Keith David Watenpaugh, *Bread from Stones: The Middle East and the Making of Modern Humanitarianism* (University of California Press: Berkeley, CA, 2015).

72. Klein quoted in Almagor, "Saving a Jewish Europe in the World." On the Madagascar Plan and the French Empire, see Eric T. Jennings, "Writing Madagascar Back into the Madagascar Plan," *Holocaust and Genocide Studies* 21, no. 2 (Fall 2007): 187–217; and Eric T. Jennings, "Last Exit from Vichy France: The Martinique Escape Route and the Ambiguities of Emigration," *Journal of Modern History* 74 (June 2002): 289–324.

73. Joseph A. Rosen, "New Neighbors in Sosúa," Survey Graphic, September 1941, Item 585752, Folder Publicity, 1936; 1939–41, DORSA, JDC Archive. For the full story of the Dominican colony in Sosúa, see Marion Kaplan, *Dominican Haven: The Jewish Refugee Settlement in Sosúa, 1940–1945* (New York: American Jewish History, 2008); and Allen Wells, *Tropical Zion: General Trujillo, FDR, and the Jews of Sosúa* (Durham, NC: Duke University Press, 2009).

74. James N. Rosenberg, "The Story of Sosúa," *American Hebrew*, November 1, 1940, Item 585777, DORSA, JDC Archive.

9

ZIONISM AND THE BRITISH LABOUR PARTY

David Feldman

WRITING IN 1959, the historian of the British Empire, Archibald Thornton, asserted "the Labour Party was always a strong supporter of Zionism."[1] His remark cannot pass without qualification. To see that Thornton disregarded significant features of an uneven history, we need only bring to mind the anger with which Zionists received the Passfield White Paper—broadcast in 1930 by the Labour government's secretary of state for the colonies—which proposed restrictions on both Jewish immigration to Palestine and land purchases, or to recall the policies pursued between 1945 and 1948 by Ernest Bevin and Clement Attlee, Labour foreign secretary and prime minister, respectively, as they resisted the Zionist drive toward independent statehood. When the Labour Party held power, the goal of keeping (or restoring) peace in Palestine and the strategic importance of relationships with Arab states could exert a powerful influence on government policy to the detriment of Zionist goals. Moreover, a strand of Labour thought drew a parallel between the impact of Jewish settlement on the Arab population in Palestine and the suffering of "indigenous natives" in Kenya at the hands of "white settlers."[2] Fenner Brockway, a redoubtable anticolonialist, wrote in 1942, "to most problems one can apply general principles but to Palestine—no. By no other question have I been so puzzled."[3] Yet Thornton was not altogether wrong. Through most of the twentieth century the sympathies of Labour Party politicians and activists were overwhelmingly with the Yishuv and then, after 1948, with Israel. This was the case even when the policies of Labour governments led them into conflict with Zionist ambitions.

In August 1917, two months in advance of the Balfour Declaration, the Labour Party's War Aims Memorandum committed the party to support for a free state in Palestine "to which such of the Jewish people as desire to do so may return."[4] This pledge, in common with the Balfour Declaration as well as the 1922 League of Nations Mandate for Palestine, expressed a commitment not only to the existing Jewish population in Palestine but to Jews the world over who wished to settle there. The British government made many promises in the course of the First World War regarding territories that endured what David Lloyd George termed the "human cancer" of Ottoman rule. To encourage uprisings in Ottoman territory, it gave assurances about Arab independence; to satisfy the French, the British agreed to divide the Arab territories of the Near East into British and French spheres of influence; and to rally the Jewish masses in Russia and Jewish financiers elsewhere, they promised Jews a homeland in Palestine.[5] These pledges were, at best, difficult to reconcile. Equally significant for this essay, the pledges resonated to different degrees with different audiences in Britain. It was the Balfour Declaration that had special appeal for the Labour Party. Between 1920 and 1945 the Labour Party's annual conference endorsed the goal of a Jewish national home in Palestine on as many as eleven separate occasions.

Leading Labour politicians such as Ramsay Macdonald and Herbert Morrison, future prime minister and home secretary, respectively, visited Palestine in the interwar years and spoke enthusiastically about the Jewish presence there. Sympathy for Jewish settlers and the project of building a Jewish national home in Palestine was reproduced among the next two generations of leading Labour politicians, shaping the opinions of figures such as Hugh Dalton and Aneurin Bevan, Richard Crossman and Michael Foot. Following the Second World War, knowledge of Nazi crimes against the Jews generated further support for the Zionists. Moreover, despite hostile public statements, the Labour government quickly moved to recognize the new state of Israel. June Edmunds writes, "By 1956 Labour was the most pro-Israel of the [British] political parties": something the Suez crisis did not alter.[6] The Labour government and the Labour Party responded to the 1967 war with support for Israel. Official neutrality masked overwhelming partisanship within the cabinet while the party's members of Parliament (MPS) were unconstrained in expressing their sentiments. Indeed, by this time Labour Friends of Israel had grown to include two hundred Labour MPS–two-thirds of the parliamentary Labour Party.[7] It was not until after the 1973 war that some Labour Party constituency activists and the Labour left organized around the weekly newspaper *Tribune* called for Israel to withdraw to its pre-1967 boundaries, to cease building settlements on occupied land, and for Palestinians to be included in peace negotiations. Yet even this criticism remained a minority current easily marginalized by the party's leaders.[8]

Elsewhere—within the Soviet bloc and postcolonial states in the Third World as well as within revolutionary and extraparliamentary movements— criticisms of Israel became more influential and far-reaching. Most notably, on

　　　　　　　Feldman

November 10, 1975, UN General Assembly Resolution 3379 declared Zionism to be "a form of racism and racial discrimination" and was approved by seventy-two votes to thirty-five, with thirty-two abstentions.[9] In Britain, too, there were signs of support for anti-Zionism. By the end of 1977 revolutionary and radical activists in several British universities had used the National Union of Students policy of "no platform for racists" to try to restrict Zionist activity.[10] However, it was not until after Israel's invasion of Lebanon in 1982 that there was significant change within the Labour Party. Some constituency Labour parties and Labour-controlled local councils, especially in London and Scotland, now promoted perspectives and policies that supported the Palestinians. Trade union views also underwent a shift. The 1982 Trades Union Congress gave overwhelming support to a resolution censuring the "death and destruction" caused by Israel's invasion of Lebanon and called for recognition of Palestinian national rights. The same year, for the first time, the Labour Party's National Executive Committee adopted a resolution that called for direct negotiation with the Palestine Liberation Organization (PLO) and the creation of a Palestinian state.[11] By the 1980s, then, not only the Trotskyite left but also large sections of the mainstream left connected to the Labour Party and the trade unions stood in opposition to Israeli policy, expressed sympathy for the Palestinians, and supported, in the face of official Israeli opposition, the Palestinians' claim to national self-determination.

This development raises several historical questions; here I want to focus on just two. For, if criticism of Israel from the Labour Party and trade unions had become commonplace by the 1980s, it can prompt us to ask anew why things had ever been different. First, why did the mainstream British left support Zionism for so long? And, second, why did a more negative attitude to Israel develop from the early 1980s?

It is the second of these issues that has attracted most attention. There are three main explanations on offer. One sort of explanation gives causal primacy to changes in Israel. Paul Keleman argues that "the British left's realignment from support to an increasingly critical stance . . . has developed primarily in response to Israel's occupation of the West Bank and Gaza."[12] Shlomo Avineri proposes two developments as crucial in leading to decreasing support for Israel among those whom he terms "middle ground liberals." First, there was the victory in the 1967 war, which led to the circulation of images of Israeli soldiers as an occupying force. Second, he points to the change of government in 1977 and the accession to power of Likud.[13] The changes these writers highlight are significant. Nevertheless, we need to keep in mind that political opinion in Britain shifted decisively a decade and a half after the 1967 war and five years after the election of a government in which Likud was the predominant party. This suggests that we need to consider not only developments in the Middle East but also political culture in Britain and in Europe.

A second explanation does focus on British political culture and, in particular, emphasizes its susceptibility to antisemitism. According to Robert Wistrich, "since 1967 anti-Semitism has re-entered leftist discourse [in Britain] not only through its obsessive focus on the sins of Israel but its ideologically-driven singling out of Jews, Judaism and Zionism as dire impediments to revolutionary progress." By 1980, not only had "Britain's radical Left become explicitly or implicitly antisemitic in its demonization of Jews, its equation of Zionism with racism or Nazism and its malevolent undermining of any moral basis for Israel's existence" but "whole swathes of educated opinion in the media, British politics and academia... have bought heavily into this demonization of Israel and America."[14] Anthony Julius broadly agrees. Antisemitic anti-Zionism, he states, "first emerged in the late 1960s and early 1970s in consequence of the Six Day War, but became hegemonic in the 1990s and 2000s."[15] These accounts are poorly equipped to account for the major discontinuity in attitudes to Israel in the mainstream British left. Even if we were to agree that hostility to Israel in Britain since the 1980s has been invariably antisemitic, we would still face the challenge of accounting both for the rise of antisemitism at this time and, second, for the earlier sympathy that Zionism had evoked in the Labour Party from the First World War until the 1970s. Our original questions would not have been answered; they would merely have been reformulated.[16]

A third sort of explanation sensibly suggests we attend to the interaction of political developments in Britain with events in the Middle East in generating changing attitudes in the Labour Party and the Left more broadly. So far as Israel is concerned, these accounts proceed on familiar lines, pointing out the victories of the Israel Defense Forces in 1967 and of Likud a decade later. They also highlight the more aggressive settlement policy pursued after 1977 and Israel's production of nuclear weapons. When they turn to developments in Britain, however, they do not dwell on antisemitism but highlight a more general current of thought. Colin Shindler observes that "there was a gradual awakening in British society to the damage caused by colonialism."[17] June Edmunds, too, has pointed to the significance of "an ideological current... supportive of Third-World anti-colonialist movements and opposing American intervention."[18] In suggesting that recent attitudes to Israel are embedded in a more wide-ranging discourse on colonialism and its legacies, these scholars open a fruitful line for inquiry. Their argument that recent responses to Zionism are bound to the legacy of colonialism could lead us to ask a new question: does the imperial context also inform previous positive responses to Zionism on the British Left? Were these earlier outlooks also embedded in thinking about empire? The next section surveys the history of Labour Party support for Zionism and Israel in the context of ideas and arguments about empire. Having done so, I shall then ask to what extent recoil from empire and colonialism can help account for the criticism of Israel in the last decades of the twentieth century.

*   *   *

Political Zionism made its way in a world of empires. Theodor Herzl traveled from one imperial capital to another, trying to further his objective. The best he achieved was the ill-fated proposal from the British government that the Zionists purchase a part of Kenya.[19] It was the British who also gave the Zionists their second and greater success: the Balfour Declaration. This was further consolidated in 1922 when the League of Nations Mandate for Palestine carried forward the earlier British commitment to "the establishment in Palestine of a national home for the Jewish people." Zionism in the first half of the twentieth century became a fateful meeting point of Jewish history with the history of the British Empire.[20]

British governance in Palestine reverberated with the hopes and fears invested in empire from within the domestic political arena.[21] *A Socialist in Palestine* is a pamphlet published in 1922 by the leader of the Labour Party and future prime minister, Ramsay Macdonald. It illustrates the way in which Zionism conjoined domestic struggles with an imperial vision. Enthused by his visit to Palestine, Macdonald reflected on the similarity between the social conflicts he found there and those he knew in Britain: "I found changes with which I was familiar producing reactions with which I was equally familiar. The land of Palestine is held by large owners, and the same class has concentrated in its hands the employment of labour, and trade. More than that, it has ruled, collected taxes, led an obedient people. All this is threatened. Palestinian social economics has had its foundations removed by the ending of the Turkish occupation."[22] It was a struggle between privilege and monopoly on the one side, democracy and social justice on the other. These were the rhetorical oppositions that Labour summoned to rally a coalition of support at home and which Macdonald now invoked as he surveyed Palestine.[23] This sort of progressive politics was easily aligned with an elevated and moralized vision of Britain's imperial mission. It would be an error to assume that socialists and radicals in the Labour Party were invariably aligned with anticolonialists. Conservatives accused socialists of wanting to do away with the empire, but this was a misrepresentation: empire was the field in which many Labour politicians believed socialism could be applied.[24] Macdonald aligned Zionism with progress and the ethical mission of the British Empire. Opposition in Palestine to the British and their support for Zionism was identified by him with base self-interest. "The 'Moslem–Christian' deputations that come to state the case against the Jews, always at some point, attack the British Government more than the Jews. They rally the Arabs in their own sectional self-defence rather than that of the Arab people or of Moslemism. The wind of Europe is cutting in upon them and they cannot stand the blast."[25]

The connection between the interests of the empire and the promotion of the Jewish national home was commonplace among Labour politicians who considered the subject in the interwar years. For Josiah Wedgwood, the Labour MP for Newcastle, this became a political passion. In 1928 he published a book proposing that the Jewish national home should become the seventh dominion within the empire, and in the following year he inaugurated the Seventh Dominion League, with himself as chairman.[26] Wedgwood was a radical who had entered Parliament as a Liberal in 1906 and, along with many others, joined the Labour Party in 1919. His radicalism ran alongside an elevated understanding of imperial patriotism. In the preface to *The Seventh Dominion* he reflected on this conjunction:

> They will say on reading this book that I am an imperialist. That is not a charge that seriously perturbs a Labour Member of Parliament . . . if it be Imperialism to be convinced that the race that spread from, and came to, these islands is the finest on earth and in history, then I am an imperialist, though I hardly think that my reasons for the faith would appeal to the fascist, fox-hunting, nigger-kicking people who too often annex the name and tarnish the lustre.[27]

Wedgwood wanted to see a Jewish Palestine added to a British Commonwealth of free democratic nations. He discovered in Jews the same "traits" he was pleased to find among his own people: "an inclination to lend money and take risks, a passion for wandering over the earth, a dislike of working for a master (called independence) and a lamentable preference for the Old Testament with its doctrine of 'hit him first and hit him hard' to the New Testament and pacifism."[28] Not only were Jews and the English cast from a similar mold, Palestine had generated bonds of mutual interest. In part, these ties were commercial. Drawing a homely analogy to a South London railway hub, Wedgwood explained "Palestine is the Clapham Junction of the Commonwealth." It was the central point for air and rail communications and for oil pipelines. Crucially, however, commercial bonds were augmented by strategic ties. Arab opposition and Italian fascist imperialism in North Africa had left the Yishuv dependent on the British, and this was something that could be used to the empire's advantage: "Egypt does not want us; we have no friends there. Palestine is emphatically a place where we do want a friendly and efficient population—men on whom we can depend, if only because they depend on us."[29]

For Wedgwood, it was not only in Britain but also in Palestine and the empire more broadly where the antinomies of the radical political drama were played out. In a vision that was similar to Macdonald's, he described class conflict not along the lines imagined by Marx but between productive and unproductive classes: idle landowners and effete clerics who lived parasitically from the hard work of laborers, farmers, and capitalists. He was a lifelong follower of Henry George and an advocate of the taxation of land values. He understood hostility to Zionism, whether it emanated from the English and other Europeans in Palestine or from the Arabs, in terms of this overarching confrontation between modernity and archaism, between patronage and an informed, independent demos.[30] Arab resentment was dismissed. Muslim merchants were too busy making money to resent Jews and the fellaheen and town workers prospered. Opposition was orchestrated by a reactionary and corrupt leadership composed largely of the two very worst sorts of person in the moral universe of an English radical: Roman Catholics and absentee landlords.[31]

Wedgwood and his allies had a notable record of defending the interests of the Kenyan population against exploitation by white settlers who chose not to toil. But in this case the settlers were productive modernizers, and the indigenous population was composed of decadent Orientals not noble Maasai warriors. "To the Zionist," Wedgwood wrote, "Palestine is a land to be filled with prosperous settlers and teeming factories, the banner of the West pushed forward into the sleepy East."[32]

Wedgwood's vision of a Jewish national home nestling cozily within the British Commonwealth came to nothing. The League of Nations mandate required Britain to prepare Palestine for self-government, so Wedgwood's proposal opened up major international issues that no British government could easily contemplate.[33] Yet, if his scheme proved an outlier, Wedgwood's response to Jewish settlers, the Yishuv, and the Arab population was typical of Labour Party idealism in the 1920s and 1930s. Here the choices in Palestine were characterized as between innovation and custom, progress and backwardness. It was this secular vision, rather than the feeling for the Holy Land and its ancient people that was a legacy of evangelical Protestantism, that most shaped Labour thinking. To be sure, Ramsay Macdonald, when in Nazareth, mused that "after far wanderings I seem to have come home, for I feel as familiar with this place as I do with the benty hillocks of Lossiemouth."[34] But he also advised the Jewish trade unions in Palestine in these terms: "Do not come to us with the historic rights of an ancient people to Palestine. You must say you have come to solve the problem of labour and socialism. If the English workers know what you are doing in this field, this will have a greater impact than the argument about historic rights."[35] According to Macdonald, "the Arab population do not and cannot use or develop the resources of Palestine. . . . Palestine not only offers room for hundreds and thousands of Jews, it loudly cries out for more labour and more skill."[36] Arthur Creech Jones, who as secretary of state for the colonies after 1945 became the diffident accomplice of a policy devised by Ernest Bevin, called on the Labour Party conference in 1939 to reaffirm its support for "the establishment of a National Home in Palestine." The conflict there, he explained, was not one between Jews and Arabs but between "the new order which the Jews stand for in Palestine and the old crumbling feudal system for which a few rich Arab landlords stand."[37] Labour support for the mandate was easily accommodated with a vision of the empire as a global mission to extend modernity and social justice. Backing for the Jewish national home followed easily from this larger vision. It did not require and, indeed, rarely enjoyed a basis in an appreciation of Jewish nationalism and the Zionists' desire for a transformation in the Jews' collective existence.[38]

* * *

Labour Party support for the Zionists came under stress whenever the party had to take responsibility for the governance of Palestine. Yet, below the level of government, Labour Party sentiment continued to flow in support of Zionism. This is illustrated if we consider some of the policies and actions of the second Labour government between 1929 and 1931 and those of Labour in power after 1945.

The Labour government of 1929 faced a structural dilemma when it confronted the problem of governing Palestine. It envisioned its role as one in which it should be even-handed between Jews and Arabs.[39] However, this objective was fatally compromised by the way in which the goals of Zionism were written into the League of Nations mandate: goals that the party had embraced.[40] To be sure, the mandate tempered commitment to build a Jewish national home by also acknowledging the civil and religious rights of non-Jews. Nevertheless, the mandate and Labour Party policy recognized the historic connection of the Jewish people with Palestine and accepted that this was linked to their right to build there a national home. In other words, the British mandatory power's obligation and desire to be even-handed between Jews and Arabs in Palestine was qualified and at times overridden by its obligation to consider not only the Jews living in Palestine but also those Jews elsewhere who might want to live there. In the interwar years, this was a matter of strategic as well as ideological importance. In 1931 there were just 180,000 Jews in the Yishuv amid roughly 850,000 Arabs. For Zionists, continued immigration was the key to a viable future.

In 1929 tension between Arabs and Jews in Jerusalem erupted in violence as Arabs attacked Jews and the British police attempted to suppress the riots: 133 Jews and 116 Arabs died in the fighting. The colonial secretary, Lord Passfield, formerly Sidney Webb, appointed two investigating commissions. They concluded that the violence had been caused by Arab fears at the consequences of Jewish immigration and that there was insufficient agricultural land in Palestine to render mass Jewish settlement viable. These findings then gave shape to the white paper published in October 1930. By suggesting that Jewish immigration should be limited by the absorptive capacity of the economy in Palestine as a whole, and not just the Jewish portion, and by seeking to limit land sales to Jews, the new policy sought, in effect, to redefine the mandatory power's obligations. It tried to narrow Britain's commitment from one to the Jewish people as a whole to those among them currently living in Palestine, and it did so by giving precedence to social and political conditions in Palestine as a whole.[41]

Yet by February 1931 the Passfield White Paper had been overturned. In a letter to Chaim Weizmann, Prime Minister Ramsay Macdonald stated that the government neither contemplated any reduction in Jewish immigration nor any stop on land sales. Weizmann's intense diplomacy—a combination of charm and harassment directed at key ministers—provides a partial explanation for the reversal.[42] Equally significant was the political frailty of the Labour government that left it vulnerable to pressure from within and beyond the party. The government did not command a majority of votes in the House of Commons and, moreover, was struggling to retain unity in the face of economic crisis and rising unemployment. This gravely weakened its capacity to face down opposition among its own MPs and supporters. The prospect of a by-election for the Labour-held seat of Whitechapel, in the heart of the Jewish East End of London, heightened the capacity of Zionists to generate dissent that could weaken the minority government. In Parliament too, Labour MPs criticized the government's proposals. They vaunted the idealism of Jewish settlers who had successfully drained swamps, fought malaria, built towns, developed electricity, and brought "a new spirit to cultivation on the land" that benefited Jews and the fellaheen alike.[43] Not only did the party contain a well of sympathy for the Zionist project but also many MPs and supporters were strongly attached to the ideals of the League of Nations. The latter point was significant because the white paper appeared to step back from the terms of the Palestine Mandate. By aiming to "crystallize" the Jewish population in Palestine, it threatened to throw the Labour government into dispute with the League and its Permanent Mandates Commission.[44] Attachment within the Labour Party to Zionist goals had not prevented the Labour government from bringing forward the white paper; however, it did play an important part in the subsequent climb down.

The Labour government fell in 1931. A series of Conservative-dominated coalitions held power from that year until 1945. In the wake of the Arab revolt that commenced in 1936, Italian aggression in North Africa, and the growing likelihood of war in Europe, the British government's interests separated decisively from those of the Zionists. The strategic need for Arab support both in Palestine and throughout the Middle East led the British in 1939 to place a strict limit on Jewish immigration to Palestine: just 75,000 were to enter over the next five years. That year a new white paper stipulated that the Jewish population of Palestine had reached a level—450,000—that meant that a Jewish national home had been established. It looked forward to the creation of a binational state. It was thus not a Labour government but a Conservative-dominated administration that abandoned Britain's commitment to the mandate in a form that Zionists could accept.[45] In the House of Commons, Herbert Morrison, the dominant Labour figure in London who was to become home secretary in Winston Churchill's wartime coalition government, denounced the 1939 White Paper as "evil" and "a breach of faith."[46]

The Labour Party's policy for Palestine at this time was framed by its twin commitments to the Jewish national home and to reconciliation between "Arab and Jew." Support for Zionist ambitions ran alongside concern to raise "the extremely primitive [Arab] workers and peasants closer to the level of the Jews." To this end, in 1937 the Palestine subcommittee of the party's international department deprecated "communalism" and proposed a series of measures to promote collaboration between Jews and Arabs in both the economy and local self-government.[47] The imperial context remained a powerful element in Labour thinking on Palestine and provided the subcommittee grounds for optimism: "Analogies are dangerous and deceptive, but the situation is somewhat similar to that which existed in Canada when disruption was threatened owing to the antipathies political, cultural and religious between French and British Canadian and to that which existed between Boer and Britain in South Africa before and after the Boer War. In each case a remarkably successful solution was achieved by granting self-government and the blessed burden of responsibility to the antagonists."[48]

Victories in wartime stimulated visionary plans for reconstruction both at home and in the empire. The Jewish national home continued to figure in Labour's global vision. However, the contribution of national minorities to the outbreak of war in Europe, as well as conflict in India between Muslims and Hindus, radically diminished belief in the capacity of local self-government to overcome communal enmity. The Labour Party now entertained a more swingeing solution to the situation in Palestine. In 1944 the National Executive Committee document *The International Postwar Settlement* looked forward to the emergence of a Jewish majority created by means of Jewish immigration and transfer elsewhere for the Arab population.[49]

Yet, despite this continuing current of support for Zionist goals, when in 1945 the Labour Party returned to power, policy once again failed to reflect Labour's longstanding affinity with the Jewish national movement. Contrary to the hopes of Zionists, the government did not repudiate the 1939 white paper. Instead, British policy was guided by geopolitical considerations in the Middle East and by Britain's economic dependence on the United States. Even so, back-bench Labour MPs, free from the burdens of statecraft, remained ideologically committed to supporting the Jewish state.

Within weeks of taking office as foreign secretary, Bevin told Attlee, "Clem, about Palestine, according to the boys in the office we've got it wrong. We've got to think again."[50] There were compelling reasons to do so. The Middle East was the central point in a system of imperial communications with India, Australia, and the Far East, and it remained the empire's main reservoir of oil. The coopera-tion of Arab leaders and masses was a vital element in this strategic network. The transformation of the Jewish national home into a Jewish state, ministers feared, would have grave repercussions not only for Britain in the Middle East but also among Muslims in India. Indeed, it was India, not the future of the mandate in Palestine, that figured most powerfully in the government's deliberations. Within these constraints, Labour government policy was to maintain order and to be even-handed.[51] Responding in Parliament to criticism from the Zionist Labour MP Sidney Silverman, the prime minister answered tartly, "One would almost have thought from Mr. Silverman's speech that we were in Palestine in partner-ship with the Jewish Agency."[52]

Attlee's response reflected the way the relationship between Zionism and the British Empire had been transformed. For the first two decades after the Balfour Declaration there were powerful connections between support for colonialism in the Labour Party and support for Zionism. For a figure such as Weizmann, the alignment of British imperial and Zionist interests was the key to success. The 1939 White Paper and the peril to Europe's Jews following the outbreak of war changed all of this. With David Ben-Gurion now the dominant figure, in 1942 the Zionist movement for the first time called for the creation of a Jewish common-wealth in Palestine, not merely a national home. Politically, Zionism ceased to be a movement seeking partnership with the leading colonial power. Ben-Gurion planned to effect a revolution.[53] The restrictions on Jewish immigration to Pales-tine imposed by the Labour government, the radicalizing effect on Zionism of the Nazi campaign against Jewish existence, and, from 1945, the congregation of so many remnants of European Jewry in displaced person camps, led Jews in Palestine to engage in armed rebellion as the British tried to prevent illegal im-migration. They were now engaged in an anticolonial war.[54]

Anglo-American relations added an insuperable difficulty for Attlee and Bevin as they confronted the Zionist insurgency in Palestine and refused demands to open Palestine to Jewish immigration. United States support for Jewish immigration to Palestine and for the Jews already there undermined the Labour government's negotiating position in Palestine. Yet the alliance with the United States was also the bedrock of Labour's postwar economic and international policy. Without US support, the policy of evenhandedness became impossible to sustain. It was with a sense of relief as well as failure that in February 1947 the government announced that responsibility for Palestine would be passed to the United Nations.[55]

And yet, despite the shifting dynamics of the Middle East and global power politics, backbench Labour MPs and the Labour Party's National Executive Committee continued to express support for Zionism.[56] Although the war had changed much, there remained a fundamental continuity insofar as Labour support for the Jewish national home emerged from a combined domestic and global vision of a moralized and socialist politics. *A Palestine Munich* is an uncompromisingly pro-Zionist pamphlet written in 1946 by the Labour MPs Richard Crossman and Michael Foot. Crossman was an Oxford don who taught philosophy and politics before he entered public life. Foot, a future leader of the Labour Party, had been one of three journalists who, in 1940, had written *The Guilty Men* under the pseudonym Cato. That book was a celebrated polemic that denounced fifteen politicians and public figures for their appeasement of Germany, Italy, and Japan. *A Palestine Munich* used the concept of appeasement to yoke Neville Chamberlain's discredited foreign policy of the 1930s to Britain's abandonment of the Balfour Declaration that had been implicit in the 1939 White Paper—"our first Middle Eastern Munich." More urgently, the pamphlet went on to link both of these prewar debacles to the postwar Palestine policy of the Labour government. Attlee and Bevin were accused of abandoning the Labour Party's consistent support for the development of "the National Home" "in order to purchase the friendship of the Mufti Ibn Saud and the other Princes and politicians who dominate Arab politics."[57] The main arguments turned on "the corrupt and undemocratic character of the feudal Arab leadership" and Labour's longstanding commitment to the Jewish national home, which the authors set out in great detail.[58] But in this respect Crossman and Foot were less concerned with the Jewish nation than with British honor. The Jews in Palestine should not be abandoned as Czechoslovakia had been at Munich. Any reflection on the Jews as a nation, their right to self-determination, or any other basis for Zionism is strikingly absent from the pamphlet.

Only with these considerations in mind can we understand Crossman's consistent support for Israel. His attachment was first to the activity undertaken in the Yishuv and then to the state of Israel rather than to the Zionist idea. When he actually encountered Zionists, while a member of the Anglo-American mission to Palestine in 1946, he disliked them as individuals but was drawn to their "strong, powerful, virile, socialist movement."[59] Insofar as he considered Jewish nationality at all, he regarded it as a contingent outcome of recent European history: "a Jewish nation has developed out of Hitler's persecutions in Europe today." Crossman claimed, "Those Jews who did not feel themselves members of a Jewish spiritual community perished in the concentration camps. It was the group that was explicitly and consciously Zionist which lived not merely physically but spiritually."[60] Whereas Crossman's response to Jews was equivocal, his identification with Zionism's civilizational mission was not. The Labour Party's postwar program to "build Jerusalem in England's green and pleasant land," instituting the welfare state and nationalizing the coalfields and railways, he believed, was a domestic variant of the Zionists' own ambitions for Jerusalem itself.[61] The postwar Labour government and the Yishuv shared this common-sense approach to socialism. The implicit point of contrast was the ideologically driven deformation of socialism in the Soviet Union. At the same time, democratic socialism in Israel provided Crossman a way of spreading the benefits of Western civilization without the evils that had befallen other settler peoples. "Why did the Jewish people in Palestine develop this collective form of society? Because they were determined neither to exterminate the indigenous people nor to exploit them. If they had permitted the enterprises in the country the free use of cheap Arab labour there would have been exploitation, there would have been the white settler with the backward people, and all the evils of which we are now having the legacy in our Colonial empire."[62] Crossman saw Zionism as an expression of the noble side of European colonialism. Its historic mission became fully apparent when considered alongside the disordered and backward state of Arab society.[63]

Labour support for Israel as a pioneer of progressive civilization and socialist practice in the Middle East proved easily transferrable from a Jewish national home located within the British Empire to an independent Jewish state. The burdensome mandate had gone, but Israel continued to demonstrate its superiority of Western over Arab society and, as a socialist society, it represented the very best of Western progress. At the party conference in 1955 Sam Watson, general secretary of the National Union of Mineworkers, speaking on behalf of the Labour Party's National Executive Committee, lauded Israel as a beacon of modernity and socialism in the midst of Arab reaction.

There is a socialist state growing up in the Middle East, and that socialist state contains within itself some of the finest creative impulses mankind has ever seen. If you want idealism go to the Negev and see the young men and women, some of them only

16 years old, making grass grow where it has never grown before. Go out and watch men who are giving up every possibility of high position, without thought of self or reward, and dedicating themselves to turning sand into soil. Go out and watch the greatest trade union organisation the world has ever seen—Histadruth—which owns and controls one third of Israel's economy and assists private enterprise by loaning money to develop other forms of control in industry. The state of Israel is a beacon of light in the Middle East. Here right on the verge of poverty and in the face of terrific exploitation, is a social experiment going on the like of which we have not seen before.[64]

In these postwar decades at the height of the Cold War, the prospect of Israel as a state that was both democratic and socialist served as an inspiration to many Labour MPs and trade unionists—an inspiration that the Israeli government and labor movement was able to consolidate through personal connections, visits, and links between the British Trades Union Congress and the Histadrut.[65] This was a moral and progressive global outlook that, so far as Labour was concerned, not only stood in contrast to the Soviet Union but also to the Conservatives' unprincipled devotion to oil that led them into alliances with "feudal rulers," and to threaten military intervention on their behalf in Jordan and Kuwait.[66]

* * *

Following the First World War, Zionism was colonialism, and that was precisely why the commitment to the Jewish national home received support from the Labour Party. Zionism was seen as an instance of the elevated colonialism that Labour espoused. This support for the Jewish national home did not stem from an appreciation of the necessity of Zionism for the Jews. Rather, Labour support for Zionism was based on the notion that Zionists were European colonists who brought a higher level of civilization to a part of the world that remained medieval in its level of economic development, its political organization, its religious practices, and its social organization. Under the mandate, this meant that British superintendence in Palestine was being used to promote economic progress and social justice. The fact that the Zionists appeared to combine technological progress with socialist organization, both on the kibbutzim and in the trade unions, rendered them especially attractive allies in Britain's global mission.

This longstanding political engagement with Zionism survived the decades of decolonization after the Second World War. Labour foreign policy in the Middle East, though necessarily shaped by strategic and economic interests, continued to be presented in idealistic and moralized terms. In 1967, as Arab armies retreated in the face of the Israel Defense Force, Raymond Fletcher, MP for a safe Labour seat in Derbyshire, told the House of Commons, "I support the socialist dockers of Haifa, the socialist builders of Beersheba, the socialist farmers on the shores of the Galilee, the socialist major of Nazareth, who has given his Arab people better houses and better conditions than they would get in Jordan."[67] In October 1973 the Conservative government responded to the Egyptian and Syrian assault on Israel by suspending arms shipments to Israel, Egypt, and Jordan. The breach of contract hit Israel the hardest and was, among other things, an attempt to forestall an oil embargo by Arab states. Harold Wilson, the leader of the Labour Party, declared his opposition to government policy, and in the House of Commons on October 18, more than two hundred Labour MPs voted against the suspension. Although fifteen Labour MPs did support the arms embargo and seventy others abstained, the pro-Israel consensus in the party remained unassailable. Wilson dismissed from the shadow cabinet Andrew Faulds, the most senior and vocal pro-Arab Labour MP. Moreover, Faulds's attempt to register the Labour Middle East Council, a group of MPs sympathetic to the Arab states, as a society affiliated of the Labour Party was disallowed on the ground that its goals were contrary to those of the party.[68]

The parliamentary debate on the embargo was notable for a series of fervent statements of faith in Israel as a democratic and socialist state. However, now—as the Labour Party's aspirations to transform British society were undermined by electoral defeats and the nation's economic frailty—for Charles Pannell, an MP for a predominantly working-class constituency in Leeds, Israel provided a glimpse of what Britain might look like one day. "I passionately believe in the State of Israel . . . it is a democratic Socialist State. When I went there I marvelled because so many of the things that we in this country see as dim in the future are coming true there now. I recognise the dynamism of its citizens who serve not only in war but in peace too. One of the things that we lack in this country is that we do great things in time of war but appear to disunite in times of peace."[69] Harold Wilson too expressed his support for Israel in elevated language. The mission to bring civilization to the torpid Orient was here articulated as a project for social democracy: "Israel is a democratic socialist country. More than that, it is a community with a national wealth as well as national burden shared in common. It is a country which, despite her prodigious arms burden, has established a remarkable record in social services and care for better facilities for educating Arabs than they ever had before 1967. . . . Therefore I believe that something is owed by some of us to the only democratic social State in that region."[70] For these Labour MPs, support for Israel was both ideological and contingent. They did not support Israel in the first instance because they were committed to building the Jewish nation. They were sympathetic to Zionism because Israel was a democratic socialist state. In a telling vignette, a decade later Wilson refused an invitation issued to attend a "World Assembly" in Israel to celebrate the fortieth anniversary of the defeat of Nazism. "This is not a political occasion but . . . [an] assembly of Israelis—not me," he complained to his secretary.[71] It was not Israelis in general but the socialists among them to whom Wilson felt attached.

If Labour Party support for Zionism emerged from a synthesis of progressive politics, colonialism, and Orientalism, does it then follow that the rising tide of criticism directed at Israel since the 1980s from the British Labour Party reflects the changing relationship of the Left to Britain's colonial past, as some historians have argued?[72] There is some evidence that supports this interpretation. The critique of Israel as an illegitimate, colonialist, and inherently racist state was an argument made among the Marxist, revolutionary, and radical Left from the 1960s onward. By the 1980s we can find this view articulated by some Trotskyite groups that had infiltrated the Labour Party.[73] More significant was the emergence of a new cohort of middle-class Labour Party activists, with bases of strength in local government, and trade union militants. They gained momentum from what they saw as the shortcomings of the Labour governments of the late 1970s, and they were provoked into campaigns of protest and resistance by the victory of the Conservative Party led by Margaret Thatcher in the general election of May 1979 and the rapid rise in unemployment in the early 1980s. In London, the new Labour leader of the Greater London Council, Ken Livingstone, argued that Labour had to gather support beyond the organized working class. Within this political context Labour sought alliances with an array of single-issue campaigns—for example, the campaigns in favor of nuclear disarmament, lesbian and gay rights, and a united Ireland, as well as those that mobilized against racism at home and apartheid in South Africa. The Palestinian cause gathered support in this environment of militancy and mobilization. It was a milieu in which there were some expressions of categorical anti-Zionism as well as some instances, notably in the wake of the invasion of Lebanon, when Israel's policies were likened to those of Nazi Germany.[74]

Yet neither categorical anti-Zionism nor antisemitism figured in the greater part of the criticism directed at Israel from the Labour Party in these years. The continuing belief of the Labour left in the legitimacy of Israel was made clear in a 1984 interview with the Labour MP Tony Benn, published in the Labour Movement Campaign for Palestine *Newsletter*. In the 1980s Benn was a talismanic figure on the Labour Left who strived to ally the party with the militant extraparliamentary opposition to the Conservative government led by Thatcher. Inevitably this brought him into contact with the revolutionary left. The interview published in the newsletter was an example of one such contact. Benn's interlocutors tried to persuade him that Israel and Zionism have "always acted . . . as an ally of imperialism." Benn had resigned from Labour Friends of Israel two years earlier, yet he refused to disavow the state. He maintained, "I am in favour of a Jewish state and I believe the Jews are entitled to have security in Israel. I don't believe that a criticism of individual items of policy can be used to see Israel destroyed." He went on to reject the idea of a binational state. He firmly believed the Jews were entitled to a land of their own.[75] Benn's position was that Palestinians as well as Jews required self-determination and a homeland.

This was not anti-Zionism in any meaningful sense of the term. The notion that these years witnessed "a divorce" between Zionism and the British Labour Party is misleading. Historians who claim that the Labour Party's anti-Zionism has been shaped by the anticolonialism of the New Left or, indeed, by antisemitism provide an explanation for a phenomenon that did not take place to any great extent. Labour Party discourse on Israel in the early 1980s was characterized not by anti-Zionism or antisemitism but by growing and increasingly vocal support for a Palestinian state as a goal and for direct negotiations with the PLO as the means to that end. We have already noted that in 1982 the party's National Executive Committee declared itself in favor of both. In 1988 and 1989 the Labour Party conference approved motions, brought forward in the context of the First Intifada, that called for recognition of the Palestinian *and* Israeli peoples' right to self-determination.

The legitimacy accorded both to the claims of the Palestinians and of the PLO to represent them extended far beyond the revolutionary left and its allies in the Labour Party. By 1983 the influence of Benn's supporters on policy making had been checked, and by the end of the decade commitments to withdrawal from the European Economic Community and to unilateral nuclear disarmament had been abandoned. Yet support for a Palestinian state and criticism of Israel continued to flourish and extended to leading figures on the right wing of the Labour Party such as Denis Healy and Gerald Kaufman.[76]

Criticism of Israel's policies and support for the Palestinians was shared widely across the political spectrum. In 1980 the European Economic Community Venice Declaration, signed by the British Conservative government among others, had recognized the Palestinians' right to self-determination, criticized Israeli settlements in the occupied territories, and saw a necessary role for the PLO as the representative of the Palestinian people.[77] Nevertheless, in the case of the Labour Party, support for the Palestinians had a particular coloring. It was conveyed in language that decried injustice and expressed the continuing significance in the Labour Party of a desire to moralize and improve the world.

It is perhaps not surprising that 1967 did not immediately shake the Labour Party's support for Israel. The war's devastating success seemed only to confirm

Israel's status as a beacon of modernity in a sea of underdevelopment. By the 1980s, however, resistance to occupation, from both within and beyond Israel's borders, and the response to this resistance by the Israel Defense Forces meant that to most in the Labour Party, Israel no longer seemed a credible vehicle for the material and moral improvement of the Middle East. In 1988 Gerald Kaufman, the Labour Party's leading spokesman on foreign affairs declared "we [Labour] should express our solidarity with the Palestinian people in their struggle. I have been to the West Bank and Gaza and in the town and the camps and I have seen that struggle at first hand. . . . We condemn the brutality with which Israeli forces are attempting, but failing, to suppress the [Palestinian] uprising."[78]

The continuing significance of a desire to infuse Britain's international role with a moral dimension became clear in 1997 when the Labour Party next formed a government. The new foreign secretary, Robin Cook, issued "a mission statement." Cook's intention, he explained, was "to make Britain once again a force for good in the world." The statement itself promised to work "to spread the values of human rights, civil liberties and democracy which we demand of ourselves."[79] This was the language of liberalism and of individual rights, not of the postcolonial New Left. Its capacity to inform criticism of Israel and support for Palestinians became clear when Cook traveled to Israel in March 1998. Cook insisted on visiting Har Homa, a hilltop on the edge of East Jerusalem and the site for a new Jewish settlement. Shortly before arriving in Israel, Cook had made clear his conviction that "settlement expansion is wrong" and had lamented the decline in Palestinian living standards since the Oslo Accords had been signed. The visit to Har Homa was decried by the Israeli government spokesman and by Binyamin Netanyahu, the prime minister. They perceived correctly that Cook had enacted a piece of theater designed to demonstrate solidarity with the Palestinians in the face of Israeli policy.[80]

The Labour Party became increasingly critical of Israel because the state had departed from ideals that, rightly or wrongly, the party had long invested in the Jewish national home. This was neither antisemitism nor anticolonialism. In many cases it was disappointment at hopes dashed. It stemmed not from a perception of Jews or of Israel as fundamentally different—either because they are Jews or neocolonialists—but from an identification with Israel as a progressive and modern state and a sense that that identification had been betrayed. Anticolonialism, then, reveals relatively little of the reasons why the British Left turned against Israel in the 1980s. Colonialism and its legacies, however, can tell us much about something that now seems strange: why the British Left ever identified itself with the Jewish national home in the first place.

Notes

1. Archibald Thornton, *The Imperial Idea and Its Enemies: A Study in British Power* (London: Macmillan, 1959).

2. Beatrice Webb, *The Diary of Beatrice Webb*, vol. 4, *1924–43: The Wheel of Life*, ed. Norman and Jeanne Mackenzie (London: Virago, 1985), 190.

3. Brockway, quoted in Stephen Howe, *Anticolonialism in British Politics: The Left and the End of Empire, 1918–1964* (Oxford: Clarendon, 1993), 149.

4. Joseph Gorny, *The British Labour Movement and Zionism, 1917–48* (London: Totowa, 1983), 7.

5. David Reynolds, *Britannia Overruled: British Policy and World Power in the 20th Century* (London: Longman, 1991), 103; and James Renton, *The Zionist Masquerade: The Birth of the Anglo-Zionist Alliance, 1914–1918* (New York: Palgrave Macmillan, 2007).

6. June Edmunds, "The Evolution of British Labour Party Policy on Israel from 1967 to the Intifada," *Twentieth Century British History*, 11, no. 1 (2000): 23–41.

7. J. Edmunds, *The Left and Israel: Party Policy Change and Internal Democracy* (Basingstoke: Macmillan, 2000), 66.

8. Ibid.; See too William Roger Louis, "The Ghost of Suez and Resolution 242," in *The 1967 Arab-Israeli War: Origins and Consequences,* ed. William Roger Louis and Avi Shlaim, 219–46 (Cambridge: Cambridge University Press, 2012). On *Tribune,* see James R. Vaughan, " 'Keep Left for Israel': *Tribune,* Zionism and the Middle East, 1937–67," *Contemporary British History,* 27, no. 1 (2013): 1–21.

9. United Nations General Assembly, Resolutions adopted by the General Assembly during its Thirtieth Session, accessed 4 July 2016, http://www.un.org/documents/ga/res/30/ares30.htm.

10. Dave Rich, "Zionists and Anti-Zionists: Political Protest and Student Activism in Britain, 1968–86" (Ph.D. diss., Birkbeck, University of London, 2015).

11. Edmunds, "Evolution of British Labour Party Policy," 30–32.

12. Paul Keleman, *The British Left and Zionism: History of a Divorce* (Manchester: Manchester University Press, 2012), 203. The interpretation offered in this essay differs from Keleman's in some significant respects, as I indicate in the notes, but it is similar in others. It is all the more important, therefore, to acknowledge that Keleman's important book stands as the most extensively researched work on the subject.

13. Shlomo Avineri, "Western Anti-Zionism: The Middle Ground," in *Anti-Zionism and Antisemitism in the Contemporary World,* ed. R. Wistrich (New York: New York University Press, 1990), 173–74.

14. Robert S. Wistrich, *A Lethal Obsession: Anti-Semitism from Antiquity to Global Jihad* (New York: Random House, 2010), 383, 386.

15. Anthony Julius, *Trials of the Diaspora: A History of Anti-Semitism in England* (Oxford: Oxford University Press, 2010), 441. See also G. Alderman, *The Jewish Community and London Politics, 1889–1986* (London: Routledge, 1989), 117.

16. These accounts also betray a weak understanding of the British Left. Wistrich, for example, pays inordinate attention to marginal Trotskyite groups such as the Workers Revolutionary Party and their Libyan-funded newspaper *News Line.*

17. Colin Shindler, *Israel and the European Left: Between Solidarity and Delegitimization* (London: Continuum, 2011), 244.

18. Edmunds, "Evolution of British Labour Party Policy," 34; see also *Left,* 2012, p. 244; and Toby Greene, *Blair, Labour and Palestine: Conflicting views on Middle East peace after 9/11* (New York: Bloomsbury Academic, 2013). Keleman, in *The British Left,* dwells neither on political culture nor on issues connected to empire. Instead he offers an interpretation that places emphasis on organization: in this case on the rise and fall of the influence of Poale Zion as an affiliated society within the British Labour Party. Keleman, however, does not manage to demonstrate the impact of Poale Zion either on Labour Party thinking or policy making. There is a need for more research on this point.

19. The proposal was ill-fated not only because the Zionists turned down the offer but also because it has been forever misnamed the "Uganda" offer, perhaps because of the proximity to the Uganda railway of the first parcel of land the British offered. Robert Weisbord, *African Zion: The Attempt to Establish a Jewish Colony in the East Africa Protectorate, 1903–1905* (Philadelphia: Jewish Publication Society of America, 1968).

20. More broadly on this point, see Derek J. Penslar, "Is Zionism a Colonial Movement?," chapter 12 of the present volume.

21. On British policy, see Bernard Wasserstein, *The British in Palestine: The Mandatory Government and the Arab-Jewish Conflict, 1917–1929* (London: Royal Historical Society, 1978); and Rory Miller, ed., *Britain, Palestine and the Empire: The Mandate Years* (Farnham, UK: Ashgate, 2010).

22. James Ramsay MacDonald, *A Socialist in Palestine* (London: Jewish Socialist Labour Confederation Poale-Zion, 1922). I am very grateful to Andrew Whitehead for allowing me to see his copy of this pamphlet. On Labour ideology and Zionism in this period, see Paul Keleman, "Zionism and the British Labour Party, 1917–39," *Social History* 21 (1996): 71–87.

23. Jon Lawrence, "Labour and the Politics of Class," in *Structures and Transformations in Modern British History*, ed. David Feldman and Jon Lawrence, 237–61 (Cambridge: Cambridge University Press, 2011).

24. On this, see Thornton, *The Imperial Idea*, 276–78; Gregory Claeys, *Imperial Sceptics: British Critics of Empire, 1850–1920* (New York: Cambridge University Press, 2010), chap. 2; and David Fieldhouse, "The Labour Governments and the Empire-Commonwealth," in *The Foreign Policy of the British Labour Governments, 1945–51*, ed. Ritchie Ovendale (Leicester: Leicester University Press, 1984).

25. Macdonald, *A Socialist in Palestine*.

26. Josiah Wedgwood, *The Seventh Dominion* (London: Labour Pub. Co., 1928). See also Norman Rose, "The Seventh Dominion," *Historical Journal* 14, no. 2 (1971): 397–416; and Paul Mulvey, *The Political Life of Josiah C. Wedgwood: Land, Liberty and Empire, 1872–1943* (Woodbridge, UK: Boydell, 2010). I have also learned from Arie Dubnov, "The Dream of the Seventh Dominion: British Liberal Imperialism and the Palestine Question," unpublished paper.

27. Wedgwood, *The Seventh Dominion*, ix.

28. Ibid., 2.

29. Ibid., 3–4.

30. Wedgwood reserved special contempt for missionaries "whose very environment and profession makes them anti-Jew if not anti-Semite. Their every political instinct is against the new prospects opening up for the land that they have made their own. To them Palestine is the Holy Land, a land of shrines and memories, to be preserved, as it was in the time of Our Saviour, unsullied by modernism and materialism." Ibid., 5.

31. Ibid., 10. On Catholic landownership among Arabs, see Seth J. Frantzman and Ruth Kark, "The Catholic Church in Palestine/Israel: Real Estate in *terra sancta*," *Middle Eastern Studies* 50, no. 3 (2014): 370–96.

32. Ibid., 7.

33. Rose, "The Seventh Dominion," 403.

34. Macdonald, *A Socialist in Palestine*, 9

35. Quotation in Gorny, *British Labour Movement*, 33–34. The significance of Christian Zionism in shaping British responses Zionist ambitions up to 1917 is a point of controversy. For contrasting views, see Eitan Bar-Yosef, *The Holy Land in English Culture, 1799–1917: Palestine and the Question of Orientalism* (Oxford: Clarendon, 2005); and Donald Lewis, *The Origins of Christian Zionism: Lord Shaftesbury and Evangelical Support for a Jewish Homeland* (Cambridge: Cambridge University Press, 2010). The point here, however, concerns the influence—or lack thereof—of forms of nonconformist Christianity within the interwar Labour Party. In addition to Macdonald's comment we can note that Ernest Bevin's years as Baptist Sunday school teacher and lay preacher did not leave a proto-Zionist imprint. C. Wrigley, "Bevin,

Ernest (1881–1951)," in *Oxford Dictionary of National Biography* (Oxford: Oxford University Press, 2004), online edn., 2008.

36. Macdonald, *A Socialist in Palestine*, 18.

37. Schneour Levenberg, *The Jews and Palestine: A Study in Labour Zionism* (London: Poale Zion, 1945), 234.

38. Aside from Keleman's *The British Left and Zionism*, the most detailed account of the relationship of British socialists to Zionism is Gorny's *The British Labour Movement and Zionism*, which provides a valuable and detailed account of attitudes and policies within the Labour Party. However, Gorny's view that "British labour's relationship with Zionism was founded not on general socialist principles but on sympathy on the part of the British" stands in contrast to the argument presented here and is based on a misunderstanding of what socialism signified in Labour Party circles. See Gorny, *British Labour Movement*, xii–xiii.

39. In this regard there was a fundamental continuity with preceding policy. See Wasserstein, *British in Palestine*.

40. On the League of Nations and the mandate see Susan Pedersen, *The Guardians: The League of Nations and the Crisis of Empire* (Oxford: Oxford University Press, 2015); Natasha Wheatley, "Mandatory Interpretation: Legal Hermeneutics and the New International Order in Arab and Jewish Petitions to the League of Nations," *Past and Present*, vol. 227, no.1 (2015): 205–48.

41. Michael Joseph Cohen, *Britain's Moment in Palestine: Retrospect and Perspectives, 1917-48* (London: Routledge, 2014), 216–28.

42. Chaim Weizmann, *The Letters and Papers of Chaim Weizmann*, vol. 15, series A, *October 1930–June 1933*, ed. Camilio Dresner (New Brunswick, NJ: Transaction, 1978).

43. Parliamentary Debates: Official Report, fifth series, Commons, 1930–31, vol. 245, (London: Her Majesty's Stationery Office), 148, 183–84; and Geoffrey Alderman, *The Jewish Community in British Politics* (Oxford: Clarendon, 1983), 112–14.

44. Cohen, *Britain's Moment in Palestine*, 229–35; Carly Beckerman-Boys, "British Foreign Policy Decision-Making Towards Palestine During the Mandate (1917–1948): A Polihueristic Perspective" (Ph.D. thesis, University of Birmingham, 2013), 136–73; and Susan Pedersen, "The Impact of League Oversight on British Policy," in *Palestine, Britain and Empire*, ed. Rory Miller, 39–65 (Farnham, UK: Ashgate, 2010).

45. Cohen, *Britain's Moment in Palestine*, 300–304.

46. Parliamentary Debates, Commons, 1938–39, 347, col. 2143–44.

47. Labour Party Archive, People's History Museum Manchester, Labour Party Advisory Committee on Imperial Questions. "Palestine," Miss A. Susan Lawrence, January 1937; and Palestine Sub-Committee, Memorandum adopted at the House of Commons February 10th 1937. While Keleman claims in *The British Left and Zionism* that Poale Zion strongly influenced the formation of Labour Party thinking on Palestine, these committee papers only provide evidence that Poale Zion was consulted, but nothing more than that.

48. Labour Party Advisory Committee on Imperial Questions. "Palestine," Miss A. Susan Lawrence, January, 1937; Palestine Sub-Committee, Memorandum adopted at the House of Commons February 10, 1937.

49. Ben Pimlott, *Hugh Dalton* (London: J. Cape, 1985), 389–91.

50. Quoted in Kenneth Harris, *Attlee* (London: Methuen, 1982), 390.

51. Alan Bullock, *Ernest Bevin, Foreign Secretary, 1945–51* (New York, Norton, 1983), 168–71, 254–58.

52. Quoted in Harris, *Attlee*, 394.

53. Ritchie Ovendale, *Britain, the United States and the End of the Palestine Mandate, 1942–1948* (Woodbridge, UK: Boydell, 1989).

54. Alan Bullock, *Ernest Bevin, foreign secretary, 1945–51* (London, 1983), 47.

55. Ibid., esp. 171, 366–67.

56. See the report of the National Executive Committee lobbying ministers Central Zionist Archives, Z4/302/30, reproduced in Michael Joseph Cohen, ed., *The Rise of Israel: A Documentary Record from the Nineteenth Century to 1948*, vol. 31 (New York: Garland, 1987), 166.

57. Richard Crossman and Michael Foot, *A Palestine Munich?* (London: Gollancz, 1946), 7, 29.

58. Ibid., 4–6.

59. Middle East Centre Archive, Oxford, Crossman, RHS GB165-0068, file 1/101, The Palestine Report—address given at Chatham House, June 13, 1946.

60. Richard Crossman, *An Englishman Looks at Palestine* (Johannesburg: S.A. Zionist Federation, 1950), 5–6.

61. The quote comes from the concluding lines of William Blake's poem "Jerusalem" and was used as a campaign slogan by the party in the 1945 general election.

62. Crossman, *An Englishman*, 18–19.

63. Crossman and Foot, *A Palestine Munich*, 25.

64. Watson quoted in John Callaghan, *The Labour Party and Foreign Policy: A History* (London: Routledge, 2007), 231.

65. Edmunds, *The Left and Israel*, 71–72.

66. Callaghan, *The Labour Party*, 235–36.

67. Edmunds, *The Left and Israel*, 71–72.

68. Keleman, *British Left and Zionism*, 162; and Vaughan, " 'Keep Left,'" 14.

69. Parliamentary Debates, Commons, 1972–73, 5th series, vol. 861, col. 484–85.

70. Ibid., col. 440.

71. Bodleian Library, Special Collections, Harold Wilson papers, c 1629, November 15, 1984, Israel.

72. In addition to those mentioned above, see Greene, *Blair, Labour and Palestine*, 40.

73. June Edmunds, "The British Labour Party in the 1980s: The Battle over the Palestinian Israeli Conflict," *Politics* 18, no. 2 (1998): 114.

74. Edmunds, *The Left and Israel*, 87–89, 95–107; Geoff Eley, *Forging Democracy: the History of the Left in Europe, 1850–2000* (Oxford: Oxford University Press, 2002), 461; and Alderman, *The Jewish Community*, 125–36.

75. "Labour Party Campaign for Palestine," *Newsletter*, no.1 (1984): 3.

76. Edmunds, *Israel and the Left*, 105; and Martin Pugh, *Speak for Britain! A New History of the Labour Party* (London: Bodley Head, 2010), 372–82.

77. Greene, *Blair, Labour and Palestine*, 20.

78. Kaufmann, quoted in ibid., 40.

79. Cook, quoted in Mark Wickham-Jones, "Labour's Trajectory in Foreign Affairs: The Moral Crusade of a Pivotal Power?" in *New Labour's Foreign Policy: a New Moral Crusade?*, ed. Richard Little and Mark Wickham-Jones, 3–32 (Manchester: Manchester University Press, 2000), 3, 9–11. The best account of Labour and Israel in the Blair years can be found in Tom Cordiner, "Zionism and Political Culture since 1945" (PhD thesis, University of Cambridge, 2012).

80. Rosemary Hollis, *Britain and the Middle East in the 9/11 Era* (London: Chatham House, 2010), 73–74; and "Middle East: Robin Cook to Go Ahead with Housing Project Visit," video, March 16, 1998, AP Archive, http://www.aparchive.com/metadata/MIDDLE-EAST-ROBIN-COOK-TO-GO-AHEAD -WITH-HOUSING-PROJECT-VISIT-2-/90a914c284d7d38a6333cdc809a23fd8?query=MIDDLE +EAST&current=5&orderBy=Relevance&hits=1622&referrer=search&search=%2Fsearch%3Fquery% 3DMIDDLE%2520EAST%26allFilters%3DHosni%2520Mubarak%3APeople&allFilters =Hosni+Mubarak%3APeople&productType=IncludedProducts&page=1&b=a23fd8.

10

VICHY IN MOROCCO

THE RESIDENCY, MOHAMMED V, AND
HIS INDIGENOUS JEWISH SUBJECTS

Daniel Schroeter

In May of 1941 René Touraine, a journalist from the Agence française d'information de presse, sent a telegram to Vichy about the mounting tensions between the sultan of Morocco Mohammed Ben Youssef and the French Protectorate authorities since the implementation of the anti-Jewish measures:

> We have learned from a reliable source that the relations between the Sultan of Morocco and the French authorities have been quite tense since the day the residency [the central Protectorate administration] applied the decree concerning the "measures against the Jews," despite the formal objection of the Sultan. The Sultan had refused to distinguish between his subjects, saying that all were "loyal." Annoyed at seeing his authority thwarted by the French authorities, the Sultan decided to show publicly that he rejected the measures against the Jews: he waited for the Throne Day (*fête du trône*) to do so. On that occasion, it was the custom for the Sultan to hold a great banquet that was attended by French officials, and distinguished Moroccan natives. For the first time, the Sultan invited representatives of the Jewish community to the banquet and placed them prominently in the best seats, right next to the French officials. The Sultan had wanted personally to introduce the Jewish individuals present. When the French officials expressed their surprise at the presence of Jews at the meeting, the Sultan told them: "I in no way approve of the new anti-Semitic laws and I refuse to be associated with any measure of which I disapprove. I wish to inform you that, as in the past, the Jews remain under my protection and I refuse to allow any distinction to be made between my subjects."
>
> This sensational declaration was highly commented on by the entire French and indigenous population.[1]

After the document was discovered in the Ministère des affaires étrangères archives at the Quai d'Orsay, Haïm Zafrani, a leader of the Alliance israélite universelle in Morocco after independence and later a professor at the Université

Paris VIII–Vincennes and preeminent scholar of Moroccan Judaism, presented the document to the Royal Academy of Morocco in 1985, thus promoting the growth of an official narrative of Mohammed V's benevolence toward the Jews during World War II.[2] It is widely believed that the efforts of the sultan and future king of independent Morocco attenuated the impact of the Vichy-instigated antisemitic legislation that he himself had been obligated to sign.[3]

No corroborating evidence has been produced of this defiant declaration of the young sultan, a symbolic figurehead of the 'Alawid dynasty who was granted no real independent governing powers and who rubber-stamped royal decrees (*dahirs*) drafted by the French authorities. The mere presence of Jews for the first time at the Throne Day banquet following the implementation of the anti-Jewish Vichy laws would have been an act of defiance; the sultan's declaration could have been a cause for the French deposing him from the throne. The second-hand report itself appears to be well scripted, produced by a journalist in the French press service that served as an instrument of censorship and the controlled dissemination of German propaganda under Vichy.[4] It is plausible that Touraine may have had a hidden agenda to discredit the sultan by portraying him as rebellious and to embarrass the resident-general, Charles Noguès (note: he concluded the telegram with the remark that the "sensational declaration" had caused quite a stir). Many colonialists had long sought to rule Morocco more directly and saw the indigenous apparatus that had been created by the first resident-general, Marshal Hubert Lyautey, to be an encumbrance, while the initial, albeit hesitant, steps of the sultan in the 1930s in support of nationalism were construed as a challenge to colonial rule. Noguès saw himself in the Lyautey colonial school—considering Lyautey as his mentor—with its espoused respect for native traditions, which had been abandoned to a certain extent by the former's predecessors. Following in the Lyautey tradition, Noguès nurtured a close relationship with the young sultan, Mohammed Ben Youssef.[5] There was little love lost between Noguès and the Vichy authorities, though the latter probably saw him as an able administrator, and Noguès himself implemented Vichy's policy, including the anti-Jewish laws. The image of a defiant sultan flouting French authority could only discredit the resident-general, who staunchly supported the protectorate system and its policy of indirect rule. If indeed the event and declaration actually occurred as reported, Noguès would have had little interest in bringing it to the attention of the Vichy authorities. This might account for the lack of corroborating evidence in the archives, for nowhere in the nearly daily reports and documents sent to Vichy by the French Residency in Morocco, often signed by Noguès himself, is the incident of 1941 reported. Still, it is surprising that the incident received no other mention in the Protectorate archives, nor in the accounts of meetings with the sultan written by

Jewish leaders during the war years or after. Finally, Throne Day, which marked the accession of the Moroccan monarch, was on November 18, so if there were any kind of official banquet in May of 1941, it would have been for another occasion. This suggests that the whole story was a complete fabrication, a probability that has escaped scholars and public figures alike who cite the document uncritically as an accurate description of what happened.[6]

The frequent reference to the alleged Throne Day incident, whether or not it actually occurred, is a reflection of Moroccan national and Moroccan Jewish identity of recent decades. It forms also part of a larger debate regarding the position of Muslims, and especially Muslim Arabs, toward Jews and Nazi Germany in World War II, which in turn reflects the contemporary divide of the Israeli–Palestinian conflict. The polemics about Mohammed V's benevolence toward the Jews during World War II or, more generally, the argument over Muslims as "good" or "bad," which has shaped most of the interpretation of the Vichy period and the Jews of Morocco, tells us much about present political debates but obfuscates a more complex set of historical circumstances.[7]

A better understanding of the situation of the Jews of Morocco during World War II can be achieved if we shift our focus to the particular historical conjuncture of late colonialism and the emergence of nationalism in Morocco. The short-lived colonial Vichy regime marked a critical period during which the contradictions of colonialism, increasingly apparent at the twilight of French Empire, were being played out. As Eric Jennings writes about other parts of the empire: "Vichy's imperial episode represents at once the coming to power and the last spasm of essentialist French colonialism."[8] During the Vichy period in Morocco, Jews were situated at the nexus of a fourfold matrix of power: the Vichy government in metropolitan France and Algeria; the French residency; the sultan and Makhzan; and the Spanish protectorate authorities in the North. All four of these elements in the colonial power structure had differing or competing political agendas that shaped the way in which they positioned themselves with regard to Vichy's Jewish policy. As a consequence, the implementation of the anti-Jewish laws was contested and unevenly applied in Morocco.

The Statut des Juifs in Morocco

It is commonly understood that Vichy's anti-Jewish statutes of 1940–41 were willingly promulgated in Morocco by the French Protectorate authorities and reluctantly signed by the relatively powerless Sultan Mohammed Ben Youssef. This account of the residency dutifully implementing the anti-Jewish legislation of the central Vichy authorities, and of the sultan insisting on the protection of his Jewish subjects and attempting to impede the implementation of the statutes, belies a much more complicated reality.

While Morocco never fell under direct Nazi occupation, the French authorities of Morocco, as elsewhere in the French Empire, became a part of the Vichy government and thus the indigenous administration—the Makhzan and the 'Alawid dynasty—continued to be the instruments of French imperial control. Though Noguès considered resigning, he continued as resident-general, often clashing with Maxime Weygand, Vichy's delegate-general and commander in chief in Africa.[9] Noguès was first appointed resident-general in 1936 by the Popular Front government of Léon Blum to replace his right-wing and anti-Socialist predecessor, Marcel Peyrouton, whose tenure had lasted only a few months.[10] Although an authoritarian military man, Noguès was viewed with suspicion or even disdain by the French settler community who saw the resident-general during the Vichy period as associated with the old regime, and he was frequently denounced to Vichy and Weygand in Algiers.[11] Noguès, and much of his appointed French administration, did not share in the ideology of the "National Revolution" program espoused by Vichy's leaders and a significant segment of the French settler population, and resented what they considered to be the undermining of the residency's authority by the Vichy government, which they saw as dangerous for French rule in Morocco.

As chief representative of the Vichy government in Morocco, Noguès was obligated to implement the racist and discriminatory Statut des Juifs (Statute on the Jews, Jewish Statute, or Jewish Law) that was promulgated in France. But as defender of French imperial interests in Morocco, Noguès was concerned about the ramifications of the Vichy-instigated anti-Jewish laws. On the one hand, the residency saw these laws as disrupting the power structure and the economic and political interests on which the French Protectorate depended for maintaining its control of Morocco. On the other hand, European settlers (whose number had greatly increased after the colonial conquest[12]), who often supported the extremist antisemitic ideology of Vichy, considered the discriminatory legislation to be to their advantage, enabling them to eliminate Jewish competitors from professions and to seize expropriated Jewish property and assets, and therefore put pressure on the residency to fully implement the laws. The strategies pursued by Noguès and the residency, which appeared to be contradictory, reflected the tensions between the longer-term interests in maintaining French imperial control of Morocco and the immediate goals of the Vichy authorities in France and Algeria and their European settler supporters in Morocco.[13]

Short of resigning, the sultan had to sign the anti-Jewish *dahirs* but, like the residency, was concerned about how the laws would affect his own position. The sultan was also caught between opposing pressures. With only fictitious legislative powers, the little symbolic capital that the sultan had rested on his position as sovereign Muslim ruler "commander of the faithful" (*amir al-mu'minin*), of the sharifian (meaning descendant of the Prophet Muhammad) 'Alawid dynasty. The spiritual realm was one sphere of power where the 'Alawids were allowed some measure of real control by the French authorities, and conferring religious authority to the sultan in turn helped legitimize the protectorate system as a whole. As Islamic head of state, the sultan found his authority challenged by the anti-Jewish laws since they undermined his ability to fulfill his duty to protect his subjects, which included Jews. On a symbolic level, the ability of the Muslim ruler to protect his "weaker" subjects, the *dhimmis*, was the litmus test of his ability to rule. Through the legal separation of Jews from Muslims and the discriminatory laws that made *dhimmis* unprotected, the sultan became emasculated, deprived of his symbolic role as protector of his subjects. This came during a period when the sultan had begun to take the first tentative steps toward asserting himself as national leader. While some Muslims as well saw Jews as competitors and stood to gain in their exclusion from liberal professions and businesses, there is little evidence that the anti-Jewish laws were greeted with a clamor of support. So embedded were Jews in the economy of Morocco that their marginalization could also be seen as harmful to society as a whole.[14]

The *dahir* issued on October 31, 1940, applied the Vichy Statut des Juifs of October 3, 1940 (the Alibert law), which excluded Jews from a wide range of occupations and imposed the *numerus clausus* restricting the number of Jews in public schools.[15] Although there was a degree of flexibility in the Moroccan law, in particular in a provision that allowed Jews to hold positions in Jewish organizations and institutions, the *dahir* was similar to the Statut des Juifs in metropolitan France in most other respects. However, there was one significant and highly symbolic difference from the metropolitan law. The *dahir* defined a Jew as "(1) every Moroccan Jew (*israélite*) or (2) every non-Moroccan residing in this zone with three grandparents of the Jewish race or two grandparents of the same race if his or her spouse is also Jewish." In other words, the law distinguished between non-Moroccan Jews defined by race and Moroccan Jews defined by religion.[16] The crucial distinction from the French law was in the religious rather than racial definition of indigenous Moroccan Jews.

In his panegyric account of Mohammed V during Vichy, Robert Assaraf asserts that the time gap between the promulgation of the Alibert law of 1940 and its adaptation in Morocco was because of the sultan's opposition to the legislation. Knowing that the sultan was not in a position to refuse signing the *dahir*, Assaraf believes that the sultan nevertheless negotiated with Resident-General Noguès, resulting in the softening of the severity of the original text and the elimination of the racial definition for indigenous Moroccan Jews.[17]

Although the change from a racial to a religious definition of the Jews seems to have come at the last minute, it was unlikely the result of the sultan's influence.[18] No evidence has yet been discovered regarding what, if any, negotiation took place between Mohammed Ben Youssef and Noguès for the *dahir* of 1940. Though there may have been some consultation between the French residency and the Makhzan, there were also bureaucratic reasons that would have accounted for the delay: the time required to draft and translate the *dahir* to Arabic and to circulate drafts to the necessary administrative offices. More significantly, the promulgation of the anti-Jewish statute in Morocco as well as in Tunisia, which was also a French Protectorate, would have involved negotiations between the central Vichy government and the residencies. The logic of differentiating Moroccan (or Tunisian) Jews defined by religion and foreign Jews defined by race thus had less to do with concern for the welfare of the Jews than with preserving the existing legal hierarchies and categories of exclusion that would better serve the interests of colonial domination in the Protectorate. Had the racial definition been applied to Moroccan Jews, it would have challenged their legal status as "indigenous" subjects of the sultan by placing them in the same category as French or foreign Jews. This can account for why, in Algeria, legally considered a part of France, the Alibert law was applied without any modification, while in both the protectorates of Tunisia and Morocco, the racial definition, which had been originally proposed and part of the first drafts of the legislation, was changed. Transforming the way the Jews' indigenous status was determined would have undermined the foundations upon which the Protectorate rested.[19]

Maintaining Jews as indigenous subjects of the sultan was therefore an important organizing principle of the colonial authorities. The Jews' "indigenous" status in Morocco was based on a clause in the 1880 Madrid Convention that established the principle of "perpetual allegiance" to the sultan, often cited by legal scholars of the Protectorate to justify the Jews' exclusion from French nationality. The Madrid Convention of 1880, the outcome of a meeting in which European powers, in an unsuccessful effort to curb the abuse of the protection system (referred to in the Ottoman Empire as the "Capitulations"), introduced the principle of perpetual, inalienable allegiance (de facto nationality). This appeared in an article of the treaty that stated: "Every Moroccan subject naturalized abroad who shall return to Morocco must after a period of residence equal in time to that which was legally necessary to obtain naturalization, choose between his complete submission to the laws of the Empire and the obligation to leave Morocco, unless it be proven that the foreign naturalization was obtained with the consent of the Moroccan government."[20] This stipulation was the result of the growing number of Jews from Morocco obtaining foreign nationality abroad and then returning to Morocco with their newly acquired status as "foreigners," a development that the Moroccan authorities found particularly frustrating.[21] While at the time it did not entail any change in the Moroccan legal system or the development of the legal concept of citizenship, this article of the Madrid Convention did provide the principle from which the concept of Moroccan nationality was later to develop, which became the legal justification of the French for exclusion of Jews from acquiring French citizenship and maintaining their status as indigenous subjects of the sultan.

Anti-Jewish Legislation Intensifies

The colonial logic that was able to maintain the indigenous status of Moroccan Jews in the 1940 *dahir* was unable to withstand the intensification of Vichy antisemitic policy. The second anti-Jewish *dahir* of August 5, 1941, based on the Vallat law of June 2, 1941, replaced the Statut des Juifs of the previous year. It applied anti-Jewish discrimination with an even greater degree of severity, especially increasing the range and scope of professions from which Jews were excluded.[22] Importantly, the distinction between non-Moroccan Jews defined by race and Moroccan Jews defined by religion in the 1940 *dahir* was missing in the 1941 *dahir*. The definition of a Jew in the *dahir* replicated, verbatim, the metropolitan law, further tightening the racial criteria.[23]

Another *dahir*, promulgated on August 5, 1941, simultaneously with the new Jewish Statute, ordered a census of Moroccan Jews to be submitted to the pashas (urban governors) and *caids* (rural governors) of their place of residence, listing their civil and family status, profession, and property within three months.[24] The intention of this and other measures was the eventual expropriation ("Aryanization," as it was called) of Jewish property, which included the closure of various Jewish-owned commercial and industrial businesses.

These decrees were followed by other specific discriminatory *dahirs* and by vizierial ordinances further defining the anti-Jewish laws and specifying the time frame in which they were to be implemented. Particularly egregious was a *dahir* of August 19, 1941, which ordered Moroccan Jewish subjects to evacuate their residences in the European sectors of cities in one month's time if they were unable to prove that they had lived there before September 1939; those residing in the European sectors before 1939 would be ordered to evacuate their residences at a date to be established by the grand vizier. Exceptions were only made for individuals who had records of highly meritorious or decorated military service.[25]

The escalation of the anti-Jewish measures followed the creation of the Commissariat général aux questions juives (CGQ J), with Xavier Vallat at its

head. Noguès appointed a commission presided by the grand vizier, Mohammed El Mokri, and the minister plenipotentiary delegate to the general residency, Jacques Meyrier, to examine how to adapt the French law to Morocco.[26]
In the case of the second *dahir*, the negotiation between the residency and the
Makhzan, first through a commission with the long-term grand vizier and then
with the sultan, may only have been to gain the Makhzan's acquiescence to a
measure that some French officials in Morocco were reluctant to apply. After the
issuance of the new Jewish statute in France, Noguès appealed to Weygand to
consider maintaining the distinction between Moroccan and non-Moroccan
Jews as in the 1940 *dahir*. He also expressed concern about how the new laws
might impact the traditional economy and demanded specific stipulations that
there would be no restriction on the traditional occupations of Moroccan Jews.
Here Noguès underlined the economic impact if Jews were no longer allowed to
practice certain professions that Islam prohibited to Muslims and alluded to the
fact that interest is forbidden in Islam and thus Jewish moneylenders served an
important economic role as intermediaries.[27] Both the Vichy authorities in Algiers and the residency in Morocco acknowledged that a distinction needed to
be made between Moroccan and non-Moroccan Jews (French and foreign Jews)
and that, for the latter, the full extent of the French law would be applied without
any modification; but the residency believed that for the indigenous Moroccan
Jews, some adaptation and modification was needed. Indeed, Noguès assured
the president of the Jewish community of Casablanca and former inspecteur des
institutions israélites, Yahia Zagury, "that the need to establish for Moroccan
Jews a special status has not escaped notice of the Government of the Protectorate which is concerned with distinguishing between French Jews settled in Morocco and those who for centuries have been an integral part of the Moroccan
population." Noguès noted to Zagury that the concerns of the Jewish communities had been communicated to the Makhzan, with whom the Protectorate authorities were jointly working on drafting the texts of the *dahir* for the new Statut
des Juifs.[28] Another report, citing Noguès, further warned of the economic consequences of the measures if adopted: "Indeed, due to the religious prohibitions
and the traditional economy, the Muslims resort to the services of Jews for all
money trade, for anything concerning the concept of interest. Undermining this
age-old equilibrium of activities might cause a major disruption, in the absence
of Muslims who could fulfill the role previously played by Jews."[29] Although the
argument that only Jews were involved in the money trade was exaggerated and
reflected stereotypical notions of both the usurious Jew and the archaic inflexi-
bility of Islamic law—for Muslims as well found ways around the prohibition of
lending money with interest—there was a recognized reliance on Jews for
commerce and money-lending and a concern that their removal would be

devastating to the economic stability of the Protectorate, especially during wartime.[30]

The sultan shared with the residency the concern about the economic impact of the new measures. Reporting on holding court with the sultan, the French authorities explained that His Majesty raised questions about the professions from which Jews were now barred. But even more strongly, he objected to the redefinition of the Jews' status. For the sultan as "commander of the faithful," the most critical issue raised by a racial definition of Jews was that of Jewish-born converts to Islam. The sultan was reported to have argued that any legislative clause that defined the Jews' status would impact the question of conversion to Islam "and that his quality as the religious leader prohibits any possibility of legislating on this point." He argued that it would not be possible for him to discriminate between Muslims. To assuage the French advisor, however, he pointed out, in somewhat contradictory terms, that one should not exaggerate the danger of the conversions, since many of the professions forbidden to Jews were already prohibited by Muslim law, and that Moroccan Jews, once converting to Islam, lose all respect of the Jewish community.[31] While emphasizing his defense of Jewish converts to Islam, he also wanted to make clear in his appeal to the French authorities that, once Muslims, the converts would no longer maintain connections to the Jewish community, nor would they be able to continue to practice professions associated to Jews.

Assuming the sultan's arguments were well represented in the report, then his (somewhat muted) response did reveal something fundamental to his position. If the racial criteria were legislated, it would undermine the role of the sultan as Muslim ruler. Through its racial definition of Jews, which implied that Muslim converts and their offspring would be regarded as Jews and subject to the anti-Jewish legislation, the proposed statute challenged the sultan's sovereignty and even Islam itself. It also crossed a sacrosanct line: once embracing Islam, it was a taboo (formerly a capital crime) to revert back to one's old religion. The sultan's objection to defining Jews racially was not so much an antiracist stance in defense of the Jews, as some would have it, but a defense of Islam and Moroccan sovereignty.

The *dahir* of 1941 stripped the sultan of a symbolically important role as Muslim ruler: the protection of his *dhimmi* subjects. Literally, *dhimmi* signifies "a protected person," which refers to non-Muslims entitled to the protection of the Islamic state. In the absence of indigenous Christians in the Maghrib, *dhimmis* were understood to mean Jews. Intent on maintaining the Jews as indigenous subjects of the sultan, whose preservation, in turn, legitimized the Protectorate, the *dhimma* system had not been abolished. While the specific legal disabilities associated to *dhimmi* status in Islamic law—payment of the annual poll tax (*jizya*) and the various humiliating conditions specified in the Pact of Umar intended to symbolize the *dhimmis'* inferiority—stopped being applied after the colonial conquest of Morocco, this was by default rather than decree. The Protectorate authorities had greatly reduced, at least in theory, the powers of the Jewish and Muslim religious courts—rabbinical and sharia. In both cases, their competence was greatly limited, primarily to matters concerning personal status. Much of the power of the religious courts—both criminal and civil—was transferred to the governmental courts of the pashas (in the cities) and *caids* (in rural regions), expanding the jurisdiction previously enjoyed by the Makhzan courts, but now under the supervision and surveillance of the French colonial authorities. The result of these changes was that the Jews, while no longer subject to the humiliating disabilities of the *dhimma* system, also lost much of their previous juridical autonomy and complained about discrimination in the new Makhzan courts.[32]

In the early years of the Protectorate, many Moroccan Jewish leaders, especially among the French-educated elite, sought to obtain French citizenship, as their co-religionists in Algeria had achieved en masse by the Crémieux Decree of 1870. But the French colonial authorities, shaped by the first resident-general, Lyautey, were opposed because many had felt that the policy in Algeria had been a serious error—only fanning the flames of settler antisemitism—and in order not to provoke the opposition of the Muslim population, who might object to the Jews receiving privileged status. The idea, rather, was to rule the Moroccan population through discreet though nonetheless firm paternalistic control.[33] The French colonial authorities had little interest in either disrupting Morocco's symbolic religious hierarchy, or in undermining the very justification of the Protectorate, which was based on the contradictory principle of preserving the "*vieux Maroc*," which meant respecting the religious authority of Muslims and Jews while reforming the system at the same time.

Whatever misgivings Jewish community leaders had in their status as indigenous subjects in the colonial/Makhzan system, the changes wrought by the Vichy laws made things immeasurably worse. They were alarmed at the impending anti-Jewish legislation and warned of the long-term consequences for the future of French rule in Morocco were the measures adopted. Invoking their unflinching loyalty to France, they also saw the advantages of reclaiming their position as *dhimmi* subjects of the sultan. In a secret memorandum submitted by two high French officials to the resident-general, it was reported that the [Jewish leaders] "refrained from questioning the legal ground [of the laws] because of their unwavering devotion to France, but were aware that His Majesty, the Sultan, would be violating Islamic law if he were to ratify, by *dahir*, measures contrary to the letter and spirit of the Qur'an. Christians and Jews can, in effect, live in Muslim territory and exercise all of the non-canonical [non-Islamic] occupations, provided that they pay taxes and respect the Muslim religion."[34] Thus, while attesting to their loyalty to France, the Jewish leaders invoked their indigenous, *dhimmi* status and appealed to the economic arguments that the residency was making in favor of allowing Jews to continue to practice traditional occupations not allowed to Muslims.[35]

Once the residency realized that it could not significantly change the stipulations of the new decree, representatives of Vichy could only seek to gain the sultan's acquiescence. Despite the sultan's strong objections to certain aspects of the *dahir*, he was obligated to sign it with its new racial definition included. An exemption was made for traditional artisanal activities and retail trade out of concern that banning Jews from these professions would destabilize the economy.[36] Although the racial definition was clearly legislated in the *dahir* of 1941, the question of whether Jews could escape their new status by conversion to Islam was still being posed.[37]

Vallat and the Vichy authorities made it clear that the residency had to conform to the new directives and that the Jewish policy in France had to be strictly implemented in the colonies. Weygand wrote to Noguès that he considered it "indispensable that all the measures taken or envisaged be coordinated for all of North Africa," and insisted on consultation and that "any new text must obtain my prior consent before being implemented."[38] Vallat later visited Morocco in August of 1941 and met with the sultan. At Vallat's insistence, a delegate of the CGQ J was dispatched to Morocco to strengthen the ties between the office and the residency "at the moment when the application in Morocco of the Statute of the Jews had entered into an acute phase."[39] Noguès and the resident-general of Tunisia, Adm. Jean-Pierre Esteva, where a delegate was also to be dispatched, objected to the appointment. Hearing of their protest, Vallat wrote that the agent could serve as a liaison while the two protectorates could "benefit from the experiences of the *métropole*, particularly in the field of economic Aryanization."[40] Yet Noguès may well have been concerned about the effects that an antisemitic campaign led by the commissariat could have on Muslim–Jewish relations. Already in September 1940, he had warned Vichy that the anti-Jewish measures could provoke Muslim hostility toward the Jews, causing unnecessary disruption. Maintaining stability among the dominated colonial subjects, especially during wartime, was an important priority for Noguès.[41]

Both the sultan and the residency understood that the *dahirs* that promulgated the Statut des Juifs, especially the one of August 1941, undermined an important foundation on which the Protectorate rested. While the colonial authorities reformed the system of justice by claiming that they were implementing greater equality for all the sultan's subjects, including the Jews, the reforms were justified by the idea that they were preserving Moroccan institutions and respecting traditional practice, which meant that the Jews would remain as indigenous subjects under the protection of the sultan. The French relied on the symbolic capital of the dynasty to justify their presence, deploying the dynastic nomenclature for the various governmental offices (Office chérifienne, etc.). The Moroccan institutions that were preserved, invented, recreated, and controlled by the colonial state—as disempowered as they may have been—were nonetheless the national edifice through which authority was exercised on a day-to-day level through the representatives of the Makhzan and which formed the Moroccan political elite. It was a card that Mohammed Ben Youssef was beginning to play during this period, invoking his symbolic role as sharifian monarch. The sultan's position with regard to his Jewish subjects thus constituted a subtle reclamation of his role as Muslim ruler, which had been effectively limited by the colonial authorities. It was a means also for the sultan to assert himself as leader of the Moroccan nation following the emergence of the nationalist movement in the 1930s and in anticipation of Morocco's independence movement that was to follow the war.

While the Throne Day incident may not have occurred—such a public defiance of Vichy seems unlikely—it is known that Mohammed Ben Youssef did unofficially meet with Jewish leaders in 1941 and 1942, at times clandestinely, reassuring them that they were to remain his protected subjects.[42] A source from the period refers to Jews invoking the sultan's protection by sacrificing four bulls according to Moroccan custom, followed by a delegation of Moroccan Jewish leaders, Elie Danan, El Alouf, and Isaac Cohen of Fez, and Mardochée Dahan of Casablanca, who were received by the sultan. The Jewish delegation was concerned about the *dahirs* affecting them, especially the census and declaration of property. The sultan ensured the delegation that the Jews were regarded as Moroccans like Muslims, and their property would not be touched. Subsequent delegations of Jewish community leaders also received reassurances from the sultan.[43] Accounts of the sultan's meetings with Jewish leaders during the Vichy period continued to be produced later during the war. Community leaders from Fez reported in 1944:

> On August 10, 1942, receiving in his palace in Rabat a delegation of the Jewish community of Fez, his Majesty Sidi Mohamed (may God strengthen and prolong his reign) declared without hesitation—despite the Vichy regime and the presence in Morocco of German and Italian commissions—that there could be no differences between his Moroccan subjects, Muslims or Jews, and during these tragic times, he would particularly watch over his Jewish subjects. His Majesty Sidi Mohamed recommends to the members of the Fez delegation to calm the Moroccan Jews that they can expect nothing wrong to happen.[44]

The Ambivalence of the Residency toward
Vichy's Jewish Policy

For the residency, the status of Jews as indigenous subjects of the sultan was an important organizing principle. Racist and antisemitic attitudes often reinforced this policy as well as what were deemed as political and practical issues, for it was believed that granting Jews French citizenship would inflame the Muslim population as well as the European settlers, making it more difficult for French rule in Morocco. The colonial authorities also believed or at least argued that Jews were ill-prepared for French citizenship; those who were able to advance in the colonial society and economy—for example, in business, civil service, liberal professions— it was argued, took advantage and abused their status. Yet neither could they be excluded, since owing to the growing numbers of those educated in the Alliance israélite universelle and Western schools, Jews could serve as useful intermediaries.

This ambivalence toward the Jews' advancement in colonial society, and the particular intermediary role that they played, explains in part the uneven application of the discriminatory anti-Jewish laws in Morocco. The *numerus clausus* that restricted Jewish access to schools and professions was readily accepted by at least some of the French administration in Morocco since they saw it as an important check on Jews who had become too haughty in their advancement; they could also argue that the Jews should continue to work as artisans, shopkeepers, and peddlers, exempting these latter traditional occupations from the banned professions.

This also accounts for the fact that the Protectorate authorities during Vichy had little hesitation in barring Jews from holding public positions but permitted them to continue to work in Jewish institutions and organizations.[45] The Alliance was allowed to continue to provide education to Jews. This did not meet with the approval of the Légion française des anciens combattants, the veterans' organization that served as a spearhead for Vichy's "National Revolution." The organization was a thorn in the side of Noguès, making political demands of the residency at the encouragement of Weygand and attempting to circumvent Noguès's authority.[46] Responding to an inquiry from the organization about Jews in the educational system in North Africa, in light of the *numerus clausus* restricting Jewish students to 10 percent in both secondary and primary schools, the French administration strongly urged that the Alliance school system be supported, even to increase its subvention, while adhering to the quotas regarding French schools. Furthermore, Noguès himself sought to ensure that all Jews, even if they had French citizenship, be removed from all committees of parents' associations of French lycées and colleges in Morocco.[47] But the Alliance was another matter. The directeur de l'instruction publique for Morocco, Robert Ricard wrote: "Even if we consider it prudent to limit the number of pupils in *Lycées* and in the European primary schools, it would be perilous to leave a mass of Jewish children unschooled, which would quickly form a disturbing proletariat. It would therefore be opportune to increase the assistance given by the Government to the Alliance israélite universelle, in a manner that would allow it to better pay its teachers and to open schools when circumstances warranted it."[48] The Alliance had long been seen as promoting French interests in Morocco, even prior to the establishment of the Protectorate, and dismantling the system was understood to be detrimental to French control. Early during the protectorate period official Franco-Jewish primary schools were opened, intended to parallel the opening of Franco-Muslim schools. But in 1924 it was decided to discontinue the development of these official Jewish schools and instead to encourage the Alliance primary schools to expand under the Protectorate's surveillance. Meanwhile, French secondary schools were opened to Jewish and Muslim children, resulting in Jews obtaining employment at a disproportionately higher rate than Muslims.[49]

Educating indigenous Jews was an important priority for colonial rule, but with limitations. The French advisor to the Makhzan (Conseiller du Gouvernement Chérifien) wrote:

> It should be noted that after thirty years of the Protectorate, the Jewish economy in Morocco had, before the implementation of the Jewish Statute, a clear tendency to evolve in the same direction as in Europe: capitalism and intellectualism had begun to occupy too prominent a place. One could already blame them, for whatever the reasons, for the abnormal character of their occupational structure, and to admonish them not to engage in unproductive and parasitic trades. However, the *Statut des Juifs*, whose goal is to fight against their domination of the liberal professions and as middlemen, could also have the counter-effect of aggravating the situation of a proletariat that would rapidly become a heavy burden on society. It therefore seems that a restructuring of the Jewish economy is needed, and demands a thoughtful social policy whose first concern would be to divert an important part of the Jewish youth away from concentration in the commercial professions and towards a diversity of productive trades.

Cooperation with the Jewish community through their schools was needed for the long process of transforming their social and economic structure.[50]

The French authorities for the most part were ambivalent if not hostile to the advancement of Moroccan Jews; yet at the same time it was recognized that they played an important role in the colonial economy, and their exclusion in some cases could be detrimental to the ability of the Protectorate to rule. The French authorities did, in some circumstances, ease the restrictive measures and, though unevenly, did make exceptions in the application of the laws and in some places simply did not implement them, or did so moderately. Article 10 of the *dahir* of 1941 allowed for individual exemption when exceptional service to Morocco (meaning France or French interests in Morocco) had been rendered, which could include those engaged in professions considered vital.[51] The residency received numerous petitions from Jews requesting exemptions from the anti-Jewish restrictions. However, the Vichy authorities were officious in ensuring that the residency enforced the anti-Jewish laws and that the procedures were scrupulously followed. While a few applicants were able to secure exemption because of their noteworthy service to Morocco, especially if it involved meritorious and decorated military service during World War I, most petitioners were rejected. The oft-cited reason was the failure to demonstrate any particular noteworthy service to "Morocco," often adding that the exclusion of the individual would have no major economic consequences or political repercussions. Some officials strictly adhered to the requisites of the exemptions, concerned that the floodgate of petitions would be opened were they too liberal in their interpretation of the law.[52] Yet other local authorities were willing to make exceptions based purely on economic considerations, especially considering the importance of Jews in certain sectors of the colonial economy and fears of the detrimental effect that exclusionary laws might have on the wartime economy.[53]

Despite the relatively high proportion of rejections of those who applied for exemptions, it is also likely that in many places there was less of a need to apply for exemption if the exclusionary laws on professions were not applied that rigorously. The residency itself remarked that local officials and administrators interpreted their obligations in implementing the Jewish Statute in contradictory ways, but as a matter of policy, the control in applying the legislation relied on regional and local authorities.[54] Some local officials may have been responding to the unpopularity of the anti-Jewish measures in their locales among some sectors of the Muslim population, although there were other Muslims who profited from the anti-Jewish measures, filling positions vacated by Jews, or benefiting from the remittance of debts owed to Jews that was also a part of the economic measures of this period.[55] The treatment of the Jews by local Makhzan officials and French *contrôleurs civils* in response to the anti-Jewish laws was therefore inconsistent, with some severely implementing the new laws, or even taking advantage of the Jews out of antipathy or for personal gain, while others all but ignored some measures whether due to sympathy or more practical considerations. In some locales, Jewish leaders used their personal ties to Makhzan authorities to lessen the impact of the measures while receiving assurances from the sultan following the plan for the 1941 *dahir* that Jews would continue to be regarded equally as his subjects.[56]

An extensive report on the Jews of Morocco, written in December 1941 and intended for military and civilian administrators in training for service in North Africa at the Centre de hautes études d'administration musulmane in Paris, asserts that the sultan and the central Makhzan greatly regretted the rigor in which the anti-Jewish measures were adopted and sought by various means to attenuate the consequences.[57] The report continued that the Protectorate government also did not implement "to the letter" some of the provisions, by way of delaying the moving of Jews to the *mellahs* or not firmly fixing a deadline for the declaration of property.[58] While the report may not have been wholly accurate, it probably did reflect a certain truth: both the residency and the sultan saw it in their interest to soften the impact of *some aspects* of the anti-Jewish Vichy laws, which they viewed as undermining their authority and the legitimacy of the Protectorate and the dynasty. Once again, this was not about their concern for the welfare of the Jews—both Noguès and Mohammed Ben Youssef favored aspects of the laws that were seen as restoring Jews to their traditional subordinate place in society, and hence, maintaining the ethnoreligious hierarchy of the Protectorate. The "Aryanization" of the economy, however, could potentially disrupt the colonial structure, further crippling the war-torn economy and destabilizing Muslim–Jewish relations.

Concerned about the economic consequences that the rapid elimination of Jews from the economy would have on French control of Morocco, yet under pressure from both the CGQ J and European settlers, the residency dragged its feet about adopting measures. With Jews banned from a wide range of professions by the Jewish Statute of 1941 and, consequently, the activities of many business enterprises suspended, French settler applicants wasted little time in offering their services and applying to become trustees of Jewish property and businesses. A branch of the Légion française des combattants in Oujda presented a list to the residency of potential legionnaire candidates desirous of becoming trustees.[59] But a metropolitan law of July 22, 1941, to place Jewish property under non-Jewish trustees, "*administrateurs provisoires,*" and other anti-Jewish laws to take control of Jewish real estate and commerce were never put into effect in Morocco.[60] Despite the enthusiasm of some of the Europeans settlers to gain control of Jewish property in Morocco, the Protectorate authorities probably saw the measures as impractical or even economically or politically destabilizing, and delayed implementing so that the law was never put into effect. Also, Vichy laws to control Jewish business assets and landed property that were promulgated in the metropole remained "under consideration" and ultimately were never applied in Morocco.[61] The Légion française des combattants was highly critical of the residency for not fully implementing all the anti-Jewish legislation and for not rigorously enforcing the census and declaration of Jewish property.[62]

Whether these measures would have been eventually implemented or more rigorously enforced if the Vichy regime had lasted for a longer period of time in Morocco will never be known.

Up until the very last months before the Allied landing in North Africa in November 1942, the authorities in Vichy were concerned about the difficulties at the local level of applying the anti-Jewish laws. Still, in the summer of 1942 Noguès was considering some modification in the *dahirs* of 1941 because of the practical difficulties in their application and was requesting that the police authorities investigate the economic repercussions and potential danger to the economy of the Protectorate if the metropolitan legislation that followed the Statut des Juifs of June 2, 1941, was fully put into effect in Morocco.[63]

Once the Allies disembarked in Morocco, the residency quickly began to consider how best to reposition itself with the interest of maintaining French colonial control. The American authorities in North Africa, mainly concerned about the military campaign and control of North Africa, initially worked in collaboration with the Vichy officials, striking a deal with the commander in chief of Vichy's armed forces, Adm. François Darlan, to keep the French administration in control.

The Jewish question presented a particularly vexing problem for both the French authorities and the Americans. There was concern about how the Muslim population might react if Jews were seen as being restored to their former social and economic status by the French authorities, which could be detrimental for the continued legitimacy of French colonial rule in the Maghreb. The American authorities themselves urged caution in revoking the anti-Jewish decrees while the military campaign was still under way, fearing the effect of Nazi propaganda on the Arabs. But there was public criticism in the Allied press on the deal with Darlan, and President Roosevelt gave a speech demanding the release of prisoners (referring to foreign Jewish refugees who were interned in labor camps across North Africa) and the abrogation of the Vichy laws. The North African Jewish leaders mobilized the support of the American Jewish leadership in denouncing Allied collaboration with Darlan and demanded the repeal of the anti-Jewish laws and the reinstatement of the Crémieux Decree in Algeria, which had been abrogated on October 7, 1940. Gen. Henri Giraud, who became the French high commissioner for French North Africa after the assassination of Darlan in late December 1942, advised Noguès that while Jews should no longer be eliminated from liberal professions, he should exercise discretion in authorizing Jews to return to positions from which they had been removed and in restoring seized property, concerned about the war effort and destabilizing the population that could occur with the massive reintegration of the Jews.[64]

While Giraud repealed the anti-Jewish legislation in North Africa on March 14, 1943, he was opposed to reinstating the Crémieux Decree, claiming that Jews should be treated no differently from Muslims. Moroccan Jewish leaders complained that despite the repeal of the anti-Jewish laws in March, the pro-Vichy officials that were still in place were systematically obstructing the reintegration of the Jews.[65] It was not until October 1943, after pressures from many leading French political figures and French, American, and international Jewish organizations, that the Comité français de libération nationale declared that the Crémieux Decree was reinstated.[66] By then the Gaullists were restored to power in French North Africa; in June 1943 Noguès resigned and went into exile in Portugal.[67]

Nationality Questions: Between Morocco and Algeria

French colonial authorities had followed closely the reactions in Morocco to the abrogation of the Crémieux Decree of 1870, which revoked the citizenship rights of Algerian Jews, and were equally concerned about its restitution in 1943. Although, in contrast to Algeria, the French Protectorate in Morocco had adhered to its policy of maintaining the Jews' indigenous status, many Jews of Moroccan descent, whether through migration, marriage to foreigners, or particular service to France, had managed to become French citizens or citizens of other countries. Algeria, especially, was the route to acquiring French nationality, both because of its proximity to Morocco and because of the large numbers of Moroccan Jews who had for centuries migrated back and forth especially between eastern Morocco and western Algeria.[68] Moroccan Jews who had acquired French nationality in Algeria, and who had returned to Morocco as French citizens, added another layer of complications to the problem of Jewish status during the war. The vexing question of how the abrogation of the Crémieux Decree of 1870 affected these French citizens of Moroccan origin became a preoccupation of the French authorities and the Jews.

Some Jews successfully petitioned the residency, arguing that their status as French citizens be recognized by virtue of the fact that they were Moroccans naturalized in Algeria subsequent to the Crémieux Decree (and therefore its abrogation should not affect them).[69] The president of the North African branch of the Légion française des combattants complained to the CGQ J about this "anomaly" of Jews of Moroccan origin born in Algeria, who were considered offspring of foreigners born in French territory and thus enjoyed the political rights of French citizens, which they acquired when they reached the age of majority.[70] Noguès similarly informed Vallat that both Jews of Moroccan origin and numerous Algerian Jews were claiming to have Moroccan descent and thus be entitled to remain French citizens as foreigners (citing the laws of 1839 and 1927, which regarded those born in France or Algeria of foreign parents as French). He pointed out that there were Algerian Jews who could also circumvent the law and be regarded as subjects of the sultan because of the law of perpetual allegiance, apparently implying that at least some saw it as advantageous to be indigenous subjects of the sultan of Morocco rather than non-Moroccan Jews and subject to the unadulterated racist laws of Vichy France. Furthermore, the French Protectorate authorities sometimes clashed with other countries in Morocco who claimed Moroccan Jews as citizens of their country, while the French, by dint of the clause on perpetual allegiance from the nineteenth century, considered them Moroccan. Noguès proposed changing this paradoxical situation so that the "nationals of a country under the Protectorate of France should not be regarded as aliens under the laws of nationality, not having ever lost their original nationality." Such a provision, which would be applied retroactively, would allow for the review of the situation of many Jews who had been able, by false statements, to be taken for French citizens.[71] The issue was taken up by Vichy in reforming the law pertaining to the status of Algerian Jews of October 7, 1940, which had abrogated the Crémieux Decree. The revised law of February 18, 1942 stipulated that Moroccan or Tunisian Jews who acquired French nationality as a result of their birth or residence in Algeria were henceforth to be subject to the same status as Algerian Jews, effectively the removal of their French citizenship.[72]

The French authorities in Morocco were concerned about the abrogation of the Crémieux Decree not only due to the numerous legal complications it posed for the large numbers of Algerian Jews with French citizenship in Morocco but also because of how it might affect the educated Muslim population, whom officials regarded as susceptible to Nazi propaganda, which tended to be anti-French and emboldened the nationalists. It was perhaps hoped that the revocation of the Crémieux Decree might garner greater support for the colonial government. French authorities reported that Muslims, especially Algerians living in Morocco, welcomed the abrogation of the Crémieux Decree since it was a blow to Jewish ascendancy, especially in educated and nationalist circles.[73] Likewise, reports elicited after the Allied invasion revealed that many Muslims were opposed to the restitution of the decree mainly because it would show favoritism to Jews and disregard for Muslims who were hoping for an improvement of their civil status.[74]

It is difficult to gauge how much the denigration of the Jews was applauded by the Muslim educated elite in Morocco. In Algeria many educated Muslims had long sought to gain the rights accorded to French citizens, and revoking the rights of Algerian Jews would hardly bode well for improving their own status.

Some Muslim leaders expressed their sympathy for the denial of rights of their Jewish compatriots.[75] To the extent that there was subsequent opposition to reinstating the decree in Algeria, it may have been less about their general approval of its abrogation and more about the idea that reinstating the decree should be accompanied with Muslims also gaining equal citizenship. In Morocco, on the other hand, since Jews were legally designated as indigenous and, in some respects, subordinate to Muslims, the abrogation of the Crémieux Decree would have had little direct impact. However, many Jews sought to gain French citizenship as their co-religionists had in Algeria, and some Moroccan Muslims believed that Jews had gained an upper hand and thus welcomed the abrogation of the Crémieux Decree as a blow to Jewish privilege in the colonial system. Overall, it is unlikely that the Crémieux Decree and its abrogation elicited much response from the Moroccan Muslim population. Yet the French authorities were concerned enough to systematically investigate and monitor Muslim reactions to the abrogation and subsequently to the reinstallation of the Crémieux Decree. The residency, both during the Vichy period and after, sought to maintain and strengthen its hold on Morocco and feared the growth of the independence movement that was encouraged by the defeat of France. France's Jewish policy in its North African colonies was of significance in determining its relationship to the Muslim population and its acquiescence to the continuation of colonial rule.

Nationalism, National Identity, and the Jewish Question

The defeat of France and the complicity of the residency with Vichy, on the one hand, and the emerging role of the sultan as a national leader, on the other, questioned the very legitimacy of the French Protectorate. The cause of self-determination advocated by Roosevelt, already declared in the Atlantic Charter of 1941, was further advanced at the Anfa conference in Casablanca in January 1943, where the Allied leaders, including Roosevelt, Churchill, de Gaulle and Giraud, met to determine the future course of the North African campaign. Defying protocol, Mohammed Ben Youssef met privately with Roosevelt, Churchill, and Robert Murphy (Roosevelt's personal representative in North Africa), without the presence of the residence general and French officials. Moroccans were later to claim that Roosevelt promised the sultan American support for the cause of Moroccan independence once the war ended. As David Stenner convincingly argues, the "Roosevelt myth" was instrumental in the nationalists' efforts to enlist US support for Morocco's independence after the war. While it remains unknown what exactly Roosevelt said to Mohammed Ben Youssef, his "unauthorized" meeting reflected the sultan's growing assertiveness in his relationship to the residency, a strategic positioning in anticipation of his role as nationalist leader.[76]

The Jewish question became an important issue for both the residency and the sultan in their respective efforts to regain authority in Morocco. During the Vichy period, Noguès would have had little to gain if the sultan were perceived as obstructing the implementation of the anti-Jewish policy in light of pressures from both the settlers and from the Vichy government. But with mounting pressures to rescind the discriminatory legislation that followed the Allied landings of 1942—"the abrogation of all laws and decrees inspired by Nazi Governments or Nazi ideologies," as President Roosevelt had declared in his speech on North Africa of November 17, 1942[77]—the residency was quick to reposition itself. With Noguès and the residency officials still in place, the French administration now had every interest in promoting the image of a benevolent monarch, protective of his Jewish subjects during the wartime, which could serve to legitimize the continuation of the French Protectorate. At the same time, there was concern of how the restitution of Jewish rights might agitate the Arab population in their own struggle for independence. However, if it were perceived that it was the sultan himself, a Muslim ruler and emerging national leader who sought to impede the impact of the anti-Jewish laws, then the restoration of the old order would be met with little opposition. The renowned sociologist Robert Montagne, founder and director of the Centre de hautes études d'administration musulmane whom Noguès had recruited to head the political department of the general staff in 1940, wrote soon after the Allied landing in November 1942: "In Morocco, the Sultan's authority has limited the impact of the anti-Jewish laws, and it seems that at the price of a few concessions at the local level, of which the resident-general would be the best judge, peace can easily be maintained."[78] Montagne's concessions hinted at allowing some Muslims to keep property or jobs taken from Jews. It is unknown whether this astute observer of Moroccan society actually believed that Mohammed Ben Youssef had any real impact in attenuating the effect of the anti-Jewish laws, but he could certainly understand the symbolic power of promoting the "Sultan as protector" image.

The French authorities were quick to underscore that the legislation in Morocco was not as zealously applied as it was in France. It was reported that Jews were able to obtain from the Protectorate authorities numerous extensions, still pending in November 1942, which enabled them to continue their professional activities undisturbed. Jews, it was claimed, recognized the moderation of the Protectorate authorities that had resisted the demands of the Commissariat général aux questions juives and were able to curb the activities of its official representative in Rabat.[79]

The Jews seemingly saw no contradiction between their professed love of France and their loyalty to the sultan as their ruler, even during the Vichy era, though they had no illusions about where real power lay in the Protectorate. The 'Alawid monarch was no doubt perceived as an integral part of the reality and power structure of the French Protectorate, yet nonetheless the symbol of the country, a ruler with his Muslim and Jewish subjects. At the same time that this loyalty and devotion to France was growing among the educated, Jews also thought of themselves as "Moroccans"—that they constituted part of a larger collectivity circumscribed by the boundaries of the country in which they lived, an identity whose origins could already be seen among some of the educated, Westernized elite of the late nineteenth century.[80] During the Protectorate, this identity was reinforced by an institutional structure, invented under the auspices of the French authorities that created for the first time national institutions consisting of religious and lay leaders.[81] Paradoxically, this identity as Moroccan Jews was rooted in the same period and circumstances that produced a growing identification with France (or Spain). Both identities were derived from modern, especially French, education, although Spanish was becoming more important in northern Morocco. The educated elites understood belonging to a nation as a prerequisite for being modern, and this could be translated both into professing loyalty to France, in part the result of being inculcated in French patriotism in the schools of the Alliance, and into imagining themselves as part of a larger collectivity of Moroccan Jews. Significantly this "national" identity did not translate into participation in the national movement with Muslim Moroccans, except for a relatively small number of Jews. The challenges of the Vichy period and the lingering restrictions on the Jewish population, mounting tensions with the authorities, and increasing conflicts with the Muslim population that followed the Allied liberation at the end of 1942, accentuated the overlapping and increasingly conflicted loyalties.[82] Despite, on the one hand, the Jews' expressions of love for France, which had betrayed them, and, on the other hand, their embrace of their historic position as *dhimmis* whom a Muslim ruler had to treat with justice—a status which symbolized inferiority and from which many had aspired to be free—the Jewish leadership was quick to represent Moroccan Jewry in simpler terms, as both patriotic to France and as loyal subjects of the sultan.

> Moroccan Jews understand all that they owe to France, homeland of human rights and liberty and, if sometimes clashes occur, it is often the doings of traitors and bad Frenchmen. The dark months—from June 1940 to November 1942, are already forgotten, and Moroccan Jews are well aware that Vichy was Germany and if a few supporters of the fascist regime are still in the administration, we are convinced that they will soon be definitively removed and that Morocco will again turn to a republican

and democratic regime equal to all, under the aegis of the eternal France and the sovereignty of his Majesty Sidi Mohammed Ben Yousef, the chivalric and venerable Sultan of Morocco who, in the dark days of the Vichy regime, never ceased to address the plight of the Jews of his empire, reminding his Moroccan subjects, who were exposed night and day to Nazi and anti-Jewish propaganda, of the precepts of the Qur'an which formally urge not to mistreat the Jew.[83]

Thus reported the Committee of the Jewish community of Fez to the World Jewish Congress in August 1944.

From hindsight, scholars often speak of Moroccan Jews forced to choose between conflicting positions and identities: loyalties to a future independent Morocco or to Zionism.[84] This was indeed the dilemma with which Moroccan Jews were faced in the postwar years of decolonization. Yet for those living in Morocco under Vichy rule, neither the birth of an independent Moroccan state nor the birth of Israel could be anticipated. Despite their sense of French betrayal during World War II, the attestation of loyalty to France by many Jews in their petitions to the French authorities in Morocco was not only a short-term strategy of survival but also reflected the conviction that French Morocco was to remain. Patriotism to France and attachments to French culture, support for Zionism, and identification with Morocco and loyalty to the sultan were not necessarily seen as irreconcilable in this period.[85] The experience of Vichy—the betrayal of France and the inability of the sultan ultimately to protect his Jewish subjects, despite his good intentions and assurances—did not turn most Moroccan Jews away from France and Morocco and toward Zionism, either during the war or immediately after, nor can the Jews' experience during Vichy account for the mass movement of emigration that began in the 1950s.[86]

Although the Jews' disillusionment with France and Morocco during Vichy was not the principal reason for the denouement of the community in the years that followed, the experience of the war was nevertheless an important turning point for the future of Jews in Morocco for two important reasons: it began the process of decolonization, and it marked the emergence of Mohammed Ben Youssef as the national leader who was to lead Morocco to independence. While decolonization was arguably the most important cause of the mass emigration of Jews in the decades following the war, the fact that a sizable Jewish community remained in Morocco after independence—more robust than anywhere else in the Arab world—can be attributed to the restoration and refashioning of the historical role of the dynasty and its ruler, in which the symbolism of the king (the title assumed after independence) as protector of the Jews was an important component. Indeed, one of the anomalies of Moroccan history is how a dynasty that had been a subservient instrument of oppression by the French occupiers not only survived but was able to take the lead in the national liberation of

Morocco rather than being displaced by nationalists untarnished by complicity with the colonial regime. The actions of a seemingly obsequious sultan during Vichy, I suggest, were crucial for the emergence of Mohammed V from the shadows of the Protectorate to become the symbol of the nation: his secret meetings with nationalists in 1942 and the cultivation of his image as an Islamic ruler shielding the Jews from Vichy's discriminatory legislation.[87]

In the 1930s, when the nationalist movement was in its incipient stage of development, nationalist elites began to approach the sultan for support when protesting decisions of the colonial administration, a development that the Protectorate authorities attempted to block. In 1934 the future leader of the Istiqlal (Independence Party), Allal el-Fassi was invited to the royal palace to meet with the sultan, followed by a visit to Fez where nationalists organized a mass welcoming of the sultan to demonstrate their support for the king in conjunction with a protest against French colonialism.[88] Mohammed Ben Youssef was becoming an important nationalist symbol. The occasion that strengthened the tie between nationalists and the sultan was the *fête du trône* (Throne Day), commemorating the accession of the sultan to the throne, which began in 1933 and was officially institutionalized in 1934. Promoted by notables and intellectuals, the occasion was used to mobilize nationalist activities, linking the ruler to the nation. For Moroccan Jews, the Throne Day also connected diverse communities in the country to the sultan. The president of the Jewish community of Rabat ordered that a prayer of the king be read in synagogues throughout the country. The sultan's "speech of the throne" on the occasion also marked a shift where the ruler, for the first time, addressed the Moroccan people as a whole and not just one particular constituency.[89] The French authorities took note, with increasing alarm, of the development of Throne Day as the rallying locus for Moroccan nationalists, which may offer some explanation for René Touraine's telegram intended to discredit the sultan.

Paradoxically, the survival of the 'Alawid dynasty and the emergence of the sultan as national leader can be attributed to the French Protectorate's carefully engineered policy of preserving the old order, originally under the direction of Lyautey. Noguès, an adherent to the philosophy of respecting native institutions and indirect rule, endeavored to renew and improve relations with the Fasi notables, the traditional political elite from Fez, and strengthen the image of the sultan, which contributed unwittingly to the growth of the nationalist opposition to French rule.[90] Yet whatever nationalist aspirations the sultan had in the 1930s, his throne was an integral part of what Jonathan Wyrtzen has so aptly termed the "neo-Makhzan" structure of the Protectorate, and was still dependent on the French for its existence.[91] The residency took action against the nationalists and their movement (Kutlat al-Amal al-Watani, the National Action

Schroeter

Block, or "Comité d'action marocaine") in 1937, banning the movement and arresting and exiling a number of its leaders.[92] The seeming inability of the sultan to offer his support weakened his ties to the nationalists. The received wisdom was that toward the end of the war, when the Istiqlal was founded and began its campaign for independence, the ties were again strengthened between the nationalists and Mohammed Ben Youssef, ultimately leading to the sultan's exile in 1953 and his triumphant return leading Morocco to independence.

Practically ignored in these accounts were the critical years under Vichy when, I would argue, Mohammed Ben Youssef's position regarding the Jewish statutes constituted a reassertion of the sultan's role as national leader of a sovereign nation, a Muslim ruler and protector of all his subjects, Muslim and Jewish.[93] While he continued to proclaim his unswerving loyalty to France, he nevertheless began to subtly use the reliance of the French authorities on his symbolism to legitimize the Protectorate for the purpose of advancing his position as Moroccan leader. The fact that, even as he signed the *dahirs*, the sultan appeared to oppose the Vichy anti-Jewish statutes, an image certainly known to the French administration, can only be understood in this context.[94]

The Sultan, Spanish Colonialism, and the Jewish Question

The confrontation over the Jewish question may also have given the sultan a strategic advantage over some of the nationalists who were critical of the sultan for too close a connection to the French authorities since he, unlike the nationalist opposition, could invoke his symbolic role as Islamic head of state. Some of the leading figures in the incipient nationalist movement, with the growing conflict in Palestine, the antisemitic propaganda campaign of the Germans, and sympathy for Germany perceived as the enemy of the colonial power, applauded the fall of France and may have supported the anti-Jewish legislation. Moroccan nationalists were allowed more freedom to publish in the Spanish northern zone and in Tangier, which served as a channel for disseminating publications into the French zone.[95] Following the suppression of the nationalist leadership in 1936–37, some of its leaders found more fertile ground to express their opposition in the Spanish northern zone of Morocco and in Tangier. Tangier had become an international zone in 1923 but was occupied by Spain in 1940 with the fall of France. Some of the nationalists made common cause with Spanish fascists in their opposition both to the French and the Jews and expressed sympathy for Germany with the objective of gaining support for the Moroccan nationalist cause.[96] When the 1941 anti-Jewish *dahir* was issued, Abdel Khalek Torrès, the leader of the Moroccan nationalist movement Hizb al-Islah al-Watani (National Reform Party) in the Spanish zone, published an article in the party's newspaper, *al-Hurriya*, in Tetouan, as reported by the French consul in Tetouan to Vichy. The article mentions that the *dahir* was "purely a French act . . . willy-nilly to put an end to the actions of Jews in its country." Torrès highlighted disparagingly the exceptions that were made for Jews who rendered service or fought for France (rather than Morocco), allowing, in his view, most Jews to escape the consequences of the legislation; he denounced how the French had allowed the evils of Jewish influence to grow during the Protectorate. In short, he saw the law as a long-needed first step to restrain Jewish activities but contended it did not go far enough.[97]

Yet Spain, the ruling power in the region, officially represented itself as protectors of the Sephardic Jews, stressing its close connections to the Jews in the Middle Ages regarding their descendants in exile as members of the Spanish race as distinct from "international Jewry." This ideology was mobilized as an instrument of expanding Spanish imperial interests in Morocco and a counterfoil to the French, a factor observed with some alarm by the Vichy and Protectorate authorities.[98] In theory, and according to agreements reached between Spain and France, the sultan's authority extended over the Spanish zone through his appointed khalifa resident in Tetouan and his agents, a means by which the French hoped to exercise some control. But tensions between the two zones worsened during Franco's dictatorship, as the khalifa's authority was strengthened and gestures were made for increasing the autonomy of Moroccan leaders in the Spanish Protectorate in order to weaken the influence of the sultan and the French.[99] During the Vichy period, the Spanish further undermined French influence in the northern zone and Tangier, demanding the abolition of the sultan's authority from these regions.[100]

The Vichy-instigated anti-Jewish *dahirs* were not applied by the Spanish authorities. The official Spanish press reported critically on France's anti-Jewish measures, indicating that in Fez and Meknes the Jews sought the protection of the Makhzan, while many fled to America as well as to the Spanish zone, especially in Tangier.[101] Because of the discrimination imposed upon them by Vichy, Spain even invited Sephardic Jews in occupied Europe and in the French Protectorate to apply for Spanish nationality.[102]

This was a remarkable turnabout from a few years earlier. Since the 1930s, Jews in the Spanish zone had been subjected to the worse excesses of antisemitism. During the Spanish Civil War, the Spanish Nationalists had taken immediate control of the Spanish Protectorate, and the Jews, accused of supporting the Spanish Republic, were terrorized by Falangists, who led a campaign against the Jews by boycotting businesses, expropriating property, and committing acts of violence. The fascists also enlisted Muslim Moroccan soldiers in their cause, offering inducements of autonomy and encouraging Moroccan nationalists as well.[103] The consul of France in Larache, a major town in the Spanish zone, reported on the favorable reception of the Muslim population in Larache and El Ksar of the anti-Jewish legislation in the French zone, while the nationalists reacted by showing their sympathy for Germany by spreading rumors that the measures were only taken because they were imposed on France and Morocco by the Third Reich; the Spanish authorities reassured the Jewish population of the good disposition of Spain towards them and toward all their "brothers of the Sephardic race."[104]

On the part of both Vichy and the Makhzan, there was concern that Spain could take advantage of the anti-Jewish laws to expand its own presence in Morocco by presenting itself as protectors of the Jews. Thus, the interests of both Mohammed Ben Youssef and the residency converged in representing the sultan as a benevolent monarch and protector of the Jews, albeit for somewhat different reasons. For the residency, the sultan was still seen as a bulwark against Spanish imperial expansion at the expense of the French. For the sultan, it was a way to outmaneuver the antisemitic nationalist opposition, who were using the Spanish zone to strengthen their position, and to undermine Spain's claim as protectors of the Jews.

Conclusion

The sultan and the Makhzan probably recognized that a liberated France would offer a better prospect for national independence and that a revolt against French rule would further weaken this goal. Furthermore, there were many mobilized Moroccan soldiers, some of whom continued to serve after the armistice and who would have felt abandoned had the sultan been removed because of his opposition, while some nationalist leaders hoped that the Moroccan recruits' support for the war effort might later earn French recognition of their cause.[105] This can also account for Mohammed Ben Youssef signing the very anti-Jewish laws that he was known to oppose, for his refusal would have been tantamount to re-signing his position; better to subtly demonstrate his opposition while giving his formal stamp of approval. The sultan's strategic positioning was probably approved by many in the French administration in Morocco, including Noguès himself who, despite his pedestrian antisemitic beliefs, saw at least parts of the legislation as counter to colonial interests in Morocco and its *politique indigène*. The sultan's stance brought him greater legitimacy as a national leader by asserting his credentials as protector of all Moroccan subjects, including the Jews, while not undermining his integral role in the French Protectorate. At the same time, the residency depended on the symbolism of the dynasty and the sultan as commander of the faithful to justify its continued domination in the protectorate system; thus, it was in its interest to maintain the legitimacy of the sultan in his protector / Islamic ruler role. The sultan's protests in the negotiations over the implementation of the Jewish statutes were used by Noguès as an argument in favor of softening the harshness of the laws.

Mohammed Ben Youssef's gestures to Jewish leaders during the war therefore cannot be understood as acts of philosemitic benevolence as they have so often been represented but as assertions of the symbolic role of the 'Alawid ruler who had begun to reassert his role as national leader.[106] Jews were therefore of exceptional symbolic value for the monarchy's legitimation and continuity, and, ultimately, in the king's ability to both co-opt the nationalist parties and to reduce their influence in the years after independence.

Morocco under Vichy also reflected the complexity of the Jews' position in the French Empire, not only caught between "colonizer and colonized," as Albert Memmi famously analyzed, but also at the nexus of multiple power structures that were undergoing change.[107] The Vichy period has often been understood in terms of a decisive rupture for the Jews of North Africa, disillusioned with France and questioning the assimilationist goals of their leaders. The very idea of rupture is dependent on a linear narrative of Westernization à la française facilitated by French colonial rule. But just as important as the break with the past, the Vichy period in Morocco also revealed the importance of continuities.

The actions of the sultan and the equivocations of Noguès demonstrated the longer-term interests of each element in the power structure: maintaining the important position that the Jews occupied in the economy while limiting their advancement and preserving the indigenous status of the Jews, which was constitutive to the colonial hierarchy of the Protectorate—a system legitimized by the continuation of the dynasty and its Islamic ruler and his Jewish subjects. When Jewish leaders in effect invoked their *dhimmi* status under the protection of Mohammed Ben Youssef, they were not so much calling for a return to the Jews' inferior status traditionally determined by Islamic law, nor repudiating assimilation to France, as they were recognizing their place in Moroccan society as subjects of the sultan.

The king as protector image that was renewed during the Vichy period in Morocco was based on an older paradigm of Islamic ruler and *dhimmi*, but adapted to the framework of the nation state, as the same dynasty that began in the seventeenth century continued to rule after independence in 1956. It has also shaped the identification of Jews with Morocco ever since and the continued reverence of Moroccan Jews, even in their dispersion, to its kings. After independence, relatively few Jews became integrated into the public sphere as participants in the national culture and political life of the country. But in a certain sense, Jews remained *dhimmis* in all but name, attached to the 'Alawid sultan as their protector. When King Mohammed V died in 1961, Jews poured into the streets in grief. This cannot simply be interpreted as a public demonstration of loyalty to Morocco by a vulnerable minority group but rather as a manner for Jews to reify their timeless identity with Morocco, symbolized by their being protected subjects of the king, a ruler representing the sharifian dynasty that, as it is imagined, provided safe haven for the Sephardic Jews and guaranteed the protection of the Moroccan Jewish collectivity over the centuries. Moreover, while leaders of the remaining Moroccan Jewish community have been at the forefront of promoting the king-protector image, both Mohammed V and Hassan II (following the latter's death in 1999) have been memorialized by Jews in the larger Moroccan diaspora, especially in Israel, where Moroccan Jews have actively promoted the commemoration of both Mohammed V and Hassan II by naming public places after them.[108]

Mohammed V is today celebrated officially in Morocco for his role in protecting the Jews during the war with the claim that they were saved from the catastrophe that befell European Jewry. This retrospective elevation of Mohammed V's role during the war has little to do with the few thousand remaining Jews in Morocco in the twenty-first century and more to do with promoting the image of a tolerant Morocco, a society in which different cultures and religions can coexist. As historically the only non-Muslim indigenous group in Morocco, Jews have become conceptually essential for imagining a more open, progressive, civil society, in contrast to the exclusionary Islamist, Arab current that has greatly grown in Morocco in recent years, with its antisemitic ideology and sometime accusations against the palace for its ties to Israel and Jews. If Mohammed Ben Youssef's image as protector of the Jews during the war was once an important symbol for the king's emergence as a national leader ready to stand up to a Western colonial power, the memory of King Mohammed V during Vichy is now promoted as a symbol of the pro-Western tolerance and pluralism of Moroccan society and its rulers.[109]

Notes

Research for this essay was made possible thanks to my tenure as Ina Levine Invitational Scholar at the Jack, Joseph and Morton Mandel Center for Advanced Holocaust Studies, United States Holocaust Memorial Museum (USHMM), and from previous research conducted at the USHMM during a summer workshop on Sephardic Jewry and the Holocaust. I am grateful to Aomar Boum, Joseph Chetrit, Jessica Marglin, Yaron Tsur, Joshua Cole, and the editors of this volume, Ethan Katz, Maud Mandel, and Lisa Leff, for their insightful comments and suggestions.

1. Ministère des affaires étrangères (henceforth MAE), Archives des Relations Extérieures, Paris, Quai d'Orsay, Série Guerre 1939/45, Vichy-Maroc. Dossier 18, Juifs (Généralités), liasse 665, série corps diplomatique (Annexe I), May 24, 1941, cited in Haïm Zafrani, *Juifs d'Andalousie et du Maghreb* (Paris:

Maisonneuve et Larose, 1996), 403–4. The document is translated in *Two Thousand Years of Jewish Life in Morocco* (Jersey City: KTAV, 2005), 294–95. I have slightly revised the translation. A copy of the document is found in the US Holocaust Memorial Museum Collections Division, Archives Branch (henceforth USHMM) in RG 43.006M-1, vol. 18.

2. David Cohen discovered and first presented the document at a conference in 1985. His paper was published in the proceedings: "Ofen Yishumah shel hateḥikah ha-anti-yehudit be-maroḳo be-teḳufat memshelet Vishi 'al pi mismakhim ḥadashim me-misrad ha-ḥuts ha-tsarfati" in *Divre ha-ḳongres ha-'olami ha-teshi'i le-mada'e ha-yahadut*, div. B, vol. 2 (Jerusalem: World Union of Jewish Studies, 1985), 225–28; and David Cohen, "L'attitude de Mohammed V vis-à-vis des Juifs du Maroc du temps du gouvernement de Vichy, 1940–1942," *Information Juive* (October 1986). It is quoted in Mohammed Kenbib, *Juifs et Musulmans au Maroc, 1859–1948* (Rabat: Université Mohammed V, Publications de la Faculté des Lettres et des Sciences Humaines, 1994), 628n98, who notes that he received a copy of the document from David Cohen. Robert Assaraf reproduces the document in *Mohammed V et les Juifs du Maroc: L'époque de Vichy* (Paris: Plon, 1997), 132–33. In addition to various scholarly publications, the document is often cited in the press and internet as part of the standard narrative of the benevolent sultan. See Sophie Wagenhofer, "Contested Narratives: Contemporary Debates on Mohammed V and the Moroccan Jews under the Vichy Regime," *Quest. Issues in Contemporary Jewish History, Journal of Fondazione CDEZ*, no. 4 (November 2012), www.quest-cdecjournal.it/focus.php?id=313.

3. Different types of sources have led to widely divergent opinions about the sultan: for example, a French intelligence source claims that the Sultan passed military information to the Germans via the German vice-consul in Tangier, which might lead to the conclusion of the sultan's hostility toward Jews. Other French officials reported that the sultan attempted to attenuate the impact of the decree. See Michael M. Laskier, *Yehude ha-Magreb be-tsel Vishi ve-tselav ha-keres* (Tel-Aviv: ha-Makhon le-heker ha-tefutsot, Universitat Tel-Aviv, 1992), 44–46, 159. Some have questioned the standard narrative: Michel Abitbol argues that "no anti-Jewish measure was ever suppressed or slowed down as a result of the Sultan's intervention." Abitbol, *The Jews of North Africa during the Second World War* (Detroit: Wayne State University Press, 1989), 187n94. The same conclusion is reached by Georges Bensoussan, *Juifs en pays arabes: Le grand déracinement, 1850–1975* (Paris: Tallandier, 2012), 631–32. Jacques Dahan, a key figure in the French Protectorate Jewish administration, president of the Conseil des communautés israélites du Maroc (created in 1947), and editor of its organ, *La Voix des communautés*, is skeptical that the sultan protested the anti-Jewish laws and objects to the mythologizing of Mohammed V. See Jacques Dahan, *Regard d'un Juif marocain sur l'histoire contemporaine de son pays* (Paris: Éditions l'Harmattan, 1995), 23. On Jacques Dahan's role, and his memories of the war, see Yaron Tsur, *Ḳehilla ḳeru'a: Yehude Maroḳo veha-le'umiyut, 1943–1954* [A Torn Community: The Jews of Morocco and Nationalism, 1943–1954] (Tel Aviv, Ha-'Amuta le-Heḳer ma'arkhot ha-Ha'apala a'sh Sha'ul Avigor: Universitat Tel Aviv, Am 'Oved, 2001), 103, 132–37, 186–95, 221–22.

4. M. B. Palmer, "L'Office français d'information (1940–1944)," *Revue d'histoire de la Deuxième Guerre mondiale* 26, no. 101 (1976): 19–40; and Claude Lévy, "La presse de collaboration en France occupée: conditions d'existence," *Revue d'histoire de la Deuxième Guerre mondiale* 20, no. 8 (1970): 92, 96.

5. William A. Hoisington Jr., *The Casablanca Connection: French Colonial Policy, 1936–1943* (Chapel Hill: University of North Carolina Press, 1984), 12–13, 159–62.

6. See, e.g., Robert Satloff, *Among the Righteous: Lost Stories from the Holocaust's Long Reach into Arab Lands* (New York: Public Affairs, 2006), 109–11, who embellishes the Throne Day narrative. See Wagenhofer, "Contested Narratives."

7. On contemporary debates regarding Mohammed V, see Wagenhofer, "Contested Narratives"; and Ruth Grosrichard, "Le Maroc, une exception?" *Zamane*, October 2011, 52–55. The latter article is part of a special dossier by the author titled "Les Arabes, Hitler, et le Shoah," published in Casablanca in this iconoclastic and muckraking history magazine, founded in 2010. On conflicting narratives of Muslim–Jewish relations and their connection to debates about Muslim Arabs and the Holocaust, see

Ethan Katz, "Did the Paris Mosque Save Jews: A Mystery and Its Memory," *Jewish Quarterly Review* 102, no. 2 (2012): 264–70; and Gilbert Achcar, *The Arabs and the Holocaust: The Arab-Israeli War of Narratives* (New York: Metropolitan, 2009).

8. Eric T. Jennings, *Vichy in the Tropics: Pétain's National Revolution in Madagascar, Guadeloupe, and Indochina, 1940–1944* (Stanford, CA: Stanford University Press, 2001), 1. Cf. Ruth Ginio, *French Colonialism Unmasked: The Vichy Years in French West Africa* (Lincoln: University of Nebraska Press, 2006), 161–72.

9. Weygand was the most important figure for Vichy in North Africa. See Jacques Cantier, *L'Algérie sous le régime de Vichy* (Paris: Odile Jacob, 2002), 93–147.

10. Hoisington, *Casablanca Connection*, 26–28.

11. MAE, Archives Diplomatiques, Vichy-Maroc, vol. 18, carton 6, dossier 1, in USHMM, RG-43.006M, reel 1, Oujda, February 1941, "Situation politique au Maroc." This anonymous report forwarded to Vichy claims that "all the racketeers, profiteers of the old regime, all the freemasons and all the Jews consider him [Noguès] as their last hope." See the memoirs of Alphonse Juin, who became commander-in-chief of the armed forces during the Vichy period and later resident-general of Morocco after World War II. Alphonse Juin, *Mémoires: Alger, Tunis, Rome* (Paris: Libraire Arthème Fayard, 1959), 24–26.

12. The number of European settlers increased at proportionally a higher level than in Algeria or Tunisia in the interwar years. There were 219,000 Europeans in Morocco in 1930 and 415,000 in 1951. Daniel Rivet, *Le Maghreb à l'épreuve de la colonization* (Paris: Hachette, 2002), 273–74.

13. On the dilemma and position of Noguès and the residency vis-à-vis Vichy, the settlers, and the sultan, see Mohammed Kenbib, "Moroccan Jews and the Vichy Regime, 1940–42," *Journal of North African Studies* 19, no. 4 (2014): 544–47.

14. Kenbib, *Juifs et musulmans*, 612–13, 628–29. The reception of the anti-Jewish laws by the Muslim population is a subject that needs further research, but the relative silence of the archives, when widespread stirrings in the Muslim community would likely have been reported, is indicative of a general lack of Muslim support for the laws.

15. Michael M. Laskier, "Between Vichy Antisemitism and German Harassment: The Jews of North Africa during the Early 1940s." *Modern Judaism* 11, no. 3 (1991): 348–55.

16. The *dahir* was published in the *Bulletin Officiel*, November 8, 1940 (the *Bulletin Officiel* publishes government legislation since 1912 and is accessible online at http://www.sgg.gov.ma/Legislation/BulletinsOfficiels.aspx).

17. Assaraf, *Mohammed V*, 128–29. The author incorrectly repeats that there was a delay of two months. The author writes that "Mohammed V was spontaneously anti-racist" (65).

18. Drafts of *dahirs* circulated before being finalized and published in the *Bulletin Officiel* of the French Protectorate, and thus the archives contain the earlier version with the racial definition still intact. Bibliothèque Nationale du Royaume du Maroc, Rabat (henceforth BNR), D.432, in USHMM, RG 81.001M-2. The *dahir* promulgated on October 31, 1940, was published in the *Bulletin Officiel* of November 8, 1940.

19. While the beys in Tunisia did not have the same kind of symbolic religious authority as did the 'Alawid dynasty in Morocco, a similar colonial logic applied in Tunisia. The beys during the Vichy period (Ahmad Pasha and his successor, Moncef Bey) were obligated to sign the decrees drafted by the French while offering gestures of support "to all the population of the regency." Moncef Bey was subsequently much celebrated by Tunisian Jews. Satloff, *Among the Righteous*, 111–14.

20. Cited in Leland L. Bowie, "An Aspect of Muslim-Jewish Relations in Late Nineteenth-Century Morocco: A European Diplomatic View," *International Journal of Middle East Studies* 7 (1976): 5.

21. Ibid., 5–6; and André Chouraqui, *La condition juridique de l'Israélite marocain* (Paris : Presses du livre français, 1950), 60–62.

22. Laskier, "Vichy Antisemitism," 349–50.

23. *Bulletin Officiel*, August 8, 1941. On the new Statut des Juifs, see Michael R. Marrus and Robert O. Paxton, *Vichy France and the Jews* (New York: Schocken, 1983), 92.

24. *Bulletin Officiel*, August 8, 1941. The only known detailed report and register of the census and list of declared property that has been discovered is for Essaouira. For an analysis and the text itself, see Joseph Chetrit, "Les Juifs de Mogador (Essaouira) pendant la Seconde Guerre mondiale: La terreur de Vichy et sa gestion communautaire," in *Les Juifs d'Afrique du Nord pendant la Seconde Guerre mondiale*, ed. H. Saadon (Paris: Editions du CNRS, forthcoming).

25. *Bulletin Officiel*, August 22, 1941. It is unknown to what extent and in what cities Jews were actually forced to leave their homes in the European quarters and relocate to the *mellahs*. There is evidence that it affected Jews in Meknes and Fez, though it seems that its implementation in Casablanca proved to be much more problematic. See Daniel Rivet, *Le Maroc de Lyautey à Mohammed V: Le double visage du protectorat* (Paris: Denoël, 1999), 413; and Jonathan Wyrtzen, *Making Morocco: Colonial Intervention and the Politics of Identity* (Ithaca and London: Cornell University Press, 2015), 208. In Fez, about 14 percent of the Jewish population lived in the *ville nouvelle*, some ten times greater than Muslims. Charlotte Jelidi, "La fabrication d'une ville nouvelle sous le protectorat français au Maroc (1912–1956): Fès nouvelle" (Ph.D. thesis, Université de Tours, 2007), 126. The reference here is to thirty Jewish families who left their homes in the *ville nouvelle* for the *mellah*.

26. MAE, Archives Diplomatiques, Vichy-Maroc, vol. 18, carton 6, dossier 1, in USHMM, RG-43.006M, reel 1, Rabat, July 6, 1941, Noguès to Weygand.

27. BNR, D.298, in USHMM, RG 81.001M-7, June 27, 1941. There are two letters of the same date from Noguès to Weygand.

28. Archives Nationales, Paris (henceforth ANP), 72AJ/594, Fonds Maurice Vanikoff, in USHMM, RG-43.122, reel 2, Rabat, July 28, 1941.

29. BNR, D.298 in USHMM, RG 81.001M-7, Algiers, July 9, 1941, "Note relative au nouveau statut des juifs en Afrique du Nord."

30. Loans with interest (*ribā*) are prohibited in Islamic law. See Joseph Schacht, "Ribā." *Encyclopaedia of Islam*, ed. M. Th. Houtsma, T. W. Arnold, R. Basset, R. Hartmann, Brill Online, 2014.

31. BNR, D.298 in USHMM, RG 81.001M-7, July 26. 1941.

32. Daniel J. Schroeter and Joseph Chetrit, "Emancipation and Its Discontents: Jews at the Formative Period of Colonial Rule in Morocco," *Jewish Social Studies* 13, no. 1 (2006): 190–95.

33. Ibid., 179–80.

34. BNR, D.432, in USHMM, RG 81.001M-2, Rabat, June 20, [1941], Direction des Affaires Cherifiennes, M. Meyrier and Colonel Guillaume to the Résident-Général.

35. Kenbib, *Juifs et musulmans*, 623–24.

36. Wyrtzen, *Making Morocco*, 206–07.

37. MAE-Nantes, Direction de l'Interieur, 1MA/250, article 1, in USHMM, RG-43.154, Centre de Hautes Études d'Administration Musulmane, "Les Juifs au Maroc," December 16, 1941, M. Dutheil.

38. BNR, D.298 in USHMM, RG 81.001M-7, Algiers, July 10, 1941.

39. MAE-Paris, AD, Vichy-Maroc, vol. 18, carton 6, dossier 1, in USHMM, RG-43.006M, reel 1, Rabat, October 2, 1941, Le directeur, Cabinet Civil du Résident Général to Amédée Outrey, Conseiller d'Ambassade, Sous-Direction d'Afrique-Levant, Département des Affaires Étrangères, Vichy.

40. MAE-Paris, AD, Vichy-Maroc, vol. 18, carton 6, dossier 1, in USHMM, RG-43.006M, reel 1, Vichy, October 12, 1941, Darlan to Vallat; October 18, 1941, Vallat to Darlan.

41. Colette Zytnicki, "La politique antisémite du régime de Vichy dans les colonies," in *L'Empire colonial sous Vichy*, ed. Jacques Cantier and Eric Jennings (Paris: Odile Jacob, 2004), 162.

42. Kenbib, *Juifs et Musulmans*, 628. See, e.g., the oral testimony of a Jewish notable from Meknes, in Chetrit, "Les Juifs de Mogador"; also referring to oral testimony, see Doris Bensimon-Donath, *Évolution du judaïsme marocain sous le protectorat français, 1912–1956* (Paris: Mouton, 1968), 110; and referring to a

conversation in 2006 with Serge Berdugo, whose father participated in a secret meeting with the sultan, see Satloff, *Among the Righteous*, 110, 221n30.

43. ANP, 72AJ/594, Fonds Maurice Vanikoff, at USHMM, RG-43.122, reel 2, "Declarations de S.M. le Sultan aux délégations des communautés israélites du Maroc." The document is not dated but was likely produced in 1942. It was first published in Zafrani, *Juifs d'Andalousie*, 404–5.

44. MAE-Nantes, Protectorat Maroc, Direction de l'Interieur, Questions Juives [henceforth MAE-Nantes, DI], 1MA/250, article 16, in USHMM, RG-43.154, Fez, November 10, 1944, Comité de communauté israélite de Fès (Mimoun Ben Dahan, signature in Hebrew of the president of the committee) to the president of the World Jewish Congress in New York, in response to a questionnaire of June 19, 1944. Copies of the report were sent to the général commandant de la région de Fès and the chef des services municipaux de Fès; the report was forwarded by the general to the Political Affairs Department in Rabat, December 8, 1944. In fact, the report was probably written and sent to the World Jewish Congress in August, as indicated on a copy of the report, found in Centre de documentation juive contemporaine, LIV-31, in USHMM, RG-43.070M.

45. Abitbol, *The Jews of North Africa*, 62–64.

46. Hoisington, *Casablanca Connection*, 187–88. On the Légion, see Cantier, *L'Algérie*, 197–218.

47. BNR, D.667, in USHMM, RG 81.001M-12, Rabat, March 10, 1942, Noguès to the General Secretaries of the regions of Casablanca, Fez, Meknes, Marrakesh, Oujda, and Rabat.

48. BNR, D.667, in USHMM, RG 81.001M-12, Rabat, January 8, 1942, Ricard, "Note sur l'organisation de l'enseignement israélite au Maroc."

49. BNR, D.667, in USHMM, RG 81.001M-12, April 9, 1942, "Note sur l'enseignement israélite au Maroc." On the Alliance israélite universelle, see Michael M. Laskier, *The Alliance Israélite Universelle and the Jewish Communities of Morocco: 1862–1962* (Albany: State University of New York Press, 1983).

50. BNR, D.667, in USHMM, RG 81.001M-12, n.d. [1942], Conseiller du Gouvernement Chérifien to Secrétaire Général du Protectorat.

51. *Bulletin Officiel*, August 8, 1941; and Wyrtzen, *Making Morocco*, 206–07.

52. Files with requests for derogations are found, e.g., in BNR, D.652, in USHMM, RG 81.001M-1 and BNR, D.371, in USHMM, RG 81.001M-3.

53. Wyrtzen, *Making Morocco*, 206–8.

54. BNR, D.667, in USHMM, RG 81.001M-12, Rabat, April 20, 1942, Noguès to Chefs d'Administration et Chefs de Region.

55. Kenbib, *Juifs et Musulmans*, 628. The remittance of debts owed to Jews refers to a *dahir* that annulled mortgages held as security by Jews in 1942. Pierre Flamand, *Diaspora en terre d'Islam: Les communautés israélites du sud Marocain* (Casablanca: Imprimeries réunies, 1959 [?]), 52–53, 86–88. The author makes no connection to the anti-Jewish laws.

56. The unevenness in the implementation of the decrees is emphasized by H.Z. Hirschberg, *A History of the Jews in North Africa*, vol. 2 (Leiden: Brill, 1981), 325. This is a history that needs further investigation, examining different locales in Morocco. For Essaouira, see Chetrit, "Les Juifs de Mogador (Essaouira)." The chief rabbi and community leader from Sefrou wrote about the close ties and consultation that he had with the pasha during the war years. David Ovadia, *Kehilat Sefru*, vol. 3 (Jerusalem: Makhon le-ḥeḳer toldot ḳehilot Yehude Maroḳo, 1975), 185.

57. Founded in 1936, the Centre de hautes études d'administration musulmane was directed by Robert Montagne for training French administrators for colonial service. See Mohammed Kenbib, "Les années de guerre de Robert Montagne (1939–1944)," in *La sociologie musulmane de Robert Montagne*, ed. François Pouillon and Daniel Rivet (Paris: Maisonnneuve & Larose, 2000), 188–95.

58. MAE-Nantes, DI, 1MA/250, article 1, Centre de hautes études d'administration musulmane, "Les Juifs au Maroc," December 16, 1941, M. Dutheil.

59. BNR, D.667, in USHMM, RG 81.001M-12, February 26, 1942, Voizard to Président du Comité regional de Légion française des combattants—Oujda (sent by way of the president of the Rabat committee on December 17, 1941).

60. MAE-Nantes, DI, 1MA/250, article 1, in USHMM, RG-43.154, June 17, 1943, "Note sur la question juive au Maroc." On the measures connected to the "aryanization" of Jewish enterprises and property in France, see Marrus and Paxton, *Vichy*, 100–107, 152–60.

61. MAE-Nantes, DI, 1MA/250, article 1, in USHMM, RG-43.154, June 17, 1943, "Note sur la question juive au Maroc."

62. BNR, D.667, in USHMM, RG 81.001M-12, Note to the Resident-General, based on a report dated January 27, 1942 presented by the regional committee of the Légion française des combattants of Casablanca.

63. BNR, D.667, in USHMM, RG 81.001M-12, Rabat, August 25, 1942, Noguès to Chefs d'Administration et Chefs de Region; Rabat, September 1, 1942, Directeur des services de sécurité du publique to Sécretaire-général du Protectorat.

64. BNR, D.371, in USHMM, RG 81.001M-3, Algiers, January 6, 1943.

65. ANP, 72AJ/594, Fonds Maurice Vanikoff, at USHMM, RG-43.122, reel 2, Casablanca, May 19, 1943, Robert Schumann to Dr. Leon Kubowitski, Head of Department of European Jewish Affairs (World Jewish Congress in New York).

66. Abitbol, *Jews of North Africa*, 110–15; and Steven Uran, "Cremieux Decree," in *Encylopedia of Jews in the Islamic World* (Brill: Leiden, 2010), 688–90.

67. Hoisington, *Casablanca Connection*, 231–43.

68. Jessica Marglin, "The Two Lives of Mas'ud Amoyal: Pseudo-Algerians in Morocco, 1830–1912," *International Journal of Middle East Studies* 44 (2012): 651–70; and Daniel Schroeter, "Identity and Nation: Jewish Migration and Inter-Community Relations in the Colonial Maghreb," in *La bienvenue et l'adieu: Migrants juifs et musulmans au Maghreb (XVᵉ–XXᵉ siècle)*, ed. Frédéric Abécassis, Karima Dirèche and Rita Aouad (Casablanca: Éditions La Croisée des Chemins, 2012), 1:136–38.

69. BNR, D.317, at USHMM, RG 81.001M-9, Taza, December 19, 1940, Fridga Benhaim to the Resident Général du Maroc; and Taza, December 19, 1940, Isaac Ben Hamou to the Resident Général du Maroc.

70. BNR, D.317 at USHMM, RG 81.001M-9, Algiers, October 11, 1941, Général François, Président de la L.F.C. de l'Afrique du Nord to Monsieur le Général, Président de la L.F.C. du Maroc à Rabat.

71. BNR, D.317 at USHMM, RG 81.001M-9, October 21, 1941.

72. MAE, AD, Vichy-Maroc, vol. 18, carton 6, dossier 1, in USHMM, RG-43.006M, reel 1, Vichy, November 9, 1941, l'Amiral de la Flotte, Ministre Secretaire d'Etat aux Affaires Etrangères to Résident Général de France in Rabat and Tunis; Vichy, December 31, 1941, L'Amiral de la Flotte to Ministre Secretaire d'Etat à L'Interieur; BNR, D.317 in USHMM, RG 81.001M-9, Rabat, April 30, 1942, Le Commisaire Résident Général de France au Maroc to Directeurs et chefs d'administration.

73. The Protectorate government in Rabat elicited and received information from police and other officials throughout Morocco on reactions from the Muslim, Jewish, and French populations to the abrogation of the Crémieux Decree in 1940. MAE-Nantes, DI, 1MA/250, article 5, in USHMM, RG-43.154, Oujda, October 9, 1940, Roux; Meknes, October 10, 1940, Leandri; Taza, October 9, 1940, Palmade; Rabat, October 10, 1940, Lucet; Port Lyautey, October 11, 1940, Baldovini; Fez, October 12, 1940, Casablanca, October 12, 1940, Ninet; Marrakesh, October 15, 1940, Martin; Salé.

74. MAE-Nantes, DI, article 5 in USHMM, RG-43.154, Martinprey, November 22, 1943, Controleur Civil, Chef de l'Annexe de Martimprey du Kiss to Contrôleur Civil, Chef de la Circonscription des Beni Snassen; Oujda, December 1, 1943, Contrôleur Civil, Chef de la Region d'Oujda to Directeur des Affaires politiques.

75. Yves-Claude Aouate, "Les Algériens musulmans et les mesures antijuives du gouvernement de Vichy (1940–1942)," *Pardès* 16 (1992): 189–202.

76. David Stenner, "Did Amrika Promise Morocco's Independence? The Nationalist Movement, the Sultan, and the Making of the 'Roosevelt Myth'," *Journal of North African Studies* 19, no. 4 (2014): 524–39; Jamaâ Baïda, "The American Landing in November 1942: A Turning Point in Morocco's Contemporary History," *Journal of North African Studies* 19, no. 4 (2014): 518–23; Wyrtzen, *Making Morocco*, 170–71, 253–55; and C. R. Pennell, *Morocco since 1830: A History* (New York: New York University Press, 2000), 262–63.

77. Quoted in Abitbol, *Jews of North Africa*, 115.

78. MAE-Nantes, DI, 1MA/250, article 1, in USHMM, RG-43.154, "Note remise par M. Robert Montagne à M. Hardion," November 19, 1942.

79. MAE-Nantes, DI, 1MA/250, article 1, in USHMM, RG-43.154, June 17, 1943, "Note sur la question juive au Maroc."

80. Jessica Marglin has persuasively situated the emergence of the concept of a collective Moroccan Jewish identity in the late nineteenth century among a Westernized elite, educated in the schools of the Alliance israélite universelle, as part of the process of "becoming modern." See Jessica Marglin, "Modernizing Moroccan Jews: The AIU Alumni Association in Tangier, 1893–1913," *Jewish Quarterly Review* 101, no. 4 (2011): 574–603.

81. Schroeter and Chetrit, "Emancipation and Its Discontents," 195–97.

82. Tsur, *Ḳehilla ḳeru'a*, 15–22.

83. MAE-Nantes, DI, 1MA/250, in USHMM, RG-43.154, article 16, Fez, November 10, 1944.

84. Muḥammad Ḥātimi, "Al-Jamāʿāt al-yahūdiyat al-maghribiya wa-l-khiyār al-saʿb bayn nidāʾ al-Ṣahyuniya wa-rihān al-Maghrib al-mustaqil, 1947–1961 [The Moroccan Jewish communities and the difficult choice between the appeal of Zionism and the gamble of independent Morocco: 1947–1961]" (State doctoral thesis, Université de Fès-Saïs, 2007).

85. On the impact on the war and the overlapping political tendencies and identities of Jews in the postwar period, see Tsur, *Ḳehilla ḳeru'a*, 188–205.

86. For an argument that the Vichy period stimulated a growth in Zionism, see Michael M. Laskier, *North African Jewry in the Twentieth Century: The Jews of Morocco, Tunisia, and Algeria* (New York: New York University Press, 1994), 84–85. See also David Bensoussan, *Il était une fois le Maroc: Témoignage du passé judéo-marocain* (Montreal: Les Éditions du Lys, n.d.), 267–69.

87. Wyrtzen, *Making Morocco*, 253.

88. Hassan Rachik, *Symboliser la nation: Essai sur l'usage des identités collectives au Maroc* (Casablanca: Éditions le Fennec, 2003), 97–98; and Wyrtzen, *Making Morocco*, 161–63. For details on the official development of Throne Day and its mobilization by the nationalists, see Robert Rézette, *Les partis politiques marocains* (Paris: Librairie Armand Colin, 1955), 79–82.

89. Rachik, *Symboliser la nation*, 110–12.

90. Georges Spillman, *Du Protectorat à l'indépendance: Maroc, 1912–1955* (Paris: Plon, 1967), 83.

91. Wyrtzen, *Making Morocco*, 80–81.

92. John P. Halstead, *Rebirth of a Nation: The Origins and Rise of Moroccan Nationalism, 1912–1944* (Cambridge, MA: Distributed for the Center for Middle Eastern Studies of Harvard University by Harvard University Press, 1967), 243–50; and Mostafa Bouaziz, *Aux origines de la koutla démocratique* (Casablanca: Faculté des Lettres Aïn-Chock, 1997), 56–57. For a general discussion on the development of the the nationalist movement and its confrontation with the residency, see Susan Gilson Miller, *A History of Modern Morocco* (New York: Cambridge University Press, 2013), 129–36.

93. An exception to the silence on this question is Wyrtzen, *Making Morocco*, 205–209.

94. One of the well-known officers in the French administration in Morocco writes about the sultan's disagreement with the anti-Jewish edicts, though curiously does not mention that, nevertheless, the Sultan did sign the *dahirs*. Spillman, *Du Protectorat à l'indépendance*, 95.

95. Jamaâ Baïda, "Perception de la période nazie au Maroc: Quelques indices de l'impact de la propagande allemande sur l'état d'esprit des marocains," in *Marocains et Allemands*, ed. A. Bendaoud and

M. Berriane (Rabat: Université Mohammed V, Publications de la Faculté des Lettres et des Sciences Humaines, 1995), 15–16; On the development of nationalist activity in the Spanish zone, see Charles-André Julien, *Le Maroc face au imperialismes, 1415–1956* (Paris: Editions J. A., 1978), 173–76, 188–89.

96. Mokhtar El Harras, "La presse écrite et l'image de l'Allemagne dans la 'zone nord' du Maroc, 1934–1945," in *Marocains et Allemands,* ed. A. Bendaoud and M. Berriane, 21–36 (Rabat: Université Mohammed V, Publications de la Faculté des Lettres et des Sciences Humaines, 1995).

97. Translation of an article in *al-Ḥurriya,* sent on August 25, 1941 in MAE-Paris, AD, Vichy-Maroc, vol. 15, in USHMM, RG-43.006M, reel 1, vol. 18. On the impact of German propaganda on Moroccan nationalists and their publications in the Spanish zone, see Jamaâ Baïda, "Le Maroc et la propaganda du IIIème Reich," *Hespéris-Tamuda,* 28 (1990): 97–100. On Torrès and *al-Iṣlāḥ,* see Halstead, *Rebirth of a Nation.* Some of Torrès' writings and speeches are found in ʿAbd al-Khāliq al-Ṭurrīs, *Min turāth al-Ṭurrīs* (Rabat: Matbaʿat al-Risāla, n.d.).

98. MAE-Paris, AD, Vichy-Maroc, vol. 18, carton 6, dossier 1, in USHMM, RG-43.006M, reel 1, Vichy June 10, 1942, "Propagande espagnole auprès des Juifs marocains," Direction Politique, Afrique—Levant. BNR, D.667, in USHMM, RG 81.001M-12, Rabat May 9, 1942, Directeur des Affaires Politiques to Secrétaire Générale du Protectorat.

99. Hoisington, *Casablanca Connection,* 146–49. See also Henry Marchat, "La France et l'Espagne au Maroc pendant la période du Protectorat (1912–1956)," *Revue de l'Occident musulman et de la Méditerranée* 10 (1971): 81–109.

100. MAE-Paris, AD, Vichy-Maroc, vol. 18, carton 6, dossier 1, in USHMM, RG-43.006M, reel 14, Rabat, October 7, 1940, Noguès to French Consul General in Tangier; Vichy October 8, 1940, Ministère des Affaires Étrangères.

101. MAE-Paris, AD, Vichy-Maroc, vol. 18, carton 6, dossier 1, in USHMM, RG-43.006M, reel 1, Madrid, December 15, 1941. Communiqué on "La question juive au Maroc d'après la propagande espagnole," from the French Embassy in Spain to Darlan.

102. Wyrtzen, *Making Morocco,* 208–09.

103. Isabell Rohr, *The Spanish Right and the Jews, 1898–1945: Antisemitism and Opportunism* (Brighton: Sussex Academic Press, 2007).

104. USHMM, RG-43.070M, LIV-1 (original in Centre de Documentation Juive Contemporaine), August 22, 1941, "Position des autorités espagnoles à l'égard du problème juif." On the issue of Spain in the northern zone, the protection of Sephardic Jews, and the French authorities, see Kenbib, "Moroccan Jews and the Vichy Regime," 548–49.

105. Moshe Gershovich, *French Military Rule in Morocco: Colonialism and Its Consequences* (London: Frank Cass, 2000), 190; and Daniel Zisenwine, *The Emergence of Nationalist Politics in Morocco* (London: Tauris Academic Studies, 2010), 22–23.

106. See especially Assaraf, *Mohammed V et les Juifs du Maroc.*

107. His theory of Jews' liminal positionality is best articulated in his autobiographical novel of growing up in Tunis: Albert Memmi, *La statue de sel* (Paris: Corrêa, 1953).

108. Emanuela Trevisan-Semi, "La mise en scène de l'identité marocaine en Israël: Un cas d'"Israélianité" diasporique," *A Contrario* 5, no. 1 (2007): 40–41.

109. This idea is reflected in the new constitution of 2011, the monarchy's response to the Arab Spring, that states that Morocco is constituted by the blending of its "African, Andalusian, Jewish and Mediterranean" cultural streams. The text is found in the *Bulletin Officiel,* July 30, 2011. The reference to the Jewish influence can be seen as an official positioning of Morocco amid the rapidly changing political and cultural landscape of the Arab world, where a struggle is being played out in protests, elections, and debates over how to define the future.

11

THE POLITICS OF STREET RIOTS

ANTI-JEWISH VIOLENCE IN TUNISIA
BEFORE DECOLONIZATION

Maud S. Mandel

ON JUNE 14, 1952, a riot broke out in the Hafsia neighborhood of Tunis, situated between the Jewish and Muslim quarters of the city. According to reports of events that day, a fight began when approximately one hundred Muslim youth entered the neighborhood with the goal of destroying "a stall containing a large roulette wheel at which certain Jewish and Muslim elements regularly play."[1] Both Muslim and Jewish leaders disapproved of the roulette wheel because it tempted those with few resources to gamble. During the attack some stones fell on adjoining Jewish houses; young Jews in the neighborhood responded by launching their own stones, leading to a brawl. While the police calmed passions, Muslim youth returned in greater numbers later that day to continue the fight, only to be chased away by angry Jewish youth. During the subsequent struggle, a policeman attacked a seventeen-year-old Jewish boy, Samuel Journo, who ultimately died from the wounds.[2] Rumors circulated that the policeman was himself Muslim, although the French colonial administration refused to release any information about him. Jewish communal authorities sought to calm the agitated Jewish community and to assure Jews that Journo's murderer would be punished. Violence continued the next day when returning Muslims, "angry at having been driven back the day before by the young Jews," sought revenge.[3] Tensions in the neighborhood persisted. On June 16 Jewish merchants refused to support a nationalist strike that had been organized in response to rumors that the French had attempted to poison the Tunisian monarch. Journo's funeral that day further piqued passions. More than ten thousand people attended the funeral, including Jewish youths who shouted angrily in Arabic and Hebrew of vengeance and justice. According to the World Jewish Congress (WJC) report

251

on these events, "the atmosphere was so tense that it would have taken nothing to ignite even more serious incidents."[4]

Historians have largely overlooked this riot. However, if we follow the prevailing historiography on the Jews of Muslim lands after 1945, and particularly after 1947–48, we would be inclined to regard these events as indicative of the increasingly vulnerable position of the North African Jewish community in light of war in the Middle East and mounting Muslim antisemitism.[5] A close reading of the riot, however, makes clear that the aggressor/victim binary is not the most productive way of understanding Muslim–Jewish relations at the moment when Tunisian nationalism began to gather steam. Indeed, while Muslim aggression against their Jewish neighbors was certainly present that day, the Tunisian independence struggle was rewriting the country's ethnic landscape for *all* social and political actors: Jews were active participants in the riot, as were French police. Moreover, while the politics of contesting French rule had certainly begun to reshape interethnic relations on the ground, a complex array of social and political actors were implicated in these developments, including Jewish international organizations that were assessing the riot from abroad. The active role of such organizations itself contributed to oversimplified perceptions of Muslim aggressors and Jewish victims. Indeed, in solidifying a particular narrative about Jewish victimization and weakness in the wider Muslim milieu, Jewish nongovernmental organizations (NGO) were directly involved in shaping events as they unfolded— and not simply as objective *rapporteurs*. The wider imperial context that gave international Jewish voices a role in determining the political future of indigenous Jews in North Africa meant that Jewish NGOs were well placed to influence events.[6]

This chapter focuses on the two substantial primary sources that report on the riot and what a new reading of these sources can tell us about the state of Muslim–Jewish relations as local nationalists began challenging French rule. The first, penned by Gerhard Riegner, secretary-general and coordinating director of the WJC, details information gathered during his visit to Tunis immediately after the riot. The second has no author attributed to it but was drafted by the American Jewish Committee (AJC) several weeks after the events in question. The very specific details recounted in the report suggest that the author or authors also spent several weeks in Tunis following the riot.

The interest of the WJC and the AJC in Jewish life in Tunisia and in North Africa more generally was of fairly recent vintage. With the end of World War II and the intensification of the struggle in Palestine, international Jewish agencies that had directed their energies toward aiding European Jews began focusing on Muslim lands more actively. Most notably, in 1947 the WJC submitted a petition to the United Nations to call attention to anti-Jewish activities in the Middle

East following a wave of anti-Jewish violence in Egypt, Aden, Syria, and Bahrain.[7] French North Africa—removed as it was both from the Holocaust's worst devastations and from the center of the Middle Eastern conflict—received less attention.[8] Soon, however, the legacy of the recent destruction in Europe combined with mounting conflict in Libya and elsewhere in the Middle East meant that Jewish life in Algeria, Tunisia, and Morocco came to the attention of various Jewish NGOs, including the WJC and AJC, which began to view the religious Jewish populations of French North Africa as a new source of vitality after the devastation of the Holocaust. Deeply involved in discussions about the fate of Libyan Jews after a 1945 riot in which 130 Jews and 1 Muslim were killed, these organizations supported the flight of thousands of Jews who fled for Israel between 1949 and 1951 while also pressing for constitutional protections for those who remained following the establishment of Libyan independence in 1951.[9] Indeed, the AJC established an office in Paris in April 1947 charged with focusing on Jewish life in both Europe and North Africa, arguing that events in Libya would serve as a destabilizing force for Jewish life throughout North Africa. For the next several years, the AJC worked in the international arena to secure human rights for the region's Jewish population.[10] As one 1949 AJC memo made explicit, it was North Africa that should "assume in our future work the place held by Eastern Europe during the first 25 or 30 years of the Committee's existence."[11]

Meanwhile, because Algerian, Moroccan, and Tunisian delegates were among the founders of the WJC in 1936, the organization saw itself as particularly well placed to pressure the French government to rethink Jewish legal status in its colonial territories and protectorates.[12] Anti-Jewish riots in the Moroccan towns of Oujda and Djerada in 1948 increased the WJC's sense of urgency.[13] With its attention drawn to the region, the WJC established a section in Morocco in 1949, the head of which was Jacques Lazarus, a former member of the French resistance and the Haganah, and head of the Comité juif algérien d'études sociales, which represented Algerian Jews to the French administration. Bringing Jewish leaders in Tunisia, Morocco, and Algeria together with WJC officials from Geneva, London, Paris, and New York, the local WJC monitored the position of Jews in the region and put pressure on the French to ensure their equality and their right to emigrate. Moreover, under WJC auspices, the first conference of North African Jewish communities took place in Algiers in June 1952, shortly after the riot under discussion. The WJC and, to a somewhat lesser degree, the AJC were thus institutionally positioned to report on events that transpired in Tunisia.

Yet even though both organizations had taken an interest in North Africa more generally and in the riot in particular, their reports differed notably from one another. While both provided a fairly similar account of the details leading up to, during, and following the riot, the AJC's report repeatedly stressed the strong relations between Muslims and Jews in Tunisia and blamed a handful of ruffians for provoking the violence. It also praised the "realistic vision" of Muslim leaders that permitted the "immediate re-establishment of the cordial and harmonious atmosphere which has always existed between Jews and Muslims."[14] The WJC report, in contrast, ended with reflections on the "significant antisemitic tendencies" at the heart of a Muslim population that "could be exploited and burst into the light of day" with little provocation. Calling for "extreme vigilance," Riegner's report warned of the risk of "closing one's eyes . . . to these latent dangers" and urged emigration and the ongoing maintenance of the French colonial infrastructure.[15]

Given long-standing differences between the AJC and the WJC regarding the most efficacious and prudent approach to Jewish political engagement, these divergent perspectives may not seem all that surprising. The AJC, born in the United States in 1906 and long dominated by the well-off and well-integrated descendants of the German Jews who had left Europe for the United States in the 1840s, promoted an "assimilationist" politics that favored behind-the-scenes negotiations to protect Jewish interests over confrontational tactics. Initially hostile to Zionism, many members of the AJC came to support Jewish development in Palestine, particularly after World War II, while never accepting the WJC's claim that Jewish politics transcended national borders. Moreover, even after the State of Israel was founded, key AJC leaders feared being accused of dual loyalty and sought reassurance from Israeli politicians that the new state would do nothing to undermine the position of Jews in the diaspora.[16]

The WJC, in contrast, while born in Geneva in 1936 as a cultural body to address the fragmentation of Jewish life in the diaspora, quickly shifted its agenda to focus on the fight against Nazism. By adopting an activist and visible political stance, it lobbied governments, convened diplomatic conferences, issued press releases and petitions, and sent countless telegrams in its initial call for a boycott of German goods and the censure of the Nuremberg laws. Once war broke out, the WJC used the same tactics to fight for Allied aid to Jewish survivors and to organize rescue schemes, all while promoting settlement in Palestine.[17]

Given these differences, the AJC and WJC often came into conflict over the best approach to forwarding Jewish political interests. Their differing reports on the 1952 events in Tunis certainly reflect these perspectives, with the AJC implicitly emphasizing the comfortable integration of Jews in the wider majority-Muslim society and the WJC stressing instead the fissures and potential for rupture. And yet as Nathan Kurz has recently argued, from 1948 to the mid-1950s, the AJC and the WJC began to converge on key political priorities regarding Jewish life in North

Africa, including the importance of maintaining French control and, as that became less likely, the need for Jewish emigration.[18] Given that the WJC called for both in its assessment of events in Tunisia in 1952, despite in fact corroborating all of the AJC's narrative details of what transpired over those days, we must look again at both how the WJC came to its conclusions and the impact of its dire assessments. Put differently, since the AJC (as well as other international Jewish NGOs) came in short order to view the landscape in North Africa in much the same way as the WJC, we must revisit the differences in their interpretations of events in Tunisia to begin to understand how the WJC's assessments of the North African Jewish landscape proved more enduring and what that can tell us about Jewish life in North Africa in the era of decolonization.

To consider these issues fully, this chapter reads the AJC and WJC reports against each other as well as against their own "fault lines," following Ann Stoler's call to read colonial archives as subjects as much as sources.[19] Stoler reminds historians of the power of colonial officials to shape historical narratives of the regions they controlled, suggesting that we should read their archives not only for what they leave out but also for their "regularities, . . . logic of recall, . . . densities and distributions, . . . [and] consistencies of misinformation, omission, and mistake."[20] To view the AJC and WJC reports as constituting a "colonial archive" may seem a leap, since neither organization represented a colonial power or even a state entity. Nevertheless, in the world of mid-twentieth-century colonial politics, Jewish organizations—and particularly the WJC—had the ear of colonial officials and, hence, played a significant role in what was "known" about the Jewish populations of North Africa both at the time and subsequently.[21] Moreover, the leaps in the WJC report, which become particularly evident when reading it against the AJC report, make Stoler's caution quite relevant, particularly considering the WJC's impact in shaping the historical record of the riot and longer-term perspectives on Muslim–Jewish relations in Tunisia.

As Mary Lewis has argued in a different temporal context, to fully understand the colonial Tunisian landscape, it is necessary "to push past the closed circuit of metropole/colony" and to consider the ways in which the wider international order shaped colonial policies and practices.[22] By adopting a similar framework for analyzing the 1952 riot in Tunis, it becomes clear that if Muslim–Jewish relations were being rewritten in the context of the Tunisian independence struggle, postwar international Jewish political actors played a key role in that process. Never passive bystanders in the events they were reporting, they sought to shape international perceptions of Jewish life in the Maghreb and to conceptualize what the end of French colonial rule would mean for the region's indigenous Jewish populations. The riot itself was not fated to change the complex dynamics among various actors in Tunisia. Rather, because the riot came to feed into a broader narrative, it added to the growing sense that Jewish lives were imperiled.

* * *

There is a notable contradiction between the opening of the WJC account, which roots the riot in sociopolitical origins and the conclusions that it draws, which stress Muslim–Jewish ethnoreligious tension. The report's author, Gerhard Riegner, explains that the initial attack was directed not at Jews but at the gambling stall. Muslim leaders, he reports, had been discouraging any participation in public rejoicing or leisure activities that June as a way of expressing a sense of communal mourning over recent political events. And while Riegner provides virtually no details about the wider political context in which the riots took place, events that spring were hardly incidental to its occurrence.

The riot occurred within the broader context of the struggle for Tunisian independence from France and the violence that that struggle unleashed. In December 1951 the French government backpedaled on previous efforts to move toward Tunisian internal autonomy, insisting that the 250,000 European settlers play a significant role in Tunisian governance moving forward. Tunisian nationalist leader Habib Bourguiba rejected prior efforts to cooperate with authorities and urged his followers toward combat. Several weeks later, Tunisian nationalists lodged a complaint with the UN Security Council that France was in violation of its treaties with Tunisia. The political situation quickly deteriorated into open confrontation. In response, French officials arrested most of the nationalist leadership, including Bourguiba, inciting riots throughout the country.[23] A cycle of French repression and violence against colonial targets intensified throughout the spring as Tunisian guerrillas used mountain bases to attack French settlers and as police and nationalists clashed in Tunis and other cities.[24] In March martial law was declared, as Prime Minister Mohamed Chenik and other ministers were arrested along with several thousand supporters of Tunisian independence.[25] In April, after the UN Security Council voted against placing the Tunisian matter on its agenda, Tunisian nationalists bombed a post office in Tunis, killing five people.[26] On June 4 police arrested agitators for three bombing attempts in March and April, and on June 5 twelve demonstrators were sentenced to prison terms ranging from five to twenty years of hard labor. On June 7, four bomb explosions went off in Tunis, and on June 11 five Tunisians were sentenced to death by a French military tribunal (three of whom were later shot).[27]

The attack on the gambling wheel three days later was embedded in this mounting tension. The death sentence of prominent Tunisian nationalists evoked calls for mourning from those supporting the movement. As Riegner reported, the gambling wheel, already viewed as a source of social instability, was now "very poorly perceived"; it seemed a symbol of frivolity in a moment of national mourning when nationalists were seeking to build support for their movement. Indeed a few days prior to the riot in the Hafsia, an attack on another gambling site had taken place in another quarter of Tunis where no Jews lived, "and where racial or religious animosities were certainly not the question."[28]

Thus, the events that triggered the riot at the Hafsia gambling wheel were not driven primarily by antisemitism—either popular or planned—but rather by wider political events and a concern (shared by Muslim and Jewish leaders alike) that illicit gambling was a social vice that should be curbed. To downplay antisemitism as the sole source of the violence is not to ignore tensions in Tunis between Muslims and Jews. Beginning with the French conquest of Algeria in 1830, French expansion throughout North Africa fundamentally altered long-standing ethnoreligious relations on the ground as colonial administrators, scholars, and legislators constructed categories for understanding indigenous society that emphasized regional, ethnic, religious, social, and economic divisions over social unity.[29] Jews, in these constructions, were often held to be more intelligent and "assimilable" than the Muslims among who they lived. In Algeria, where such thinking took legal form, the 1870 Crémieux Decree granted French citizenship to nearly the entire Algerian Jewish population, juridically cutting them off from most Algerian Muslim subjects.[30] In Tunisia and Morocco, which remained nominally under Muslim control throughout the colonial period, no mass naturalizations occurred.[31] Nevertheless, the "Frenchification" of local Jewish populations took place through more informal administrative practices and the schools of the Alliance israélite universelle, meaning Jews had greater opportunities to acculturate to European social and cultural norms than the Muslim populations amidst whom they lived, contributing to the formation of new social hierarchies and new ethnoreligious tensions.[32]

Nor were these tensions cemented in time but rather changed in response to local conditions, colonial/metropolitan relations, and global politics. As Joshua Cole has shown in the case of Constantine in the interwar years, for example, tensions between Muslims and Jews increased substantially as Jewish citizens and Muslim colonial subjects found that changing terms of their political inclusion forced them to forge different alliances with the colonial state and its local administrators.[33] Yet, while anti-Jewish sentiment grew as a result, the causes of violence in 1933 and, more famously, those of the violent riots a year later cannot be attributed "simply" to antisemitism. The 1934 riot, which led to the deaths of twenty-four Jews and four Muslims and significant damage to Jewish businesses and property, emerged from the complex social, economic, and political conditions of 1930s Constantine, including the poverty of the city's Muslim shop owners and surrounding peasantry; spreading European antisemitism; growing frustration of Muslims toward the French; fears of Jewish residents regarding increased Nazi and Arab nationalist propaganda; Constantine's political milieu; the residue of prior incidents perpetrated by Jews against Muslims; and the slow response of French authorities to the actual violence during the riots themselves.[34] Likewise, as Harvey Goldberg has made clear in his analysis of the anti-Jewish riots in Libya in 1945, such violence emerged as Muslim nationalists sought to test the limits of local colonial control. The attack on Jews, then, became a "generalized call to eliminate foreign rule in terms that resonate[d] with the traditional religio-political order."[35]

As in Algeria and Libya, tensions between Muslims and Jews in Tunisia became exacerbated in the shifting political context of the interwar years. Of particular significance was the charged issue of Palestine, which inspired controversy in Tunisia due to that country's proximity to the Middle East and its greater access to regional news. As a result, local nationalist parties expressed stronger pro-Palestinian sympathies than was typical of Muslim nationalist movements elsewhere in the Maghreb. Criticizing Zionism through its organ *La Voix du Tunisien* in the early 1930s, Neo Destour, the leading Tunisian independence party, demanded that French authorities take a stand against Zionist gatherings. The result was conflict and even localized violence when Tunisian Muslim nationalists clashed with the flourishing local Zionist movement that had built a substantial press and network of philanthropic and youth organizations.[36] Muslim–Jewish tensions intensified again during World War II, when some Muslims saw the German conquest as a way to free themselves from the French and established alliances with the antisemitic Nazi regime.[37] And yet, as Robert Satloff has demonstrated, other Tunisian Muslims went out of their way to protect local Jews while most, in North Africa and elsewhere, displayed indifference to the Jewish plight.[38]

Whatever the shifting and complex range of Muslim–Jewish relations in Tunisia prior to the 1950s, Neo Destour sought to be as inclusive as possible in its public pronouncements, deemphasizing the role of Islam in Tunisian nationalism in part to encourage Jewish support for the movement.[39] And reports from American, British, and French Jewish representatives who visited Tunisia in the early 1950s insisted that the Tunisian nationalist struggle against the French rarely affected Jews.[40] In February 1952, for example, the American Jewish Joint Distribution Committee reported "no evidence of anti-Jewish policy on the part of the nationalist movement."[41] While concern was regularly voiced for Jews in the country's interior where small Jewish communities lived isolated from one another among much larger Muslim populations, the predominant sense was that Tunisian nationalism was generally tolerant toward Jews.

As this discussion suggests, then, Muslim–Jewish relations in Tunisia varied according to local, national, and global realities, and tension between the two groups was neither pervasive throughout the country nor pivotal to Neo Destour's agenda. Emphasizing antisemitism as the riot's driving force thus raises the question of why tensions emerged in Tunis at that particular moment and overlooks counter evidence of a more variegated social landscape.

Similarly revealing with regard to the state of Muslim–Jewish relations in Tunis in the early 1950s is the fact that the site targeted for destruction in the riot—the gambling stall—was a shared social space where Jews and Muslims played *together*, winning disapproval from their respective communal leaders for giving in to joint temptation. As Emily Gottreich's analysis of the *mellah* of Marrakesh makes clear, Jewish quarters in North Africa often became spaces for illicit ethnoreligious mixing around gambling, prostitution, and other social vices.[42] While such willingness to recreate together does not in itself prove the existence of a convivial interethnic landscape, the recognition of such shared leisure spaces nevertheless reminds us that historical accounts stressing the binary of Muslim aggressors and Jewish victims belies a more complex social reality. According to scholars such as Richard Parks and Paul Sebag, the Jewish quarter in Tunis, or the *hara*, while cemented in the public imagination as a strictly Jewish space carved out of the wider "Arab" *medina*, was, in fact, residentially mixed with poverty rather than ethnicity being the primary marker of residential inclusion.[43] As Sebag noted of the *hara* in the 1950s, "Jews and Muslims pursue the same professions in neighboring stalls; on the patios, their wives help one another in numerous ways; their children play together on the esplanade without the slightest incident."[44] Not only were Jews not bound to live in the *hara*'s confines but also, since the interwar years, French urban planners and colonial administrators had systematically sought to move Jewish inhabitants to other areas of the city in a wider effort to "regenerate" and Europeanize non-Muslim areas of the urban landscape.[45] The Hafsia neighborhood, where the gambling stall was located and that bordered the *hara* in the northern part of the medina of Tunis, while often understood to be a Jewish space, was ethnically mixed, particularly after World War II, when aerial bombardments had degraded the area further, causing even more Jews to move out.[46] The gambling stall thus brought together those of different religions but shared poverty.[47] To be sure, playing together did not necessarily create social fusion. As Albert Memmi's semiautobiographical novel of life in Tunis, *A Pillar of Salt*, makes clear, it only took "five hundred steps" in the *hara* to "change civilizations."[48] Nevertheless, day-to-day relations were generally peaceful, suggesting that neither antisemitism nor long embedded interethnic tension can be considered the primary trigger for the violent outburst of June 14.

Perhaps more interesting, however, is that the riot's initial escalation was not the work of anti-Jewish mobs but rather the result of *Jewish* responses to stones that had fallen on their homes.[49] Although, once agitated, Muslim youth continued to attack the neighborhood, these repeated attacks were driven, in the opinion of both the AJC and WJC reports, by having been "bested" by Jewish youth in the previous encounters.[50] Beginning in the early 1940s, the Jewish Agency had intermittently trained young Jews in self-defense as part of a wider intensification of pro-Zionist activities in Tunisia.[51] While those officially trained in self-defense were undoubtedly quite small in number, generally speaking, it was the poorest members of Tunisia's Jewish population—well represented in the *hara*—who flocked to the Zionist movement after World War II.[52]

Indeed, both the AJC and WJC pointed to a Jewish population that responded quickly when rocks landed accidentally or intentionally on their doors and windows. In Riegner's words: "The fact remains . . . that young Jews immediately took to the defense. That is how the first fight broke out and it seems that the Jews did fairly well defending themselves." As the riot spread, young Jews "vigorously defended themselves, and pushed the Arabs back fairly far, beyond the Jewish quarter, even as far as the Arab quarter."[53] According to Riegner, it was French police that prevented the Jewish fighters from chasing their opponents even further. Moreover, as noted earlier, young Jews attending Journo's funeral called out loudly for revenge. When an unfounded rumor circulated that the Jewish quarter was again under attack, hundreds of young people began running from the morgue to help defend their co-religionists. Thousands of others lined the streets to watch the coffin be carried to the cemetery. Describing the funeral as one of the most moving he ever attended, Riegner noted that "this was one of the most impressive demonstrations of the Jewish masses which reflected their determination to protect themselves and their solidarity with the victim."[54] Likewise, the AJC labeled the action of the Jewish youth as "magnificent," giving many "food for thought." Elsewhere in the report, the AJC noted the "fine attitude of Jewish youth . . . [which] showed its spirit of cooperation and its will to defend the interests of the Jewish community."[55]

These depictions reveal a Jewish population—and particularly a young Jewish population—actively taking part in the riot and in their own self-defense. As a minority in a shifting political context, they were undoubtedly also at risk. However, Jews were hardly passive bystanders or mute victims in a period in which the French authorities and the Tunisian nationalist movements were renegotiating their relationship. As scholarship on Tunisian Jews makes clear, whatever their liminal position in French-controlled Tunisia, they often were better positioned than their Muslim neighbors with regard to the French authorities.[56] Nor were they united in their response to the conflict, with some

such views had to remain confidential so as to protect Jews from nationalist retribution.[67] Subsequently, the WJC and its local Jewish supporters emphasized that support for the French was essential, even if such support had to remain behind the scenes. In November the Tunisian committee of the WJC thus asserted the "absolute necessity of maintaining a French presence in Tunisia" while urging neutrality in public. According to one attendee, "We should do nothing to make it seem as though we are maneuvering to prevent any group's access to full liberty," a stance, he believed, that would contradict the Jews' very public struggle for liberty across the ages. Rather than rejecting pro-colonial politics altogether, however, he instead urged the WJC to act "with discretion" behind the scenes to maintain French protections for Tunisian Jews.[68] The WJC took heed; following the riot, Riegner met privately with Pierre Mendès-France, then member of the French National Assembly and soon to be France's third prime minister of Jewish origin, to ask him to use his influence to help his co-religionists in Tunisia.

One might well ask why the WJC was so willing to trust France to protect Jewish interests given that country's recent antisemitic past and the WJC's own expressed distrust of French motives during the riot. Indeed, whatever the differences in interpretation between the AJC and WJC reports, they agreed on French duplicity that June. The AJC thus deplored French censorship, "which was inspired by a strange spirit and which tended rather to create a chasm between the two elements of the population than to maintain an atmosphere of peace and cordiality."[69] The WJC's report went even further, accusing the French of intentionally pushing Jewish and Muslim residents against each other as a way to distract attention from the wider independence struggle. And yet, despite the WJC's distrust of French motives, it ultimately saw the maintenance of French control to be a more surefire way to protect the Jewish future in Tunisia than the declaration of independence.

How could Riegner so easily whitewash France's recent past while so quickly assuming the racism of Tunisian society? Although the report itself supplies few answers to this question, it is notable that World War II and the rise and fall of the Vichy regime seems to have done little to shake Riegner's faith in the European civilizing mission or his belief that European governments might be viable partners in the struggle to protect Jewish rights.[70] Moreover, he used his position as an international Jewish spokesman to promote that perspective both with French authorities and with like-minded members of the Tunisian Jewish leadership with whom he was in close contact. The solution he and the wider WJC promoted encouraged a sense of Jewish distance from Tunisian nationhood by calling for emigration or the maintenance of French colonial rule.[71] As Riegner later summarized, "The WJC was the only Jewish organization that foresaw the unfolding of potentially destructive political events in the region. We had no choice but to draw the appropriate dire conclusions."[72]

Such an assessment provides a clue into the origins of the WJC's perspective. Indeed, The WJC had come of age during efforts to save European Jews from the Nazis and as Zionism was gaining popularity as an answer to antisemitism. Riegner himself became well known in Jewish circles as the author of the so-called Riegner telegram, the first official communication about the Nazi's exterminatory campaign to make it from Europe to the United States and England in August 1942. His wartime efforts to save European Jewish life permanently marked his subsequent work (and that of the WJC more generally) as he continued to defend Jews around the globe.[73] As he commented many years later in his memoirs, "The world conflict from which we [had] emerged raised far-reaching challenges to received opinion and prompted fresh reflection."[74] For him and for others with whom he worked, downplaying or ignoring anti-Jewish animosity came at great peril; it was, quite simply, a mistake the WJC was determined not to let the world make again. The fact that Jews themselves seem to have helped ignite the violence in Tunis thus received no comment in his conclusions. Rather, Riegner insisted that the key lesson to take from these events was the need for "an attitude of extreme vigilance" in order to avoid "closing our eyes to possible latent dangers."[75] Anti-Jewish violence in Libya and Iraq simply confirmed what the WJC already knew to be true: that Jews in Arab lands were the next large Jewish population to be at risk. The riot confirmed the WJC's worst fears and galvanized the organization's spokesmen to take steps to protect "endangered" Jews.

But while the WJC was the most vocal in drawing such conclusions, it was not alone. As observers from the American Jewish Joint Distribution Committee (AJDC) noted in February, even before the riot had occurred "the majority of the Jewish population feels that should the French be forced to leave Tunisia, the Jews would have to leave too."[76] While the numbers of departures after independence do not reflect an immediate or panicked flight, the fact that the AJDC and other Jewish NGOs promoted such views helped shape international perspectives on viable regional outcomes.[77] Indeed, although the WJC and AJC provided different interpretations of the riot and disagreed publicly on the best ways to protect Jewish interests, in short order, the AJC also began insisting on the Jewish right to emigrate.[78]

This focus on a Jewish exit strategy from Tunisia remained central to Jewish NGO policies as the country moved toward independence. In August 1954, for example, the WJC's political director in London, A. L. Easterman, met with Habib Bourguiba in the Ferté-Montargis fortress where he had been interned by French authorities hoping to quell the nationalist movement. Bourguiba assured

Easterman that Jews would be guaranteed equality in all civic and political rights, including the right to emigrate to Israel. The meeting established a close working relationship between Bourguiba and the WJC as the latter began directing its efforts more systematically to Morocco.[79] Yet, if with the dawning of Tunisian independence, WJC representatives continued to work with local Jewish leaders to protect the rights of Jewish Tunisian citizens, they never abandoned efforts to protect the right to emigrate to Israel. One scholar has argued that the WJC adopted a " 'constructively vague' approach" with regard to North African Jewish emigration to Israel as a way both to remain faithful to the organization's pro-Zionist heritage and to safeguard its relations with its Muslim contacts.[80] But I would argue otherwise: the WJC's consistent reiteration of the right of migration subtly emphasized Jewish distance from the Tunisian nationalist project even as the WJC sought to defend a place for Jews therein. Such a dual integration/emigration emphasis paved the way for other international Jewish NGOs to follow suit.

* * *

To emphasize the WJC's role in shaping the boundaries of Jewish political belonging in Tunisia in the early 1950s is not to argue the WJC or any other Jewish NGO was solely responsible for new ways of thinking about Jewish life in the region. As earlier scholarship has shown, French colonial expansion in North Africa, surging regional nationalist movements, and World War II all played a role in transforming Muslim–Jewish relations in Tunisia by the 1950s. What this literature has overlooked, however, is that the processes of change that came with European expansion in Tunisia and elsewhere in North Africa took new shape with French extrication from the region.[81] In other words, the process of ethno-religious renegotiation that had accompanied colonial conquest shifted again in the face of the cycle of nationalist violence and French repression. Within this volatile atmosphere, political constellations shifted and frayed, creating new political opportunities for Jewish organizations working in the region.

The AJC and WJC representatives who stepped into this space came with perspectives and political strategies honed in other contexts. AJC representatives responded to the riot by drawing on that organization's long-term commitments to Jewish integration into majority societies; the WJC focused instead on Jewish vulnerability and marginality drawn from its years of fighting Nazi racism in Europe. By telling the story of the riot as one of Jewish victimization at the hands of an aggressive Tunisian Muslim minority, WJC representatives began drawing political lines that emphasized Muslim–Jewish division. This move, while made with the best of intentions, described Jews as outsiders to the Tunisian national project and endorsed French colonialism. As other Jewish NGOs came to view Muslim–Jewish relations along similar lines, the story of ethnore-ligious tension began to dominate, erasing all signs of the complex and varie-gated landscape that had existed before.

Notes

1. G. M. Riegner, "Rapport sur la situation en Tunisie," June 20, 1952, XIX, Fonds Jacques Lazarus, Alliance israélite universelle (AIU), 1. A second major source for the riot, "General Report on the Inci-dents in the Ghetto of Tunis between Jews and Moslems," June 14 and 15, 1952, Countries Subject Files [FG 347.7.1 FAD-1]. Box 120, Folder 1, Foreign Affairs Department, American Jewish Committee Files, Center for Jewish History [hereafter, "General Report"], states instead that fighting broke out after the Muslim youth "inevitably" moved on to neighboring Jewish houses after destroying the gambling wheel. Thanks to Nathan Kurz for sharing this latter report and several other key documents with me.

2. While "Rapport sur la situation en Tunisie" reports that the policeman beat Journo, the "General Report" claims that a policeman shot Journo.

3. Riegner, "Rapport sur la situation en Tunisie," 2.

4. Ibid., 3.

5. Most accounts of Jewish life in Tunisia do not touch on the riot as such. Mostly notably, Paul Sebag's *Histoire des Juifs de Tunisie: Des origines à nos jours* (Paris: L'Harmttan, 1991), which points to the period after World War II as one of dynamic change in Tunisian Jewish economic, occupational, and educational life, does not mention the riot. Claude Nataf, "Les Mutations du judaïsme tunsien après la seconde guerre mondiale," *Archives juives* 30, no. 1 (2006): 125–36, which focuses on Tunisian Jewish re-sponses to World War II, also never mentions the riot. Unsurprisingly, Claire Rubinstein-Cohen, *Por-trait de la communauté juive de Sousse (Tunisie): De l'orientalité à l'occidentalisation—Un siècle d'histoire (1857–1957)* (Saint-Denis: Éditions Edilivre Aparis, 2011) also does not mention the riot, due to its focus on Sousse. The one detailed scholarly account of the riot can be found in Michael M. Laskier, *North African Jewry in the Twentieth Century: The Jews of Morocco, Tunisia, and Algeria* (New York: New York University Press, 1994), 260–61, in which the author argues that the June 14 riot was a turning point in Tunisian Jewish history, after which Muslim animus increased substantially. Laskier's work largely em-phasizes the decline narrative outlined above. The riot is also mentioned briefly by Abdelkrim Allaghui in "La minorité juive de Tunisie face à la decolonization au cours des années 50," in *Processus et enjeux de la décolonisation en Tunisie*, ed. Habib Belaïd (Tunis: Publications de l'institut supérieur d'histoire du movement national, 1999), 314–15. For recent examples of the broader decline narrative, see Georges Bensoussan, *Juifs en pays arabes: Le grand déracinement, 1850–1975* (Paris: Tallandier, 2012); and Shmuel Trigano, "La face cachée du nationalisme en terres d'Islam," in *La fin du judaïsme en terres d'Islam* (Paris: Denoël, 2009), 9–50.

6. This essay is indebted in part to a historiographical tradition of crediting the intervention/interfer-ence of foreign Jewish organizations—and particularly the Alliance israélite universelle—with promoting North African Jewish attraction to French colonial culture and thereby destabilizing centuries-long cul-tural connections to the region. See, notably, Mohammed Kenbib, *Juifs et Musulmans au Maroc: 1859–1948* (Rabat: Université Mohammed V, Publications de la Faculté des Lettres et des Science Humaines, 1994); and Michael M. Laskier, *The Alliance Israélite Universelle and the Jewish Communities of Morocco, 1862–1962* (Albany: State University of New York Press, 1983). For more recent assessments, see essays by Jonathan G. Katz, Joy A. Land, and Keith Walters in *Jewish Culture and Society in North Africa*, eds., Emily Benichou Gottreich and Daniel J. Schroeter (Bloomington: Indiana University Press, 2011); as well as Daniel J. Schroeter and Joseph Chetrit, "Emancipation and Its Discontents: Jews at the Forma-

tive Period of Colonial Rue in Morocco," *Jewish Social Studies* 13, no. 1 (Fall 2006): 170–206. For Tunisia, see Claude Hagège and Bernard Zarca, "Les Juifs et la France en Tunisie: Les benefices d'une relation triangulaire," *Le mouvement social* 4, no. 197 (2001): 14–15, 20–21; Yaron Tsur, "Réformistes musulmans et Juifs en Tunisie à la veille de l'occupation française," in *Juifs et musulmans en Tunisie: Fraternité et déchirements*, ed. Sonia Fellous (Paris: Somogy, 2003), 161–68. For other international organizations that affected Jewish life in North Africa, particularly after World War II, see Michael Menachem Laskier, Sara Reguer, and Haim Saadoun, "Community Leadership and Structure," in *The Jews of the Middle East and North Africa in Modern Times*, eds., Reeva Spector Simon, Michael Menachem Laskier, and Sara Reguer (New York: Columbia University Press, 2002), 57–58. For the impact in Morocco, see Jonathan Wyrtzen, "Constructing Morocco: Colonial Struggle to Define the Nation, 1912–1956" (PhD. diss., Georgetown University, 2009), 268.

7. Nathaniel A. Kurz, "'A Sphere above the Nations?': The Rise and Fall of International Jewish Human Rights Politics, 1945–1975" (PhD diss., Yale University, 2015), chap. 3. Kurz notes that the AJC and other Jewish NGOs did little of substance due to a "reigning sense of passivity and helplessness" (169).

8. The exception was the Alliance israélite universelle, which was established in Paris in 1860 to fight for Jewish political rights and modernization worldwide, and which established an educational network in French North Africa. The Alliance continued this work after World War II, expanding its mandate to a range of juridical and social issues, particularly in Morocco. Yaron Tsur, "L'AIU et le judaïsme marocain en 1949: L'émergence d'une nouvelle démarche politique," *Archives juives* 34, no. 1 (2001): 54–73. The WJC, in contrast, focused much less on North Africa. *Unity in Dispersion: A History of the World Jewish Congress* (New York City: Institute of Jewish Affairs of the WJC, 1948), for example, published in 1948, never mentions North African Jews. Devoted primarily to documenting the WJC's wartime activities, the volume ends by discussing its role elsewhere in the Arab world and in Eastern Europe. In his memoir, Gehard M. Riegner speaks of the Jewish world's "rediscovery" of North African Jews after World War II. Riegner, *Never Despair: Sixty Years in the Service of the Jewish People and the Cause of Human Rights*, trans. William Sayers (Ivan R. Dee, 2006), 354.

9. For discussions of the riot in Libya, see Harvey E. Goldberg, *Jewish Life in Muslim Libya: Rivals & Relatives* (Chicago: University of Chicago Press, 1990), 97–122.

10. For the AJC's growing role in France, see Laura Hobson Faure, *Un "Plan Marshall Juif": La présence juive américaine en France après la Shoah* (Paris: Armand Colin, 2013). For the role of the AJC, WJC, and other NGO's in Libya, see Kurz, "'A Sphere above the Nations?'", 212–26.

11. Cited in Kurz, "'A Sphere above the Nations?,'" 225–56.

12. Wyrtzen, "Constructing Morocco," 268. For more on the WJC activities in North Africa, see Kurz, "'A Sphere above the Nations?,'" 228–29; Laskier, Reguer, and Saadoun, "Community Leadership and Structure," 58; Maud S. Mandel, *Muslims and Jews in France: History of a Conflict* (Princeton, NJ: Princeton University Press, 2014), chap. 2; and Riegner, *Never Despair*, 354–65.

13. These riots, which also raised fears of regional antisemitism, were also more complex than they initially appeared to many European and American Jewish observers. Mandel, *Muslims and Jews in France*, 27–28.

14. "General Report," 11–12.

15. Riegner, "Rapport sur la situation en Tunisie," 6.

16. Marc Dollinger, *Jews and Liberalism in Modern America: Quest for Inclusion* (Princeton, NJ: Princeton University Press, 2000), 11–12, 92–97, 118–20, 123–24, 126–28. For a general history of the AJC, see Naomi Cohen, *Not Free to Desist: History of the American Jewish Committee, 1906–66* (Philadelphia: Jewish Publication Society, 1972).

17. For the WJC's early years, see WJC, *Unity in Dispersion*. For a general overview of its history, see Avi Becker, "Sixty Years of World Jewish Congress Diplomacy: From Forging Policy to the Soul of the Nation," in *Jewish Centers and Peripheries: Europe between America and Israel Fifty Years after World War II* (New Brunswick, NJ: Transaction, 1999), 373–96; and Avi Becker, "Diplomacy without Sovereignty:

The World Jewish Congress Rescue Activities," in *Organizing Rescue: Jewish National Solidarity in the Modern Period*, ed. Selwyn Ilan Troen and Benjamin Pinkus, 343–60 (London: Frank Cass, 1992).

18. Kurz, "'A Sphere above the Nations?,'" 229. As Kurz makes clear, most scholars have missed the ways in which Jewish international organizations converged on these issues.

19. Stoler provides a valuable overview of the way new scholarship encourages an examination of archives-as-subject rather than simply archives-as-source. Ann Laura Stoler, "Colonial Archives and the Arts of Governance," *Archival Science* 2 (2002): 87–109, at 109. Also see Ann Laura Stoler, *Along the Archival Grain: Epistemic Anxieties and Colonial Common Sense* (Princeton, NJ: Princeton University Press, 2010).

20. Stoler, "Colonial Archives and the Arts of Governance," 100.

21. See Sara Abrevaya Stein, *Saharan Jews and the Fate of French Algeria* (Chicago: University of Chicago Press, 2014) for an interesting parallel of the ways in which colonialism shaped what was "known" about North African Jews.

22. Mary Lewis, "Geographies of Power: The Tunisian Civic Order, Jurisdictional Politics, and Imperial Rivalry in the Mediterranean, 1881–1935," *Journal of Modern History* 80, no. 4 (2008), 798. Also see Lewis, *Divided Rule: Sovereignty and Empire in French Tunisia, 1881–1938* (Berkeley: University of California Press, 2014).

23. Kenneth Perkins, *A History of Modern Tunisia* (Cambridge: Cambridge University Press, 2004), 122–23; and Benjamin Rivlin, "The Tunisian Nationalist Movement: Four Decades of Evolution," *Middle East Journal* 6, no. 2 (Spring 1952): 189.

24. Assa Okoth, *A History of Africa*, vol. 2, *1915–1995* (Nairobi: East African Education Publishers, 2006), 233.

25. In 1950 France promised self-government to Tunisia and established a ministry headed by Mohamed Chenik and supported by Neo Destour to help govern the country. As the nationalist movement gathered steam, France back peddled on earlier commitments. Kenneth Perkins, *A History of Modern Tunisia*, 2nd ed. (Cambridge: Cambridge University Press, 2014), 110–34.

26. "Developments of the Quarter: Comment and Chronology," *Middle East Journal* 6, no. 3 (Summer 1952): 335.

27. "Developments of the Quarter: Comment and Chronology," *Middle East Journal* 6, no. 4 (Autumn 1952): 463.

28. Riegner, "Rapport sur la situation en Tunisie," 1.

29. Recent scholarship has stressed that a full understanding of Jews and Muslims within colonial North Africa can only emerge from studying them together. See, for example, Emily Benichou Gottreich, *The Mellah of Marrakesh: Jewish and Muslim Space in Morocco's Red City* (Bloomington: Indiana University Press, 2006); Joshua Schreier, *Arabs of the Jewish Faith: The Civilizing Mission in Colonial Algeria* (Piscataway, NJ: Rutgers University Press, 2010); and Benjamin Stora, *Les trois exils: Juifs d'Algérie* (Paris: Stock, 2006). For the power of French ethnic constructions in Algeria, see Patricia Lorcin, *Imperial Identities: Stereotyping, Prejudice and Race in Colonial Algeria* (London: I. B. Tauris, 1995); and Patricia Lorcin, *Kabyles, Arabs, Français: Identités coloniales* (Limoges: PULIM, 2005).

30. Schreier, *Arabs of the Jewish Faith*, argues that Jewish "worthiness" for emancipation was used to exclude Muslims who were seen as comparatively less able to become French. See Stein, *Saharan Jews*, for a notable exception to the mass naturalization of Algerian Jews.

31. In 1923 the French government passed the Morinaud Law, enabling non-French Europeans who had been in Tunisia for three years to become naturalized as part of the government's wider efforts to increase its hold over the country in the face of Italian imperialist designs in the region. Thus, despite French colonial administrators' opposition to blanket Jewish naturalization, the number of naturalized Jews grew over the next ten years. See Richard C. Parks, "Hygiene, Regeneration, and Citizenship: Jews in the Tunisian Protectorate" (Ph.D. diss. University of Minnesota, 2012), 34–37, 98–100. Fayçel Cherif reports 7,160 Jewish naturalizations from 1911 to 1940; Cherif, "Jewish-Muslim Relations in Tunisia during

World War II: Propaganda, Stereotypes, and Attitudes, 1939–1943," in *Jewish Culture and Society in North Africa*, 314. In Morocco, rules against naturalization were tighter than in Tunisia and Algeria. André Chouraqui, *Histoire des Juifs en Afrique du Nord: Le retour en Orient* (Monaco: Editions du Rocher, 1998), 39. For a helpful comparison of the processes of Jewish modernization in Tunisia and Morocco, see Michel Abitbol, "La modernité judéo-tunisienne vue du Maroc," in *Juifs et musulmans en Tunisie*, 181–90.

32. As Gottreich makes clear in *The Mellah of Marrakesh*, the impact of European expansion on Jews varied throughout the country with those in Marakesh proving quite distrustful of arriving outsiders. For scholarship on the impact of the AIU in the region, see note 6, above.

33. Joshua Cole, "Constantine before the Riots of August 1934: Civil Status, Antisemitism, and the Politics of Assimilation in Interwar French Algeria, *Journal of North African Studies* 17, no. 5 (December 2012): 839–61.

34. Charles-Robert Ageron, "Une émeute anti-juive à Constantine (août 1934)," *Revue de l'Occident musulman et de la Méditerranée*, no. 13–14 (1973): 23–40; Yves-Claude Aouate, "Constantine 1934: Un pogrom 'classique,'" *Les nouveaux cahiers* (1985); Robert Attal, *Les émeutes de Constantine: 5 août 1934* (Paris: Romillat, 2002); Richard Ayoun, "À propos du pogrom de Constantine (août 1934)," *Revue des études juives* 144 (1985): 181–86; Joshua Cole, "Antisémitisme et situation coloniale pendant l'entre-deux guerres en Algérie," *Vingtième siècle* 108 (October–December, 2010): 3–23; and Ethan Katz, "Constantine Riots (1934)," *Encyclopedia of the Jews in the Islamic World*, ed. Norman Stillman (Boston: Brill, 2010).

35. Goldberg, *Jewish Life in Muslim Libya*, 118.

36. Haïm Saadoun, "L'Influence du sionisme sur les relations judéo-musulmanes en Tunisie," in *Juifs et musulmans en Tunisie: Fraternité et déchirements*, ed., Sonia Fellous, 219–29 (Paris: Somogy, 2003); and Haïm Saadoun, "The Effect of the Palestinian Issue on Muslim-Jewish Relations in the Arab World: The Case of Tunisia (1920–1939)," in *Israel and Ishmael: Studies in Muslim–Jewish Relations*, ed., Tudor Parfitt, 105–23 (New York: St. Martin's, 2000).

37. Cherif, "Jewish–Muslim Relations," 305–20.

38. Robert Satloff, *Among the Righteous: Lost Stories from the Holocaust's Long Reach into Arab Lands* (New York: PublicAffairs, 2007). For stories of Tunisian Muslims protecting Jews, see pp. 111–37.

39. James J. Natsis, *Learning to Revolt: The Role of Students in the National Movement in Colonial Tunisia* (Lanham, MD: University Press of America, 2002), 46; Rubinstein-Cohen, *Portrait de la communauté juive de Sousse*, 246–47; and Sebag, *Histoire des Juifs de Tunisie*, 276–78.

40. Hélène Cazes-Benatar, for example, noted no anti-Jewish discrimination in Tunisia. Cazes-Benatar, "Report on the Political Situation in North-Africa," October 1, 1950, Records of the Geneva Office of the American Jewish Joint Distribution Committee, G 45-54/4/22/3, American Jewish Joint Distribution Committee [AJDC], at http://jdc.org/.

41. "Executive Meeting: North Africa and the Middle East," February 29, 1952, North Africa, Loan Kassas, 1951–1954 45/54 #10 [45/64 #13], NY AR194554/4/2/5/10, AJDC.

42. Gottreich, *Mellah of Marrakesh*, 74; 79.

43. Philippe Barbé argues that the hara was not economically homogenous, with a middle class of shopkeepers and craftsmen living within as well as a small Europeanized group of merchants, financiers, doctors, and lawyers living on its edge. Barbé, "Jewish–Muslim Syncretism in the Writings of Albert Memmi," in *Jewish Culture and Society in North Africa*, ed. Emily Benichou Gottreich and Daniel J. Schroeter, 114–17 (Bloomington: Indiana University Press, 2011). Parks, however, shows how the area grew poorer as wealthier Jews moved to more Europeanized sections of the city. Parks, "Hygiene, Regeneration, and Citizenship."

44. Paul Sebag, *La Hara de Tunis: L'évolution d'un ghetto Nord-Africain* (Paris: Presses universitaires de France, 1959), 88.

45. Parks, "Hygiene, Regeneration, and Citizenship."

46. Thanks to Richard Parks for this information.

47. For a description of Jewish poverty in the *hara* in the postwar years (although with no mention of Muslims in this area that the author labels "a city within a city"), see Sebag, *Histoire des Juifs de Tunisie*, 262.

48. Albert Memmi, *The Pillar of Salt*, trans. Edouard Roditi (Boston: Beacon Press, 1955), 97; see also Barbé, "Jewish–Muslim Syncretism," 113.

49. Jewish participation in anti-Muslim violence was also evident in Constantine in 1933 and 1934. See Cole, "Constantine before the Riots of August 1934"; and Katz, "Constantine Riots (1934)."

50. For an ethnographic analysis of the shame for Muslims associated with being "bested" by Jews, see Goldberg, *Jewish Life in Muslim Libya*, 29–31.

51. Laskier, *North African Jewry*, 280–82; and Haim Saadoun, "Tunisia," in *The Jews of the Middle East and North Africa in Modern Times*, ed. Reeva Spector Simon, Michael Menachem Laskier, and Sara Reguer (New York: Columbia University Press, 2002), 455.

52. Sebag, *Histoire des Juifs de Tunisie*, 273–74; and Nataf, "Les mutations du judaïsme tunisien," 131.

53. Riegner, "Rapport sur la situation en Tunisie," 1.

54. Ibid., 3.

55. "General Report," 8; 11.

56. See most recently, Parks, "Hygiene, Regeneration, and Citizenship."

57. Albert Memmi rather schematically described Tunisian Jews as divided among those who supported Tunisian nationalists, those who supported the French, and those who hoped to migrate to Israel. Memmi, "Le Juif colonisé," in *Juifs et Arabes* (Paris: Gallimard, 1974), 68–76. For a more detailed historical depiction of the community's political diversity, see Sebag, *Histoire des Juifs de Tunisie*, 276–77, who nevertheless argues that the great majority shied away from either supporting the Tunisians against the French or vice versa. Nataf, "Les Mutations du judaïsme tunsien," 125–36, in contrast, argues that many of those with pro-French sympathies prior to the war emerged bitter and willing to support alternative options, such as communism and Zionism. For Jewish attraction to communism as rooted in their attachment to French republican ideals, see Hagège and Zarca, "Les juifs et la France en Tunisie," 11–12. For differing views toward Tunisian independence among the Jews of Sousse, see Rubinstein-Cohen, *Portrait de la communauté juive de Sousse (Tunisie)*, 225–48.

58. Dr. Mokadem, "Communiqué," June 16, 1952, XIX, Fonds Jacques Lazarus, AIU; and "General Report," 8.

59. "Extraits de la presse arabe de Tunis," XIX, Fonds Jacques Lazarus, AIU; see also "General Report," 8. André Chouraqui, Louis D. Horwitz, and Helene Cazes-Benatar described Neo-Destour's apology as well as the sympathy expressed in the Arabic language press. In their summary, "The leaders of the Jewish communities have maintained friendly relations with both sides in the conflict." Chouraqui, Horwitz, and Cazes-Benatar, "Foreign Countries: North Africa," *American Jewish Year Book* 54 (1953), 375–76.

60. "General Report," 10–11.

61. Riegner, "Rapport sur la situation en Tunisie," 6.

62. "General Report," 11–12.

63. Ibid., 2.

64. Ibid. Rubinstein-Cohen captures the regional impact of Zionism after 1948 and the way Jewish out-migrations reflected both class differences and shifting political realities on the ground as Tunisian nationalism threatened French colonial control. Rubinstein-Cohen, *Portrait de la communauté juive de Sousse (Tunisie)*, 225–32.

65. Kurz, "'A Sphere above the Nations?,'" chap 4.

66. Riegner, "Rapport sur la situation en Tunisie," 6.

67. Perlzweig quoted in Kurz, "'A Sphere above the Nations?,'" 230. Despite the Tunisian Jewish support of the French colonial state, Riegner left the conference feeling that "most community leaders

seemed wrapped in a feeling of security, far from imagining the profound changes that would threaten their way of life." Riegner, *Never Despair*, 355.

68. Cited in André Dreyfus to Maurcie L. Perlzweig, November 12, 1952, XIX, Fonds Jacques Lazarus, AIU.

69. "General Report," 11.

70. Riegner certainly was not alone in viewing postwar France as untainted by the crimes of its Vichy predecessor, as Henry Rousso proved many years ago in his work on "the Vichy syndrome." Henry Rousso, *The Vichy Syndrome*, trans. Arthur Goldhammer (Cambridge, MA: Harvard University Press, 1991). Most Jews in France also bought into a myth that France was free of the taint of Nazi crimes due to their rapid political, economic, and social reintegration after World War II, which prevented them from calling attention to France's role in the persecution of its Jewish residents. See Maud S. Mandel, *In the Aftermath of Genocide: Armenians and Jews in Twentieth Century France* (Durham, NC: Duke University Press, 2003).

71. Kurz, " 'A Sphere above the Nations?,' " 209.

72. Rienhard, *Never Despair*, 256.

73. According to Becker, Nahum Goldmann, WJC president from 1949 to 1977, refused to draw direct comparisons between the situation in Nazi Germany and that in North Africa. Nevertheless, numerous references in WJC documents make clear the degree to which the shadow of World War II shaped assumptions and perceptions regarding Jewish life elsewhere after the war. Becker, "Diplomacy without Sovereignty," 357–58.

74. Riegner, *Never Despair*, 355.

75. Riegner, "Rapport sur la situation en Tunisie," 6.

76. "Executive Meeting: North Africa and the Middle East," February 29, 1952, North Africa, Loan Kassas, 1951–1954 45/54 #10 [45/64 #13], NY AR194554/4/2/5/10, AJDC; see also Laskier, *North African Jewry*, 262–63; and Sebag, *Histoire des Juifs de Tunisie*, 276.

77. Laskier, *North African Jewry*, 274.

78. Kurz, " 'A Sphere above the Nations?,' " chap 4.

79. Rienhard, *Never Despair*, 357–58.

80. Becker, "Diplomacy without Sovereignty," 354.

81. Scholars have begun making a similar kind of argument in the case of Algeria. See most notably Ethan Katz, *The Burdens of Brotherhood: Jews and Muslims from North Africa to France* (Cambridge, MA: Harvard University Press, 2015), chaps. 4 and 5; Mandel, *Muslims and Jews in France*, chap. 2; and Todd Shepard, *The Invention of Decolonization: The Algerian War and the Remaking of France* (Ithaca, NY: Cornell University Press, 2006), 169–82.

PART 3

ZIONISM AND COLONIALISM

12
IS ZIONISM A COLONIAL MOVEMENT?

Derek J. Penslar

THE RELATIONSHIP BETWEEN Zionism and colonialism, long a highly controversial subject among scholars throughout the world, has in recent years become
a primary source of friction between champions and opponents of revisionism
within Israeli historiography and sociology. Until the 1980s most scholars of Israel studies teaching in Israeli universities denied or qualified linkages between
Zionism and late nineteenth-century imperialism. This approach is still taken by a
number of younger scholars in Israel, but in the past fifteen years there has risen
a cohort of Israeli academics who, following the lead of Arab and Western scholarship on the modern Middle East, have made linkages between Zionism and
colonialism central to their scholarly endeavors.

Regardless of their political stance, historians of Israel have sought to recon-
struct the sensibilities and mental universe of their subjects, just as scholars of
Israeli sociology have focused on broad sociocultural and economic structures.
Traditional Zionist historiography emphasized that the founders of the State of
Israel did not think of their enterprise as colonial in nature and, in fact, abhorred
contemporary European colonialism for its parasitical profiting from the expropriation of native land and the exploitation of native labor. Classic Israeli social
science, in turn, has contended that the Zionist movement and Yishuv did not
conform to any conventional model of a colonizing state and that the structural
barriers between Jewish and Arab society before 1948 were so great as to render
impossible any consideration of the Jewish–Arab relationship as one between
colonizers and colonized.

Some of the more recent Israeli historiography, on the other hand, claims
that Zionist thinking, like that of fin-de-siècle Europeans as a whole, operated on
multiple levels and that feelings of benevolence, humanitarianism, and sympathy

could easily blend with condescending, orientalist, and racist views of the Palestinian Arabs. Israel's current crop of critical sociologists, claiming that Jews and Arabs in pre-1948 Palestine constituted a common socioeconomic and political matrix, argue that Zionism conformed closely with typical European settlement colonialism, in which, as Ronen Shamir has put it, "employers and employees belong to the same ethnic group . . . and in which that ethnic group has effective control over the land in ways that enable it to extract and utilize its resources."[1]

One serious problem with the discussion on the relationship between Zionism and colonialism is the attempt to establish complete congruence or total separation between the two phenomena. A related problem is the failure to include additional categories of analysis such as anticolonialism (Zionism as an act of resistance by a colonized people) and postcolonial state building (understanding Israel within the political and economic framework of twentieth-century Asia and Africa). This essay contends that the Zionist project was historically and conceptually situated between colonial, anticolonial, and postcolonial discourse and practice. Colonial and anticolonial elements coexisted in the Zionist project from its inception until the creation of the state in 1948. From the time of Herzl onward, the Zionist political elite was eager to appeal to the interests of the Great Powers, and the Zionist movement as a whole was shot through with orientalist conceptions of Arab degeneracy and primitiveness. At the same time, pre-state Zionism possessed anticolonial elements present in sundry national liberation movements in the modern world. Moreover, underlying Zionist thought, preceding and running alongside of it, was the European Jewish intelligentsia's historic struggle, from the time of the Jewish Enlightenment until the twentieth century, to defend Jewish culture against that of the dominant Christian society through strategies similar to those employed by the colonized intelligentsia of Asia and Africa.

After 1948 the young State of Israel, like many countries in Asia and Africa, translated the anticolonialist rhetoric of victimization into a triumphant postcolonial discourse of technical planning and state socialism. Yet colonialist elements were present as well in the treatment of Israel's Arab minority and state confiscation of its land. Israeli territorial conquests in the 1967 war, although fueled mainly by security concerns, evoked powerful feelings of manifest destiny as well as a lust for profit, thus highlighting the colonialist aspects of the Zionist project and causing many of Israel's critics to adopt a longstanding Arab discourse of Zionism as a purely colonialist movement from the start.

Unlike most of the literature on Zionism's relationship with colonialism, which tends to employ comparative models solely in order to incriminate or exculpate Zionist thought and practice, my intent here is to build a two-way street in which a comparative approach can throw new light on our understanding of not only Zionism but also the historic relationship between colonialism and nationalism throughout the globe. I draw here on some essential texts in postcolonial studies, especially the work of Partha Chatterjee, whose theoretical models of anticolonial nationalism, although based on the particular case of Bengal, suggest many intriguing points of contiguity between the Zionist project and anticolonial movements. Dialectically, however, my use of postcolonial texts to deconstruct current conceptions of Zionism's relationship with colonialism will deconstruct the texts themselves, for, I believe, scholars such as Chatterjee are prone to essentialize anticolonial movements and unjustly deny their grounding in classic European nationalism.[2] In other words, by depicting Zionism as in many ways an anticolonial movement and Israel as having resembled, at least for its first two decades, a postcolonial state—by placing Zionism in Asia, as it were—I re-place Zionism in Europe, a continent distinguished by not only the great overseas empires of the West but also a sizable body of colonized, stateless peoples, including Jews.

In this essay I draw a distinction between postcolonial discourse and post-colonial practice. When first used in the 1950s, the term "post-colonial" referred to a historical movement, when Europe's former colonial possessions became independent. Since the 1970s, however, post-colonialism has mutated from a descriptive category into a conceptual framework for critiquing Western forms and relations of power. (Thus the de-hyphenization of the term; from the delimited temporal and spatial realm of "the post-colonial world," emphasizing transition, to the diffuse and overarching intellectual field of "postcolonialism.") Whereas post-colonial states were frequently the creation of nationalist movements, post-colonialism, according to Robert Young, one of the subject's most eminent scholars, "always operates as a form of internationalism" because nationalism, in his view, is inherently oppressive, and new tricontinental (Asian/African/Latin American) states that adopt European nationalist sensibilities and practices have internalized the evils of the oppressor.[3] I do not share this view, which robs the anticolonial nationalist movements of the power of judgment and which, as I argue at the end of the essay, overlooks nationalism's transcendence of its European origins to become a global vehicle of collective identity.

Modern European colonialism took many forms, the principal ones being settler colonialism, in which substantial numbers of Europeans established permanent communities that became extensions of the homeland; penal colonialism, where Europe's dangerous classes were shipped off to distant terrain (for example, Australia); and exploitation colonialism, wherein the natural resources and indigenous population of lands in the New World, Africa, and Asia were harnessed in the service of the motherland or of a private company licensed by the state (for example, the British East India Company). The exploitation of native labor as well as the expropriation of native lands could occur in all three types of colonialism. The two phenomena were at times causally linked, in that expropriation could stimulate the formation of a landless rural population, which then provided cheap labor on plantations and in workshops and factories. On the other hand, the two could develop separately; settlement colonialism frequently displaced the native from his land so that it might be worked by members of the colonizers' nationality.

It is tempting to classify Zionism as a form of settlement colonialism not only because of the large numbers of Jews who immigrated to Palestine but also because of the speed with which they indigenized, that is, became rooted in the land and came to think of it as their native land (as opposed to an abstract, distant object of desire, a "holy land" or "land of their ancestors" to which they would return in messianic days). In this regard, the Zionist Yishuv resembled the settlement of the Boers in South Africa or the British colonists in early modern North America. Perhaps the most celebrated exponent of this view in the Western world is the late Edward Said, who in a stream of writings decried the Zionists' eagerness to ally with the great colonial powers and the rapidity with which they engulfed, and then extruded, virtually the entire Palestinian nation.[4] A far more nuanced stance was adopted by the French scholar Maxime Rodinson in his thoughtful long essay *Israel: A Colonial-Settler State*, published in 1973. Rodinson displayed considerable sympathy with the Jews' historic attachment to the Land of Israel, and he believed that the aspiration to return to Zion was not, in and of itself, tainted by colonialism. Nor did he identify Zionist courting of the European powers with colonial ambition, since Arab nationalists did exactly the same thing in order to realize their own political aspirations. What made Zionism a form of settler colonialism, in Rodinson's view, was the simple fact that Palestine was inhabited by an indigenous people and colonized by a European one.[5] Quoting the sociologist René Maunier, Rodinson wrote: "One can speak of colonization when there is, and by the very fact that there is, *occupation with domination*: when there is, and by the very fact that there is, emigration with legislation."[6] That is, Zionists immigrated to Palestine, dominated it, and then legitimated their domination through legislation such as the Law of Return.

Rodinson contends that Zionism is a form of settler colonialism but observes that colonialism has run throughout the entirety of human history, so the only real difference between Zionism and past forms of European colonialism is its relative novelty. This argument is unassailable by dint of its excessive breadth. The period between the birth of Zionism and the birth of the State of Israel corresponded more or less to the era when European colonial domination reached its zenith. It is thus not surprising that the debate about Zionism's relationship with colonialism centers around its connections with or divergence from European practices of that period.

Fin-de-siècle European colonialism was fostered by a colonizing state, a key factor missing in the early Zionist movement. Until Israel's establishment in 1948, the various international Zionist agencies and the Zionist institutions of the Yishuv exercised highly limited authority over small portions of Palestine. It is often claimed that, after the collapse of the Ottoman Empire and the establishment of the British mandate over Palestine, Britain came to play the role of colonizing state. The British Mandatory regime developed Palestine's physical infrastructure, sanctioned mass Jewish immigration, and encouraged the development of Jewish autonomous political and even military institutions.[7] Clearly, without British support, the Zionist project would have died in the cradle. Yet Britain's role was inconsistent, vacillating between promoting and throttling the Zionist project. Britain was more a stepfather than a biological parent of the Jewish state. Thus, even critics of Zionism such as Daniel Boyarin and Gershon Shafir have acknowledged that the Zionist movement lacked a "mother country" and therefore defies simplistic association with European settlement colonialism.[8]

There are apparent parallels between the Zionist movement's nation-building practices and the exploitation and displacement modes of colonial practice. The former manifested itself in the heavy reliance upon Arab labor in the Zionist plantation colonies and in certain urban industries. The level of exploitation, however, was exceedingly modest; during the mandate period, only about 5 percent of Palestine's Arabs worked in the Jewish sector, and their earnings made up only 7 percent of the Palestinian Arab national product.[9] Moreover, the use of Arab labor was not necessarily or purely colonial, as throughout the Arab world in the early twentieth century the development of capitalist agriculture tore peasants from their holdings and sent them into agricultural wage labor. Both Arabs and Jews owned citrus groves and both employed Arab laborers on similar terms. The argument that Zionism aspired from the start to displace the local population points to the Zionist national institutions' assiduous purchase of Arab-owned land and restrictive access to it to Jews alone. Indeed, there are many documented cases, from the turn of the century through the 1930s, of Jewish land purchases causing the displacement of Palestinian peasants; yet the overall dimensions of the phenomenon are difficult to determine, as is the overall importance of displacement as opposed to other factors in the movement of Palestinian laborers from the countryside to the cities during the mandate period.[10]

Critiques of Zionism as a form of displacement colonialism not only point to Jewish land purchases but also claim that from the time of Herzl onward, the

Zionist movement intended to expel the native Palestinian population. Until the intensification of the Zionist–Palestinian conflict during the mid-1930s, however, there was little discussion, public or private, of systematic removal of Arabs from Jewish-owned land.[11] A discourse of expulsion did not develop even when the Zionists explicitly invoked European nationality conflicts as models for their own actions. (Thus, for example, in 1908 the Zionist Organization (ZO) planned to establish a publicly funded colonization company along the lines of the Prussian Colonization Commission, which sought to strengthen the German presence in Prussian Poland. Zionist bureaucrats blithely cited both the Prussian commission's colonization of German settlers and Polish countermeasures, such as agricultural cooperatives to assist Polish freeholding peasants, as models of the mobilization of public direction and expertise, on the one hand, and private capital, on the other, for the public good.[12]) The tumultuous events of the years 1936–45 introduced an aggressive, militant tone into Zionist political rhetoric, which did not shy away from a possible "transfer" of Palestinians. But neither this rhetoric nor the mass expulsions that in fact did occur during the 1948 War can be assimilated within a colonialist analytical framework. The war was not a colonial uprising but rather an existential conflict between two nationalities.

Although the consequences of Zionist settlement up to World War II did not assume the grand dimensions of European colonialism, the Zionist project's means and methods, its underlying sensibilities regarding Palestine and its inhabitants, were shot through with colonial mentalities. Within a few years of its founding in 1897, the ZO tried to assume the role of a colonizing state. It overtly emulated European practices by establishing a colonial bank, funding research and experimentation in tropical agriculture, and supporting capitalist joint-stock companies that, like their counterparts in the service of European imperialism, were thought to eventually yield a profit to their shareholders. The instrumental rationality, bureaucratic procedure, and expectation of sustained profit that characterize modern colonialism (and distinguish it from mere conquest) were all present in the early Zionist project. The ZO's attempts to take on the mantle of the colonizing state, however, failed primarily due to a lack of means. Moreover, although the officers of the ZO had few qualms about linking the enterprise with European colonialism, their colonization schemes did not call for the exploitation of native labor (as was the case in the African colonial societies sponsored by the Zionist leader Otto Warburg, who hoped to set up profitable plantation colonies in Palestine but assumed that the laborers would be Jewish).

Zionist discourse conformed in many ways to the colonialist and orientalist sensibilities of fin-de-siècle European society. Zionism contained a powerful *mission civilisatrice* to awaken the Middle East from what was believed to be a narcotized Levantine torpor, to shatter the fossilized soil of the Holy Land with

European tools and technology. One of the most powerful motifs in Zionist thought, the desertification of Palestine under Arab and Turkish rule and the Zionist mission to make the desert bloom, was shared by many Europeans who attributed the naturally arid ecology of the Middle East to human malfeasance. French colonialists claimed, for example, that in antiquity Algeria had been the breadbasket of Rome but under Berber rule had become barren and malarial.[13] Moreover, Zionists, like Europeans in general, both romanticized and scorned the Middle East's native peoples. Zionists exalted the Bedouin as the true son of the desert, and some residents of the Yishuv, particularly students, laborers, and guards, dressed in Arab fashion as an expression of their sense of return to reclaim their ancient Middle Eastern patrimony. This sentimental idealization of the noble savage, however, was overlaid by powerful feelings of moral and material superiority. The Palestinian peasant was often perceived by Zionists as an ignoble savage, uncouth and backward. The most benign Zionist impulses to offer Arabs the fruits of Western technology and to present a model of bourgeois social relations were imbedded in a project to control, direct, and regulate all affairs in the Land of Israel. This blend of feelings of familial affinity and paternalist superiority was manifested in the Zionist claim that the Palestinian Arabs, or "Arabs of the Land of Israel," as they were called, were the descendants of ancient Hebrews who had been cut off from Jewish civilization and slowly devolved, preserving shards of the ancient Hebrew customs and language.

Such views toward Arabs could be understood in terms of Mary Louise Pratt's concept of the "anticonquest," "strategies of representation whereby European bourgeois subjects seek to secure their innocence in the very moment that they assert European hegemony."[14] Zionism certainly contained orientalist elements, and it constructed elaborate moral justifications for its colonization project. At the same time, its discursive framework differed from that of European overseas colonialism in intriguing ways—for example, in its assertion of familial propinquity, however distant, with the Arabs. As opposed to Joseph Conrad's nightmarish vision of the corruption of the white man who journeys into the heart of African darkness, Conrad's contemporary, the Hebrew writer Moshe Smilansky, presented Jewish contact with the Bedouin and Druze of Palestine as literally an ennobling experience. In Smilansky's writing, celebration of the Arab must be understood in terms not of Western romanticization of the utterly alien noble but rather of Russian depictions of the semi-Asiatic Caucasian Muslim as intrinsically Russian.[15] Of course, the Caucasian Muslim in imperial Russia was, no less than the Palestinian Arab, a colonized figure; what interests us here is the differing strategies of and justifications for domination.

Whereas the topos of the Arab as sexual object figured prominently in orientalist fantasy (the object was usually female but at times male, as in André

Gide's novel *The Immoralist*), the sexualized Arab rarely figured in literature or public speech as a Zionist desire.[16] Although there were surely romantic and sexual contacts between Jews and Arabs in early twentieth-century Palestine (this subject requires serious exploration), the issue of miscegenation, the source of such great anxiety and public debate in French, Dutch, and German colonialism, scarcely rippled the waters of Zionist discourse. In early-twentieth-century Germany, female colonial activists had to struggle for the legitimization of the woman as a colonizing agent in the form of the settler's wife (as opposed to the native concubine), while in the Zionist movement and the Yishuv the Jewish woman was, from the start, accorded a central role as wife and mother, and, indeed, the socialist Zionist women's movement's struggle to replace that ideal type with the female pioneer laborer attests to the significance and tenacity of the former.[17] Perhaps the difference between the two situations may be attributed to the fact that German colonialism was primarily an exploitative venture in which men sought adventure and release from the confines of the domestic sphere, whereas Zionism represented a form of settlement colonialism, which, as in North America, frequently involved families immigrating as a whole.

Our discussion thus far has focused on the Zionist movement's relation with Palestinian Arabs, with whom Zionists claimed a hazy affinity while asserting their absolute cultural superiority. This claim of propinquity came into much sharper focus when the Zionist leadership and intelligentsia, which was overwhelmingly Ashkenazi, turned its attention to Jews of the Middle East (Mizrahim). Zionists followed in the tracks of the Alliance israélite universelle, a Paris-based organization that, in the last third of the nineteenth century, established a network of schools for Jewish youth throughout the Mashriq and Maghreb. As agents of French language and culture in the Middle East, the teachers of the Alliance were suffused with a *mission civilisatrice* very much in keeping with the cultural goals of French colonialism.[18] Ashkenazi Zionists, in turn, considered their Middle Eastern brethren to be degenerate yet improvable "human material," to employ the commonly used term from the interwar period.[19] Those who had been least exposed to Western influences (for example, the Jews of Yemen) were seen as petrified exemplars of the ancient Hebrews (Galapagos Jews, as it were). Precisely because they were believed to be true Orientals, however, Yemenite Jews were also perceived as "natural laborers" who could compete successfully with Arabs, performing backbreaking agricultural work at low wages. (With this goal in mind, in 1912 the ZO's Palestine Office recruited Yemenite Jews to immigrate to Palestine; a contingent of them labored on the lands of the Kinneret training farm, only to be summarily expelled in 1930 when the land was needed for new immigrants from eastern Europe.[20]) On the other hand, the highly urbanized Jews of Iraq were perceived as degenerate because of their assimilation into Arab culture and their advanced state of secularization. Thus, during the early 1940s Histadrut emissaries in Iraq conceived of the Jews in that land as requiring not only physical rescue but also a physical and spiritual regeneration in the Land of Israel.[21] Throughout the mandate period, American and European Zionists active in a variety of social-welfare projects (for example, the Hadassah Medical Organization) conceived of Palestine's Mizrahi Jews and Arabs alike as socially and culturally backward and in need of the blessings of Western civilization.

It has become fashionable to claim that from the Zionist movement's very beginnings the Ashkenazi Zionist stance toward Middle Eastern Jews was pronouncedly colonialist.[22] There is good reason to make a claim for a colonialist policy by the Israeli state during the period of the great immigration from the Mashriq and Maghreb. Before 1948, however, Zionist institutions had limited abilities to command the fate of Jews in Palestine and virtually none in the rest of the world. To the extent that colonialist elements suffused the Zionist movement's position toward Mizrahi Jews, these were more cultural than operational. It is certainly possible to employ the term "colonial" to describe not merely physical domination but also cultural hegemony, not governmentality but collective mentality, but if we are to do so then we must be willing to apply this concept to the historic status of European, and not only Mizrahi, Jews as a colonized people. Only then can we understand why Zionism, even when espoused by an Ashkenazi elite and suffused with colonial motifs, represented the ultimate phase of a European anticolonial discourse that dated back to the early nineteenth century.

In an essay on colonial practice in fin-de-siècle French Indochina and the Dutch East Indies, Ann Stoler writes of the profound anxiety caused to colonial administrators by the phenomenon of miscegenation between European males and native females. The offspring of such unions were said to create an economic problem by producing an underclass of paupers, yet the threat that these children posed to their colonial masters was clearly cultural in nature. A child neglected by his European father but dutifully raised by his native mother was said to have been abandoned and thus subject to government action, whereas the abandoned children of native fathers were objects of neither concern nor tutelary policy. Children of mixed unions were considered potentially improvable because of their European blood; in fact, if raised as wards of the state, they could form "the bulwark of a future white settler population, acclimatized to the tropics but loyal to the state."[23] In Indochina and the East Indies, French and Dutch citizenship were granted to métis via an examination of the supplicants' racial fitness, mastery of the colonizer's language and culture, and demonstrated commitment to leave behind the world into which they had been born.

Stoler's description of French and Dutch policies and attitudes toward their colonial subjects can be easily mapped onto attitudes and policies toward Jews in eighteenth- and nineteenth-century Europe. Emancipation was granted on a quid pro quo basis. Cultural and economic regeneration—that is, mastery of the host society's language, the adoption of reigning cultural mores, and a movement from the traditional practice of peddling to livelihoods in crafts and agriculture—were considered either preconditions for citizenship (as in the German states) or immediate and necessary outcomes of the attainment of citizenship (as in France). For Jews in post-Napoleonic Prussian Poland, as for Indo-Europeans in colonial southeast Asia, citizenship was granted on a case-by-case basis, the result of a rigorous yet arbitrary examination procedure. Proposals made in the late nineteenth century by colonial officials to establish agricultural colonies for the regeneration of the Indo-European poor had their parallel in the era of enlightened absolutism, when reformist bureaucrats in Prussia, Austria, and Russia championed, and at times established, colonies to train Jews in productive labor.[24]

Much of the recent literature on the colonial encounter probes the complex reaction of the colonized intelligentsia to the blandishments of the West, the inability to achieve full acceptance, and the simultaneous desire to preserve and transform indigenous cultures. Throughout Asia and Africa, intellectuals compensated for their economic and military inferiority vis-à-vis the West by asserting the moral and spiritual superiority of the colonized nation versus the powerful but allegedly spiritually bankrupt European powers. For example, in India, Vivekananda's Ramakrishna mission, founded in 1897, refashioned Hinduism into a bulwark against the West, which allegedly inculcated spiritual discipline into its adherents through yoga and meditation and stimulated national solidarity by preaching the necessity of social action.[25] Here, as well as in such diverse lands as Thailand (Siam), Meiji Japan, and late Ottoman Egypt, the locus of collective identity was presented by intellectuals as found in the realms of culture, religion, and historical commemoration, which could lead to a purification of contemporary ways of thinking and a return to lost glory.

Moreover, colonized intellectuals in various lands claimed that the colonized peoples' material disadvantage was the result of an unjustified and tragic rejection of science and technology, which had been essential elements of the pristine sources of the indigenous culture (for example Islam, Hinduism, Buddhism). Siam's King Rama IV (1851–68) ascribed opposition to scientific inquiry within Buddhism to pollution from Hinduism, whereas in the predominantly Hindu Bengal early Indian nationalists located the source of their technological decline in Islamic influences.[26]

King Rama's distinction between Buddhism's rich spiritual heritage and the cold truths of Western science, and his well-tempered statement that each is necessary to human well-being, find their Jewish historical parallel in the Haskalah, the Jewish variant of the European Enlightenment. One of the Haskalah's pioneering texts, Naphtali Herz Wessely's *Words of Peace and Truth* (1782–85), distinguishes between the "Torah of God" and the "Torah of man" and calls for a new appreciation of the latter in Jewish education. Like Thai, Bengali, and Egyptian intellectuals in the late nineteenth century, Wessely and his fellow adherents of the late-eighteenth- and nineteenth-century Haskalah claimed that their religious culture was inherently open to scientific inquiry but had been tainted by superstition. Such arguments were made by *maskilim* throughout Europe, yet they were particularly prevalent in the German lands, which were home to ideologically rigorous movements for reform within Judaism and for the systematic study of Jewish texts following the norms of Western scholarship. In the first half of the 1800s, champions of Reform Judaism attributed the superstitions that allegedly stunted the Jews' worldly knowledge to baleful Christian influences just as Asian intellectuals besmirched neighboring or competing religions. And, like colonized Asian intellectuals who used Western methods to study their civilizations' classic texts, practitioners of the Wissenschaft des Judentums—that is, the study of the Jewish lettered tradition outside the pietistic parameters of that tradition—adumbrated Asia's colonized intelligentsia in their compensation for powerlessness by locating the essence of Jewish civilization and its justification for continued existence entirely in the realm of spiritual and literary creativity. As Susannah Heschel has argued in her study of Abraham Geiger, the founder of Liberal Judaism in Germany, Geiger's writings on the Pharisaic roots of Jesus's teaching can be interpreted "in [Edward] Said's terms as a revolt of the colonized against Christian hegemony".[27] Geiger, like the mobilized, anticolonial intellectual, turned a proud and defiant gaze toward the dominator, appropriating his discourse not merely to refute claims to superiority but also to reverse the dominator/dominated power relationship.

The division between body and spirit, between the physical and the metaphysical, that was central to post-Cartesian Christian civilization had worked its way into Jewish culture already in the seventeenth century, stimulating astronomical, medical, and (al)chemical inquiry. The Haskalah, Reform Judaism, and the Wissenschaft des Judentums, however, contained a revolutionary and totalizing agenda not found previously in the realms of Jewish thought. The modernizing movements within Judaism claimed the right to abrogate centuries of interpretive tradition and to base faith and practice entirely on a rationalistic reading of ancient authoritative texts. This transformation of Judaism was paralleled in early-nineteenth-century India by Rammohan Roy, who invented a laicized, rationalized Hinduism that drew solely on the ancient Hindu scriptures, the Upanishads, and their philosophic commentaries, the Vedanta.[28]

Abraham Geiger dismissed much of rabbinic Judaism as a lifeless husk encasing Judaism's biblical, monotheistic essence, and Leopold Zunz, the greatest of the early exponents of secular Judaic scholarship, excavated the literary riches of the Jewish past to demonstrate its superiority to contemporary arid Talmudism. The Indian parallel to the work of these men, a Wissenschaft des Hinduismus, if you will, came into its own in the 1870s with the founding by Dayananda Saraswati of the Arya Samaj. The Arya Samaj saw in the Vedanta a fixed, textual base for a rationalized Hindu religion. The Arya Samaj presented ancient Vedic religion as monotheistic and egalitarian, far superior to its degenerate Hindu successor, which had allegedly been corrupted by polytheism and the introduction of the caste system.[29] Like the proponents of Jewish Wissenschaft, Hindu reformers accepted Western scholarly methods, for a rationalized religion depended upon standardized, critical editions of sacred texts.

Among both Jews and Hindus, religious reform and textual scholarship were part of a broad movement for cultural renewal, of which education was an essential part. Like the *maskilim* in Europe, the Arya Samaj founded schools to educate Indian children as an alternative to the schools of the colonizer, in this case Western missionaries. Cultural renewal also sought to rearrange and stabilize gender relationships. According to Partha Chatterjee, Bengali literature in the late nineteenth century contained a strong criticism of the politically emasculated and feminized babu, or middle-class male. Misogynistic discourse about women as seducers of and lords over men was a projection of the babu's fears of his own loss of traditional culture and emasculation at the hand of the colonial state. The babu, then, had much in common with the *balabat*, the Jewish householder, who was presented in classic Yiddish literature as talkative but impotent, and dominated by bossy females.

Comparing Chatterjee with recent work by the Jewish historians Marion Kaplan and Paula Hyman, we see both Jewish and Indian writers in the late nineteenth century accusing women of leaping to assimilate into the colonizers' culture, thereby neglecting their duties as mothers of the nation and preservers of religious ritual. These accusations were themselves yet another form of projection, for among both Jews and Indians men comprised the bulk of the vanguard undergoing assimilation. Women, largely confined to the home, maintained religious traditions within the intimate sphere of the family while the observance of public ritual experienced decline.[30]

An essential component of both early Indian and Jewish nationalism was a defensive, secular historiography that posited the continuous existence of a united people (what Benedict Anderson calls a "bounded seriality"[31]), whose fall from divine glory was the result of random chance and human action, not divine will. Traditional Hindu historiography, like the historical consciousness of biblical and rabbinic Judaism, interpreted the course of human events as the result of divine providence, which rewarded and punished the faith community according to its observance of the divine way, be it dharma or halakha. Although Jewish historical thinking began to secularize in the sixteenth century, in the wake of the expulsion of the Jews from Spain, Hindu scholars were accounting for the Muslim and British conquests of India within this sacred-historical framework as late as the mid-1800s. But in the 1870s Hindu historiography adopted modern Western conceptual norms, with the result being a body of writing in many ways parallel to the great works of Jewish historical writing of the age. Heinrich Graetz's magisterial *History of the Jews*, like Tarnicharan Chattopadhyay's *History of India*, blended staggering erudition with protonationalist apologetics. Both authors molded history by compartmentalizing it into distinct periods separated by particular events that became synecdoches for the nation as a whole. History moved from the periphery to the center of consciousness; the nationalist project was presented as an act of restoration as much as one of revolutionary transformation.[32]

The comparisons I am offering between the Jewish and Asian intelligentsia might appear forced because, prior to the rise of Zionism, the Jewish intelligentsia rarely thought of itself as colonized but rather as members of a religious minority. Even in Russia, where the status of the Jews was hobbled by legal restrictions and governmental policy was often steeped in Judeophobia, *maskilim* believed themselves to be deeply rooted within their lands of residence and foresaw the day where, in Russia—as in most of central and western Europe—emancipation would transform Jews into enfranchised citizens and capitalism would make them into prosperous burghers. The sense of confidence in the Jewish future was far greater still in most of Austria-Hungary, the German states, and western Europe. In an environment suffused with such irenicism, one could argue, Jewish intellectuals did not engage in colonial mimicry (to employ Homi Bhabha's celebrated concept[33]); rather, they were no more or less European than their Christian fellow countrymen. There was, however, a clearly apologetic, defensive component in the Haskalah and Wissenschaft movements that differentiates them from their general European counterparts, the Enlightenment and historicism. The popularization of scientific discourse in the Jewish press was far more than an instrument of mass education through the dissemination of useful knowledge; it was seen as a vehicle for the collective transformation of a people psychically stunted by Talmudism. Jewish intellectuals in nineteenth-century Europe may have felt that time was on their side, but they were nonetheless engaged in a vigorous campaign to refashion Judaism, not merely to be accepted into European society but also to protect Jewish life from the blandishments of both Christianity and secularism, to engage in a carefully thought-out process of imitation in order to prevent assimilation. The material conditions of life for European Jews and Asians differed greatly, as did the relations of power with the European hegemonic powers, but the thought processes of Jewish and Asian intellectuals were similar, including those that led to the development of nationalist ideologies. It is no surprise, then, that aspects of Zionism resemble anticolonial national movements, although there were spectacular differences as well.

Partha Chatterjee has traced the transition in nineteenth-century Bengali thought between the rationalist and universalist trends of Hindu reform movements and the rejection of those trends late in the century by an antirational, mystical glorification of the Indian national spirit. For example, the lower-caste mystic Ramakrishna, who became the object of a cult in the 1880s, glorified the "ancient Hindu national ideal" of ecstatic asceticism.[34] Ramakrishna's emphasis on myth rather than rationality, and on myth's power to fuel nationalistic sentiment, found its counterpart in a major stream of Zionist ideology, beginning with Micha Berdichevsky and finding its most scholarly exponent in Gershom Scholem, who rejected the rationalism of the Wissenschaft des Judentums and embraced Kabbalah as the primary manifestation of Jewish vitalist spirit throughout the ages.

As Amos Funkenstein observed, the Zionist project was fueled by two contradictory conceptions of human nature: romantic and materialist. The former defined man as ineffable, spontaneous spirit, and the latter operated within grooves cut by economic laws, "stychic" social processes (to use Ber Borochov's terminology), and a search for "human material" to be shaped by Zionist apparatchiks into a productive laboring nation.[35] The nationalization of the masses had to be rationally planned even when it involved stoking irrational collective feeling. Thus, anticolonial movements, and the postcolonial states that succeeded them, feature aspects of hyper-rational, utopian planning while pooling reservoirs of tribal solidarity and fury against the colonizer.

Consider the case of women's suffrage, which was the subject of almost two centuries of debate in the West and which only came to France and Switzerland after World War II. As Sylvia Walby has noted, many postcolonial states have granted women the franchise at the time of the states' establishment. Political citizenship is granted to all adults at the time of state creation as an expression of a populist sentiment and a legitimization of the overthrow of nonrepresentative colonial rule. As Chatterjee writes of India, nationalists asserted that the entire people had been nationalized, that is, vested with a distinct and unifying Indianness. The nation, having been feminized by the colonial power, was to be emancipated in one fell swoop.[36] This conceptual framework is of benefit for the study of Zionism, for it helps account for the ZO's early granting of voting rights to women (at the Second Congress of 1898, at time when only New Zealand had national female suffrage) and the passion with which all but ultra-Orthodox members of the Yishuv advocated women's suffrage after World War I.

State building in the postcolonial world demands direction, planning, and regulation. Chatterjee's important essay on the role of planning and technical expertise in modern Indian nationalism helps us to pinpoint the point of departure between Zionism and anticolonial movements, and between Israel and postcolonial states.[37] For Chatterjee, economic planning, like women's suffrage, is a form of state legitimization through which the state appears to rise above individual interests and promotes a Gramscian "passive revolution" in which modest reforms are accomplished but precapitalist elites are not annihilated. Economic planning is outside of the politics of the state but is deeply imbricated with it. For most Third World countries, India included, such planning has focused primarily on industrialization, with agriculture more likely to be left to the private sector.

The comparisons with the situation of the Jews in the twentieth century are striking. For the Jews there has been, even after the creation of the State of Israel and certainly before it, no unifying state to orchestrate economic development. Yet world Jewry has formed a unit more cohesive than an ethnic group or stateless nationality. Thanks to their economic and philanthropic elite (often one and the same), Jews the world over have been joined up into a quasi-polity whose members, unlike those of a state, cannot be confidently tallied up and located in a particular space. Rather, this entity resembles, to use another of Benedict Anderson's terms, an "unbounded seriality," borderless yet finite. Nor did twentieth-century Jewry have to contend with precapitalist elites cluttering up the development landscape. Indeed, the Jews' elites have been among the West's princes of capitalism.

During the first half of the twentieth century, the Zionist movement created a protostate in which planning was indeed a form of legitimization, of imagining the nation by asserting the authority to set the course of the nation-building enterprise. Like postcolonial states, the Zionist movement and early State of Israel venerated technical expertise; the engineer, along with the farmer and warrior, was part of the pantheon of Zionist heroes. In Zionism, however, the position of the colonial state in Third World developmental nationalism was replaced by an opponent as amorphous and unbounded as the Jews themselves: the Diaspora, which had allegedly distorted the healthy political, economic, and spiritual structures of ancient Israel and had rendered the Jews dysfunctional.

Because Jews have constituted an unbounded nation, Zionists were not the only agents of Jewish social engineering over the last century. During the formative decades of the Yishuv, a number of international Jewish philanthropic organizations, often better funded than the Zionists, attempted mass colonization of Jews in lands as far flung as Argentina and Ukraine. Zionism's developmental ethos and its program of massive Jewish social and economic change appealed to Jewish philanthropies of virtually every stripe. Thus, in 1929 non-Zionists in the United States were mobilized to serve Zionist political goals through the expanded Jewish Agency for Palestine, while the Yishuv's material needs were attended to during the interwar period by organizations such as the Palestine Economic Corporation, which received much of its funding from the New York–based American Jewish Joint Distribution Committee. Both Zionists and the non-Zionist Jewish philanthropies shared a developmental agenda that focused not on industrial development, as was the case in postcolonial state-building projects, but rather on agricultural settlement. The reason for this reversal was ostensibly because the Jews' concentration in urban occupations, particularly commerce, and the economic needs of the sites of Jewish social engineering (for the Jewish Colonization Association, the Argentinean pampas; for the Joint Distribution Committee, Crimea and Ukraine; for the Zionists, Palestine) demanded the creation of a class of Jewish agriculturalists.[38]

Much of the motivation behind the agrarian orientation of the agents of Jewish social engineering, however, was ideological—apologetic, romantic, or socialist. In fact, the State of Israel's economic development has produced not an agricultural utopia but rather an industrialized city-state that imports raw goods and cheap labor and exports high-technology products. Israel's economic reality, which comports well with what Revisionist Zionists were calling for in the interwar period, is far removed from the Labor Zionist agrarian romance. The motives behind the Zionist project had little in common with those of Western settlement colonialism but also did not fit well with the developmental worldview of postcolonial state building.

Our discussion demonstrates that at a certain point comparisons between Zionism, on the one hand, and colonialism or postcolonial states, on the other, are no longer valuable except as tools for highlighting the eccentric, distinctive qualities of the Zionist project on the world stage. Attempts to force the Zionist project into Chatterjee's theoretical framework of an anticolonial nationalism and postcolonial state yield valuable new ways of perceiving Israel, yet ultimately they fall short not only because of Zionism's unique features, but also because Chatterjee fails to satisfactorily distinguish anticolonial nationalism and postcolonial policy from their European predecessors, which are, in fact, Zionism's true parents.

Chatterjee's desire to essentialize the colonized nation leads him to juxtapose Western, liberal politics, allegedly based on the mechanistic principles of majority rule and legitimized by atomized, individual voters, and what he claims is the consensus-based politics of postcolonial states. In fact, a politics of consensus characterized many modern European states, including Imperial Germany, in which the chancellor and cabinet were not responsible to parliament, and the Italian kingdom, which was managed through a constant process of give and take between members of a minuscule political and economic elite. The failure of the international Zionist movement or the Yishuv's representative bodies during the interwar period to function as paradigms of representative democracy, therefore, does not in any way remove the Zionist project from mainstream fin-de-siècle European statecraft, let alone the rough-and-tumble world of politics among socialists and national minorities in eastern Europe.

Chatterjee attempts to refute Anderson's claim that the modern nation-state is a Western conceptual category that predetermined the form and content of anticolonial collective identities. Chatterjee posits a distinction between Western and postcolonial states, claiming that the former, having long performed their national identities through the free exercise of power, have been sufficiently secure to leave the realms of education, religion, and familial affairs to the private realm. Post-colonial states, on the other hand, have been forced to make such matters central to state policy, for these had formed the core of the colonized people's identity during the period of struggle with the West.[39] This distinction has, of course, not historically existed; the modern state has been an increasingly invasive entity from the days of absolutism through the era of social-welfare states in the mid-twentieth century. Moreover, virtually all forms of European nationalism have stressed the cultural uniqueness of the people and the obligations of the state, or, in the case of stateless peoples, the intelligentsia, to preserve and promote the national culture.

Zionism's *mission civilisatrice* was directed primarily at Jews, not the indigenous Arabs of Palestine. It was not primarily a manifestation of a colonial will to power, nor was it merely a response to centuries of gentile criticisms of Jewish social and economic behavior. As a European nationalist movement, Zionism could not help but have a powerful pedagogic and developmental dynamic. In the late eighteenth century, German states expected Jews to undergo, as the bureaucrat Christian Friedrich Wilhelm von Dohm put it, "civil improvement," but the same expectations were held for other social groups considered to be unproductive. Hence the appearance in Germany in the 1780s of books with titles such as *On the Civil Improvement of Women* or *On the Civil Improvement of Monks*. Similarly, the demand upon the Jews in revolutionary France to undergo "regeneration" had at first been applied to the people of France as a whole as part of the revolutionary project to forge a homogenous French nation, language, and culture.[40] A century later, French Jewry's ongoing efforts to fully acculturate were paralleled by the Third Republic's gradual transformation of, to cite Eugen Weber's memorable phrase, "peasants into Frenchmen."[41] The Zionist aim of transforming "Jews into Israelis" was unique not so much in the project of nationalization as in its overwhelming difficulty, in that the nationalization of the Jews demanded the rapid and laborious creation of its own preconditions, for example, the presence of a population in situ, a rudimentary national economy, and a body of folk culture.

Chatterjee depicts the historian as the craftsman of the modern Indian nation, but of course the same can be said of any land in nineteenth-century Europe. Augustin Thierry and François Guizot in France, Johann Gustav Droysen and Heinrich von Treitschke in Germany, Pasquale Villari and Gioacchino Volpe in Italy all claimed to engage in a scholarly enterprise, based on a careful accumulation of evidence and free of prejudgments, yet still compelled, in Villari's words, not by "merely a scientific need, but a moral duty" to demonstrate the historical roots of national unification.[42] (How rare was Benedetto Croce's tart statement of 1916 that "the history of Italy is not ancient or centuries old but *recent*, not outstanding but *modest*, not radiant but *labored*."[43]) Zionist ideology was well served by the Jews' unusually high level of textual production and by the long history of Jewish communal autonomy, which provided Zionist historians such as Ben-Zion Dinur ample evidence, reproduced through the multivolume anthology *Yisra'el ba-Golah* (Israel in exile), that the Jews had, throughout the historic depth and geographic breadth of their diaspora, comprised a coherent national body, which, through Zionism, was merely fulfilling its longstanding and inevitable destiny. Villari's object of study was a predominantly peasant culture, yet he too combed through the past to locate manifestations of the united *Volksgeist*, although in his case evidence came largely from the realm of folk customs and lore.

The origins of modern European nationalism are steeped in controversy, as classic views emphasizing the centrality of nationalist ideology, created and disseminated by narrow intellectual elites, have been steadily replaced by a focus on socioeconomic transformation, uneven economic development, and the reshaping of preexisting collective identities as the prime sources of popular nationalist sentiment. Nationalism may well have had eighteenth-century manifestations outside of Europe, as Anderson has argued of the socially frustrated and independent-minded "creole pioneers" of Latin America. Even within Europe, nationalist sensibility could emerge from what was essentially a political conflict between metropole and creoles, as in Ireland at the time of the Act of Union, when Anglo-Irish landowners claimed to be true Irishmen, the natural-born stewards of the indigenous thralls. But it was precisely this sort of political conflict that stimulated the European intelligentsia to formulate nationalist ideology as early as the sixteenth century and to frame the cult of national essence within issues of cultural production. Thus, in Elizabethan England the unparalleled beauty of the English language and the unassailable virtue of English liberty were totally intertwined.[44] French nationalism, in turn, equated collective identity, morality, and culture, and it featured a defensive ethos in which England was perceived as the dominant enemy. During the Napoleonic era, German nationalism emerged as a response to French cultural and political hegemony. As the nineteenth century wore on, the chemical equation for a defensive nationalist ideology spread eastward and southward throughout the European continent.

Scholars in postcolonial studies strive to divorce the politics of the colonized from that of their colonizers. Chatterjee has devoted a dense, rich monograph (*Nationalist Thought and the Colonial World: A Derivative Discourse?*) to just this project, setting himself at the outset against the classic work of Elie Kedourie, who pronounced nationality theory to have been entirely and uniquely European in origin and to remain, in Chatterjee's words, "a prisoner of European intellectual fashions," incapable of functioning as an autonomous discourse.[45] Yet with the powerful exception of Mohandas Gandhi, the nationalist ideologues and political leaders who fill the pages of this book all espouse ideas with European equivalents and, at many times, European roots. Throughout the book, Chatterjee intimates that the problematic of nationalism lies in bourgeois modernity as such, and that anticolonial nationalisms, even while challenging "the colonial claim to political domination . . . also accepted the very intellectual premises of 'modernity' upon which colonial domination was based."[46] According to the historian and postcolonial theorist Dipesh Chakrabarty, the only way to escape from the tyranny of European thinking, or, as he puts it, to "provincialize Europe," is to divest oneself of the nationalist project altogether, and by extension to reject modern historicism, whose developmental dynamic and homogenizing yet exclusivist forms of classification manifest themselves and are sustained by nationalist sentiment. Chakrabarty concedes, however, the improbability of his project. With a Derridean flourish, he writes: "The project of provincializing Europe must realize itself within its own impossibility. . . . This is a history that will attempt the impossible: to look towards its own death by tracing that which resists and escapes the best human effort at translation across cultural and other semiotic systems, so that the world may once again be imagined as radically heterogeneous."[47] Chakrabarty's project is not only "impossible," it is also elitist, as it denies the legitimacy of the self-consciousness of hundreds of millions of humans across the globe. It is also naïve for assuming that "radical heterogeneity" is consonant with legitimacy and authenticity.

Here we come to the core of my argument. The fact that nationalism was a European cultural invention does not delegitimize or subordinate extra-European nationalist movements any more than modern mathematics in the West has been tainted by its dependence on the medieval Islamic invention of algebra. As in math and science, so too in the realms of philosophy and sensibility, certain concepts enter global circulation and become fixtures in human consciousness. One may reject the existence of universal truths or beliefs but acknowledge that substantial portions of humanity share certain conceptual categories and employ similar methods for structuring reality and locating meaning. For much of humanity, nationalism has functioned as an algebra of modernity, isolating and bringing to light the factors of ethnic solidarity and then initiating *al-jabr*, the reunion of broken parts. Jews are but one of many dependent variables in this global equation, to which Zionism is one of many possible solutions.

Thus far I have set Zionism against the background of colonialism, anticolonial movements, and postcolonial states. I have argued that Zionism is not merely a subset of the first and can, like the latter two, be simplified and rendered largely congruent with European nationalism. Zionism was a product of the age of imperialism. Its adherents shared a number of common sensibilities with European advocates of colonial expansion in the Middle East. Yet the movement was more than a form of colonial practice. Enmeshed in a matrix of religious sensibility, political ideology, and historic circumstance, Zionism realized itself in the Middle East, a space chosen not for its strategic value, natural resources, or productive capabilities but rather because of what Jews believed to be historic, religious, and cultural ties to the area known to them as the Land of Israel. Zionism's call for a persecuted religious minority to build a new society in a distant land resembled the ideology of the Puritans, who spearheaded settler colonialism in what would become the United States; but, whereas the Puritans saw North America as a tabula rasa upon which a new Jerusalem would be inscribed, Zionism was based in concepts of return, restoration, and re-inscription. The fact that these concepts were constructions of a particular time and place (nineteenth-century Europe), that they represented a profound rupture with traditional Jewish conceptions of the Land of Israel, and that Jewish political and settlement activism assaulted the longstanding Jewish discourse of eventual redemption in messianic time does not alter the assumptions of continuity and the claims of return inherent in Zionist ideology and sincerely held by its exponents. Because Zionism's *mission civilisatrice* was directed almost entirely inward, to the Jews themselves, Zionism lacked the evangelical qualities of European colonialism in North America, Asia, and Africa, where conversion of the heathen to Christianity served as a justification, consequence, and, at times, a cause of colonial expansion.

Anticolonialism's emphasis on cultural renewal, akin to cultural nationalism in nineteenth-century Poland, Bohemia, Ireland, and many other European lands, had its Jewish equivalent in the Haskalah and Wissenschaft des Judentums. These movements, which often denied Jewish national distinctiveness, were not Zionist despite themselves, playing the role of unwitting soldiers in a teleological march toward full-blown nationalism. The Haskalah and Wissenschaft des Judentums were necessary but hardly sufficient preconditions for Zionism. Without challenges to emancipation in the West and brutal, state-sanctioned antisemitism in the East, Zionism would have been stillborn, just as, say, modern Thai nationalism would not have developed from its mid-nineteenth-century Buddhist reformist roots had France not seized lands traditionally under Siamese jurisdiction in the Mekong River Valley.

The Arab Revolt of 1936–39 transformed the Palestinian Arab in the Zionist imagination from a natural part of the landscape into a coherent, hostile political force, an enemy that would have to be vanquished in the struggle to establish a Jewish state. During the 1948 War, hundreds of thousands of Palestinian Arabs were compelled to leave their homes, and after the war the Israeli state prevented the return of the refugees, carried out massive expropriations of Arab land, and subjected most of Israel's Arab citizens to harsh military rule. Palestine was but one of many places on the globe in the mid-twentieth century where indigenous nationalities were displaced in the wake of state creation. (The partition of India led to the forced migration of some 14 million souls. Ethnic cleansing and land confiscation/redistribution were widely practiced in post-1945 eastern European successor states, and more than 10 million ethnic Germans were expelled from the Soviet Union.) Thus, the most controversial aspects of Israeli actions toward Palestinians during the 1948 War and its aftermath were not specifically colonial. A colonial sensibility may, however, be detected in the young Israeli state's educational policies toward its Arab population in that a curriculum steeped in Hebrew literature, Jewish history, and Zionist ideology was imposed upon the defeated native population. Moreover, Israeli Palestinians, like other colonized peoples, responded by engaging in a complex process of refraction and manipulation of the hegemonic culture and political system (what Mary Louise Pratt has termed "transculturation"), leading to the creation of new forms of collective consciousness.

The early years of the Israeli state brought to the fore a rather different form of Zionist colonial discourse, this time directed toward Jewish immigrants from the Middle East and North Africa. As mentioned earlier, already during the mandate period European and North American Zionist leaders had looked upon the small oriental Jewish community of Palestine as culturally backward and had treated Middle Eastern Jews as a ready source of manpower that could compete with cheap Arab labor. With the mass immigration after 1948 of Jews from the Middle East and North Africa, a new colonialist dimension was added to Ashkenazi hegemony over the discrimination against Middle Eastern Jews. In the 1930s the Ashkenazi governing elite invented "oriental" (Mizrahi) Jews as a coherent ethnic category. Jewish communities of diverse provenance from Morocco to Iran were sewn into a single ethnic collective defined solely by their origins in the lands of

Islam.[48] The colonialist aspect of this action lies in the European colonial state's historic practice of hardening and standardizing borders, both territorial and ethnic. That is, just as the colonial state drew borders that threw together historically antagonistic collectives into a single polity, so it institutionalized differences between ethnic groups. As Mahmood Mamdani has written of the Rwandan genocide, although prior to Belgian colonial rule cultural distinctions between Hutu and Tutsi certainly existed, the Belgians exaggerated and hardened these distinctions, rendering them impermeable through a construction of the Tutsi as racially distinct from and superior to the Hutu and thus worthy of a favorable educational policy that groomed them for the colonial administrative elite. In the case of the Mizrahi Jews, the Israeli Ashkenazi elite experimented with ethnic fusion rather than fission, amalgamation rather than differentiation, but the result was the same: the creation of an essentialized, naturalized Other. As Mamdani puts it, "there is no middle ground, no continuum, between polarized identities. Polarized identities give rise to a kind of political difference where you must be either one or the other. You cannot partake of both. The difference becomes binary, not simply in law but in political life. It sustains no ambiguity."[49] The last words of this quotation point to the limitation as well as applicability of a colonial model to the Ashkenazi/Mizrahi dichotomy in recent Israeli history. Although discrimination against Mizrahi Jews is still a prominent feature in Israeli society, it has declined over time, and as the uniform, statist policies of David Ben-Gurion's Israel have collapsed into a bric-a-brac of separate subcultures, ethnic difference, not only between Ashkenazi and Mizrahi Jews but also within these blocks, is flourishing. More than a half century of life in Israel has effectively destroyed the Arab–Jewish culture of the Maghrebi/Mashriqi diaspora but has engendered new forms of Mizrahi political activism and cultural creativity. However problematic the position of "Mizrahiness" may continue to be in Israel, the primary site of colonial discourse in contemporary Israel is not south Tel Aviv, but the Occupied Territories, for after the 1967 War, Israel's relationship with the Arab minority changed to a bona fide form of colonialism. The demographic balance between occupier and occupied tilted increasingly toward the latter, Israel gained substantial economic profit from the Occupation, and Israel's military and security forces brutally combated Palestinian nationalism in a fashion similar to French rule in pre-Independence Algeria. Perhaps even more important, from the late 1970s onward, Jews were encouraged to move into the Occupied Territories as state-sponsored settlers, living as a minuscule minority of privileged colonists in areas that remained, unlike post-1948 Israel, overwhelmingly Arab.

Israelis justified the conquest of eastern Jerusalem and the West Bank via arguments about the religious and historical rights of Jews to sovereignty over their alleged biblical patrimony. Moreover, the seizure of the Sinai Peninsula, Gaza Strip, and the Golan Heights was attributed to bona fide security concerns. The act of conquest was arguably not motivated by a desire to subjugate a people and expropriate its land, but the speed with which the Palestinian labor force and market became tools for Israeli economic exploitation, the harshness of Israeli military occupation, and the sheer numbers of Arabs brought under Israeli control quickly created a colonial regime in the Occupied Territories.[50] Indeed, one could argue that post-1967 Israel became not only a colonial state but also an imperial one, the difference being that imperialist ideology, which emerged in late nineteenth-century Europe, posited that the nation depended for its survival upon territorial expansion and that empire was an indivisible extension of the nation.[51]

Classic Zionism and its ideological underpinnings grew out of, yet departed significantly from, European imperialism and the orientalist sensibilities that justified it. After 1967, however, Israel underwent a rapid evolution into a colonial state. We would be well served, therefore, to consider the importance of ruptures as well as continuities within the fabric of Israeli history when evaluating the relationship between Zionism and colonialism. Similarly, we must be sensitive to Zionism's multivocality, its capacity (present in all nationalist ideologies) to function within discourses of both power and powerlessness, national liberation and ethnic exclusion. The blinkered passion that leads Jewish activists to identify Zionism as a movement of national liberation and to whitewash its oppressive and racist qualities finds its counterpart in the overwrought, almost campy tone of anti-Israel discourse, both within academia as well as outside of it. (For example, Columbia University's Joseph Massad, who brooks no comparison between Zionism and Afro-Asian nationalisms, reduces the infinitely varied aspirations of millions of individuals caught up in the Zionist project to an act of sexual conquest intended to deflower the Holy Land, inseminate it with Western seed, and emasculate the Arab and Mizrahi Jew alike.[52]) Surely scholars can set an example for their students and the public by shunning the use of the word "colonial" as a universal pejorative akin to "fascism" during the heyday of the student movements of the 1960s and 1970s. Let us understand colonialism to be no more or less than a form of power, and the colonized as subjects of various forms of domination, without making facile identifications between power relations and moral qualities. Let us approach the questions "Is Zionism a colonial movement?" and "Is Israel a colonial state?" as an invitation to serious reflection, open to all possibilities, carried out according to the most stringent academic standards, albeit fraught with implications that reach far beyond the walls of academia to other walls, which run through the heart of Israel and Palestine.

Notes

Previously published in Derek J. Penslar, *Israel in History: The Jewish State in Comparative Perspective* (New York: Routledge, 2006). The author and editors have corrected small grammatical or stylistic errors from the original version.

1. Ronen Shamir, *The Colonies of Law: Colonialism, Zionism, and Law in Early Mandate Palestine* (Cambridge: Cambridge University Press, 2000), 17.

2. Compare Partha Chatterjee, *Nationalist Thought and the Colonial World: A Derivative Discourse?* (London: Zed, 1986); with Partha Chatterjee, *The Nation and Its Fragments: Colonial and Postcolonial Histories* (Princeton, NJ: Princeton University Press, 1993). Both books stress Third World nationalisms' ongoing struggle to free themselves from the Western epistemological categories that make nationalist sensibility possible in the first place. Particularly in the second book, Indian nationalism is presented as the product of a ceaseless agon with Western thought as opposed to an adaptation of it.

3. Robert J. C. Young, *Postcolonialism: An Historical Introduction* (Oxford: Blackwell, 2001), 57–69, quote at 61.

4. E.g., Edward Said, *The Question of Palestine* (New York: Vintage, 1979).

5. Maxime Rodinson, *Israel: A Colonial Settler-State?* (New York: Monad, 1973), 39. The same is true for stateless European peoples who throughout the nineteenth century presented themselves as serving the interests of the dominant powers. In the Hapsburg Empire, Poles and Czechs won autonomy and bilingualism, respectively, as rewards for their loyalty, and during World War I leaders of both national movements constantly lobbied the Great Powers just as the Zionists did.

6. Maunier quoted in ibid., 90. Emphasis added.

7. See the essays in part 2 of economic historian Nachum Gross's collected works, *Lo 'al ha-ruah levadah: 'iyunim ba-historiyah ha-kalkalit shel eretz-yisra'el ba-'et ha-hadashah* (Jerusalem: Magnes and Yad Ben-Zvi, 1999). Many of Gross's arguments were popularized by Tom Segev in *One Palestine, Complete: Jews and Arabs under the British Mandate* (New York: Metropolitan, 2000).

8. Daniel Boyarin, "Zionism, Gender and Mimicry," in *The Pre-Occupation of Postcolonial Studies*, ed. Hamid Naficy, Fawzia Afzal-Khan, and Kalpana Sheshadri (Durham, NC: Duke University Press, 2000), 256; and Gershon Shafir, "Zionism and Colonialism: A Comparative Approach," in *Israel in Comparative Perspective: Challenging the Conventional Wisdom*, ed. Michael N. Barnett, 227–42 (Albany: State University of New York Press, 1996).

9. Jacob Metser, *The Divided Economy of Mandatory Palestine* (Cambridge: Cambridge University Press, 1998), 174–75.

10. Kenneth Stein, *The Land Question in Palestine: 1917–1939* (Chapel Hill: University of North Carolina Press, 1984); and Arieh L. Avneri, *The Claim of Dispossession: Jewish Land-Settlement and the Arabs, 1878–1948* (New Brunswick, NJ: Transaction, 1984).

11. A bizarre scholarly alliance has developed between critics of Israel who believe that Zionism sought from the outset to expel the native population in the fashion of European settlement colonialisms and right-wing Israeli scholars who wish to claim a historical pedigree for their own support for "transfer," that is, the expulsion, of Arabs from the territories conquered in 1967. In fact, although there were occasional statements by Zionist activists dating back to the turn of the twentieth century supporting expelling the native population, the discourse of transfer only became serious and systematic in the wake of the 1937 Peel Commission partition proposal, whose territorial division would have left almost as many Arabs as Jews in the area allotted for the Jewish state. See Derek Penslar, "Historians, Theodor Herzl, and the Palestinian Arabs: Myth and Counter-Myth," in *Israel in History: The Jewish State in Comparative Perspective*, 52–61 (London: Routledge, 2007).

12. Derek J. Penslar, *Zionism and Technocracy: The Engineering of Jewish Settlement in Palestine, 1870–1918* (Bloomington: Indiana University Press, 1991), 94–96.

13. Yael Simpson Fletcher, " 'Irresistible Seductions': Gendered Representations of Colonial Algeria around 1930," in *Domesticating the Empire: Race, Gender and Family Life in French and Dutch Colonialism*, ed. Julia Clancy-Smith and Frances Gouda, 193–210 (Charlottesville: University of Virginia Press, 1998).

14. Mary Louise Pratt, *Imperial Eyes: Travel Writing and Transculturation* (London: Routledge, 1992), 7.

15. Yaron Peleg, *Orientalism and the Hebrew Imagination* (Ithaca, NY: Cornell University Press, 2005).

16. As Peleg explains, Smilansky's stories represent an eroticized image of the Bedouin male, but his relationship with Jews is a friendship among equals, not the domination by the older European man of the young native boy found in Gide.

17. Lora Wildenthal, *German Women for Empire, 1884–1945* (Durham, NC: Duke University Press, 2001). On women in the Yishuv, see Deborah Bernstein, *Pioneers and Homemakers: Jewish Women in Pre-State Israel* (Albany: State University of New York Press, 1992).

18. Aron Rodrigue, *Images of Sephardi and Eastern Jewries in Transition, 1860–1939: The Teachers of the Alliance Israélite Universelle* (Seattle: University of Washington Press, 1993).

19. The term "human material" (*homer enushi*) was most likely derived from the German "*Menschenmaterial*," a word popularized during the interwar period and associated with the brutal materialism of both fascism and communism.

20. Gershon Shafir, *Land, Labour, and the Origins of the Palestinian-Israeli Conflict* (Cambridge: Cambridge University Press, 1989), 91–122; Yehuda Nini, *He-hayit o-halamti halom? Temanei Kineret: Parashat hityashvutam ve-'akiratam, 1912–1930* (Tel Aviv: 'Am 'Oved, 1996); and Gabi Peterberg, "Domestic Orientalism: The Representation of 'Oriental' Jews in Zionist/Israeli Historiography," *British Journal of Middle Eastern Studies* 23, no. 2 (1996): 140–44.

21. Yehouda Shenhav, *Ha-yehudim ha-'aravim: Le'umiut, dat ve-etniut* (Tel Aviv: 'Am 'Oved, 2003), chaps. 1 and 2.

22. Ibid.; Peterberg, "Domestic Orientalism"; and Ella Shohat, "Rupture and Return: Zionist Discourse and the Study of Arab Jews," *Social Text* 75, no. 21 (2003): 49–74.

23. Ann Stoler, "Sexual Affronts and Racial Frontiers: European Identities and the Cultural Politics of Exclusion in Colonial Southeast Asia," in *Becoming National: A Reader*, ed. Geoff Eley and Ronald Grigor Suny, 286–324 (New York: Oxford University Press, 1996), 295.

24. I discuss this subject in detail in my book *Shylock's Children: Economics and Jewish Identity in Modern Europe* (Berkeley: University of California Press, 2001), chap. 1.

25. Peter van der Veer, "The Moral State: Religion, Nation, and Empire in Victorian Britain and British India," in *Nation and Religion: Perspectives on Europe and Asia*, ed. Peter van der Veer and Hartmut Lehmann, 15–43 (Princeton, NJ: Princeton University Press, 1999), 32–34.

26. Compare Thongchai Winichakul, *Siam Mapped: A History of the Geo-Body of a Nation* (Honolulu: University of Hawaii Press, 1994), 39–40; with Chatterjee's essay "Histories and Nations," in *The Nation and Its Fragments*. For a comparison of Zionist and colonial African intellectuals, see Dan Segre, "Colonization and Decolonization: The Case of Zionist and African Elites," in *Comparing Jewish Societies*, ed. Todd Endelman, 217–34 (Ann Arbor: University of Michigan Press, 1994).

27. Susannah Heschel, *Abraham Geiger and the Jewish Jesus* (Chicago: University of Chicago Press, 1998), 20–21. See also Christian Wiese, "Struggling for Normality: The Apologetics of *Wissenschaft des Judentums* in Wilhelmine Germanhy as an Anti-Colonial Intellectual Revolt against the Protestant Construction of Judaism," in *Towards Normality? Acculturation and Modern German Jewry*, ed. Rainer Liedtke and David Rechter, 77–101 (Tübingen: Mohr Siebeck, 2003).

28. Van der Veer, "Moral State," 30–31.

29. Ibid.

30. Compare Chatterjee, "The Nation and Its Women," in *The Nation and Its Fragments*; with Paula Hyman, *Gender and Assimilation in Modern Jewish History* (Seattle: University of Washington Press, 1995); and Marion Kaplan, *The Making of the Jewish Middle Class: Women, Family, and Identity in Imperial Germany* (New York: Oxford University Press, 1991).

31. Benedict Anderson, *The Spectre of Comparisons: Nationalism, Southeast Asia, and the World* (London: Verso, 1998), 30–45.

32. See Chatterjee's essays "The Nation and its Pasts" and "Histories and Nations" in *The Nation and Its Fragments*.

33. On this point Bhabha was adumbrated by Albert Memmi, whose 1957 book *The Colonizer and the Colonized (Portrait du colonisé précédé du portrait du colonisateur* [Paris: Buchet]) described Jews as a colonized minority engaging in "self-colonization" by aping the dominator. See Rachel Feldhay Brenner, *Inextricably Bonded: Israeli Arab and Jewish Writers Re-Visioning Culture* (Madison: University of Wisconsin Press, 2003), 54.

34. Discussed in Chatterjee's essay "The Nationalist Elite" in *The Nation and Its Fragments*.

35. Amos Funkenstein, "Zionism, Science, and History," in *Perceptions of Jewish History* (Berkeley: University of California Press, 1993), 347.

36. Compare Sylvia Walby, "Woman and Nation," reproduced in *Mapping the Nation*, ed. Gopal Balakrishnan, 235–54 (London: Verso, 1996), 253–54; with Chatterjee's essay, "The Nation and Its Women," in *The Nation and Its Fragments*.

37. Chatterjee, "The National State," in *The Nation and Its Fragments*.

38. These themes are further developed in Penslar, *Shylock's Children*, chap. 6.

39. Chatterjee, "Whose National Community?" in *The Nation and Its Fragments*.

40. Penslar, *Shylock's Children*, 27–32.

41. Eugen Weber, *Peasants into Frenchmen: The Modernization of Rural France* (Stanford, CA: Stanford University Press, 1976).

42. Villari, quoted in Mauro Moretti, "The Search for a 'National' History: Italian Historiographical Trends Following Unification," in *Writing National Histories: Western Europe since 1800*, ed. Stefan Berger, Mark Donovan, and Kevin Passmore, 111–22 (London: Routledge, 1999), 114.

43. Ibid., 118.

44. Despite its many problems, Liah Greenfeld's *Nationalism: Five Roads to Modernity* (Cambridge, MA: Harvard University Press, 1992) argues this point convincingly.

45. Eli Kedourie, *Nationalism* (London: Hutchinson, 1960); Chatterjee, *Nationalist Thought and the Colonial World*, 10.

46. Ibid., 30; see also 169.

47. Dipesh Chakrabarty, *Provincializing Europe: Postcolonial Thought and Historical Difference* (Princeton, NJ: Princeton University Press, 2000), 45–46.

48. Ella Shohat, "Sephardim in Israel: Zionism from the Standpoint of Its Jewish Victims," in *Dangerous Liaisons: Gender, Nation, and Postcolonial Perspectives*, ed. Anne McClintock, Aamir Mufti, and Ella Shohat, 39–68 (Minneapolis: University of Minnesota Press, 1997); Ella Shohat, *Israeli Cinema: East/West and the Politics of Representation* (Austin: University of Texas Press, 1989); and Shlomo Swirski, *Israel: The Oriental Majority* (Hebrew original 1981; London: Zed Publishers, 1989). For overviews of changing trends in Mizrahi studies over the past twenty years, see the essays by Ella Shohat, Aziza Khazzoom, Sami Shalom Chetrit, and Uri Ram in the *Israel Studies Forum* 17 (2002): 86–130.

49. Mahmood Mamdani, *When Victims Become Killers: Colonialism, Nativism, and the Genocide in Rwanda* (Princeton, NJ: Princeton University Press, 2001), 23, cited in Gil Andijar, *The Jew, the Arab: A History of the Enemy* (Stanford, CA.: Stanford University Press, 2003), xv. See also Terence Ranger, "The Invention of Tradition in Colonial Africa," in *The Invention of Tradition*, ed. Eric Hobsbawm and Terence Ranger, 211–62 (Cambridge: Cambridge University Press, 1992).

50. By the 1980s, as much as 40 percent of the Occupied Territories' labor force was employed in Israel, and their collective income comprised at least one-fourth of the Territories' total product. Metser, *Divided Economy of Mandatory Palestine*, 174–75.

51. On this point, see Young, *Postcolonialism*, chap. 2 and 3.

52. Joseph Massad, "The 'Post-Colonial' Colony: Time, Space, and Bodies in Palestine/Israel," in *The Pre-Occupation of Postcolonial Studies*.

13

DEREK PENSLAR'S "ALGEBRA OF MODERNITY"

HOW SHOULD WE UNDERSTAND THE RELATION
BETWEEN ZIONISM AND COLONIALISM?

Joshua Cole

DEREK PENSLAR'S THOUGHTFUL 2006 essay "Is Zionism a Colonial Movement?" (chapter 12 of this volume) takes a highly politicized question about the history of Zionism and offers a set of historical comparisons that he hopes will provide room for a less polemical discussion. At the very least, he would like to address the question of Zionism's relationship to colonialism in a way that does more than simply reproduce with greater urgency the irreconcilable positions between those who argue that no such relationship exists and those who argue that the former is best understood as a pure form of the latter.[1]

Let's begin with the terms invoked by his question. By "Zionism," Penslar means not only the movement to establish a Jewish state in Palestine that began in Europe in the late nineteenth century but also the various strands of Jewish thought that contributed to the birth of a Jewish nationalism in much earlier decades. His use of the term also encompasses the many different ideological currents that converged at the moment of the founding of Israel in 1948, and the diverse voices that have supported this new nation ever since. The very breadth of this inclusive definition of Zionism has implications for his argument, for it is this diversity of opinion that leads him to his nuanced answer to his question, emphasizing the multivocal and polyvalent nature of this political tradition.

What does Penslar mean by "colonial"? He does not actually define the word in his own terms, although he invokes definitions offered by others and uses familiar typologies ("settler colonialism," "penal colonies," "exploitation colonies"). We can glean a fairly specific sense of what he means by "colonial" in the concluding paragraphs of the essay, however, when he asserts that since 1967 Israel has acted as a colonial, even "imperial" power in the Occupied Territories:

[. . .] after the 1967 war, Israel's relationship with the Arab minority changed to a bona fide form of colonialism. The demographic balance between occupier and occupied tilted increasingly toward the latter, Israel gained substantial economic profit from the Occupation, and Israel's military and security forces brutally combatted Palestinian nationalism in a fashion similar to French rule in pre-Independence Algeria. Perhaps even more important, from the late 1970s onward, Jews were encouraged to move into the Occupied Territories as state-sponsored settlers, living as a minuscule minority of privileged colonists in areas that remained, unlike post-1948 Israel, overwhelmingly Arab.[2]

"Colonialism" in this sense means state-sponsored settlement of a new population in space inhabited by others, economic exploitation, and brutal military measures to make resistance impossible. The reference to French Algeria is significant here and acts as a kind of ideal type: it is a form of shorthand referring to a well-known example of a European empire that was forced by its own intransigence and the resistance of a subjugated people to unleash a punishing violence in defense of a status quo characterized by a fundamental imbalance of power and resources.

Penslar's point, then, is not to say that Zionism has never been colonial but rather to ask questions about a much longer history and to suggest that the ruptures in this history are at least as important as the continuities. He looks at the prehistory of Zionism in Europe before the 1890s to point out that the movement has its origins in traditions that share many characteristics with anticolonial movements elsewhere in the world. He notes the many similarities between Zionist activities in Palestine and European settler colonialisms between the 1890s and World War II, but he also highlights a major difference—the absence of a colonizing state as the driving force of settlement and expropriation. In looking at the earliest years of Israel's existence, on the other hand, he suggests that there is something to be gained by considering Israel in the context of postcolonial regimes in Asia and Africa. Israel, like Algeria or India, consolidated its position as a new nation in an international order shaped by migration and shifting transnational relationships in the aftermath of World War II and the ensuing Cold War. Here the comparison hinges in part on an international context that gave the victims of European empires a new legitimacy in what would soon be known as the era of decolonization.[3] In each of these three contexts, he argues, Zionism can be seen to have interesting parallels not only with colonialism but also with anticolonial traditions and with postcolonial nations.

His answer to the question posed in his title, therefore, is both yes and no. This is not equivocation but rather an attempt to address both the complexity of this long history and the particularities of this individual case. He suggests that the above comparisons are useful but concludes that their cumulative effect is to demonstrate "the eccentric, distinctive qualities of the Zionist project on the world stage."[4] Although I accept many aspects of his argument, I suggest that his implicit operating definition of what "colonial" means might at times be too narrow, and that the "eccentric" qualities of the Zionist project might not be any more peculiar than the specificities of other examples, including the seemingly archetypal case of French Algeria.

Penslar's insistence on a broad range of comparisons is nevertheless suggestive: I am persuaded that in many respects the history of Zionism before 1948 and the history of Israel itself after that date are both comparable to and different from histories of various colonial movements, anticolonial movements, and other examples of postcolonial nation-states. I agree that some, but certainly not all, elements of Zionist thought and practice before 1948 were shaped by the cultural ethos and political realities of Europe during the decades that constituted the apogee of European colonialism. The very idea that Europeans (in this case European Jews) might depart from Europe in order to found a new society in the Middle East became more plausible as a result of European imperial conquests in Africa and Asia in the nineteenth century. Many of the steps taken to realize this project—financial support and institutions to encourage settlement in Palestine, the evocation of a specifically Jewish *mission civilisatrice* in the Middle East, the connection of this civilizing mission with the implementation of Western technologies that would transform the landscape and economy of Palestine and other lands, the common orientalist tropes in Zionist writings about Arab culture—bore the imprint of their origins in a colonial mindset that imagined European solutions to "problems" of "underdevelopment" in so-called backward civilizations.

Penslar argues, however, that the differences in the case of Zionist settlement are also important: that the Jewish civilizing mission was aimed largely at other Jews, and that the absence of a colonizing state makes the situation very different from other examples of settler colonialism. Here, I think, one might push back against his argument a bit. If one compares the case of Zionist settlement in Palestine in the interwar years with French Algeria during the same period, the power of the French state certainly stands as an obvious difference; at the same time, however, the complicated politics of the colonial situation in Algeria were not completely determined by the power of the national government based in Paris or even their representatives in Algiers. First of all, much of the settler population came from places other than France—Spanish, Italian, Sardinian, and Maltese dialects were commonly heard alongside French and Arabic in the streets of Oran and Algiers in the nineteenth century. Furthermore, much of the bitterness of Algerian politics after 1870, and especially in the interwar years, came from the increasing ability of the local settler political establishment in Algeria to defy the ability of authorities in Paris to implement reform of the colonial system.

Some settler political movements in Algeria advocated outright secession from France, and this threat worked to extract significant concessions from the authorities in Paris, concessions that preserved the disproportionate political and economic power of the settler minority in French Algeria.[5]

The crucial moments in the evolution of such intransigent political movements among the settler population arose when the Parisian officials attempted to bind local Muslim and Jewish populations in Algeria more closely to the French polity by redefining their civil status. Thus, the granting of citizenship to Algerian Jews in 1870 led to the development of an entrenched antisemitism among settlers in Algeria, and attempts to extend limited suffrage rights to Algerian Muslims after World War I enraged the political representatives of Algerian settlers further. The failure of the Blum-Viollette proposal in the 1930s—which would have granted citizenship and the right to vote in parliamentary elections to a small number of Algerian Muslims—was guaranteed by massive resistance on the part of the representatives of French settlers in parliament and Algerian municipal authorities.[6]

In this context, what was "colonial" about the political dynamic in French Algeria was not necessarily those aspects of the situation that resulted from the power of the French state to enforce its will on the various populations of Algeria. It was rather the complicated triangulation that resulted from the competing interests of a metropolitan authority in a distant capital, local leadership among an increasingly defensive and at times militant settler population, and a majority population of colonial subjects who were simultaneously marked for inclusion in an imagined future polity of uncertain constitution and excluded from such participation in the present.[7] One might argue that such triangulation is also present in interwar Palestine. The fact that the distribution of powers among Jewish settlers, British mandate authorities, and Palestinian Arabs was different from French Algeria, or that the competing visions of the future polity were drastically different from those entertained by political figures in France, does not necessarily mean that we are not dealing with a "colonial situation" in Palestine during these years, one in which Zionists had their role, if not always a determining one.[8] One could obviously debate this issue at length, but my sense is that Penslar's claim that there was a qualitative difference between Zionist activities in Palestine and settler colonialisms elsewhere might lead one to underestimate the extent to which a similar dynamic may have been at work.

Frederick Cooper, Ann Stoler, Mahmood Mamdani, and others argue that it is not merely conquest, domination, and exploitation that is at the core of the "colonial" but rather the dynamic of simultaneous inclusion and differentiation that perpetuates such rule and attempts to make it a permanent state of affairs.[9] Such inclusion and differentiation occurs when a population is targeted for incorporation into a larger polity while simultaneously marked by categories of ethnic, religious, or civic difference that distinguish them from the larger population of the new entity. Close attention to this dynamic can help to understand the place of Zionism in interwar Palestine's colonial situation and the resonances of this connection after 1948. Penslar is certainly correct to note that Jewish organizations that encouraged settlement in Palestine in the interwar years were motivated by a restricted vision of their "civilizing mission" that aimed primarily at Jews, and that efforts to imagine how Palestinian Arabs might be incorporated into a larger imperial polity were largely undertaken by French or British colonial authorities. Yet that does not mean that Zionist efforts to ignore or exclude Palestinian Arabs from their plans for settlement or economic development were not shaped by the larger context of the colonial situation in ways that are also comparable to the activities of settlers in French Algeria.

Penslar himself alludes to the dynamic of inclusion and differentiation in his discussion of the ways that Mizrahi Jews were "invented" as a category by the Israeli state after their migration from North Africa. He suggests that the emergence of the Mizrahim as a category is symptomatic above all of a tendency of colonial states to "harden" or "standardize" categories of people and territory.[10] Other historians have made similar arguments—one thinks of the recent literature on Hutus and Tutsis in Rwanda, for example.[11] I would suggest that such "hardening" is only one side of a more fluid situation in colonial relationships in which the various peoples thrown together under colonialism were also in many cases able to take advantage of unexpected opportunities to adapt and even transform their situations and invest them with new meaning. In other words, although it was often true that colonial situations produced "hardened" differences that resulted in anticolonial nationalisms or bitter civil conflict between ethnic groups whose destinies were shaped by colonial relationships, it is also true that colonial situations created an unpredictable environment for reshaping such notions of difference in surprising ways.

Attention to such a possibility has opened up interesting avenues of research in colonial history and might help to explain or contextualize the many contradictions of colonial societies, especially those populated by groups who, like the Jews in Palestine, found themselves at the intersection of colonial and anticolonial allegiances. Eve Troutt Powell describes the fascinating case of Egyptian nationalism in the late nineteenth and early twentieth century, where a distinctive anticolonial posture regarding the British was combined with a highly racialized attitude toward the Sudanese, who were subject to Egypt's own colonial ambitions.[12] Likewise, Douglas Northrop has identified equally contradictory elements in the Soviet empire in Central Asia. On the one hand, the Soviets adopted the anticolonial posture of Marxist-Leninism to distinguish themselves from the

Tsarist regime that preceded them, but at the same time they sought to capture and mold the particular identities of Uzbeks and others to a new kind of transnational empire that was committed to the cause of proletarian revolution.[13] I raise these examples not to suggest that they are in any way the same as Penslar's treatment of Zionism but merely to point out that the intersection of colonialism and nationalism in various parts of the world often produced seemingly "eccentric" and distinctive cases as a result of the unpredictable combination of local circumstance and contingent events. Such eccentricity should not in itself be a part of the criteria that we use to judge whether a situation is "colonial" or not.

Let's look more closely at the case of French Algeria, which functioned as a touchstone for Penslar's implicit definition of what "colonial" might mean. He is certainly correct to emphasize the violence of the French colonial regime in Algeria, which was evident at all stages of the colony's evolution, including the initial conquest, the decades of settlement, and the bitter war of independence.[14] The dynamic of inclusion and differentiation identified by Frederick Cooper and Ann Stoler was also characteristic of French policy in Algeria, having been built into the justifications that successive governments in France gave for creating and maintaining their empire in North Africa.[15] The fact that the French civilizing mission envisioned the eventual assimilation of Africans and Asians into a French imperial polity did not prevent the government from excluding both Algerian Muslims and Algerian Jews from active citizenship in the early decades of the conquest, or of endorsing doctrines of racial difference in determining which peoples among the heterogeneous population of Arabs and Berbers were best suited for labor recruitment.

On the one hand, one might point to these well-documented "tensions of Empire" to support what Penslar identifies as a colonial state's tendency to "[throw] together historically antagonistic collectives" while also maintaining rigid categories of exclusion that "institutionalized differences between ethnic groups."[16] On the other hand, the institutions that enforced differentiation between different groups in Algeria were themselves subject to evolution and negotiation throughout the colonial period. In other words, prolonged coexistence within the colonial situation in French Algeria meant that the allegedly fundamental categories that underlay political relationships were also subject to a slow evolution or even recomposition, and this process was never fully controlled or determined by the powers of the colonial state, in spite of its best efforts.

The history of Algerian Jews provides a clear example of this. In the 1830s, soon after the conquest of Algeria began, the French state lumped Algerian Jews into the catch-all category of "indigenous" people that included Algerian Muslims. In 1870, however, this very same population of Algerian Jews was granted citizenship as a result of the Crémieux Decree that accompanied the foundation of the

Third Republic, an act that provides an unusual example of a people crossing the boundary that was elsewhere used to separate the colonized from colonizer, the African from the European. As Joshua Schreier has recently demonstrated, the Crémieux Decree was controversial in almost all respects: Algerian Jews debated among themselves whether their new civil status violated their traditional allegiances, and they faced hostility, from settler antisemites who believed it to have been a mistake, as well as from Muslims who resented the new closeness between Jewish citizens and a government that was viewed as a foreign occupier.[17] To complicate the matter further, there remained a small group of Saharan Jews who never received citizenship because they lived in an area that was still subject to military authority at the time the Crémieux Decree was implemented.[18] (This oversight was only remedied in the closing stages of the French-Algerian War, one year before independence.[19]) Throughout these decades Algerian Jews were targeted by international organizations that had embraced a version of a Jewish civilizing mission such as the Alliance israélite universelle, but it was largely under the auspices of local leadership that Jewish communities in Algeria underwent a significant evolution during the colonial period, eventually developing a notable attachment to republican ideas about education and the place of religion in daily life.[20] It is also true that Algerian Jews remained vulnerable to periodic outbursts of violent anti-Jewish sentiment during these decades from both settler antisemites and, more rarely, from their Muslim neighbors, but this was rooted less in atavistic tribal allegiances than in very contemporary conflicts about the inclusion of Algeria's Muslims and Jews in the French imperial polity.[21]

In spite of the many controversies associated with the Crémieux Decree, however, the measure was largely successful in winning the loyalty of Algerian Jews to the Republic. Algeria's Jews volunteered for military service in World War I at rates comparable to non-Jews among the population of Algerian citizens, and Zionism subsequently won few adherents in Algeria, in contrast with neighboring Tunisia.[22] The bulk of Algeria's Jews ended up in France rather than Israel when the settler population emigrated after Algerian independence in 1962. The enduring loyalty of Algeria's Jews to France is all the more surprising considering the fact that their citizenship was revoked in 1940 under the Vichy regime, only to be restored three years later after the allied military invasion of North Africa. The success of the Crémieux Decree was, in any case, not merely a "hardening" of preexisting ethnic solidarities that already existed before the arrival of the French. Nor was the outcome entirely the effect of state power. To characterize this history in such terms is to underestimate the realignment of religious and civic identities that took place in the crucible of a colonial situation, and to ignore the ways in which the experience of being Jewish shifted in relation to understandings of what it meant to be French or North African.[23]

Something similar about the realignment or recomposition of ethnic or religious identities might also be said of the fate of Muslim Algerians under French rule, and a look at this example might help us understand more about how what was "colonial" about French Algeria was not clearly determined by the power of the colonial state. For almost the entire colonial period in Algeria, the French state justified the exclusion of Algerian Muslims from citizenship by arguing that their religious practices were incompatible with the civil code. (The same argument was used against Algerian Jews until the Crémieux Decree in 1870). Muslims were granted a specific personal civil status that allowed them to continue practicing their religion without direct interference from the state—a policy that was obviously necessary to preserve some semblance of social peace—and the French state was therefore forced to exert its influence over religious life in Algeria through less direct means, by a gradual reform of Muslim schools and legal institutions that placed them under the jurisdiction of the French. As Allan Christelow documents, French efforts to bureaucratize Muslim law courts in Algeria beginning in the 1850s succeeded in transforming a decentralized and loosely organized system into a highly centralized one that was subject to French control through an appeal process. At the same time, however, Algerian Muslims took advantage of these new institutions to express themselves politically. When the settler establishment realized this and subsequently attempted to abolish the courts and Muslim law schools in the 1880s, the result was what Christelow calls "the first concerted political action in sixty years of colonial domination," a protest by Muslim urban notables that drew sympathy from politicians in metropolitan France and eventually also from some settler politicians. The effort to ban the Muslim courts and schools failed, and they evolved into permanent and influential institutions, which effectively transferred authority over Islamic practice from rural tribal leadership to an urban elite.[24] As James McDougall's work shows, these quasi-official Islamic associations flourished in the first decades of the twentieth century, eventually becoming instrumental in the development of a separate political realm in which Algerians were negotiating among themselves what it might mean to be Muslim and Algerian *and French* within the colonial situation.[25] An understanding of this complex story has long been neglected within the historiography because the first impulse after 1962 was to explain the outcome of French Algeria's bitter history, the emergence of a successful Algerian national movement. But this new research has helped to account for the surprising combination of confidence and solicitousness that at times characterized French policy toward its Muslim subjects in the 1920s, a combination that was evident in the use of state funds to construct an imposing mosque in the heart of Paris's Latin Quarter.[26]

As in the case of Algeria's Jews, then, the gradual evolution that followed the violence of the early conquest and subsequent civic exclusion of Muslims was marked by shifts in the meaning of being French, Algerian, and Muslim under colonial rule. Most significantly, by the first decades of the twentieth century, it had become possible to claim to be all three simultaneously. As Todd Shepard points out, this was a situation that both Algerians and the French were at pains to forget at the moment of decolonization.[27] The point of these examples is to show that the colonial situation in Algeria was not merely about the power of the state to impose "hardened" categories on a resistant people, even if it is relatively easy to cite examples of attempts to do just that. It is also about the ways that the need to adapt and live within the colonial situation produced sometimes surprising opportunities for people to express older identities in new ways, transforming them in the process.

These peculiarities of the Algerian case support the point that Penslar makes about colonial and anticolonial nationalisms in the twentieth century, that these doctrines were all a part of the "algebra of modernity, isolating and bringing to light the factors of ethnic solidarity and then initiating *al-jabr*, the reunion of broken parts."[28] I would suggest, however, that Penslar's argument might remain too attentive to inputs (strong or weak states, coherent ethnic solidarities that are resistant to change) and outcomes (national independence) in defining when and where to use the label "colonial." It may be that what is most instructive about the comparison between Israel/Palestine and French Algeria is neither the inputs nor the bitter outcomes but rather the shifting relationships engendered by occupation and settlement in the context of simultaneous inclusion and differentiation.

My own inclination after pursuing this line of thought would have been to ask some further questions about how historians use the term "colonial." Historians of colonialism have recently been at pains to underscore the ways that colonial powers have not always exercised unlimited power, pointing out that it was precisely the weakness of colonial states that often gave subjugated populations indirect ways of shaping and adapting the circumstances of their lives. Laurent Dubois's work on the Haitian Revolution argues, for example, that the slaves in Saint-Domingue in the 1790s played an important role in shaping ideas about citizenship and political liberty in France.[29] Frederick Cooper identifies ways in which West African politicians, trade unions, and their representatives in French West Africa after 1945 challenged the French government to redefine the scope of the postwar welfare state, even as these same trade unions contributed to the mobilization that would lead to national independence for Côte d'Ivoire and Senegal.[30] One would not have to assert that Israel is a "colonial" power exactly like France or Britain to look for ways in which the history of Israel/Palestine has also been subject to similar shaping from below, whether from Palestinian Arabs or from newly arrived populations of Mizrahi or Sephardic Jews.

Penslar chose to conclude his essay, however, not with a reconsideration of what we mean by "colonial" but rather with a different argument about nationalism aimed primarily at the work of Partha Chatterjee and Dipesh Chakrabarty, both important members of the influential Subaltern Studies group that energized academic research on colonial history beginning in the early 1980s. Penslar goes so far as to announce that his disagreement with Chatterjee and Chakrabarty is in fact at the "core" of his thinking, in spite of the fact that this debate is neither about Zionism nor about colonialism as such but rather about the apparent universality of nationalism in the contemporary world. Penslar's argument is this: that extra-European nationalist movements are in no way lacking in legitimacy simply because the ideal that they strive for—a "nation" of people that is congruent with the institutions of a nation-state—is a European cultural invention. He seems most incensed by Chakrabarty's suggestion that the goal of historians should be to "provincialize Europe," that is, to escape from the tyranny of a Euro-centric vision of history that sees nations as the natural outcome of human development. Since millions of people outside of Europe have insisted on the integrity of their own nationalist aspirations, he claims, it is "elitist" of Chakrabarty to criticize them simply because nations first emerged in their modern form in Europe.

Penslar's charge of "elitism," as he must know, is bound to hurt. One of the most fundamental claims of the Subaltern Studies group has been that a history of subjugated peoples outside of Europe must necessarily break with the conceptual universe produced by "elitist" documents in European colonial archives. Since these sources were produced by the very same colonial officials who were responsible for maintaining the subjugation of colonized peoples, so the argument goes, the information contained within them must necessarily be tainted by the ideologies and concepts that shaped and justified colonial control. Given this inherent discursive bias at the heart of colonial archives, historians influenced by the Subaltern Studies group embarked on a two-pronged agenda: on the one hand, a critical reading of official documents produced by colonial states, and on the other, a search for sources that would allow for a rereading of colonial histories from below—that is, from the position of the powerless, the excluded, and the despised, the "subaltern" subjects of colonial power.[31]

In the end, Penslar's disagreement with Chatterjee and Chakrabarty is not merely about nationalism but rather about the relationship between "nations" and various bureaucracies and instrumental rationalities that are associated with modern nation-states. For Penslar, the author of a perceptive book on Zionism and technocracy, modern states build this relationship from the ground up by combining technological expertise for addressing social problems with ideological definitions of national belonging that are subject to their own evolution. His 1991 book describes the emergence of the technical engineer as a "Zionist ideal type" by 1948 through a complex merging of Central European (and largely German) ideas about statist social policy with Eastern European ideas about regenerating Jewish lives through labor and settlement in rural Palestine.[32] Penslar emphasizes that the emergence of the Zionist technician had important political consequences in organizing settlement in Palestine, in conceiving of a new and specifically Jewish economy there, and in shaping Israel's military leaders, for example. He does not, however, indicate that such interpenetration of expertise and politics is necessarily fatal to the legitimacy of the nation-state. On the contrary, in his view this combination of political and technological aspirations is what makes Zionist technocracy "like its counterparts throughout the Western world."[33]

Chatterjee and Chakrabarty, on the other hand, take a less sanguine view of the ways that expertise and politics have become entwined in the modern world, and their unease with this has everything to do with two things: their reading of Michel Foucault and a set of perceptions about the timing of national movements. From Foucault, Chatterjee and Chakrabarty borrowed a skepticism toward the promise of emancipation embodied in liberal political institutions, finding that the freedoms (from oppression, from want, from ill health, etc.) promised by such institutions came with strings attached, new forms of constraint whose disciplinary effects were found not merely in institutions of social control but also in the very forms of knowledge about human bodies and collectivities that made political institutions possible.

For Chatterjee and Chakrabarty, the question of timing matters as well, because the western European nations that were most involved in colonial expansion developed their specific vocabularies for expressing national belonging simultaneously with a period of rapid development of bureaucratic definitions of social welfare, public health, and notions of economic productivity between the late eighteenth and the first decades of the nineteenth century, years that also saw expansions in the realm of political rights and representative institutions. This meant that debates within Europe about democracy, the economy and the state's responsibility for the care and protection of a national population took place in a context where it was possible to imagine that the relationship between state and nation, between bureaucracy and people was an organic one. Within the various traditions of European liberalism, such an assumption functions as a kind of a priori given, and it is this assumption, in fact, that gives weight to assertions about the "legitimacy" of a given nation-state. Of course, there was nothing truly organic about this relationship—it was as historical as claims for national solidarity elsewhere, but the fact that it was possible to imagine the relationship between people and nation-state as organic was important.[34]

For those parts of the world that were colonized by European nations in the nineteenth century, however, no such presumption about an organic relationship between "nation-state" and "people" was possible because their first experience of these bureaucracies, of these technocratic definitions of well-being that were so much a part of the creation of the modern state, came in the form of disruptive powers that violently imposed new amalgamations upon historic collectivities that had other notions of legitimacy or well-being. It was only natural, then, that when they sought to develop a vocabulary for expressing what they felt to be organic about their own collectivities, they would seek to define these claims at least in part in opposition to what they saw as a foreign imposition.[35]

One of the singular contributions of historians associated with the Subaltern Studies group has been to lay bare the various ways in which coercive assumptions about bodies, their well-being, and their amalgamation into nations have been built into the institutions of colonial rule as well as into the disciplines of the human sciences. Some, like Chakrabarty, have taken an extreme view, finding the contamination to be complete. Penslar rejects this view, insisting on at least the possibility of a legitimately democratic politics emerging from traditions of nation building that emerge alongside more technocratic visions of population management and economic organization. Penslar is absolutely right to assert that historians need to tackle the complicated stories behind such traditions, but the task of a critical history is not necessarily to judge which claims are "legitimate" and which are not. It is rather to examine the processes and contexts that give meaning to *any* claims of national belonging and exclusion. Penslar is certainly correct to assert that we have no choice but to take seriously the national aspirations of peoples in all parts of the world, but once he brings up the question of "legitimacy" he is leaving the realm of critical history and entering into a more overtly political realm.

This complexity makes me wonder if the question Penslar poses (is Zionism a colonial movement?) is necessarily the right one to answer persistent questions about possible relationships between the history of Israel/Palestine and the history of European colonialism in the nineteenth and twentieth centuries. If anything, his focus on a particular movement over a broad span of time has shown us that terms such as "colonial" and "anticolonial" have context-specific valences; these words are more helpful to our understanding when they are understood to apply to dynamic relationships rather than to coherent identities that persist over time, institutions, or political movements.

The logical endpoint of this line of thought may be that the dynamic of inclusion and differentiation is not merely characteristic of colonial regimes during the imperial age but of modern nations in general. Most nations, after all, have extended their boundaries over new territories and incorporated different peoples at some point or another in their history, and this extension and incorporation is often accompanied by violence and exploitation that is dependent on and justified by descriptions of irreconcilable difference. Historians are nevertheless selective about which of these many situations deserve the label "colonial." People calling themselves Bretons, Basques, or Occitans periodically claim that their struggles for cultural integrity and political autonomy are "anticolonial" struggles, but asserting that contemporary France is a "colonial" power within the hexagon is not at all a majority view. Simultaneously, of course, certain arguably "colonial" dynamics persist in the French nation's unusual relationships with its overseas territories in Guiana, the Antilles, or the islands of Réunion and Mayotte. Has Penslar's essay offered us a way of deciding when it is appropriate to use the term "colonial" when speaking of such things? I wonder, as it seems inevitable that the ultimate context for claiming whether "colonial" is the appropriate term for a movement such as Zionism is in fact, political, and this puts us squarely back in the polemical hothouse that his valuable essay seeks to avoid.

Notes

1. For summary of this debate that comes to a different conclusion than does Penslar, see Gabriel Piterberg, *The Returns of Zionism: Myths, Politics and Scholarship in Israel* (New York: Verso, 2008), esp. chap. 2, "The Zionist Colonization of Palestine in the Comparative Context of Settler Colonialism," 51–92.

2. Derek J. Penslar, "Is Zionism a Colonial Movement?," chap. 12 of the present volume, 296. Penslar also states that this colonial outcome may not have been the intent of the original occupation in 1967. In the case of the Sinai Peninsula, Gaza Strip, and Golan Heights, he argues, the occupation was essentially motived by security concerns. Nevertheless, he argues, "the speed with which the Palestinian labor force and market became tools for Israeli economic exploitation, the harshness of the Israeli military occupation, and the sheer numbers of Arabs brought under Israeli control quickly created a colonial regime in the Occupied Territories" (ibid., 297).

3. This notion finds support in a recent trend in German historiography that seeks to see the extension of Nazi power over central and eastern Europe as an essentially colonial project. See, for example, Mark Mazower, *Hitler's Empire: How the Nazis Ruled Europe* (New York: Penguin, 2009).

4. Penslar, "Is Zionism a Colonial Movement?," 270.

5. The classic account in English of the emergence of a distinct colonial culture in Algeria is David Prochaska, *Making Algeria French: Colonialism in Bône, 1870–1920* (New York: Cambridge University Press, 1990). For an account of the secessionist impulse in Algerian politics in the late nineteenth century, see Daniel Rivet, *Le Maghreb à l'épreuve de la colonisation* (Paris: Hachette, 2002), 188–90.

6. On Maurice Viollette and the reforms of the interwar period, see Charles-Robert Ageron, *Histoire de l'Algérie contemporaine*, vol. 2 (Paris: Presses universitaires de France, 1979), 389–402.

7. A recent study that explores this triangulation in a particularly detailed fashion is Didier Guignard, *L'Abus de pouvoir dans l'Algérie colonial* (Paris: Presses universitaires de Paris ouest, 2010).

8. My use of the term "colonial situation" is of course rooted in the arguments of Georges Balandier. See Georges Balandier, "La Situation coloniale: Approche théorique," *Cahiers internationaux de sociologie* 11 (1951): 44–79.

9. See the essays in Frederick Cooper and Ann Stoler, eds., *Tensions of Empire: Colonial Cultures in a Bourgeois World* (Berkeley: University of California Press, 1997); Mahmood Mamdani, *Citizen and Subject: Contemporary Africa and the Legacy of Late Colonialism* (Princeton: Princeton University Press, 1996); and Frederick Cooper, *Colonialism in Question: Theory, Knowledge, History* (Berkeley: University of California Press, 2005).

10. He argues that "Jewish communities of diverse provenance, from Morocco to Iran, were sewn into a single ethnic collective defined solely by their origins in the lands of Islam. The colonialist aspect of this action lies in the European colonial state's historic practice of hardening and standardizing borders, both territorial and ethnic. That is, just as the colonial state drew borders that threw together historically antagonistic collectives into a single polity, so it institutionalized differences between ethnic group." (Penslar, "Is Zionism a Colonial Movement?," 295–96).

11. Mahmood Mamdani, *When Victims Become Killers: Colonialism, Nativism, and the Genocide in Rwanda* (Princeton, NJ: Princeton University Press, 2002).

12. Eve Troutt Powell, *A Different Shade of Colonialism: Egypt, Great Britain, and the Mastery of the Sudan* (Berkeley: University of California Press, 2003).

13. Douglas Northrop, *Veiled Empire: Gender and Power in Stalinist Central Asia* (Ithaca, NY: Cornell University Press, 2003). On Leninist nationality policy and the Soviet Empire, see also Terry Martin, *The Affirmative Action Empire: Nations and Nationalism in the Soviet Union, 1923–1939* (Ithaca, NY: Cornell University Press, 2001) and Ron Suny, *The Revenge of the Past: Nationalism, Revolution, and the Collapse of the Soviet Union* (Stanford, CA: Stanford University Press, 1993).

14. On the question of violence in the conquest of Algeria, see Benjamin Brower, *A Desert Named Peace: The Violence of France's Empire in the Algerian Sahara, 1844–1902* (New York: Columbia University Press, 2009). On violence in the French-Algerian war of 1954–1962, see especially two books by Raphaëlle Branche: *La Torture et l'armée pendant la guerre d'Algérie, 1954–1962* (Paris: Gallimard, 2001) and *L'Embuscade de Palestro: Algérie 1956* (Paris: A. Colin, 2010). An especially helpful overview of the persistence of violent social relations in Algeria and their complex relation to politics is James McDougall, "Savage Wars? Codes of Violence in Algeria, 1830s–1990s," *Third World Quarterly* 26, no. 1 (2005): 117–31. See also Joshua Cole, "Intimate Acts and Unspeakable Relations: Remembering Torture and the War for Algerian Independence," in *Memory, Empire, and Postcolonialism: Legacies of French Colonialism*, ed. Alec Hargreaves, 125–41 (New York: Lexington, 2005); and Joshua Cole, "Massacres and their Historians: Recent Histories of State Violence in France and Algeria in the Twentieth Century," *French Politics, Culture & Society* 28, no. 1 (Spring 2010): 106–26.

15. On racial ideologies and colonization in Algeria, see Patricia Lorcin, *Imperial Identities: Stereotyping, Prejudice and Race in Colonial Algeria* (New York: I. B. Tauris, 1999); and Brower, *A Desert Named Peace*. On the decision to turn Algeria into a colony of settlement, see Jennifer Sessions, *By Sword and Plow: France and the Conquest of Algeria* (Ithaca, NY: Cornell University Press, 2011). A recent account of the relationship between power and culture in colonial Algeria is George Trumbull, *An Empire of Facts: Colonial Power, Cultural Knowledge and Islam in Algeria, 1870–1914* (New York: Cambridge University Press, 2009). Finally, on the French civilizing mission, see the instructive disagreements between Alice Conklin, *A Mission to Civilize: The Republican Idea of Empire in France and West Africa, 1895–1930* (Stanford, CA: Stanford University Press, 1997); and Gary Wilder, *The French Imperial Nation-State: Negritude and Colonial Humanism between the Two World Wars* (Chicago: University of Chicago Press, 2005).

16. Penslar, "Is Zionism a Colonial Movement?, 296".

17. Joshua Schreier, *Arabs of the Jewish Faith: The Civilizing Mission in Colonial Algeria* (New Brunswick, NJ: Rutgers University Press, 2010). For an equally valuable but more personal account, see Benjamin Stora, *Les trois exils: Juifs d'Algérie* (Paris: Stock, 2006).

18. Sarah Stein, *Saharan Jews and the Fate of French Algeria* (Chicago: University of Chicago Press, 2014). See also Rebecca Wall, "The Jews of the Desert: Colonialism, Zionism, and the Jews of the Algerian M'zab, 1882–1962" (Ph.D. diss., University of Michigan, 2014).

19. Moreover, Todd Shepard, *The Invention of Decolonization: The Algerian War and the Remaking of France* (Ithaca, NY: Cornell University Press, 2008), 242–47, has argued persuasively that the enfranchisement of the Jews of the M'zab occurred at this late date in significant part as a means of further marking the hardening boundaries between Jewish inclusion and Muslim exclusion in the emerging post-Algerian French nation-state.

20. On the Alliance israélite universelle, see Lisa Leff, *Sacred Bonds of Solidarity: The Rise of Jewish Internationalism in Nineteenth-Century France* (Stanford, CA: Stanford University Press, 2006).

21. Joshua Cole, "Antisémitisme et situation coloniale pendant l'entre-deux guerres en Algérie," *Vingtième siècle*, no. 108 (October–December 2010): 3–23.

22. On Zionism in North Africa, see Michael Laskier, *North African Jewry in the Twentieth Century: The Jews of Morocco, Tunisia, and Algeria* (New York: New York University Press, 1994). On the participation of Algerian and French Jews in World War I, see Ethan Katz, *The Burdens of Brotherhood: Jews and Muslims from North Africa to France* (Cambridge, MA: Harvard University Press, 2015), chap. 1.

23. The story of North African Jews in France and their loyalty to the Republic continued to evolve after decolonization, especially after the effects of the 1967 war between Israel and its Arab neighbors began to be felt among the many different populations in France who had very specific experiences of colonialism and migration. On this evolution, see Maud S. Mandel, *Muslims and Jews in France: History of a Conflict* (Princeton, NJ: Princeton University Press, 2014); and Katz, *Burdens of Brotherhood*.

24. Allan Christelow, *Muslim Law Courts and the French Colonial State in Algeria* (Princeton, NJ: Princeton University Press, 1985), 9–10. For a general history of France's policy toward Muslim colonial subjects before decolonization, see Pascal Le Pautremat, *La Politique musulmane de la France au XXe siècle: De l'Hexagone aux terres d'islam: espoirs, réussites, échecs* (Paris: Maisonneuve & Larose, 2003).

25. James McDougall, "The Secular State's Islamic Empire: Muslim Spaces and Subjects of Jurisdiction in Paris and Algiers, 1905–1957," *Comparative Studies in Society and History* 52, no. 3 (July 2010): 553–80.

26. On the history of the Paris mosque, see especially Naomi Davidson, *Only Muslim: Embodying Islam in Twentieth-Century France* (Ithaca, NY: Cornell University Press, 2012).

27. Shepard, *Invention of Decolonization*.

28. Penslar, "Is Zionism a Colonial Movement?," 294.

29. Laurent Dubois, *Avengers of the New World: The Story of the Haitian Revolution* (Cambridge, MA: Harvard University Press, Belknap, 2004).

30. Frederick Cooper, "Citizenship and the Politics of Difference in French Africa, 1946–1960," in *Empires and Boundaries: Race, Class, and Gender in Colonial Settings*, ed. Harald Fischer-Tiné and Susanne Gehrmann, 107–28 (New York: Routledge, 2010). On the complex linkages between labor struggles and the evolution of anticolonial nationalism in colonial Africa, see Frederick Cooper, *Decolonization and African Society: The Labor Question in French and British Africa* (Cambridge: Cambridge University Press, 1996). On the postwar moment as one of uncertain possibilities for realignment in the French empire wherein the political claims of the colonized played a central role, see Frederick Cooper, *Citizenship between Empire and Nation: Remaking France and French Africa, 1945–1960* (Princeton University Press, 2014).

31. A useful introduction to these arguments, listing the primary contributions of several members of the group up to the late 1990s is Partha Chatterjee, "A Brief History of *Subaltern Studies*," in *Empire and Nation: Selected Essays* (New York: Columbia University Press, 2010), 288–301.

32. Derek J. Penslar, *Zionism and Technocracy* (Bloomington: Indiana University Press, 1991), 154.

33. Ibid.

34. Partha Chatterjee, "Whose Imagined Community? (1991)" in *Empire and Nation*, 23–36.

35. Chatterjee, in particular, sees this evolution as crucial to the development of ethnic politics in the postcolonial world, with many of his examples coming from the study of populist parties in India. See Partha Chatterjee, *The Politics of the Governed: Reflections on Popular Politics in Most of the World* (New York: Columbia University Press, 2004); and more recently Partha Chatterjee, *Lineages of Political Society: Studies in Postcolonial Democracy* (New York: Columbia University Press, 2011).

14

MOVING ZIONISM TO ASIA

TEXTS AND TACTICS OF COLONIAL SETTLEMENT,
1917–1921

Elizabeth F. Thompson

AS A HISTORIAN of the modern Middle East, I welcome Derek Penslar's effort to "plac[e] Zionism in Asia."[1] First, he argues that Zionism as practiced in West Asia (Palestine) was not true settlement colonialism because settlers were not citizens of the colonial power ruling the territory (Britain). Then he turns to South Asia and to cultural analysis to argue that European Zionism shared similar roots and ideological values with Indian anticolonial nationalism. On these bases, Penslar concludes that Zionists cannot be considered fully colonialist until after they founded the State of Israel in 1948.

My critique focuses on two related points. The first considers the argument's key methodological pivot, Penslar's distinction between practice and discourse, between sociology and history, and between sensibility and structure. His structural analysis of Zionism in Palestine remains distinct from his discourse analysis of Jewish nationalist writing in Europe. This spatial separation of method introduces critical distortions to Penslar's presentation of Zionism in Palestine. If we look at what Zionists both said *and* did in Palestine before 1948, we find little European anticolonialism and an intimate alliance of settlers with the British mandatory (colonial) state.

My second point addresses the problematic limits to Penslar's move of Zionism into West Asia. Colonialism is generally understood as a relationship— that is, the institutionalization of practices that perpetuate the subordination of one people to another in a differentiated space.[2] Penslar, however, neglects the other half of the Zionists' encounter in Palestine: the indigenous peoples, including Arabic-speaking Jews, Muslims, and Christians. Any assessment of whether their encounter was colonial must take into account indigenous responses to the settlers.

317

Redressing the historical distortion wrought by these two methodological problems requires that we study texts produced by Zionists and Arabs within the context of events in West Asia. I draw on my own research on colonialism after World War I to examine the seminal years between 1917 and 1922, when the Balfour declaration officially became international law as part the League of Nations Mandate for Palestine.[3] The evidence presented here suggests that we must date Zionism's full embrace of settler colonialism to 1917, not 1948. Not only did Zionists cooperate more fully with the British state than Penslar suggests but the anticolonialism he describes among intellectuals did not dominate Zionist practice within Palestine.

Zionism in West Asia

Penslar's decision to situate Zionism in Asia is brilliant—on more than one level. He makes the move in order to challenge Partha Chatterjee, a leading post-colonial historian of India who argued that anticolonial movements do not owe their origins to European nationalism. Penslar argues that European Jews and Indians shared common roots in European nationalism, which ascribed their people's subordinate status to European (Christian) dominance and the lingering influence of traditional elites, and which advocated national revival through education and political independence.

On another level, Penslar's move of Zionism into Asia is fruitful for understanding how Zionists behaved in West Asia (Palestine), especially at the time of the Jewish home's founding at the end of World War I. Zionism resembled emergent nationalisms among Armenians, Kurds and Arabs, who feared annihilation by the Ottoman military regime. By war's end, as victorious Allies occupied the region, even ordinary Turks feared they would be wiped from the map, if not from the face of the earth. Similar fears of state-sponsored violence motivated European Jews to flee to Palestine (and in greater numbers to North America). Zionism shared the zero-sum, Darwinian spirit of other national movements in Palestine and Greater Syria.[4]

Penslar's structural analysis of Zionism as colonialism, however, neglects the political and cultural processes that shaped it at the critical moment of the founding of the Jewish home. He therefore elides the fact that Jewish settlement depended vitally on the British Empire. The Jewish population had surged in Palestine to 85,000 by 1914, but then slumped to 55,000 by the time Gen. Edmund Allenby's troops occupied Jerusalem in December 1917. Many Jews fled persecution under martial law and hunger. Zionist leaders were forcibly expelled in early 1915. The Ottoman military governor, Jemal Pasha, had learned of their intention to build a state on Ottoman territory and deemed it treason. Among those expelled was David Ben-Gurion, the future founder of the State of Israel in 1948.

In 1915 Ben-Gurion sailed to New York City and launched a recruitment drive for a Jewish brigade in the British army. "A ray of light pierces through the abysmal darkness that shrouds our people at this critical hour," he told a New York audience in September 1915. "The urge for redemption is searing a path for itself in the heart of the nation." He reassured socialists that building a Jewish state was not an act of imperialism. In language that echoes other settler-colonial movements, he declared, "We do not ask for the Land of Israel for the sake of ruling over its Arabs, nor seek a market to sell Jewish goods produced in the Diaspora. It is a Homeland that we seek, where we may cast off the curse of exile, attach ourselves to the soil." Like the pioneers who settled America, he vowed, we will fight "wild nature and wilder redskins" in Palestine.[5]

But Jews saw no future in such a war-torn land. After campaigning in dozens of American cities, Ben-Gurion found only one hundred volunteers for the brigade. Unknown to Ben-Gurion, however, a group of Zionists in Britain pursued a higher road to Palestine. At its center was Chaim Weizmann, a chemist who met the future prime ministers David Lloyd George and Winston Churchill when he invented a process for the mass production of artillery shells.[6] Weizmann had already met Arthur Balfour, foreign minister in 1917. Weizmann and other Zionists convinced the cabinet that a Zionist Palestine would serve British imperial interests. Lloyd George, an evangelical Christian, embraced the religious implication of a Jewish return to the Holy Land. He dismissed objections that Palestine's Muslim population might oppose the idea.[7]

On November 2, 1917, Lord Balfour issued his famous declaration, promising that Britain would support "the establishment in Palestine of a national home for the Jewish people," provided that "nothing shall be done which may prejudice the civil and religious rights of existing non-Jewish communities in Palestine."[8] Overnight, Zionism's fortunes reversed. Jews around the world celebrated with parades and speeches. By month's end, Ben-Gurion convinced a crowd of 2,000 at the Cooper Union Hall to pledge to devote their energy to building a national home in Eretz Israel. He launched another fundraising tour and found 1,500 volunteers to depart immediately for Palestine.[9] "The fortunes of Zionism were transformed by World War I," writes historian David Vital.[10] Penslar agrees that "clearly, without British support the Zionist project would have died in the cradle."[11]

Any evaluation of the colonial nature of Zionism in western Asia must account for this close link to the British state. Penslar, however, minimizes the degree to which Zionists wedded their movement to the British imperial state. He argues that Zionism lacked the "key factor" of settlement colonialism because its settlers were not citizens of the colonizing state. In addition, he argues, Zionists wielded only "limited authority over small portions of Palestine."[12] Penslar rests these claims, however, on a peculiarly narrow definition of settler colonialism and a selective reading of the historical record. Scholars of settler colonialism generally employ a wider definition that permits a range of relationships between settlers and their supposed—and always distant and defied—"mother" state. Editors of a leading volume on global settler colonialism argue that Zionism differed from other settler movements mainly in that it aimed from the outset to build a state— and succeeded in doing so.[13]

And the historical record suggests a direct link between Zionists' success and their ties to the British imperial state. Under British sponsorship, Weizmann brought the Zionist Commission to Palestine in March 1918 to implement the Balfour Declaration's guarantees: unobstructed immigration, Hebrew as an official language of government, and privileged access to the highest British officials. Zionists also worked closely with British officials to craft propaganda on Palestine. One British film, produced by Zionist advisor Albert Hyamson, is titled "The British Conquering Palestine for the Jews." Other propaganda promised that the British–Zionist alliance would bring "European science, culture and civilization to the East."[14]

In 1922 the Anglo-Zionist alliance was institutionalized in international law, with the ratification of the League of Nations Mandate for Palestine, incorporating the Balfour Declaration. Winston Churchill also promised to ensure continued immigration.[15] Within a decade the Jewish population of Palestine surpassed one hundred thousand.

In this context, Penslar's claim that Zionists wielded limited authority in Palestine must be qualified. By 1922 the Yishuv was already becoming a quasi-state under the legal aegis of the British Mandate. It ran its own schools and social welfare system under the Histadrut, the labor federation organized by Ben-Gurion and Berl Katznelson. Ben-Gurion rose to prominence as its leader and eventually to the political leadership of the Yishuv.

And like other settler movements, Zionism in West Asia aimed to build a separate, autarkic, and superior economy tied to the metropole. With foreign capital, the Yishuv industrialized and expanded a capitalist agricultural market that far outpaced the indigenous economy. The Histadrut worked diligently to break up cooperation between Jewish and Arab workers in what several scholars call pure settlement colonialism (distinct from the earlier settlers' use of Arab labor).[16]

Zionist leaders also wooed Arabic-speaking, indigenous Jews away from their Muslim and Christian neighbors, marking a clearer social line between the Yishuv and the "non-Jewish communities." Before 1914, elite Arabic-speaking Jews played the role of mediators between Europeans and Arabs, advocating an inclusive Zionism and coexistence, against Europeans' exclusive Zionism. But their loyalties and social ties shifted under pressures of war and, as Penslar notes, of Zionists' "civilizing mission" toward their backward cousins of the East. Arab Jews were drawn into international Jewish charity and business networks, and after the war began intermarrying with European Jews and speaking Hebrew.[17]

Penslar agrees with René Maunier's definition of settler colonialism: "One can speak of colonization when there is, and by the very fact that there is, *occupation with domination* ... emigration with legislation."[18] But Penslar mentions only the 1950 Law of Return as an example of Zionists' domination through legislation. Given the realities recited here, this is misleading. By 1922 Zionists had legitimated their domination under the 1917 Balfour Declaration and the British Mandate. With direct aid of the British state, they expanded their settlement as a separate and superior society tied directly to the metropole, fulfilling the definition of settlement colonialism.

Anticolonialism's Move from Europe to Asia

At this point Penslar moves from structural analysis to a textual analysis of nationalist writing by Jews in Europe and Indians in South Asia, leaving the realities of Palestine behind. He notes only in passing that Jewish settlers wielded an ideology "shot through with colonial mentalities," and emphasizes that their Orientalism differed from European colonialism because Zionists claimed a "familial propinquity" with Arabs.[19]

If we place those settlers' texts back into their Asian context, however, we see a different story. European Zionists' ideas about national regeneration and liberation jettisoned their anticolonial packaging upon ships' arrival at the port of Jaffa. Indeed, the dominant powers in the Yishuv actively opposed anticolonialism: Weizmann's Zionist Commission and Ben-Gurion's mainstream Labor Zionism. Because of space limitations, I present here just two examples, drawn from Zionist responses to the 1921 May Day riots that began in Jaffa and ended with dozens of Jews and Arabs dead. The violence was a wake-up call to the British and Zionists that Arabs massively opposed plans for a Jewish home. Critics intervened at this crucial moment, before the Balfour Declaration was officially written into the mandate.

After the riots, Judah Magnes, a leading American Zionist who later became Hebrew University's first president, warned against the use of Balfour for imperial ends. "You begin by thinking that the Balfour Declaration confers political primacy upon you and places the bayonets on your side," he wrote. "Because of this you think you can afford to bear, if you must, the resentment of your neighbours which is the inevitable result everywhere of the political privilege granted to a minority from without." Zionists must instead implement the Declaration to conform with Jewish ethics, he argued: "We do not want the Jews to be a privileged class in Palestine, even if this be offered to us . . . We want equal rights for everyone."[20] Magnes was viciously attacked for advocating coexistence in a binational Arab-Jewish state and was eventually forced out of his university post and out of Palestine in the 1948 War.

Likewise, Martin Buber, a principal Zionist thinker of the World War I era, warned the Zionist Congress of 1921 that aggressive nationalism would undermine national dignity and spiritual renewal. "The immediate logical consequence of the Balfour Declaration would have been negotiations with the non-Jewish population of Palestine," he declared. Buber met fierce opposition, however, when he offered a resolution rejecting "methods of nationalistic domination" and calling for cooperation with Arabs. Zionist leaders rewrote the resolution to emphasize their anger about the 1921 riots. Buber said he felt shocked and emasculated, and withdrew from party politics.[21] But he continued to exhort Jews to revise their European Zionism to meet social reality in Asia.[22] "Settlement 'alongside,' when two nations inhabit the same country, which fails to become settlement 'together with' must necessarily become a state of 'against.' "[23] Like Magnes, Buber continued to meet opposition from Zionist leaders after he moved to Palestine. They dismissed his view that the only viable state is one based on solid relationships with Arabs.[24]

By juxtaposing separate analyses of Jewish anticolonial thought in Europe and Jewish actions in Palestine, Penslar's essay gives the impression that anticolonialism remained an enduring component of Zionism until 1948. By combining cultural and social analysis of Zionism *within* Palestine, we see instead that European anticolonialism did not condition Jewish nationalism in the Yishuv. Binationalists like Buber and Magnes were dismissed as unrealistic precisely because their ideas did not fit the political goals of the settler colonialists.

Zionists' Encounter with Arabs

Zionist colonialism cannot be assessed solely from Jewish action and self-narrative, as Penslar's essay pretends. It must take account of Arab responses, which equally defined the nature of the encounter.

The manner in which Arabs learned of the Balfour Declaration set the future terms to their relationship with Jewish settlers. Before 1914 they had heard, read, and translated Zionist programs to build a Jewish state in Palestine. But because of military censorship, few Ottoman Arabs had learned of the Balfour Declaration by well into 1918. After the British occupied southern Palestine in December 1917, their military authority issued no formal proclamation of the declaration.

Even Jews learned of it only by word of mouth, likely from General Allenby's troops. The editor of a top Arab newspaper, *Filastin*, learned about Balfour only after the Ottoman defeat in late October 1918.[25]

Shortly thereafter, on November 2, 1918, the Zionist Commission sponsored a parade in Jerusalem to celebrate the declaration's first anniversary. Arab residents of the city were shocked, especially because Jews publicly claimed all of Palestine as their national home. The next day a delegation of more than one hundred Arab notables visited the office of the British military governor, Ronald Storrs. At their head was Mayor Musa Kazim Pasha al-Husayni, a retired Ottoman governor who had served in many Arab districts of the empire. He presented Storrs with a petition: "We have noticed yesterday a large crowd of Jews carrying banners and overrunning the streets shouting words which hurt the feelings and wound the soul. They pretend with open voice that Palestine, which is the Holy Land of our Fathers and the graveyard of our ancestors, which had been inhabited by the Arabs for long ages who loved it and died in defending it, is now a national home for them." The petition expressed the Darwinian fear of collective annihilation sparked by the Armenian genocide. As a remedy, it proposed a return to prewar Ottoman pluralism, based on fraternity and equality in one state: "[We] expect that a Power like Great Britain well known for justice and progress will put a stop to the Zionists' cry. Furthermore, it will establish a just ruling for immigration to Palestine by Muslims, Christians and Jews equally, in order that the country may be saved from being lost and the inhabitants from being persecuted. In conclusion, we Muslims and Christians desire to live with our brothers the Jews of Palestine in peace and happiness and with equal rights. Our privileges are theirs, and their duties ours."[26] The British responded only with vague promises of liberation and national governments in the Joint Anglo-French declaration of November 7.

With no sign of British action, Palestinian Arabs organized cross-sectarian Muslim–Christian associations in every major city. In February 1919 the first annual Palestinian Arab Congress passed resolutions demanding sovereignty, affirming Palestine's links with Syria, and rejecting the Balfour Declaration: "In accordance with the rule laid down by President Wilson, we consider invalid every promise or treaty made regarding our country."[27]

Arabs in Egypt, Iraq, and Syria also embraced President Woodrow Wilson's promise of rights to even the smallest nations.[28] In Damascus, Prince Faysal established an Arab government of Greater Syria, including Palestine. He believed that Britain had promised such a state in return for the Arab Revolt's help in defeating the Ottomans. Britain now betrayed that promise (made by mail in 1915 to Faysal's father, Sharif Husayn) in favor of its 1917 promise to Jews in Palestine and the 1916 secret Sykes-Picot Agreement that granted France control of much of Greater Syria. The Paris Peace Conference consequently denied Faysal's appeal for an independent Arab state. Faysal then placed his final hopes in Wilson's call for government by consent. He convened an Arab congress that summer to meet with an American delegation that polled Arabs on their political preferences.

Palestinians sent delegates to the Syrian Arab Congress in Damascus, which told the American King-Crane commission that Palestine was historically a southern district of Greater Syria and that the majority the population desired a unified, independent state. When Britain and France ignored the commission's report, the congress responded with defiance but not violence. In March 1920 Izzat Darwazeh, congress secretary and native of the Palestinian city of Nablus, proclaimed Faysal king of an independent state. In July the congress ratified a democratic constitution that proclaimed all citizens of Greater Syria, regardless of religion, equal. Two weeks later, however, French tanks bulldozed into Damascus and replaced the Syrian Arab Kingdom with a French mandate.

At the same time, High Commissioner Herbert Samuel arrived to establish a civilian government in Palestine. He proposed a constitution with a joint legislative assembly that would guarantee Britain and Zionists a majority of votes. Kazim and other Arab groups rejected participation in a government that limited the 88 percent majority of the population to minority representation. Samuel responded harshly, repressing Arab political associations.

In a last-ditch effort, Kazim led a delegation to London in late 1921 to argue against incorporating the Balfour Declaration into the mandate. Churchill refused to meet him and in June 1922 issued a white paper calling for a mandate based on Balfour and on guarantees of continued Jewish immigration. In the summer of 1922 the League of Nations complied with Churchill's wishes and authorized British mandates as well in Iraq and Transjordan, along with French mandates in Syria and Lebanon. The only Arabs to escape European colonial rule after World War I were the Saudis of Arabia.

Arabs' encounter with Zionism was conditioned by this history of force and exclusion from the due process set in motion at the Paris Peace Conference. While Zionists had been granted ample opportunity to present their case to the conference, Faysal was the only Arab permitted to speak, and then only on behalf of his father in Arabia, not as a representative of Greater Syria. In the end, the mandates were imposed by brute force. Churchill had suppressed the 1920 Iraqi revolt with a terrifying campaign of carpet bombing.[29] The French responded similarly to revolt in Syria.

Conclusion

To aggravate inequities in the process of founding a Jewish home in the British Mandate, Britain subsequently failed to fulfill Balfour's promise that the Jewish home would not harm the civil and social rights of non-Jews. Britain's postwar debt limited their means. While the Yishuv drew on foreign funds to build an impressive social network for employment, health care, and education, Arabs of Palestine lived under a meager mandatory budget spent largely on policing and repression. They had wholly inadequate schooling and health care, and their farms remained undercapitalized. Relative deprivation fueled Arab violence in the 1929 riots, the 1936–39 revolt, and again in 1948.

Penslar's final claim that the 1948 War was not an anticolonial uprising therefore rings hollow. It was the culmination of a conflict conditioned by a colonial regime of domination. Zionists' privileged status fueled their ambition, and at the end of World War II Jews of the Yishuv launched an anticolonial war of terror against Britain. Arabs turned to war in 1947 as a continuation of earlier anticolonial revolts in Palestine, Syria, and Iraq. Arabs from all of these countries joined the Palestine war in 1948 because they saw it as the culmination of their own suffering. They fought Jews as local representatives of an international regime—first the League of Nations and now the United Nations—that sanctioned their second-class status under international law. In their eyes, the forceful imposition of the interests of foreign-born settlers over longtime residents of Palestine did not constitute what Penslar calls "existential conflict between two nationalities."

Notes

1. Derek J. Penslar, "Is Zionism a Colonial Movement?," chap. 12 of the present volume, 277.

2. Frederick Cooper, *Colonialism in Question: Theory, Knowledge, History* (Berkeley: University of California Press, 2005), 26–27. Of course there are many definitions of colonialism. I use Cooper's from this volume because it is a widely read, highly regarded critique of the state of the field, and it was published before Penslar's essay.

3. I draw on my own research in the period in my two books: Elizabeth Thompson, *Colonial Citizens: Republican Rights, Paternal Privilege, and Gender in French Syria and Lebanon* (New York: Columbia University Press, 2000); and Elizabeth F. Thompson, *Justice Interrupted: The Struggle for Constitutional Government in the Middle East* (Cambridge, MD: Harvard University Press, 2014).

4. Thompson, *Justice Interrupted*, 117–23.

5. David Ben-Gurion, "Earning a Homeland," *Rebirth and Destiny of Israel*, trans. M. Nurock (New York: Philosophical Library, 1954), 3–6.

6. Jehuda Reinharz, *Chaim Weizmann: The Making of a Statesman* (New York: Oxford University Press, 1993), 1–59.

7. Chaim Weizmann, *The Letters and Papers of Chaim Weizmann*, vol. VII-A, ed. Leonard Stein (Jerusalem: Israel Universities Press, 1975), 81–83, 114–15; Jonathan Schneer, *The Balfour Declaration* (New York: Random House, 2010), 333–46; and Jehuda Reinharz, "The Balfour Declaration and Its Maker: A Reassessment," *Journal of Modern History* 64 (September 1994): 455–99.

8. Yale Law School, Lilian Goldman Law Library, The Avalon Project, Documents in Law, History and Diplomacy, http://avalon.law.yale.edu/20th_century/balfour.asp.

9. Shabtai Teveth, *Ben-Gurion: The Burning Ground, 1886–1948* (Boston: Houghton-Mifflin, 1987), 114–17; "Peace Army for Palestine," *New York Times*, April 27, 1917, 11.

10. David Vital, *Zionism: The Crucial Phase* (Oxford: Clarendon, 1987), 89–162, 211–35; and Anita Shapira, *Land and Power: The Zionist Resort to Force, 1881–1948* (Stanford, CA: Stanford University Press, 1999), 83.

11. Penslar, "Is Zionism a Colonial Movement?," 279.

12. Ibid.

13. Caroline Elkins and Susan Pedersen, *Settler Colonialism in the Twentieth Century* (New York: Routledge, 2005), 2–3.

14. James Renton, "Changing Languages of Empire and the Orient: Britain and the Invention of the Middle East, 1917–1918," *Historical Journal* 50, no. 3 (2007): 661–64.

15. Correspondence with the Palestine Arab Delegation and the Zionist Organisation 1922. Viewed July 14, 2012 at the World War I Document Archive, http://www.gwpda.org/1918p/palestine_zionist_1922.html; and Churchill White Paper of 1922, viewed July 18, 2012 at the Avalon Project, Yale Law School, Lillian Goldman Law Library, http://avalon.law.yale.edu/20th_century/brwh1922.asp.

16. Gabriel Piterberg, *The Returns of Zionism* (New York: Verso, 2008), 62–73. See also Gershon Shafir, *Land, Labor, and the Origins of the Israeli–Palestinian Conflict, 1882–1914* (Berkeley: University of California Press, 1988).

17. LeVine, *Overthrowing Geography: Jaffa, Tel Aviv, and the Struggle for Palestine, 1880–1948* (Berkeley: University of California Press, 2005), 60–84; Abigail Jacobson, *From Empire to Empire: Jerusalem Between Ottoman and British Rule* (Syracuse, NY: Syracuse University Press, 2011), 82–116, 172–77; Adam Lebor, *City of Oranges: An Intimate History of Arabs and Jews in Jaffa* (New York: W. W. Norton, 2006), 179–81; and Tom Segev, *One Palestine, Complete: Jews and Arabs under the British Mandate* (New York: Henry Holt, 1999).

18. René Maunier, quoted in Maxime Rodinson, *Israel: A Colonial Settler-State?* (New York: Monad, 1973), 90. Emphasis added.

19. Penslar, "Is Zionism a Colonial Movement?," 280–81.

20. J.L. Magnes, "Zionist Politics: New York, August 26, 1921," reprinted in *Like All the Nations?* (Jerusalem, 1930), 45–58.

21. Martin Buber, *A Land of Two Peoples: Martin Buber on Jews and Arabs*, ed. Paul Mendes-Flohr, (Chicago: University of Chicago Press, 2005), 60–61, 63. See also commentary by Mendes-Flohr at 47, 58–59, 62–63, 64.

22. Ibid., 70–72.

23. Ibid., 91.

24. Haim Gordon, *The Other Martin Buber* (Columbus: Ohio University Press, 1988), 80, 102, 104–5, 134, 137, 160.

25. Rashid Khalidi, *The Iron Cage: The Story of the Palestinian Struggle for Statehood* (Boston: Beacon, 2006), 96.

26. Reprinted in Ann Mosely Lesch, *Arab Politics in Palestine, 1917–1939* (Ithaca, NY: Cornell University Press, 1979), 85–86. Alternate translation in Yehoshuah Porath, *The Emergence of the Palestinian-Arab National Movement 1918–1929* (London: Frank Cass, 1974), 60–61.

27. Muhammad Muslih, *Origins of Palestinian Nationalism* (New York: Columbia University Press, 1989), 181–82; see also Muslih, *Origins*, 178–85; Jacobson, *Empire to Empire*, 156–57; and Porath, *Emergence of the Palestinian–Arab National Movement*, 40, 42, 71.

28. Erez Manela, *The Wilsonian Moment: Self-Determination and the International Origins of Anticolonial Nationalism* (New York: Oxford University Press, 2007).

29. Priya Satia, *Spies in Arabia: The Great War and the Cultural Foundations of Britain's Covert Empire in the Middle East* (New York: Oxford University Press, 2008), 239–62.

15

WHAT WE TALK ABOUT WHEN WE TALK ABOUT COLONIALISM

A RESPONSE TO JOSHUA COLE
AND ELIZABETH THOMPSON

Derek J. Penslar

"Is Zionism a Colonial Movement?" was a child of the Second Intifada. In the spring of 2001, I was a research fellow at the newly opened Yitzhak Rabin Center in Ramat Aviv. Israel and the Occupied Territories were in turmoil. I walked past the Dolphinarium discotheque just hours before the suicide bombing on June 1 that killed twenty-five people. During that terrible time, I sought serenity in reflection and emotional detachment, like a patient who believes that understanding his illness will mitigate his pain and endow him with agency. Sitting in my spare but quiet office in the old Petroleum Institute (the Rabin Center had not yet moved to its grand, permanent domicile), I mulled over the Zionist project's fundamental contradiction, between the liberation of one nation and the oppression of the other. My main source of intellectual sustenance was not the historiography on Zionism and Israel but rather a body of literature in subaltern and postcolonial studies, a literature with which I had become familiar through teaching graduate seminars on nationality theory and national movements. I found Partha Chatterjee's work particularly inspiring, although I read it against the grain, finding greater similarities between Western and subaltern collective identifications than Chatterjee himself contended, and locating the Zionist project within the realms of both the colonizer and the colonized.

This intellectual exercise places Zionism in a global matrix of nationality movements and conflicts in the twentieth and twenty-first centuries. Doing so in no way minimizes Zionism's internal contradictions and the wrongdoings perpetrated in its name. But it does acknowledge that acts of oppression, subjugation, and violence committed by state actors can occur within a great variety of political systems and matrices of power. They should not be equated solely with the consequences of what is usually understood as modern colonialism, that is,

327

the geopolitical system in which for several centuries a handful of Western powers controlled, directly or indirectly, much of the earth's population and resources.

My article was published late in 2001 under the title "Zionism, Colonialism and Postcolonialism" in *The Journal of Israeli History*. (The following year, that issue of the journal was published as a standalone book.) In 2005, I revised and expanded the article for inclusion in my book *Israel in History*, filling in analytical gaps in the argument and dealing more squarely with Israel's colonial dimensions, particularly since 1967.[1] Although it had been almost forty years since Israel's conquest of the West Bank and Gaza, I continued to conceive of the Zionist project as separable from the Occupation by viewing it over an expanse of almost 120 years, during most of which the impetus to expropriate or subjugate a native population was weak (up to 1948) or checked by mitigating forces (between 1948 and 1967). Perhaps even more significant was that I prepared the revised article around the time of the Gaza withdrawal, which allowed me, like many others, to think of the Occupation as still reversible. In 2016, it is increasingly difficult to maintain this point of view.

I have of late found it helpful to conceive of the Occupation as what the Russian literary theorist Mikhail Bakhtin called a chronotope, a "time-space" in which time is visible and space is perceived through the lens of history. For several decades, the chronotope of an occupation that began in 1967 enabled conceiving of it as an irregularity in not only time (with 1948–67 as the norm) but also space. The establishment of Jewish settlements in the West Bank and Gaza did not result in annexation, leaving the whole enterprise in a state of suspense. Under the radically different influences of the Oslo Peace Process and the two intifadas, Israeli Jews who identified with what in Israel is called the "left" (that is, those who are receptive to territorial compromise and recognition of Palestinian national rights) began to conceive of "Palestine" as something separate from "Israel." Although I was not fully aware of it at the time, the original and revised versions of my article were written within this conceptual framework.

In the wake of the Second Intifada, among Israeli Jews memories of pre-1967 Israel have faded, animosity toward the Palestinians has grown, and the price of maintaining the Occupation has declined drastically. In the dominant political discourse in Israel, the Occupation has assumed a new form as lacking a clear historical beginning and therefore having no end. The chronotope of eternal mastery over the land in turn blurs territorial distinctions between what used to be divided by the 1949 Armistice lines. Thus, many Israelis and Palestinians concur that there should be one state between the Mediterranean and the Jordan and that 1967 is of far less significance than 1948 because the latter marked the onset of both an Israeli state-building project and a Palestinian *nakba* (catastrophe) that continue to this day.

Periodization still matters, however. The fledgling Zionist movement of the decades before World War I is vastly different from the nation-building project of the mandate period, and the State of Israel's formative first two decades did have distinct features, as did the period from 1967 to 1987, and arguably the one from 1987 to 2005. Understanding continuities and ruptures across these periods requires conceptual clarity. One may bemoan the current impasse between Israel and the Palestinians and decry Israeli actions, but the indiscriminate use of the term "colonial" to describe those actions has little explanatory power. The utility of applying the concept of colonialism to any or all periods within the history of the Zionist project depends upon how one defines colonialism, and the responses to my article by Joshua Cole and Elizabeth Thompson conceive of the term in substantively different ways. In my remarks I will highlight the strengths and limits of each of their approaches, keeping in mind that although the present surely influences our perception of the past, the past has to be understood in its own terms, and that conceptual frameworks are meant to illuminate, not obscure, historical events.

For Cole, colonialism involves not only projections of state power but also a dynamic interaction between the metropole, settlers, and natives. Drawing on the case of French Algeria, Cole sees in colonialism a discourse and practice of "inclusion and differentiation." Cole describes colonial subjects as excluded from the body politic yet imagined by French authorities as possibly included at some future date. (Cole's observation reminds us of Dipesh Chakrabarty's concept of indefinitely delayed recognition of native rights, the "not yet" of the hierarchical and tutelary colonial regime.[2]) While settlers pursued their own agendas, often at odds with the metropole, natives exerted agency in the formulation of new identities and even in shaping the parameters of colonial policy.

Cole's paradigm of colonialism offers many applications to the Zionist project and the State of Israel. In Mandate Palestine, Jews and the British authorities had both common and clashing interests, leading to relationships as complex as those between Algeria's European settlers, the *pieds-noirs,* and the French state administration. The fractiousness of a population of alleged clients is apparent as well in the post-1967 Israeli settlement enterprise in the Occupied Territories. Throughout the period of Israeli statehood, the government has attempted both the fusion of Jewish communities (particularly *edot ha-mizrah,* Jews from the Muslim world) and the fission of Arab minorities (for example, subjecting only the Druze to military conscription in return for a somewhat greater level of rights and privileges than those of Christian and Muslim Arabs[3]). The dynamic of inclusion and differentiation within a liberal settler-state is at the center of Shira Robinson's important monograph on Israel's Arab citizens during the 1950s.[4] In keeping with Cole's argument about Algeria, however, the invention of a unified "oriental" Jewry during Israel's first decade stimulated the construction a generation later of new political, religious, and cultural identities by activists among what came to be known as Mizrahi or Sephardi Jews. The latter appellation is an extension of the term for Jews of Iberian descent to include virtually all of Israel's non-Ashkenazi Jews. Sephardi/Mizrahi activists both rejected and incorporated the collective ascription that had been invented by the state's governing elite.

One of the contradictions within much of the critical literature on Israeli society is the depiction of Palestinian or Mizrahi Jewish identities as complex, variegated, and multivectored while reducing the country's Ashkenazic Jewish population to a homogenous mass. Why would European Jewish immigrants to pre-1948 Palestine or the newly formed State of Israel, immigrants hailing from a vast spatial and cultural expanse, be any less divided by class and outlook, any less prone to multiple subethnic particularities than newcomers in any settler-colonial project, be it North America, Australasia, South Africa, or Algeria? In my article I refer to the "complex process of refraction and manipulation of the hegemonic culture and political system" by Israeli Palestinians. The same can be said for European Jewish immigrants who maintained a variety of national and subethnic habitus (e.g., Polish, Hungarian, German) while performing a "sabra" identity that did not obliterate so much as displace and conceal ongoing difference. Speaking of new Yemenite immigrants to the State of Israel, David Ben-Gurion proclaimed that they should forget that they are Yemenite just as he had forgotten that he was Polish.[5] Such a statement testifies to the limitations as well as successes of the Zionist project to invent a culturally homogeneous new Hebrew. Not only did secular Zionists never truly forget that they were "Polish," the revolutionary transformation of the self and the collective that lay at the center of the Zionist project left entire swaths of Jewish society, such as the ultra-Orthodox, virtually untouched or had unintended consequences that ran far afield of what the founders of the state had envisioned. The Zionist project was a matrix with many points of entrance and exit, including people who would, or who would come to, define themselves as non- or anti-Zionist, and inhabiting myriad points along spectra of religiosity and political ideology.

By presenting colonialism as an encounter rather than a unidirectional projection, we open the way to understanding the formation of new sensibilities among colonizers and colonized alike. This approach can take us beyond the focus in the vast majority of scholarship on the relationship between Zionism and colonialism on the expropriation of the Palestinians. Expropriation or subjugation of natives is an essential component of settlement colonialism, but also worthy of attention is the indigenization of the colonizer. Like European settlers in the New World, Jews arriving in Palestine cast off some forms of identification and behavior, retained or modified others, and developed new ones as well. In short, Jewish immigrants became creoles, and their descendants became natives.[6]

Many scholars, particularly in the field of Middle Eastern Studies, have argued that from its beginnings Zionism epitomized settlement colonialism in its claim of title to land inhabited by an indigenous population. Israel is often compared with colonial North America and Australasia, modern South Africa, and Algeria under French rule. One can indeed draw broad similarities between all these cases. The Zionist quest to create a "New Hebrew" can be likened to the New England Puritan colonists' vision of a New Jerusalem and to the self-aggrandizing discourse of Algerian *pied-noir* activists as the "Latins of Africa," said to comprise a new race, fair of form, committed to hard labor and to reviving the land from neglect at the hands of ostensibly indolent and fanatical Arabs and Berbers.[7] Like various forms of settlement colonialism, Zionism featured a dual sense of compassion and condescension toward the natives, a *mission civilisatrice* and a compulsion to separate from them, and faith in Western technology to revive a once fertile but now desertified land. The hallowed Zionist principle of "Hebrew labor" has parallels as far-flung in space and time as colonial North America, where colonists vowed to toil the land by the sweat of their brow, and South Africa in the 1920s, when Afrikaner mineworkers campaigned against cheap black labor under the slogan "Workers of the World Unite, and Fight for a White South Africa!"[8]

In settler-colonial societies' formative years, worry lest the colonists meld into the aboriginals led the former to separate themselves from the latter, to dominate, marginalize, or eradicate them, all while extolling the newcomers' own indigeneity.

In late-seventeenth-century New England the fiery preacher Cotton Mather nervously described his son Increase and his native-born peers as "tame Indians." In response to the prospect of falling into what Mather called "criolian degeneracy," Mather invented a no less creolized English-American persona, both highly cultured and plainspoken.[9] There is a clear resemblance to the twentieth-century native-born Palestinian/Israeli Jew, the *sabra*, who remained attached to European culture while being a child of the Land of Israel. Colonial American plain speech was an antecedent of the blunt, direct Hebrew speaking style known as *dugri*. Colonial American and Zionist anxieties about native peoples also characterized modern Afrikaners, who, fearing being "swamped" by the black majority, developed a pioneering culture centered around self-reliance and self-defense. Given these points of contact between the Zionist project and varieties of settlement colonialism, I must respectfully disagree with the anthropologist Zali Gurevitch, who, in a classic essay from 1992, claimed that most peoples take their nativity for granted and that Israeli Jewish identity was unusually mediated, reflective, and overwrought, defined by doubt and insecurity. Gurevitch's observations pertain, in fact, to settler-colonial societies as a whole.[10]

These comparisons are suggestive, yet we may not take for granted the presentation of entities as diverse as colonial North America, pre-1962 Algeria, pre-1994 South Africa, and the State of Israel as fitting into a unified matrix of "settler states." As Cole observes, every form of settlement colonialism had distinct qualities. The purpose of comparison is to gain insight from the understanding of difference as well as similarity across time and space. Sympathizers of Israel are wont to separate the Zionist project from colonialism as such, whereas a more rigorous and scholarly approach would be to adopt the Wittgensteinian concept of familial resemblance, according to which each member of a set bears some resemblance to one or more other members, but each may have unique features as well. Not all forms of settlement colonialism, for example, require a metropole; South Africa did not have one prior to the establishment of British hegemony. Some types of settlement colonialism depend upon native labor, whereas others shun it. Although Zionism has been overwhelmingly bent on separation from Arabs, Zionism has not developed elaborate racial categorizations that in South Africa were known as theoretical apartheid. And finally, the Zionist project featured many distinct qualities among settler-colonial ventures, for example, the concept of return to an ancient patrimony; the mission to foster mass migration of persecuted and impoverished members of a single community; the top-down construction of a new polity, national economy, and culture; and a zealous secularism (at least in its formative decades).

Another problem with a comparative approach is the setting of too broad or narrow a comparison situation. Should our concept of colonialism be limited to the Western world? Awet Tewelde Weldemichael argues that in the post-1945 era African and Asian powers have practiced what he calls "secondary colonialism" in lands adjacent to their borders. In his comparative study of the Ethiopian annexation of Eritrea and Indonesia's occupation of East Timor, Weldemichael argues that these states' practices are just as illegal, brutal, and destructive of the native culture and economy as those of Western colonialism.[11] A second, related question is whether Israel is best understood within a framework of modern Western settlement colonialism or whether instead Israel should be compared to countries anywhere in the world that practice demographic engineering—that is, moving dominant or favored populations from one territory to another within its borders.

As Johannes Becke has argued, in recent decades a variety of non-Western states have employed demographic engineering as a tool of state expansion. Becke compares Israel's development of Jewish settlements in the West Bank with, among other cases, Moroccan settlement in Western Sahara. Both settlement projects are illicit in the eyes of the international community.[12] "Illicit" practices are, however, not necessarily colonial in the strict meaning of the word. Intriguingly, the term "colonial" barely appears in a new essay collection, edited by Oded Haklai and Neophytos Loizides, on demographic engineering in comparative perspective.[13] Essays on Israeli, Moroccan, Indonesian, and Turkish settlement projects in the West Bank, Western Sahara, East Timor, and northern Cyprus, respectively, are placed alongside essays on internal demographic engineering, such as Baathist Iraqi attempts to Arabize Kirkuk or Sinhalese settlement in Tamil and Muslim areas of eastern Sri Lanka. The irredentist fervor of the Gush Emunim may be likened to Indonesian fantasies of restoring the territorial integrity of the early modern Majapahit Empire, but perhaps a closer comparison would be with the fanaticism of Buddhist monks who see the entire island of Sri Lanka as a Sinhalese patrimony.

In the twentieth century, the widest-ranging attempt at state-directed demographic engineering was not made by any Western colonial empire, nor by any of the countries analyzed in Haklai's and Loizides's volume, but rather by the Soviets in Kazakhstan. During the 1930s, due to the collectivization of agriculture and an ensuing famine, some two million Kazakhs died and another half million fled. While over half the native population was killed or deracinated, some 1.5 million Poles, Chechens, Germans, Turks, and Koreans were deported from the Soviet Union's borderlands and sent to Kazakhstan. Thanks to high levels of intermarriage and the heavy hand of Stalinist education, the immigrants, and even more their children, came to see themselves as Soviet pioneers, charged with taming a wild frontier.[14] In Kazakhstan, as in many other lands where demographic engineering has been practiced, the identities of settlers and natives alike have undergone constant shifting and reevaluation.

Settler colonialism may have been a purely Western phenomenon, but demographic engineering is a global one. Moreover, just as state expansion, occupation, and settlement are not limited to the "West," so is the sensibility of being colonized not limited to the "rest." The stateless peoples of pre-1914 Europe's polyglot empires were not necessarily beneficiaries of liberal political institutions, or at least they did not perceive themselves as such. European imperialism was continental as well as transoceanic, and great swaths of people, not only in the distant reaches of Central Asia but also in southern and eastern Europe, were caught up in its wake. Cole is correct that modern social policy could benefit even the stateless and dispossessed within Europe, whereas colonized peoples in

Asia or Africa bore the brunt of an externally imposed force that was economically exploitative and culturally alien. Yet the same sense of the artificiality of imperial rule, of deprivation and exclusion, was found in the heart of nineteenth- and twentieth-century Europe as well as in Asia and Africa. Cole himself admits that the "dynamic of inclusion and differentiation is not merely characteristic of colonial regimes during the imperial age but of modern nations in general."

What, then, is left of the term "colonial"? Cole observes that whether and how the term is used ultimately depends upon specific political contexts, which trap us all in a "polemical hothouse." In the case of pre-1948 Zionism, the principal historical issue is as specific as our discussion thus far has been general: that under the mandate, the British ruled—and the Zionists aspired to rule— without the consent of the governed, and that both parties applied brute force when the indigenous population attempted to assert its rights to self-determination. Scholarship on this issue is particularly prone to slippage between the analytical/ explanatory and the normative dimensions of the term "colonialism." In Elizabeth Thompson's critique of my article, the spatial and temporal specificity of her conceptualization of colonialism produces some important correctives to my original argument. But that specificity leads as well to a certain analytical rigidity that fails to capture the complexity of the Zionist project and its relationship with the Jewish diaspora from which it emerged.

Focusing on Palestine during the period of the British mandate, Thompson argues that if we take into account the full range of the Yishuv leadership's thoughts and deeds, the Zionist project clearly emerges as a settler-colonial movement allied with the British colonial regime. Zionist leaders such as Theodor Herzl, Chaim Weizmann, and Vladimir Jabotinsky explicitly linked the fortunes of Zionism to those of the British Empire, to which, they claimed, a Jewish national home could bring great strategic benefit. What is more, Zionism benefited directly from the Great Powers' suppression of Arab nationalism at the end of World War I and particularly from the structure of the mandate, which incorporated the terms of the Balfour Declaration. Like Cole, Thompson observes that settlers can have a distant, even conflicted, relationship with the metropole, so the many disagreements with Palestine's British rulers, which by the 1940s led to armed clashes, did not weaken Zionism's deep colonial roots. Last but not least, Thompson widens my focus from that of the colonizers to include the sensibilities of the natives, for "any assessment of whether their encounter was colonial must take into account indigenous responses to the settlers."

Thompson's arguments are clear, perhaps a bit too much so. After all, stateless or oppressed peoples often seek alliances with powerful patrons, claiming to offer them some tangible or strategic benefit. During the last decades of the Ottoman Empire, nationalist movements in the Balkans used these strategies to win support from the Great Powers. During World War I, Mohandas Gandhi was firmly pro-British and mobilized South Africa's Indian community in support of the Entente.[15] The subaltern's assertion of utility as a means for enhancing agency is not in and of itself a display of mimicry or the behavior of a lackey. Moreover, it is inaccurate to equate the story of pre-1948 Zionism with the British mandate. Over half of its history took place before 1917, when the Zionist movement had no sponsoring state but rather operated independently, engaging in sporadic yet increasingly organized settlement activity, particularly after the establishment of the Zionist Organization's (ZO) Palestine Office in 1908.

Between 1896 and 1904, the ZO's founder and president, Theodor Herzl, ran from one Great Power capital to another, offering the Jews as loyal subjects of any state—including the Ottoman Empire—that would grant the Jews the right to construct, as the ZO's Basel Program put it, "a national home secured by public law." The vagueness of this wording was not, as some scholars have argued, a rejection of Herzl's own clear desire for an independent Jewish state. Herzl himself was open to myriad possibilities falling well short of statehood for a Jewish polity.[16] Like most political leaders, Herzl was pragmatic and opportunist, and his objectives are best understood in terms of a matrix rather than a fixed point. All the more so for Herzl's successor as ZO leader, Chaim Weizmann, who shepherded the ZO for almost three decades, navigating between clashing political forces within the Zionist movement, severe economic constraints on the development of the Jewish National Home, and Britain's shifting Middle Eastern strategies. The relationship between interwar Zionism and the British Empire was thus somewhat more strained than Thompson suggests. Although the British certainly fostered the growth of the Yishuv through granting autonomy to its governing institutions, tolerating immigration and land purchase (with periodic reversals of policy), and building national infrastructure, it is simply not true that by the early 1920s the Yishuv had become a protostate.

The most significant respect in which the meeting of minds between Zionists and the British assumed a colonial hue was the denial of the native majority's claims to self-determination. In this sense Weizmann and Gandhi, both of whom during the 1920s argued for the fulfillment of their collective aspirations within a liberal British empire, fell into opposite camps. Zionists' guilty conscience about their intrusion into a land claimed by a preexisting population led to the creation of fanciful apologetic arguments, such as claims that the Palestinian Arabs were in fact devolved Hebrews from biblical times, or that Palestinian resistance to Zionism was being led by "reactionary effendis" who wanted to shield the fellaheen from the message of class liberation preached by Labor Zionism.

Were these arguments conscious lies, convenient but sincere fabrications, or something else altogether? Answering that question demands listening critically to and interrogating the voices of our subjects, regardless of nationality, subject position, or place in the hierarchies of power. For example, immediately after World War I anticolonial movements claimed to employ Wilsonian language of self-determination, yet when Wilson spoke of consent of the governed in non-European environments, he had no desire to oversee the end of empires in Asia and Africa. As Erez Manela has written, Wilson became a symbol and a vehicle for political movements for which he had little sympathy.[17] A similar level of sophistication is required when reading Zionist discourse.

On the one hand, the Mandatory government and Zionists often enjoyed close relations, and the British and Zionists were military allies from the mid-1930s until the end of World War II. Zionists had no reason to disavow this alliance so long as it was beneficial to them. At the same time, throughout the interwar period Zionists attempted to forge relations with anticolonial movements worldwide but were usually rebuffed. (When asked by Zionist leaders for their support, Gandhi demurred, calling instead for European Jewry to engage in passive resistance to Nazism.) A meeting of minds did form, however, between Zionism and Irish nationalism, which shared a common heritage of persecution and a common goal to free themselves from British rule. Labor Zionism claimed kinship between the new Hebrew laboring class in Palestine and the toiling masses of the world. Given that the Zionist labor movement was determined to keep Arabs away from the embryonic Jewish national economy, the contradictions within this rhetoric are striking. I referred earlier to Afrikaner miners who invoked the language of international labor solidarity to protect their own jobs against blacks. What may appear to us as racist hypocrisy was perceived differently by impoverished men struggling to earn a livelihood or Zionists striving to create the economic preconditions of a Jewish commonwealth. Contradiction is no more indicative of mendacity than is logical or cohesive argumentation.

Varieties of perspective illuminate one of Thompson's final points, about whether the 1948 Palestine war should be defined as an anticolonial uprising. To Arabs throughout the Middle East, the war was "a continuation of earlier anticolonial revolts in Palestine, Syria, and Iraq." True enough. But this emotionally powerful term obscures more than it explains the Arab world's highly limited support for this uprising. The volunteer Arab Liberation Army was brought together by the Arab League not so much to liberate Palestine on behalf of its indigenous inhabitants as to thwart the expansionist aspirations of Abdullah, king of Jordan. The regimes of the Arab states that bordered Palestine had little desire for Palestinian statehood, and they throttled the flow of volunteers seeking to fight alongside of Palestinian militias.[18] Not only was this uprising internally fractured, by mid-May of 1948 it had no clear colonial target, as the British mandate had been terminated and the British armed forces had withdrawn from

Palestine. Support from the United States to Israel was guarded and limited to diplomatic assistance.

Meanwhile, Palestine's Jews were fighting what they perceived as a war of liberation, although just as Arabs had no colonial power against whom to direct an anticolonial uprising, it is not clear from whom the Jews were seeking independence, as by May of 1948 Palestine had no suzerain. In 1948 Arabs and Jews fought on two levels—on an earthly, material level against each other for control of the land, and on an affective and psychological level as an assault against decades, if not centuries, of humiliation and depredation. Arabs fought against "colonialism" just as Jews fought against their own historic condition of statelessness and disempowerment. Hence, Israel conventionally calls the 1948 war one for "independence" or "liberation" (*milhemet ha-atsma'ut/ha-shihrur*). A more accurate, but less often used and less easily translatable, term for the war was *milhemet ha-komemiyut. Komemiyut* comes from Leviticus 26:13 and refers to the redemption of the Israelites from Egypt, God's removal of the yoke of slavery from their shoulders and causing them to walk upright (*komemiyut*) toward freedom. The words *atsma'ut* and *shihrur* connote a struggle against an antagonist, a force from which one has been liberated, thus allowing for independence and autonomy, but *komemiyut* suggests an action that, even if initiated by transcendent forces, is ultimately reflexive and self-directed.[19] A similar reflexivity characterizes the official name of Israel's foundational document, which is commonly referred to as the "Declaration of Independence" but in fact was formally titled the "Declaration of the Establishment of the State of Israel."

Throughout most of the fighting, Palestine's Jews enjoyed military superiority, but they also lived with the existential fear that their backs were to the wall and they had nowhere to run. The 700,000 Palestinian refugees who were driven from their homes or fled in panic in 1948 are a testimony to the collective human tragedy known as the *nakba* and to the cruel and simple fact that there were no places to which the fleeing masses could go. In contrast, the infant State of Israel had about 70,000 Jewish refugees who were uprooted from their homes but remained within the country. Small numbers of Jews fled the war-torn country by sea, but few had the means or the will to do so.

Understanding these complicated realities calls for terms and concepts not normally found in scholarship on the Zionist project and the Israel/Palestine conflict. The early Zionist movement sought close ties with colonial powers, but the State of Israel was born in the era of decolonization in the wake of World War II, and in its birth struggles it developed means of revenue extraction, weapons procurement, and governance that resembled those of anticolonial movements throughout the world in the first half of the twentieth century. As I have argued elsewhere, the Irish Republican Army during the interwar period, and the

Viet Minh and Algerian Front de Libération Nationale (FLN) during the 1950s, knew that they could not possibly succeed without money and weapons, and they mobilized their own populations as well as ethnic diasporas and supporters abroad. Israel did the same, albeit far less successfully in terms of winning the support of patron states; no state gave Israel arms in 1948, although the USSR allowed Czechoslovakia to sell it aircraft and weaponry. Israel compensated for its lack of a patron state by achieving far higher levels of financial support from the Jewish diaspora than the Irish Republican Army received from Irish Americans, or the FLN from the Jeanson network in France, or the Viet Minh from the Vietnamese diaspora in Thailand.[20]

This comparison may appear forced because Israel in 1948 fought against an indigenous majority as well as external foes. For this reason, the more conventional comparison would be between Zionists and *pied-noir* settlers rather than the FLN. In fact, both sets of comparisons are valid. In this spirit, the South African historian Hermann Giliomee has written of the Afrikaners as a pioneer people who fought the first anticolonial war in modern history (the Anglo-Boer War) but then went on to champion apartheid and become the "pole cat of the world."[21] Historical analysis must adapt itself to the contours and contradictions of lived reality, not file them down into straight lines and right angles. The purpose of comparison is not to establish phenomenal identity, let alone moral congruence, between different situations. It is, rather, to distinguish between essential and nonessential causal factors, to isolate the variables that lead to common outcomes across diverse situations or diverse outcomes across similar situations.

Reflecting upon these two perceptive critiques of my article, I appreciate the attractiveness of the term "colonialism" as an analytical and explanatory term, but it has limitations, and there are many aspects of the Zionist project for which it does not account. As a general tool of historical analysis, the term runs the risk of being at the same time too broad, too narrow, and too schematic. It encompasses acts of conquest and settlement on a global scale yet presents the fin-de-siècle European encounter with Asia and Africa as unique. It depicts Zionism as a form of settlement colonialism yet acknowledges the vast differences between settler-colonial societies as diverse as the United States, Canada, Australia, Algeria, and South Africa. It purports to describe a concept, a process, and a discourse, yet it all too often devolves into a normative term with a uniformly pejorative connotation. It does not account for the often precarious situation of world Jewry in the late nineteenth and twentieth centuries, the wellsprings of Jewish nationalism in eastern Europe, the creation of a modern Hebrew culture, and global Jewish solidarity, all of which have been essential for the fruition and survival of the Zionist project.

The most promising recent scholarship on the Zionist project either offers a clear, specific, and situationally relevant definition of colonialism or avoids the term in favor of more capacious categories of encounters and interactions (which are by no means always pleasant or on equal terms).[22] We would all do well to avoid employing "colonialism" in an axiomatic or unreflective way, keeping in mind Nietzsche's celebrated warning that those concepts that humans routinely assume to be truths are "metaphors which are worn out and without sensuous power; coins which have lost their pictures and now matter only as metal."[23] Reflecting on what we are talking about when we talk about colonialism and striving to imbue it with concrete meaning will make critique of the Zionist project more accurate, nuanced, and amenable to productive comparative analysis.

Notes

Thanks to Johannes Becke for his comments on an earlier draft of this essay.

1. Derek J. Penslar, *Israel in History: The Jewish State in Comparative Perspective* (New York: Routledge, 2007).

2. Dipesh Chakrabarty, *Provincializing Europe: Postcolonial Thought and Historical Difference* (Princeton, NJ: Princeton University Press, 2000).

3. Randall Geller, "Non-Jewish Minorities and the Question of Military Service in the Israel Defense Forces, 1948–1958" (Ph.D. thesis, Brandeis University, 2011).

4. Shira Robinson, *Citizen Strangers: Palestinians and the Birth of Israel's Liberal Settler State* (Stanford, CA: Stanford University Press, 2014).

5. Ben-Gurion before the Knesset, reproduced in Tom Segev, *1949: The First Israelis* (New York: Free Press, 1985), 167–68.

6. For more on these themes, see Derek J. Penslar, "What if a Christian State Had Been Established in Palestine?," in *What Ifs of Jewish History: From Abraham to Zionism*, ed. Gavriel Rosenfeld, 142–64 (New York: Cambridge University Press, 2016).

7. David Prochaska, *Making Algeria French: Colonialism in Bône, 1870–1920* (New York: Cambridge University Press, 2004).

8. Leonard Thompson, *A History of South Africa* (New Haven, CT: Yale University Press, 2000).

9. John Canup, *Out of the Wilderness: The Emergence of American Identity in Colonial New England* (Middletown, CT: Wesleyan University Press, 1990), 219.

10. On this issue, see the valuable book by Uriel Abulof, *The Mortality and Morality of Nations* (Cambridge: Cambridge University Press, 2015), which examines Israeli Jews, Afrikaners, and Quebecois under the rubric of what he calls "ontological and epistemic insecurity."

11. Awet Tewelde Weldemichael, *Third World Colonialism and Strategies of Liberation: Eritrea and East Timor Compared* (Cambridge: Cambridge University Press, 2013).

12. Johannes Becke, "Towards a De-Occidentalist Perspective on Israel: The Case of the Occupation," *Journal of Israeli History* 33 (2013): 1–23.

13. Oded Haklai and Neophytos Loizides, eds., *Settlers in Contested Lands: Territorial Disputes and Ethnic Conflicts* (Stanford, CA: Stanford University Press, 2015).

14. Kate Brown, *A Biography of No Place: From Ethnic Borderland to Soviet Heartland* (Cambridge, MA: Harvard University Press, 2004), chap. 7.

15. On Gandhi's attitudes toward the British Empire, which were far from uniformly hostile, see Faisal Devji, *Gandhi: The Impossible Indian* (London: Hurst, 2012).

16. I explore these themes in a book I am currently writing, a biography of Herzl for Yale University Press Jewish Lives series.

17. Erez Manela, *The Wilsonian Moment* (New York: Oxford University Press, 2007).

18. Joshua Landis, "Syria in the 1948 Palestine War: Fighting King Abdullah's Greater Syria Plan," in *Rewriting the Palestine War: 1948 and the History of the Arab-Israeli Conflict*, ed. Eugene Rogan and Avi Shlaim (Cambridge: Cambridge University Press, 2001), 178–205; Benny Morris, *1948: A History of the First Arab-Israeli War* (New Haven, CT: Yale University Press, 2008), 84–85, 88–93; and Ronen Yitzhak, "Fauzi al-Qawuqji and the Arab Liberation Army in the 1948 War: Toward the Attainment of King 'Abdullah's Political Ambitions in Palestine," *Comparative Studies of South Asia, Africa and the Middle East* 28 (2008): 459–66.

19. Sidney Tarrow, *The Language of Contention: Revolutions in Words, 1688–2012* (Cambridge: Cambridge University Press, 2013), 160–61. Thanks to Arie Dubnov for our e-communications on this point.

20. Derek J. Penslar, "Rebels without a Patron State: How Israel Financed the 1948 War," in *Purchasing Power: The Economics of Modern Jewish History*, ed. Rebecca Kobrin and Adam Teller, 171–91 (Philadelphia: University of Pennsylvania Press, 2015).

21. Hermann Giliomee, *The Afrikaners: Biography of a People* (Richmond, VA: University of Virgina Press, 2010), xiv.

22. Tami Razi, " 'Aravim-yehudim? Etniyut, le'umiyut, u-migdar be-Tel Aviv ha-mandatorit." *Teoriyah u-vikoret* (2011), 38–39; Robinson, *Citizen Strangers*; Jonathan Gribetz, *Defining Neighbors: Religion, Race, and the Early Zionist-Arab Encounter* (Princeton, NJ: Princeton University Press, 2014); and Liora Halperin, *Babel in Zion: Jews, Nationalism, and Language Diversity in Palestine, 1920–1948* (New Haven, CT: Yale University Press, 2014).

23. Friedrich Nietzsche, "On Truth and Lie in an Extra-Moral Sense" (1873), available at Oregon State University website, http://oregonstate.edu/instruct/phl201/modules/Philosophers/Nietzsche/Truth_and_Lie_in_an_Extra-Moral_Sense.htm. Accessed December 23, 2014.

ISRAEL BARTAL

is Avraham Harman Professor of Jewish History, member of the
Israel Academy of Sciences, and former Dean of the Faculty of
Humanities at the Hebrew University (2006–10). From 2007 to 2015, he
was the chair of the Historical Society of Israel. Professor Bartal has
taught at Harvard, McGill, University of Pennsylvania, Rutgers, and
Johns Hopkins, as well as at Moscow State University. Bartal is one of
the founders of *Cathedra*, the leading scholarly journal on the history
of the Land of Israel, and served as its co-editor for over twenty years.

Since 1998 he has been the editor of *Vestnik*, a scholarly journal of
Jewish studies in Russian. Among his publications are *Poles and Jews:
A Failed Brotherhood* (with Magdalena Opalski, University Press of
New England, 1992); *Exile in the Land* (ha-Sifriya ha-Tsiyonit, 1994);
The Jews of Eastern Europe. 1772–1881 (University of Pennsylvania
Press, 2005, published also in Russian and German); *The Varieties of
Haskalah* (editor, with Shmuel Feiner, Hebrew University Magnes
Press, 2005); *Cossack and Bedouin: Land and People in Jewish Nation-
alism* (Am Oved Publishers, 2007); and *The History of Jerusalem: The
Late Ottoman Period (1800–1917)* (editor, with Haim Goren, Yad
Ben-Zvi Press, 2010).

341

Joshua Cole

Professor of History at the University of Michigan, is the author of *The Power of Large Numbers: Population, Politics, and Gender in Nineteenth-Century France* (Ithaca NY: Cornell University Press, 2000). His research and teaching deal primarily with the social and cultural history of France in the nineteenth and twentieth centuries, and he has published work on gender and the history of the population sciences, colonial violence, and the politics of memory in France, Algeria, and Germany. He is currently writing a book entitled *The Empire of Fear: A Story of Provocation and Colonial Violence in Algeria, 1919–1940*, an archival investigation of an episode of anti-Jewish violence in Constantine, Algeria, in August 1934.

David Feldman

is Director of the Pears Institute for the study of Antisemitism and also Professor of History at Birkbeck, University of London. He is the author of *Englishmen and Jews: Social Relations and Political Culture, 1840–1914* (Yale University Press, 1994). His published essays include "Jews and the British Empire c. 1900" in *History Workshop Journal* (2007). He is the co-editor of a number of volumes including *Post-War Reconstruction in Europe: International Perspectives, 1945–49* (Oxford University Press, 2011), *Structures and Transformations in Modern British History* (Cambridge University Press, 2011) and *Blood: Reflections on What Unites and Divides Us* (Shire, 2015). In 2016 he was a Vice-Chair of the Chakrabarti Inquiry into Antisemitism and other forms of Racism in the [British] Labour Party.

Susannah Heschel

is the Eli Black Professor of Jewish Studies at Dartmouth College. She is the author of *Abraham Geiger and the Jewish Jesus* (University of Chicago Press, 1998) and *The Aryan Jesus: Christian Theologians and the Bible in Nazi Germany* (Princeton University Press, 2008). Her work has been supported by Guggenheim, Ford Foundation, National Humanities Center, Carnegie Foundation and the Wissenschaftskolleg zu Berlin fellowships. She is currently writing a book on the history of Jewish scholarship on Islam.

Ethan B. Katz

is Associate Professor of History at the University of Cincinnati and a specialist in modern France and its empire and modern Jewish history. Katz is the author of *The Burdens of Brotherhood: Jews and Muslims from North Africa to France* (Harvard University Press, 2015), for which he won a National Jewish Book Award and the David H. Pinkney Prize for the best book in French history. He is also the co-editor of *Secularism in Question: Jews and Judaism in Modern Times* (University of Pennsylvania Press, 2015). His work has been supported by fellowships from the Herbert D. Katz Center for Advanced Judaic Studies at the University of Pennsylvania, the Charles Phelps Taft Research Center at the University of Cincinnati, the Yad HaNadiv Beracha Foundation, and the Lady Davis Trust of the Hebrew University. He is currently writing a book on the Algiers underground during World War II.

Lisa Moses Leff

is Professor of History at American University and an expert in modern French Jewish history. She is author of *Sacred Bonds of Solidarity: The Rise of Jewish Internationalism in Nineteenth Century France* (Stanford University Press, 2006) and *The Archive Thief: The Man Who Salvaged French Jewish History in the Wake of the Holocaust* (Oxford University Press, 2015), for which she was awarded the 2016 Sami Rohr Prize for Jewish Literature. She is currently writing a book on the Panama Affair.

Frances Malino

is the Sophia Moses Robison Professor of Jewish Studies and History at Wellesley College and Chair of the Jewish Studies Program. She is author of *The Sephardic Jews of Bordeaux: Assimilation and Emancipation in Revolutionary and Napoleonic France* (University of Alabama Press, 1978) and *A Jew in the French Revolution: The Life of Zalkind Hourwitz* (Blackwell, 1996) and co-editor of *Essays in Modern Jewish History: A Tribute to Ben Halpern* (Fairleigh Dickinson University Press, 1982), *The Jews in Modern France* (Brandeis, 1985), *Profiles in Diversity: Jews in a Changing Europe* (Wayne State University Press,

1998), and *Voices of the Diaspora: Jewish Women Writing in the New Europe* (Northwestern University Press, 2005). Her newest project is titled *Teaching Freedom: Jewish Sisters in Muslim Lands*. In 2012 she was named Chevalier dans l'Ordre des Palmes académiques by the French Ministry of Education.

Maud S. Mandel

is Dean of the College and Professor of History and Judaic Studies at Brown University. She is author of *In the Aftermath of Genocide: Armenians and Jews in Twentieth Century France* (Duke University Press, 2003), which won the Herbert Katzki book award from the American Jewish Joint Distribution Committee and *Muslims and Jews in France: History of a Conflict* (Princeton University Press, 2014). She has been awarded fellowships from the American Council of Learned Societies and the American Philosophical Society. In 2016, she was elected a fellow of the American Academy for Jewish Research.

Adam Mendelsohn

is Director of the Kaplan Centre for Jewish Studies and Research at the University of Cape Town, South Africa, and former Director of the Pearlstine/Lipov Center for Southern Jewish Culture at the College of Charleston, South Carolina. Much of his research focuses on the relationship between Jews in America and the British Empire prior to mass eastern European migration, at a time when these fledgling communities were beginning to grapple with the challenges of living in liberal societies. He is the author of *The Rag Race: How Jews Sewed Their Way to Success in America and the British Empire* (New York University Press, 2015), winner of the National Jewish Book Award in American Jewish Studies and of the Best First Book Prize from Immigration and Ethnic History Society, and co-editor of *Jews and the Civil War: A Reader* (with Jonathan D. Sarna, New York University Press, 2010) and *Transnational Traditions: New Perspectives on American Jewish History* (with Ava Kahn, Wayne State University Press, 2014).

Derek J. Penslar

is the the Samuel Zacks Professor of Jewish History at the University of Toronto. He is also a Visiting Professor of History at Harvard

University and the Stanley Lewis Visiting Professor of Modern Israel Studies at the University of Oxford. Penslar's books include *Shylock's Children: Economics and Jewish Identity in Modern Europe* (University of California Press, 2001), *Israel in History: The Jewish State in Comparative Perspective* (Routledge, 2007), and *Jews and the Military: A History* (Princeton University Press, 2013). Penslar is currently writing a biography of Theodor Herzl for the Yale University Press Jewish Lives series and a book on Zionism for the Rutgers University Press series Keywords in Jewish Studies. Penslar is co-editor of the *Journal of Israeli History* and is an elected fellow of the Royal Society of Canada and the American Academy for Jewish Research.

DANIEL SCHROETER

is the Amos S. Deinard Memorial Chair in Jewish History at the University of Minnesota. His works include *The Sultan's Jew: Morocco and the Sephardi World* (Stanford University Press, 2002), and *Merchants of Essaouira: Urban Society and Imperialism in Southwestern Morocco, 1844–1886* (Cambridge University Press, 1988); both books were translated to Arabic and published in Morocco. He is co-editor of *Jewish Culture and Society in North Africa* (Indiana University Press, 2011), and an editor and contributor to the *Encyclopedia of the Jews in the Islamic World* (Brill, 2010). He was the 2014–15 Ina Levine Scholar-in-Residence at the Jack, Joseph and Morton Mandel Center for Advanced Holocaust Studies of the United States Holocaust Memorial Museum, and is currently at work on a book with Aomar Boum on Morocco and the Holocaust.

ELIZABETH F. THOMPSON

holds the Farsi Chair in Islamic Peace at American University. She is currently writing a study of the defeat of liberalism and subsequent birth of Islamism in the Middle East after World War I, to be published by Grove Atlantic in 2018. She is author of *Justice Interrupted: The Struggle for Constitutional Government in the Middle East* (Harvard University Press, 2013), a history of constitutional movements against tyranny and inequality in the Middle East since 1839, culminating in the Arab uprisings of 2011. Her first book, *Colonial Citizens: Republican Rights, Paternal Privilege and Gender in French*

Syria and Lebanon (Columbia University Press, 2000), won book prizes from the American Historical Association and the Berkshire Conference of Women Historians. Thompson has also won research awards from the Carnegie Corporation of New York, the Social Science Research Council, the US Institute of Peace, and the Library of Congress. She has served as Middle East co-editor of the new 1914–18 Online Encyclopedia of the First World War and co-director of the National Endowment for Humanities Summer Seminar for Faculty, "World War I in the Middle East."

TARA ZAHRA

is Professor of History at the University of Chicago. Her research focuses on the transnational history of modern Europe, migration, the family, nationalism, and humanitarianism. Zahra is the author of *The Lost Children: Reconstructing Europe's Families after World War II* (Harvard University Press, 2011), *Kidnapped Souls: National Indifference and the Battle for Children in the Bohemian Lands* (Cornell University Press, 2008), and *The Great Departure: Mass Migration and the Making of the "Free World"* (Norton, 2016).

COLETTE ZYTNICKI

is Professor Emerita of Contemporary History at Toulouse University (Jean-Jaurès). She is the author of *Les Juifs à Toulouse de 1945 à 1970: Une communauté toujours recommencée* (Presses universitaires du Mirail, 1998) and *Les Juifs du Maghreb. Naissance d'une historiographie coloniale* (Presses universitaires de Paris Sorbonne, 2011), and most recently, *L'Algérie, terre de tourisme. Histoire d'un loisir colonial* (Paris: Vendémiaire, 2016). She is editor of *Terre d'exil, terre d'asile: Migrations juives en France aux XIXe et XXe siècles* (Éditions de l'Éclat, 2010) and has also published several co-edited collections. She is currently completing a new book entitled *Draria, un village de colonisation algérien.*

INDEX

Bourgeois, Léon, 137

Bourguiba, Habib, 256, 264–65

Boyarin, Daniel, 279

Brazil, 173, 174

Britain: antisemitism in, 196; attitudes toward colonialism/imperialism in, 196–200; Jewish colonials' return to, 81–83, 85–96; Jewish commercial activities in, 83; Labour Party's relations with Zionism, 193–210; and Palestine, 197–206, 279, 318–25, 334–36; promises concerning Middle East made during WWI, 194, 323; U.S. relations with, 204; Zionism and, 318–21, 335–36

Brit Shalom, 72

Brockway, Fenner, 193

Brunot, Louis, 38

Buber, Martin, 80n72, 181, 322

Buber, Salomon, 74

Buddhism, 284

Bukovina, 171

Burma, 99n32

Burton, Richard, 58

Caetani, Leone, 71

Cagnat, André, 33

Cahen, Abraham, 33, 44, 46, 49

Canada, 180

Cape Town, South Africa, 84–85

Caro, Leopold, 170, 172, 174

Carthage, 31, 39–41

Cassin, René, 130–32, 148–58, 165n120

Catherine II (the Great), empress of Russia, 118

Cato (pseudonym of Michael Foot), *The Guilty Men*, 204

cave dwellers, 35

Cazès, David, 46

Central America, 176

Central Asia, 305–6

Central Committee of Liberated Jews, 177

Centre de hautes études d'administration musulmane, Paris, 230, 247n57

Certeau, Michel de, 30

Césaire, Aimé, 10, 165n120

CGQJ. *See* Commissariat général aux questions juives

Chakrabarty, Dipesh, 293, 310–12, 329

Chamberlain, Neville, 204

Charvit, Yossef, 9

Chatterjee, Partha, 277, 286, 288–90, 292–93, 298n2, 310–11, 318, 327

Chattopadhyay, Tarnicharan, *History of India*, 287

Chenik, Mohamed, 256

Chetrit, Joseph, 9

Cheyette, Bryan, 11–12

child marriage, 103, 113n9

Choate, Mark, 167

Chouraqui, André, 40, 47–50

Christelow, Allan, 308

Christianity: Islam in relation to, 60, 72–74; Judaism in relation to, 61–62, 70; views on Islam, 57, 67; views on Judaism, 57

Christian Social party (Vienna), 171

chronotopes, 328

Churchill, Winston, 234, 319, 320, 324

civil improvement, 291

civilizing mission: AIU and, 37, 44–45, 101, 104, 110–12, 159n9, 282, 307; in Algeria, 131, 157–58; concept of, 6; of France, 153, 157–58, 306; of French Jews to co-religionists, 32–33, 46; of Germany, 291; international intent of, 137; paradox of, 110; Reinach and, 132; Russia influenced by, 124; Zionism and, 205, 206, 280–82, 291–92, 294, 303, 305, 321, 331

Clark, Linda, 107

clothing, 108–9

Cochini Jews, 91

Cohen, Hermann, 71

Cohen, Isaac, 226

Cohen, Rabbi Haim, 37

Cole, Joshua, 17, 257, 329–30, 332–34

Colet, Louise, 58

Collection of Semitic Inscriptions, 31–32

colonial archives, 255, 310

colonial historiography, 10–15, 18, 23n43

colonialism: border/category "hardening" as component of, 296, 305–9; defining, 301–2, 304–5, 309–10, 312, 334, 338–39; eastern European settlement, 167, 170–71, 173–74, 180, 183; emigrant, 167–68, 170–71, 173–74, 177–82, 180–81; exploitation associated with, 181, 183, 277–79, 297; forms of power and agency in, 306–9, 330–31; ideological underpinnings of, 3; inclusion and differentiation characteristic of, 304–6, colonialism (*cont.*)

312–13, 329–30, 334; Jewish participation in/ identification with, 11, 75, 120–21; Jews in relation to, 1–4, 175–76; politics associated with, 290–91; reform efforts of Jews in, 130–58; settler, 277–78, 294, 302–4, 318, 320–21, 331–32; and social/demographic engineering, 124, 289–90, 311, 332–33; as term of reproach, 297, 338; types of, 95n3, 277–78; Zionism and, 1–2, 17, 175–76, 206, 275–97, 301–13, 317–25, 327–39

Comité français de libération nationale, 232

Commissariat général aux questions juives (CGQJ), 221, 225, 232

Conférence internationale des associations de mutilés et anciens combattants, 149

Conrad, Joseph, 281

Constantine, anti-Jewish violence in, 257–58

Cook, Robin, 210

Cooper, Frederick, 2, 11, 18, 23n43, 158, 304, 306, 309

Coriat, Messody, 107

Côte d'Ivoire, 309

Crémieux, Adolphe, 107, 110, 132, 134, 154

Crémieux Decree, 129, 224, 231–34, 257, 306–8

Creully, Colonel, 33

Croce, Benedetto, 292

Crossman, Richard, 194; *A Palestine Munich*, 204–5

Czartoryski, Adam, 119

Czechoslovakia, 169, 183, 184, 338

Dahan, Mardochée, 226

Dalton, Hugh, 194

Damascus Affair, 132

Danan, Elie, 226

Darlan, François, 231

Darwazeh, Izzat, 324

Davis, Elias, 87

De Gaulle, Charles, 148, 151–54, 157, 234

demographic engineering. *See* social engineering

De Pass, Aaron and Elias, 84

Depreux, Édouard, 148

Derzhavin, Gavrila, 119

dhimmis (protected person), 219, 223–26, 242

Dilthey, Wilhelm, 71

Dinur, Ben-Zion, 292

Disraeli, Benjamin, 6, 63

Dohm, Christian Friedrich Wilhelm von, 291

Dominican Republic, 187

dress. *See* clothing

Dreyfus, Alfred, 134, 160n20

Dreyfus, Marguerite, 135

Dreyfus, Mathieu, 135

Dreyfus Affair, 133–36, 140–42, 160n20, 162n50, 171

Droysen, Johann Gustav, 292

Druze, 281

Dubois, Laurent, 309

Duff-Gordon, Lady, 85

Durand, Marguerite, 108

Easterman, A. L., 264–65

eastern Europe, 5; colonialism of, 167–71, 173–74, 179–84; concerns about emigration from, 172–73; emigration from, 166–67, 169–74, 177–82, 185–86; exploitation of emigrants from, 181, 183; German imperialism linked to, 168; nationalism in, 168–69; Zionism and, 168–69, 184–85; Zionism compared to settlement projects of, 170–71, 179–81

East India Company, 88, 91

Éboué, Félix, 153

economic history, 14

Edmunds, June, 194, 196

Edrehi, Moses, 35–36

Egypt, 305, 323

Eisenbeth, Maurice, 33, 34, 42, 44, 46, 49

Elkin, Benjamin, 87

Elmaleh, Amram, 102

Elmaleh, Edmond Amran, 104, 113n12

emancipation/liberation: of Algerian Jews, 132; in French context, 7, 114n29, 123, 151–52; imperialism as means of, 124; Jewish liberal advocacy of, 139; modernization as means of, 4; of Muslims, 133, 135–36, 140–41, 146–47, 150; of women, 102, 108; WWI and, 133, 137–40; WWII and, 152

emigrant colonialism, 167–68, 170–71, 173–74, 177–82

emigration: colonialism linked to, 166–67, 170–71, 173–74, 177–82; controlled, as response to social and political problems, 177–79, 185; from eastern Europe, 166–67,

169–74, 177–82; nationalism linked to, 177–81, 184; from Palestine/Israel, 177; Zionism and, 166–69, 175–79

Encaoua, Chief Rabbi Abraham, 37, 52n35

England. *See* Britain

Enlightenment: absolutism and, 118; Haskalah in relation to, 6; ideals of, 43; Russian adoption of ideals of, 118–19

E. Solomon and Sons, 91

Espagne, Michel, 29

Esquer, Gabriel, 33

Esteva, Jean-Pierre, 225

Ettinghausen, Richard, 72

Ewald, Heinrich, 64

Expositions Universelles (Paris), 105

Eyal, Gil, 75

Fadeuhecht, O., 166

Fanon, Frantz, 10, 165n120

Farahi, Hamiduddin, 71

fascism, 144

fashion. *See* clothing

El-Fassi, Allal, 238

Faulds, Andrew, 207

Faysal, Prince of Greater Syria, 323–24

Feldman, David, 16

feminism: familial (equality in difference) vs. individualist, 106–7, 110; *institutrices* and, 101–2, 106–8

Filastin (newspaper), 323

Flaubert, Gustav, 58

Fleischer, Heinrich Leberecht, 65

Fletcher, Raymond, 206–7

Foot, Michael, 194; *A Palestine Munich*, 204

Formstecher, Salomon, 70

Foucauld, Charles de, 36

Foucault, Michel, 311

France: and Algerian War, 156–57; anti-Jewish legislation in, 219; and assimilation of the Jews, 4; civilizing mission of, 153, 157–58, 306; and federalist system for colonies, 155–56, 165n119; governance of, 118; and Greater Syria, 323–24; historiographic focus on, 5; and Jewish efforts at colonial reform, 130–58; Jewish involvement in politics of, 130; Jews in, 3, 4, 116–19, 122–26; Orientalist scholarship in, 29, 31–38; recruitment of eastern Europeans for colonies of, 183; as

republic vs. empire, 144–45; revolutionary ideals of, 123–26, 130, 131, 133, 142, 152–53; Russia in comparison with, 116–19; and Tunisian independence, 256, 262–65, 268n25; universalist vs. particularist logics underlying, 4–6

Franco, Francisco, 240

Franco-Judaism, 131

Frederick the Great, king of Prussia, 118

Free France, 148, 151–54

French Communist Party, 144

French Section of the Workers' International (SFIO, Socialist Party (France)), 142, 144

French Union, 148, 156

Frere, Bartle, 89–90

Freud, Sigmund, 58

Freytag, Gustav, 60

Fried, Alfred, 158

Friedlaender, Israel, 57

Fromm, Erich, 80n72

Front de Libération Nationale (FLN), 338

Funkenstein, Amos, 288

Galicia, 169, 171, 174, 178

Gambetta, Léon, 132, 134

Gandhi, Mohandas, 293, 335, 336

Gargas, Sigismund, 173

Gastfreund, Isaac, 60

Gaxotte, Pierre, 143

Geiger, Abraham, 6, 56, 60–63, 73, 285–86

George, Henry, 199

German Settlement Commission, 174

Germany: colonialism of, 74, 170, 183; cultural/ civilizing mission of, 291; and eastern Europe, 168; scholarship on Islam in, 56–68, 71–77; treatment of Jews and the colonized by, 15

Ghriba Synagogue, Djerba, 39

Gide, André, 281–82

Giliomee, Hermann, 338

Giraud, Henri, 154, 231–32, 234

Goitein, Shlomo Dov, 54–55, 69, 71, 72, 74, 76

Goldberg, Harvey, 258

Goldziher, Ignaz, 58, 59, 62, 65–66, 68

Gordon, Judah Leib, 125

Gorny, Joseph, 213n38

Gottreich, Emily Benichou, 8, 9, 259

253; elements of the colonial power in, 217; Muslim-Jewish relations in, 225; nationalism in, 226, 234–39; scholarly institutions in, 34–38; sultan's role in, 216, 218–20, 223–24, 226, 234–43; Vichy regime in, 215–20

Morrison, Herbert, 194, 202

Moss, Kenneth, 169

Moutet, Marius, 146

Muhammad (prophet), 60–66, 74, 76

Muir, William, 65, 67

Müller, Friedrich Max, 75

Munk, Salomon, 60

Murphy, Robert, 234

Muslims. *See* Islam and Muslims

Mussolini, Benito, 150, 183

Napoleon, 7, 123

nationalism: in Algeria, 129; anticolonial vs. European, 293–94, 310; in eastern Europe, 168–69; emigration linked to, 177–81, 184; formations of, 292–93; historiography and, 292; Indian, 284, 286–89; Irish, 336; in Morocco, 226, 234–39; and settlement colonies, 173–74; state apparatus in relation to, 310–12; in Tunisia, 252, 256, 258, 261; Zionism and, 318. *See also* Zionism

National Union of Students, 195

nation-states: historiographic focus on, 1, 2, 4–5; inclusion and differentiation characteristic of, 312–13; nationalism and, 311–12; as Western concept, 291

Nazism, 185, 264

Neo Destour, 258–59, 261–62

neo-Hasidism, 70

Nerval, Gérard de, 58

Netanyahu, Binyamin, 210

New Jewish Woman, 102

New Woman, 108, 112–13

Nicholas I, emperor of Russia, 118

Nietzsche, Friedrich, 339

1939 White Paper, 202–4

1948 Arab-Israeli War, 280, 295, 322, 325, 336–38

Nobel Peace Prize, 150

Noguès, Charles, 216, 218–20, 222, 225, 227, 235, 238, 241–42

Nöldeke, Theodor, 63, 71

nongovernmental organizations (NGOs), Jewish, 251–52, 255, 264–66

Nordau, Max, 80n72, 182

Norden, Benjamin, 85, 86, 97n17

North African Jews, 30–50; as bridge between East and West, 45–48; citizenship of, 268n31; Eastern identity of, 38–42, 47–50; ethnic status of, 12–13; European Jews' perceptions of, 42–45; identification of, with colonizers, 13; Jewish scholars' views of, 31–50; origins of, 39–42; revisions of historiography on, 8–9; traditions of, 37–38; violence against, 252–53, 257–58. *See also* Algerian Jews

Northrop, Douglas, 305

Occupied Territories, 296–97, 328

orientales (Eastern Jewish students), 105–6, 113n2

Orientalism: colonial scholarship in the discipline of, 32–34; *institutrices* and, 101–13; Jewish, 31–38, 56–59; Jews' role in, 29–30, 58, 69–70, 74–76; meanings of, 6–7, 29, 58; Said's theory of, 23n47; as scholarly discipline, 29, 31–38, 49; utilitarian purpose of, 29, 32, 34; Zionism and, 70, 75–76, 280–82

Oslo Peace Process, 328

pacifism, 143–44

Pact of Umar, 224

Palestine and Palestinians: Arab-Jewish relations in, 200–201, 320–25, 337; binationalism/pluralism in, 72, 76, 202, 322–23; Britain and, 197–206, 279, 318–25, 334–36; British Labour Party and, 193–210, 213n47; colonialism and, 304–5, 309–10; cultural response of, to Israel, 295; desertification of, 281; emigration from, 177; Israeli colonization of, 296–97; Mandate for, 143, 194, 197, 199–201, 204, 279, 318, 320–21, 334–36; as national home for Jews, 168–69, 171, 178, 194, 197–200, 202–4, 206, 319, 323; support for, 209–10; Tunisian response to, 258; Zionism and, 166, 168–69, 175–77, 180, 305, 317–25

Palestine Economic Corporation, 290

Palestine Liberation Organization (PLO), 195, 209

Pannell, Charles, 207

World War II: UN Declaration on, 164n104; as war of liberation, 152

Wyrtzen, Jonathan, 238

Yemeni Jewry, 92, 100n50, 282

Young, Robert, 277

Youssef, Mohammed Ben (sultan of Morocco; later King Mohammed V), 215–20, 223–26, 244n3

Zadoc-Kahn, Edmond, 140, 162n50

Zafrani, Haïm, 215–16

Zagury, Yahia, 222

Zahra, Tara, 16

Zangwill, Israel, 175

Zionism: and anticolonialism, 276, 284–88, 318, 321–22, 336–37; and Arabs, 181, 182, 279, 281–83, 295, 298n11, 305, 320–25; Ashkenazi Jews and, 282–83, 330; British Empire and, 318–21, 335–36; and British Labour Party, 193–210, 213n38; civilizing mission of, 182, 280–82, 291–92, 294, 303, 305, 321, 331; and colonialism, 1–2, 17, 175–76, 206, 275–97, 301–13, 317–25, 327–39; competing emigrant destinations for, 175–77, 180, 289–90; complex identities within, 330–31; criticisms of, 139, 208–9, 279–80; dual Palestine-Europe focus of, 168–69; early history of, 319, 335; and eastern Europe, 168–69, 184–85; eastern European settlement projects compared to, 170–71, 179–81; and emigration, 166–69, 175–79; and equality, 288–89; historiography and, 9, 15, 275–76, 292; ideological conflicts within, 179; Labor Zionism, 181, 290, 321, 336; meaning of, 301; motivations for, 166, 170–71, 175, 181; mystic strand of, 288; and nationalism, 318; oriental identity and, 70, 75–76; and Orientalist themes, 280–83; and Palestine, 166, 168–69, 175–77, 180, 305, 317–25; and postcolonialism, 276–77; as racism, 195; "return" as fundamental principle of, 171, 278, 294, 319; romantic vs. materialist conceptions of human nature, 288; secular perspective on, 199–200; and settlement colonies, 173–74, 278, 320, 331–32; supporters of, 143; technical expertise in, 289, 311; Tunisian opposition to, 258

Zionist Commission, 320, 321, 323

Zionist Organization (ZO), 280, 282, 288, 335

Zola, Émile, 142

Zunz, Leopold, 286

Zytnicki, Colette, 16